IS
Management
HANDBOOK
7TH EDITION

I.N.

IS
Management
HANDBOOK
7TH EDITION

Carol V. Brown
EDITOR

with
Heikki Topi

AUERBACH

Boca Raton London New York Washington, D.C.

Library of Congress Cataloging-in-Publication Data

IS management handbook / Carol V. Brown, Heikki Topi, editors. -- 7th.
    ed.
        p.   cm.
    Includes bibliographical references and index.
    ISBN 0-8493-9820-7 (alk. paper)
    1. Information resources management Handbooks, manuals, etc.
    2. Information technology--Management Handbooks, manuals, etc.
    I. Brown, Carol V. (Carol Vanderbilt), 1945- . II. Topi, Heikki.
    T58.64.I83   1999
    658.4'038--dc21   99-41254
                                                                              CIP

© 2000 by CRC Press LLC
Auerbach is an imprint of CRC Press LLC

No claim to original U.S. Government works
International Standard Book Number 0-8493-9820-7
Printed in the United State of America 1 2 3 4 5 6 7 8 9 0
Printed on acid-free paper

Contributors

SAMI J. ALBANNA, *Chief Architect, CSC, Catalyst Methodology, Newton, MA*

SANDRA ALLEN-SENFT, *Corporate IS Audit Manager, Farmers Insurance, Alta Loma, CA*

ANN S. ANGEL, *President, Technologies Training of the Triad, Inc., Winston-Salem, NC*

WILLIAM J. BEAUMONT, *Vice President, Marketing, DecisionOne Corp., Frazer, PA*

EILEEN BIRGE, *Research Director, The Concours Group, Houston, TX*

BERNARD H. BOAR, *Information Business Strategist, NCR, Lincroft, NJ*

BIJOY BORDOLOI, *Professor, College of Business Administration, University of Texas at Arlington, Arlington, TX*

JOE R. BRIONES, *Manager, Computer Services, Computer Sciences Corp., Fort Worth, TX*

CAROL V. BROWN, *Professor, Kelley School of Business, Indiana University, Indianapolis, IN*

MICHAEL J. CERULLO, *Professor, Southwest Missouri State University, Springfield, MO*

VIRGINIA CERULLO, *Professor, Southwest Missouri State University, Springfield, MO*

AMY Y. CHOU, *Instructor, College of Business, St. Cloud University, St. Cloud, MN*

DAVID C. CHOU, *Professor, College of Business, St. Cloud University, St. Cloud, MN*

THOMAS B. CLARK, *Professor, College of Business Administration, Georgia State University, Atlanta, GA*

DALE COHEN, *Team Manager, Electronic Messaging Team, R.R. Donnelley & Sons Co., Chicago, IL*

RICHARD H. DEANE, *Professor, College of Business Administration, Georgia State University, Atlanta, GA*

NICHOLAS ECONOMIDES, *Professor, Stern School of Business, New York University, New York, NY*

G.A. FLANAGAN, *MJC Communications, Hales Corner, WI*

LEE A. FREEMAN, *Kelley School of Business, Indiana University, Bloomington, IN*

Louis Fried, *Chief Information Officer, TELLUS Corp. Palo Alto, CA*

Frederick Gallegos, *IS Audit Advisor and Faculty Member, College of Business Administration, California State Polytechnic University, Pomona, CA*

James E. Gaskin, *Consultant, Mesquite, TX*

Robert L. Glass, *President, Computing Trends, Bloomington, IN*

Varun Grover, *Professor, College of Business Administration, University of South Carolina, Columbia, SC*

Uma G. Gupta, *Professor, College of Business Administration, Creighton University, Omaha, NE*

Steve Guynes, *Professor, College of Business Administration, University of North Texas, Denton, TX*

Ron Hale, *Senior Manager, Deloitte & Touche LLP, Chicago, IL*

Richard D. Hays, *President, Hays Consulting, Sarasota, FL*

Robert Heckman, *Professor, School of Information Studies, Syracuse University, Syracuse, NY*

Ray Hoving, *IT Management Consultant, Ray Hoving and Associates, New Tripoli, PA*

Philip N. James, *President, Strategic Management Services, Northridge, CA*

Seung Ryul Jeong, *Reengineering Consultant, Samsung Corp., Seoul, Korea*

Leonard M. Jessup, *Professor, Kelley School of Business, Indiana University, Bloomington, IN*

R.C. Johnson, Jr., *MJC Communications, Hales Corner, WI*

Diana Jovin, *Market Development Manager, NetDynamics, Inc., Menlo Park, CA*

Michael C. Kettelhut, *Associate Director, Data Administration, Alcon Laboratories, Dallas, TX*

William R. King, *Professor, Katz Graduate School of Business, University of Pittsburgh, Pittsburgh, PA*

Christopher Klaus, *Chief Technology Officer, Internet Security Systems, Atlanta, GA*

James J. Kubie, *MJC Communications, Hales Corner, WI*

Carol L. Larson, *Freelance Desktop Publisher, Beaverton, OR*

James A. Larson, *Senior Software Engineer, Intel Architecture Lab, Beaverton, OR*

Phillip Q. Maier, *Program Manager, Secure Network Initiative, Lockheed Martin Corp., Sunnyvale, CA*

Patrick McBrayer, *Project Manager, ATM Specialist, First Consulting Group, Long Beach, CA*

Ephraim R. McLean, *Professor, College of Business Administration, Georgia State University, Atlanta, GA*

L.A. Melkus, *Consultant, MJC Communications, Hales Corner, WI*

N. Dean Meyer, *President, N. Dean Meyer Associates, Ridgefield, CT*

John P. Murray, *IT Consultant, Madison, WI*

WILLIAM HUGH MURRAY, *Executive Consultant, Information Systems Security, Deloitte & Touche, Wilton, CT*

ALI H. MURTAZA, *Senior Consultant, Data Warehousing, Deloitte & Touche Consulting Group, Toronto, Ontario, Canada*

STEFAN M. NEIKES, *Data Analyst, Tandy Corp., Watuga, TX*

JOE OSTERHAUS, *Associate Architect, CSC Catalyst Program, CSC, Newton, MA*

YANNIS A. POLLALIS, *Professor, School of Information Studies, Syracuse University, Syracuse, NY*

RICHARD L. PTAK, *Director, Systems Management Research, D.H. Brown Associates, Inc., Port Chester, NY*

SANJIV PURBA, *Senior Manager, Deloitte & Touche Consulting Group, Toronto, Ontario, Canada*

V. RAMESH, *Professor, Kelley School of Business, Indiana University, Bloomington, IN*

VASANT RAVAL, *Professor, College of Business Administration, Creighton University, Omaha, NE*

JOHN F. ROCKART, *Director, Center for Information Systems Research, Sloan School of Management, Massachusetts Institute of Technology, Cambridge, MA*

JEANNE W. ROSS, *Principal Research Scientist, Center for Information Systems Research, Sloan School of Management, Massachusetts Institute of Technology, Cambridge, MA*

RICHARD ROSS, *Principal, CSC Index, New York, NY*

RANDALL H. RUSSELL, *Senior Manager, Ernst & Young Center for Business Innovation, Ernst & Young, Boston, MA*

HUGH W. RYAN, *Partner, Andersen Consulting, Chicago, IL*

S. YVONNE SCOTT, *Assistant Director, Corporate Information Systems, GATX Corp., Chicago, IL*

JAMES A. SENN, *Director, Information Technology Management Group, College of Business Administration, Georgia State University, Atlanta, GA*

JAMES E. SHOWALTER, *Consultant, Enterprise Computing, Automotive Industry Business Development, Sun Microsystems, Greenwood, IN*

JANICE C. SIPIOR, *Professor, College of Commerce and Finance, Villanova University, Villanova, PA*

SUMIT SIRCAR, *Director, Center for Information Technologies Management, University of Texas at Arlington, Arlington, TX*

STANLEY H. STAHL, *President, Solution Dynamics, Los Angeles, CA*

STEWART L. STOKES, JR., *National Practice Director, Behavioral Skills Management, PLATINUM Technology Solutions, Inc., Wellesley, MA*

DETMAR W. STRAUB, *Professor, College of Business Administration, Georgia State University, Atlanta, GA*

CHRISTINE B. TAYNTOR, *Manager, Corporate Staff Applications, Allied Signal, Inc., New Providence, NJ*

JAMES T.C. TENG, *Professor, College of Business Administration, University of South Carolina, Columbia, SC*

HEIKKI TOPI, *Visiting Professor, Kelley School of Business, Indiana University, Bloomington, IN*

ANDREW URBACZEWSKI, *Professor, College of Business and Economics, Washington State University, Pullman, WA*

JOHN VAN DEN HOVEN, *Manager, Architecture Planning, Noranda, Inc., Toronto, Ontario, Canada*

ROBERTO VINAJA, *Assistant Director, Center for Information Technologies Management, University of Texas at Arlington, Arlington, TX*

SHOUHONG WANG, *Professor, College of Business and Industry, University of Massachusetts, Dartmouth, Dartmouth, MA*

BURKE T. WARD, *Professor, College of Commerce and Finance, Villanova University, Villanova, PA*

TRENTON WATERHOUSE, *Marketing Manager, LAN Switching Systems, Cabletron Systems, Rochester, NY*

JASON WEIR, *Technical Writer, Data-Mirror Corporation, Markham, Ontario, Toronto, Canada*

STEVEN M. WILLIFORD, *President, Franklin Services Group, Inc., Pataskala, OH*

JOHN WINDSOR, *Professor, College of Business Administration, University of North Texas, Denton, TX*

LEO WROBEL, *President, Premiere Network Services, Inc., DeSoto, TX*

A.P. (DENNIS) YOUNG, *President, Young, Clark & Associates, Inc., Atlanta, GA*

MICHAEL ZIMMER, *Senior Data Administrator, Ministry of Health, Victoria, British Columbia, Canada*

Contents

INTRODUCTION xv

SECTION 1   ACHIEVING STRATEGIC IT ALIGNMENT 1
IT LEADERSHIP ROLES
   1 The New Enabling Role of the IT Infrastructure 5
      Jeanne W. Ross and John F. Rockart
   2 Partnering Roles of the IS Executive 19
      Carol V. Brown, Ephraim R. McLean, and Detmar W. Straub
   3 Knowledge Management — Coming Up the
      Learning Curve 27
      Ray Hoving
   4 The CIO Role in the Era of Dislocation 41
      James E. Showalter
STRATEGIC IT CAPABILITIES
   5 The IS Executive and Strategic Planning 49
      Philip N. James
   6 Integrated Systems Planning: A Holistic Model 63
      Yannis A. Pollalis
   7 Strategic Information Technology Planning and the
      Line Manager's Role 73
      Robert Heckman
   8 Managing Advanced Information Technology 83
      Louis Fried
   9 Moving the IT Work Force to a Client/Server
      Environment 95
      Eileen Birge
  10 Redesigning the IT Organization for the
      Information Age 109
      Bernard H. Boar
  11 Successfully Hiring and Retaining IT Personnel 121
      John P. Murray
OUTSOURCING VS. INTERNAL PROVISIONING
  12 Preparing for the Outsourcing Challenge 133
      N. Dean Meyer

13 IT Performance Turnaround — The Outsourcing
    Alternative 143
    Richard D. Hays

14 Support Services Outsourcing 151
    William J. Beaumont

15 Managing the IT Procurement Process 157
    Robert Heckman

16 Control of Information Systems Outsourcing 173
    S. Yvonne Scott

**SECTION 2 DESIGNING AND OPERATING AN ENTERPRISE
INFRASTRUCTURE** 185

Distributed Computing Environments

17 Client/Server Computing: Politics and Solutions 191
    Steve Guynes and John Windsor

18 Culture Change: A Client/Server Enabler 201
    Stewart L. Stokes, Jr.

19 Shifting to Distributed Computing 211
    Richard Ross

20 Improving Data Center Productivity and Effectiveness 225
    John P. Murray

TELECOMMUNICATIONS MANAGEMENT

21 U.S. Telecommunications Today 233
    Nicholas Economides

22 Operating Standards for LANs 249
    Leo Wrobel

23 Virtual Networking Management and Planning 257
    Trenton Waterhouse

24 Successful Network Implementations 269
    Patrick McBrayer

25 Integrating Electronic Messaging Systems
    and Infrastructures 279
    Dale Cohen

DATA WAREHOUSING

26 Data Warehousing Concepts and Strategies 295
    Stefan M. Neikes, Sumit Sircar, and Bijoy Bordoloi

27 Data Marts: Plan Big, Build Small 315
    John van den Hoven

28 A Framework for Developing Enterprise Data
    Warehouses 321
    Ali H. Murtaza

29 Data Mining: Exploring the Corporate Asset 331
    Jason Weir

30 Data Conversion Fundamentals 339
    Michael Zimmer
QUALITY ASSURANCE AND CONTROL
31 Quality Information Services 355
    Joe R. Briones
32 Information Systems Audits: What's in It for
    Executives? 365
    Vasant Raval and Uma G. Gupta
SECURITY AND RISK MANAGEMENT
33 Key Factors to Strengthen the Disaster Contingency
    and Recovery Planning Process 373
    Michael J. Cerullo and Virginia Cerullo
34 Taking an Adaptive Approach to IS Security 383
    Christopher Klaus

SECTION 3   PROVIDING APPLICATION SOLUTIONS 395
NEW TOOLS AND APPLICATIONS
35 IT-Enhanced Productivity and Profitability 399
    William R. King
36 The Use of Intelligent Agents for Decision-Making: An
    Analysis of the State of the Art 405
    Roberto Vinaja and Sumit Sircar
37 Analyzing Agents for Electronic Commerce 419
    Shouhong Wang
38 Java™: The Language and Its Supporting Technologies.... 431
    V. Ramesh
SYSTEMS DEVELOPMENT APPROACHES
39 The Methodology Evolution: From None, to
    One-Size-Fits-All, to Eclectic.. 443
    Robert L. Glass
40 Strategic Use of JAD 451
    Michael C. Kettelhut
41 User-Centered Design 463
    James J. Kubie, L.A. Melkus, R. C. Johnson, Jr., and
    G.A. Flanagan
42 Database Development Methodology and Organization ... 481
    Sanjiv Purba
PROJECT MANAGEMENT
43 Project Success and Customer Needs 491
    Richard H. Deane, Thomas B. Clark, and A.P. (Dennis) Young
44 Win-Win Projects 501
    Stanley H. Stahl
45 Managing the User/IS Relationship 509
    Ann S. Angel

46 Reengineering Project Challenges 517
   Varun Grover, Seung Ryul Jeong, and James T.C. Teng
47 Managing Development in the Era of Complex Systems 527
   Hugh W. Ryan

SOFTWARE QUALITY ASSURANCE
48 Meeting the Software Challenge 533
   Sami J. Albanna and Joe Osterhaus
49 Analyses of Software Quality and Auditing 549
   David C. Chou and Amy Y. Chou
50 Software Testing Basics and Guidelines 563
   Christine B. Tayntor
51 Ethical Responsibility for Software Development...............575
   Janice C. Sipior and Burke T. Ward

SECTION 4   EXPLOITING WEB TECHNOLOGIES 585
E-COMMERCE OPPORTUNITIES AND CHALLENGES
52 Creating Electronic Markets in Business-to-Business
   Commerce..589
   James A. Senn
53 E-Commerce Issues for External Web Sites 605
   Andrew Urbaczewski and Leonard M. Jessup
INTRANET APPLICATIONS
54 Developing Corporate Intranets 613
   Diana Jovin
55 Designing a Business-Justified Intranet Project...................623
   Richard L. Ptak
EXTRANET APPLICATIONS
56 Expanding the Reach of Electronic Commerce:
   The Internet EDI Alternative 635
   James A. Senn
57 Implementing and Supporting Extranets..............................649
   Phillip Q. Maier
POLICY AND DEVELOPMENT ISSUES
58 Internet Security and Firewall Policies 661
   William Hugh Murray
59 Implementing the First Web Site...681
   Lee A. Freeman and Leonard M. Jessup
60 Internet Acceptable Usage Policies......................................687
   James E. Gaskin

SECTION 5   FACILITATING KNOWLEDGE WORK 697
SUPPORT FOR END USERS
61 Helping Users Help Themselves 699
   James A. Larson and Carol L. Larson

62 Supporting Telework 707
Heikki Topi
63 Information Sharing Within Organizations 719
Randall H. Russell
CONTROLS FOR USER-DEVELOPED APPLICATIONS
64 End-User Computing Control Guidelines 727
Ron Hale
65 Control Issues in End-User Computing and Applications .. 739
Sandra D. Allen-Senft and Frederick Gallegos
66 Reviewing End-User Applications 749
Steven M. Williford

INDEX 767

Introduction

BY THE END OF THE 1990s, the information technology (IT) industry had become the largest U.S. industry and IT had become an enabling technology in most U.S.-based organizations — permeating nearly all major business activities. Many IT organizations have become agents of change within their own enterprises. Yet according to recent assessments by IT managers, consultants, and academics, much can still be done to improve their effectiveness today and preparedness for tomorrow.

Whether or not you believe that we are now living in the information age, IT-related topics are certainly at the forefront. Indeed, as we enter the new millennium, businesses as well as local, national, and global communities are focused on the operational reliability of computers, networks, and embedded processors. The Year 2000 (Y2K) bug is a part of the vernacular and the layman on the street has become aware of the unprecedented dependence on nonhuman machinery within the industrial society. This is truly an exciting time to be a member of the IT community — but the opportunity exists to become both heroes and scapegoats.

Organizations that have most of their Y2K preparedness behind them, however, are already refocusing on the role of IT as an enabler and sometimes a potential driver — a catalyst for strategic change. Yet along with this strategic IT role comes the challenge of meeting growing expectations by the user community. Many business managers today no longer need to be persuaded about the importance of tracking the capabilities of new types of IT applications or the value of training on personal productivity tools for new hires. Client/server architectures, Web technologies, and network standards are likely to be IT concepts that already have face validity within the top management suite. Yet too few IT organizations have developed the skill sets and expertise to confidently achieve the performance levels required by their information age customers. In some of these organizations, IT may even be viewed as a constraint to competitiveness and the gap between expected and actual IT performance may be significant.

The objective of this edition of the *IS Management Handbook* is to provide a resource that will help you, as a practicing IT manager, develop the IT competencies needed for your organization to exploit the opportunities and navigate around some of the pitfalls of managing IT. Our target audience is not only senior IT leaders but also other members of the IT management team, as well as those who consult on IT management issues.

The five themes addressed by the 66 articles that have been crafted by more than 80 practicing managers, consultants, and academics are briefly introduced next. Readers interested in some guidelines for using the handbook can forward to the end of this "Introduction."

SECTION 1: ACHIEVING STRATEGIC IT ALIGNMENT

IT alignment has been a top management issue for more than a decade. Given the fast-changing business and technology environments as we enter the new millennium, achieving strategic alignment between the IT function and the business is expected to continue to be a top issue. The chapters in this section provide some IT management frameworks, stimulating scenarios, as well as specific guidelines.

The three topics covered in this section are IT leadership roles, strategic IT capabilities, and outsourcing vs. internal provisioning.

SECTION 2: DESIGNING AND OPERATING AN ENTERPRISE INFRASTRUCTURE

The intensifying speed of change in the IT industry has not only increased the importance of IT infrastructure planning but also the complexity of IT operational responsibilities. Designing an enterprise infrastructure today typically requires distributed architectures and involves decisions that affect the firm's IT alignment. The unprecedented dependence on IT applications for business operations has also only heightened the criticality of IT operational decisions. The chapters in this section provide models, guidelines, and advice for infrastructure management, including data warehousing issues.

The five topics covered in this section are distributed computing environments, telecommunications management, data warehousing, quality assurance and control, and security and risk management.

SECTION 3: PROVIDING APPLICATION SOLUTIONS

Today's IT industry offers an increasing array of software development tools and commercial software packages. User organizations are increasingly likely to seek a packaged solution for common functions or processes. Effective IT applications management requires not only a knowledge of systems development methodologies and project management skills, but also an awareness of new types of business applications and techniques. The chapters in this section discuss what's ahead in terms of application solutions, provide guidelines for meeting today's software development and implementation challenges, and offer some basic quality assurance solutions.

The four topics covered in this section are new tools and applications, systems development approaches, project management, and software quality assurance.

SECTION 4: EXPLOITING WEB TECHNOLOGIES

Although Web technologies are still considered to be in their infancy, they have already become a part of the IT architecture of many enterprises. In particular, electronic commerce applications are one of the most exciting IT stories of the second half of the 1990s. Today's IT manager needs to understand the opportunities that Web technologies offer for the development and operation of information systems, both today and tomorrow. The chapters in this section discuss the opportunities and potential pitfalls from today's vantage point.

The four topics covered in this section are E-commerce opportunities and challenges, intranet applications, extranet applications, and policy and development issues.

SECTION 5: FACILITATING KNOWLEDGE WORK

End-user technologies continue to be moving targets, and facilitating the use of these tools by knowledge workers is more critical than ever. An organization's knowledge workers can include savvy computer users who require information access and support both at the desktop and anytime, anywhere, as well as plant managers learning how to use a mouse device and graphical user interface for the first time. The chapters in this section remind us that technical solutions alone are not enough: End-user computing effectiveness typically also requires investments in people and work design solutions.

The two overall topics covered in this section are support for end users and controls for user-developed applications.

HOW TO USE THIS HANDBOOK

The handbook is a resource for those responsible for managing and guiding the planning and use of information technology within organizations, both large and small. Like previous editions, it is written for the practicing IT manager. We think it contains some useful food for thought for senior IT executives in organizations of any size, as well as for those IT managers closer to the trenches. In the past, some IT leaders have used this handbook as a management development tool, sometimes as a source of readings for seminar-style discussions. Among our authors are former CIOs at Fortune 500 companies now in consulting, other practicing IT managers, consultants, and academics who conduct practice-oriented research.

To help our readers find the sections and information nuggets most useful to them, the selected articles have been organized into the above 18 topics under five themes. In the preceding paragraphs we have introduced these themes and pointed you to our topical coverage. This same organization scheme should be evident in our Contents pages.

- For those of you interested in browsing chapters in a particular section or a particular topic, we recommend reading first the section introduction that appears at the beginning of each of the five sections.
- For those of you interested in gleaning specific knowledge about a narrow topical area, we recommend an old-fashioned manual search of our alphabetical subject index at the end of the handbook.

For both new and old readers of the *IS Management Handbook*, we welcome your input! As new editors of the Handbook we have put our own "spin" on both the content and format. We would welcome any feedback you would like to provide to us about the selected topics and organization of this handbook as well as recommendations for potential topics and authors for future editions. (Our contact information is provided below.)

ACKNOWLEDGMENTS

It is a privilege to be tapped for the editorship of the *IS Management Handbook*. We believe that our prior work experiences in the IT field, our experiences as educators seeking to respond to the curriculum needs of senior IT executives, and our experiences as researchers tracking industry trends and identifying best practices for IT management have prepared us well for this editorial challenge.

Our thanks to the many authors who responded to our requests for new material and our editorial critiques. We hope that all authors are delighted with the end product to which they have contributed. Each chapter in the handbook has been reviewed by us multiple times in pursuit of currency, accuracy, and presentation clarity.

Special thanks are due to the publisher, Richard O'Hanley, who has shepherded us through the process via telephone and electronic communications and trustingly waited for the first fruits of this new collaboration.

As we complete our writing of this "Introduction," the IT community is faced with not only the opportunity to be at the forefront of IT innovation and development worldwide but also a global IT work force shortage. We encourage our readers not only to invest in the development of their current IT work force, but also to participate in local, regional, and national initiatives to better secure the future by increasing the IT talent pipeline.

CAROL V. BROWN	HEIKKI TOPI	BLOOMINGTON, IN
cbrown@iupui.edu	hetopi@indiana.edu	JUNE 1999

Section 1
Achieving Strategic IT Alignment

For more than a decade, achieving strategic alignment between the IS organization and the business has been a top IS management issue. Today's hypercompetitive business environments only heighten the need for strategic alignment to be the top goal of IS management. But strategic IT alignment cannot be achieved through a periodic planning process; it needs to be an ongoing goal. It also requires highly effective IT leaders.

IT LEADERSHIP ROLES

We begin this new section of the Handbook with four chapters that address today's (and tomorrow's) IT leadership roles. In a global world, powerful, flexible IT infrastructures are a prerequisite for doing business. Chapter 1, "The New Enabling Role of the IT Infrastructure," describes the four key elements of an IT infrastructure and three partnership processes to recreate an IT infrastructure for an IT-dependent, wired world. This research is based on fifteen contemporary case studies, including many leading organizations.

Chapter 2, "Partnering Roles of the IS Executive," describes a model of four different IT leadership roles. Two transactional leadership roles are required for operational and organizational excellence; the two transformational roles are required for technology innovation and enterprise reengineering. The authors highlight the need for IT leaders to build and sustain strong partnering relationships with not only internal customers and top management but also strategic vendors and leaders in the IT industry.

The remaining two chapters look ahead to tomorrow. Knowledge management (KM) has become one of the hottest business buzzwords as we enter the new millennium. Chapter 3, "Knowledge Management–Coming Up the Learning Curve," defines what this trend means for IS leaders and discusses the organizational barriers. Examples of best practices are shared via three mini-case descriptions of KM initiatives in leading manufacturing and service companies.

1

The final chapter on IT leadership issues, "The CIO Role in the Era of Dislocation," is intended to stimulate your thinking about what lies ahead for the IT industry, IS professionals, and you. Based on insights as a former CIO and now a consultant with access to leading thinkers, the author paints his own picture of the coming landscape and what it means for the CIO role. He challenges IT leaders to ensure that their own organizations are among the survivors in a new era of pervasive computing and dislocating technologies.

STRATEGIC IT CAPABILITIES

As we enter this new information age, what strategic IT capabilities are needed?

Strategic IS planning capabilities are the focus of the first three chapters. Chapter 5, "The IS Executive and Strategic Planning," describes an integrated IS and business planning process and the IS executive's role. The following chapter, "Integrated Systems Planning: A Holistic Model," describes an IS strategic planning model that integrates business process reengineering (BPR) and total quality management (TQM) initiatives. Several success stories using this holistic model are also presented. Both of these chapters emphasize the critical role of senior IS managers. In contrast, the critical role played by line managers in strategic IT initiatives is the focus of Chapter 7, "Strategic Information Technology and the Line Manager's Role."

As the introduction of new technologies has accelerated over the past decade, IS organizations have developed a capability to effectively bring in new emerging technologies. How to introduce and nurture new technologies in business organizations is the thrust of the Chapter 8, "Managing Advanced Information Technology." As the author warns, the tracking and acquisition of new technologies needs to be in alignment with both technology strategy and business strategy.

The final three chapters in this section focus on a strategic IT capability no organization today can afford to overlook: how to build, retain, and allocate skilled human resources for today's and tomorrow's IT work. Chapter 9, "Moving the IT Work Force to a Client/Server Environment," offers specific tactics for moving a mainframe-based work force to a client/server environment. How to reposition the IS organization to better exploit its strategic IS resources is the focus of Chapter 10, "Redesigning the IT Organization for the Information Age." A design solution based on centers of competency — groups of employees with a logically related set of skills — that produce and sell products and services within an internal marketplace is argued to be the best way for an IT organization to fulfill its strategic potential.

Increasing the global supply of IT professionals is an issue being addressed today by governments and businesses alike. For those organizations experiencing an IT work force shortage, Chapter 11, "Successfully Hiring and Retaining IT Personnel," provides a welcome success story.

OUTSOURCING VS. INTERNAL PROVISIONING

The topic of this section has received increasing attention in prior editions of this Handbook: the internal versus external provisioning choices, with a focus on outsourcing issues. All the chapters provide evidence that IS outsourcing is a reality in today's world. Some chapters focus on improving the performance of the IS organization to make good selective outsourcing decisions; others focus on how to manage outsourcing relationships and contracts. For those readers with new dependencies on major software package vendors, such as the providers of enterprise resource planning systems, successfully managing such contracts is of critical importance.

The authors of the first two chapters in this section argue that dissatisfaction with the performance of the internal IS unit is the single most common reason for turning to an outsourcing vendor. In Chapter 12, "Preparing for the Outsourcing Challenge," useful guidelines are provided for preventing a bad outsourcing decision. The author describes how to improve perceptions of strategic value and details some methods to help ensure fair service and cost comparisons between internal staff and outsourcing vendors. Chapter 13, "IT Performance Turnaround: The Outsourcing Alternative," focuses on how to assess the need for, gain buy-in to, and launch an IT performance turnaround.

The remaining three chapters provide detailed suggestions for managing outsourcing situations. The outsourcing of desktop support services is the focus of Chapter 14, "Support Services Outsourcing." A process model for IT procurement developed by a Society for Information Management working group is described in Chapter 15, "Managing the IT Procurement Process."

Chapter 16, "Control of Information Systems Outsourcing," begins with a succinct recap of the primary drivers for outsourcing and the selective outsourcing option and then turns to a discussion of the key components of outsourcing agreements from an IS management perspective. As the author points out, IS outsourcing does not mean the abdication of responsibility, and good contractual agreements are the first step toward effective IS management of outsourcing arrangements.

Chapter 1
The New Enabling Role of the IT Infrastructure

Jeanne W. Ross
John F. Rockart

RECENTLY, some large companies have made some very large investments in their information technology (IT) infrastructures. For example:

- Citicorp invested over $750 million for a new global database system.
- Dow Corning and most other Fortune 500 companies invested tens of millions of dollars or more to purchase and install enterprisewide resource planning systems.
- Johnson & Johnson broke with tradition by committing corporate funds to help its individual operating companies acquire standard desktop equipment.
- Statoil presented all 15,000 of its employees with a high-end computer for home or office use.

At firms all over the world senior executives in a broad cross-section of industries are investing their time and money to shore up corporate infrastructures. In the past, many of these same executives had, in effect, given their IT units a generous allowance and admonished them to spend it wisely. Now, in contrast, they are engaging in intense negotiations over network capabilities, data standards, IT architectures, and IT funding limits. The difficulty of assessing the value of an IT infrastructure, coupled with technical jargon and business uncertainties, has made these conversations uncomfortable for most executives, to say the least. But the recognition that global markets are creating enormous demands for increased information sharing within and across firms has led to the realization that a powerful, flexible IT infrastructure has become a prerequisite for doing business.

The capabilities built into an infrastructure can either limit or enhance a firm's ability to respond to market conditions (Davenport and Linder,

0-8493-9820-7/00/$0.00+$.50
© 2000 by CRC Press LLC

1993). To target a firm's strategic priorities, senior executives must shepherd the development of the infrastructure (Broadbent and Weill, 1997). Sadly, most senior executives do not feel qualified to do so. As one CEO described it: "I've been reading on IT, but I'm terrified. It's the one area where I don't feel competent."

New infrastructure technologies are enabling new organizational forms and, in the process, creating a competitive environment that increasingly demands both standardization for cost-effectiveness and customization for responsiveness. Most firms' infrastructures are not capable of addressing these requirements. Accordingly, firms are ripping out their old infrastructures in an attempt to provide features such as fast networks, easily accessible data, integrated supply chain applications, and reliable desktop support. At the firms that appear to be weathering this transition most successfully, senior management is leading the charge.

Over the past three years, we have done in-depth studies of the development of the IT infrastructure at 15 major firms. We have examined their changing market conditions and business imperatives, and we have observed how they have recreated their IT infrastructures to meet these demands. This chapter reports on our observations and develops a framework for thinking about IT infrastructure development. It first defines IT infrastructure and its role in organizations. It then describes how some major corporations are planning, building, and leveraging new infrastructures. Finally, it describes the roles of senior, IT, and line managers in ensuring the development of a value-adding IT infrastructure.

WHAT IS AN IT INFRASTRUCTURE?

Traditionally, the IT infrastructure consisted primarily of an organization's data center, which supported mainframe transaction processing. (See Exhibit 1.1.) Effectiveness was assessed in terms of reliability and efficiency in processing transactions and storing vast amounts of data. Running a data center was not very mysterious, and most large organizations became good at it. Consequently, although the data center was mission critical at most large organizations, it was not strategic.

Some companies, such as Frito-Lay (Mead and Linder, 1987) and Otis Elevator (McFarlan and Stoddard, 1986), benefited from a particularly clear vision of the value of this infrastructure and converted transaction processing data into decision-making information. But even these exemplary infrastructures supported traditional organizational structures, consolidating data for hierarchical decision-making purposes. IT infrastructures in the data center era tended to reinforce existing organizational forms rather than enable entirely new ones.

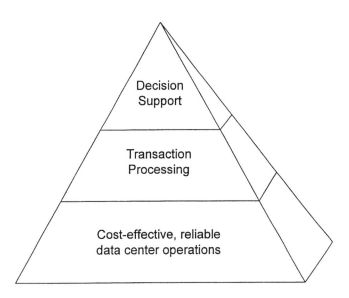

Exhibit 1.1. The role of IT infrastructure in traditional firms

In the current distributed processing era, the IT infrastructure has become the set of IT services shared across business units (Broadbent and Weill, 1997). Typically, these services include mainframe processing, network management, messaging services, data management, and systems security. While still expected to deliver reliable, efficient transaction processing, the IT infrastructure must also deliver capabilities, such as facilitating intraorganizational communications, providing ready access to data, integrating business processes, and establishing customer linkages.

Delivering capabilities through IT infrastructure is much more difficult than managing a data center. Part of the challenge is technological because many of the individual components are immature, making them both unreliable and difficult to integrate. The bigger challenge, however, is organizational, because process integration requires that individuals change how they do their jobs and, in most cases, how they think about them.

CHANGING ORGANIZATIONAL FORMS AND THE ROLE OF INFRASTRUCTURE

Historically, most organizations could be characterized as either centralized or decentralized in their organizational structures. While centralization and decentralization were viewed as essentially opposite organizational structures, they were, in fact, different manifestations of hierarchical structures in which decisions made at the top of the organization were carried out at lower levels. (See Exhibit 1.2.) Decentralized

Decentralized   Centralized

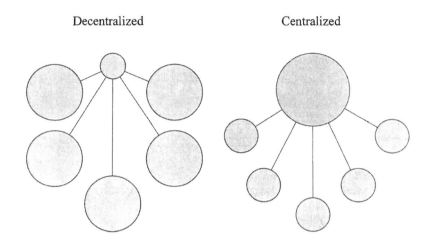

Exhibit 1.2. Traditional organizational models

organizations differed from centralized in that more decision making was pushed down the hierarchy but communication patterns were still vertical and decisions involving two business units were usually made at a higher level, so that business units rarely recognized any interdependencies.Centralization and decentralization posed significant trade-offs in terms of their costs and benefits. Simply stated, centralization offered economies of scale while decentralization allowed firms to be more responsive to individual customers. Thus, the degree to which any firm was centralized or decentralized depended on which of these benefits offered the most value. As global markets have forced firms to speed up decision making and to simultaneously recognize both the global scope of their customers and their unique demands, firms have found it increasingly important to garner the benefits of both centralization and decentralization simultaneously. Johnson & Johnson and Schneider National demonstrate how firms are addressing this challenge.

Johnson & Johnson

For almost 100 years Johnson & Johnson (J&J), a global consumer and health care company, achieved success as a decentralized firm (Ross, 1995a). Both J&J management and external analysts credited the autonomy of the firm's approximately 160 operating companies with stimulating innovation and growth. In the late 1980s, however, top management observed that a new breed of customer was emerging, and those customers had no patience for the multiple salespersons, invoices, and shipments characteristic of doing business with multiple J&J companies. For example, executives at Wal-Mart, the most powerful of the US retailers, noted that J&J companies were sending as many as 17 different account representatives in a single month. In the future, Wal-Mart mandated, J&J should send just one.

In response, J&J created customer teams to service each of its largest multibusiness accounts. The teams consolidated data on sales, distribution, accounts receivable, and customer service from the operating companies and presented a single face to the customer. Initially, much of the reconciliation among the businesses required manipulating spreadsheets populated with manually entered data. Ultimately, it meant that J&J would introduce complex structural changes that would link its independent operating companies through franchise management, regional organizations, and market-focused umbrella companies.

Schneider National

In contrast, Schneider National, following deregulation of the U.S. trucking industry in 1980, relied on a highly centralized organizational structure to become one of the country's most successful trucking companies. Schneider leveraged its efficient mainframe environment, innovative operations models, centralized databases, and, later, satellite tracking capabilities to provide its customers with on-time service at competitive prices. By the early 1990s, however, truckload delivery had become a commodity. Intense price competition convinced Schneider management that it would be increasingly difficult to grow sales and profits.

Schneider responded by moving aggressively into third-party logistics, taking on the transportation management function of large manufacturing companies (Ross, 1995b). To succeed in this market, management recognized the need to organize around customer-focused teams where operating decisions were made at the customer interface. To make this work, Schneider installed some of its systems and people at customer sites, provided customer interface teams with powerful desktop machines to localize customer support, and increasingly bought services from competitors to meet the demands of its customers.

Pressures toward Federalist Forms

These two firms are rather dramatic examples of a phenomenon that most large firms are encountering. New customer demands and global competition require that business firms combine the cost efficiency and tight integration afforded by centralized structures with the creativity and customer intimacy afforded by decentralized structures. Consequently, many firms are adopting "federalist" structures (Handy, 1992) in which they push out much decision making to local sites. In federalist firms, individuals at the customer interface become accountable for meeting customer needs, while the corporate unit evolves to become the "core" rather than headquarters. (See Exhibit 1.3.) The role of the core unit in these firms

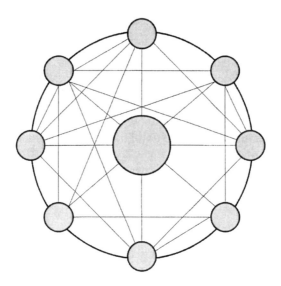

Exhibit 1.3. Federalist organizational model

is to specify and develop the core competencies that enable the firm to foster a unique identity and generate economies of scale (Hamel and Prahalad, 1990; Stalk, Evans, and Shulman, 1992).

Federalist firms require much more horizontal decision making to apply shared expertise to complex problems and to permit shared resources among interdependent business units (Quinn, 1992). Rather than relying on hierarchical processes to coordinate the interdependencies of teams, these firms utilize shared goals, dual reporting relationships, incentive systems that recognize competing objectives, and common processes (Handy, 1992). Management techniques such as these require greatly increased information sharing in organizations, and it is the IT infrastructure that is expected to enable the necessary information sharing. However, an edict to increase information sharing does not, in itself, enable effective horizontal processes. To ensure that investments in information technology generate the anticipated benefits, IT infrastructure must become a top management issue.

ELEMENTS OF INFRASTRUCTURE MANAGEMENT

At the firms in our study we observed four key elements in the design and implementation of the IT infrastructure: organizational systems and processes, infrastructure services, the IT architecture, and corporate strategy. These build on one another (as shown in Exhibit 1.4) such that corporate strategy provides the basis for establishment of the architecture

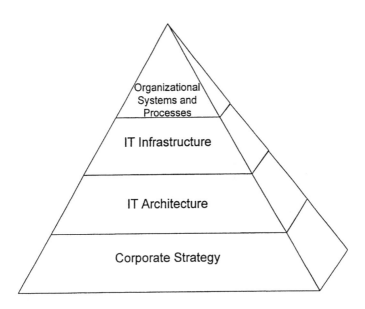

Exhibit 1.4. The IT infrastructure pyramid

while the architecture guides decisions on the infrastructure, which provides the foundation for the organizational systems and processes.

Corporate Strategy

The starting point for designing and implementing an effective infrastructure is the corporate strategy. The strategy defines the firm's key competencies and how the firm will deliver them to customers. Many large decentralized firms such as J&J have traditionally had general corporate strategies that defined a firm-wide mission and financial performance goals, but they allowed individual business units to define their own strategies for meeting customer needs. In the global economy these firms are focusing on developing firm-wide strategies for addressing global customer demands and responding to global competition.

For purposes of developing the IT infrastructure, senior management must have an absolutely clear vision of how the organization will deliver on its core competencies. General statements of financial and marketing goals do not provide the necessary precision to develop a blueprint for the foundation that will enable new organizational processes. The necessary vision is a process vision in which senior management actually "roughs out" the steps involved in key decision-making and operational processes.

Based on a clear vision of how it would service customers, Federal Express developed its Powership product, which allows any customer — be it an individual or a major corporation — to electronically place and track an order. Similarly, JC Penney's internal management support system evolved from a clear vision of the process by which store managers would make decisions about inventory and sales strategies. This process included an understanding of how individual store managers could learn from one another's experiences. Such a clear vision of how the firm will function provides clear prescriptions for the IT infrastructure.

A corporate strategy that articulates key processes is absolutely essential for designing an IT infrastructure because otherwise neither IT nor business management can define priorities. The vision peels back corporate complexities so that the infrastructure is built around simple, core processes. This peeling provides a solid foundation that can adapt to the dynamics of the business environment.

Some firms have attempted to compensate for a lack of clarity in corporate goals by spending more money on their infrastructures. Rather than determining what kinds of communications they most need to enable, they invest in state-of-the-art technologies that should allow them to communicate with "anyone, anytime, anywhere." Rather than determining what data standards are most crucial for meeting immediate customer needs, they attempt to design all-encompassing data models. This approach to infrastructure building is expensive and generally not fruitful. Money is not a good substitute for direction.

IT Architecture

The development of an IT architecture involves converting the corporate strategy into a technology plan. It defines both the key capabilities required from the technology infrastructure and the places where the technologies, the management responsibility, and the support will be located. Drawing on the vision of the core operating and decision-making processes, the IT architecture identifies what data must be standardized corporate-wide and what will be standardized at a regional level. It then specifies where data will be located and how they will be accessed. Similarly, the architecture differentiates between processes that must be standardized across locations and processes that must be integrated.

The architecture debate is a critical one for most companies because the natural tendency, where needed capabilities are unclear, is to assume that extensive technology and data standards and firm-wide implementation of common systems will prepare the firm for any eventuality. In other words, standard setting serves as a substitute for architecture. Standards and common systems support many kinds of cross-business integration and provide economies of scale by permitting central support of technologies. However, unnecessary standards and common systems limit business unit flexibility, create resistance and possibly ill will during implementation, prove difficult to sustain, and are expensive to implement.

The elaboration of the architecture should help firms distinguish between capabilities that are competitive necessities and those that offer strategic advantage. It guides decisions on trade-offs between reliability and state-of-the art, between function and cost, and between buying and building. Capabilities recognized as strategic are those for which a firm can justify using state-of-the-art technologies, de-emphasizing standards in favor of function, and building rather than buying.

IT Infrastructure

Although firms' architectures are orderly plans of the capabilities that their infrastructures should provide, infrastructures themselves tend to be in a constant state of upheaval. At many firms key elements of the IT infrastructure have been in place for 20 to 30 years. Part of the infrastructure rebuilding process is recognizing that the fast pace of business change means that such enduring infrastructure components will be less common.

Architectures evolve slowly in response to major changes in business needs and technological capabilities, but infrastructures are implemented in pieces with each change introducing the opportunity for more change. Moreover, because infrastructures are the base on which many individual systems are built, changes to the infrastructure often disrupt an uneasy equilibrium. For example, as firms implement enterprisewide systems, they often temporarily replace automated processes with manual processes (Ross, 1997a). They may need to construct temporary bridges between systems as they deliver individual pieces of large, integrated systems or foundation databases. Some organizations have tried to avoid the chaos created by temporary fixes by totally replacing big pieces of infrastructure at one time. But infrastructure implementations require time for organizational learning as the firm adapts to new capabilities. "Big bang" approaches to infrastructure implementations are extremely risky. Successful companies often rely on incremental changes to move them toward their defined architectures, minimizing the number of major changes that they must absorb.

For example, Travelers Property & Casualty grasped the value of incremental implementations while developing its object-oriented infrastructure. In attempting to reuse some early objects, developers sometimes had to reengineer existing objects because new applications clarified their conceptualizations. But developers at Travelers note that had they waited to develop objects until they had perfected the model, they never would have implemented anything (Ross, 1997c). Stopping, starting, and even backing up are part of the learning process inherent in building an infrastructure.

Organizational Systems and Processes

Traditionally, organizations viewed their key systems and processes from a functional perspective. Managers developed efficiencies and sought continuous improvement within the sales and marketing, manufacturing, and finance functions, and slack resources filled the gaps between the functions. New technological capabilities and global markets have emphasized three very different processes: (1) supply chain integration, (2) customer and supplier linkages, and (3) leveraging of organizational learning and experience.

For many manufacturing firms, supply chain integration is the initial concern. To be competitive they must remove the excess cost and time between the placement of an order and the delivery of the product and receipt of payment. The widespread purchase of all-encompassing enterprisewide resource planning (ERP) systems is testament to both the perceived importance of supply chain integration to these firms and the conviction that their existing infrastructures are inadequate. Supply chain integration requires a tight marriage between organizational processes and information systems. An ERP provides the scaffolding for global integration, but a system cannot be implemented until management can describe the process apart from the technology.

At the same time, firms are recognizing the emergence of new channels for doing business with both customers and suppliers. Where technology allows faster or better customer service, firms are innovating rapidly. Thus being competitive means gaining enough organizational experience to be able to leverage such technologies as electronic data interchange and the World Wide Web and sometimes even installing and supporting homegrown systems at customers' sites.

Finally, many firms are looking for ways to capture and leverage organizational learning. As distributed employees attempt to customize a firm's core competencies for individual customers, they can increase their effectiveness if they can learn from the firm's accumulated experiences. The technologies for storing and retrieving these experiences are at hand, but the processes for making that happen are still elusive.

Firms that adapt and improve on these three processes can be expected to outperform their competitors. It is clear that to do so will require a unique combination of a visionary senior management team, a proactive IT unit, and a resourceful work force. Together they can iteratively build, evaluate, redesign, and enhance their processes and supporting systems.

IMPLEMENTING AND SUSTAINING THE INFRASTRUCTURE

It is clear that the top and bottom layers of the IT pyramid are primarily the responsibility of business managers, whereas the middle layers are the

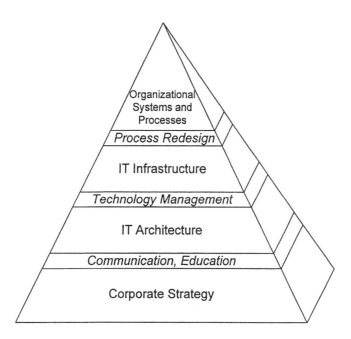

Organizational
Systems and
Processes

Process Redesign

IT Infrastructure

Technology Management

IT Architecture

Communication, Education

Corporate Strategy

Exhibit 1.5. Partnership processes in infrastructure development

responsibility of IT managers. Three partnership processes provide the glue between the layers as shown in Exhibit 1.5.

Communication and Education

The process of moving from a strategy to an IT architecture involves mutual education of senior business and IT managers. Traditional approaches to education, such as lectures, courses, conferences, and readings, are all useful. Most important, however, is that management schedules IT-business contact time in which the focus of the discussion is business strategy and IT capability. For example, at Schneider Logistics, senior business managers meet formally with IT managers for two hours each week. This allows IT management to identify opportunities while senior management specifies priorities and targets IT resources accordingly.

Thus, the IT architecture debate is a discussion among senior managers with insights and advice from the IT unit. Senior management articulates evolving strategies for organizational processes, whereas IT clarifies capabilities of the technologies. A key role of IT becomes one of explaining the potential costs of new capabilities. Typical return-on-investment computations are often not meaningful in discussions of infrastructure development, but senior managers need to know the size of an investment and the accompanying annual support costs for new capabilities before they commit to large infrastructure investments.

To avoid getting bogged down in arguments over who would pay for new capabilities, some firms have made "speed bump" investments. Texas Instruments (TI), for example, traditionally funded infrastructure by attaching the cost of incremental infrastructure requirements to the application development project that initiated the need. But when the corporate network proved inadequate for a host of capabilities, senior management separately funded the investment (Ross, 1997b). In this way TI avoided the inherent delays that result from investing in infrastructure only when the business units can see specific benefits that warrant their individual votes in favor of additional corporate taxes.

Technology Management

Moving from the architecture to the infrastructure involves making technology choices. Senior managers need not be involved in discussions of the technologies themselves as long as they understand the approximate costs and risks of introducing new capabilities. Instead, core IT works with local IT or business liaisons who can discuss the implications of technology choices. Selecting specific technologies for the corporate infrastructure involves setting standards. Local IT staff must understand those choices so that they can, on the one hand, comply with standards and, on the other hand, communicate any negative impacts of those choices.

Standards will necessarily limit the range of technologies that corporate IT will support. This enables the IT unit to develop expertise in key technologies and limits the costs of supporting the IT infrastructure. However, some business units have unique needs that corporate standards do not address. Negotiation between corporate and local IT managers should allow them to recognize when deviations from standards can enhance business unit operations without compromising corporate-wide goals. IT units that clearly understand their costs have an edge in managing technologies because they are able to discuss with business managers the value of adherence to standards and the trade-offs inherent in noncompliance (Ross, Vitale, and Beath, 1997).

Process Redesign

Although the infrastructure can enable new organizational forms and processes, the implementation of those new processes is dependent on the joint efforts of business unit and IT management. Successful process redesign demands that IT and business unit management share responsibility and accountability for such processes as implementing common systems, establishing appropriate customer linkages, defining requirements for knowledge management, and even supporting desktop technologies. The

16

joint accountability is critical to successful implementation because the IT unit can only provide the tools. Business unit management needs to provide the vision and leadership for implementing the redesigned processes (Davenport, 1992).

Many process changes are wrenching. In one firm we studied autonomous general managers lost responsibility for manufacturing in order to enable global rationalization of production. Initially, these managers felt they had been demoted to sales managers. A fast-food firm closed the regional offices from which the firm had audited and supported local restaurants. Regional managers reorganized into cross-functional teams and, armed with portable computers, took to the road to spend their time visiting local sites. In these and other firms changes rarely unfolded as expected. In most cases, major process changes take longer to implement, demand more resources, and encounter more resistance than management expects.

IMPLICATIONS OF INFRASTRUCTURE REBUILDING

We observed significant obstacles to organizations' attempts to build IT infrastructures to enable new federalist structures. Most of the changes these firms were implementing involved some power shifts, which led to political resistance. Even more difficult to overcome, however, was the challenge of clarifying the firm's strategic vision and defining IT priorities. This process proved to be highly iterative. Senior management would articulate a vision and then IT management would work through the apparent technological priorities that the strategy implied. IT could then estimate time, cost, and both capabilities and limitations. This would normally lead to an awareness that the strategy was not clear enough to formulate an IT architecture. When the organization had the necessary fortitude, management would continue to iterate the strategy and architecture, but most abandoned the task midstream and the IT unit was left trying to establish priorities and implement an architecture that lacked clear management support. This would lead either to expensive efforts to install an infrastructure that met all possible needs or to limited investment in infrastructure that was not strategically aligned with the business (Henderson and Venkatraman, 1993).

Although it is difficult to hammer out a clear architecture based on corporate strategy and then incrementally install an IT infrastructure that supports redesigned organizational processes, the benefits appear to be worth the effort. At Travelers, the early adoption of an object environment has helped it retain a high-quality IT staff and allowed it to anticipate and respond to changing market opportunities. Johnson & Johnson's development of a corporate-wide infrastructure has allowed it to address global cost pressures and to respond to the demands of global customers. Senior management sponsorship of global systems implementations at Dow Corning has enabled the firm to meet due dates for implementation and anticipate potential process redesign.

As firms look for opportunities to develop competitive advantage, they find it is rarely possible to do so through technological innovations (Clark, 1989). However, the firms in this study were attempting to develop infrastructures that positioned them to implement new processes faster and more cost effectively than their competitors. This kind of capability is valuable, rare, and difficult for competitors to imitate. Thus, it offers the potential for long-term competitive advantage (Collis and Montgomery, 1995). Rebuilding an infrastructure is a slow process. Firms that wait to see how others fare in their efforts may reduce their chances for having the opportunity to do so.

Notes

Broadbent, M., and Weill, P. 1997. Management by maxim: How business and IT managers can create IT infrastructures. *Sloan Management Review* 38(3): 77–92.

Clark, K.B. 1989. What strategy can do for technology. *Harvard Business Review* (November–December): 94–98.

Collis, D.J., and Montgomery, C.A. 1995. Competing on resources: Strategy in the 1990s. *Harvard Business Review* 73 (July-August): 118–129.

Davenport, T.H. 1992. *Process innovation: Reengineering work through information technology.* Boston: Harvard Business School Press.

Davenport, T.H., and Linder, J. 1993. Information management infrastructure: The new competitive weapon? Ernst & Young Center for Business Innovation Working Paper CITA33.

Hamel, G., and Prahalad, C.K. 1990. The Core Competence of the Corporation, *Harvard Business Review* 68 (May-June).

Handy, C. 1992. Balancing corporate power: A new federalist paper. *Harvard Business Review* 70 (November-December): 59–72.

Henderson, J.C., and Venkatraman, N. 1993. Strategic alignment: Leveraging information technology for transforming organizations. *IBM Systems Journal* 32(1): 4–16.

McFarlan, F.W., and Stoddard, D.B. 1986. Otisline. Harvard Business School Case No. 9-186-304.

Mead, M., and Linder, J. 1987. Frito-Lay, Inc.: A strategic transition. Harvard Business School Case No. 9-187-065.

Quinn, J.B. 1992. *Intelligent enterprise: A knowledge and service paradigm for industry.* New York: Free Press.

Ross, J.W. 1995a. Johnson & Johnson: Building an infrastructure to support global operations. CISR Working Paper No. 283.

Ross, J. W. 1995b. Schneider National, Inc.: Building networks to add customer value. CISR Working Paper No. 285.

Ross, J.W. 1997a. Dow Corning: Business processes and information technology. CISR Working Paper No. 298.

Ross, J.W. 1997b. Texas Instruments: Service levels agreements and cultural change. CISR Working Paper No. 299.

Ross, J.W. 1997c. The Travelers: Building an object environment. CISR Working Paper No. 301.

Ross, J.W., Vitale, M.R., and Beath, C.M. 1997. The untapped potential of IT chargeback. CISR Working Paper No. 300.

Stalk, G., Evans, P., and Schulman, L.E. 1992. Competing on Capabilities: The new rules of corporate strategy. *Harvard Business Review* 70 (March-April): 57–69.

Chapter 2
Partnering Roles of the IS Executive

Carol V. Brown
Ephraim R. McLean
Detmar W. Straub

IS PARTNERING — the formation of linkages with managers both internal and external to the IS department — is critical to effective leadership in today's strategically focused organizations. This chapter discusses the leadership and partnering roles essential to IS managers as well as to an ideal IS management team.

Partnering relationships are increasingly being recognized as a critical component of IS leadership. The trend toward sharing the ownership and management of systems projects with line management, begun in the 1980s, is expected to continue. In addition, the recent trends toward increased outsourcing, inter-organizational systems, and strategic vendor alliances point to an expanded group of partners, both within and outside of the organization.

This new emphasis on IS partnering parallels some of the evolutionary changes in the nature of the IS organization itself. During the past two decades, the role of IS has changed from providing back-office support to becoming a prove valued asset, viewed by many organizations as a key part of their strategic competency. A similar change can be seen in the role of IS managers. Early in the evolution of business computing, many IS managers believed that their role was simply to manage the technology itself. Their job, it was assumed, was to ensure that the technology performed efficiently and that the engines of production were as reliable as possible. To be sure, several mission-critical application systems were developed in this era; but because the primary focus of IS was on operating hardware and completing software projects on time and within budget, few IS managers saw the need to venture too far outside of the IS department.

0-8493-9820-7/00/$0.00+$.50
© 2000 by CRC Press LLC

Today, however, there is growing realization that IS managers and professionals need to forge linkages with managers in other parts of the firm, as well as with strategic vendors, consultants, and others external to the firm to optimize the utilization of the information resource. This phenomenon is IS partnering.

This chapter discusses the forms that internal and external IS partnerships can take. First, it presents a model of the types of leadership and roles necessary to today's IS management. It then discusses the ingredients of successful partnering relationships and the four partnering roles crucial to effective IS leadership.

AN IS LEADERSHIP MODEL

A recent model of IS leadership roles delineates two distinctive yet complementary types of leadership: transactional leadership and transformational leadership. Transactional leadership is concerned with coping with complexity through planning and budgeting, organizing and staffing, controlling and problem solving. Without good transactional leadership, complex enterprises tend to become chaotic in ways that threaten their existence. On the other hand, transformational leadership is concerned with coping with change through setting direction, aligning people to a vision of an alternative future, and empowering and motivating them to meet the challenges created by the vision. Both types of leadership are essential for managing today's IS functions: transactional leadership to produce stability and efficiency and transformational leadership to produce innovation and effectiveness.

Exhibit 2.1 presents a graphical representation of this IS leadership model. The vertical axis depicts the environmental dimension (i.e., the business climate). Transactional leadership is most often associated with stable, static environments, while transformational leadership is associated with more dynamic and turbulent environments.

The horizontal axis of the model captures the second dimension, one that has posed a challenge for IS managers for more than a decade: how to provide both technology and organizational leadership. For example, much has been written about the IS human resource challenge of selecting, developing, and motivating IS personnel to develop needed technology and business skills — whether individually or in project teams. Many senior IS executives face a similar dilemma as chief information officers (CIOs); they must balance the roles of general manager and information technology specialist.

The IS leadership model suggests that four IS leadership roles are essential for success in today's strategically focused organizations: technologist, enabler, innovator, and strategist. IS leaders must play both transactional

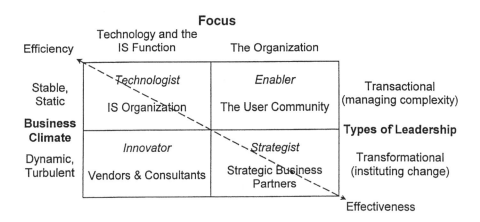

Exhibit 2.1. A Model of IS Leadership Roles. Source: E.R. McLean and S.J. Smits, "The IS Leader as Innovator," Proceedings of the Twenty-Fifth Hawaii International Conference on Systems Sciences IV (January 1993), pp. 352-358.

(complexity) and transformational (change) roles simultaneously to meet the organization's needs for efficiency and effectiveness, for stability and innovation. The four roles are therefore viewed as interdependent, although mastery of the transactional roles is a prerequisite for success in the transformational roles.

The model also suggests that although individuals may assume varying roles as they move along a career path to the role of strategist, the IS organization as a whole should have strengths in all of the roles. In other words, the model sketches out the profile of an ideal IS management team that can lead the firm in both stable and dynamic environments and in internal and external relationships. At any point in time, a given firm may stress one or another of the roles in its team profile, but some strength in all the roles ensures that the firm will be able to cope regardless of what the future holds.

IS PARTNERING RELATIONSHIPS

Today's IS managers, then, must be effective technological and organizational leaders in both stable and turbulent environments. But, to achieve this success, IS managers must be able to develop and sustain partnering relationships with other managers both internal and external to the IS department. Partnering does not refer to the intra-organizational relationships mandated by organizational reporting structures or to the inter-organizational relationships described in formal contractual agreements with outside suppliers or consultants. Rather, the focus is on cooperative, interpersonal relationships that are built and sustained by IS managers outside of the traditional hierarchical reporting arrangements and outside of inter-organizational contractual agreements.

Furthermore, there are at least three important ingredients for building and sustaining such IS partnering relationships.

Mutual Benefits

First, a partnership must be perceived as providing mutual benefits. External partnerships are formed with an expectation of a win-win outcome: both partners perceive benefits for their own organizations. This is because each partner holds expertise or offers resources that are not possessed by the other partner. Similarly, internal business IS partnerships imply a win-win outcome for both organizational stakeholders, as well as for the company as a whole.

Cooperation and Trust

Second, partnerships require cooperation and trust between the partners. In the case of new partnerships or new organizational players, trust may initially be based on perceived expertise and credibility of the partner owing to a past track record unrelated to the partnership. However, to sustain a partnership, trust between the players must grow based on the track record of the partnership itself.

Commitment

Third, commitment to the partnership must be perceived over some extended period of time. Successful partnerships take time to be nurtured and developed. Each partner must assume a measure of responsibility and accountability and be committed to sustaining the relationship over a long enough period of time to achieve the expected benefits for both partners.

FOUR FORMS OF IS PARTNERSHIPS

The IS leadership model suggests that four forms of IS partnering relationships are critical to effective IS leadership (see Exhibit 2.2). The two transactional management roles focus on relationships among the technology providers within the organization and with the user community. In the two transformational management roles, the emphasis changes to internal and external IS partnering roles that facilitate innovative reengineering initiatives.

The Technologist

The technologist role is concerned with technology leadership. The objective of this role is to develop a stable, reliable infrastructure and to promote organizational efficiencies. In earlier days when mainframes

	Leadership Roles	Partners	Leadership Focus	Anticipated Benefits
Transactional Roles	Technologist	IS providers throughout the organization	Technology excellence and reliability	Effective coordination among IS providers; shared expertise
	Enabler	User and line management	Organizational effectiveness	Applications responsive to customer needs
Transformational Roles	Innovator	Vendors, outsourcers, and consultants	Technological Innovations	Leading-edge applications of IT; renovation of the IS function
	Strategist	Top management and corporate customers and partners	Business reengineering	Information systems to support business process reengineering; competitive advantage

Exhibit 2.2. Four Forms of IS Partnering

dominated the environment, this responsibility was solely the domain of the corporate IS function; little "serious" computing occurred outside of the central IS department.

Now, all this has changed. In companies such as Hughes Aircraft and IBM, less than 20% of the total IS activity has been under the direct control of the corporate IS director. Whether these other IS providers fall under the rubric of divisional computing (and the emerging title of DIO — divisional information officer) or end-user computing, the corporate IS executive must now learn to partner with them. Senior corporate management looks to the CIO to provide leadership in all matters pertaining to information technology — but does not provide the CIO the authority to mandate compliance to this leadership vision. The only way the IS executive can ensure a broad-based success for the organization's use of IT is by engendering a close partnership with these various IS providers.

The Enabler

The enabler is concerned with organizational leadership and responsiveness to the firm's internal customers. The critical partnering relationships here are with the user community. The goal is to create and maintain a climate conducive to point responsibility and accountability for systems development initiatives. For example, line managers need to be encouraged to become the champions and sponsors for new systems projects by taking a formal role in the management of the project. These cross-functional partnerships require a mutual appreciation of the expertise and experience that both IS and non-IS partners bring to the table; and, as a result, a mutual dependence on the expertise and resources offered by both of the partners. Systems projects developed with such partnerships are much more likely to be successfully implemented; that is, the partnerships provide a win-win situation for both partners. Successful systems implementation, in turn, builds trust and confidence between IS and non-IS management, and a long-term commitment to this user–IS partnership.

The Innovator

The innovator role is concerned with cooperative partnering with one or more external IT service providers. These strategic IT vendors — whether equipment manufacturers, software houses, outsourcers, or consultants — can provide IT expertise and technologies that may not otherwise be available to the firm. Naturally, both the firm and the vendor must perceive mutual benefits from this cooperative venture to commit to such a partnership, which frequently requires the sharing of in-house and advanced knowledge. For the vendor, this benefit may be a long-term supplier contract or a new technology or application that can be marketed to other firms.

The insurance company USAA, for example, entered into a partnership with IBM to develop a major imaging system for its Property & Casualty Division (Lasher et al., 1991). The major benefit for USAA was to be one of the first in the financial services industry to implement an advanced imaging system. For IBM, the venture provided the opportunity to learn about the insurance applications for imaging from a firm that had already been experimenting with this emerging technology, as well as with the development of new hardware and software products.

Partnerships with outsourcers also characterize the innovator role when a reengineering of the IS functions is the objective. For example, Equifax's multiyear contract with Integrated Systems Solutions Corporation, IBM's outsourcing subsidiary, and Xerox's contract with EDS are both illustrations of such long-term associations. Of course, partnering with a vendor may appear suspect to some, perhaps akin to hiring the fox to guard the hen house. Clearly, such partnerships must be approached carefully, with both parties perceiving a direct benefit and expressing a willingness to build the mutual trust necessary to sustain a long-term relationship. When successful, such partnerships can provide significant competitive advantage, allowing companies to bypass their competition.

The Strategist

Whereas the innovator role is concerned with the reengineering of the IS function to take advantage of innovative technologies, the strategist role is concerned with the reengineering of mainline business processes. Given the cross-functional nature of such redesign efforts, a critical partnership must be established with top management. Strong interpersonal relationships with top management are essential to build the shared vision that underlies successful reengineering projects (and other strategic information systems). Also, a sustained IS-top management partnership is needed to ensure the success of such projects, which often take several years to complete. Furthermore, systems directed at building and sustaining competitive competencies often involve large capital investments without hard numbers to support ROI calculations, frequently entail technological risks, and almost always result in major changes in organizational structures and responsibilities. For such major undertakings to be successful, close communication and cooperation — that is, partnering — are essential. For some firms, a strong partnership between the CEO and CIO may be adequate; for others, a partnership among all the members of the firm's top management team may be required.

It is even possible for this partnering to extend beyond the boundaries of the firm. In Xerox, the concept of customer is just that — the person or organization that buys Xerox products, not an internal consumer of information services. Thus IS managers and executives regularly meet with Xerox customers to identify opportunities where-by IS can "delight the customer." As John Hammet, the former CIO of Pillsbury, has said: "If you're not serving your customers directly, you'd better be serving someone who is."

CONCLUSION

Although each of the four partnering roles is essential for successful IS management today, not all organizations provide a context conducive to these partnering relationships. Several characteristics of the overall organization, and of the IS organization itself, affect the ability to realize the benefits of partnering. For example, a firm's structure, culture, and reward system, including the degree to which business units are autonomous, affect the extent to which a cooperative climate exists for internal and external partnering in each of the leadership roles. Similarly, the demand for reengineering and change — although continuing to deliver dependable and cost-effective systems — creates a difficult balancing act for the IS executive. Where once the IS department had both the responsibility and the resources to be the primary provider of information services, there are now many such providers within organizations, among them end users, outsourcers, and divisional computing facilities. Without effective partnering with these other suppliers — and consumers — the chances of success are greatly reduced.

Successful IS management of the 1990s requires IS managers with both technical and interpersonal competencies. Skillful partnering, for example, requires communication and negotiation skills, the ability to tolerate ambiguity, and other broad, general management skills. Career paths that provide cross-functional and line and staff experiences for IS managers help build some of these personal competencies. Forward-looking IS managers should seek out such development opportunities both for themselves as well as for their staffs. Finally, all parties must recognize that a successful partnership is not so much an endproduct as a process — a process that must be constantly nurtured and fine tuned to deal with the many challenges facing today's organizations.

Reference

Lasher, D.R., B. Ives, and S.L. Jarvenpaa, "USAA-IBM Partnerships in Information Technology: Managing the Image Project," *MIS Quarterly* 15 (December 1991), pp. 551-566.

Chapter 3
Knowledge Management — Coming Up the Learning Curve

Ray Hoving

A NEW LEVEL OF IT capability is emerging, knowledge management. With KM, the intellectual assets as well as the information assets of the firm are maintained and applied through information technology. By capturing and organizing the pockets of knowledge within a company, the firm's core competencies can be developed and maintained. Once stored and made accessible on computer, this know-how can be shared as needed among employees and business partners.

KM can enhance organizational effectiveness in numerous ways. The following examples are based on my research of KM practices in several corporations:

- A major food company captures extensive market research information to understand consumer preferences and then applies its marketing know-how to respond with the right products, packaging, and advertising programs.
- A large financial services company provides superior customer service by giving its customer representatives the information at their fingertips to immediately respond to questions from their investors.
- A construction materials company captures manufacturing know-how to ensure consistent, quality, low-cost production.
- A global electronics firm links its research and development activities throughout the world in order to accelerate the time to market new products.

0-8493-9820-7/00/$0.00+$.50
© 2000 by CRC Press LLC

- A consulting company creates a repository of the insights gained from its various engagements across time in order to reapply this know-how for new clients.
- A large group of hospitals combine the know-how of its many specialists to provide computer-assisted diagnosis and treatment of chronic diseases.
- A major reinsurance company combines the knowledge of actuarial science with interpretation of the latest medical research in order to precisely predict trends in health care costs.
- A large chemical company taps the knowledge of their scientists, engineers, and manufacturing personnel to develop health, safety, and environmental programs along with emergency response preparedness.
- A major pharmaceutical company provides a systematic way to document clinical research to accelerate FDA approval.

THE DEFINITION OF KNOWLEDGE MANAGEMENT

Emerging topics are often difficult to clearly define in pragmatic terms at first. The clients in my consulting practice have been seeking a simple definition of KM. I offer one of 25 words or less:

> The effective creation, use, and preservation of organizational know-how;
>
> In a collaborative business environment;
>
> Enabled by use of advanced information technology tools and methods.

Several key points are built into this definition. The emphasis is on *organizational* know-how vs. *individual* know-how. While the knowledge of individuals within a company makes up its organizational capability, the power of an organization comes from its ability to integrate each employee's knowledge and build it into its fabric. Although more difficult to master, the collective organizational know-how of the firm represents its true core competency.

The definition emphasizes preservation of knowledge as much as its creation and use. Useful knowledge atrophies quickly when not organized and maintained systemically. Organizational knowledge transforms into folklore and then into a distant memory, only to be reinvented by the next team assigned to the job. Preservation requires diligent effort to keep the knowledge fresh and applicable.

The definition also requires an important organizational context: a company culture and business environment that supports, expects, and rewards for collaborative behaviors. The natural resistance of individuals to share knowledge must be overcome by a superordinate goal of cooperation for the good of the whole. Although IT can enhance collaboration by providing easy-to-use tools for sharing know-how across geographic and organizational boundaries, the company must have this strong desire for teamwork through information built into its culture.

The third element of the definition calls for the use of advanced information technology. Some may argue that KM can take place without computers. However, I believe its use would be limited in most organizations of any significant size. The ability to provide instant access to shared information and to enable rapid communication among employees, its customers, and business partners, is fundamental to successful KM.

The simplest way to think of KM is as the next level of capability in the application of computers for business solutions. Exhibit 3.1 depicts the eras of computing across the past four decades.

The earlier computer systems could only deal with hard data such as accounting records. Now, thanks to the tremendous strides in areas such as electronic document management, information retrieval and library science, and image processing, we can store less defined unstructured data and still make sense of it. The unstructured world is where most thinking and communication takes place (see Exhibit 3.2). It is said that only about 20 percent of the knowledge of an organization is captured in traditional transaction-oriented computer systems. The other 80 percent can be found in memos, lab notebooks, engineering diagrams, e-mail exchanges, sales contact reports, work procedures, and educational material. Most of this has been captured electronically in one way or another. The challenge of KM is to organize this unstructured material in a way to make it come alive for the organization.

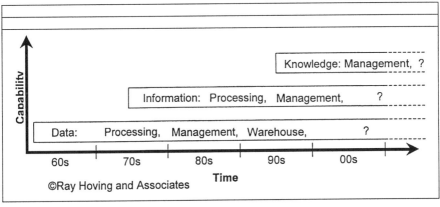

Exhibit 3.1. KM: The Next Significant Plateau

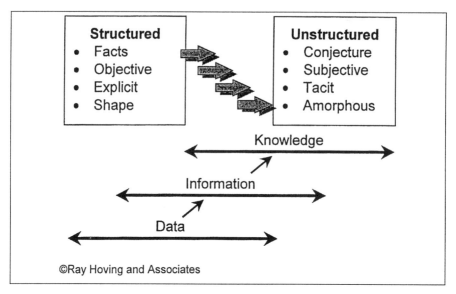

Exhibit 3.2. The Context for Knowledge Management

THE BUSINESS CASE FOR KNOWLEDGE MANAGEMENT

Based on my research, I have derived four compelling reasons for an organization to invest in KM. Each is discussed in the following paragraphs.

1. The only sustainable competitive advantage of a company is the organization's ability to learn, remember, and change. One of the first companies to develop the concept of a learning organization was Royal Dutch Shell. Management believed the only truly sustainable competitive advantage of a firm is its organization's ability to learn. This thinking was further enhanced by Peter Senge's work on the learning organization in the late 1980s.

My statement takes this thinking a step further. Granted, it is necessary for a successful organization to be continuously learning about things such as the dynamics of its marketplace and the best way to invent, produce, and deliver products and services. However, although learning is necessary, it is not sufficient. An organization must have the means to apply its knowledge and change positively as a result. KM provides a consistent, organized way to capture learning in a way that encourages the organization to make positive improvements.

A third element of this principle, remembering, is also necessary to sustain success. Organizational memory can atrophy quickly if not cared for. KM provides the means to retrieve what is relevant at the right time. The blending of man and machine through KM application provides an organization with an extremely powerful resource. Humans are wonderfully creative but terribly forgetful. Computers have yet to become inventive, but once stored and categorized properly, they do not forget one bit of information.

2. Employees will be changing companies and careers more in the future. Organizational memory will deteriorate faster unless overtly preserved. The career model of the work force is undergoing revolutionary change. Today's worker is being motivated by *employability* more than by *employment.* They are switching jobs and careers much more often than their previous generation. The people you had expected to stay in your company to perform in key positions to invent, make, and sell your products; to provide work process leadership; and to preserve core competencies cannot be counted on to stay. Most of the time, when they leave, their know-how goes with them. By building KM into a company's culture, it is expected that this know-how is to be shared among the minds of its employees and owned and maintained by the corporation through use of information technology.

3. High-performance companies embed genuine teamwork in their culture. Organizations like to think they perform as a team, although unfortunately, many do not. The context for greatness through teamwork is found in its company's culture. A positive culture comes from the behaviors of its senior leaders: those who walk the talk, by demonstrating through their own actions, that cooperation and active mutual support among employees yields the best return for customers and shareholders.

With organizational culture as it context, communications is the tool for achieving teamwork. KM offers a systematic way for employees to communicate among each other, sharing their know-how, and cooperatively inventing new solutions to improve organizational effectiveness.

4. Information technology has reached a level of capability, ease of use, and cost performance to enable collaborative computing across distance and time. IT is now enabling an extended reach for organizational communication with the advent of personal computers, easy-to-use software, and sophisticated communications networks. A meeting of the minds previously required a physical gathering. Now, information, ideas, and action plans can be communicated as effectively across distance and time, as down the hall in the same building. If applied properly, IT enables large-scale, diverse global corporations to have the intimacy of people working closely together for the good of the company. The trouble is this powerful tool can be as easily misused. Information overload has run rampant. People can spend an entire day just reading and responding to e-mail. People seem to be following the motto: "When in doubt, send it out." The process discipline found in KM makes sure the right information is available to the right people at the right time.

KM plays an important role in a company regardless of its industry. Knowledge fits directly into the value proposition of the service sector, where it is embedded in the products sold to the consumer. Major consulting organizations such as PricewaterhouseCoopers, Andersen Consulting, and Ernst & Young, began concerted efforts to manage their intellectual property several years ago. Today, they have sophisticated KM systems to capture and preserve their know-how derived from research and previous engagements, and extend it into their future business.

In the manufacturing sector, knowledge is applied more internally for research and development (R&D) production, distribution, and marketing excellence. Exhibit 3.3 depicts, in chart form, the contrast of the application of knowledge by industry.

Let's take a commodity industry, farming for example, and explore its use of KM. I live in the country in an old farmhouse on five acres. There is a 15-acre tract of land adjacent to my property, farmed by a neighbor. Each year, we wonder whether the crop is going to be corn, hay, or soybeans. The farmer rotates these crops depending on soil conditions and economic predictions of demand. He uses "no-till" planting to avoid erosion. Through the use of seed genetics, he is able to select varieties that are herbicide resistant and provide maximum yield in our Pennsylvania climate. Knowledge is certainly not embedded in the product sold (I don't believe anyone has declared soybeans a brain food), but the know-how to be a successful farmer is quite sophisticated.

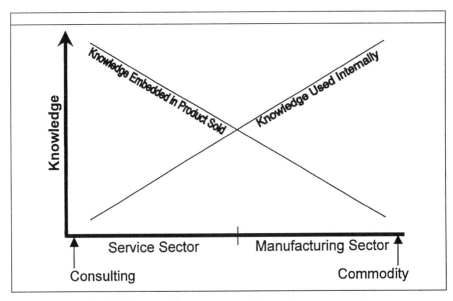

Exhibit 3.3. Knowledge Application by Industry Sector

The success and survival of any company are predicated on its knowing how to do something better than its competition. An organized approach to developing, applying, and sustaining this know-how is a competitive necessity.

SENIOR IT MANAGEMENT PERCEPTIONS

During the spring of 1998, Ray Hoving and Associates was engaged by Lotus Development Corporation to read the pulse of the marketplace in the emerging field of KM and to reach conclusions on best methods for deployment in corporations. Interviews were conducted within 13 firms (11 onsite) across a variety of industries; 21 individuals, mostly CIOs, participated.

The research objectives were to do the following:

- Understand the current perception of KM from CIO's and business users.
- Identify some leading pragmatic thinking and best practices for KM planning and implementation.
- Identify key issues affecting growth of the KM market and the role of Lotus in it.

Most of the CIOs saw the power and importance of KM applications for their companies. Eight of the CIOs strongly agreed (5 on 5-point scale) that KM would be high on their own priority lists within five years, but only one respondent said that KM was currently high on the priority list of his CEO. When asked what IT initiatives today were more important than KM, these were the responses:

- Y2K date change (7).
- ERP (5).
- Core transaction systems (4).
- Basic infrastructure technology rollouts (3).
- Automation of basic processes (2).

There are, however, several barriers to effective KM deployment that must be overcome. The participants were asked to rate 12 potential barriers to KM deployment, in response to the following question: To what extent do you believe each of these barriers holds back implementation of KM in your organization? Exhibit 3.4 presents the six most significant barriers (from greatest to least barrier).

Not surprisingly, the top two barriers have to do with the lack of a compelling business case and executive understanding and support. The champions of KM within a company must use hard facts, not faith, to secure the resources for KM investment. Passion will not win out over pocketbooks.

	1	2	3	4	5	Mean*
Lack of a compelling business case with clearly understood benefits	0	1	1	4	11	4.47
Lack of executive understanding and support for Knowledge Management initiatives	0	1	3	4	8	4.19
Management attention is diverted to other initiatives such as Y2K and ERP	0	0	3	7	6	4.19
Cultural resistance to sharing knowledge	0	1	4	7	5	3.94
Lack of work processes that embed Knowledge Management efforts into routine activities	1	1	2	7	5	3.88
Lack of motivational incentives to encourage knowledge sharing in the organization	1	2	2	5	5	3.75

* Responses were on 5-point scale: 1-None, 2-Little, 3-Some, 4-Great, 5-Very Great

Exhibit 3.4. Barriers to Deployment

The third barrier, management attention being diverted to Y2K, ERP, and so on, has CIOs focusing on "blocking and tackling" for their companies. In due time, these will consume less energy.

The next three barriers have to do with overcoming individual and organizational behavioral resistance to knowledge sharing. These have the most long-term impact on the successful deployment of KM within an organization. Companies whose culture supports and requires knowledge sharing among team members will reap the benefits of KM. Developing such a culture requires hard work and bold leadership. Changes in attitudes, internal work processes, and rewards and incentives will need to be made and reinforced.

The key conclusion from the research can be summarized as follows. The question is when KM, not whether KM. Companies will actively promote KM when (1) the business benefits of KM are obvious to executives, (2) teamwork through electronic collaboration is commonplace within the company, and (3) corporate computing infrastructure and transaction application systems are in good shape.

BEST PRACTICES

My research identified three companies that are excellent examples of best practices in thinking and deployment of KM.

Creating Organizational Readiness

Kraft Foods North America is the $17 billion a year food business of Phillip Morris. With its 70 major brands, the food company is the leading marketplace innovator in the food industry, having more than 300 new patents granted since 1990. Each day, more than 100 million consumers across

North America enjoy at least one Kraft product. One out of every 10 cows do their work for Kraft.

Jim Kinney, the CIO at Kraft Foods is both a visionary and a pragmatist. Like most CIOs of large corporations, today's emphasis is on blocking and tackling by getting over the Y2K hump and completing the implementation of large-scale transaction systems. However, Jim makes sure he and his organization will be prepared for significant new waves of IT application, such as KM.

Kraft has created the beginnings of knowledge repositories under the directions of its Chief Marketing Officer, Paula Sneed. They are amassing a history of milti-media marketing campaigns to emphasize brand awaremenss, providing on-line access to consumer research, and creating a comprehensive technical research library for use throughout Kraft

Kraft's vision for KM focuses on four areas:

- Preserving and sharing internal knowledge about the business.
- Promoting team-based initiatives across geographies and time.
- Reading the pulse of the consumer.
- Reducing time to market.

Kraft has an extreme consumer orientation in which its culture and essence are driven by understanding and responding to consumer preferences. It has targeted the research and development organization as an early adopter of KM application, both with regard to food science and consumer needs. CIO Kinney is ensuring that the IT-based environment to support KM will be ready to respond to the business drivers coming out of the vision.

Weaving KM Into Strategic Intent

The Lincoln National Reassurance Company (Lincoln Re) is a subsidiary of Lincoln Financial Group, located in Fort Wayne, Indiana. It provides insurance to insurance companies, enabling these insurers to manage their life-health insurance risk and capital portfolios. Insurance companies have traditionally been information-intensive companies. Their success depends heavily on actuarial knowledge and risk predictability for customer segments. Reinsurance services require an even greater precision to achieve growth and profitability.

Lincoln Re views KM as strategic to their business as evidenced by the 1997 annual report titled "Lincoln Re-Knowledge Management." Art DeTore is Vice President of Strategic Planning and Knowledge Management for Lincoln Re. Larry Rowland is the President and CEO. As Art puts it: "Knowledge Management is the heart and soul of our organization. It is strategic to our business and woven into all of our work processes." Larry Rowland further emphasizes the importance: "Most companies focus on economies of scale; at Lincoln Re we focus on economies of knowledge."

Application of KM in Lincoln Re has produced strong business results. Management of structured knowledge in the form of expert systems rules and unstructured knowledge, usually found in documents, has become a core competency. The evidence of its success is overwhelming. Results of an independent study comparing more than a dozen of the leading reinsurance companies clearly differentiated Lincoln Re as providing the greatest value in the eyes of the consumer. One third of its new business comes from extensions of the value chain beyond classic reinsurance sales.

Lincoln Re's success can be attributed to several reasons: (1) a sustained investment in IT and KM for over a decade, (2) a broad view of KM which is shared by all executives and employees, (3) embedding KM directly into business work processes, and (4) establishing performance measures that directly relate the KM activities to the income statement.

Overcoming Barriers to Knowledge Sharing

Air Products and Chemicals, Inc. is a $4.5 billion, Fortune 250 manufacturer of products separated from air (e.g., nitrogen, oxygen, carbon dioxide, and argon), hydrogen, gases-related equipment, and intermediate chemicals. Its chemicals business has grown to exceed $1 billion of sales annually.

The chemicals group of the company is an innovator with the use of collaborative computing technologies and methods. Glenn Beck, the director of chemicals group IT, reflected on the evolution of KM applications in chemicals: "Our Knowledge Management journey has proceeded in four stages of experiential learning: We first began by using DEC's All-In-One for our scientific community on the VAX platform. We then phased out All-In-One with Notes Mail and discussion databases. In our third stage of learning we found out what true collaborative computing is all about. We are just now beginning to understand the social and cultural issues/opportunities of collaboration. We see the fourth stage, which we are just entering now, as true Knowledge Management where we are preserving and sharing our intellectual capital."

Vince Grassi, the manager of chemicals process modeling and control, has been a strong proponent of collaborative computing throughout the process technology community in the chemicals group. This group represents more than 400 people in engineering, R&D, and manufacturing plant sites worldwide. All documentation related to its engineering efforts is kept electronically in discussion forums and databases. This has enabled a tremendous amount of knowledge to be captured and redeployed as needed.

As Vince puts it, "We follow a simple principle: 'If it's not in the database, it never happened...' "

The practices resulting from this firm leadership have generated many early successes for the chemicals group:

- *Electronic conferences create good ideas.* Traditional meetings with everyone present in the same time and space are biased toward those who can speak up spontaneously. Although this is great for bold and garrulous participants, ideas from those less spontaneously eloquent often get suppressed. Vince Grassi related an example: "We had a meeting of plant and home office engineers to discuss production improvements. It was a well-run classic jousting session that created some good ideas. The best idea, however, came two hours later when an engineer, usually quiet in meetings, crafted his thoughts as an entry in the electronic discussion database. This idea yielded a $200,000 benefit by changing the instrumentation system and workflow in the plant. We have seen how electronic forums such as these open up new avenues for employee innovation."
- *Knowledge of the whole organization exceeds the capabilities of the best individuals.* The 400 scientists and engineers in the chemicals group contribute to over 100 project knowledge databases, which have been established around key products and processes. All related documentation and communication are kept in the knowledge repository. Vince stated, "If knowledge resides in each individual, the organizational knowledge is very limited. By leveraging our knowledge, we can exceed the capabilities of our best experts and make it available to all."
- *Impact of staff turnover is minimized.* An engineer, who had been working for three years on a process model for polymer manufacturing, had transferred to a different group to take on a new assignment for the company. Although this was an important career move, there was great concern that his work would be lost. The engineer who took over for him was not nearly as familiar with the process modeling tools. However, after reading over all the well-organized notes in the knowledge database, the new engineer came up to speed in record time. This truly amazed the scientific community, made believers in KM out of many of them, and, most important, enabled the polymer modeling program to continue without any loss of knowledge.
- *Product introduction time is greatly reduced.* Air Products' Specialty Chemicals business acquired technology of a new product from another company. This intellectual property had to be translated into English, understood, and used as a base for creating manufacturing capacity in three plants located in three different countries. Use of Notes and the KM practices in place at Air Products, enabled manufacturing of this product to go online and on budget in record time.

Leadership in the business community has been enthusiastic, unwavering, and even forgiving to an extent. This atmosphere, where employees believe in such principles as "if it's not in the database, it doesn't exist," has made a significant difference in successful deployment. Employees have no choice but to share knowledge because the only accepted repositories are in shared databases. The natural resistance to sharing knowledge has been overcome through use of this tool along with appropriate rewards and incentives from management.

Attention to quality is also extremely important. Each of the 100 knowledge databases has an assigned moderator. Guidelines for content management have been published and discussion forums are monitored for quality and consistency. These hygienic approaches are critical to achieving successful deployment of KM initiatives. Overall progress and conformance to strategic intent are ensured through a "collaborative business solutions steering team" of key senior managers. User ownership and accountability are clear.

GETTING STARTED WITH KNOWLEDGE MANAGEMENT

KM is the next significant extension of IT capability in organizations. Corporations should prepare for widespread use by planning the KM architecture and experimenting with pilot applications.

There are, however, four prerequisites to achieving success with KM:

1. *The basic computing and telecommunications infrastructure needs to be in good shape, including broad use of office tools and e-mail for collaboration.* KM requires a computer-literate work force utilizing tools that enable them to easily communicate and share information with each other. This process requires a foundational infrastructure to be established, standardized, and made operationally sound. The building blocks to KM include a telecommunications network with the capacity to handle transfer of fairly large amounts of information, a PC and server environment which can readily handle introduction of new applications, and a database environment for consistent storage and retrieval of corporate data. In addition, fundamental office tools for document preparation, spreadsheets, and presentations need to be consistent throughout the firm. And, finally, an e-mail capability with the capacity and ease of use to encourage widespread collaboration is a must.

2. *The company's transaction-based applications and databases need to be extensive, timely, and accurate.* Given the premise that KM is a culmination of both structured and unstructured information, it is necessary for a company to have the basic transactions of its business enabled through IT. If KM programs within a firm only concentrate on high-level subjective information derived from the intuition of its

leaders, the program would be missing the essential ingredients of the analytical data needed to make the right decisions. The results of many years of investment in the fundamental transactional systems of a corporation will yield new insights as companies get a handle on a system's operating details in order to derive knowledge from the evidence.

3. *Senior management needs to be educated on the concepts and benefit potential in order to endorse KM investment.* They say that education is the key to understanding. Most enlightened senior managers welcome the opportunity to become educated regarding new concepts of value to their company. However, in our time-constrained world, education must be accomplished efficiently. Short, to-the-point educational experiences that weave the theory and concepts with practical examples relevant to their company are just what an executive seeks. As stated earlier, emphasis on benefit potential must be given the highest attention.

   It is difficult to relate any IT investment directly to bottom-line results such as return on investment and return on equity. IT is so pervasive and integrated with work processes that the direct cause and effect of IT alone are difficult to measure. Given this, many people shy away from doing benefit analysis of IT investments. However, it is much better to be approximately right than to be precisely wrong. Linking KM investment proposals to nonmonetary operating indicators, such as cycle time reduction, reduced error rates, and improved yields, will enable executives to relate these key operating indicators to their intuitive feel of bottom-line return.

4. *The culture and reward structures of the organization must be supportive of knowledge sharing among employees.* This is the toughest nut to crack. It is not that people do not want to change; it is just that they do not want to be changed. This makes behavioral modification the most difficult to achieve in individuals, and it is further compounded when the objective is organizational behavioral change. People will take the path of least resistance virtually every time. When the pain of change is less than the pain of staying where they are, people will move to the new state. If a company's culture allows people to hoard their knowledge and compete within the firm, people will go right on doing it. When people see that their performance and their careers are in jeopardy if they do not get with the new program of collaborative team-based business conduct, they will choose the new path. The Air Products case cited provides an excellent example.

Once the prerequisite conditions are met, proceeding with KM is a much less daunting task. However, the best way to assimilate new technologies and work processes is through planned experimentation and piloting before full-blown implementation. Experiments are small proof-of-concept applications which demonstrate the value of a new initiative to the company. Pilots are live use of the initiative on a small scale. Pilots should be done before full implementation to understand implementation requirements and target true benefit potential.

KM should follow these principles of technology assimilation. Selection of the right demonstration projects with the right executive champion is critical to achieving the momentum required for full-scale implementation. Bear in mind that use by proactive early adopters is the easiest to achieve. The tough part comes in winning over the silent majority. Given that the power of KM comes through its ubiquitous application across company boundaries, the end game is not achieved until widespread deployment is achieved.

Recommended Reading

Davenport, T.H., and Prusak, L. 1998. *Working knowledge: How organizations manage what they know.* Boston: Harvard Business School Press.
Senge, P.M. 1990. *The fifth discipline: The art & practice of the learning organization.* New York: Doubleday/Currency.
Stewart, T.A. 1997. *Intellectual capital: The new wealth of organizations.* New York: Doubleday.

Chapter 4
The CIO Role in the Era of Dislocation

James E. Showalter

PETER DRUCKER has suggested that the role of the CIO has become obsolete. His argument suggests that information technology has become so mission critical for reaching the company's strategic goals that its responsibility will be ultimately subsumed by the CEO or the CFO. After years of viewing information technology as an excessive but "necessary cost," executive management has now awakened to the recognition that failing to embrace and manage "dislocating" information technologies can mean extinction.

A dislocating technology is defined as a technological event that enables development of products and services whose impact creates completely different lifestyles and/or commerce. The Internet has been such a dislocating force, and others are on the horizon. Navigating these dislocations requires leadership and vision that must span the total executive staff, not just the CIO. This, I believe, is Drucker's point: The management of dislocating technologies transcends any individual or organization and must become integral to the corporate fabric. However, I also believe there is still an important role, albeit a different role, for the CIO in the 21st-century enterprise.

In his recent book, *The Innovator's Dilemma — When New Technologies Cause Great Firms to Fail*, Clayton Christensen provides a superb argument for corporate leadership that takes the company to new enhanced states enabled by technological dislocations. The Silicon Valley success stories have been *entrepreneurs* who recognize the market potential of dislocations created by technology. I believe the 21st-century CIO's most important role is to provide *entrepreneurial leadership* during these periods of dislocation for the company.

FROM PUNCTUATED EQUILIBRIUM TO PUNCTUATED CHAOS?

Evolutionary biologist Stephen Jay Gould theorizes that the continuum of time is periodically "punctuated" with massive events or discoveries that create dislocations of the existing state of equilibrium to a new level of

0-8493-9820-7/00/$0.00+$.50

prolonged continuous improvement (i.e., *punctuated equilibrium*). The dinosaurs became painfully aware of this concept following the impact of the meteorite into the Yucatan peninsula. In an evolutionary sense, the environment has been formed and shaped between cataclysmic dislocations — meteorites, earthquakes, droughts, plagues, volcanoes, and so on. Although exact scenarios are debatable, the concept is plausible even from events occurring in our lifetime.

There are many examples of analogous technological discoveries and innovations (the internal combustion engine, antibodies, telephone service, interstate highway system, etc.), which promoted whole new arrays of products and possibilities that forever changed commerce and lifestyles. In each of these examples our quality of life improved through the conveniences these technologies enabled. The periods between dislocations are getting shorter. For example, the periods between the horse, the internal combustion engine, and the fuel cell took a century whereas the transformations between centralized computing, distributed computing, desktop computing, network computing, and ubiquitous computing have occurred in about 40 years.

In the next century, technological dislocations in communications, genetics, biotechnology, energy, transportation, and other areas will occur in even shorter intervals. In fact, change is expected so frequently that Bill Gates has suggested that our environment is actually in constant change or upheaval marked by brief respites — "*punctuated chaos*" rather than punctuated equilibrium. We are currently in the vortex of a dislocation or transition period that many companies will not survive into the 21st century. With certainty, many new companies, yet unidentified, will surface and replace many of the companies currently familiar to us. No company is exempt from this threat, even the largest and most profitable today. The successes will be those that best leverage the dislocating technologies. To protect their companies from extinction, CIOs must understand the economic potentials and consequences of dislocating technologies.

THE ERA OF NETWORK COMPUTING

We are currently experiencing a new technological dislocation that embodies the equivalent or possibly greater potential of any previous innovation. This new dislocation is *network computing,* or perhaps a better nomenclature, *ubiquitous communications.* Network computing involves the collaborative exchange of information between objects, both human and inanimate, through the use of electronic media and technologies. Although network computing could arguably be attributed to early telecommunications applications in which unsophisticated display terminals were attached to mainframe computers through a highly proprietary communications network, the more realistic definition begins with the Internet.

Moreover, thinking must now focus on anything-to-anything interchange and not be limited only to human interaction. Navigating this transition will challenge every company — a mission for the CIO.

From today's vantage, networking computing includes (1) the Internet and Internet technologies and (2) pervasive computing and agent technologies.

The Internet and Internet Technologies

The compelling and seductive power of the Internet has motivated all major worldwide enterprises to adopt and apply Internet technologies within their internal networks under local auspices. These private networks, called intranets, are rapidly becoming the standard communications infrastructure spanning the total enterprise. Intranets are indigenous and restricted to the business units that comprise the enterprise. They are designed to be used exclusively by employees and authorized agents of the enterprise in such a way that the confidentiality of the enterprise's data and operating procedures are protected. Ingress and egress to and from intranets are controlled and protected by special gateway computers called firewalls. Soon additional gateway services, called portal services, will enable the enterprise to create a single portal to its network of internal Web sites representing specific points of interest that the company allows for limited or public access.

In general, the development and stewardship of intranets are under the auspices of the CIO. Whereas the Internet conceptually initiated the possibilities afforded by network computing to an enterprise, it is the intranets that have enabled the restructuring or reengineering of the enterprise.

Essentially all major enterprises have launched intranet initiatives. Due largely to ease of implementation and low investment requirements, enterprises are chartering their CIOs to implement intranets posthaste and without time-consuming cost justifications. In most cases, enterprises are initially implementing intranets to provide a plethora of "self-service" capabilities available to all or most employees. In addition to the classic collaboration services (e-mail, project management, document management, and calendaring), administrative services such as human resource management and financial services are being added which enable employees to manage their respective portfolios without the intervention of service staffs. This notion enables former administrative staffs to be transformed into internal consultants, process specialists, and other more useful positions for assisting in the successful implementation of major restructuring issues, staff retraining, and, most important, the development of a new corporate culture. Over time, all applications, including mission-critical applications, will become part of the intranet. Increasingly, these duties are being outsourced to trusted professional intranet specialists. Clearly, CIOs must provide the leadership in the creation and implementation of the company's intranet.

Companies in the 21st century will be a network of trusted partners. Each partner will offer specific expertise and capabilities unavailable and impractical to maintain within the host or nameplate company. Firms producing multiple products will become a federation of subsidiaries each specific to the product and/or services within its market segment. Each company will likely require different network relationships with different expert providers. This fluidity is impossible within the classical organizational forms of the past.

To meet these growing requirements and to remain profitable, companies are forced to reduce operating costs and develop innovative supply chain approaches and innovative sales channels. Further, in both the business-to-business (buy side) and the business-to-customer (sell side) supply chains, new "trusted" relationships are being formed to leverage supplier expertise such that finished products can be expedited to the customer. Initially, this requirement has motivated enterprises to "open" their intranets to trusted suppliers (buy side) and to dealers, brokers, and customers (sell side) to reduce cycle times and cost. These extended networks are called extranets. However, the cost of maintaining extranets is extreme and generally limited to large host companies. In addition, lower-tier suppliers and partners understandably resist being "hard wired," maintaining multiple proprietary relationships with multiple host companies. This form of extranet is unlikely to persist and will be replaced by a more open approach.

Industry associations such as SITA (Societe Internationa de Telecommunications Aeronautiques) for the aerospace industry and the Automotive Network Exchange (ANX) for the automotive industry have recognized the need for a shared environment in which companies within a specific industry could safely and efficiently conduct commerce. Specifically, an environment is needed in which multiple trusted "virtual networks" can simultaneously coexist. In addition, common services indigenous to the industry, such as baggage handling for airlines, could be offered as a saving to each subscribing member. These industry-specific services — "community-of-interest-networks" (COINS) — are evolving in every major industry. COINS are analogous to the concept of an exchange. For example, the New York Stock Exchange is an environment in which participating companies subscribe to a set of services that enable their securities to be traded safely and efficiently.

For all the same reasons that intranets were created (manageability, availability, performance, and security), exchanges will evolve across entire industries and reshape the mode and means of interenterprise commerce. Supply and sales chain participants within the same industry are agreeing on infrastructure and, in some noncompetitive areas, on data and transaction standards. In theory, duplicate infrastructure investments are eliminated and competitiveness becomes based on product/customer relationships. The automotive industry, for example, has cooperatively developed and implemented the ANX for all major original equipment manufacturers and (eventually) all suppliers. In addition, ANX will potentially include other automotive-related market segments, such as financial institutions, worldwide dealers, product development and research centers, and similar participants. Industries such as aerospace, pharmaceuticals, retail merchandising, textiles, consumer electronics, and so on will also embrace industry-specific exchanges.

Unlike the public-accessible Internet, which is essentially free to users, exchanges are not free to participants. By agreement, subscription fees are required to support the infrastructure capable of providing service levels required for safe, effective, and efficient commerce. The new "global internet" or "information highway" (or whatever name is ultimately attached) will become an archipelago of networks, one of which is free and open (Internet) while the others are private industry and enterprise subscription networks. The resulting architecture is analogous to today's television paradigm — free channels (public Internet), cable channels (industry-specific exchange), and pay-for-view channels (one off service, such as a video teleconference).

Regardless of how this eventually occurs, intranets are predicted to forever change the internal operations of enterprises, and exchanges are predicted to change commerce among participants within an industry. Again, the CIO must provide the leadership for his or her firm to participate in this evolving environment.

Pervasive Computing and Agent Technology

The second dislocation is ubiquitous or pervasive computing. Currently there are an estimated 200 million computers in the world. By 2002, Andy Grove of Intel estimates there will be 500 million. In most cases, today's computers are physically located in fixed locations, in controlled environments, on desktops, and under airline seats. They are hardly "personal" in that they are usually away from where we are, similar to our automobiles. But this will change dramatically.

Although there are "only" 200 million computers today, there are already 6 billion pulsating noncomputer chips embedded in other objects, such as our cars, thermostats, and hotel door locks throughout the world. Called "jelly beans" by Kevin Kelly in his book *Out of Control and New Rules for the New Economy*, these will explode to over 10 billion by 2005. Also known as "bots," these simple chips will become so inexpensive that they can affordably be attached to everything we use and even discarded along with the item when we are finished using it, such as clothing and perishables. Once the items we use in daily life become "smart" and are capable of "participating" in our daily lives, the age of personal computing will have arrived.

Programmable objects or agents are the next technological dislocation. Although admittedly sounding futuristic and even a bit alarming, there is little doubt that technology will enable the interaction of "real objects" containing embedded processors in the very near future. Java, Jini, Java chip, next-generation (real-time) operating systems are enabling information collection and processing to be embedded within the "real-life" objects. For example, a contemporary automobile contains between 40 and 70 microprocessors performing a vast array of monitoring, control, guidance, and driver information services. Coupled with initiatives for intelligent highway systems (ITS), the next-generation vehicles will become substantially safer, more convenient, more efficient, and more environmentally friendly than our current vehicles. This same scenario is also true of our homes, transportation systems, communications systems (cellular phones), and even our children and persons

Every physical object we encounter and/or employ within our lifestyles can be represented by a software entity embedded within the object or representing the object as its "agent." Behavioral response to recognizable stimuli can be "programmed" into these embedded processors to serve as our "agents" (e.g., light switches that sense the absence of people in the room and turn off to save energy and automobiles that sense other automobiles or objects in our path and warn or even take evasive actions). Many other types of agents perform a plethora of other routine tasks that are not specific to particular objects, such as searching databases for information of interest to the reader. The miniaturization of processors (jelly beans), network programming languages (Java), network connectivity (Jini), and appliance manufacturers' commitment will propel this new era to heights yet unknown. Fixed process systems will be replaced by self-aligning systems enabled by agent technology. These phenomena will not occur naturally but, rather, must be directed as carefully as all other corporate resources. In my judgment, this is the role of the 21st-century CIO.

SUMMARY

In summary, the Internet has helped launch the information age and has become the harbinger for the concepts and structure that will enable international communication, collaboration, and knowledge access for commerce and personal growth. Although the Internet is not a universal solution to all commerce needs, it has, in an exemplary manner, established the direction for the global information utility. It will remain an ever-expanding and vibrant source for information, personal communication, and individual consumer retailing. Intranets, developed by enterprises, are reshaping the manner in which all companies will structure themselves for the challenging and perilous journey into the 21st century. Complete industries will share a common exchange infrastructure for exchanging information among their supply, demand, product, and management support chains.

Pervasive computing will emerge with thunder and lightning over the next few years and offer a dazzling array of products that will profoundly enrich our standard of living. Agent technology coupled with embedded intelligence in 10 billion processors will enable self-aligning processes that adapt to existing environmental conditions.

CIOs who focus on the business opportunities afforded by dislocating information technologies will be the ones who succeed. Even if the CIO title changes in the future, an officer of the company must provide leadership in navigating the company through technological transitions or dislocations. As we enter the new millennium, however, there is a lot of work to be done to create the environment discussed in this chapter. As Kevin Kelly observes:

> "…wealth in this new regime flows directly from innovation, not optimization: that is, wealth is not gained by perfecting the known, but by imperfectly seizing the unknown."

Successful CIOs will adopt this advice as their credo.

Recommended Reading

Christensen, C. 1997. *The innovator's dilemma: When new technologies cause great firms to fail.* Boston: Harvard Business School Press.

Drucker, P. 1994. Introduction. In *Techno vision,* edited by C. Wang. New York: McGraw Hill.

Gates, B. 1999. *Business @ the speed of thought*, New York: Warner Books.

Kelly, K. 1997. The new rules for the new economy - twelve dependable principles for thriving in a turbulent world. *Wired,* September, 140.

Schlender, B. 1999. E-business according to Gates. *Fortune*, 12 April.

Chapter 5
The IS Executive and Strategic Planning

Philip N. James

TODAY'S MANDATE TO CREATE THE FUTURE underscores both the need for effective, continuous planning and the vital role information plays in today's businesses and their planning processes. Business and IT planning allow corporations to achieve the nimbleness necessary for competitive advantage. They also provide people and organizations with an anchor or center that conveys a much needed sense of stability amid constant change.

Although the planning process never ends, the strategic plan must be managed. Conventional project management tools generally work best with a fixed plan, not with one that changes. Newer tools are needed that provide managers with an easily visible and modifiable framework.

After reviewing the basics of strategic IS planning, this chapter examines the products of the planning process and their role in ensuring effective management of the information resource. An overview of an integrated IS and business planning process is provided, including a detailed discussion of the role chief information officers (CIOs) or senior IS executives play.

STRATEGIC BUSINESS PLANNING: THE BASIS FOR STRATEGIC IS PLANNING

Responsibility for the future well-being of a company rests with the CEO and his or her executive team. Each member of the team, including the CIO or senior IS executive, should be fluent in modern strategic planning: its concepts, methodologies, and tools. These include SWOT analysis, Porter's contributions (e.g., five market forces, three generic strategies, and value chain analysis), portfolio analysis (e.g., the Boston Consulting Group's growth/share matrix), and critical success factors analysis.

The executive team should possess thorough knowledge of the business — its marketplace, customers and prospects, and competitors. Although the CEO has earned the right to provide the strategic vision, every member of the team must work at articulating it in a way that can be unanimously supported and so that it drives every decision in the company.

Strategic planning is most effective when it is never far from immediate concerns. It should keep the strategic vision alive in day-to-day decision-making.

Although each member of the executive team applies strategic thinking from the perspective of his or her function and the resources managed through that function, each must also apply it from the perspective of the company as a whole, considering and integrating all six organizational resources to create a dynamic future. Most executives are used to thinking about three such resources — *money, people,* and *things*; but only a few consider *information, time,* and *relationships* as important resources as well. It is particularly important that the senior IS executive helps colleagues understand the role of information as a resource and to recognize information opportunities for the company.

ELEMENTS OF STRATEGIC BUSINESS PLANNING

The Planning Process

Organizations that plan successfully and outperform their competitors view planning not only as a process, but also as a way of life. Their line managers keep the strategic vision, planning issues, and trends in mind for even the most routine daily operational decisions. They meet frequently to refine their understanding of changes in the business environment and the implications of those changes for current strategies. Such an organization is fine-tuned to respond effectively to change; its strategic plan serves as a compass that guides its responses.

Strategic Planning Retreats

Because it is difficult for even the most-effective planning organizations to remain focused on the future in the face of day-to-day problems, the executive team should occasionally isolate itself from its usual environment to renew and refine its focus. These retreats, generally lasting two or three days, provide opportunities to explore concerns that may be suppressed in the regular business environment and to reinforce team members' relationships with one another.

Retreats are often held when a significant opportunity or threat is perceived; they give the team a chance to remold the company to respond effectively. Rarely held more often than two or three times a year, retreats nevertheless play a key role in keeping a company effective.

The Products of Planning

The most valuable products of the strategic planning process are *intangible*: a more cohesive executive team, a sense of knowing where the company is going and how to get there, and sounder decisions. The most *tangible* products are the plans, which should include a mission and vision, an information architecture, and an information infrastructure.

Importance of Producing a Written Plan. Regardless of its size, a company is a complex collection of resources, configured in a particular way. It is impossible for any one person to keep all aspects in mind. A written plan that describes the company, its resources, and how it is expected to change over time provides guidance for people at all levels in carrying out their work.

A written plan is most valuable when opportunities or threats arise. Responses to these changes require the reallocation of resources. Because the written plan reminds everyone how resources are allocated at the time of the change, the reassessment of priorities and reallocation become reasonable tasks. To expect executives to be able to assess the enterprisewide consequences of any particular reallocation in the absence of a written plan is unreasonable.

Need for a Continuous Planning and Review Process. Plans are obsolete as soon as they are published. Organizations successful at planning recognize that future results are conceived through the process, which enables everyone to keep abreast of the organization's direction and to commit to support it. The written plans are snapshots of the process at a point in time that provide interim guidelines only and must be constantly reviewed.

The way an organization treats its plans is a clue to the effectiveness of its planning process. All too often, after much energy and resources have been invested in a planning process, the plans are put on a shelf and forgotten. The usual reason given is that the business changed so much that the plan became irrelevant.

If that fate befalls a plan, it is not only the plan that is irrelevant, but the planning process as well. Too many companies begin the planning task with great enthusiasm, but abandon it when it reaches a meaningful stage. This is one of the primary reasons why a continuous planning process, supported by all managers involved, is the most effective kind of planning.

In addition to plans, the planning process yields action plans for specific activities by specific units or individuals and allocates resources to them. The priorities of these activities and allocations should be reviewed with some frequency, usually more often than once a year.

ROLE OF THE TOP IS EXECUTIVE

Strategic planning is now more than ever a process that depends on good relationships. If the senior IS executive is not accepted as a full member of the team, he or she receives the output from the planning process and has to adapt to it. If a full member of the team, the IS executive influences the output and optimizes the role of information in furthering the company's success.

The relationship between the senior IS executive and the CEO can be crucial. If it is excellent, it helps create good relationships with the rest of the senior executive team. More importantly, it helps the CIOs develop the critical ability to understand how the CEO thinks and how information can enable the CEO's vision.

Educating the Executive Team

The most effective planning for the strategic use of the information resource occurs when every member of the executive team recognizes information opportunities. If the relationships between the senior IS executive and his or her colleagues are solid enough, the IS executive will be able to educate them, usually informally, to understand the role of information as a resource.

Unfortunately, many executives resist learning things they do not feel they need to know. They will, however, learn from a friend and colleague, particularly if the education is provided subtly and in small doses.

Developing the Vision for the IS Function

Functional or program executives are each responsible for developing a vision for their individual functions and their resources that is based on the company's strategic vision. The IS executive is no different.

The current focus on the reengineering of business processes acknowledges the newly recognized importance of the information resource. Because most business processes are stable over time — more stable than organizational units — IS development is based on business processes rather than on organizational units. The evolution of information technology has provided new ways to manage information, and business processes must be brought current to take advantage of them.

Knowing which business processes to reengineer first requires a vision of how information is used by the organization. This information vision is a high-level, conceptual framework and philosophy that govern the management of information in the company. It forms the superstructure on which the enterprisewide information architecture is developed. It also defines relationships among various kinds of information and the responsibilities of the various executives and managers who are engaged in the task of managing information.

Identifying Information Megatrends

Information megatrends are important to the strategic planning process because, among other things, they help determine the structure of the information vision. Following are examples of the better-known information megatrends:

- *Power, size, cost.* Information technology hardware is growing in capability and power while shrinking in cost and size. There is little evidence that this trend will level off in the foreseeable future.
- *Application availability and ease of use.* Software and applications are becoming easier to use, and more applications for many common business processes are becoming readily available as off-the-shelf items.
- *Growing sophistication of information management.* As software becomes more readily available and easier to use, the complexity of the support infrastructure and the technical sophistication needed to serve the growing applications portfolio have burgeoned.
- *Communications capacity.* The speed and capacity of public and private communications networks are growing, increasing the ability of businesses to deliver information anywhere, anytime, any way.

The role of the IS executive is to keep abreast of such megatrends through many channels, including reading the trade and research literature, participating in trade and professional organizations, attending seminars, and studying the uses of information technology by customers and competitors.

Strategic IS Decisions

Among the most important strategic IS decisions are those that help the company capitalize on information opportunities. Key strategic information management decisions in business today include the following:

- *Reengineering.* What technologies can help a business process improve its relationships with customers?
- *Outsourcing.* What aspects of information management could be done better by another company that specializes in a particular aspect? How does the organization develop the right kinds of relationships with outsourcing vendors?
- *Legacy systems.* How can current technologies be applied to better manage the information now managed by legacy systems?
- *Client/server.* Where, how, and when should information management be moved to distributed client/server architectures?

- *Groupware.* How can groupware improve communication and the use of information for competitive advantage?
- *Systems integration.* How does one make sure that information systems throughout the company work well together?
- *The Internet.* What kind of Internet presence would improve the business? Should the company implement an intranet?
- *Emerging technologies.* Where and when does an organization apply such technologies as data warehousing, electronic data interchange (EDI), object-oriented approaches, new applications development tools, and multimedia to improve pockets of information management? How does the organization learn to migrate useful technologies throughout the company where appropriate?

Leading the Delivery of Information Services

The role of the senior IS executive increasingly lies in the development of a strategic information infrastructure that is matched to the way the company does business and uses information. Parts of the infrastructure include building the enterprisewide information architecture, enforcing open systems and other standards enterprisewide, and implementing a backbone communications network with sufficient capacity to meet today's needs and sufficient flexibility to add capacity as needs grow. Even if ancillary information executives report to heads of their business divisions, the senior IS executive should oversee their activities in the context of enterprisewide leadership. The senior IS executive retains residual responsibility to ensure that the company is using information technology effectively, that its costs are not excessive, and that the company can respond with agility to new opportunities without being hindered by rigid applications.

Planning in the Absence of a Formal Procedure

In an effective planning process, IS planning and business planning are both part of a single process. As a respected full partner on the executive team, the CIO or senior IS executive is an influential participant in this integrated process. But what if the CIO is not a full partner in the business planning process? In the worst case, what if there is no recognizable planning process, and the senior IS executive must discover or invent the business plan?

These situations create a loose integration between business and IS planning. Loose integration fails to facilitate full use of the information resource and often leaves both the company's business executives and the CIOs frustrated. Information plays only a small role in helping to ensure the company's success, information opportunities are overlooked, and goals and objectives may be difficult to support because they were formulated without input about information needs. Furthermore, if relationships between senior IS executives and business executives are not good, they may adversely affect attitudes about information technology.

PRODUCTS OF THE IS PLANNING PROCESS

The planning process has four major tangible products that together constitute the IS strategic plan:

- The information mission and vision.
- The enterprisewide information architecture.
- The enterprisewide support infrastructure.
- An allocation of resources to projects.

The Information Mission and Vision

The information mission documents the role of the IS organization within the company. In all companies, the mission includes supporting business objectives; in some companies, the mission also includes providing information services outside the company for profit. The mission may encompass a single IS organization, a collection of several relatively independent organizations that serve the major units of the company, or one or more independent vendors to whom information services have been outsourced. Each independent IS unit may have its own mission; in that case, the mission of the corporate IS organization is to coordinate the efforts of all of these units, ensure adherence to standards and preferred practices, and maintain the overall corporate philosophy governing information resource management.

The mission also describes the scope of the information management role. In most companies, the IS organization focuses on managing machine-readable information inside the company. Many IS organizations also manage the accessing of online marketplace information in public, trade, or private data base and its integration with company information to provide perspective on the company's competitive position. A few leading companies have taken on the challenge of managing information that is relatively difficult to manage, including paper documents in file cabinets and telephone conversations. The most strategic information a company acquires is usually received verbally, often in nonbusiness settings. Few companies have learned how to systematically capture and use this information.

The Enterprisewide Information Architecture

It is increasingly recognized that the best way to ensure that all parts of the organization work effectively together and remain agile from an information perspective is to develop an architecture for the company's information. An architecture is a collection of documents that together represent a structure. A building architecture includes sketches, renderings, blueprints, construction drawings, and sometimes models. Some of these documents are useful for the building's owner, who is usually not an architect or engineer, and others are useful for the builder or the tradespeople who contract with the builder. In a sense, the building itself is part of the documentation of its architecture.

An information architecture is similar. Documents show the relationships of the parts to each other and to the whole, with respect to the business. Some documents are designed for the users, some for executive management, and some for the builders of the information systems that support the architecture.

The Enterprisewide Support Infrastructure

Once the information architecture—the entity—is in place, it must be maintained and kept effective. The information architecture focuses on information, not technology. The infrastructure focuses on both technology and the human processes that support the enterprise. The infrastructure includes conduits for information (communications), engines for processing it (computers) and storing it (such as disks and tapes), and the standards, procedures, and guidelines that connect information with the people who manage it.

Training is another important component of the infrastructure. Both those who build and maintain the infrastructure and those who use it need to be trained. After training is completed, help should still be readily available. It may be delivered through a help desk that allocates problems to those most qualified to solve them or through consulting support that helps trained users accomplish a particularly difficult or complex task.

Allocating Resources to Projects

The process of allocating resources to projects involves three steps:

- Conducting an information requirements analysis.
- Justifying IT investments.
- Making the allocations.

Conducting an Information Requirements Analysis. The results of the information requirements analysis are necessary for planning the projects that enable the company to remain agile with respect to change. In many ways, the information requirements analysis should be an ongoing process. In practice, however, it is done infrequently, usually when the company is first developing an information architecture or approaching the infrastructure systematically and strategically. It is also done when major changes to either the architecture or the infrastructure are anticipated.

Conducting an information requirements analysis is similar to conducting a systems analysis for a new application. The analysis involves reviewing documentation, administering questionnaires, conducting interviews, making observations, and documenting the results. The difference in an information requirements analysis is that the focus of the activity is the enterprise as a whole, not just a business process or functional area. In addition, the activity is conducted with a strategic perspective intended to highlight areas where information is not being used or managed effectively and suggest techniques for improvement.

Defining Business Processes. The analysis begins with definitions of the company's business processes, a task that may constitute the most valuable aspect of the analysis process. Although understanding of what a business process is and how to identify a complete process, regardless of how many organizational units implement it, has grown enormously with the advent of reengineering, it may take several iterations with knowledgeable executives and managers and the help of a perceptive consultant to reach agreement on the set of business processes that constitute the company. In one organization, for example, four studies by four different consultants led to four different lists of business processes. The differences among the lists were not merely semantic, but substantive and conceptual.

Delineating Information Requirements. Once the business processes are defined, their information requirements are sought. This is done through interviews with the managers involved in the processes and individuals or organizations involved in feeding the processes (suppliers) and acquiring their products (customers). The importance and availability of the information is then rated, and an information/process matrix is produced with information/availability scores in the cells. This kind of information helps focus attention on high-payoff areas of the information architecture, the infrastructure, or reengineering that should be pursued.

Planning Methodologies. Many approaches to information resource planning have been developed over the years. Each has strengths and weaknesses, and none is entirely correct for any one organization. Most companies adopt elements from several of these approaches, tailoring the set to fit their individual circumstances.

A methodology is a detailed set of procedures for carrying out a process. It is not a cookbook or recipe for success but rather a checklist for experienced professionals to ensure that no significant part of the process is overlooked. A methodology cannot be effectively applied by someone lacking the requisite experience.

It is important to remember that it is the planning process, particularly its team-building and relationship-building aspects, that is most important for successful planning. If the right people are meeting at the right frequency to discuss the right issues, then nearly any planning methodology will be successful. If those elements are not present, then success will be hard to achieve regardless of which methodology is used.

The following approaches have been found effective in many planning situations in the past. To a greater or lesser degree, each of them has been associated with a specific methodology.

- *BSP (IBM's Business Systems Planning methodology).* Among BSP's strengths are its focus on the management of information and data (as opposed to processing) and on business processes (as opposed to organizational units). Among its weaknesses is its complexity.
- *CSF (critical success factors).* Popularized by John Rockart of the Massachusetts Institute of Technology, this approach is valuable because it is nearly intuitive, works well with senior executives, and facilitates prioritization.
- *Stages of growth.* This approach builds on a discovery by C.R. Gibson and R.L. Nolan that the most effective IT management strategy depends on which of four stages of growth a company is in regarding its use of technology. Over the years, as understanding of the management of the information resource has become more sophisticated, the number of stages has increased to eight.
- *Resource reallocation.* Another Nolan strategy compares actual allocation of IT resources with an ideal allocation based on the company's business and other factors. The approach aims to reach the ideal through reallocation.
- *Ends/means analysis.* In this approach, required outputs are identified, and then inputs and processes that will produce the outputs are sought.
- *Strategy-set transformation.* This approach seeks to transform the business strategy set (i.e., mission, vision, goals, and objectives) to a corresponding IT strategy set.

Justifying IT Investments. In the early days of information technology, justifying investments was not difficult. Because applications were developed to increase productivity, they were justified by the numbers of people they displaced. Today, however, applications of information technology are justified on the basis of their effectiveness in terms of, for example, providing strategic advantage and improving customer service.

Measures of successful IT investments are few and far between. Quite often, investments in information technology are championed by a visionary senior executive who believes that the investment is important for the company. Many of the success stories regarding competitive advantage attest to the effectiveness of this approach. But what if the champion is wrong? Failures usually are undocumented, and there probably are many more failures than successes resulting from the champion approach.

It is desirable to have one or more methods of project analysis to support the champion or justify a project on its own merits. The usual capital budgeting approaches of cost/benefit analysis, payback analysis, and financial return (i.e., ROI, ROA, ROE) provide useful information even if they do not fully justify a project. In today's world of often-intangible benefits, these approaches can often be modified to include an assessment of intangible value, something on which executives can agree. Unfortunately, the most strategic projects involve great risk, and a company unprepared to take the risk foregoes the value.

Making the Allocations. All planning activities ultimately produce a set of projects to be carried out in a particular order. Early in the IS planning era, these projects were usually large applications supporting a portion of a business process. Today's projects are smaller, modular, and much more varied.

Although projects need not be defined during the planning phase in the detail necessary for project management purposes, some definition of resources required over time is necessary, usually in the form of a budget and an action plan, or schedule. Defining projects in this way can be done only by experienced people familiar with the technology, the organization (i.e., both the one that will carry out the project and the one that will use its results), and the culture. Although it is more accurate to define a project's budget and schedule later on when more detailed information about it becomes available, the initial high-level budget and schedule are important.

It is particularly important that the planned budget for a project be large enough to cover the possibility of significant change and yet not so large as to cause an important project to be deemed unfeasible. The budget figure and schedule set during the planning process are the ones that are remembered as the project comes to a close. No matter how many revisions are completed with care through a formal change process during the project, the initial schedule and budget will be the performance measurements that many people may use to assess whether or not the project was overbudget and behind schedule.

THE CHANGING NATURE OF TODAY'S PROJECTS

The classic approach to planning just described ends with a set of prioritized projects, a result necessary even in today's fast-paced business world. The projects carried out today differ from their predecessors in terms of their size, ease with which they are changed, and general nature.

Project Size

Projects are generally much smaller than projects used to be. What used to be large projects encompassing two or three years are now collections of modular projects, which, taken together, produce similar end results. Building modules rarely takes more than six months. Because benefits are realized as each module comes online, there is a stream of increasing benefits over two or three years.

Ease of Change

The modular project approach makes the introduction of change much easier than it used to be. Priorities can be reviewed continuously and continuously changed. New competitive forces can be recognized and accommodated as they arise. New technologies can be incorporated as soon as their effectiveness has been satisfactorily proven.

Nature of Projects

New applications development was the major activity of IS departments through the 1980s. In the late 1980s, when management of data separately from its processing was fully implemented, cross-functional applications became possible. Although business processes were defined in IBM's BSP methodology, the concept of a business process was not refined until the introduction of the reengineering concept in the early 1990s.

Reengineering business processes using current technologies has enabled revolutionary thinking about cross-functional applications and data management. The concept of the enterprisewide information architecture emerged and then broadened to encompass suppliers and customers through electronic data interchange (EDI). Innovations in communications exploded and client-server architectures emerged. All of these forces led to new kinds of projects.

The result of this accelerating revolution in information technology is that projects are rarely new applications today. The concept of an application changed first, and the subsequent availability of some of the more traditional applications in excellent commercial packages meant that they need no longer be developed. As a result, today's projects include many new kinds of activities, among them:

- Creating a communications backbone.
- Creating a data warehouse.
- Designing/implementing an information architecture.
- Reengineering a business process.
- Building/improving a support infrastructure.
- Changing an organizational culture.
- Implementing an executive information system.
- Building a presence on the Internet to improve customer service.

Traditional applications development projects are now few and far between and usually involve modification of a commercially available package rather than custom building a new one.

CONCLUSION

Strategic IS planning is a challenging undertaking. The following guidelines aim to help IS executives achieve the goal of effective and strategic management of the information resource:

- *Build relationships.* Implementation of a strategic plan is as dependent on relationships as is the plan's development. The planning products document agreements, but relationships make them work.
- *Stay strategic.* Success depends on the executive team's ability to understand how information enhances structure and strategy. Although "the devil is in the details," no one will pay attention to the devil unless they are shown his strategic position.
- *Use the planning products to improve the quality of information services.* The architecture illustrates how to deploy information; the support infrastructure ensures that the information is provided by those who acquire it and available to those who need it.
- *Exploit emerging technologies, but maintain a business focus.* IS executives should not ignore exciting emerging technologies, but carefully manage their introduction.
- *Remain alert to what is going on outside the company.* It is important to remain current with business and technology developments. Other information leaders, academicians, or consultants are all potential resources for strategic IS planning.

References

Allen, B.R., and Boynton, A.C. "Information Architecture: In Search of Efficient Flexibility." *MIS Quarterly* 15, no. 4 (1991).
Bergeron, F., Buteau, C., and Raymond, L. "Identification of Strategic Information Systems Opportunities." *MIS Quarterly* 15, no. 1 (1991).
Earl, M.J. "Experiences in Strategic Information Systems Planning." *MIS Quarterly* 17, no. 1 (1993).
Feeny, D.F., Edwards, B.R., and Simpson, K.M., "Understanding the CEO/CIO Relationship." *MIS Quarterly* 16, no. 4 (1992).
Hammer, M. and Champy, J. *Reengineering the Corporation.* New York: Harper Business, 1993.
King, W.R. "Creating a Strategic Capabilities Architecture." *Information Systems Management* 12, no. 1, 1995 (only one of many articles on strategic planning written by this author).
Koch, C. "Enter the Power Elite." *CIO* 9, no. 14, 1996.
Martin, B.L. et al. "The End of Delegation? Information Technology and the CEO" *Harvard Business Review* 73, no. 5, 1995.
Niederman, F., Brancheau, J.C., and Wetherbe, J.C. "Information Systems Management Issues for the 1990s." *MIS Quarterly* 15, vol. 4 (1991).
Thompson, A.A., and Strickland, A. J., III. *Strategic Management: Concepts and Cases.* 8th ed. Chicago: Richard D. Irwin, 1995.
Wetherbe, J.C. "Executive Information Requirements: Getting it Right." *MIS Quarterly* 15, no. 1 (1991).
Whitman, M.E., and Gibson, M.L. "Enterprise Modeling for Strategic Support." *Information Systems Management* 13, no. 2 (1996).

Chapter 6
Integrated Systems Planning: A Holistic Model

Yannis A. Pollalis

BUSINESS PROCESS REENGINEERING (BPR) has become one of this decade's most cited management issues in the managerial, academic, and trade press. It has also been listed as a top priority by most surveys of corporate executives, business planners, and management consultants. The BPR concept was introduced during the late 1980s primarily by a few influential consultants and academics. BPR uses information technology (IT) to radically change (or redesign) the business processes within organizations to dramatically increase their efficiency and effectiveness. Although some of the concepts and methods of previous management practices are similar to those of BPR (e.g., total quality management and activity value analysis), BPR is still perceived by some advocates as a different way of management thinking. Thus many of the mistakes committed with BPR's predecessor concepts and methods have been repeated.

Furthermore, evidence indicates that a great percentage of BPR efforts have failed. Research on these failures produced a list of critical failure factors that include lack of management commitment and leadership, resistance to change, unclear specifications, inadequate resources, technocentricism, a lack of user/customer involvement, and failure to address the human aspect of planned change.

Although BPR reflects a relatively new way of thinking about process change, similar efforts have already taken place in the areas of information systems planning (ISP) and total quality management (TQM). Thus, integrating BPR, ISP, and TQM into a holistic model capitalizes on the lessons learned from ISP and TQM efforts and avoids repetition of past mistakes.

ISP AS PLATFORM FOR INTEGRATING BPR AND TQM

TQM's main goal is to improve the processes within an organization and the organization's ability to meet the needs of the customer by emphasizing continuous quality improvement and responsiveness to customer demands. Overall, TQM activities involve improving business processes and implementing incremental change by:

- Focusing on satisfying customer needs.
- Analyzing business processes continuously to increase efficiency and customer service.
- Emphasizing teamwork and employee empowerment across and within the firm to ensure the previous two activities.

ISP activities include

- Identifying information resources that support or redefine the goals of the firm and the IS organization.
- Identifying opportunities to use IT and improve the firm's competitive advantage.
- Implementing process change through IT.
- Meeting the systems requirements of internal and external users.

More specifically, ISP aims to reduce the uncertainty associated with the internal and external business environments. Uncertainty in the internal environment is generated by process changes in an organization. Its successful resolution depends on the ability of IS management to understand the interrelationships among the various organizational functions and processes and minimize redundancy and inefficiencies. This type of uncertainty requires that ISP consider process quality improvements along with user satisfaction goals.

Uncertainty in the external environment results from IT developments and competitive market pressures. ISP's role in this arena is to identify opportunities and threats in the environment and successfully integrate them with the IS organization's goals.

Thus, ISP can be defined as a proactive process that emphasizes IT-based process change to improve an organization's ability to:

- Respond successfully to external threats and opportunities.
- Strategically apply its own capabilities and competencies through information resources.

Based on this definition, ISP focuses on three areas common to both BPR and TQM:

- *Technological improvement* — which reflects the IT focus of BPR's process redesign and innovation efforts.

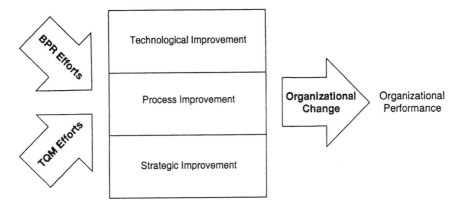

Exhibit 6.1.   Planning as a platform for integrating BPR and TQM efforts.

- *Process improvement* — which emphasizes both the redesign of exist
  ing organizational processes and the employee empowerment con
  cepts used in TQM's cross-functional and coordination activities.
- *Strategic improvement* — which concentrates on BPR's and TQM's
  alignment with corporate objectives.

Thus, as illustrated in Exhibit 6.1, IS planning can act as a platform that
integrates an organization's BPR and TQM process change efforts.

COMMON DIMENSIONS OF ISP, BPR, AND TQM

IS planning has four major components that overlap with the objectives
of BPR and TQM.

Alignment of Corporate and IS Goals

In IS planning, information resources are used to support business goals
(usually efficiency, effectiveness, and competitive uniqueness), as well as
to lead corporate strategic efforts to capitalize on external opportunities
and internal competencies derived from IT. For example, Wal-Mart's integrated distribution network and United Services Automobile Association's
(USAA) state-of-the-art document-handling system represent two such IT-
based distinctive competencies. These competencies were aligned with corporate strategies and brought competitive advantage to the two companies.

Customer Focus

The ultimate goal of ISP should not be to use IT to implement organizational change for the sake of technology's potential capabilities. Rather, ISP
should address various concerns of quality and customer needs, and im-

prove and sustain linkages between the organization and its internal and external customers. In general, IT systems that help the customer to order, choose among alternatives, and purchase products and services contribute to both BPR's radical change and TQM's continuous improvement efforts. Thus, IS planning becomes the hub for a value-added network that includes linkages to both external customers (e.g., suppliers, buyers, and competitors) and internal customers (e.g., functional departments and divisions).

For example, the legendary systems of American Airlines' SABRE, American Hospital Supply's ASAP, and McKesson's ECONOMOST have helped to build strong ties with external customers (i.e., travel agents, hospitals, and drugstores, respectively) owing to their user friendliness, convenience, and value-added services offered with the total package.

Similarly, ISP can facilitate relations and linkages among an organization's internal customers (e.g., accounting, purchasing, production, and marketing) by improving the quality and efficiency of IS services. Examples of such cases include Charles Schwab's integrated account environment (called cashiering), which allows faster and more reliable retrieval of customer/investor account information by the various Schwab brokers; and Citicorp's work-group computing environment, which integrates the business divisions of leasing, retail banking, institutional banking, capital markets, and real estate loans to promote reliable information and overall organizational effectiveness.

IT-Based Process Change

By changing, updating, or replacing existing information systems and processes within a firm, ISP facilitates restructuring of a firm's business processes. Prerequisites of such planned IT-based change include management support, strong IT leadership, involvement of IS executives in corporate planning, and systems thinking. The efforts of Pacific Bell, Xerox, and Texas Instruments in this area are discussed in the section on successful integrations.

Organizational Learning

By forcing its participants to understand a firm's various processes, their critical success factors, and the way IT can improve them, the ISP function becomes a facilitator for learning about organizational processes. Various techniques, such as scenario-based planning and simulations of internal or external crises, promote such learning and prevent unexpected disasters. Among the classic examples of such efforts toward organizational learning through strategic planning is Shell's crisis management simulations, in which what-if exercises resulted in major redesign and process changes that helped the company anticipate and prevent market- and technology-based disasters.

Major Components of IS Planning	Interrelated BPR Efforts	Interrelated TQM Efforts
Strategic Alignment: Dynamic relationship between corporate and IS goals; focus on capitalizing on external opportunities and internal capabilities and cornpetencies derived from IT.	Reengineering efforts begin with the corporate objectives and aim to realign operational capabilities with corporate strategic goals.	TQM's efforts include alignment with the IS organization's goals to improve IS operations (e.g., introduce new software tools and promote acceptance by organizational users).
Customer Focus: Introduction or adoption of IT to increase customer satisfaction and create value-added services.	Reengineering is driven by customer demands and is taking advantage of the market opportunities derived from customer needs.	TQM is focusing on both internal customers (e.g., business divisions) and external customers (e.g., buyers, suppliers, competitors, support institutions).
Process Change: Changing, updating, or replacing existing IT-based processes to improve organizational effectiveness and efficiency (i.e., change management and systems planning).	BPR asks whether organizational processes can be redesigned to increase their effectiveness and looks at the interrelationships among the organizational processes affected by IT.	TQM emphasizes coordination among IS professionals and the rest of the organizational functions and continuous improvement of the processes across the organization's value chain.
Organizational Learning: Understanding the firm's critical success factors, the relationships among its cross-functional processes, and its capacity to prevent crises and disasters (i.e., scenario-based planning).	Reengineering examines the possibility of changing organizational members' business mental models by challenging management's existing assumptions and learning both from past failures and successes and from new IT developments.	TQM focuses on incremental changes similar to prototyping systems development methodology and learning by completing small steps in implementing change, using work groups, and sharing information across functional areas.

Exhibit 6.2.   Integrating BPR and TQM with IS planning.

Exhibit 6.2 depicts the integration of an organization's BPR and TQM process change efforts with IS planning.

INTEGRATED PROCESS CHANGE MANAGEMENT

Recent research and case studies confirm the similarities between ISP, BPR, and TQM. Organizations that engage in uncoordinated and sometimes concurrent efforts for ISP, BPR, and TQM engender the following problems and concerns:

- Different organizational members advocate and participate in often similar ISP, BPR, and TQM change initiatives, which result in redundancy, inefficiency, and inconsistency in organizational projects and goals.
- Some organizational members participate in more than one of the three initiatives, resulting in confusion and inability to define clear and consistent goals across the organization. In addition, because participants in ISP and TQM activities often fear that the reengineers will eliminate or ignore their efforts in the eagerness to start with a clean slate, they are reluctant to commit needed resources to ISP and TQM activities.
- Because of the confusion and lack of trust among the participants in the preceding two scenarios, very few ISP, BPR, and TQM projects can be successfully implemented.
- There are no clear and compatible measures or criteria of success for ISP, BPR, and TQM projects, resulting in inadequate evaluation of efforts to implement organizational change. Furthermore, although BPR advocates might view organizational change as strategic, TQM and ISP advocates might regard it as simply operational, thus making it almost impossible to set priorities for projects and coordinate change efforts across a firm.

Success Stories

Companies such as Pacific Bell, Xerox, and Texas Instruments (TI) are among the few firms that, under the concept of process management, have integrated traditional TQM procedures with IS process-modeling and BPR techniques. In these organizations, in contrast to what Michael Hammer and James Champy preached in *Reengineering the Corporation* (New York: Harper Business, 1993), BPR and TQM are viewed as two sides of the same coin and IS planning is integrated with their efforts toward process change management. For example, Pacific Bell and TI created central process-management teams responsible for providing tools and methods to concurrent BPR efforts and for ensuring that IS, TQM, and BPR teams are coordinated and learn from each other's successes and failures.

More specifically, at Pacific Bell, process management efforts include IS projects responsible for aligning systems development strategies and tools with the current needs of BPR projects. At Texas Instruments, various process-capture tools allow continuous improvement methods to be integrated with BPR and IS development processes; similarly, Xerox has created the concept of process owners who decide what kind of change needs to be performed in a broad business process (e.g., tweaking vs. a major overhaul) and how IS, TQM, and BPR groups can work together to provide the necessary tools and methodologies.

In contrast to these integrated environments, some companies continue to view BPR as a radically different type of activity for IT planning and TQM. Such companies take a more top-down approach that allows BPR consultants to identify specific projects and procedures and ignore any organizational learning accrued before their involvement. The problem with uncoordinated approaches, however, can be traced back to TQM efforts that attempted to deliver competitive advantage without considering key external and organizational factors (i.e., technology developments, market conditions, and corporate strategy), focusing instead on internal improvements and process changes.

BPR is not an entirely new activity, different from ISP and TQM. As Exhibit 6.3 illustrates, all three are complementary elements of efforts toward process change management. Although ISP, BPR, and TQM should be coordinated within an organization, certain activities are unique to each of them. These activities are shown as the nonoverlapping areas in Exhibit 6.3 and include the following:

- TQM usually involves bottom-up, incremental design changes focusing on specific processes.
- BPR usually involves a top-down orientation, focusing on innovation and radical change.
- ISP can be both top-down (i.e., strategic) and bottom-up (tactical) to identify corporate strategies as well as IS implementation problems. Successful ISP practice involves both top-down and bottom-up orientations to anticipate short-term organizational changes and long-term technology developments and market forces that could affect corporate goals.

STEPS FOR INTEGRATING ISP, BPR, AND TQM

The following steps form the basis for process change management and will help IS professionals integrate ISP, BPR, and TQM.

Determining priorities and organizational goals for each initiative. For example, does process change mean the same for ISP, BPR, and TQM groups? Organizational priorities can be established through the techniques of critical success factors (CSFs) and benchmarking, or be based on the organization's distinctive competencies (IT-based or otherwise). ISP, BPR, and TQM task forces should collaborate with top management in this stage.

Bringing participants from each initiative together to discuss their projects and identify similarities and differences among them. The shared dimensions of the three initiatives as delineated in Exhibit 6.1 should be used in this step.

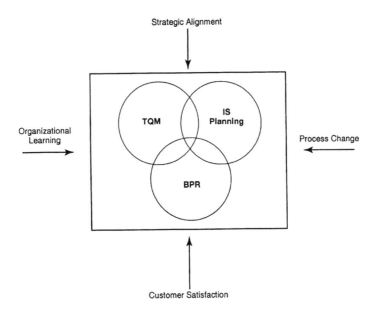

Exhibit 6.3.   ISP, TQM, and BPR as complementary efforts of process change management.

Establishing collaborative meetings or groups to discuss organizational learning issues over the course of ISP, BPR, and TQM efforts. Such groups discuss what the organization has learned from each initiative so far to make use of successful processes and avoid repetition of past mistakes. *Avoiding redundant activities.* Scheduling regular informative meetings at which teams disclose their findings helps ensure that activities are complementary rather than redundant.
Setting synchronous and clear goals. This step is accomplished by having teams agree on measurement criteria or participate in one another's evaluation procedures.

ROLE OF IS MANAGEMENT

The importance of IT resources in any BPR and TQM effort gives IS management a central and sensitive role in the integration process. By conveying the following key concepts to the BPR and TQM groups, IS managers clarify the necessity of integration as well as the IS function's supportive role in the effort toward organizational change.

Shared Resources and Expertise

The whole organization benefits when teams share resources and expertise while working toward process innovation (BPR), continuous process improvement (TQM), and IT-based strategic advantage (ISP). Stressing the common goals among the three initiatives (e.g., alignment, customer satisfaction, process improvement, and organizational learning) helps clarify this concept. IS managers can also play the role of the outside IT consultant for both BPR and TQM initiatives.

Alignment of Technology with Corporate and Customer Needs

Teamwork and inclusion of IS managers in BPR and TQM decision processes and projects increases the likelihood that the systems delivered by IS will be aligned with corporate goals, as well as with customer (internal and external) specifications. Furthermore, senior executives are more likely to accept and support recommendations for organizational change when participants from all three initiatives are involved in and accountable for final process change results.

Commitment and Accountability

Integrating ISP, BPR, and TQM efforts is not about giving more control to the IS organization and management. It is about commitment and accountability — both at the individual and group levels — to build a platform for shared expertise and organizational goals.

Strategic Advantage

The ISP-BPR-TQM think tank promotes competency-based strategies and creates processes and systems that optimize the organization's unique capabilities and resources.

Prototyping for Success

Prototyping procedures in which pilot systems and processes are tested before full-scale implementation and full commitment of resources increases the success rate for the perspective change and enhances the learning capacity of the ISP, BPR, and TQM groups.

Common Measurement Criteria

Consistent measurement criteria across all three initiatives ease the transition from independence and redundancy to integration and sharing. Common criteria among BPR, ISP, and TQM include process quality, product quality, system quality, customer satisfaction, cost reduction, faster delivery, and value-added service to customers.

Measurement should not be based on a bottom-line approach that continuously monitors costs and benefits. Such an approach eventually results in micro savings and demoralization of the ISP-BPR-TQM alliance. Measurement should be flexible, because there is no guaranteed way to include or predict all benefits and costs from a system or process, and allow for innovation and guided risk taking. This approach gives participants a certain degree of responsibility for decision making and brings better results in the long run. In summary, measurement should be able to see both the forest and the trees in regard to the short- and long-range goals of a BPR, ISP, and TQM alliance.

CONCLUSION

Organizations that quickly jump from one management trend to another without first learning from past experience have high failure rates in their efforts toward process change management. In contrast, organizations that have a universal management philosophy embedded in all activities related to improvement and change compete successfully. In an age when global competition and continuous technology developments are the norm, the ISP-BPR-TQM holistic model capitalizes on and integrates the learning that occurs in IS planning, business process reengineering, and total quality management.

Chapter 7

Strategic Information Technology Planning and the Line Manager's Role

Robert Heckman

How can a company gain the benefits of entrepreneurial IT decision making by line managers without permitting the IT environment to become a high-cost, low-performance, disconnected collection of independent systems? This chapter proposes an approach to IT planning that includes a formal role and responsibility for line managers. When combined with centralized IT architecture planning, this planning technique creates an approach to information management that is simultaneously top-down and bottom-up.

The pendulum is swinging back. For more than a decade the responsibility for managing and deploying information resources has ebbed away from the centralized Information Management (IM) department and into line departments. The end-user computing revolution of the eighties was followed by the client-server revolution of the nineties. In both cases the hoped-for outcome was the location of information resources closer to the customer and closer to marketplace decisions, which in turn would lead to better customer service, reduced cycle time, and greater empowerment of users.

The reality, however, was often quite different. Costs for information technology spiraled out of control, as up to half the money a company spent on information technology was hidden in line managers' budgets. In addition to higher costs, distributed architectures often resulted in information systems with poor performance and low reliability. Because the disciplines that had been developed for centralized mainframe systems were lacking, experienced technologists were not surprised when client-server systems performed poorly. Many client-server systems lacked (and still

0-8493-9820-7/00/$0.00+$.50
© 2000 by CRC Press LLC

lack) effective back-up and recovery procedures, capacity planning procedures, or performance analysis metrics. With costs up and performance down, CEOs are once again calling for greater centralized control over information resources.

The growing movement toward enterprise resource planning (ERP) systems such as those offered by SAP, PeopleSoft, and Baan has also increased awareness of the need for careful management of the IT infrastructure. The architectures of the client-server versions of these systems paradoxically create a need for stronger centralized control of the IT infrastructure. Large companies such as Kodak (SAP) and Corning (PeoplSoft) have created single infrastructure development teams with integrated responsibilities for technical architecture, database administration, site assessment, and planning.

Finally, the diffusion of Internet and intranet resources has suggested to many that a more centralized approach to control of network resources is also desirable — in fact, even necessary. Recent discussions about the network computer, one which obtains virtually all application and data resources from a central node, have reminded more than one observer of the IBM 3270 "dumb terminal" era.

THE IT MANAGEMENT CHALLENGE

Despite these drivers toward re-centralization, the forces which originally led to diffusion of IT management responsibility still exist. Certainly, the impact of information technology continues to grow and at the same time becomes more widely diffused throughout organizations. Likewise, the need to respond quickly to competitive thrusts continues to increase the value of independent IT decision making by line managers. As technologies become more user-friendly and the work force becomes more IT literate, it is inevitable that line managers will face more and more technology-related decisions.

The challenge, then, is how to gain the benefits of entrepreneurial IT decision making by line managers without permitting the IT environment to become a high-cost, low-performance, fragmented, and disconnected collection of independent systems.

One solution to the IT management challenge is better IT planning. Information systems planning is an idea which has been with us for some time, and numerous systems planning methodologies have been developed and published. However, most IT planning methodologies are based on a top-down, centralized approach and are motivated more by technology issues than by business issues. They tend to be driven or facilitated by technologists within the centralized IM organization, or by outside consultants engaged by IM. Ownership of the process and the responsibility for its success are vested in the IM analyst's role.

Top-down centralized planning conducted by the IM department has an important, even critical role, especially in large organizations. The construction of a single, standardized IT architecture and infrastructure is a crucial step for the successful integration of systems throughout the organization. It provides the foundation upon which aligned business and technology strategies can be built. The development and management of the infrastructure is clearly a centralized IM responsibility. However, it only solves one-half of the IT management and planning problem. Top-down, centralized IT planning is unlikely to result in a portfolio of IT investments which effectively *use* the infrastructure to achieve business objectives.

A DIALECTICAL APPROACH

A more comprehensive view of IT planning is needed to address the simultaneous needs for centralized coordination and diffused decision making. The first step is to recognize that such planning will necessarily be dialectical — that is, it will involve conflict. To say that a process is dialectical implies tension or opposition between two interacting forces. A dialectical planning process systematically juxtaposes contradictory ideas and seeks to resolve the conflict between them.

This expanded view of planning is based on the idea that effective planning can be neither exclusively top-down nor exclusively bottom-up. It must be both. The key to success using this planning philosophy is the creation of a formal role for line managers in the IT planning process. The top-down/bottom-up IT planning approach shown in Exhibit 7.1 is built on three fundamental principles:

1. *Push responsibility for IT planning down and out into the organization.* The ability to manage and plan for information resources must be a normal and expected skill for every line manager, equal in importance to the management of human and financial resources.
2. *Integrate the IT planning activities of line managers through the role of a chief information officer (CIO).* By emphasizing the benefits of entrepreneurial IT decision making by the line manager responsible for business strategy, organizations run the risk of the IT environment becoming fragmented and unresponsive. The CIO, as leader of the Information Management Department, must be responsible for integration and control of IM throughout the organization.
3. *View the IT environment as an information market economy.* Line managers are free to acquire resources from the information market as they choose. However, just as the federal government regulates

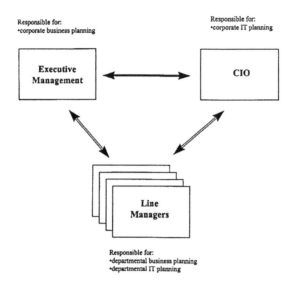

Exhibit 7.1. Responsibilities in a Dialectical Planning Process

activities in the national economy through guidelines, policies, and standards, the CIO establishes the information infrastructure within which line managers make information market decisions (Boynton and Zmud, 1987).

This emphasis on departmental strategy as opposed to corporate strategy is intentional. It does not deny the critical importance of unified corporate-level business and IT strategies. Rather, it acknowledges that there are often departmental strategies that are not identified in corporate strategy or that may, to some degree, conflict with corporate strategy. A top-down/bottom-up planning process recognizes the possibility that corporate-level business and IT strategies may be influenced over time by the strategic choices made in the sub-units.

THE LINE MANAGER'S ROLE

Since much attention both in literature and in practice has been given to the top-down component of IT planning, procedures for this kind of work are widely understood in the community of technologists. IT planning, however, is likely to be an unfamiliar job for many line managers. The following simplified planning process (shown in Exhibit 7.2) may provide a useful framework for line managers to follow when beginning departmental IT planning.

Unlike many detailed processes which are more suitable for project-level planning, this streamlined approach is valuable because it ensures that

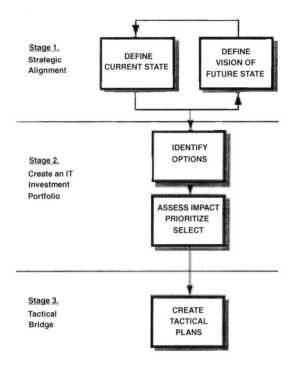

Exhibit 7.2. An IT Planning Process for Line Management

line managers focus their attention at the strategic and tactical levels rather than at the detailed project level. The process is also highly flexible and adaptable. Within each of the three stages any number of techniques may be adopted and combined to create a customized process which is comfortable to each organizational culture.

Stage 1: Strategic Alignment

The overall objective of Stage 1 is to ensure alignment between business and technology strategies. It contains two basic tasks: developing an understanding of the current technology situation and creating a motivating vision statement describing a desired future state. In addition to understanding and documenting the current business and technology contexts, this stage has the goal of generating enthusiasm and support from senior management and generating commitment, buy-in, and appropriate expectation levels in all stakeholders.

One technique for creating a rich description of the current business and technology situation is the BASEline analysis. The four steps in the BASEline analysis procedure are shown in Exhibit 7.3. Additional tech-

Every planning process should begin with a clear understanding of the current situation. The purpose of a BASEline Analysis is to define the current state in a systematic way. To insure comprehensiveness, it draws on multiple sources of information. While it is true that the process of intelligence gathering should be ongoing, proactive, and systematic, the formal planning exercise provides an opportunity to review and reflect on information already compiled. In addition, gaps in the current knowledge base can be identified and filled.

The BASEline analysis procedure explores the current state in terms of four dimensions:

Business Strategy: If the IT strategy is to be in alignment with the business strategy, it is crucial the business strategy be clearly articulated and understood by all members of the planning team.

Assets: If the IT strategy is to be implementable, it must be realistic. That is, it must be based on an objective assessment of the assets currently available or realistically obtainable by the organization. Included in this analysis are tangible assets such as hardware and software, databases, capital, and people. In addition, invisible assets such as management skills, technical skills, proprietary applications, core competencies, marketplace position, customer loyalty, also provide a foundation for future strategic moves.

System Strategy: To avoid fragmentation, duplication, and incompatibility, a departmental IT plan must recognize the opportunities and constraints provided by corporate IT policies and infrastructure. The departmental planning team must be knowledgeable about corporate standards and plans to effectively integrate its initiatives.

Environments: External environments often create important constraints and opportunities for IT planners. Relevant strategic planning assumptions about future technological, regulatory, economic and social environments must be brought to the surface, and agreed upon by the planning team.

Exhibit 7.3. BASEline Analysis

niques which can be used in Stage 1 are scenario creation, stakeholder interviews, brainstorming, and nominal group techniques.

Stage 2: Create an IT Investment Portfolio

In this stage the objective is to identify a rich set of options for future information technology investments. In addition to generating potential investment options, in this stage it is also important to understand which options will have the greatest impact on the business, to assess the risk associated with each option, and to estimate the resources required to implement the impact options.

Techniques which may be used in this stage are the strategic option generator (Wiseman, 1988), value chain analysis (Porter & Millar, 1985), critical success factor analysis (Shank et al., 1985), brainstorming, and nominal group techniques. It may also be useful in this stage to systematize the evaluation process through the use of some form of scoring model. A scoring model enables the planning team to integrate considerations such as financial benefit, strategic impact, and risk.

Stage 3: Tactical Bridge

In this stage the line manager takes the crucial actions necessary to ensure that the strategic IT investment portfolio is actually implemented. To overcome the greatest single threat to strategic technology planning — a plan that is put on the shelf and never looked at again — it is important to ensure that resources are made available to implement the projects which comprise the investment portfolio. To do this, it is necessary to integrate the work accomplished in strategic planning with the ongoing, periodic tactical planning which occurs in most organizations.

The most important tactical planning activities are often financial. It is imperative that money be allocated in the annual budgeting cycle to execute the strategic projects identified in the IT investment portfolio. While this may seem obvious, companies often fail to make this link. It is assumed that the operating budget will automatically take into account the strategic work done six months earlier, but in the political process of budget allocation, the ideas in the strategic plan can easily be forgotten. Human resources are also often taken for granted. However, careful tactical planning is usually necessary to insure that the right blend of skills will be available to implement the projects called for in the strategic plan. Once appropriate resources (time, money, people) have been allocated, then intermediate milestones and criteria for evaluation should be developed.

Finally, effective communication of the strategic and tactical work that has been done is a crucial step. Dissemination of the planning work through management and staff presentations and publications will ensure that organizational learning occurs. Thus, attention should be devoted in Stage 3 not only to ensure that strategic plans are implementable, but that they continue to affect the organization's strategic thinking in the future.

PLANNING PROCEDURES

When beginning the process of IT planning for the first time, a number of basic procedural issues will have to be addressed and resolved. Who is the line manager responsible for developing an IT plan? Who should be involved in the IT planning process? How formal should the process be? What deliverables should be produced? What is an appropriate planning horizon? What is the right planning cycle?

There is no one right answer to these questions. The culture and the leadership style of the company and the department will to a great degree influence how planning processes are executed. There are, however, several procedural guidelines which may be useful for line managers who are undertaking the task of IT planning:

Who Is the Line Manager?

The key role in this process is played by the department or business unit manager. In smaller companies, no more than two or three senior executives may play the line manager role as described here. Larger corporations may have as many as 20 or 30 business units with a scope that warrants independent IT planning. Regardless of who occupies the role of line manager, it is absolutely critical that this individual take an active interest in IT planning and be personally involved in the process. He or she is the only one who can ensure that directly reporting managers view planning for information resources as an integral part of their job accountability.

Who Should Be Involved?

Composition of a planning team is a delicate art. We may think of representation on the planning team both horizontally and vertically. Attention to horizontal representation ensures that all sub-units are represented in the planning process. Attention to vertical representation ensures that employees at all levels of the organization have the opportunity to provide input to the planning process. It is also critical that departmental IT planning has a link to corporate IT planning. Thus it is usually beneficial to include a member of the central IM staff on the departmental planning team. Other outside members may also be appropriate, especially those who can provide needed technical expertise in areas such as emerging technologies where the line management team may not have the necessary technical expertise.

Process and Deliverables

As the business environment becomes more dynamic and volatile, the technology planning process must be more flexible and responsive. Thus the planning process should not be too rigid or too formal. It should provide the opportunity for numerous face-to-face encounters between the important participants. Structure for the process should provide well-defined forums for interaction rather than a rigidly specified set of planning documents. Perhaps a more effective mechanism for delivering the work of planning teams is for the line manager to periodically present the departmental IT plan to other senior managers, the CIO, and to members of his own staff.

Planning Horizon

The planning horizon must also be determined with the dynamic nature of the information technology environment in mind. Although here are exceptions, it is usually unrealistic for a department manager to plan with any precision beyond two years. Corporate IT planning, on the other hand, must look further when considering the corporate system's infrastructure and policies. This long-term IT direction must be well understood by departmental managers, for it is critical to line planning activities.

Planning Cycle: A Continuous Process

Plans must be monitored and updated frequently. It may be sufficient to go through a formal planning exercise annually, including all three steps mentioned earlier. Checkpoint sessions, however, may occur at various intervals throughout the year. Major evaluations—such as the purchase of a large software package or the choice of a service provider—are likely to occur at any time in the cycle and should be carefully integrated with planning assumptions. It is absolutely critical that the strategic IT plan be integrated into other strategic and tactical planning processes, such as strategic business planning and annual budgeting for the department. Unless this linkage is formally established, it is very unlikely that strategic IT planning will have much influence on subsequent activities.

CONCLUSION

Regardless of the procedures chosen, the goal is for all members of the organization to understand that strategic IT planning is a critical component of business success. Everyone should be aware of the decisions reached and the linkage between business strategy and technology strategy. In the future, when all members of line management recognize that strategic technology planning is an essential component of strategic business planning, then an emphasis on strategic IT planning as a stand-alone activity may not be necessary.

For now, however, as the pendulum swings back from decentralized to centralized control of information resources, there is a risk that line managers may not recognize the need for strategic IT planning. As we better understand the importance of centralized control of the IT infrastructure, we must not forget that the integration of IT into business strategy remains the province of every line manager who runs a business unit.

REFERENCES

Boynton, A.C. and Zmud, R., "Information Technology Planning in the 1990s: Directions for Practice and Research," *MIS Quarterly,* 11(1), 1987, 59-71.

Porter, M. and Millar, V., "How Information Gives You Competitive Advantage," *Harvard Business Review,* July, 1985.

Shank, E. M., Boynton, A. C, and Zmud, R., "Critical Success Factors as a Methodology for MIS planning," *MIS Quarterly,* June 1985, pp. 121-129.

Wiseman, C. 1988. *Strategic Information Systems,* Irwin Publishing, Toronto, Ontario, Canada.

Chapter 8
Managing Advanced Information Technology
Louis Fried

THE DRIVE TO SEEK IMPROVEMENT has resulted in a burgeoning interest in technology management ranging from acquisition through exploitation of new technologies. Although many technologies are of primary interest to one or two industries, all industries have a common interest in information technology.

Most major corporations would not be able to operate their businesses without computer systems. Executives have awakened to the fact that technology management is as important for their information systems as it is for their manufacturing facilities and their products. This chapter details the objectives of technology management and the link between the introduction of new information technology and business process redesign.

TECHNOLOGY MANAGEMENT

Two major issues, inexorably linked together, trouble IS directors of major corporations. These issues are

- Supporting the redesign of company business processes.
- Replacing legacy systems that are impeding the IS function's ability to respond flexibly to business needs.

The link between these two issues is the ability of the IS function to plan for, acquire, and deploy new information technology for the development and operation of new applications.

The internal needs of IS — better price/performance ratios, faster software development paradigms, specialized application capabilities, smaller increments of capacity increases, and improved architectural flexibility — generally require a substantial short-term increase in new technology costs before the long-term benefits can be realized. Although business needs have spurred the adoption of new information technology, in many cases, IS departments are poorly equipped to deal with the entire scope of managing the introduction of new technology to the organization. Technology management is not only a problem for IS in fast-paced industries such as bio-technology or electronics, technology management is critical to continued survival.

The scope of technology management includes a broad range of activities such as:

- Strategic technology positioning.
- Tracking technology trends.
- Aligning technology needs with business needs.
- Identifying appropriate new technology.
- Identifying the technology rendezvous (i.e., the relative importance of technologies to the business compared with the time at which the technology should be adopted by the company).
- Justifying technology acquisition.
- Acquiring new technology.
- Introducing new technology.
- Adapting technology to the business needs.
- Deploying technology.

This chapter offers a strategic perspective on some of these issues.

STRATEGIC TECHNOLOGY POSITIONING

Although many aspects of technology management could be assumed under this activity, this chapter takes a narrower view. Strategic technology positioning consists of adopting policies and procedures that set forth the management position regarding technology. An organization may determine that its competitive position is best served by being an adopter, an adapter, or an inventor of technology. Adopters frequently use off-the-shelf products and thus trail others in technology acquisition. Adapters make technology acquisitions. Adapters make technology an essential element of their value-based planning and use new technology in innovative ways. Inventors seek opportunities through creating new or innovative uses of technology to stay far ahead of competition.

Furthermore, producers must align the feedback of technology opportunities with the business plans. Strategic business plans developed without regard to the competitive threats and opportunities supported by technology advances can be blind-sided by more aggressive users of technology.

TRACKING TECHNOLOGY TRENDS

Large IS groups frequently have specific positions created to track technology. Technology tracking activities are often part of a technology planning or systems architecture group within the IS division. Although some managers feel that technology tracking is a part of every systems analyst's job, more successful results are obtained when the effort is not so diffused. Because successful technology planning must be continuous, specific assignment of responsibility is necessary. In smaller companies that cannot dedicate full-time personnel to this task, the responsibility should be made explicit for one or two individuals as a part-time function with defined results expected.

Technology tracking can only work properly in the framework of strategic technology positioning. It is futile to track emerging technologies if the company's position is that of an adopter. However, for technology adapters and inventors, a vision and understanding of the future and of technology life cycles are imperative. This understanding of the technology life cycle serves as a means to determine areas where skills need to be developed, to identify new projects, to improve productivity and quality, and to anticipate potential competitive advantages and disadvantages. A technology's life cycle consists of six stages:

1. *Breakthrough and basic research.* The technology is invented and advanced to a stage at which product development is feasible.
2. *Research and development.* Initial products are developed.
3. *Emergence.* Products are introduced and the market is educated to accept the products.
4. *Growth.* New products using the technology continue to be offered at a rapid pace.
5. *Maturity.* The market for the technology stabilizes and products become commonly applied.
6. *Decline.* The technology is superseded by newer technologies that have functional cost, or performance advantages.

Usually, businesses must consider technology applications rather than simply individual technologies. Technology applications are generally constructed by blending individual technologies; personal computing, for example, was made possible by technology trends in miniaturization, local area networking, and graphical user interfaces, among other technologies. By monitoring the stages of information technologies, which develop at different paces, a company can observe the applications to which technologies are applied.

ALIGNING TECHNOLOGY STRATEGY WITH BUSINESS NEEDS

Tracking technology without regard to the needs of the business can waste a lot of time and money. It is absolutely critical that those tracking the technology be aware of its potential uses in the processes and products or services of the company. This knowledge enables technology planners to:

- Appraise those technologies that may be used immediately for competitive advantage.
- Appraise changes or new developments that may be used for competitive advantage over the next three to five years.
- Identify potential applications of current and future technology and how such applications may affect the competition.
- Identify potential changes in current applications driven by market demands or technology developments.

Aligning technology strategy with business needs is one of the most frequently identified problems facing corporate IS executives. This alignment requires knowledge of the business operations of each strategic business unit in the corporation, their competitive business strategies, and the best available information on the technology and business strategies of their competitors. In addition, it requires the active participation of both information technologists and users to develop an understanding of the potential for use of information technology and a consistent vision of the future.

Research in technology management and product development has shown the success of triad management. Triad management techniques create teams of marketing, technology suppliers (e.g., engineering or R&D), and manufacturing representatives to rapidly introduce new technologies or bring new products to market. Similarly, most successful IS implementations are those that were required and driven by the users. To achieve alignment, IS must form alliances and occasional task forces or teams with user organizations. Technology planning is no exception if the alignment of technology and business strategy is the goal.

Alignment of technology strategy with business strategy requires two modes of operations:

- The technology strategy must be able to respond quickly to changing business needs.
- The technology potential and vision must be able to influence the development of business strategy.

Technology Planning Specialists

Even though the profusion of personal computers has forced employees and managers to become more computer literate, there are still noncomputing professionals who do not have insights into the full potential of computing and communications technology.

Technology planners should make a point of meeting with user managers, not only to educate them informally, but to learn about their business operations and needs. Most people are flattered to be asked about their jobs, and most line managers will readily respond to requests from IS personnel to learn more about their business operations.

Technology planners also need to discover how competing companies are using information technology. This does not imply industrial espionage, but simply tracking the trade press, attending industry or information technology conferences, and talking with prospective vendors and suppliers. Innovative applications can arise outside the company's industry and be applicable to company needs, so this intelligence effort should not be confined to the company's industry.

Increasingly, close cooperation with both suppliers and customers is needed to be competitive and to respond to market conditions. It is now necessary to view the organization and its business processes as part of an extended enterprise composed of the organization, its allies, suppliers, and major customers. Technology planners must either create relationships within the businesses that will provide the perspective of the extended enterprise or they must initiate relationships with key suppliers and customers to understand their uses of information technology and how the company's processes need to interface those of its business partners.

Building the Business Case

As technology planners acquire a knowledge of the industry and the business, they must document this knowledge so it may be used to build a business case for new applications. They also need to find a way to translate the needs of strategic business units into a projection of when and how new or emerging technologies will influence the company's industry.

First, with a knowledge of the industry's business processes, technology planners can construct a value chain. For example, in a manufacturing company, the value chain may contain the major elements of R&D, engineering, logistics, operations and manufacturing, marketing, distribution, sales, and service. New technology can affect any aspect of this chain through such areas as product design tools, materials or components procurement, inventory management, manufacturing methods and controls, maintenance of plant and equipment, packaging processes, and sales and service tracking. The potential applications that can provide leverage and maximize the contribution to the corporation from technology investment can be recognized. In addition, the technologies capable of supporting those applications can be identified.

Working with user managers, technology planners can gain an understanding of both the leverage points and the perceived priorities of managers. These factors determine the relative importance of various technologies to the organization compared to the time at which the technology should be adopted by the company.

The time of *technology rendezvous* is important for meeting strategic alignment objectives. When constructed on the basis of knowledge of the industry and the competition, it provides a senior executive view of the needs for introducing new technology or extending the use of currently available technology to remain competitive, thus influencing corporate business strategy. Simultaneously, it provides IS with a view of when and how it should anticipate training, experimentation, and application development using these technologies. This knowledge directly influences long-range application planning, IS budgeting, and hardware and software selection.

INFORMATION TECHNOLOGY DEVELOPMENT

Professionals involved in technology management have discovered that technology per se is rarely deployable. Instead, technology is deployed through application.

For example, a new technology for the manufacture of integrated circuits is deployed through the change of processes and equipment on the production line; a new materials technology for manufacturing automobile fenders will be deployed through changes in the molding equipment and the manufacturing and assembly processes. Similarly, new information technology is deployed through its application for the benefit of the company and its processes and users.

Information technology deployment through applications means changes and requisite training for the application designers and developers as well as for the users. The processes that will change may include requirements definition, systems design specification, programming, user documentation development, application testing, system installation, system support, and end-user business processes. These changes may result in an organizational change to the systems development and maintenance function to permit more rapid applications development and better field support to users. Substantive changes that allow companies to take full advantage of enabling information systems technology almost invariably require changes in the business processes and in the organizations that perform these processes.

Up to this point, this chapter has dealt primarily with technology planning, including identification of business needs and identification of appropriate new technologies to support those needs. The actual acquisition of new technology requires justification in terms that meet the approval of senior management. Even if the planning stages have been carried out with appropriate approval by senior management, the introduction of specific elements of the plan requires detailed planning and justification based on the benefits of applications to the business.

Two types of technology introduction predominate: those that do not have an impact visible to the users and those that have a direct effect on the user. In the first case, for example, an IS department may introduce a subsystem for massive parallel processing that adds capacity to process additional transactions of the same nature and, in the same apparent manner, as current transactions. Such a technology introduction may be invisible to the users of the systems (other than the impact from system testing before implementation). However, it would be highly visible to the IS department as new design and programming techniques are introduced. Many other introductions of new technology inevitably change the way employees who use the applications perform their tasks.

Reengineering

The goal of many organizations is to replace old systems with new ones that are easier to maintain and modify, support the types of user interfaces to which users of personal computers have become accustomed, and support new modes of business operation. For many applications, downsizing of equipment and the introduction of client/server architectures will provide significantly lower operating costs.

One reason that apparently successful systems development projects have not achieved expected benefits is that the applications were designed to support existing business processes. When existing business processes form the foundation for the requirements definition, even anticipated gains in efficiency may be unrealized. The result: companies have begun using a collection of methods and tools under the general name of business process redesign (BPR), or reengineering.

Many consulting firms have adopted variations of the BPR methods. SRI International defines BPR as a methodology for transforming the business process of an enterprise to achieve breakthroughs in the quality, responsiveness, flexibility, and cost of those processes to compete more effectively and efficiently in the enterprise's chosen market. BPR uses a combination of industrial engineering, operations research, management theory, performance measurement, quality management, and systems analysis techniques and tools simultaneously to redesign business processes and to harness the power of information technology to support these restructured business processes more effectively.

BPR projects are designed to take a fresh look at a major business process from a customer perspective. The customer of a process may be the external customer of its products or services or may be the internal recipient of the process output.

Redesigning business processes using new technology benefits the company by improving efficiency and making business processes more responsive to customer needs. In the end, it represents a clear manner in which technology influences the strategy of the company.

SRI's seven-step BPR methodology and some of the associated elements, tools, and techniques used are outlined in Exhibit 8.1. By using this or similar BPR or reengineering approaches, organizations can overcome resistance to change and the problems of maintaining the effectiveness of employees during the period of transition to the new systems and business processes that affect the way employees perform their jobs.

Guidelines for Successful Technology Deployment

Project Framework. Few companies succeed with projects that massively change the entire company's operating structure. New technology introduced within such a project framework runs a high risk of adding to the company's problems rather than solving them. Generally, projects that address a single process (e.g., materials procurement, loan approval processing, or claims processing) have a greater likelihood of success. Success in the initial project that introduces new technology is crucial to expanding the use of the technology in the organization. In fact, it may be critical to the entire process of acceptance of new technology by management and employees.

Keep Employees Well Informed. All affected or potentially affected company personnel should be provided with regular information about the BPR project's purpose, status, effect on existing processes and employees, training schedules, and interface needs. This information should be delivered within the context of the expected benefits to the company's competitive positions so that everyone involved retains a focus on the value of the change.

Acknowledge Downsizing Effects. If staff reductions are anticipated, employees should receive a statement from senior management at the beginning of the project about how such reductions will be managed. For example, a statement that all staff reductions will be managed through normal attrition can make a major difference in employee cooperation. Management positions on how employees will be retrained, what options exist for transfer or early retirement, or what types of outplacement support will be provided should be publicized. Some companies have offered bonuses to employees facing displacement so that they will remain at their positions until new systems or processes are completely installed.

Continuity. The implementation time for redesigning a major business process and introducing new technology that enables the new process may be two or more years. It is vital to the success of the project that the senior management sponsors of the project be committed to this time

1. *Taking the Customer's View.* Identifying factors that lead to customer satisfaction, from the customer's perspective.
   - Customer focus groups.
   - Customer surveys.
   - Customer interviews.
   - Customer evaluation.
   - Transaction analysis.

2. *Taking Management's View.* Identifying management's perspective of factors that lead to customer satisfaction and the differences between the two perspectives.
   - Management interviews.
   - Management focus groups.

3. *Current Process Definition and Measurement.* Documenting the current business process; measuring output of the process and subprocess to develop a foundation for the redesign.
   - Work flow observation.
   - Structured interviews.
   - Process flow diagramming.
   - Data and Control flow diagramming.
   - CASE tools.
   - PERT tools.
   - Process cycle time analysis.
   - Intermediate and output measurement.
   - Statistical analysis of output production.
   - Problem root-cause analysis.

4. *Working Group Education.* Educating client's BPR participants about the potentials of process restructuring and IT as applicable to the problem domain.
   - Presentations on:
     — Process redesign methods.
     — Process definition and tools.
     — IT capabilities.
     — Business cases.
   - Workbook of articles and papers.

Exhibit 8.1. Seven-step BPR methodology.

---

frame and that they be kept informed of progress throughout the implementation.

Coordinated Assistance. Advice or assistance should be sought and encouraged from both management and the employees involved in the project during implementation; for example, it may be appropriate to seek

5. *Identifying Change Opportunities.* Brainstorming with BPR team members to create a new business process.
   - Process and data/control flow diagrams.
   - CASE tools.
   - Measurement results interpretation.
   - Process walkthrough methods.
   - Alternative evaluation methods.
   - Redesign requirements analysis and deployment.
   - Measurement and metrics design.
   - PERT tools

6. *Analysis of Recommended Action.* Conducting detailed planning of the new process; identifying IT implications, new technology trends, new system architectures; developing cost/benefit estimates; and preparing a proposal to management for the business process change.
   - Management and organizational change analysis.
   - Business case for redesign.
   - System architecture.
   - Technology forecasting.
   - Project cost estimating (including training).
   - Hardware/software cost estimating.
   - Cost/benefit analysis.
   - Project planning.
   - Risk analysis.
   - Presentation preparation tools.

7. *Approval, Commitment, and Implementation.* Obtaining management approval and detailed project planning.
   - Presentation preparation tools (implementation is not covered by the BPR methodology).

SOURCE: SRI International

Exhibit 8.1. (continued)

---

the assistance of the human resources or personnel functions to deal with changes that affect employees. Furthermore, coordination with the managers of functions that use the output of the redesigned process must be maintained to ensure that new interfaces operate smoothly. If the process involves external suppliers or distributors, it may be necessary to set up a help desk or hotline during the implementation phase or train field representatives to assist such external participants.

Evaluate and Monitor the New Process. Where possible, it is essential to set up and evaluate a pilot operation of the redesigned business process.

Debugging is always easier when only a limited part of the company's activities have been committed.

The results of the process change should be monitored in terms of the measures and goals established during the analysis phase, and these results should be periodically reported for at least the first year or more of the implementation. The measurement devices should be built into the new process to provide continuous measurement and to form a basis for further evolution in the future.

CONCLUSION

Acquiring appropriate technology that can advance an organization's competitive position requires a dedicated and continuing effort. Acquisition of appropriate technology first requires that the technology planners understand the needs of the business and the strategic technology position that senior management has adopted.

Second, technology planners must maintain an awareness of technology trends to ensure the organization's ability to support its business needs and technology position. Technology planners must position IS not only to support the organization's business directions but to influence company or business strategy. Next, IS and technology planners must justify the adoption of new technology in terms of the new or improved business processes that the new systems will support. The key to successful introduction and deployment of new information technology is business process redesign that combines the business strategy, the process improvement justification, and the technology into a coherent approach that can be readily conveyed to senior management.

Chapter 9
Moving the IT Work Force to a Client/Server Environment

Eileen Birge

TRANSFORMING CURRENT MAINFRAME development and operations staff to a client/server environment is an intensive process. During the first year of the move to client/server technology, the IS department makes critical decisions — decisions that will affect the systems development and operating environments for years to come.

GAINING COMMITMENT FOR STAFF RETRAINING

Companies have taken several approaches to acquiring client/server skills:

- Laying off existing resources and hiring personnel with the new skills.
- Using systems integrators to develop the initial applications and transferring knowledge to the current staff.
- Independently retraining the current staff and hiring (or contracting for) a minimum number of new skill resources.

Recruiting fees, reduced productivity while learning the organization's structure, culture and products, management time to recruit and interview, and high turnover from a work force with limited company loyalty are just a few of the costs associated with replacing current employees.

Most companies moving to client/server have looked at the costs and the benefits of transforming their current staff and elected to retrain and retain. What are the benefits of retaining?

- *Employee loyalty.* Systems work often requires extra effort. Employees who recognize the investment the company has made in them will respond appropriately.
- *Retention of knowledge.* This includes retention of knowledge about the company and its values.
- *Knowledge of systems development process, audit trails, security, and controls.* Many of the skills associated with good development are not specifically technology related. It is usually less expensive to retain these skills and add the technology component than to buy pure technology knowledge and build development skills.

One research company has estimated the cost of retraining for a standard 200-person department at $5.5 million. Management must thoroughly understand that transformation is a process and that not all benefits of the new technology will be realized in the first few months. This whole project should be treated as a major capital expenditure with the same types of approvals and reviews that a company would give to a capital project of this magnitude.

MAKING THE PARTNERING DECISION

Early in the transformation process, the organization must determine the extent of involvement of outside resources. At one end of the spectrum is a partnership arrangement where the experienced outside resource has a long-term commitment throughout the process and provides or contracts for nearly all services. At the other extreme, an organization uses outside resources only in a limited manner, with an internal commitment to do it themselves, rather than use outsiders (i.e., make rather than buy) whenever possible. Regardless of the choice, the approach to a partnering decision should be articulated at the beginning. If the organization chooses significant partner involvement, time and effort should be spent in choosing the partner carefully. Key items to look for include the following:

- *Depth of commitment.* Does the prospect practice internally the methods, technologies, and organizational behavior of interest to the organization?
- *Corporate culture.* Is the prospect's culture one with which the organization feels comfortable?
- *Flexibility.* Will the prospect truly study the organization, or is the prospect wedded to one approach and ready to advocate that solution? For example, do they sell one particular vendor's products or only sell their own proprietary approach?
- *Track record.* How has the prospect performed in assisting other companies?
- *Risk acceptance.* Is the prospect willing to tie financial reward to successful outcomes?

CREATING AN ATMOSPHERE OF CHANGE

There is an anecdote on change. The chair of a meeting says: "Change is good. Change is exciting. Let the change begin." Meanwhile all the meeting participants are thinking: "Who's getting fired?" If this anecdote represents thinking of the organization to be transformed, attitudes must be adjusted before proceeding.

The process of creating the right atmosphere for change is a major project in itself and beyond the scope of this chapter. Key points for creating this atmosphere, however, include the following:

- Allowing room for participation.
- Leaving choices.
- Providing a clear picture.
- Sharing information.
- Taking a small step first.
- Minimizing surprises.
- Allowing for digestion.
- Demonstrating IS management commitment repeatedly.
- Making standards and requirements clear.
- Offering positive reinforcement.
- Looking for and rewarding pioneers.
- Compensating extra time and energy.
- Avoiding creating obvious losers.
- Creating excitement about the future.

ESTABLISHING THE VISION OF THE IS GROUP OF THE FUTURE

The Vision Statement

What will be the role of IS in the future of the organization? How will success be measured? Are the mission and strategy of the IS department in concert with that of the organization as a whole? Regardless of how client/server technology is implemented, it will be a major financial commitment. Before that commitment is made, the role of IS should be reexamined and optimal use of financial resources ensured.

A Functional Organization Chart for the IS Department

The current organization probably reflects many assumptions from mainframe technology roots, with offshoots reflective of the growth of LAN technology. For the transition to client/server to be effective, an organization must do more than merely layer technology onto the existing organization. A sample new functional client/server-legacy organization chart is shown in Exhibit 9.1.

The sample organization emphasizes tools and methods. The client/server environment can be an intensively productive environment —

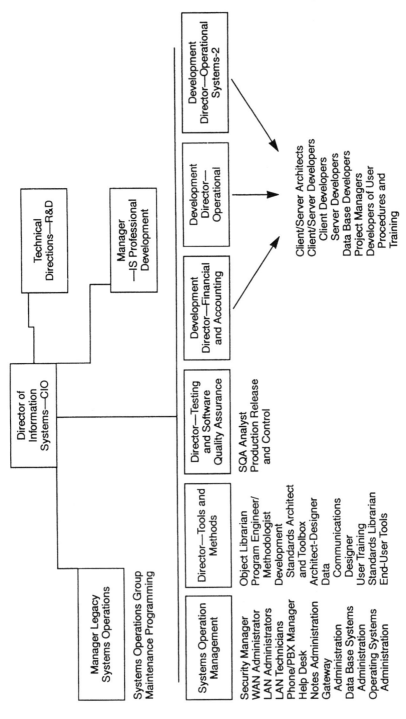

Exhibit 9.1. Sample functional client/server legacy organization chart

some companies have reported throughput improvements of two to four times in the effort to design and implement systems, with similar increases in user satisfaction. Companies can only realize these gains when the developers have an understanding of the tools they are to use, the design guidelines to follow, data base standards, and version control procedures, among other issues. It is also important to note the position of Manager — IS Professional Development — in the exhibit. Transitioning the staff, updating the plan, tracking progress, and managing a multimillion dollar budget requires full-time commitment.

Position Descriptions for the Future Department

IS managers should create a picture of what their staff will be doing in the not-so-distant future. To create the transformation plan, they must know where they are going. They should write descriptions that are as clear as possible, giving serious thought to how performance will be measured for each item on the position description (a sample is included in Exhibit 9.2). Managers should make a preliminary estimate of how many of each type of skill set they will need. They should focus on what the person in the position will be doing as opposed to the place in the organizational hierarchy.

In developing position descriptions and estimated staffing quantities, IS managers should consider the following:

- Client/server development teams should be kept as small as possible. Teams of five to seven are optimal, eight to 10 are manageable.
- A development team requires a full-time manager, three to four developers, a part-time or full-time data base analyst, a part-time or full-time client/server architect, and (in the latter stages of the project) a full-time user procedure analyst/training specialist. (If the project affects a large number of users and has a significant training component, these metrics do not apply. The project to design and deliver the training material may dwarf the systems project.) One architect and one data base analyst can be assumed for eight developers.
- Client/server developers work with users to identify requirements, reengineer processes, design, code, and test. Development methodologies in this environment are most effective when they stress iterative prototyping and refinement. For optimal efficiency, the roles of analyst and programmer should not be separated.
- A client/server architect works with members of the tools and methods group to set up development environments and to identify components of production environments. If a production environment will involve use of previously untested products or new releases of prod-

COMPANY ABC
POSITION DESCRIPTION

Date: 8/1/98   Position Title: Client/Server Developer

Primary Function

Develop and maintain ABC business applications.

General Description of Work Performed

1. Design logical data bases using ABC development platforms.
2. Work with data administration staff to implement and tune data bases.
3. Conduct and record facilitated joint application sessions.
4. Lead prototyping sessions and implement user requests.
5. Interview users and document user requirements.
6. Create detailed program specification packages and test plans.
7. Code and unit test programs.
8. Create and implement systems test plans.
9. Implement conversion plans.
10. Provide quality assurance testing of programs coded by others.
11. Create systems documentation.
12. Design and implement user interfaces in compliance with CUA and ABC standards.
13. Provide user support on ABC business applications.
14. Provide assistance to user procedure/training analysts in the development of user training and documentation manuals.
15. Interview and assist in the recruiting of S professional staff.
16. Participate in staff and status meetings.

Key Measures of Success

1. Customer satisfaction with usability and quality of delivered software.
2. Programming accuracy and completeness.
3. Timely completion of assigned tasks.
4. Compliance with ABC design and development standards.
5. Customer and project manager assessment of ability to function successfully as a member of a team.

Education and Experience

BA or BS in Computer Science or Business Degree with IS minor
2 years development experience
ABC's Client/Server Technology Series
Organizational development training (as specified by Human Resources)

Exhibit 9.2.   Sample position description: Client/server developer.

ucts, the architect tests the technical architecture before significant development efforts are expended.

- The tools and methods group can be highly leveraged. One tool builder-designer should be assumed for each 50 developers-architects-analysts.
- If software is being developed for internal use only, one tester should be assumed for every two developers.
- One LAN administrator should be assumed for every 200 users and one groupware administrator for every 400 users. Growth in management tools should reduce staffing requirements over time.

This is an area where most organizations look to consultants for assistance — both for identifying the responsibilities and to work with human resources to determine the impact on pay scales and incentive plans.

Skills and Performance Needed

In the preceding step, responsibilities and work performed were defined by each position. In this step, they are translated into the types of skills and levels of proficiency required. For example, a client/server developer position description may include some of the following responsibilities:

- Interviewing users and documenting user requirements.
- Preparing logical data models.
- Preparing unit-test plans and executing plans.
- Managing own time against task deadlines.

Those responsibilities can then be translated into skills. Interviewing users requires the following:

- Interviewing techniques.
- Effective listening.
- Interview planning.

Documenting user requirements requires:

- Effective writing skills.
- Understanding of the selected methodology and associated documentation techniques.

It is tempting to declare that all staff be expert in all skills required for their positions, but that is both unrealistic and unaffordable. It is necessary to identify the minimal skill level needed to perform in the position in a satisfactory manner.

The translation of job responsibilities into skills requirements is difficult. Doing this job well, however, has a tremendous payoff. It affects the evaluation process and has a dramatic effect on explaining the role of training and staff development to senior management. It focuses the work force. Setting the expected skill levels assists staff in planning their own self-study activities.

Hiring and Arranging for Skills from the Outside

At this stage, IS managers should have an initial feel for the skills that are likely candidates for acquisition from new hires or consultants. They should start the process for acquiring these skills now so that the candidates will be on board when they are ready to start implementing the plan. The hiring and acquisition process will continue at the same time as the next seven steps.

CREATING THE PLAN

After establishing the environment needed for success and also establishing the vision of the IS group of the future, companies are ready to tackle the nuts and bolts of the transformation to a client/server environment.

Mapping Current Staff to Future Positions

For this task, managers must look at their current organization and personnel and attempt to fit the individuals and positions into their future roles. During the mapping operation, interests and individuals should be matched rather than it being assumed that programmers will become client/server developers. All staff members should have access to materials developed so far. The position descriptions help staff identify what roles they believe are most suited to their own abilities.

How do managers decide who is best suited to be a client/server developer? A client/server architect? No fixed rules exist, but there are some guidelines. The client/server architect will typically be more technical than his or her developer counterparts. The architect usually has less user involvement and interacts more with the development team. Managers should look for persons and development positions that focus on the technical vs. the functional aspects of the work.

Aptitude should be considered. One report concluded that 26% of existing mainframe personnel could not be converted to client/server. In other experiences, this figure has been closer to 35%. These persons are clearly the candidates to maintain legacy systems during a transition period.

Skills Analysis

The positions of the future and the skills they require have been identified. The probable candidates for each position have also been identified. In this step, managers identify what skills the candidates already have to avoid wasting training dollars.

A skills assessment document should be prepared. The document asks individuals to rate themselves as 0 (no knowledge), 1 (conceptual), and so forth. Guidelines are given so that the staff understands the indicators for these levels. Guidelines are not meant to be all-inclusive (i.e., the guidelines should help individuals assess themselves, not delineate the total knowledge requirements for that level).

First, each staff member should self-assess without knowledge of the suggested skill levels for the proposed positions. Next, an independent party should assess each individual. Managers should meet with the staff member to discuss any significant variations between the self-assessment and the independent assessment. The final, agreed-upon skill level should be documented.

The manager responsible for implementing the transition plan now has a picture of each individual: current skills, current skill levels, and the target skills and levels needed to perform in the future. Managers must analyze and summarize to develop the profile of the typical staff person slotted for any position for which six or more staff will be assigned. These positions may include: project managers, client/server developers, data base administrators, client/server architects, LAN administrators, and software quality assurance testers. For such positions as WAN administrator or object librarian, plans can be tailored to individual needs. Little benefit will be gained from summarization because there will be only a few candidates for each position.

The Training or Job Assignment Plan

Armed with the profile of typical current skill levels and the target skill levels, a training assignment plan designed to raise skill levels to the targets can be created. The following rules apply:

- Training alone cannot create level 3 (works independently) or level 4 (expert) personnel. Although training often only creates a level 1 (conceptual understanding) rating, effective training can create a level 2 (works under supervision) rating. Training also helps level 3 and 4 performers maintain currency in their skills.
- Within two months after training and using a major new tool on a daily basis, productivity should be at 50% of target. By six months, productivity should be at 100% (and skill level should be at 3).
- Training not followed quickly by job-reinforcing experience is wasted.

Given these rules, it is helpful to look at a sample training or assignment plan for an organization's first group of client/server developers.

1. *Form a team of 6–8 people.* Provide a high-level description of the system to be implemented (people learn best when they can relate the knowledge to what they need to know — so as they take classes,

they can relate the concepts taught to the system they will work on). Plan on training the team together.

2. *Provide initial technology awareness training and needed soft skills training in the following areas:*
   - Client/server and LAN basics (e.g., terminology and theory).
   - Client and server operating systems.
   - Office suite productivity training (e.g., for word processors, spreadsheets, and graphics tools — tailored to the documentation and probable uses).
   - Data analysis and documentation tool (relational or object oriented).
   - Effective listening and writing.
   - Methodology orientation.
   - Facilitation (developers only).
   - LAN administration (LAN administrators only).

3. *Assign the first job.* The first job assignment within the department should not be a mission-critical system nor have a deadline that is critical to success. One company elected to make its first client/server implementation a companywide budgeting system, to be delivered in September to coincide with the beginning of the annual budget cycle. Not surprisingly, the system failed to make the deadline: everyone in the company knew and IS's judgment was seriously questioned. Preferably, the project should have some kind of high impact when delivered so that the first client/server application helps fuel the excitement about the change to this architecture. The assignment should be sufficiently complex to test most aspects of the technical architecture and reinforce the needed technical skills.

   Plan to have this team conduct the initial user-requirements definition — using the data design tool, methodology, and writing techniques. The LAN administrators should set up the development environment and productivity tools.

4. *Provide second-level training after the requirements.* Typically, the developers and architects will need training in user-interface design, the specific development tool, and prototyping. The architect may require additional training on the components of the technical architecture assumed for use in this application. Other members of the team may require training in data base administration and performance tuning.

5. *Build prototypes and the technical architecture.* Plan to have the team return to the project and conduct prototyping sessions with the user. Critical functional ability and performance features should be developed to the point where the technical architecture can be tested and modified, if necessary.

6. *Complete the system.* Integrate the completion with methodology training appropriate for the project phase.

An Infrastructure to Manage the Plan

With a 200+ person department, a three-year plan, dozens of vendors, more than 2,500 person-skill combinations, as much as $2 million in hard costs to budget, classrooms to equip and schedule, and as many as 300 official and unofficial training courses to track, management is a challenge. For the typical Fortune 1,000 company, executing this plan requires a full-time commitment and appropriate systems support.

TESTING AND EXECUTING THE PLAN

Testing and Refining the Plan

A plan has already been developed for the first team. Now, the plan must be executed. The manager responsible for all professional development should participate in as much of the training as possible to observe the participants and the material. Participants should be debriefed after each training session to determine strengths and weaknesses. Participants should also be interviewed at intervals after the training to find out what worked and what did not. The project managers can help determine how job-ready the participants were after returning from training. The suggestions from the first project team should be incorporated into the training plan.

Executing the Plan with the Remaining Staff

The remaining staff should be scheduled into the refined training plan. Again, the mode of training development teams together should be followed once a project has been identified. It should be assumed that a new group can be started through the process every four to eight weeks. The schedule should be modified to reflect current assignments.

Refining the Training Plan

Feedback should be collected from system users regarding satisfaction levels. Additional feedback can be obtained from staff going through the plan and incorporated into the plan on a continuing basis. Staff who went through the training earlier may need refresher or catch-up topics to reflect new thinking or new technology. The plan should be verified at least quarterly with the group responsible for technology to update tools and architecture information.

Incorporating Continuing Change and Development into the Culture

The environment will continue to change. Business and strategies will change faster. It is important for the IS staff to realize that the transformation process will never end. At least semi-annually, each staff member should reassess current skill levels, create new targets for performance,

1. Establishing the environment needed for success, including
   - Making the partnering decision.
   - Establishing the technical architecture and operating environment.
   - Gaining management commitment to the staff transformation approach. Creating an atmosphere of change.

2. Establishing the vision of the IS group of the future, including
   - Creating a vision statement for IS.
   - Creating an organization chart for the EUC department in the future.
   - Creating position descriptions for the future department.
   - Identifying the skills and performance levels that will be needed.

3. Creating the plan, including
   - Making a preliminary cap of current personnel to future positions.
   - Performing a skills analysis
   - Determining which skills must be acquired vs. built.
   - Creating a training and job assignment plan.
   - Creating an infrastructure to help manage the plan.
   - Initiating hiring or arranging for skills from the outside.

4. Testing and executing the plan, including
   - Testing the plan.
   - Executing the plan with the remaining staff.
   - Evaluating and refining the training plan.
   - Incorporating continuing change and development into the culture.

Exhibit 9.3. Major tasks in moving to a client/server environment.

---

and identify the combinations of job experience, self-development, and formal training needed to achieve those skills. Preferably, achievement of skill development goals should be a component of the bonus or raise process.

CONCLUSION

As can be seen, moving a staff to client/server is just like most systems projects: Managers must determine what they want, refine the requirements, create a plan to implement the requirements, and then test and refine the plan. What seems to be a monumental task can be broken down into manageable and measurable steps; see Exhibit 9.3 for a review of the steps and Exhibit 9.4 for a Gantt chart depicting their timeline.

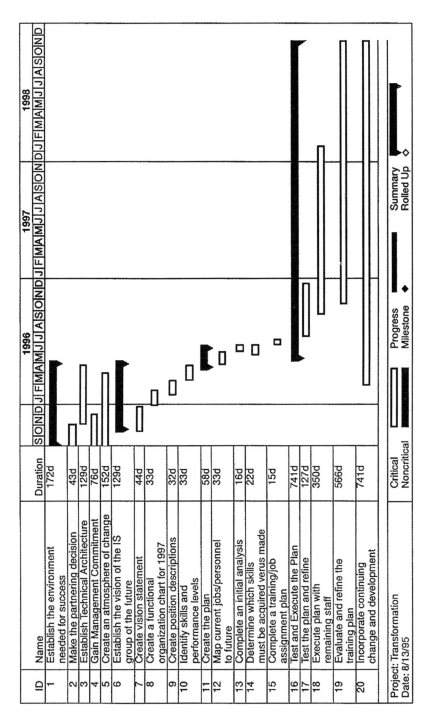

Exhibit 9.4. Gantt chart for transformation process

Chapter 10
Redesigning the IT Organization for the Information Age
Bernard H. Boar

ORGANIZATIONAL DESIGN is a critical facilitator of strategic information age initiatives. Yet traditional IT structures are misaligned with the information age because they cannot cope with continual change and the rapid horizontal introduction and utilization of gregarious information technologies. An organizational structure that combines the ideas of minibusinesses and the internal marketplace can provide a dynamic balance between stability and productivity and flexibility and innovation, replace a history of episodic and misguided restructuring with continuous restructuring, and position the IT organization to fulfill its strategic potential.

To most employees, strategy is equal to organizational structure or, more precisely, the changing of organizational structure. Although employees most often are not privy to the grand strategy of the business or are presented with only isolated and disjointed pieces of it, they personally observe and feel the impact of reorganizations. For most people, the announcement of another reorganization signifies business strategy going into motion. Organizing and reorganizing to align and realign is the most common and visible sign of strategy to the organizational rank and file.

Astute strategists recognize that organizational structure is critical to facilitating strategy. The organizational design defines the structural distribution of resources that need to be mobilized to execute a strategy. At the same time, it is important to emphasize that structure follows strategy; it is not strategy but the facilitation of strategy. In general, organizational restructuring is the last issue to be addressed when developing a strategic plan. Management first focuses on what is to be achieved and the required actions to accomplish ends and then, and only then, addresses how to organize to facilitate those ends. Setting an organizational structure in place before the process of strategic thinking is completed unnecessarily constrains the degrees of freedom.

Although organizational design is the first result of strategy, not the aim of it, people often believe that the reorganization that they are going through for the nth time is literally the business strategy. If they are right, the IT manager is probably in a great deal of trouble.

OBJECTIVES OF THE INFORMATION AGE DESIGN

It is virtually impossible for an IT executive or manager to execute a strategy if the IT organization's structure stands in direct opposition to it. To a large degree, strategy is not a problem of managing a large group but a problem of orchestrating advantageous coordination across groups. It is not surprising, therefore, that organizational design is a strategic configuration of power. To allow the business to engage in IT-enabled strategic initiatives, IT organizational design for today's information age should achieve the following pressing objectives:

- Heightened collaboration. The design should help the various organizational units work harmoniously together toward shared competitive aims.
- Speed in everything. The design should enable the business to execute all actions with swiftness.
- Responsiveness. The design should permit the business to react promptly to changing times and circumstances.
- Flexibility. The design should permit the organization to be adaptive.
- Innovation. The design should leave room for people to be innovative in solving customer problems.
- Permeability. The design should enable new ideas to enter and disperse throughout the organization. In other words, it should enable the business to learn.
- Leverage. The design should permit the business to achieve economies of scale and reuse where appropriate.
- Execution. The design should facilitate doing by lubricating action and eliminating the exhausting resistance of friction.
- Spontaneity. The design should permit the organization to evolve dynamically to stay in harmony with the changing environment. This is called spontaneous self-reorganization.
- Accountability. The design should delineate who is responsible for what.
- Authority. The design should make clear who has the authority to make decisions and allocate resources.
- Control. The design should balance spontaneity with the need for control.

Organizational design remains an art. It is usually necessary to select a strategic dimension that is most relevant to the current times and circumstances (e.g., geography, function, process, or market) as dictated by a strategy. The selected dimension is set as the anchor of the design and the remaining design choices are made by revolving them about this primary factor.

In addition to speed and flexibility, it is important to underscore the need to eliminate friction. In most organizations today, if nothing was done but eliminating the massive organizational drag on action, most organizations would experience tremendous increases in productivity. The retarding resistance of organizational friction to doing slows any and all actions except the boldest, those characterized by indirection or surprise maneuvers. So what must often be overcome in redesigning IT organizations to permit graceful maneuverability is to remove the ingrained structures that promote friction.

The history of IT organizational design is the history of a structure in place; the whistle blows, a game of musical chairs ensues, a new structure is created, and the game continues until the next whistle. As organizations strive to balance stability and productivity against flexibility and innovation, they periodically restructure in mass to respond to the environmental stimuli. An IT organizational structure that combines the ideas of minibusinesses and the internal marketplace can provide a dynamic balance, replace episodic restructuring with continuous restructuring, and position the IT organization in the desired state of potentiality.

BASIC AND ALTERNATIVE ORGANIZATIONAL DESIGNS

Designing an information age structure for the IT organization poses challenges at two levels: the macro and the micro. The macrodesign problem addresses the number of IT organizations and their roles and sibilities, placement relative to the business units they serve, and governance relationship to other IT entities within the business. The microdesign problem addresses the question of how a specific IT organization should organize itself internally to efficiently and effectively deliver its products and services to its customers.

The Macroproblem of IT Organizational Structure

The basic organizing unit of the modern enterprise is the strategic business unit (SBU). As the foundational building block of a global enterprise structure, a strategic business unit has the following characteristics:

- It is a collection of related business.
- It has a distinct mission.
- It serves well-defined markets.

- It has a distinct set of competitors.
- It has the resources and opportunity to deliver value to its market.
- It has a distinct management team.
- It has profit and loss responsibility.

The distinct business units may cooperate extensively with each other or be quite independent in their actions. The degree of collaboration is referred to as a strategic position along a continuum between a pure union and a pure multistate strategy. In a union strategy, the business units collaborate extensively in terms of sharing and leveraging processes, competencies, product development, and marketing initiatives. In a multistate strategy, each business addresses its marketplace unilaterally. The design point for the union/multistate decision is strongly influenced by the following factors:

- Market position. To what extent do market segments across SBUs and product lines overlap? To what extent will the business share brand names, advertising, customer image, and other marketing elements across products/markets?
- Product/service position. To what extent is there synergy between SBU product lines?
- Competitive moves. To what extent is advantage accrued by linking competitive moves across SBUs?
- Cost position. To what extent does cross-SBU collaboration lead to cost advantage (i.e., reuse, leverage, economies of scale)?

After analysis, a business takes a considered position somewhere along the continuum between the extremes of a pure multistate and a pure union.

Against the background of this macroorganizational structure of the business, a corresponding IT organizational structure must be designed. An IT organization provides two broad sets of products and services to its customers — life cycle applications development and support services and production operations. For each of these, there are three basic structures (with endless mutations) to choose from:

1. Centralized. A single and centralized IT organization provides these services to the SBUs.
2. Dispersed. Independent IT organizations provide these services to designated SBUs.
3. Integrated. Independent but coordinated IT organizations provide these services to designated SBUs.

For each considered alternative macrodesign, centralized, dispersed, integrated, or mixed, it is necessary to consider the following four basic questions:

Domain of System	Transaction Processing	Information Analysis	Type of System Information Sharing	Workgroup Productivity	Individual Productivity
Corporate					
Shared SBU					
Divisional					
Department					
Personal					

Exhibit 10.1 Taxonomy of Information Systems for Determining Roles and Responsibilities

1. How many IT organizations will the corporation have? Will each SBU have its own or will they share IT service providers?
2. What will be the roles and responsibilities of each IT organization? Exhibit 10.1 shows a simple taxonomy of information systems. Which cells are each IT entity responsible for, and are they responsible for development and/or operations? A similar mapping must be done in terms of allocation of databases.
3. Will the IT entities be separate from the SBUs they serve or will they be entities within the business units? If they are apart, what will be the economic rules for exchanging goods and services?
4. How will multiple IT entities be governed? For issues of common concern, such as architecture, corporate communications networks, and human resource policies, what governance mechanisms will be deployed to maintain synergy?

In this way, a macro-IT organizational structure, whether centralized, dispersed, integrated, or mutated, is designed for both development and operations that align itself with the macro-SBU structure and union/multistate strategy of the business.

The Microproblem of IT Organizational Structure

The microproblem of IT organizational design starts where the macroproblem ends. Each IT entity that will exist needs an internal structure that lets it deliver operations and development in a fast, flexible, and friction-free manner. If the internal structure does not become a strategic configuration of power, then all efforts to make IT maneuverable will fail because it will not be possible to mobilize IT resources effectively and efficiently.

Although there are endless mutations and variations, there are six basic microdesign structures to choose from:

1. Functional structure. Employees are grouped strictly vertically based on functional skills and expertise.

Organizational Structure	Advantages	Challenges
Functional	• Efficiency • Centers of excellence • Focus • Ease of management	• Efficient decision making • End-to-end accountability • Functional loyalty • Lack of flexibility
Matrix	• Provides attention to multiple dimensions of organization design • Coordination • Considered allocation of resources • Horizontal communications	• Difficult to implement and manage • Power battles • Delineation of authority • Costs of communication
Product	• Product/customer focused • Accountability • High product-level coordination • Decision making at product level	• Cost inefficiencies • Horizontal product coordination • Responsiveness to local needs
Geographic	• Market sensitivity • Decision making and authority at market level	• Cost inefficiencies • Cross-geographic • Local loyalties
Front End/Back End	• Single customer interface • Customer responsive • Promotes many-to-many relationships	• Linking front ends to back end efficiently and effectively • Cost allocations • Decision making
Process	• Efficiency • Customer focus • Productivity	• Process leadership • Cross-process coordination • Functional expertise • Process fiefdoms

Exhibit 10.2 Advantages and Challenges of Microorganizational Design

2. Matrix structure. Employees are grouped in a gridlike structure with multiple chains of authority. These reporting arrangements are defined to integrate vertical function with horizontal processes.
3. Product structure. Employees are grouped into self-contained product-driven structures with end-to-end responsibility for a given family of products.
4. Geography structure. Employees are grouped into self-contained structures that deliver all products and services to a geographical region.
5. Front-end/back-end structure. Employees are grouped into customer-facing functions that serve customers and use products and services developed and supported by back-end functions.
6. Process structure. Employees are grouped into horizontal teams that deliver products and services by process.

Exhibit 10.2 summarizes the generic advantages and challenges of each structure.

The problem for the information age IT organization is to define a structure that balances conflicting needs. Although stability and formality are needed for short-term efficiencies, flexibility and spontaneity are needed to cope with the surrounding turbulence characterizing today's businesses. IT organizations need to be organic rather than bureaucratic.

PROBLEMS WITH TRADITIONAL IT ORGANIZATIONAL DESIGNS

Most traditional IT organizations are a structural combination of functional and product design structures. MVS people supported the mainframe environment, and UNIX people supported the UNIX environment. Operations people supported specific technological smokestacks. Developers were organized by product teams to serve specific customers.

This structure made reasonably good sense during the industrial age of IT. Because the IT technology platforms were segregated vertically, functional centers of excellence to achieve stability and efficiency were a good choice. Each functional unit could strive to optimize its individual environment for the welfare of the customer and the corporation. There was little need for cross-environment collaboration, coordination, and information flow.

Two things have gone wrong with this model. First, the technology organizations wish to deploy (i.e., interactive multimedia across distributed and heterogeneous computing environments) is horizontal in nature. Making this technology work requires extensive horizontal collaboration and coordination across functional specialties. The traditional IT hierarchical smokestack structure is not only inappropriate for this collaboration, it also actively works against it because employees are loyal to their specific vertical technological environment rather than cross-environment needs.

Second, the traditional smokestack IT organization was designed for stability and predictability. Its structure was designed to preserve rather than change. During the mainframe era of the industrial age, change was slow and predictable. The smokestack structure took on a mechanistic and bureaucratic flavor as it ponderously introduced or experimented with new technologies. Change was routinely viewed as a threat rather than an opportunity.

The problems with the traditional IT structure do not therefore require elaborate or extensive debate. Its shortcomings are dual: It was designed to optimize, through economies of scale, the delivery of vertical IT products and services, and it was designed not to change but to preserve.

The result of this is obvious to everyone in the IT field. IT organizations are viewed as slow, inflexible, and a business obstacle to be overcome. They are not strategic configurations of power because their inherent microorganizational structure is misaligned with the horizontal technological needs of the information age. They are misaligned because they create tremendous friction to change for the business. They cannot cope with continual change and the rapid horizontal introduction and utilization of gregarious information technologies.

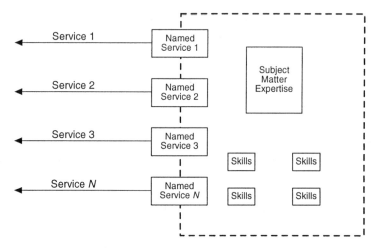

Exhibit 10.3. Centers of Competency

THE PROPOSED SOLUTION

The proposed solution to this problem is to design a new micro-IT organizational structure built on three interrelated ideas:

- Centers of competency. This concept logically groups employees into related sets of skills.
- Process. In this approach, all work gets done through processes.
- Internal marketplace. An internal marketplace is established in which centers of competency buy and sell products and services to each other.

The following sections discuss how the three ideas combine to form the proposed microorganizational design structure.

Centers of Competency

A center of competency is a group of employees with a logically related set of skills. It is often also referred to as a center of excellence or a knowledge center. The center of competency provides an administrative home for employees, a place to learn skills and receive specialty mentoring, and a facility to investigate and develop best practices.

A center of competency is a minibusiness or a boutique service provider. As shown in Exhibit 10.3, it provides a group of services to other IT centers of competency. Its manager or coach is the business manager responsible for developing the center of competency so that its employees can find work. The coach/manager, like any other business person, owns capabilities and must find utilization opportunities for them. So a center of competency is a minibusiness, not unlike an SBU: it has products to sell, a

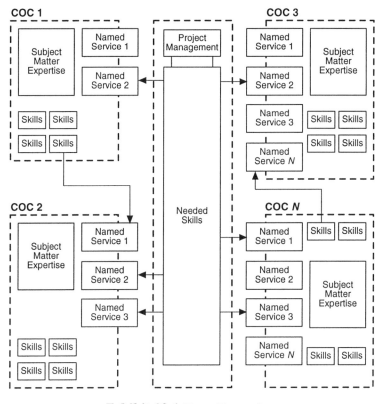

Exhibit 10.4. Team Formation

marketplace, the need to earn revenue, and the need to upgrade continually its products and services to maintain its customer base.

Process

In this view, all work is the result of executing processes. Process owners hire individuals from centers of competency and form teams to develop processes. Product managers, marketing/sales managers, and senior management hire members of the centers of competency to execute processes. Exhibit 10.4 shows how a team is formed. The buyer hires individuals with the necessary skills from each center of competency.

Internal Marketplace

In this idea, shown in Exhibit 10.5, the IT organization runs on the model of an internal marketplace. The marketplace works as follows:

- Senior management negotiates budgets with product managers, marketing/sales, and process owners.

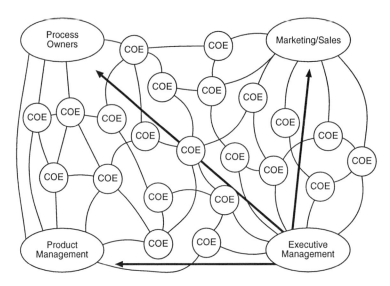

Exhibit 10.5. The Internal Marketplace Model

- Centers of competency are minibusinesses that need to earn revenue. They do not receive a budget, and they have a cost and earning projection.
- The four centers (i.e., product managers, marketing/sales, process owners, and senior management) run the economy with budgeted money, buying products and services from the centers of competency. This generally involves the hiring of a project manager who, in turn, shops for desired services in the internal marketplace. Centers of competency, in turn, also buy products and services from other centers of competency.

In this way, the traditional hierarchical, mechanistic, and bureaucratic IT organization is transformed into a vibrant and dynamic economic entity with buyers, sellers, and a sustainable strong motivation to cooperate and continually improve products and services.

An internal marketplace built on boutique centers of competency is a desirable structure for the information age IT organization for the following reasons:

- The IT organization is no longer shielded from marketplace realities. It also experiences the day-to-day pressures to continually upgrade its products and services. If a center of competency wants to stay in business, it must continually improve its products and services to other centers of competency.
- The core structure for execution is a horizontal team. This team is formed using marketplace mechanisms.

- The normal marketplace mechanism of how money is spent is used to foster alignment. As management, product managers, marketing, and process owners shift their spending patterns, the centers of competency must respond or they will lose revenue.
- The structure lends itself to spontaneous reorganization. As spending patterns shift or centers of competency develop new products or services, the structure naturally adjusts to the new realities. Reorganization in the internal marketplace is occurring dynamically as some products and services win and others lose.
- The structure is highly scalable. Successful centers of competency can be grown, shrunk, or replicated as needed.
- There is a marketplace and everyone has a customer. Centers of competency will thrive only if they can find buyers for their services. Product managers and marketing will thrive only if they employ processes to deliver products and services that SBU customers want.
- Customers can evaluate, measure, and negotiate terms and conditions of purchase. Suppliers need to continually refine their offerings to maintain satisfied customers. Members of a center of competency work for their customer, not their vertical boss.
- The structure lends itself to virtual structures or, if desired, outsourcing. In both cases, the decision is made as to which service offerings are better performed by noninternal providers, but those services must be designed into the overall internal economy.
- Centers of competency are extremely motivated to cooperate with each other. Only through horizontal collaboration on customer-focused teams are they able to accrue revenue.
- Centers of competency improve value for buyers by integrating products and services across centers. Buyers can buy basic products and services or more finished goods.

The traditional IT organizational structure suffers from a gross inconsistency. External customer-facing business units have to cope with the marketplace every day and be adaptive and fast. The mechanisms that cause concern for speed, flexibility, service, value, and quality are the marketplace mechanisms of choice and selection. Traditional IT organization units have functioned bureaucratically in the comfort of entitlement. They deliver products and services but do not have to win the business. The boutique structure of centers of competency integrated with the notion of an internal marketplace addresses this shortcoming.

CONCLUSION

Designing an information age structure for the IT organization is a challenge of coordination. The micro-IT organization should be designed so that horizontal products and services can be delivered rapidly, flexibly, and without friction. The best mechanism for doing so is an internal marketplace based on center-of-competency boutiques that are subject to marketplace mechanisms. Speed and agility in the IT organization depend on submitting the organization to marketplace pressures.

Specifically, the proposed design addresses the stated objectives in the following way:

- *Heightened collaboration.* The unit of delivered work is the team. Centers of competency remain effective only if they can work together on successful teams.
- *Speed in everything.* The internal marketplace rewards efficiency and speed. Centers of competency are motivated to continually improve their offerings with speed being a prime buying factor of purchases.
- *Responsiveness.* Centers of competency earn their living. As with any supplier in a marketplace, urgency in meeting customer needs is critical.
- *Flexibility.* Centers of competency adapt to meet the current and emerging needs that buyers will pay for. The problem for the center of competency is not what it wants to provide but what a customer will pay for.
- *Innovation.* Centers of competency are rewarded for constantly upgrading and innovating by the growth of their center.
- *Permeability.* There is little advantage to maintaining the status quo. Centers of competency search for new ideas and ways to remain prosperous.
- *Leverage.* Centers of competency mentor and teach their preferred skills to others. Processes are reused and tuned to promote efficiency in execution.
- *Execution.* Execution is accomplished through the unit of the team. Noncooperation is rewarded by replacement.
- *Spontaneity.* The design lends itself to spontaneous self-reorganization. As money and opportunities are made available, entrepreneurial centers of competency hustle to the new opportunity.
- *Accountability.* Buyers are accountable for what they buy.
- *Authority.* Buyers make informed purchase decisions.
- *Control.* Management can expand, contract, or reposition the internal economy at will, based on how it changes its spending patterns.

The internal marketplace structure is superior to the other six structures discussed in this chapter because it is fast and flexible and removes friction. It repositions the IT organizational structure as a strategic configuration of power.

Chapter 11

Successfully Hiring and Retaining IT Personnel

John P. Murray

DESPITE THE CURRENT SHORTAGE of qualified IT professionals, a midwestern consulting agency more than tripled its number of employees. The hiring practices of the agency are credited for their ability to attract and retain talent. These practices successfully manage technology, candidates' qualifications, competitive pay, openness about the culture of the firm, and candidates' expectations.

This chapter examines hiring techniques for attracting and keeping IT talent. These techniques have been successfully used by a Midwest consulting agency to aggressively increase its headcount. Despite a tight IT labor market, the total headcount for the branch had increased from 75 in mid-1995 to 230 employees by mid-1998. The branch has enjoyed the benefits of its hiring model, which is applicable to many IT organizations.

The hiring record of the branch is impressive. However, it is more impressive when considered within the context of the hiring standards established in the branch. The hiring goal is based upon interviewing only those candidates who appear to be within the top 20 percent of all prospective candidates. The selection of candidates is based upon clearly defined hiring criteria. Those criteria form the basis for deciding whether or not the candidate will invited to a formal interview. Therefore, the process focuses on increasing the headcount within the branch, but only within the established hiring standards.

ACKNOWLEDGING THE COMPETITION FOR INFORMATION TECHNOLOGY PERSONNEL

When considering IT hiring and retaining issues, the place to begin is with the recognition that prospective employers face a "seller's market."

0-8493-9820-7/00/$0.00+$.50

Because there are many more employment opportunities for IT people than there are people available, prospective employment candidates enjoy the luxury of being selective with regard to their next employer. That circumstance is particularly valid for the high-quality candidates. The favorable job climate for IT people is a reality that is likely to continue to exist for some time. Given that reality, it is mandatory that organizations interested in finding and retaining high-quality IT people adopt more creative methods to address IT hiring and retention concerns.

It is important to recognize the value of focusing on, and hiring, high-quality IT people. Again, given the strong market for IT employees, there is often not going to be much difference in terms of salary between the highest-quality people and people in the second rank. While the difference in salary expense between the best and the next tier of employees may not be great, the difference in quality can be significant. The best, the brightest people will often make a considerably higher contribution over time. That being the case, it should be easy to justify extra compensation where needed, to attract those people.

Quality is an important factor in the decision to hire an individual, but the topic transcends individual hiring concerns. Good IT people are attracted and challenged by association with IT professionals of the same caliber. An organization that has built a strong IT department is going to have an advantage in hiring candidates, because those candidates will be able to see that the organization cares about the IT effort within the organization. When an organization can point to an IT environment that both stresses and delivers high-quality work, the best people are going to be interested in coming on board.

Because people with IT skills are at a premium, the market for people with those skills is very aggressive. One result of that circumstance is that IT people have an understanding of the market value of their skills; they understand the competitive nature of the marketplace. Therefore, the process of attracting, hiring, and retaining skilled IT people has become increasingly aggressive and competitive. Organizations that fail to recognize the realities of the marketplace and to make a strong commitment to compete are not going to succeed in the race to find and retain good people.

It may come down to a simple business consideration about whether or not a willingness to make the appropriate commitment exists within the organization. When a commitment to the technology is not in place, attempting to hire and retain good IT people is simply going to be futile.

Many IT people receive a constant stream of calls from recruiters attempting to persuade them to change employers. In most instances, those callers are making very tempting proposals. Items such as signing bonuses, large salary increases, and additional time off become routine offers to encourage job changes. In addition, there will be promises that the candidates will be working in areas that use the newest technology. Promises will be made about the willingness of the employer to provide technology-related educational opportunities. There will be references to the potential opportunity to manage interesting IT projects.

Hearing those blandishments sets high levels of expectation in the minds of those being recruited. Sometimes the candidate, upon joining the organization, finds that the promises are not honored. When that happens, it is likely the person will move on to something else. The concern here is not with the keeping of promises, but with the expectations those promises raised in the minds of the candidates. Those expectations, valid or not, become a baseline for IT people considering changing jobs. Poorly managed employee expectations ultimately encourage the employee to move on to something else. Obviously, when good employees leave the organization, everyone involved loses.

THE FRAGILE NATURE OF THE TECHNOLOGY-BASED HIRING PROCESS

Success in the hiring of IT personnel must be based upon a clear understanding of the marketplace and the needs and desires of the IT candidates. Like it or not, technical people often do tend to have a different set of goals and interests than other types of employees. The purpose here is not to pass judgment on those differences, but to make it clear that a successful hiring and retention program must acknowledge those differences and use them to the advantage of the potential employer.

The first item to be recognized is that of the ability of the particular organization to offer competitive salaries. Again, given the realities of the marketplace, a failure to become and remain competitive with salaries is simply going to exacerbate the problems associated with hiring and keeping IT personnel. This is a dual problem, in that competitive salaries will attract good employees, but it will also require competitive salary adjustments to retain those employees. There is another aspect of the salary issue in that salaries for existing IT employees are going to have to be reviewed and, where appropriate, adjusted. Absent a continuing review of salaries for all IT employees, retention difficulties will increase.

One aspect of the salary issue is to consider moving away from the traditional process of annual salaries to a nine-month review cycle. If that change occurs, it will be important to advise all IT employees of the change as part of an approach to forestall offers from competitors. Making a salary review timing change will create some level of difficulty with other departments within the organization; however, doing so will help the IT retention effort. Whether or not the improvement is worth the additional difficulty is an issue for each organization, but doing so represents an effective approach to the problem.

Although it may be a difficult concept to sell within the organization, because it disrupts the traditional human relations structure, it is worthwhile to give serious thought to adopting a new approach to IT hiring. The approach taken will depend upon the size of the organization and the particular IT installation. In medium and larger organizations, the responsibility for the hiring and retention of IT personnel should be within the IT department. Again, given the size of the IT department, it might have its human resources section within the department.

In smaller organizations, several approaches should be considered. One approach would be to work out an agreement between the IT department and the human resources department to work very closely in hiring IT people, with someone from the IT department accepting primary responsibility for the effort. Another approach would be to engage the assistance of an outside consultant to assume responsibility for finding, hiring, and retaining IT employees. Of course, any approach can only be successfully developed with the support and cooperation of the human resources department, but making such a change is worth considering.

The idea here is not to circumvent the human resources department, nor to lessen the importance of that department in any way. Usually the human resources department has involvement in all hiring decisions across the organization. As a result, given the magnitude of the hiring effort, the process can be lengthy. When the hiring process takes too long, the candidates will move on to other opportunities. It is imperative, when a good IT candidate is identified, that an offer be made as quickly as possible. One way to deal with that reality is to shift the primary responsibility and focus for IT hiring to the IT department.

There are several valid reasons for taking a different approach to IT hiring. First, being in a position to talk comfortably about technology-related issues with candidates will send a signal that the organization is interested in them as technicians and will put them at ease. Organizations do sometimes send IT candidates the wrong signal in that several of the primary hiring contacts tend to be with people who have little practical understanding of the technology. Being involved early on with someone who can relate to the candidate and the associated technology constitutes a hiring plus. Second, a person with a technical background is going to be more sensitive to the interests and needs of the candidates. An important aspect of a successful IT hiring campaign is that a strong relationship is developed between the candidate and the person doing the hiring. The existence of a mutual understanding of the technology will work to strengthen that relationship.

Many times the decision to join a particular organization occurs as the result of subtle issues that arise during the interview process. In that regard, having someone who can make the candidate comfortable and to whom the candidate can relate is going to be a benefit. In addition, taking such an approach will help to set the organization apart from those where the approach is simply to hire everyone through the human relations department. Being able to send a signal that the organization really does care about its IT effort represents a hiring strength.

SUCCESSFUL HIRING CRITERIA

There are four basic components associated with the process of the successful hiring of IT personnel. To be successful the hiring process must be rapid, focused, candid, and decisive. An examination of each of the components, the ways they affect the hiring process, and their relationship to each other will provide guidelines for dealing with the hiring issues.

A salient reason employers fail in their effort to hire IT people has to do with using standard hiring approaches for all types of employees. It is not unusual to find organizations where it takes an average of 15 or more working days to respond to a résumé after it comes into the office. In responding to the résumé the first interview may be scheduled for several weeks in the future. To make matters worse, an offer may be contingent on multiple interviews involving a number of people. When that amount of time constitutes the normal hiring schedule, any hope of finding good IT candidates is unrealistic; in today's market, they will have gone somewhere else. It should be obvious then that, in today's hiring market, the ability to react quickly to good IT candidates is imperative. That approach can only be used when the organization is well prepared.

Like it or not, a "one size fits all" approach is not going to produce success in hiring IT people. One way to look at the current situation as it applies to hiring IT personnel is to think of it as a commodities business. With high demand and low supply, those prospects who are available are going to be hired quickly. Expecting that a lengthy hiring cycle will not affect hiring IT people is incorrect. The reality is that there are just too many jobs available and while the organization is grinding through the employment process, someone else, who is more nimble, is going to hire the candidate.

An important component of moving to a successful hiring effort in such an organization is to reduce the IT hiring cycle from weeks to days. Doing so may, given the current status in many organizations, seem a difficult, if not impossible, cultural change. However, if the organization is serious about the IT hiring effort, this is a change that is going to have to be accommodated.

The realities of the marketplace have to be acknowledged. A candidate, having a number of job opportunities available, is not going to be very patient waiting for an organization to respond. Those other organizations making offers are going to put pressure on the candidate to accept, which works against the slow-moving organization. When an organization moves quickly with the hiring process, there are two positive results. First, the organization sends the candidate a signal that it values the candidate and wants the candidate to join the organization. Second, moving rapidly sends a message that this is an organization where decisions are made quickly.

Success in hiring IT people is contingent upon the development of a focused hiring approach. Understanding the requirement for speed with IT hiring is critical, but doing so is only possible within the framework of a clear process. Those doing the hiring must be comfortable with two sets of criteria. Those criteria are (1) the existence of the appropriate technical skills needed to do the work and (2) the personal traits that fit the culture of the organization.

The technical skills may vary with the needs of different departments or projects; so specific technical skill and experience will vary. However, within the general context of the organization, there should be a baseline of technical skills. As an example, if the organization operates in a UNIX environment, UNIX experience is going to be an important factor. Beyond the basics, there will often be some "nice to have" skills or experience that adds to the attractiveness of the particular candidate. Perhaps there is a need for Access experience in the marketing department; obviously, someone with that skill and experience would be of interest.

As the technology needs of the organization change, those doing the hiring have to be made aware of those changes. With a clear technology focus, people not meeting the hiring criteria will be bypassed, saving time and effort for everyone. There may be some gray area in that people with a strong technology interest and aptitude, yet without the identified specific skills, will be considered. The idea here is to come to a clear understanding about the needs in the technical area and to focus the recruiting effort on that area.

Again, the importance of having someone who understands the technology at the beginning of the process needs to be stressed. Sometimes a candidate without the exact skills required, but with good experience and adaptability surfaces. When that happens, an interviewer with a good technology basis will be in a position to make an offer that otherwise would be passed over.

Developing and maintaining a strong understanding of the current and anticipated uses of the technology within the organization is a strong IT hiring factor. Having a person with a strong technology background (and appropriate people skills) directly involved in IT hiring process will smooth the process. That involvement will also forestall future disappointments on the part of candidates who feel they did not receive a clear picture of the technology used within the organization.

The model used to identify personal traits considered in hiring IT personal is more general. In determining the personality criteria, the place to begin is with an understanding of the culture of the organization. Just as all organizations differ, the same is true of their cultures. The values of the organization must be clearly understood by those doing the interviewing. The interviewer has to be in a position to explain the organizational values to the candidate so that he or she has a clear understanding of what is going to be expected if the candidate is hired.

As an example, the culture of the organization may be based upon a high level of structure and control. In that environment, people usually receive specific instructions about their assignments and about the anticipated results. If the candidate has a strong interest in being "creative," i.e., wants to go ahead and do things on his or her own, with very limited supervision or direction, the environment within the organization is probably not going to provide a good fit.

One of the mandates of the IT department may be to develop and maintain high levels of customer service. In such an environment, the interviewer must make certain the candidate understands the importance of customer service and is going to be comfortable in such a culture. If that is not the case, it will be much better for everyone to come to that decision quickly and for both parties to recognize that not going forward is the most appropriate choice for everyone.

To move the hiring process along, it is important that someone directly involved with interviewing have the authority to make an offer or to reject a candidate. If the appropriate hiring model is in place and carefully followed, it will ease the hiring decision. Again, any delay through the hiring process represents a risk. Failing to close the hiring loop quickly means that the candidate remains available to the competition. If the proper hiring structure is in place, there is no need to prolong the decision to hire or to reject a particular candidate. To speed the process, a reasonable approach is to make offers contingent upon acceptable reference checks. Again, in a well-managed hiring process, checking references should not consume too much time.

In moving to a more focused, more rapid process of interviewing and hiring IT candidates the risk associated with making a hiring mistake is going to increase. It may happen that an unsatisfactory candidate is hired who, in a more structured, more traditional environment would not have been considered. However, if the hiring focus and criteria are clear and if the proper discipline is in place, such mistakes will be rare. Success in the hiring process is worth the risk of a mistake from time to time.

MANAGING THE EXPECTATIONS OF THE CANDIDATES

A substantial number of the people interviewed for IT positions are going to have a definite set of ideas about what it is they expect from a job and from an employer. The people doing the interviewing need to anticipate that the candidates will be willing to express their views about those interests. One aspect of the interviewing process should be to talk with candidates about precisely what it is they consider important with regard to their work.

In so far as practical, the concerns of the candidate should be separated into technology-related and quality-of-life issues. Without that separation, it is too easy to glide over the technology interests and talk about the standard benefits offered by the organization. The importance of the technology-related items to the candidates has to be recognized and covered in sufficient detail.

There are two goals here; one is to determine if the interests of the candidate can be met by the IT department. The second goal is to set the expectations of the candidate correctly as they relate to the realities of the job and the organization. It is important that an open and candid environment be established so that, should an offer be made and accepted, all parties understand what is expected.

Although there can be a number of answers to the question about the candidates' work interests, some basic issues are likely to be raised. Usually, candidates will want to know about the technology currently being used within the organization. They will want information about the role of the IT function within the organization and how it is viewed by the rest of the organization. They will also want to know about the future course of the technology within the organization.

Candidates will have an interest in the existence of career ladders within the organization. This is an area where candor is going to be important. If the candidate raises the issue of career development, the person doing the interview should ask questions that will identify the specific interests behind the questions. The goal here is to determine the basis for the question, i.e., is there really an interest in moving into a management role, or is the interest in moving to management based upon the desire to move to a higher salary level. If the answer has to do with salary and the organization rewards strong technical performance with increased salary, that point should be discussed with the candidate.

An important issue is going to be that of continuing training. Many candidates, particularly good candidates, are going to want to know whether or not the organization supports continuing IT training and the level of that support. The rapid changes in IT technology mandate a continual upgrading of skills for people who want to make a strong contribution. If the organization makes an effort to hire the best possible people, there has to be an understanding that those people will have a strong interest in education.

Educational support should be seen as a critical component of the hiring approach. If the organization is supportive of education, that should be seen as a strong point and stressed as such in the interview. Conversely, if the organization does not value continuing education, the interviewer should be candid about that fact.

It is important to recognize that IT training, given that it is appropriately managed, represents an investment, not an expense. The rapid changes in IT technology require a continuing upgrading of technical skills. Training good people in the current technologies is in the best interest of the individual and the organization. A linkage exists between a strong IT training program and the retention of high-quality IT people; that linkage should be seen as a critical component in the success of the IT effort.

Dealing with high-quality IT people raises the bar for the IT department. Well-motivated employees are going to work hard at their careers. The managers of the IT department have to recognize that high-quality people are likely to take an aggressive approach to their continuing education. If there are representations about educational commitments to employees, those commitments must be honored.

In answering the questions from the IT candidates, the only policy that will serve the organization well over time is the use of candor. It is a mistake to allow the pressure to fill open IT positions encourage those doing the hiring to be less than forthcoming about the ability within the organization to meet the desires of the candidates. Of course, it is important to make the hire, but that hire should not be made based upon a set of false assumptions on the part of the candidate. In today's market it is likely, once the candidate faces the realities of the job, if there has been misrepresentation, he or she will to move on to something else. When a good employee leaves, everyone loses.

Even though presenting a less-than-candid scenario is an obvious mistake, in today's competitive hiring environment, it does happen. Taking that approach can be seen as having an upside in that it will improve the hiring success rate. Conversely, the approach carries a downside, in that the mistake of being less than candid will generate unrest within the IT department and will result in a high rate of department resignations.

"SELLING" THE CANDIDATES ON THE ORGANIZATION

Being candid with prospective employees does not preclude opportunities to sell the organization. It will pay to take the time to identify the positive aspects of the organization and to explain those aspects when talking to candidates. Again, it is important the person doing the interviewing takes the time to find out the interests of the particular candidates. Having that understanding, they will be in a position to emphasize those positive aspects of the organization that fit the interests of the particular candidate. It is important to recognize the level of pressure that exists to find and hire strong IT candidates. Making an effort to sell the organization is simply one way to counteract that pressure.

Clearly, any area where the organization can support the interests of the candidate represents an opportunity to encourage the employee to join the organization. Beyond that, there should be concentration on what it is that sets the organization apart from others.

Some examples of ancillary selling points would include the values of the company, the culture under which the organization operates, and attractive benefits that are not commonly found in other organizations. Taking the time to understand those components that make the organization a good place to work and to emphasize those strengths in the hiring process is an appropriate and effective hiring tool.

As an example, in the case of the success of the branch office used in this chapter, one of the strong points of that organization is the commitment to "doing the right thing." Taking the time with candidates to talk about that commitment and to use examples of how the process works within the branch has been a very effective tool in helping people make up their minds to join the branch.

DEALING WITH THE ISSUE OF RETENTION

IT organizations are generally uncomfortable with the issue of employee turnover. While keeping good IT people is important, indeed critical, to the health of the IT installation, some limited turnover is not a bad circumstance. There are benefits to bringing in people with different perspectives and ideas, people familiar with new technologies, who can infuse a higher level of energy and excitement into the IT installation.

Conversely, people do become stale; they grow restless, and they may develop an interest in moving on to something else for a variety of reasons. When that occurs, if the organization cannot meet the changed needs of those employees, it is in the best interest of all concerned for that employee to move on to something else.

The goal, concerning turnover, should be to keep total turnover low, to concentrate on retaining the good people within the IT installation. Beyond that, an additional emphasis should be placed on retaining the most valuable people, the perceived "stars" of the installation. Just as with hiring, it is going to be important to understand the needs and goals of the currently employed IT professionals and to work to accommodate those needs and goals. Again, those needs and goals will change based upon changes in technology and upon the pressures applied by competitors to lure the employees away.

It is critical, with regard to the development of a retention effort, that someone remains in close contact with the IT employees and is alert to their changing needs and interests. The absence of continuing open communication within the IT department is going to create opportunities for people to be lured away.

Again, the issue of IT retention begins with the hiring process. Those items identified within the hiring model will lay the groundwork for a continuing employment relationship. The model works; it should be seen as the basis not only for successful hiring, but also for improved retention.

CONCLUSION

One way to look at the issue of the hiring and retaining of IT personnel is to consider the process as a project. As with any project, success is dependent upon the ability to develop processes that work and, once developed, to adhere consistently to those processes. Having developed a project approach provides the ability to install a hiring/retention model, to improve the IT success record.

Of course, over time circumstances are going to change and what works today will no longer be effective. Obviously, when that happens, it will be time to review the model and to make the appropriate changes. The technology- and money-related sections of the model will be the most likely to change. The idea is to remember that changes will occur and to be in position to shift the appropriate hiring criteria as those changes occur.

An important aspect of the use of the hiring model is that it formalizes the hiring process. Given that the model is used to address IT hiring issues, modifications can be made as changes occur within the industry. That ability allows the organization to remain current with whatever may be occurring within the organization itself, or within the IT industry.

Following the usual hiring practices will not work in the pursuit of IT personnel. That is not to say that IT people will not be found and hired; they probably will, but they are not likely to be the best candidates. Even when good hiring practices are in place and work well, finding IT candidates is expensive. To obtain the best return on the hiring investment, it is important to hire, and to retain, the best possible candidates.

The first step in the process, as is the case with any project, is to decide whether or not the organization is willing to make the commitment to developing a successful IT hiring and retention program. If the answer to that question is yes, the opportunity exists to make significant progress in a relatively short time.

While hiring IT candidates is expensive, moving to a more effective IT hiring process need not require additional expense. What it does require is the development of a particular culture within the organization, focused on the goal of attracting, hiring, and retaining high-quality IT professionals. Again, the idea of a model is an appropriate way to think about the issues involved. The points considered in this chapter cover the issues required to move to a strong IT hiring and retention environment. This process has been tested and found to be very effective. Attracting and retaining high-quality IT people is a process that can be improved in any organization; whether or not that happens is up to those charged with the task.

Two IT hiring scenarios exist. A certain level of pain is going to be associated with either approach. Not making any changes to the current process will lessen the stress on the culture that would be associated with developing a new hiring model. The pain in that approach will be the inability of the organization to find and retain high-quality IT people. Conversely, moving to the IT hiring model is going to create disruption within the organization. The benefit to be found in moving to the new model will be that the experience associated with IT hiring and retention is going to improve.

It is in the best interest of every organization to find and retain high-quality IT people. Doing that may require change, and it may bring about some stress within the organization. Each organization has to decide about its willingness to make the changes and to act or not, as it sees fit.

Chapter 12
Preparing for the Outsourcing Challenge

N. Dean Meyer

THE DIFFERENCE BETWEEN fruitful partnerships with vendors and outsourcing nightmares is not simply how well you select the vendor and negotiate the deal. It has more to do with how you decide when to use vendors (vs. internal staff) and how well someone manages those vendors once you have hired them.

To use vendors effectively, executives must see through the hype of sales pitches and the confusion of budget numbers to understand the fundamental trade-offs between vendors and internal staff and the unique value that each delivers.

Our research shows that it requires healthy internal organizations, in which same-profession staff decide "make-vs.-buy" in a fact-based manner, case by case, day after day, and in which staff use their specialized expertise to manage vendors to internal standards of excellence. In other words, successful management of vendors starts with the effective management of internal staff.

This thesis may be counterintuitive, because outsourcing is generally viewed as an alternative to internal staff. It differs from much of the "common wisdom" about outsourcing for the following reason: It is a perspective on outsourcing from someone who is not in the outsourcing business and who has no vested interest in selling outsourcing. It is written from the vantage of someone who has spent decades helping executives solve the problems of poorly performing organizations, including enhancing their partnerships with vendors.

Excerpted and adapted from: *Outsourcing: How to Make Vendors Work for Your Shareholders,* copyright 1999 NDMA Publishing, Ridgefield, CT.

Recognizing that business executives' interest in outsourcing often reflects frustration with internal IT operations, this chapter looks at the typical sources of dissatisfaction. Such a look leads to an understanding of what it takes to make internal service providers competitive alternatives to outsourcing, and how they can help a corporation get the best value from vendors. But, first, it examines vendors' claims to put the alternative into perspective.

CLAIMS AND REALITY

Outsourcing vendors have promised dramatic cost savings, along with enhanced flexibility and the claim that line executives will have more time to focus on their core businesses. Although economies of scale can theoretically reduce costs, outsourcing vendors also introduce new costs, not the least of which is profits for their shareholders. Cost savings are typically real only when there are significant economies of scale that cross corporate boundaries. Similarly, the sought-after ability to shift fixed costs (such as people) to variable costs is diminished by vendors' requirements for long-term contracts for basic services that provide them with stable revenues over time.

Performance claims beyond costs are also suspect. For example, the improved client accountability for the use of services that comes from clear invoicing can usually be achieved at lower cost by improving internal accounting. Similarly, outsourcing vendors rarely have better access to new technologies as claimed. How often do you hear of technology vendors holding products back from the market simply to give an outsourcing customer an advantage?

As Tom Peters and Robert Waterman said years ago, successful companies "stick to their knitting."[1] Vendors claim that outsourcing leaves business managers more time to focus on the company's primary lines of business. But this is only true if the people who used to manage the outsourced function are transferred into other business units. On the other hand, if these managers are fired or transferred to the outsourcing vendor, there will be no more managers focusing on the "knitting" than before outsourcing.

Moreover, managing outsourcing vendors is no easier (in fact, it may be more difficult) than managing internal staff. Contracts and legal interpretations are involved, and it is challenging to try to guide people when you do not write their performance appraisals.

Our research reveals that, contrary to conventional wisdom, many executives pursue outsourcing with or without fundamental economic benefits. Their real motivation is dissatisfaction with internal service functions.

THE REAL MOTIVATION

Our analysis shows that there are four main reasons why executives might be willing to pay more to replace internal service providers with external vendors:

- *Customer focus*. Internal providers may not treat their clients as customers and may attempt to dictate corporate solutions or audit clients' decisions. External providers, of course, recognize these clients as customers and work hard to please them.
- *Tailoring*. Corporate staff may believe they only serve corporatewide objectives, as if "one size fits all." Of course, every business unit has a unique mission and a unique role in strategy, and hence unique requirements. Outsourcers are quite pleased to tailor their products and services to what is unique about their customers (for a price).
- *Control over priorities*. To get internal providers to do any work may require a convoluted project-approval process, sometimes even requiring justifications to an executive committee. In other cases, it requires begging the internal providers, who set their own priorities. With outsourcing, on the other hand, all it takes is money. You buy what you want, when you want, with no need for approvals other than that of your boss who gave you the money to spend on your business.
- *Response time*. Sometimes, internal staff develop long backlogs, and acquiring their services requires waiting in line for an untenably long time. By contrast, outsourcers can be very responsive (as long as the customer pays for the needed resources).

When internal service providers address these four concerns, outsourcing must compete on its own merits — that is, on fundamental economics. If there is any good that comes from the threat of "losing the business" to an outsourcing company, it is that a complacent staff department is forced to respond to these legitimate concerns.

The following sections discuss, first, a practical approach to improving the performance of an internal service function; and, second, methods needed to make fair service and cost comparisons between internal staff and outsourcing vendors.

BUILDING COMPETITIVE INTERNAL SERVICE ORGANIZATIONS

To improve internal service performance to competitive levels, the starting point is data collection. Client interviews and staff feedback reveal problems that need to be addressed. These symptoms provide impetus to change and guidance on what needs to be changed.

Next, it is vital to create a practical vision of the ideal organization. A useful way to approach this is to brainstorm answers to the following question: "What should be expected of a world-class service provider?" Examples include the following:

- The provider is expected to designate an "account executive" for each business unit who is available to answer questions, participate in clients' meetings, and facilitate their relationships with the function.
- The provider is expected to proactively approach key opinion leaders and help them identify breakthrough opportunities for the function's products in an unbiased, strategy-driven manner.
- The provider is expected to proactively facilitate the formation and operation of consortia of clients with like needs.
- The provider is expected to help clients plan and defend budgets to buy the function's products.
- In response to clients' requests, the provider is expected to proactively offer a range of viable alternatives (as in Chevrolet, Cadillac, or Rolls Royce) and supply all the information clients need to choose.
- Whenever possible, the provider is expected to design products using common components and standards to facilitate integration (without sacrificing its ability to tailor results to clients' unique needs).
- The provider is expected to assign to each project the right mix of skills and utilize a diversity of vendors whenever others offer more cost-effective solutions.

Such a brainstorming stretches leaders' thinking about what is expected of them, and builds a common vision of the organization they wish to build.

These vision statements can also teach clients to demand more of their suppliers, internal and external. Clearly, when clients express interest in outsourcing, there is a good chance that they see it as a commodity rather than a core competence of the company. On the other hand, when its strategic value is appreciated, a function may be kept internal even if its costs are a bit higher. The price premium is more than repaid by the incremental strategic value that internal staff can contribute (and outside vendors cannot).

Next, leaders assess the current performance of the organization against their vision. This reaffirms the need for change and identifies additional concerns to be addressed.

A plan is then developed by analyzing the root causes of the concerns identified in the self-assessment and by identifying the right sequence of changes needed to build a high-performance organization that delivers visible strategic value.[2]

RESPONDING TO AN OUTSOURCING CHALLENGE

It is generally difficult to compare an internal service provider's budget to a vendor's outsourcing proposal. This is the probably the greatest problem faced by internal service providers when they attempt to respond to an outsourcing challenge.

There are two primary causes for this confusion: First, internal budgets are customarily presented in a fashion that makes it difficult to match costs to individual deliverables. Second, internal staff are generally funded to do things that external vendors do not have to (and should not) do.

Budgeting by Deliverables

Most internal budgets are presented in a manner that does not give clients an understanding of what they are buying. To permit a fair comparison of costs, an internal service provider must change the way it presents its budget.

Consider a budget spreadsheet, where the columns represent cost factors such as salaries, travel expenses, professional development, etc. The rows represent deliverables (i.e., specific projects and services).

	Salaries	Travel	Training
Project 1	$	$	$
Project 2	$	$	$
Service 4	$	$	$
Service 4	$	$	$

This sort of spreadsheet is a common, and sensible, way to develop a budget. The problem is, after filling in the cells in this spreadsheet, most organizations total the columns instead of the rows, presenting the budget in terms of cost factors.

This, of course, invites the wrong kind of dialogue during the budget process. Executives debate the organization's travel budget, micromanaging staff in a way that they never would an outsourcing vendor.

Even worse, executives lose sight of the linkage between the organization's budget and the deliverables they expect to receive during the year. They do not know what they are getting for their money, so the function seems expensive.

At the same time, this approach leads clients to expect that they will get whatever they need within the given budget, making it the staff's problem to figure out how to fulfill clients' unlimited demands. Put simply, clients are led to expect infinite products and services for a fixed price!

Success in this situation is, of course, impossible. As hard as staff try, the internal service provider gets blamed for both high costs and unresponsiveness.

Meanwhile, outsourcing vendors can offer bids that appear less costly simply by promising less. Executives have no way of knowing if the proposed level of service is comparable to what they are receiving internally.

While vendors are generally quite clear about the deliverables within their proposed contracts, the internal organization's deliverables remain undocumented. When comparing a short list of outsourced services to a long but undocumented list of internal services, the vendor may very well appear less expensive.

Of course, comparing "apples to oranges" is quite misleading and unfair. The answer to this predicament is simply presenting the internal budget in a different way. The internal service provider should total the rows, not the columns. This is termed "budget by deliverables," the opposite of budgeting by cost factors.

With a budget presented in terms of deliverables, executives are often surprised to learn just how much an internal service provider is doing to earn its keep. Budget by deliverables permits a fair comparison of the cost of buying each product and service from internal staff vs. an outsourcing vendor. In many cases, clients learn that, although the vendor appears to be less expensive in total, it is offering fewer services and perhaps a lower quality of service than internal staff currently provide. It is unfortunate that it often takes an outsourcing challenge to motivate the consideration of a budget-by-deliverables approach, as it is broadly useful.

One key benefit is that the debate during the budget process becomes much more constructive. Instead of demanding that staff do more with less, executives decide what products and services they will and won't buy. Trimming the budget is driven by clients, not staff, and, as a result, is better linked to business priorities.

Once a budget by deliverables is agreed on, another ongoing benefit is that clients understand exactly what they can expect from staff. Of course, if they want more, internal staff should willingly supply it — at an additional cost. This is one critical part of an "internal economy" that balances supply and demand.

Recognizing Subsidies

Staff do some activities for the common good (to benefit any and all clients). Because these deliverables are done on behalf of the entire firm, they are often "taken for granted" or not noticed at all by clients. Nonetheless, these important "corporate good" activities must be funded. We call these "subsidies."

One example is the service of facilitating the development of corporate standards and policies. Another example of a subsidy activity is commodity-product research and advice (a "consumers' report"). For example, in IS, staff may research the best configurations of personal computers for various uses. This research service helps clients make the right choices, whether they buy PCs through mail order or internal staff. Corporate-good activities should not be delegated to vendors who have different shareholders in mind. In a budget by deliverables, subsidies should be highlighted as separate rows. Their costs should not be buried within the price of other deliverables.

If the costs of these services were spread across other internal products, they would inflate the price of the rest of staff's product line and put them at an unfair disadvantage when compared to external competitors who do not do these things.

In our IS example, if the costs of the PC research were buried in the price of PCs, then mail-order vendors would outcompete the internal IS department (even though staff's bulk purchasing might negotiate an even better deal for the firm). As more clients bought directly from external vendors, the fixed costs of PC research would have to be spread across fewer units, and the price of a PC would rise further — chasing even more business away. Eventually, this drives the internal IS department out of the business of supplying PCs.

This distortion is particularly critical during an outsourcing study. If subsidies are not separated from the cost of competitive products, the outsourcing vendor may win the business, even though its true unit costs may be higher. Later, the corporation will find that critical corporate-good activities do not get done.

Funding subsidies individually separate the outsourcing decision (which focuses on ongoing products and services) from the decision to invest in the subsidies. It permits a fair comparison with competitors of the prices of specific products and services. It also encourages a thoughtful decision process around each such activity, leading to an appropriate level of corporate-good efforts.

It is worth noting that once we compare "apples to apples" in this way, many internal service providers are found to offer a very competitive deal. Making sure that clients are aware of this is a key to a permanent role as "supplier of choice."

Activity-Based Costing Analysis

While the logic of budget by deliverables is straightforward and compelling, the mechanics are not so simple. Identifying an organization's products and services — not tasks, but deliverables — is, in itself, a challenge. The level of detail must be carefully managed so that each row represents a meaningful client purchase decision, without inundating clients with more than they can comprehend.

Once the products are identified, allocating myriad indirect costs to a specific set of deliverables is a challenge in "activity-based costing." Many have found an activity-based costing analysis difficult for even one or two lines of business. To prepare a budget by deliverables requires a comprehensive analysis across all products and services. This adds unique problems, such as "circles," where two groups within the organization serve one another, and hence each is part of the other's cost structure and neither can determine its price until the other does.

Fortunately, there is a step-by-step process that resolves such complications and leads to a clear result.[3] The budget-by-deliverables process begins with the identification of lines of business and deliverables. For each deliverable, a unit of costing (such as hours or clients supported) is identified, and a forecast of the number of units required to produce the deliverable is made.

Next, indirect costs are estimated and allocated to each row (each deliverable). Direct costs are added to each row as well. Overhead costs (initially their own rows) are "taxed" to the other deliverables. Then, all the groups within the organization combine their spreadsheets, and the total cost for each deliverable is summed.

With minor modifications to the budget-by-deliverables process, the analysis can produce unit prices (fees for services) at the same time as the budget. The result of the budget-by-deliverables process is a proposal that estimates the true cost to shareholders of each staff deliverable, making for fact-based budgeting decisions and fair (and, hopefully, favorable) comparisons with outsourcing vendors' proposals.

VENDOR PRICING: LESSONS FROM THE PAST

When comparing a staff's budget with an outsourcing proposal, some additional considerations are important to note. Even if internal costs are lower than outsourcing, comparisons may be distorted by some common vendor tactics.

Outsourcing vendors sometimes "buy the business" by offering favorable rates for the first few years of a contract and making up for the loss of profits throughout the rest of the relationship.

This tactic may be supported by excess capacity that the vendor can afford to sell (for a short while) below full costs. Or, the vendor may be generating sufficient profits from other companies to afford a loss for a certain period. Neither enabling factor lasts for long. In the long run, this leads to higher costs, even in discounted-present-value terms, because entrepreneurs will always find ways to be compensated for taking such risks. A similar technique is pricing basic services at or below costs, and then making up the profits on add-on business.

Tricks that make outsourcing appear less expensive are best countered by demanding a comparison of all costs over a longer period. Costs should include all activities of the function, itemized in a way that permits comparisons under different scenarios, forecasting increased and decreased demands.

The term need not be limited to the initial proposed contract. A longer time frame is justifiable, because an outsourcing decision is difficult to reverse. It takes years to rebuild an internal capability and transition competencies from a vendor back to staff. Thus, it makes sense to ask vendors to commit to prices for 10 or more years.

EXTENDED STAFFING

Too often, if a staff function is not working right, outsourcing has simply been a method of paying someone else to take the pain. It is a way to avoid expending the time and energy to build a high-performance internal service provider.

But paying profits to other shareholders is short-sighted because it sacrifices a potentially valuable component of business strategy and drives up long-term costs.

Shirking tough leadership duties in this manner is also mean-spirited. It destroys careers, with little appreciation for people's efforts and the obstacles they faced, and it creates an environment of fear and destroys morale for those who remain.

Even partial outsourcing — sometimes buying from vendors and at other times from staff — is not constructive in the long term because it allows internal service groups to deteriorate. As they lose market share, internal organizations shrink, lose critical mass, and get worse and worse.

There is no substitute for proper resolution of clients' concerns by investing in building an internal service provider that earns clients' business. This, of course, does not mean that outside vendors are avoided where they can contribute significant and unique value. In fact, one aspect of a healthy internal service provider is its proactive use of vendors. We call this approach to managing vendors extended staffing.

A healthy organization divides itself into clearly defined lines of business, each run by an entrepreneur. Each entrepreneur should know his or her competitors and continually benchmark price and performance against them. This is not tough to do. Those very competitors are also potential extensions to the internal staff. If demand goes up, every entrepreneur should have vendors and contractors lined up, ready to go. And whenever they bid a deal, staff should propose a "buy" alternative along side their "make" option.

By treating vendors and contractors as extensions to internal staff — rather than replacements for them — extended staffing enhances, rather than undermines, internal service providers. And by bringing in vendors through (not around) internal staff, extended staffing gives employees a chance to learn and grow.

When internal staff proactively use vendors, making educated decisions on when it makes sense to do so, the firm always gets the best deal. With confidence in their niche, ethical vendors are happy to compete for business on the merits of their products rather than attempt to replace internal staff with theirs. Furthermore, by using the people who best know the profession to manage vendors and contractors, extended staffing also ensures that external vendors live up to internal standards of excellence.

Extended staffing automatically balances the many trade-offs between making and buying goods and services. It leads to the right decisions, in context, day after day.

Notes

Peters, T.J., and Waterman Jr., R. H. 1982. *In search of excellence.* New York: Harper & Row.
A tested, effective process of systemic change is discussed in detail in Meyer, N. D. 1998. *Road map: How to understand, diagnose, and fix your organization.* Ridgefield, CT : NDMA Publishing.
Meyer, N. D. 1998. *The internal economy: A market approach.* Ridgefield, CT: NDMA Publishing.

Chapter 13
IT Performance Turnaround —
The Outsourcing Alternative
Richard D. Hays

MANY OF THE DISAPPOINTMENTS in IT outsourcing are the result of misguided drivers, especially the flight from a poorly performing and frustrating IT unit. Investing time and energy in turning around the performance of an internal IT unit before making the outsourcing decision provides direct identification and confrontation of fundamental problems that must be dealt with anyway, a sounder basis for evaluating outsourcing options, and the possibility of a healthy internal IT unit that can provide services better and cheaper than an outsider can.

Before the last decade, "outsourcing" was a term rarely heard and even more rarely used. Outsourcing now has grown to become a primary force shaping business. Currently, over 2500 books and articles focus on outsourcing — how to do it, how not to do it, what functions to outsource, traps to avoid, etc. A recent A. T. Kearney study revealed that over 86% of major corporations are now outsourcing some functions. Many early successes fueled interest and encouraged others to consider their own outsourcing possibilities. The Information Technology function has been an especially tempting outsourcing target due to its high cost, service that is often viewed as unresponsive and frustrating, and a willingness to see it as an easily substitutable commodity. Many IT executives have realized only too late that their efforts to optimize internal technology may have been eclipsed by the pressing need to deal with external communications and service effectiveness issues.

OUTSOURCING RESULTS: A MIXED BAG

Many outsourcers have reduced costs and improved service levels. Others have found that their strategic focus has been sharpened by eliminating an IT function that was not central to their core technology. Still others have achieved improved access to information technology and expertise as a result of their outsourcing move.

However, for some organizations, the shift to outsourcing their IT function has been much less positive. Horror stories have resulted from the lack of flexibility and control that accompanies this shift. Old problems and complaints that were to have disappeared with the introduction of a new IT supplier remained. New limitations on control and flexibility have hampered strategic actions and some have awakened to rude shocks as unanticipated parts of their agreement forced sudden and unpleasant learning about the contracting process. For these companies, the promise of IT outsourcing is severely tarnished.

Many of these disappointed volunteers in the outsourcing movement share a common original motivation and entry process. They were propelled into outsourcing primarily as a flight from a poorly performing internal IT unit (the more satisfied outsourcing companies are more likely to have had an original motivation rooted in broader strategic concerns). Frustration with cost and/or service quality within the existing IT unit and with repeated unsuccessful attempts to "fix the problem" have often precipitated a headlong jump to an outsourcing option. With no existing positive model of a well-functioning IT unit available, these organizations have been much more likely to jump into outsourcing for inadequate reasons or to have negotiated less favorable contracts and conditions. In addition, a quick move directly into outsourcing often means that fundamental factors that helped create the initial unsatisfactory IT performance remain unidentified and unaddressed — the seeds of future discontent, even in an outsourcing mode. To determine the level of concern about existing internal service performance within one's own organization, check the following listing of major symptoms:

- *Conflict.* A high state of conflict and disagreement between IT and customer units is a continuing and dominant feature of the ongoing relationship.
- *Complaints.* Customer units complain loudly and insistently about poor IT service or high IT costs.
- *Duplicating service.* Customer units attempt to build their own internal duplicates of IT-provided services in order to gain better control.
- *Executive frustration.* Senior corporate executives are very frustrated with seemingly uncontrolled IT costs and the continuing need to "referee" conflicts between IT and its customer units.
- *Organizational energy.* Considerable executive and managerial time, energy, and effort are being expended in dealing with interdepartmental conflict issues or in "positioning" for possible future conflicts.

- *Customer impact.* The internal conflicts over IT costs or service quality are beginning to have an impact on the interface with external customers.

WHY THE "TURNAROUND" OPTION MAKES SENSE

The risk and uncertainty surrounding IT outsourcing can be significantly reduced through accomplishment of a performance turnaround in the existing IT unit prior to formal consideration of outsourcing. Effecting such a turnaround requires commitment of substantial resources and effort, but three important payoffs exist for the organization that can bring it off successfully.

Confront Key Performance Limiting Issues

If an existing IT unit is performing poorly, it is doing so for specific reasons. All too frequently, these reasons have to do with fundamental structural factors that seriously impede the unit's ability to yield solid cost-effective service. For example, a major source of difficulty for many internal IT units is the fuzzy or conflicting service expectations that exist. Lack of specific articulation and agreement between supplier and user of IT services breeds violation of unstated (but strongly held) expectations. In addition, senior management may want low cost while line customer units want premium service. The IT function is caught in the middle and can satisfy neither. If these conflicts have not been addressed and resolved, moving to outsourcing may only exacerbate problems. It has been noted that "if the IT activity has been badly managed in the first place, will the IT managers be any better at managing an external provider? Indeed, does executive management want to give the benefits of improving an inefficient operation to the marketplace? In this situation, there are at least two possible responses. A company can (1) hire better IT managers or (2) turn around internal performance before subcontracting to the marketplace. These are sensible precautions and probably should precede any outsourcing based on dissatisfaction with operations."[1] Fundamental problem issues such as these, if left unresolved, will only migrate into the new outsourcing arrangement and continue to cause problems there (but in a way that is much more difficult to resolve).

Create a Solid Comparison Basis for Outsourcing

When moving directly from a poorly performing internal IT unit to outsourcing, a company has a very ill-formed basis for structuring and negotiating a contract. Significant evidence is emerging that IT performance gains have much more to do with the adoption of good management practices than with economies of scale.[2] Can your organization afford to give away an unknown (but probably large) premium to an outsider, based simply on their ability to bring in good management? Without the existence of a well-

145

functioning internal IT unit operating within the unique variables and constraints of a particular company, that company has little basis for structuring the contract. The outsourcing contractor is much more experienced and knowledgeable about the factors that will determine final cost and performance — a rather one-sided basis for negotiations!

Achieve Better Cost/Service Than Outsiders Can Offer

A well-known study carefully examined six firms with IT units that were judged by their own company to be performing unsatisfactorily.[3] Each firm placed their IT function out to bid in an outsourcing mode but, after considering both external bids *and* a bid from their own internal IT unit, elected to grant a "contract" to their internal unit (a practice of "insourcing"). The performance of each unit was then monitored as changes were made — changes that were more extensive than were possible in the old mode of a totally captive unit. The performance results were impressive. Costs were reduced from 20 to 54% and, in many cases, service improved as well. They concluded that internal IS departments, given the freedom and capability to change, often possess strong cost advantages over any outsider and offer greater insight into the unique organizational service needs as well. The emerging success stories in "insourcing" are causing new questioning as to why an external agent, using essentially the same people and equipment as the internal unit, should be able to deliver more cost-effective service and produce a profit as well. In fact, once internal IT units start to see the overall problem from this perspective, the challenge to use their own resources to exceed what an outsider could offer can become a very positive and motivational vision. They already have the basic resources that would become available to an outside supplier — why not work on the revised perspective, practices, and processes that will provide the same cost and service benefits? Achieving this objective requires a strong challenge of the existing systems and mentality; but if an outsider can do it, why can we not do it?

Each of these three benefits can be substantial, but the combination of all three provides a commanding reason to seriously consider the turnaround option. Many companies have avoided the turnaround option because of the difficulty in designing and executing such a complex organizational change. However, the change technology and experience base is available that can help structure an IT performance turnaround that is highly likely to succeed (even in cases with low reform success in the past).

IS A TURNAROUND ATTEMPT RIGHT FOR YOU?

Factors surrounding any individual organization will determine whether or not a turnaround attempt should be made prior to outsourcing. While no simple answer exists, affirmative responses to the following questions should bias one's thinking toward investing in a turnaround effort.

Is IT central to the core business and strategy? IT is often viewed as a substitutable and replaceable commodity, particularly if historical performance has been poor. However, a more in-depth analysis may reveal that IT is more central to the effectiveness of strategic actions than is apparent on the surface. If the overall strategy of the business depends to any substantial degree on IT functioning and performance, outsourcing could mean loss of control and flexibility in a key area — actions that could seriously blunt the overall strategic impact.

Could IT become a source of competitive advantage? For many companies, IT is more than just crucial to strategic action — it is a fundamental source of external competitive advantage. American Airlines, Otis Elevator, USAA Insurance, FedEx, and Frito Lay all gain primary competitive advantage from their IT competence. Envisioning how IT could move to a role of providing a basic competitive advantage may be extremely difficult if present IT issues center around the adequacy of basic functioning.

Are your IT needs complex, relatively unique, and dynamic? An outsourcing contract can be most effective with fairly straightforward service needs and a moderately steady-state situation. The loss of flexibility as conditions change (one's needs change or the technology changes) can become a substantial limitation with a rigid contract.

Is frustration with the present IT function a primary outsourcing motivator? Successful outsourcing arrangements tend to be grounded in strategic analysis rather than based on a flight from a frustrating existing internal unit. Identification of, and assault on, the fundamental issues creating the present performance problems are going to be necessary, even in an outsourcing mode.

SETTING UP THE TURNAROUND

If attempting a turnaround seems appropriate and beneficial, several actions need to be taken to set the stage for a successful effort. These include

- *Situational assessment.* Analyze the initial situation to determine the need for change, the general extent of changes needed, and the capability of the parties involved to manage and embrace the change. Asking pointed questions about the general need, the IT unit, and the customer units can help focus thinking about the need to change and making this need more salient to all.
- *Enrollment of stakeholders.* Ensure the continuing understanding and support of senior managers, customer managers, and IT leadership in the organizational change process. Top managers and customer unit leaders must have specific information on the need for change, the

benefits of a successful effort, required resources, impact on others, and schedule. The IT leadership needs to grapple with the significant issues involved with a major change process.

- *Final commitment.* Commit all of this setup work to a specific and written document that serves as a public agreement on the need for the change, the goals of the turnaround, the general process to be used, etc. Top management, customer unit leaders, and IT leadership all need to have a shared understanding and agreement about the important organizational changes ahead. The team that will actually manage the change process will need to organize itself to ensure effective project management.

BUILDING THE INFORMATION BASE

Any successful organizational change effort must be grounded in firm information and analysis. An IT turnaround effort requires a clear vision of the existing problem situation and its causation, detailed insights into the real service needs of customer units, and a deep understanding of their own internal processes and procedures. An effective change plan must be founded on this solid information base.

The process of constructing the needed information base can serve as the launch of a new IT culture that is centered on "internal customers" — units that have service needs that must be identified and filled if IT is to be successful. Extracting the views of these internal customers and other stakeholders regarding the following issues is essential to the construction of an effective IT change plan. Questions to be asked include

- How is present IT service seen?
- How is the present IT function seen?
- What are their service needs?
- What specific topics are now causing the most "pain" within internal customer units?
- What is the desired balance between cost and service responsiveness?
- How strongly is a need for basic change felt?

Surveys and interviews can provide important insights into the causal forces that shape today's problem situation. Focused exploration of customer unit service expectations can reveal the nature and form of their service beliefs (and provide an opportunity to identify those that may be unreasonable or excessively costly).

DESIGNING THE TURNAROUND PLAN

Once the information base regarding the existing problem, the customer service expectations, and existing processes is understood in depth, a plan to direct the IT turnaround effort can be constructed. The plan needs to set specific and measurable goals, define the needed changes, and identify the required processes for change.

Many of the goals of the plan will be derived from newly defined IT performance standards. Considerable work needs to be expended on working directly with customer units to define these standards. They will reflect both the specific service expectations of the customer units and the practical and professional pragmatics of the IT unit. The standards need to be as specific and measurable as possible and to be explicitly agreed upon by all as the definition of excellent service. This definition of excellence will serve as the guide for the efforts of the IT unit as well as the judgment standard to be used by the customer units. The process of negotiating and defining these standards may be one of the most difficult tasks of the entire turnaround, but it is also one of the most important. A survey of information systems departments in a variety of industries for factors that contribute to high internal customer satisfaction revealed that IT units ranking high on service satisfaction had significantly better and more precise specifications regarding the service to be performed than did their less well-rated counterparts.[4] For these IT units, the considerable investment in defining expectations and clarifying standards paid off strongly in service satisfaction.

MOVING THE PLAN ON TO AN IMPLEMENTATION SUCCESS

Supporting elements are key to converting a turnaround plan from an abstract concept to an implementation success. Supporting elements include

- *Align the IT culture.* Customer-centeredness must become the driving force of the IT culture. Most poorly performing IT units have an internal culture centered on the enhancement of their own technology or processes. The conversion of this well-established culture to an entirely new focus, which gives pre-eminent attention to the service needs of customer units, is a prodigious task that is unlikely to respond to gentle prodding. Gaining an explicit understanding of the functioning of the present internal IT culture and producing a specific articulation of the desired culture are necessary, but difficult and foreign processes for most IT units. Designing the actual cultural changes and reinforcements may be even more foreign.
- *Develop "Service People."* Building the skills and attitudes that will be necessary to have truly "service-oriented people" in the IT unit is also a necessary support step for the change plan. Being skillfully solicitous of, and receptive to, customer feedback (particularly negative feedback) is a trainable skill. This skill escapes even many external service companies, but is no less crucial to an IT unit dealing with in-

ternal customers. IT agents must provide respectful and responsive service interactions with internal customer units and must be able and willing to gain feedback on service rendered — an invaluable element in improving future service.

- *Assure Capability for "Service Recovery."* Many IT units deliver service adequately but destroy their relationship with customer units when they face "service recovery" situations. Even the best of service will sometimes fail, and the skill that the IT unit has built to recover positively from these unanticipated shortfalls will heavily shape the customer's view of the service received. Recovery situations are particularly difficult because of the higher interpersonal skill level and service commitment needed to handle disgruntled and emotionally charged customers who have just received service that violates their expectations.

LOOKING AT OUTSOURCING OPTIONS

At the completion of a successful IT performance turnaround, the company has a greatly expanded range of alternatives. With a cost-effective and service-sensitive IT unit in place, the motivation for outsourcing erodes. The loss of flexibility and control associated with outsourcing is just too great a cost without the negative prod of poor and costly existing service. The process of creating a truly effective internal IT unit has caused fundamental problems to be addressed and, at a minimum, establishes an excellent basis for negotiating an outsourcing contract. If outsourcing is still to be considered, the outsourcing options themselves become richer as new performance experience is gained. A more sophisticated view moves from asking a simple "outsource or not?" question and to looking at the effectiveness of selective outsourcing of very specific functions. A performance turnaround is, indeed, the viable alternative to outsourcing.

Notes

1. Michael J. Earl. "The Risks of Outsourcing IT," *Sloan Management Review,* Spring 1996, p. 27.
2. Mary C. Lacity and Rudy Hirschheim. *Beyond the Information Systems Outsourcing Bandwagon: The Insourcing Response,* John Wiley, New York, 1995, p. 168.
3. Lacity and Hirschheim, p. 36.
4. Bruce Pfau, Denis Detzel, and Andrew Geller. "Satisfy Your Internal Customer," *The Journal of Business Strategy,* November/December 1991, p. 11.

Chapter 14
Support Services Outsourcing
William J. Beaumont

MANY IS ORGANIZATIONS struggle to control the skyrocketing costs associated with desktop assets. Companies that have traditionally relied on large, distributed systems as the backbone of their information systems are increasingly dependent on desktop systems. Although the use of desktop computers has grown dramatically, only recently have PCs and LANs been entrusted with mission-critical tasks.

As a business tool, a computer helps users increase productivity by performing tasks cheaper, better, and faster than alternate methods; if it does not, it is not worth buying. Whether or not a piece of equipment is a sound investment depends partly on what the cost is and how it is measured.

TOTAL COST OF OWNERSHIP

For the past decade, the Gartner Group has compiled data on a measuring concept now widely adopted by the IT industry known as Total Cost of Ownership (TCO). TCO is defined as the total cost of the computer asset, including the hard costs of purchasing hardware plus the soft costs of labor associated with supporting and maintaining the asset.

As much as 85% of a PC's total cost of ownership is associated with soft costs, which can be as much as $10,000 per machine, per year. By the mid-1990s, the TCO of a typical desktop PC was approximately $44,000 over the PC lifecycle (i.e., a period of five years). A fully networked PC was even more expensive at almost $12,000 per node, per year for hardware, software, support, administrative services, and end-user operations.

Although processors are now extremely fast for a great deal less than before, increases in labor costs have been massive. Administrative expenditures have quadrupled and those for end users have doubled, prompting the urgent need to bring distributed computing costs under control.

INTEGRATION OF DESKTOP SUPPORT SERVICES

The only way to control the escalating costs of desktop computing is through greater coordination of desktop support services, since that is where the majority of corporate IT money is spent. Any company hoping to gain control of its IT environment must be able to measure and justify all of the expenses associated with end-user computing.

This justification can best be achieved with a fully integrated desktop management solution for identifying, controlling, and reducing TCO, which should include ways to analyze improvement plans, implement optimization plans, and audit results to ensure that reductions are being achieved.

Savings of several thousand dollars per PC can be achieved by organizations committed to a serious, companywide cost-reduction effort. Even greater savings are possible—from 25% to as much as 50%—when the effort is managed at the enterprise level.

OUTSOURCING SUPPORT SERVICES

The use of third-party support services continues to grow at a rapid pace as companies struggle to keep up with growing user demands within multivendor, multiplatform environments. Soft costs are escalating beyond affordable rates, making outsourcing of support services an efficient and practical way of supporting employees. In addition, outsourcing these services allows companies to focus on business issues at hand instead of addressing individual problems that could be handled more effectively by another party.

The increase in outsourcing support services can largely be attributed to complex processing environments. IT managers are challenged by the sophistication of today's networks and application software, the shortage of skills needed to support their users, and increased pressure from day-to-day business issues. It has become more difficult for even the largest in-house support center to stay abreast of new applications and technologies to support their own base of users and keep them satisfied.

Mixed PC/work station environments spend more than $400 per user, per year on problem resolution. Multiplied throughout an organization with hundreds or thousands of users, the cost of providing effective support becomes substantial.

Third-party organizations that focus on support services can leverage their investments in technology and staffing across a broad base of clients to obtain economies of scale that allow them to provide cost-effective solutions. A single point of contact to handle multiple support issues, ranging from software applications through operating systems through hardware problems, has become a more cost-effective way to resolve problems on a per-user basis.

The most practical solution helps customers optimize their investments in IT by taking on some or all support tasks. This allows IS to focus on strategic functions such as developing new systems and introducing new technology that benefit their businesses.

Key characteristics of the third-party service provider that need to be evaluated are

- *Vendor neutral.* The third party should support all brands, or make explicit any vendor alliances or biases.
- *Simple to deal with.* The third-party service should be a virtual extension of in-house support and coordinate activities across the enterprise.
- *Proven resource.* To minimize risks, the vendor selected should have an established track record.
- *Measurable performance.* Third-party providers should have mechanisms in place to demonstrate the performance benefits being sought—such as to reduce costs, enhance control, maximize systems availability, and increase end-user satisfaction.

A STRATEGIC, COMPREHENSIVE APPROACH TO CONTROLLING COSTS

Most organizations need a strategy for controlling costs at the desktop, including the following integrated services.

Planning and Consulting Services

Planning support services help organizations define their environments, set targets for improvement, and monitor progress against plans. These services should be available either as a one-time service or used over the course of a project.

Consultants should be used on ad hoc projects. Sometimes the greatest value of outside consultants is having an independent, unbiased party review internal operational or organizational approaches to problems.

Hardware Services

Both remedial and preventive maintenance, with optional on-site staff support, should be provided for a variety of products. Almost every desktop unit undergoes at least one or two changes per year. Moves, adds, and changes to any system should be supported, providing a comprehensive solution.

153

Asset Management Services

Asset management contributes to service effectiveness in large organizations. Accurate information is vital to cost control. Companies that engage in IT asset management stand to reap significant savings and boost end-user productivity.

An effective asset management service inventories a customer's IT environment and creates an asset data base through a combination of automated and manual data collection activities. Once completed, the data base should contain information detailing the customer's IT assets from several perspectives including hardware, software, end users, location, and cost centers.

To ensure that all facts are up to date, it is a good idea for a client support team to apply specialized software to probe the network for new, moved, or changed devices and see that all changes are captured in the data base. Periodic audits of the IT environment should be performed.

End-User Support Services (Help Desk).

Round-the-clock support services, more commonly known as the help desk, aid users with the navigation and resolution of computer technology questions, as well as supporting hardware, software, and system-related activities. Services should meet the growing needs of multivendor processing environments, offering solutions that are responsive to a customer's needs.

Contracted support services can include

- *Call management* (including a problem triage service).
- *Basic end-user support* (popular shrink-wrapped applications and suites).
- *Network end-user support* (network operating systems).
- *Customized support* (support for software packages unique to a function or industry).
- *Advanced end-user support* (complex products such as Lotus Notes).

Network Support Services

IS organizations spend approximately 40% of their time on networking issues and 60% of their tools budget on network management. A customer's environment should be remotely monitored 24 hours a day, seven days a week, to improve costs, boost user productivity, and increase systems availability. Round-the-clock monitoring allows for the identification of potential trouble spots and enhances network performance by helping to highlight areas for improvement.

Tailored Program

Some organizations need support for individual projects while others need complete management of their desktop environment. In either case, a tailored program should be designed, allowing companies to focus their resources on their core competencies.

Support Partner Services

When an organization requires additional services such as leasing, procurement, or disaster recovery, it is ideal if the vendor can respond with an integrated solution through support partners. These preferred vendor relationships offer quick, comprehensive responses to a customer's business requirements.

CONCLUSION

Technology is changing at a rapid pace, and companies are struggling to come to grips with managing their desktop assets. They are seeking innovative solutions to lowering the total cost of ownership of their IT environment.

To improve operational performance, service and support must be integrated. A tightly integrated suite of services to support desktop systems is often the best solution for controlling the exploding costs of desktop computing.

155

Chapter 15
Managing the IT Procurement Process

Robert Heckman

THIS CHAPTER PRESENTS a process model of IT procurement which was developed by a group of senior managers who make up the Society for Information Management (SIM) Working Group on IT Procurement. The model systematically describes the processes involved in IT procurement and is a useful tool for bringing managerial discipline to the increasingly important activity of IT procurement.

An IT procurement process, formal or informal, exists in every organization that acquires information technology. As users of information systems increasingly find themselves in roles as customers of multiple technology vendors, this IT procurement process assumes greater management significance. In addition to hardware, operating system software, and telecommunications equipment and services –– information resources traditionally acquired in the marketplace — organizations now turn to outside providers for many components of their application systems, application development and integration, and a broad variety of system management services. Yet despite this trend, there has to date been little, if any, research investigating the IT procurement process. While IS development activities are represented by at least 120 terms in the keyword classification scheme for IS research literature, market-oriented strategies for information resource acquisition are represented by a single term — "Outsourcing of IS."

Several studies of IT procurement issues have recently been commissioned by the Society for Information Management (SIM) Working Group on IT Procurement. These studies are an attempt to begin a systematic investigation of critical IT procurement issues. This chapter presents a model of the IT procurement process which was developed by the SIM Working

0-8493-9820-7/00/$0.00+$.50
© 2000 by CRC Press LLC

Group to provide a framework for studying IT procurement. This model has provided the conceptual context for the Working Group's empirical research projects, and a framework for organizing key issues and questions. The model represents IT procurement as consisting of six major processes. Contained within each major process is a series of sub-processes and a set of key questions.

BACKGROUND

IT procurement is an interdisciplinary process, typically involving staff members from the IS organization, purchasing, legal, financial/treasury, and end users from all departments and services available. The speed with which new products are introduced to the marketplace make IT procurement an extremely intricate and volatile process. Two relatively recent trends suggest that a disciplined, process-oriented framework might be needed to help us better understand and manage the complex IT procurement activity. The first trend is the *evolution of the information resource acquisition process* from an internal, unstructured, craft-like activity to a more structured, market-oriented discipline. The second trend is the recent expanded focus on *business process analysis and design.*

EVOLUTION OF THE INFORMATION RESOURCE ACQUISITION PROCESS

Heckman and Sawyer (1996) have described an information resource (IR) acquisition model which characterizes the acquisition process using two dimensions: *source* and *process*. Exhibit 15.1 shows the model, which illustrates that an IR can be acquired from an internal throughout the firm. This complex organization structure, the great number of different products (hierarchy) or external (market) source, and the acquisition process can be either structured or unstructured. Exhibit 15.1 also shows how the model can be used to illustrate the evolution of information resource acquisition in organizations over time.

Exhibit 15.1 suggests that in the early years of computing, organizations developed many of their systems internally using relatively unstructured processes. As experience with systems development grew, more structured methods of analysis, design and programming were developed, and software construction began to evolve from a craft-like activity to an engineering discipline. As information technology price performance dramatically improved and microcomputers became available, the era of end-user computing began. In this era, organizations tended to turn outward to the market to meet more of their information resource needs, but they did so with relatively little structure or discipline in the process. Finally, in the current era, organizations are recognizing the need to bring more order to

Source

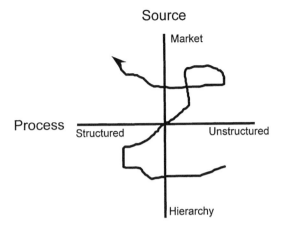

Exhibit 15.1. Information Resource Acquisition Model: The Evolution of IT Acquisition.

their IR acquisition activities. As client/server architectures become more complex and interconnected, the need for more disciplined management of the procurement process will also grow. The IS literature has begun to indirectly address this need in debates about the appropriate management of IT outsourcing relationships.

One way to impose discipline or structure on a process is to develop a framework, which allows the process to be analyzed and managed in a systematic way. An example of such a framework is the traditional systems development life cycle (SDLC). The SDLC framework allowed discipline to be introduced to the process of systems analysis and design, and laid the groundwork for the development of methodologies intended to improve reliability and productivity (Reifer, 1994; Thayer, 1988; Rook, 1986; Vaughn and Parkinson, 1994). It enabled not only the creation of structured analysis and design tools, but also made possible systems development approaches which transcend the traditional SDLC. It can be argued that the SDLC was an essential evolutionary step, which made possible the more advanced approaches of rapid prototyping, object-oriented analysis, joint application development (JAD), etc. The IT Procurement Process framework might provide a similar evolutionary function.

BUSINESS PROCESS ANALYSIS AND DESIGN

Business process analysis and redesign have become an important management tools for both American and global businesses. Davenport and Short define a business process as *a set of logically related tasks performed to achieve a defined business outcome.* Business processes are generally independent of organizational structure, and this attribute has led to great interest in business process redesign (BPR). In BPR, important business processes are decomposed and reassembled in ways that are intended to be more efficient and effective. Techniques and principles for the analysis and design of business processes have been widely promulgated; however, all have in common the necessity to identify, understand, and measure the components or sub-processes which comprise a critical business process.

The process framework described below attempts to accomplish this objective in the IT procurement domain. It provides a comprehensive description of the processes and sub-processes that are involved in procuring IT products and services. By identifying and describing the process in detail, efforts to analyze, measure, and redesign IT procurement activities can begin from a firm foundation.

DEVELOPMENT OF THE FRAMEWORK

In January, 1994 the Society for Information Management (SIM) Working Group on Information Technology Procurement was formed to exchange information on managing IT procurement, and to foster collaboration among the different professions participating in the IT procurement process. The IT Procurement Process Framework was developed by a twelve-member subgroup comprised of senior IT procurement executives from large North American companies.

The task of developing the framework took place over the course of several meetings and lasted approximately one year. A modified nominal group process was used, in which individual members independently developed frameworks which described the IT procurement process as they understood it.

In a series of several work sessions, these individual models were synthesized and combined to produce the six-process framework presented below. Once the six major procurement processes had been identified, a modified nominal group process was once again followed to elicit the sub-processes to be included under each major process. Finally, a nominal group process was once again used to elicit a set of key issues, which the group felt presented managerial challenges in each of the six processes. The key issues were conceived of as the critical questions which must be successfully addressed to effectively manage each process. Thus they represent the most important issues faced by those executives responsible for the management of the IT procurement function.

The process framework and key issues were reviewed by the Working Group approximately one year later (Summer, 1996), and modifications to definitions, sub-processes and key issues were made at that time. The key issue content analysis described below was conducted following the most recent Working Group review in early 1997.

160

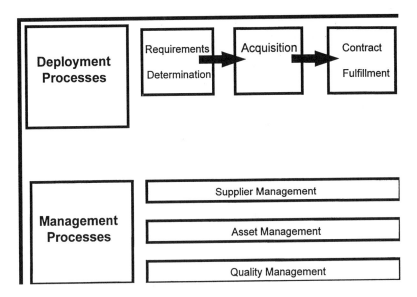

Exhibit 15.2. Major Processes in IT Procurement

THE IT PROCUREMENT FRAMEWORK: PROCESSES, SUB-PROCESSES, AND KEY ISSUES

The IT Procurement Process Framework provides a vehicle to systematically describe the processes and sub-processes involved in IT procurement. Exhibit 15.2 illustrates six major processes in IT procurement activities. Each of these major processes consists of a number of sub-processes. Exhibits 15.3 through 15.8 list the sub-processes included in each of the major processes. They also include the key issues identified by the Working Group. Procurement activities can be divided into two distinct types of processes: *deployment processes and management processes.*

Deployment processes

Deployment processes consist of activities which are performed (to a greater or lesser extent) each time an IT product or service is acquired. Each individual procurement can be thought of in terms of a life cycle which begins with requirements determination, proceeds through activities involved in the actual acquisition of a product or service, and is completed as the terms specified in the contract are fulfilled. Each IT product or service that is acquired has its own individual iteration of this deployment life cycle.

Requirements Determination is the process of determining the business justification, requirements, specifications and approvals to proceed with the procurement process. It includes sub-processes

Definition

The process of determining the business justification, requirements, specifications, and approvals to proceed with the procurement process.

Subprocesses

☐ Identify need.

☐ Put together cross-functional team and identify roles and responsibilities.

☐ Continuously refine requirements and specifications in accordance with user needs.

☐ Gather information regarding alternative solutions.

☐ Perform cost-benefit analysis or other analytic technique to justify expenditure.

☐ Evaluate alternative solutions (including build/buy, in-house/outsource, etc.) and associated risk and benefits.

☐ Develop procurement plans that are integrated with project plans.

☐ Gain approval for the expenditure.

☐ Develop preliminary negotiation strategies.

Key Issues

☐ What are the important components of an appropriate procurement plan? [S]

☐ How much planning (front-end loading) is appropriate or necessary for different types of acquisitions (e.g., commodity purchases versus complex, unique acquisitions)? [S]

☐ How should project teams be configured for different types of acquisitions (appropriate internal and external resources, project leader, etc.)? [IR]

☐ How should changes in scope and changes in orders be handled? [P]

☐ What are the important costs versus budget considerations? [F]

☐ What are the most effective methods of obtaining executive commitment? [E]

☐ Can requirements be separated from wants? [P]

☐ Should performance specifications and other outputs be captured for use in later phases such as quality management? [P]

Exhibit 15.3 Requirements Determination Process

such as organizing project teams, using cost–benefit or other analytic techniques to justify investments, defining alternatives, assessing relative risks and benefits defining specifications, and obtaining necessary approvals to proceed with the procurement process (See Exhibit 15.3.)

Acquisition is the process of evaluating and selecting appropriate suppliers and completing procurement arrangements for the required products and services. It includes identification of sourcing alternatives, generating communications (such as RFPs and RFQ) to suppliers, evaluating supplier proposals, and negotiating contracts with suppliers. (See Exhibit 15.4.)

Contract Fulfillment is the process of managing and coordinating all activities involved in fulfilling contract requirements. It includes ex-

Definition

The process of evaluating and selecting appropriate suppliers and completing procurement arrangements for the required products and services

Subprocesses

☐ Develop sourcing strategy including the short list of suitable suppliers.

☐ Generate appropriate communication to suppliers (RFP, RFQ, etc.) including financing alternatives.

☐ Analyze and evaluate supplier responses and proposals.

☐ Plan formal negotiation strategy.

☐ Negotiate contract.

☐ Review contract terms and conditions.

☐ Award contract and execute documents.

☐ Identify value added from the negotiation using appropriate metrics.

Key Issues

☐ Is there support of corporate purchasing programs, policies, and guidelines (which can be based on technology, financing, accounting, competitive impacts, social impacts, etc.)? [E]

☐ What tools optimize the procurement process? [P]

– EDI

– Autofax

– Procurement Cards

☐ What processes in the acquisition phase can be eliminated, automated, or minimized? [P]

☐ Is it wise to be outsourcing all or part of the procurement process? [IR]

☐ What are the appropriate roles of users, legal, purchasing, and IS in the procurement process? [IR]

Exhibit 15.4 Acquisition Process

pediting of orders, acceptance of products or services, installation of systems, contract administration, management of post-installation services such as warranty and maintenance, and disposal of obsolete assets. (See Exhibit 15.5.)

Management processes

Management processes consist of those activities involved in the overall governance of IT procurement. These activities are not specific to any particular procurement event, but rather are generalized across all such events. Three general classes of IT procurement management processes are Supplier Management, Asset Management, and Quality Management.

Supplier Management is the process of optimizing customer-supplier relationships to add value to the business. It includes activities such as development of a supplier portfolio strategy, development of relationship strategies for key suppliers, assessing and influencing

Definition

The process of managing and coordinating all activities involved in fulfilling contract requirements

Subprocesses

- Expedite orders and facilitate required changes
- Receive material and supplies, update databases, and reconcile discrepancies
- Acceptance of hardware, software, or services
- Deliver materials and services as required, either direct or to drop-off points
- Handle returns
- Installation of hardware, software, or services
- Contract administration
- Process invoices and issue payment to suppliers
- Resolve payment problems
- Manage post-installation services (e.g., warranty, maintenance, etc.)
- Resolve financial status and physical disposal of excess or obsolete assets
- Maintain quality records

Key Issues

- What are some provisions for early termination and renewals? [L]
- What are the best methods for assessing vendor strategies for ongoing maintenance costs? [ER]
- What interaction between various internal departments aids the processes? [IR]

Exhibit 15.5 Contract Fulfillment Process

supplier performance, and managing communication with suppliers. (See Exhibit 15.6.)

Asset Management is the process of optimizing the utilization of all IT assets throughout their entire life cycle to meet the needs of the business. It includes activities such as development of asset management strategies and policies, development and maintenance of asset management information systems, evaluation of the life cycle cost of IT asset ownership, and management of asset redeployment and disposal policies. (See Exhibit 15.7.)

Quality Management is the process of assuring continuous improvement in the IT procurement process and in all products and services acquired for IT purposes in an organization. It includes activities such as product testing, statistical process control, acceptance testing, quality reviews with suppliers and facility audits. (See Exhibit 15.8.)

KEY IT PROCUREMENT MANAGEMENT ISSUES

Exhibits 15.3 through 15.8 contain 76 key IT procurement management issues identified by the members of the Working Group. These issues represent the beliefs of these domain experts concerning the most serious

Definition

The process of optimizing customer-supplier relationships to add value to the business

Subprocesses

❑ Categorize suppliers by value to the organization (e.g., volume, sole source, commodity, strategic alliance). Allocate resources to most important (key) suppliers.

❑ Develop and maintain a relationship strategy for each category of supplier.

❑ Establish and communicate performance expectations that are realistic and measurable.

❑ Monitor, measure, and assess vendor performance.

❑ Provide vendor feedback on performance metrics.

❑ Work with suppliers to improve performance continuously. Know when to say when.

❑ Continuously assess supplier qualifications against requirements (existing and potential suppliers).

❑ Ensure relationship roles and responsibilities are well defined.

❑ Participate in industry/technology information sharing with key suppliers.

Key Issues

❑ How does anyone distinguish between transactional/tactical and strategic relationships? [ER]

❑ How can expectations on both sides be managed most effectively? Should relationships be based on people-to-people understandings or solely upon the contractual agreement (get it in writing)? What is the right balance? [ER]

❑ How can discretionary collaborative behavior — cooperation above and beyond the letter of the contract — be encouraged? Are true partnerships with vendors possible, or does it take too long? What defines a partnership? [ER]

❑ How should multiple vendor relationships be managed? [ER]

❑ How should communication networks (both internal and external) be structured to optimize effective information exchange? Where are the most important roles and contact points? [IR]

❑ How formal should a measurement system be? What kind of report card is effective? What are appropriate metrics for delivery and quality? [M]

❑ What is the best way continuously to assess the ability of a vendor to go forward with new technologies? [M]

❑ What legal aspects of the relationship are of most concern (e.g., nondisclosure, affirmative action, intellectual property, etc.)? [L]

❑ What is the best way to keep current with IT vendor practices and trends? What role does maintaining market knowledge play in supplier management? [M]

❑ What is the optimal supplier-management strategy for a given environment? [S]

❑ How important is the development of master contract language? [L]

❑ In some sectors there is an increasing number of suppliers and technologies, although in the others vendor consolidation is occurring. In what circumstances should the number of relationships be expanded or reduced? [ER]

❑ What are the best ways to get suppliers to buy into master agreements? [L]

❑ What are the best ways continuously to judge vendor financial stability? [M]

❑ Where is the supplier positioned in the product life cycle? [M]

❑ How should suppliers be categorized (e.g., strategic, key, new, etc.) to allow for prioritization of efforts? [M]

❑ What are the opportunities and concerns to watch for when one IT supplier is acquired by another? [M]

Exhibit 15.6 Supplier Management Process

Definition

The process of optimizing the utilization of all IT assets throughout their entire life cycle to meet the needs of the business

Subprocesses

☐ Develop and maintain asset management strategies and policies. Identify and determine which assets to track they may include hardware, software licenses, and related services.

☐ Implement and maintain appropriate asset management databases, systems, and tools.

☐ Develop a disciplined process to track and control inventory to facilitate such things as budgeting, help desk, life-cycle management, software release distribution, capital accounting, compliance monitoring, configuration planning, procurement leverage, redeployment planning, change management, disaster recovery planning, software maintenance, warranty coverage, lease management, and agreement management.

☐ Identify the factors that make up the total life cycle cost of ownership.

☐ Communicate a software license compliance policy throughout the organization.

Key Issues

☐ What assets are included in IT asset management (e.g., data, human resources, consumables, courseware)? [F]

☐ How can legal department holdups be reduced? [P]

☐ What is the best way to communicate corporatewide agreements? [IR]

☐ How should small ticket assets be handled? [P]

☐ How does a company move from reactive to proactive contracting? [S]

☐ Are there ways of dealing with licenses that require counts of users? [L]

☐ What are the best ways of managing concurrent software licensing? [L]

☐ Can one be contracting for efficiency using national contracts for purchase, servicing, licensing? [P]

☐ How can software be managed and tracked as an asset? [F]

☐ How can the workload in software contracting be reduced? [P]

☐ Are there ways to encourage contract administration to be handled by the vendor? [P]

☐ Is it possible to manage all three life cycles simultaneously: technical, functional, and economical? [S]

☐ How does a company become proactive in risk management? [S]

☐ What is the appropriate assignment of internal responsibilities (e.g., compliance)? [IR]

☐ Do all items need to be tracked? [P]

☐ How much control (a) can the company afford? (b) does the company need? (c) does the company want? [F]

☐ What are the critical success factors for effective asset management? [S]

☐ What practices are most effective for the redeployment of assets? [P]

☐ Are there adequate systems available to track both hard and soft assets? Are there any integrated solutions (support, tracking, and contract management)? [P]

☐ What are the best ways to handle the rapid increase in volume and rapid changes in technology? [P]

☐ What is the appropriate reaction to dwindling centralized control of the desktop with nonconformance to guidelines and procedures? [IR]

☐ Is there a true business understanding of the total cost of ownership over the entire life cycle of an asset? [F]

☐ What are the impacts on organizational structure? [IR]

☐ What kind of reporting is most effective? [P]

☐ How can one manage tax issues–indemnification, payments, and insurance issues? [F]

☐ What issues should be considered in end-of-lease processes? [P]

Exhibit 15.7 Asset Management Process

Definition

The process of assuring continuous improvement in all elements of the IT procurement framework

Subprocesses

☐ Define and track meaningful process metrics on an ongoing basis.

☐ Conduct periodic quality reviews with suppliers.
- Provide formal feedback to vendors on their performance.
- Facilitate open and honest communication in the process.

☐ Collect and prioritize ideas for process improvement.

☐ Use formal quality improvement efforts involving the appropriate people.
- Participants may include both internal resources and vendor personnel.

☐ Recognize and reward quality improvement results on an ongoing basis.
- Recognize nonperformance/unsatisfactory results.

☐ Audit vendors' facilities and capabilities.

☐ Conduct ongoing performance tests against agreed upon standards.
- e.g., acceptance test, stress test, regression test, etc.

☐ Utilize appropriate industry standards (e.g., ISO 900, SEI Capability Maturity).

☐ Periodically review vendors' statistical process control data.

Key Issues

☐ What is the best way to drive supplier quality management systems? [ER]

☐ What is the appropriate mix of audits (supplier/site/regional, etc.) for quality and procedural conformance?[M]

☐ What is the importance of relating this process to the earliest stages of the requirement determination process? [P]

☐ What corrective actions are effective? [P]

☐ When and how is it appropriate to audit a supplier's financials? [M]

☐ What is an effective way to audit material or services received? [M]

☐ What is the best way to build quality assurance into the process, as opposed to inspecting for quality after the fact? [P]

☐ What metrics are the most meaningful quantitative measures? [M]

☐ How can one best measure qualitative information, such as client satisfaction? [M]

☐ When should one use surveys, and how can they be designed effectively? [M]

☐ How often should measurements be done? [M]

☐ How does one ensure that the data collected is valid, current, and relevant? [M]

☐ What is the best medium and format to deliver the data to those who need it? [P]

☐ What are used performance and quality metrics for the IT procurement function? [M]

☐ How does one effectively recognize and reward quality improvement? [ER]

☐ When is it time to reengineer a process rather than just improve it? [P]

☐ How much communication between vendor and customer is needed to be effective? [ER]

Exhibit 15.8 Quality Management Process

challenges facing managers of the IT Procurement function. To better understand the key issues, a content analysis was performed to determine if there were a few main themes underlying these questions. The content analysis identified eight themes, which are shown in Exhibit 15.9, ranked according to the number of times each theme occurred in the key issue list. (Each theme in Exhibit 15.9 is labeled by a one- or two-letter code. These codes also appear in Exhibits 15.3 through 15.8 to indicate how each key issue was categorized.) The following themes were those which the rankings in Exhibit 15.9 suggest are most important to the senior procurement managers in the SIM Working Group.

Process Management, Design, and Efficiency

Practicing IT procurement managers are most concerned with the issue of how to make the procurement process more efficient. The questions that reflect this theme address the use of automated tools such as EDI and procurement cards, reduction of cycle time in contracting processes, development and use of asset tracking systems and other reporting systems, and the integration of sub-processes at early and later stages of the procurement life cycle. The emergence of process efficiency as the leading issue may indicate that procurement managers are under pressure to demonstrate the economic value of their organizational contribution, and thus follow the last decade's broad management trend of rigorously managing costs.

Measurement, Assessment, Evaluation

The second most important theme concerns the search for reliable and valid ways to evaluate and assess performance. This search for useful assessment methods and measures is directed both at external suppliers and at the internal procurement process itself. The latter focus is consistent with the notion that procurement managers are looking for objective ways to assess and demonstrate their contribution. The focus on supplier assessment reflects an understanding that successful supplier relationships must be built on a foundation of high quality supplier performance.

Internal and External Relationships

The third and fourth most frequently cited themes deal with the issue of creating effective working relationships. The importance of such relationships is an outgrowth of the cross-functional nature of the IT procurement process within organizations and the general transition from internal to external sources for information resource (IR) acquisition. Venkatraman and Loh (1994) characterize the IR acquisition process as having evolved from managing a portfolio of technologies to managing a portfolio of relationships, and the results of this analysis suggest that practicing managers agree.

168

Rank	[Code]	Theme	No. Key Issues Containing This Theme
1	[P]	Process management, design, and efficiency	21
2	[M]	Measurement, assessment, evaluation (of vendor and self)	16
3	[ER]	External relationships (with supplier)	9
4	[IR]	Internal relationships (internal teams, roles, communication)	9
5	[S]	Strategy and planning	7
6	[L]	Legal issues	6
7	[F]	Financial, total cost of ownership (TCO) issues	6
8	[E]	Executive support for procurement function	2

Exhibit 15.9 Ranked Themes in Key Issues

Other Themes

The other issues which concern senior procurement managers are planning to develop an effective procurement strategy, legal problems, financial and total cost of ownership (TCO) concerns, and obtaining executive support for their activities.

A MANAGEMENT AGENDA FOR THE IT PROCUREMENT PROCESS

The process framework and key issues identified by the SIM IT Procurement Working Group suggest an agenda for future efforts to improve the management of the IT procurement process. The agenda contains five action items which may best be carried out through a collaboration between practicing IT procurement managers and academic researchers. The action items are

1. Develop IT procurement performance metrics and use them to benchmark the IT procurement process.
2. Clarify roles in the procurement process to build effective internal and external relationships.
3. Use the procurement process framework as a tool to assist in reengineering the IT procurement process.
4. Use the framework as a guide for future research.
5. Use the framework to structure IT procurement training and education.

Develop IT Procurement Performance Metrics and Use Them to Benchmark the IT Procurement Process.

Disciplined management of any process requires appropriate performance metrics, and members of the Working Group have noted that good metrics for the IT procurement processes are in short supply. The process framework is currently providing structure to an effort by the Working Group to collect a rich set of performance metrics which can be used to raise the level of IT procurement management. In this effort, four classes of performance metrics have been identified:

- Effectiveness metrics
- Efficiency metrics
- Quality metrics
- Cycle time metrics

Closely related to the metrics development issue is the need felt by many procurement professionals to benchmark critical procurement processes. The framework provides a guide to the process selection activity in the benchmarking planning stage. For example, the framework has been used by several companies to identify supplier management and asset management sub-processes for benchmarking.

Clarify Roles in the Procurement Process to Build Effective Internal and External Relationships

IT procurement will continue to be a cross-funtional process which depends on the effective collaboration of many different organizational actors for success. Inside the customer organization, representatives of IS, legal, purchasing, finance, and user departments must work together to buy, install, and use IT products and services. Partnerships and alliances with supplier and other organizations outside the boundaries of one's own firm are more necessary than ever as long-term outsourcing and consortia arrangements become more common. The key question is how these multifaceted relationships should be structured and managed.

Internally, organizational structures, roles, standards, policies and procedures must be developed which facilitate effective cooperation. Externally, contracts must be crafted which clarify expectations and responsibilities between the parties. Recent research, however, suggests that formal mechanisms are not always the best means to stimulate collaboration. The most useful forms of collaboration are often discretionary — that is, they may be contributed or withheld without concern for formal reward or sanction (Heckman and Guskey, 1997). Formal job descriptions, procedures, and contracts will never cover all the eventualities which may arise in complex relationships. Therefore, managers must find the cultural and other mechanisms which create environments which elicit discretionary collaboration both internally and externally.

Use the Procurement Process Framework as a Tool to Assist in Reengineering the IT Procurement Process.

Another exciting use for the framework is to serve as the foundation for efforts to reengineer procurement processes. One firm analyzed the sub-processes involved in the requirements analysis and acquisition stages of the procurement life cycle to reduce procurement and contracting cycle time. Instead of looking at the deployment sub-processes as a linear sequence of activities, this innovative company used the framework to analyze and develop a compression strategy to reduce the cycle time in its IT contracting process by performing a number of sub-processes in parallel.

Use the Framework as a Guide for Future Research

The framework has been used by the SIM IT Procurement Working Group to identify topics of greatest interest for empirical research. For example, survey research investigating *acquisition* (software contracting practices and contracting efficiency), *asset management* (total life cycle cost of ownership and asset tracking systems), and *supplier management* (supplier evaluation) has been recently completed. The key issues identified in the current chapter can likewise be used to frame a research agenda which will have practical relevance to practitioners.

Use the Framework to Structure IT Procurement Training and Education

The framework has been used to provide the underlying structure for a university course covering IT procurement. It also provides the basis for shorter practitioner workshops, and can be used by companies developing in-house training in IT procurement for users, technologists and procurement specialists.

This five-item agenda provides a foundation for the professionalization of the IT procurement discipline. As the acquisition of information resources becomes more market oriented and less a function of internal development, the role of the IT professional will necessarily change. The IT professional of the future will need fewer technology skills because these skills will be provided by external vendors who specialize in supplying them. The skills which will be critical to the IT organization of the future are those marketplace skills which will be found in IT procurement organizations. The management agenda described in this chapter provides a first step toward the effective leadership of such organizations.

NOTES

Barki, H., Rivard, S., and Talbot, J. (1993), "A Keyword Classification Scheme for IS Research Literature: An Update," *MIS Quarterly,* (1 7:2) June, 1993, 209–226.
Davenport, T., and Short, J. (1990), "The New Industrial Engineering: Information Technology and Business Process Redesign," *Sloan Management Review,* Summer, 11–27.
Hammer, M. (1 990), "Reengineering Work: Don't Automate, Obliterate," *Harvard Business Review,* July/August, 104–112.
Heckman, R., and Guskey, A. "The Relationship Between University and Alumni: Toward a Theory of Discretionary Collaborative Behavior," *Journal of Marketing Theory and Practice, forthcoming.*

Heckman, R., and Sawyer, S. (1996), "A Model of Information Resource Acquisition," *Proceedings of the Second Annual American Conference on Information Systems,* Phoenix, AZ.

Lacity, M. C., Willcocks, L. P., and Feeny, D. F., "IT Outsourcing: Maximize Flexibility and Control," *Harvard Business Review,* May–June 1995, p. 84–93.

McFarlan, F. W. and Nolan, R. L., (1995). "How to Manage an IT Outsourcing Alliance," *Sloan Management Review* (3 6:2), Winter, p. 9–23.

Reifer, D. (1994*) Software Management,* Los Alamitos CA: IEEE Press.

Rook, P. (1986) "Controlling Software Projects," *Software Engineering Journal,* pp. 79–87.

Sampler, J. and Short, J. (1994), "An Examination of Information Technology's Impact on the Value of Information and Expertise: Implications for Organizational Change," *Journal of Management Information Systems (I* 1:2), Fall, 59–73.

Teng, J., Grover, V., and Fiedler, K. (1994), "Business Process Reengineering: Charting a Strategic Path for the Information Age," *California Management Review,* Spring, 9–31.

Thayer, R. (1988), "Software Engineering Project Management: A Top–Down View," in R. Thayer (ed.), *IEEE Proceedings on Project Management,* Los Alamitos CA: IEEE Press, pp. 15–53.

Vaughn, M. and Parkinson, G. (1994*) Development Effectiveness,* New York: John Wiley & Sons.

Venkatraman, N. and Loh, L. (1994), "The Shifting Logic of the IS Organization: from Technical Portfolio to Relationship Portfolio," *Information Strategy: The Executive's Journal,* Winter, pp. 5–11.

Chapter 16

Control of Information Systems Outsourcing

S. Yvonne Scott

IS OUTSOURCING is not a new trend. Today, it is a mature concept—a reality. The use of service bureaus, contract programmers, disaster recovery sites, data storage vendors, and value-added networks are all examples of outsourcing. There are even examples of entire large IS organizations being outsourced as early as 25 years ago. Today, IS functions such as time-sharing, network management, software maintenance, applications processing, limited facilities management, full facility management, and EDI services are all potentially outsourced functions.

However, outsourcing is not a transfer of responsibility. Tasks and duties can be delegated, *but responsibility remains with the organization's management.* Therefore, outsourcing does not relieve the organization or management of the responsibility to provide IS services for internal operations and, in some cases, for customers.

Outsourcing is not an excuse for substandard customer service, regardless of whether or not the customers are internal or external to the organization. Customers do not care how or by whom services are provided. Their concern is that they receive the quality services they need, when they are needed.

The most successful outsourcing deals are tailored relationships that are built around specific business needs and strategies. There has been a definite shift from an all-or-nothing approach to a more *selective* application of outsourcing. In many cases, deals have been structured to more closely resemble partnerships or alliances rather than service agreements. For example, some of these deals include agreements to share in the profits and products that result from the alliance.

Outsourcing also does not eliminate the need to audit the outsourced services. It is the auditor's responsibility to safeguard all the assets of an organization. Because information is clearly an asset, the organization must ensure that information confidentiality, integrity, and availability are preserved.

OUTSOURCING SERVICES

Any agreement to obtain services from an outside vendor rather than to provide them internally meets the definition of outsourcing. The following list includes the types of IS outsourcing service contracts that the IS community is being required to address:

- Time-sharing and applications processing.
- Contract programming.
- Software and hardware maintenance.
- Contingency planning and disaster recovery planning and services.
- Systems development and project management.
- Electronic data interchange services.
- Network management.
- Reengineering services.
- Transitional services.
- Limited facilities management.
- Full facility management.
- Remote LAN management.
- Help desk services.

It should be noted that the first six services in this list have been outsourced for at least 20 years. The remainder of the list represents expansions of the other services. For example, facilities management is the use of time-sharing on a broader basis, and remote LAN management can include hardware maintenance on a distributed basis.

WHY OUTSOURCE?

Outsourcing should be specifically tailored to the business needs of an organization. It appears to be most feasible for those organizations with the following characteristics:

- *Organizations in which IS is not a competitive tool.* If there is little opportunity for an organization to distinguish itself from its competition through systems applications or operations, there is less concern over entrusting the execution of these services to a third party.
- *Organizations in which short-term IS interruptions do not diminish the organization's ability to compete or remain in business.* An outsourcing vendor should be able to recover operations in one to two days. It is probably not reasonable to rely on a third party to recover complex

systems within one to two hours. Contracts can be structured to specify that the outsourcer must recover within a one- to two-hour time frame or incur severe penalties. However, if the outsourcer fails to comply with the contract, it is unlikely that the penalty adequately compensates the organization for the long-term effects of losing customers. Therefore, the shorter the tolerable window of exposure, the less viable outsourcing becomes.

- *Organizations in which outsourcing does not eliminate critical internal knowledge.* If outsourcing eliminates internal resources that are key to the future innovations or products of the organization, the risk may be too great to assume.
- *Organizations in which existing IS capabilities are limited or ineffective.* If this is the case and the organization is considering outsourcing, management has probably determined that additional investments must be made in the area of IS. In this situation, it may make more sense to buy the required expertise than to build it.
- *Organizations in which there is a low reward for IS excellence.* In this case, even if the organization developed and operated the most effective and efficient information systems the payback would be minimal. Because every organization must capitalize on its assets to survive, the effort that would be expended could probably be spent more wisely in other areas.

MOTIVATING FACTORS

Companies have various reasons for outsourcing. Just as the outsourcing agreement itself should be tailored to the individual circumstances, the factors that cause an organization to achieve its objectives through outsourcing are unique.

It is important to understand these motivating factors when evaluating whether or not a particular solution meets an organization's objectives. In addition, as in all cases in which the IS manager has an opportunity to participate in the solution of a business problem (e.g., systems development audits), it is important to understand the overall objectives. To add value to the process, these objectives and their potential shortcomings should be considered when evaluating whether or not the outsourcing agreement maximizes asset use and maintains the control environment. For this reason, the motivating factors often cited by management, as well as some of the reasons why these objectives may not be readily met, are

- *Cost Savings.* As the global economy grows, management faces increased competition on reduced budgets. The savings are generally believed to be achievable through outsourcing by increasing efficiency (e.g., staff reductions, shared resources); however, several factors may preclude cost savings. Comparable reductions in service levels and product quality may occur, and comparable staff reductions may not be reflected in decreased fees to outsourcers. In addition, vendors may not achieve the economies of scale previously gained through shared hardware because many software vendors have changed licensing agreements to vary with the size of the hardware and third-party use.

- *Fixed Cost vs. Variable Cost.* In some cases, management has been driven to a fixed-cost contract for its predictability; however, service levels may decrease as the cost of providing those services increases. In addition, should business needs dictate a reduction in information systems, the company may be committed to contracted fees.
- *Flexible IS Costs.* Management may have indicated that outsourcing is preferred because it allows management to adjust its IS costs as business circumstances change; however, necessary revisions in service levels and offerings may not be readily available through the vendor at prices comparable to those agreed on for existing services.
- *Dissatisfaction with Internal Performance.* Dissatisfaction is often cited by senior management because it has not seen the increases in revenue and market share nor the increased productivity and cost reductions used to justify projects. Many outsourcing agreements, however, include provisions to transfer employees to the outsourcer. The net result may be that the personnel resources do not change significantly.
- *Competitive Climate.* Speed, flexibility, and efficiency are often considered the keys to competitive advantage. By outsourcing the IS function, personnel resources can be quickly adjusted to respond to business peaks and valleys, and as a result, solutions may be implemented more quickly. However, the personnel assigned to respond to the business needs that determine the organization's competitive position may not be well acquainted with the company's business and its objectives. In addition, short-term cost and time savings achieved through reactive systems development may lead to a long-term deficiencies in the anticipation of the information systems needs of both internal and external customers.
- *Focus on Core Business.* Outsourcing support functions such as IS allows management to focus on its primary business. If IS is integral to the product offering or the competitive advantage of the organization, however, a shift in focus away from this component of the core business may lead to long-term competitive disadvantage.
- *Capital Availability and Emerging Technologies.* Senior management does not want to increase debt or use available capital to improve or maintain the IS function. If IS is proactive and necessary to support the strategic direction of the organization, however, delaying such investments may result in a competitive disadvantage. In addition, precau-

tions must be taken to ensure that the outsourcing vendor continues to provide state-of-the-art technology.

- *Staff Management and Training.* Outsourcing eliminates the need to recruit, retain, and train IS personnel. This becomes the responsibility of the vendor. But regardless of who these individuals report to, IS personnel need to receive training on the latest technologies to remain effective. After control over this process is turned over to a vendor, provisions should be made to ensure that training continues. In addition, the cost of this training is not actually eliminated. Because the vendor is in business to turn a profit, the cost of training is included in the price proposal. In addition, this cost is likely to be inflated by the vendor's desired profit margin.
- *Transition Management.* As mergers and acquisitions take place, senior management views outsourcing as a means to facilitate the integration of several different hardware platforms and application programs. In addition, some managers are using outsourcing as a means to facilitate the organization's move to a new processing environment (e.g., client/server). However, knowledge of strategic information systems should not be allowed to shift to an outside vendor if the long-term intention is to retain this expertise within the organization. In such cases, the maintenance of existing systems should be transferred to the outsourcer during the transition period.
- *Reduction of Risk.* Outsourcing can shift some of the business risks associated with capital investment, technological change, and staffing to the vendor. Because of decreased hands-on control, however, security risks may increase.
- *Accounting Treatment.* Outsourcing allows the organization to remove IS assets from the balance sheet and begin to report these resources as a nondepreciable line item (e.g., rent). The organization should ensure that outsourcing is not being used as a means of obtaining a capital infusion that does not appear as balance sheet debt. This can be achieved if the outsource vendor buys the organization's IS assets at book (rather than market) value. The difference is paid back through the contract and, therefore, represents a creative means of borrowing funds.

All these driving forces can be valid reasons for senior management to enter into an outsourcing arrangement. It should be noted that the cautions discussed in the previous sections are not intended to imply that outsourcing is undesirable. Rather, they are highlighted here to allow the reader to enter into the most advantageous outsourcing agreement possible. As a result, these cautions should be kept in mind when control measures are considered.

OUTSOURCING AGREEMENTS

Although it is desirable to build a business partnership with the outsource vendor, it is incumbent on the organization to ensure that the outsourcer is legally bound to take care of the company's needs. Standard contracts are generally written to protect the originator (i.e., the vendor). Therefore, it is important to critically review these agreements and ensure that they are modified to include provisions that adequately address the following issues.

Retention of Adequate Audit Rights

It is not sufficient to generically specify that the client has the right to audit the vendor. If the specific rights are not detailed in the contract, the scope of a review may be subject to debate. To avoid this confusion and the time delays that it may cause, it is suggested that, at a minimum, the following specific rights be detailed in the contract:

- Who can audit the outsourcer (i.e., client internal auditors, outsourcer internal auditors, independent auditors, user-controlled audit authority)?
- What is subject to audit (e.g., vendor invoices, physical security, operating system security, communications costs, and disaster recovery tests)?
- When the outsourcer can or cannot be audited.
- Where the audit is to be conducted (e.g., at the outsourcer's facility, remotely by communications).
- How the audit is conducted (i.e., what tools and facilities are available).
- Guaranteed access to the vendor's records, including those that substantiate billing.
- Read-only access to all of the client company's data.
- Assurance that audit software can be executed.
- Access to documentation.
- Long-term retention of vendor records to prevent destruction.

Continuity of Operations and Timely Recovery

The time frames within which specified operations must be recovered, as well as each party's responsibilities to facilitate the recovery, should be specified in the contract. In addition, the contract should specify the recourse that is available to the client, as well as who is responsible for the cost of carrying out any alternative action, should the outsourcer fail to comply with the contract requirements. Special consideration should be given to whether or not these requirements are reasonable and likely to be carried out successfully.

Cost and Billing Verification

Only those costs applicable to the client's processing should be included in invoices. This issue is particularly important for those entering into outsourcing agreements that are not on a fixed-charge basis. Adequate documentation should be made available to allow the billed client to determine the appropriateness and accuracy of invoices. However, documentation is also important to those clients who enter into a fixed invoice arrangement. In such cases, knowing the actual cost incurred by the outsourcer allows the client to effectively negotiate a fair price when prices are open for renegotiation. It should also be noted that, although long-term fixed costs are beneficial in those cases in which costs and use continue to increase, they are equally detrimental in those situations in which costs and use are declining. Therefore, it is beneficial to include contract clauses that allow rates to be reviewed at specified intervals throughout the life of the contract, or in the event of a business downturn (e.g., sale of a division).

Security Administration

Outsourcing may be used as an agent for change and, therefore, may represent an opportunity to enhance the security environment. In any case, decisions must be made regarding whether the administration (i.e., granting access to data) and the monitoring (i.e., violation reporting and follow-up) should be retained internally or delegated to the outsourcer. In making this decision, it is imperative that the company have confidence that it can maintain control over the determination of who should be granted access and in what capacity (e.g., read, write, delete, execute) to both its data and that of its customers.

Confidentiality, Integrity, and Availability

Care must be taken to ensure that both data and programs are kept confidential, retain their integrity, and are available when needed. These requirements are complicated when the systems are no longer under the physical control of the owning entity. In addition, the concerns that this situation poses are further compounded when applications are stored and executed on systems that are shared with other customers of the outsourcer. Of particular concern is the possibility that proprietary data and programs may be resident on the same physical devices as those of a competitor. Fortunately, technology has provided us with the ability to logically control and separate these environments with virtual machines (e.g., IBM's Processor Resource/System Management). It should also be noted that the importance of confidentiality does not necessarily terminate with the vendor relationship. Therefore, it is important to obtain nondisclosure and noncompete agreements from the vendor as a means of protecting the company after the contract expires. Similarly, adequate data retention and destruction requirements must be specified.

Program Change Control and Testing

The policies and standards surrounding these functions should not be relaxed in the outsourced environment. These controls determine whether or not confidence can be placed in the integrity of the organization's computer applications.

Vendor Controls

The physical security of the data center should meet the requirements set by the American Society for Industrial Security. In addition, there should be close compatibility between the vendor and the customer with regard to control standards.

Network Controls

Because the network is only as secure as its weakest link, care must be taken to ensure that the network is adequately secured. It should be noted that dial-up capabilities and network monitors can be used to circumvent established controls. Therefore, even if the company's operating data is not proprietary, measures should be taken to ensure that unauthorized users cannot gain access to the system. This should minimize the risks associated with unauthorized data, program modifications, and unauthorized use of company resources (e.g., computer time, phone lines).

Personnel

Measures should be taken to ensure that personnel standards are not relaxed after the function is turned over to a vendor. As was noted earlier, in many cases the same individuals who were employed by the company are hired by the vendor to service that contract. Provided these individuals are competent, this should not pose any concern. If, however, a reason cited for outsourcing is to improve the quality of personnel, this situation may not be acceptable. In addition, care should be taken to ensure that the client company is notified of any significant personnel changes, security awareness training is continued, and the client company is not held responsible should the vendor make promises (e.g., benefits, salary levels, job security) to the transitional employees that it does not subsequently keep.

Vendor Stability

To protect itself from the possibility that the vendor may withdraw from the business or the contract, it is imperative that the company maintain ownership of its programs and data. Otherwise, the client may experience an unexpected interruption in its ability to service its customers or the loss of proprietary information.

Strategic Planning

Because planning is integral to the success of any organization, this function should be performed by company employees. Although it may be necessary to include vendor representatives in these discussions, it is important to ensure that the company retains control over the use of IS in achieving its objectives. Because many of these contracts are long term and business climates often change, this requires that some flexibility be built into the agreement to allow for the expansion or contraction of IS resources.

In addition to these specific areas, the following areas should also be addressed in the contract language:

- Definition and assignment of responsibilities.
- Performance requirements and the means by which compliance is measured.
- Recourse for nonperformance.
- Contract termination provisions and vendor support during any related migration to another vendor or in-house party.
- Warranties and limitations of liability.
- Vendor reporting requirements.

PROTECTIVE MEASURES DURING TRANSITION

After it has been determined that the contractual agreement is in order, a third-party review should be performed to verify vender representations. After the contract has been signed and as functions are being moved from internal departments to the vendor, an organization can enhance the process by performing the following:

- Meeting frequently with the vendor and employees.
- Involving users in the implementation.
- Developing transition teams and providing them with well-defined responsibilities, objectives, and target dates.
- Increasing security awareness programs for both management and employees.
- Considering a phased implementation that includes employee bonuses for phase completion.
- Providing outplacement services and severance pay to displaced employees.

CONTINUING PROTECTIVE MEASURES

As the outsourcing relationship continues, the client should continue to take proactive measures to protect its interests. These measures may include continued security administration involvement, budget reviews, ongoing reviews and testing of environment changes, periodic audits and security reviews, and letters of agreement and supplements to the contract. Each of these client rights should be specified in the contract. In addition, a continuing review and control effort typically includes the following types of audit objectives:

- Establishing the validity of billings (IBM's Systems Management Facility type-30 records can be used).
- Evaluating system effectiveness and performance. (IBM's Resource Management Facility indicates the percentage of time the central processing unit is busy. As use increases, costs may rise because of higher paging requirements.)
- Reviewing the integrity, confidentiality, and availability of programs and data.
- Verifying that adequate measures have been made to ensure continuity of operations.
- Reviewing the adequacy of the overall security environment.
- Determining the accuracy of program functionality.

AUDIT ALTERNATIVES

It should be noted that resource sharing (i.e., the sharing of common resources with other customers of the vendor) may lead to the vendor's insistence that the audit rights of individual clients be limited. This may be reasonable. However, performance review by the internal audit group of the client is only one means of approaching the control requirement. The following alternative measures can be taken to ensure that adequate control can be maintained.

- *Internal Reviews by the Vendor.* In this case, the outsourcing vendor's own internal audit staff would perform the reviews and report their results to the customer base. Auditing costs are included in the price, the auditor is familiar with the operations, and it is less disruptive to the outsourcer's operations. However, auditors are employees of the audited entity; this may limit independence and objectivity, and clients may not be able to dictate audit areas, scope, or timing.
- *External Auditor or Third-Party Review.* These types of audits are normally performed by an independent accounting firm. This firm may or may not be the same firm that performs the annual audit of the vendor's financial statements. In addition, the third-party reviewer may be hired by the client or the vendor. External auditors may be more independent than employees of the vendor. In addition, the client can

negotiate for the ability to exercise some control over the selection of the third-party auditors and the audit areas, scope, and timing, and the cost can be shared among participating clients. The scope of external reviews, however, tends to be more general in nature than those performed by internal auditors. In addition, if the auditor is hired by the vendor, the perceived level of independence of the auditor may be impaired. If the auditor is hired by each individual client, the costs may be duplicated by each client and the duplicate effort may disrupt vendor operations.

- *User-Controlled Audit Authority.* The audit authority typically consists of a supervisory board comprising representatives from each participating client company, the vendor, and the vendor's independent accounting firm and a staff comprising some permanent and temporary members who are assigned from each of the participating organizations. The staff then performs audits at the direction of the supervisory board. In addition, a charter, detailing the rights and responsibilities of the user-controlled audit authority, should be developed and accepted by the participants before commissioning the first review.

This approach to auditing the outsourcing vendor appears to combine the advantages and minimize the disadvantages previously discussed. In addition, this approach can benefit the vendor by providing a marketing advantage, supporting its internal audit needs, and minimizing operational disruptions.

CONCLUSION

Outsourcing arrangements are as unique as those companies seeking outsourcing services. Although outsourcing implies that some control must be turned over to the vendor, many measures can be taken to maintain an acceptable control environment and adequate review. Some basic rules can be followed to ensure a successful arrangement. These measures include

- Segmenting the organization's IS activities into potential outsource modules (e.g., by technology, types of processing, or businesses served).
- Using analysis techniques to identify those modules that should be outsourced.
- Controlling technology direction setting.
- Treating outsourcing as a partnership, but remembering that the partner's objective is to maximize its own profits.
- Matching the organization's business needs with the outsource partner's current and prospective capabilities (e.g., long-term viability,

corporate culture, management philosophy, business and industry knowledge, flexibility, technology leadership, and global presence).
- Ensuring that all agreements are in writing.
- Providing for continuing review and control.

The guidelines discussed in this chapter should be combined with the client's own objectives to develop individualized and effective control.

Section 2
Designing and Operating an Enterprise Infrastructure

DESIGNING, IMPLEMENTING, AND MAINTAINING the enterprise IT infrastructure has become one of the most important tasks for corporate IS management, and the intensifying speed of technology change has made these responsibilities both increasingly important and increasingly difficult. An IS manager in charge of infrastructure development faces myriad influential factors that have an impact on strategic and operational decisions. The purpose of this section is to discuss a variety of key issues related to IT infrastructure management and to provide support for decision making. The chapters in this section cover the following topics:

- Managing a distributed computing environment.
- Designing, implementing, and maintaining the telecommunications infrastructure.
- Data warehousing.
- Quality assurance and control.
- Security and risk management.

DISTRIBUTED COMPUTING ENVIRONMENTS

The fundamental characteristics of client/server computing continue to be widely applied even though the model often has other names (e.g., netcentric computing). The main management issue has, however, stayed the same: how best to distribute computing responsibilities across a variety of computers performing different tasks on different platforms optimized for the task. In addition to the technical changes involved with moving from centralized to distributed data and processing, both client/server computing and, more currently, netcentric computing have had a strong impact on the allocation of organizational responsibilities. Client/server computing has enabled a greater flexibility for divisions and departments to assume IS development responsibilities. At the same time, these technologies have increased the need for centralized standards and controls.

Chapters 17, "Client/Server Computing: Politics and Solutions," and 18, "Culture Change: A Client/Server Enabler," address the political issues associated with the new distributed environment. Chapter 17 introduces the client/server model from both the technical and organizational perspectives; Chapter 18 discusses the overall cultural changes associated with the move to a client/server architecture. Chapter 18 makes several excellent points about cultural change that can in fact be applied to a variety of situations involving technology changes.

One of the most difficult challenges in managing a distributed computing environment is the need to maintain a balance between architectural integrity and the continuously changing needs of user departments. Chapter 19, "Shifting to Distributed Computing," presents a model for service delivery that analyzes service levels from three different perspectives: risk, cost, and quality. The author provides guidelines for reducing risk and cost and increasing quality in distributed computing while maintaining a balance between the needs of the business units and the corporation.

During these times of continuous and rapid change, operational efficiency remains critical. Chapter 20, "Improving Data Center Productivity and Effectiveness," is an excellent reminder of straightforward but essential issues of high productivity, operational efficiency, and cost control especially in the less dynamic parts of the computing infrastructure. IS managers are being asked to simultaneously improve service and keep costs under control, and Chapter 20 provides excellent advice for this task.

TELECOMMUNICATIONS MANAGEMENT

Telecommunications infrastructure has become an inseparable part of enterprise IT infrastructure; in fact, they can no longer be managed separately. Therefore, it is essential for IT executives and managers to have a strong understanding of telecommunications industry issues. Chapter 21, "U.S. Telecommunications Today," provides a macro-level view of the forces transforming the telecommunications industry in the United States today and the impact of these changes on the availability, pricing, and quality of services available to businesses and consumers. The coverage includes Internet telephony, the Telecommunications Act of 1996 and its effects (or lack of them), wireless telecommunications, and accelerated merger and acquisition activities within the industry.

The development of operating standards for local area networks (LANs) has been a long-standing battle for managers responsible for infrastructure development. Many LANs have evolved over time, rather than been designed, in response to the changing needs of organizational units. In addition to resulting in weaker architectures than desired, this situation has often led to the assumption that few rules apply to LANs. At the same time, LANs have become essential parts of the IT infrastructure that support, among other things, mission-critical applications and time-critical messaging. Chapter 22, "Operating Standards for LANs," addresses the need for developing, maintaining, and implementing LAN operating standards to ensure the efficiency, cost-effectiveness, security, and reliability of LAN environments and provides practical guidelines for achieving these goals.

One of the most recent technical advances in enterprise networking has been the use of virtual networking technologies. These technologies allow network mangers to manage the configuration of and access to networks with software controls that communicate with switches, the main components of virtual networks. Virtual networks are discussed at a detailed level in Chapter 23, "Virtual Networking Management and Planning." This chapter focuses on the most modern and scalable networking technology, asynchronous transfer mode (ATM). This chapter also provides an excellent introduction to the advantages of virtual networking and the services that genuine virtual networks offer.

IT managers responsible for data communications are increasingly required to update the existing networking infrastructure or implement an entirely new one. This requires a systematic approach such as described in Chapter 24, "Successful Network Implementations." This chapter also compares two of the most important backbone technologies, ATM and Gigabit Ethernet, and discusses the criteria organizations can use to choose between them. The author also pays special attention to testing, which is an issue too often neglected in network implementation.

One of the most difficult integration tasks in enterprise infrastructure development is the development of an integrated, synergistic messaging system that allows an organization to use a large number of different messaging systems. Chapter 25, "Integrating Electronic Messaging Systems and Infrastructures," provides a comprehensive coverage of the challenges faced when integrating message systems across an enterprise and various models that can be used in messaging system implementation.

DATA WAREHOUSING

Data warehousing has become an essential component of enterprise information infrastructure in most large organizations today, and it is also becoming increasingly important in middle-size companies as a means to provide high-quality decision support data. Chapter 26, "Data Warehousing Concepts and Strategies," provides an introduction to data warehousing and covers issues related to the fundamental characteristics, design and construction, and organizational utilization. The authors remind us that data warehousing entails not only technical issues; successful implementation requires attention to a variety of organizational and managerial issues as well. In particular, both financial and support personnel resources must be made available, and sufficiently strong attention must be paid to the quality of data at the conceptual level.

Data marts, scaled-down versions of data warehouses that have a narrower (departmental) scope, can be an alternative to full-scale data warehousing. Chapter 27, "Data Marts: Plan Big, Build Small," discusses how data marts can be used by organizations as initial steps on the way toward a centralized data warehouse. This approach requires a clear view of the eventual goal and careful planning. When implemented properly, data marts can be both a cost-effective and organizationally acceptable solution to providing organizational decision makers with high-quality decision support data. The author also provides an excellent introduction to the difference between data marts and data warehouses that could be useful for communications with business managers.

Chapter 28, "A Framework for Developing Enterprise Data Warehouses," provides a set of guidelines for making an enterprise data warehouse an operational reality. It directs the reader through the steps of business requirements definition, data sourcing, target architecture definition, access tool selection, and finally the administration of the operational data warehouse. The author also emphasizes the importance of a conceptual data model in helping users understand the data available in an enterprise data warehouse.

Data mining applications use data stored in data warehouses and transactional databases to identify previously unknown patterns and relationships. The introduction to data mining techniques and applications provided in Chapter 29, "Data Mining: Exploring the Corporate Asset," convincingly shows why traditional verification-based mechanisms are insufficient when analyzing very large databases. Data mining can help organizations get the full value out of the data that they collect and store. This chapter gives an excellent rationale for investing in the tools, knowledge, and skills that are required to make data mining work.

The conversion of data from one format to another is a challenging task that is necessary when an organization moves from one data management platform to another or starts to build a data warehouse and wants to preserve old data. Chapter 30, "Data Conversion Fundamentals," is a practical introduction to the process of data conversion and the decisions the group responsible for the conversion may face. After guiding the reader carefully through a 10-step process of conversion, the author points out the importance of ensuring data quality during the process and the potentially serious consequences if data quality is ignored. This is especially important when moving data from transaction processing systems to the data warehouse.

QUALITY ASSURANCE AND CONTROL

Included here are two chapters that focus of achieving, maintaining, and measuring information systems quality. Chapter 31, "Quality Information Services," emphasizes the need to understand and meet customer requirements and expectations. Doing so requires nurturing continuous open communication between the internal customer and the IS unit and a flexible IT architecture that makes it possible to respond to changing business needs. Service-level agreements between the IS unit and its customers define the expected quality level in measurable terms. Although this chapter focuses on centralized operations, the principles that are presented are also applicable in distributed environments.

Information systems audits are an important management tool for maintaining high IT standards. Chapter 32, "Information Systems Audits: What's in It for Executives?," presents an overview of the IS audit function and its role in organizations. Traditionally, audits have been viewed by nonauditors as negative events that are "done to" an organizational unit. This chapter presents a more contemporary, value-added approach in which auditing is performed in cooperation with business personnel and in support of the business unit's quest for excellence in IS quality. This chapter shows how regular, successfully implemented IS audits lead to significant benefits for the entire organization.

SECURITY AND RISK MANAGEMENT

The final two chapters in this section focus on vitally important security management and risk management issues. It is essential that every organization is prepared for natural and man-made disasters. Chapter 33, "Key Factors to Strengthen the Disaster Contingency and Recovery Planning Process," provides a comprehensive overview of the planning required for an organization to be prepared to face even the most unexpected events and survive a severe crisis. The chapter emphasizes the importance of a comprehensive disaster contingency and recovery plan (DCRP) because the plan as a whole is only as strong as its weakest link.

The importance of a comprehensive and holistic approach to security is one of the key ideas underlying Chapter 34, "Taking an Adaptive Approach to IS Security," also. The author argues that it is not sufficient to view IS security as a collection of direct technical countermeasures against potential intruders. Risk analysis, security policies, and security audits will not be sufficient if the organization's approach to security is not also adaptive — capable of reacting to external events and being a step ahead of potential violators of security.

Chapter 17
Client/Server Computing: Politics and Solutions

Steve Guynes
John Windsor

A POLITICAL SITUATION is developing in corporate America that will have a major impact on corporate information systems (IS) departments. The IS department's role within the corporation is changing — especially in its interaction with corporate end users, who are demanding increased control over corporate data. IS departments must voluntarily begin to move in a new direction, or they risk encountering serious problems with top management. For example, the increased interest in outsourcing is one indication of the many problems that now must be addressed.

Client/server computing is another such issue. Client/server has become increasingly popular because top management believes it saves money, and end users believe it solves all their computing needs. Unfortunately, neither of the above is completely true.

The major problem is neither top management nor end users fully understand all that is involved in corporate computing. Top management easily understands that the hardware for a client/server system costs less than a mainframe but has a more difficult time understanding the costs involved in client/server multiplatform software or controls to protect data integrity. In addition, end users may have little understanding of why they cannot upload their local data to the corporate data base.

The IS department is committed to protecting the systems and data that are the lifeblood of the organization. For their part, IS managers are concerned with where corporate data are being downloaded and with the stability of the networking systems that are installed throughout the organization. Historically, data centers have been charged with maintaining the integrity of the corporate data base and have established extensive controls to protect the data. They view client/server systems as additional problems to an already complex situation. So, it seems that IS management, top management, and corporate end users are working at cross purposes.

This chapter suggests some ways to implement client/server systems that will satisfy all three. Terms associated with client/server computing are defined. The advantages attainable from a successful implementation are identified, and some of the problems are addressed. Finally, some suggestions for implementation are presented.

CLIENT/SERVER DEFINITIONS

Client/server computing is still being defined by the computer industry. Even though client/server is still evolving, however, there are some fundamental concepts in place. The main force behind client/server computing is the empowerment of end users through delivery of data, programs, and processing power to their desktops.

The distinguishing feature of client/server is that it contains cooperative processing capabilities. This means client (i.e., work station or desktop PC) processing is split from server processing, while presenting a single logical picture to the user.

Clients have processing capabilities and make requests to servers. The server is the machine on which a process or set of processes resides; it is made available to the clients via a local area network (LAN). Software applications tie the three components — client, server, and network — together to form the client/server architecture.

At the work station, the user can manipulate data and execute the programs received from the server. The client addresses the server by way of queries or commands and waits for the appropriate response from the server. The server, for its part, never initiates contact with clients; rather, it monitors the network, waiting for requests from clients. Depending on the specific implementation, the queries can be performed synchronously or asynchronously.

When it receives data from the server, the client performs data analysis and presentation locally. In a heterogeneous client/server environment, the server and the clients can run on several operating system platforms including Windows 95/98, Windows NT, Linux, and other UNIX variants.

The Server's Varied Tasks

The nature of the server depends on the goal of the client/server system. The server could be

- A print server, which requires low machine power.

- A file server, which requires medium machine resources.
- A data base server, which requires a high amount of machine resources — usually DASD and I/O.
- An application server, which also requires a high amount of machine resources — usually processing speed and memory.

These types of servers are not mutually exclusive. It is possible, for example, for a server to be a print server for one client, a file server for another, and a data base server running the data base application for yet another.

Ideally, servers hide the composite client/server system from clients and users. As long as the server is transparent, its configuration (e.g., the underlying hardware platform and operating system) disappears from the client view of the system. If a data base server uses an SQL interface, for example, the clients do not need to know if the server is running UNIX, OS/2, Windows NT, or any other type of operating system. The client is just concerned about the SQL interface.

In many large corporations that have data residing on a mainframe computer, the server provides a gateway from the clients to the mainframe. The server must have adequate disk space to serve the clients, since in many client/server systems, the server is the central location for data. In other large computer installations, the mainframe operates as the server.

In addition, the client/server relationship can be hierarchical. For example, a client to one server may be a server to another client. However, to qualify as true client/server computing, a system must have the ability to install the client and server on two separate platforms. Either the client or the server hardware platform can be upgraded without having to upgrade the other platform. The user must be able to change one of the nodes in the client/server system without having to change the other nodes. Each node is independent of the others, with the server able to service multiple clients concurrently.

BENEFITS FROM CLIENT/SERVER

In client/server environments, the user begins to feel direct involvement with the software, data, hardware, and the system performance. This sense of ownership has long been an objective of data centers. It allows users to define the critical needs of the information system and allocate the resources they are willing to spend on those needs. One implication of this benefit is that user involvement with the process of developing their information system is considered key to the success of any new development project. There are other benefits that appeal to top management, however, including cost savings, boosts in efficiency, and extended life span of existing equipment. These are discussed in the sections that follow.

Keeping Costs Down

If installed properly, client/server reduces the operating costs of information systems departments; one reason is that the hardware typically uses replicated configurations, thereby allowing greater coverage of the sophisticated support environment.

Client/server systems also permit applications to be put on PCs or work station servers, which are less expensive than mainframe and midrange systems. Additionally, client/server data base management systems are less expensive than mainframe DBMSs.

Server performance is cheaper than equivalent mainframe performance. The client/server model provides faster performance because the processing is done locally and does not have to compete for mainframe central processing unit (CPU) time. PC MIPS (millions of instructions per second) can provide a cost advantage of several hundred to one, compared with mainframe MIPS. The response time to complex queries on a mainframe takes from three to five seconds. With a client/server system, those same responses are sub-second. This allows users to customize complex queries that were difficult in the mainframe environment.

In addition, client/server provides a better return on technology investment because it allows niche or specialized technology to be configured as common resources widely available within the computing environment. If the proper controls are in place, client/server computing allows greater access to corporate data and information while providing for appropriate data security.

Increasing Efficiency

The work station controls the user interface in the client/server environment. Most commonly, user interface commands are processed on the client. Because the server is free of user-interface and other types of computations performed by the client, the server is able to devote more resources to specific computing tasks, such as intensive number crunching or large data base searches. Only answers to requests from the clients are sent. Full data files do not need to be sent to another work station for processing, as in networked, PC-based environments. Also, because the user interface is controlled at the client, not every keystroke is sent through the network. Both of these cut down network traffic dramatically.

Client/server systems can speed up the application development process, as the developers do not have to compete for mainframe resources. This provides faster response time due to fewer bottlenecks and may reduce the systems development backlogs found in most companies. Because the client receives only the data requested, network traffic is reduced and performance is improved. Access is also easier because resources are transparent to users.

Powerful PCs and work stations can run applications that are impractical to run on the mainframe. Central processing unit-intensive applications, such as graphics and data analysis, require client/server's distributed processing and shared data to be efficient. By running these applications on PCs or work stations, the server is freed up to process other applications.

Data base servers centralize the data that allows remote access to the data. Client/server computing allows multiuser access to shared data bases. With client/server computing, users can access the data that were stored in their departments in the past and any other corporate data that they need to access. Besides access to more data, users have broader access to expensive resources, can use data and applications on systems purchased from different vendors, and tap the power of larger systems. Client/server end users also have access to large data bases, printers, and high-speed processors, all of which improve user productivity and quality.

Reallocating Resources

Client/server computing allows organizations to extend the life span of existing computer equipment. The existing mainframes can be kept to perform as servers and to process some of the existing applications that cannot be converted to client/server applications. Mainframes can also be used as enterprise data management and storage systems after most daily activity is moved to lower-cost servers. The users' PCs can be kept to act as front-end processors.

Client/server computing is flexible in that either the client or the server platform can be independently upgraded at any time. As processing needs change, servers can be upgraded or downgraded without having to develop new front-end applications. As the number of users increases, client machines can be added without affecting the other clients or the servers.

PROBLEMS ASSOCIATED WITH CLIENT/SERVER

Companies either moving from a mainframe environment to client/server computing or adding client/server to an existing environment face several problems. Client/server technology requires more diverse technical support, as it allows a company to use hardware and software from many different vendors. Support contracts are required with each of these vendors. To minimize the difficulties of having multiple vendors, a company must establish internal hardware and software standards. The full-scale implementation of client/server computing also requires either reorganizing existing departments or creating new ones.

Staffing Changes

Client/server systems require more staff experts because of the diversity of technologies that must be brought together to create an effective system. For example, most developers understand either the mainframe system or the PC, but not both. Because there is a shortage of skilled and experienced developers, there is more trial and error in developing client/server applications than for older, well-understood mainframe applications. Developers need to go through extensive training to learn the new technology.

In addition to retraining current employees, a company may need to hire specialists in LAN administration, data base administration, application development, project management, and technical support for users.

Lack of Standardization

As with most developing technology, client/server computing does not have agreed-on industry standards. Currently no standard exists for retrieving, manipulating, and maintaining such complex data as graphics, text, and images.

Standards must be established for client/server to allow the use of products from different vendors. SQL is one such standardized data-access language; however, each DBMS vendor has its own SQL dialect. This adds to the complexity of building transparent links between front-end tools and back-end data base servers.

Communications Barriers. If the company is to take advantage of its investment in existing computing resources — typically a mainframe — during the move into a client/server environment, a set of communications problems is introduced. The ability to communicate with the mainframe as a server is available through several protocols, most typically TCP/IP. Fortunately, client software increasingly uses this protocol as well.

The network hardware needed to include the mainframe in the system is an expenditure generally not included in the prices quoted by the software vendors. Additionally, most client/server software that is compatible with the mainframe links only to a specific software package on the mainframe. The company must either have current versions of that software or maintain both platforms at compatible levels.

Security Issues

There are serious security and access control issues to be considered. Since the server is usually the central location for critical data, adequate physical security and operational security measures need to be taken to ensure data safety. Backup and recovery procedures are improving, but logging procedures are still lacking.

A large number of tools exist that perform security and control functions on mainframe systems. All of them can help with the client/server effort, but they are not designed specifically for client/server computing. The lack of automatic backup and recovery tools is a problem. Until these tools are developed, companies should not place mission-critical applications on a client/server system.

Performance monitoring and capacity planning tools are a low priority for many client/server administrators. Buying a new server and adding it to the system is much less expensive than spending a lot of time on capacity and performance analysis.

Tools

The tools necessary to support client/servers are not yet fully developed. There is a lack of client/server-oriented communications, diagnostic, and applications tools. These troubleshooting tools are more powerful than they were three years ago, but they are less robust than those readily available for mainframes. There is also a lack of tools for converting existing applications to client/server routines. This forces client/server users to either write new applications or use the existing applications on the mainframe. But because most companies have invested in millions of lines of mainframe code that cannot be converted to client/server use, mainframes will not be turned off for many years.

Ownership Problems

The sense of ownership that can be such a positive for user involvement in application development may also create major problems. Systems may be viewed as "belonging to" the user departments, creating situations in which hardware and software expenditures introduce products that are incompatible with the existing system. Users may well develop the attitude that the system must be modified to meet their design decisions, rather than the users adhering to company standards.

The ownership problem can also extend to user-developed software and data. Data and data bases must be viewed as a corporatewide resource to be used effectively. As the data become associated with a department, the development of private data bases can be a major problem. In addition, the rest of an organization depends on timely data. As a department develops private data bases, the updates to the corporate data base become less critical, in their eyes, and the data used for decision making by the rest of the organization become out of date. The ownership of software creates the same type of problem. As a department develops software that provides enhanced decision-making capabilities, department members' willingness to share the software may well decline. In addition, the private software bank creates situations in which other users are forced to develop the same tools on their own. This increases the potential cost of new applications.

IMPLEMENTATION CONSIDERATIONS

The successful implementation of client/server systems requires involvement by top management, representatives from user groups, and key IS representatives. It is possible for the IS group to become so involved in the selection and decision process that it ignores the business strategic concerns. Also, the business users may not see the value of careful and reasoned selection and end up with a solution that at the beginning may seem to meet their requirements but in reality may not solve their business needs.

Therefore, the major issues to be considered include ways that the system would improve efficiency, reduce costs, provide a competitive advantage, and reduce cycle time. Users should build a model of the organization's work flow and data flow. This helps in designing networks and will help determine how data should be distributed.

The front-end tools that are selected (i.e., SQL-based, user interface builders, and integrated development tools) are determined by the data and systems requirements and require a great deal of investigation to decide which application suits the system's particular needs.

The users must be made aware of the client/server technology and the benefits it can provide, and a knowledge of the proposed client/server solution should be disseminated to all concerned groups. This knowledge is key to the proper use of the technology, as it puts users in a better position to evaluate the technology. If the users can make use of the system, and it solves the business problem, the chance for acceptance is high.

Training

Training is another key to the successful implementation of a client/server solution. Without proper training, the risk of failure is high. If the information systems personnel are not aware of the fundamental limits of current client/server technology, they can either exceed the system's limits or underuse the system, which would seriously damage the success of the project.

Checklist

There are several key decisions that must be made before implementing a client/server system. Technical questions include

1. What operating systems will be used?
2. What graphical user interface will be used?

3. What hardware platforms will be used?
4. What online transaction processing monitors will be used?

Political questions include

1. Who owns the data?
2. Who owns the applications?
3. Who is responsible for maintenance?
4. How are the standards established and enforced?

CONCLUSION

The changes occurring in the IS environment are the result of the increasing desire to move the technology beyond its present state. With the availability of new and cheaper personal technologies, the drive for direct exploitation of available information is increasing. IS managers should approach client/server with a clear view of the lasting business benefits that it can bring rather than opposing or resisting the migration. However, to accommodate this change, IS managers must also recognize that in client/server computing, no answer is perfect. Technology that is selected now may not be the solution in the future, and IS managers should realize that some custom components may have a limited lifetime.

IS managers' responsibilities have shifted to the establishment and management of infrastructures, services, and data quality. It is no longer appropriate for them to position themselves between the end user and the technology. Most of the issues presented by client/server systems are similar to those presented by mainframe computing. For this reason, IS managers are uniquely positioned to lead in the correct implementation of client/server systems. Top management, end users, and the IS group must work together to solve the types of business problems for which client/server is best suited.

The leadership in implementing client/server computing should be placed with the user. However, implementation must be guided and supported by IS. All the knowledge gained from years of dealing with problems of standardization, documentation, maintenance, and performance should be shared with the rest of the organization.

Chapter 18
Culture Change: A Client/Server Enabler

Stewart L. Stokes, Jr.

CLIENT/SERVER computing emerged in the 1980s during what is described as the era of information innovation and support. Spawned by the development of the personal computer (PC) and the explosion of telecommunications technologies and fueled by frustrations over the rigidities of centralized computing, distributed computing promised to liberate users from the mainframe. The new computing paradigm of client/server computing emphasizes innovation and integration over centralization and control.

The move to client/server computing, although rich with promise, brings major technical and cultural changes for information systems (IS) professionals. These changes accompany the transition from older transaction systems supporting standalone applications in functional business units to newer cross-functional information systems supporting the more contemporary emphasis on process redesign and management. The changes also involve the adoption of collaborative, cross-functional teams as the vehicle for client/server applications development.

Although culture change is only one of the four major domains of change (the others are structural, technical, and personal), it is important as both the enabling change agent and the most difficult domain to accomplish. Technical change is designed and implemented. Structural change is mandated. Personal change is encouraged and reinforced. Yet to the frustration of those who would drive it, culture change too often moves at glacial speed.

0-8493-9820-7/00/$0.00+$.50
© 2000 by CRC Press LLC

CLIENT/SERVER CHANGES

Technical Changes

On the technical side, client/server computing combines the best features of mainframe, PC, and local area network (LAN) architecture. It brings unique end-user functions and processes to client work stations while locating common processes and data management on shared (i.e., server) platforms.

These technical shifts require new skills development in a multitude of areas, including object-oriented analysis and programming, graphical user interface (GUI) presentation, structured query language (SQL) data bases, systems integration, and networking. The technical training needs accompanying the transition to client/server computing are well understood; the non-technical education needs, less so.

Culture Changes

On the non-technical or cultural side, the move to client/server computing changes how individuals and teams work with each other and with their internal customers. Many of the changes are grounded in departmental and organizational politics, because internal power equations shift as client/server applications are constructed and implemented.

As the locus of control of information processing shifts from traditional centralized and closed technology environments into distributed, open environments, IS professionals find themselves experiencing new roles, relationships, expectations, work styles, and accountabilities. In addition, the traditional motivators for IS professionals change. The following list summarizes the 11 culture changes IS professionals face as they engage in the transition to client/server computing. Most of the changes are political in nature, involving issues of control, status, and influence. The implementation of client/server solutions will be improved as these culture changes are recognized and managed.

1. Client/server applications are oriented to cross-functional business processes (as contrasted with traditional functional orientations) and often are implemented in concert with business process reengineering.
2. Business units become the drivers and managers of client/server projects.
3. The locus of responsibility and control for client/server projects shifts from the traditional, centralized information processing facility to the business units.
4. Internal customers are empowered through use of client/server technologies; this empowerment may contribute to adversarial relations with more traditionally managed IS colleagues.

5. New performance expectations from internal customers are placed on IS staff and management.
6. The decision-making style regarding the use of IT within the enterprise shifts from hierarchical decision making within vertical, functional units or silos to horizontal, collaborative decision making within cross-functional teams.
7. Individual technical contributors evolve into internal consultants.
8. Work styles shift from solo performer to collaborative contributor in customer-driven, team-based environments.
9. Pressure is exerted on IS professionals and their business unit customers to augment individual accountability with team accountability.
10. The need for increased levels of risk tolerance on the part of decision makers and the ability to learn from mistakes and failure becomes critical.
11. The traditional IS motivators (i.e., solo applications development) are replaced with such new motivators as collaborative teamwork, partnering with business customers, and making joint decisions regarding the use of information technology.

These culture-based people issues may seem less tangible (and perhaps less obvious) than the technical issues accompanying client/server computing. But they are no less important. Cultures have a major influence on human behavior, and changes in culture require as much unlearning and relearning as do changes in technology.

Organizations are still very much on the learning curve regarding successful client/server application development and implementation. Early applications of client/server technology were developed for workgroups and business units, and some of the 11 culture changes were — and are — less evident at these stages than they are in more complex enterprise client/server computing initiatives. Client/server solutions will be the technical enablers of relationships characterizing the rapidly approaching era of interenterprise alliances.

This is not to say that all client/server initiatives have had to contend with many of the culture changes noted. As new toolsets are developed and more ambitious (and risky) enterprisewide projects are undertaken, more of these culture change issues will emerge.[1]

THE IMPORTANCE OF CROSS-FUNCTIONAL TEAMS

Collaborative, cross-functional teams have the potential to enhance the creation and implementation of successful client/server solutions. Collaborative teams differ from cooperative groups in several significant ways, and it is these differences that give collaborative teams the potential to outperform groups of individuals working together. Collaborative teams are teams whose members:

- Are committed to shared productivity goals (which is not always true with work groups).
- Understand their interdependencies (which is less of a priority with work groups).
- Agree to be evaluated as a team and not as separate individuals (something that may be problematic for work groups).
- Behave as each other's internal customers (work groups may not recognize that they are each other's customers, let alone behave that way).

Cross-functional team success is a derivative of the departmental and business unit cultures from which team members are drawn. As representatives of their own functional areas and departments, cross-functional team members bring to the team all the biases, perceptions, and assumptions that characterize their home turf. Although these beliefs or mental models are seldom acknowledged or discussed, their presence affects individual behaviors and team interaction. Team members may waste large amounts of time and energy defending issues that seem inconsequential to the team but important to individuals. Team leaders must develop skills in conflict management, influencing, and negotiation and apply these skills in what are often highly charged situations.

Although team-based environments pre-date client/server computing, the open, cross-functional nature of client/server computing makes the development of collaborative teams a critical success factor to the use of the technology. This is a critical point, because many IS professionals are reluctant to make the commitment to developing team-based skills. They tend to be uncomfortable working in team settings and prefer individual accountability. In comparison to the ubiquitous project teams, which themselves pose behavioral challenges, the dynamics of cross-functional teams are highly complex. The importance of teams to client/server computing reiterates the need for IS managers and professionals to understand and resolve issues of culture.

THE CREATION AND CONTRIBUTION OF CULTURE

To appreciate the importance of culture change to the success of client/server initiatives, it is helpful to define culture and discuss its contribution to organizational life. The more understanding IS change agents have of their culture's characteristics and opportunities to reposition these characteristics, the greater the likelihood of a successful cultural transition.

Organizational cultures are like human personalities: ingrained, controlling, and difficult to change. The family culture within which individuals are raised contributes greatly to how they perceive and understand the world. Similarly, the culture of an organization contributes to how individuals perceive and understand the workplace and its environment.

Organizational culture reflects the shared values and beliefs that permeate an organization and its components. A strong but often unspoken understanding of shared values is the glue that binds a culture together. The beliefs or mental models that accompany these shared values help account for that most common of all definitions of culture: "This is the way we do things around here." Cultures also consist of assumptions, attitudes, expectations, policies, and practices that influence behaviors and ways to get work done.

Mental models easily become sacred cows. Most organizations have sacred cows, or enshrined beliefs about what is important. The sacred cows in an organization are often quick to bellow when the organization rethinks its business processes and practices. One person's expendable process is another's sacred cow that is not to be tampered with under any circumstances.

Icons and Culture Shifts: The Systems Development Example

A good example of a cultural icon that qualifies for sacred cow status in some IS shops is the traditional linear systems development cycle with its often complex value analyses. Although few people quarrel with the importance of a thorough needs analysis/requirements definition, some individuals question the usefulness of overly lengthy requirements analyses.[2]

Today's emphasis on internal and external customer service and speedier time to market of IS products and services is being realized through iterative prototyping, which is helping to change the culture surrounding requirements definition. Rapid application development (RAD) software is being used by cross-functional collaborative teams with representatives from the IS and business unit communities to speed up the systems development life cycle process.

Although some organizational cultures have long supported a major role for users/internal customers in the systems development process, more have not than have. Market pressures, flatter organizational structures, and enabling RAD software are all contributing to major culture change regarding the relationship between IS and customers. Partnering with users/customers is near the top of IS agendas today.

Organizational History: The Centralized Computing Legacy

A major contributor to an organization's culture is its history, usually complete with accompanying stories, myths, and heroes. Histories can be both a source of pride and inspiration and a hindrance to progress.

Enterprises that have a strong history of host-based, transaction processing and a centralized computing structure may find that their history gets in the way of attempts to change the culture of computing. Although it is not uncommon to find users/clients to be more technically knowledgeable than their IS colleagues, users often have only a narrow view of the enterprisewide costs and benefits accruing from a particular client/server system. This means that IS professionals need to become effective coaches so that they can help scope and shape client/server applications to benefit the entire enterprise.

Systems professionals assuming leadership roles in client/server computing are developing high levels of business savvy that let them converse easily with their business partners regarding a client/server project's business drivers. IS professionals have to learn new interpersonal communication skills, including how to probe and drill down through discussions to unearth the real business problems. Effective communication skills are more highly valued today, because time-to-market pressures do not give applications developers the luxury of long development times. Performance expectations from the business sectors are being ratcheted up.

Silo Cultures and the Move toward Interdependence

As enterprises flatten their structures, their people experience a major shift in their relationships and behaviors from independence to interdependence. Enterprises have historically been organized by function, in vertical, parallel line departments or silos (e.g., manufacturing/production, marketing, and finance). These functional entities have been supported by staff departments, such as human resources and information systems. In some instances, the staff departments have provided enterprisewide support; in other cases, line departments have enjoyed the benefits of their own dedicated staff resources. In still other situations, especially in the IS area in recent years, people have migrated from centralized units into line departments.

Functionally oriented silo entities tend to be characterized by the command and control management model and cultures that believe in structure, procedures, and predictability. Although these are laudable attributes, they have contributed to the creation of ponderous bureaucracies. With the demands of worldwide competition, the need for faster time to market of products and services, and the promise of an expanding supply of productivity-enhancing software, enterprises of all sizes are evolving from silo structures into flatter, less bureaucratic, and more technologically intensive structures. These flatter structures are process oriented. In silo cultures, managers own vertical functions; in process cultures, professionals (i.e., teams) own horizontal processes.

Just as a defining cultural attribute of functional management is independence (tempered with cooperation), a defining attribute of process management is interdependence (enhanced by collaboration). As enterprises attempt to evolve their structures from a functional focus to a process focus, they encounter the mental models or sacred cows that have characterized their cultures and determined peoples' behaviors. If the prevalent mental models are oriented toward independent behaviors (e.g., the belief that the only objectives that matter are those of an individual's own department or business unit or that the only performance reviews that count are those done by an individual's own functional manager), then little in the way of culture change will occur until the mental models have been challenged and determined to impede progress and growth, and champions have been secured to spearhead the change.

STRATEGIES FOR ACHIEVING CULTURE CHANGE

Culture change is best approached in the spirit of patient impatience. Histories do not change; heroes live on, shared values are deeply ingrained, and attitudes, beliefs, and behaviors die hard. Yet, although the artifacts of culture remain highly visible on peoples' walls and on their desks, these characteristics are the raw material of culture change.

There is no formula or detailed methodology for achieving culture change, and there is no guarantee of success (witness the number of mergers that either suffer or fail because of the inability to blend and resolve cultural differences). There are, however, tactical and operational strategies and techniques that can be incorporated in the change management process to stimulate and enhance culture change. These strategies aim to facilitate change in the key components of organizational culture: the shared values, beliefs, mental models, and assumptions. They are

- Securing support from the top, by champions, through words and most importantly through deeds.
- Formulating a clear and concise vision statement of what culture changes are necessary, why they are necessary, how they are going to be implemented, and what is expected of everyone in the process.
- Creating dissatisfaction with the values and beliefs that are no longer desirable, in part by explaining why they are no longer valued.
- Providing visible examples of the changed values and beliefs the organization wishes to live by, described and modeled by senior managers and staff.
- Demonstrating in real time the values, attitudes, and behaviors desired instead of merely presenting them in training sessions.

- Revising the recognition and reward structure to support the values, attitudes, and behaviors desired (i.e., walking the talk).
- Creating new heroes, stories, and legends that embody the desired values, then recounting these at every opportunity (like the salespeople heroes of Johnson and Johnson who became living role models of the company's credo by demonstrating its values during the Tylenol contamination incident).
- Changing the management style and, if necessary, the organizational structure to support the desired values.
- Holding many formal and informal meetings to explain, recognize, and reinforce the desired values and the progress made toward living them on a daily basis.
- Providing well-organized and timely training and education that explains, demonstrates, and reinforces the desired behaviors.
- Ceasing to reward behaviors that exhibit the no-longer-desired values.
- Making staff changes when necessary to reinforce the values, attitudes, and behaviors that have been articulated and to demonstrate that culture change is a total team effort.

These strategies should be implemented within the larger context of enterprisewide and business-unit goals and objectives. Although business units have always been involved in systems development requirements definition, they have traditionally been relegated to the role of users. Today, no term is more archaic.

CONCLUSION

It should be apparent from the menu of tactical and operational change strategies that much "walking the talk" is required to achieve cultural change. Technical reskilling efforts are sometimes accompanied by pronouncements extolling the virtues of change. Occasionally these pronouncements include a paragraph or two describing the benefits for the organization when the technical changes are implemented. Once in a while, there are even statements describing the benefits of change for those actually doing the work.

What often happens, however, is that there is more talk than walk. It is easier and less risky to make pronouncements than to back them up with action. As one honest and introspective senior systems manager said, "We have the tendency around here to believe that when we've talked enough about doing something, it's tantamount to having done it. We're good at strategizing; we're not so good at executing."

The cost of talking about the importance of changing the organizational culture is usually less than the cost of actually doing it. Talk is cheap, but the price of change is steep and often paid in the currency of status, reputation, and maybe even one's job. Rhetoric to the contrary, organizations, like people, tend not to change until the price of not changing is higher than the price of changing. Niccolo Machiavelli said it well hundreds of years ago in *The Prince*: "There is nothing more difficult to take in hand, more perilous to conduct, or more uncertain in its success, than to take the lead in the introduction of a new order of things." In other words, to change.

Notes

Executive Guide To Client/Server, Chicago: SIM International, 1995.
Radosevich, "Beat the Clock," *CIO Magazine*, November 15, 1995.

Chapter 19
Shifting to Distributed Computing

Richard Ross

MANY OF THE TOP CONCERNS of senior IS managers relate directly to the issues of distributing information technology to end users. The explosive rate at which information technology has found its way into the front office, combined with the lack of control by the IS organization (ostensibly the group chartered with managing the corporation's IT investment), has left many IS managers at a loss as to how they should best respond. The following issues are of special concern:

- Where should increasingly scarce people and monetary resources be invested?
- What skills will be required to implement and support the new environment?
- How fast should the transition from a centralized computing environment to a distributed computing environment occur?
- What will be the long-term impact of actions taken today to meet short-term needs?
- What will be the overall ability of the central IS group to deliver to new standards of service created by changing user expectations in a distributed computer environment?

The inability to resolve these issues is causing a conflict in many organizations. Particularly in large companies during the past decade, the rule of thumb for technology investment has been that the cost of not being able to respond to market needs will always outweigh the savings accruing from constraining technology deployment. This has resulted in a plethora of diverse and incompatible systems, often supported by independent IS organizations. In turn, these developments have brought to light another, even greater risk — that the opportunity cost to the corporation of not being

0-8493-9820-7/00/$0.00+$.50
© 2000 by CRC Press LLC

able to act as a single entity will always outweigh the benefit of local flexibility.

This conflict was demonstrated by a global retailer with sales and marketing organizations in many countries. To meet local market needs, each country had its own management structure with independent manufacturing, distribution, and systems organizations. The result was that the company's supply chain became clogged — raw materials sat in warehouses in one country while factories in another went idle; finished goods piled up in one country while store shelves were empty in others; costs rose as the number of basic patterns proliferated. Perhaps most important, the incompatibility of the systems prevented management from gaining an understanding of the problem and from being able to pull it all together at the points of maximum leverage, while leaving the marketing and sale functions a degree of freedom.

Another example comes from a financial service firm. The rush to place technology into the hands of traders has resulted in a total inability to effectively manage risk across the firm or to perform single-point client service or multi-product portfolio management.

WANTED — A NEW FRAMEWORK FOR MANAGING

The problem for IS managers is that a distributed computing environment cannot be managed according to the lessons learned during the last 20 years of centralized computing. First and foremost, the distributed computing environment is largely a result of the loss of control by the central IS group because of its inability to deliver appropriate levels of service to the business units. Arguments about the ever-declining cost of desktop technology are all well and good, but the fact of the matter is that managing and digesting technology is not the job function of users. If central IS could have met their needs, it is possible users would have been more inclined to forego managing their own systems.

Central IS's inability to meet those needs while stubbornly trying to deliver with centralized computing has caused users to go their own way. It is not just the technology that is at fault. The centralized computing skills themselves are not fully applicable to a distributed computing environment. For example, the underlying factors governing risk, cost, and quality of service have changed. IS managers need a new framework, one that helps them to balance the opportunity cost to the business unit against that to the company while optimizing overall service delivery.

DEFINING THE PROBLEM: A MODEL FOR DCE SERVICE DELIVERY

To help IS managers get a grip on the problem, this chapter proposes a model of service delivery for the distributed computing environment (DCE). This model focuses on three factors that have the most important

212

influence on service as well as on the needs of the business units vs. the corporation — risk, cost, and quality (Exhibit 19.1). Each factor is analyzed to understand its cause and then to determine how best to reduce it (in the case of risk and cost) or increase it (as in quality).

Risk in any systems architecture is due primarily to the number of independent elements in the architecture (Exhibit19.2). Each element carries its own risk, say for failure, and this is compounded by the risk associated with the interface between each element.

This is the reason that a distributed computing environment will have a greater operational risk than a centralized one — there are more independent elements in a DCE. However, because each element tends to be smaller and simpler to construct, a DCE tends to have a much lower project risk than a centralized environment. Thus, one point to consider in rightsizing should be how soon a system is needed. For example, a Wall Street system that is needed right away and has a useful competitive life of only a few years would be best built in a distributed computing environment to ensure that it gets online quickly. Conversely, a manufacturing system that is not needed right away but will remain in service for years is probably better suited for centralization. One other difference between a distributed environment and a centralized environment is the impact of a particular risk. Even though a DCE is much more likely to have a system component failure, each component controls such a small portion of the overall system that the potential impact of any one failure is greatly reduced. This is important to take into account when performing disaster planning for the new environment.

Cost is largely a function of staffing levels (Exhibit 19.3). As the need for service increases, the number of staff members invariably increases as well. People are flexible and can provide a level of service far beyond that of automation. Particularly in a dynamic environment, in which the needs for response are ill-defined and can change from moment to moment, people are the only solution.

Unfortunately, staff is usually viewed as a variable cost, to be cut when the need for budget reductions arises. This results in a decrease in service delivered that is often disproportionately larger than the savings incurred through staff reductions.

Finally, quality is a subjective judgment, impossible to quantify, but the factor most directly related to the user's perception of service where information technology is concerned. In essence, the perception of quality is proportional to the user's response to three questions:

- Can I accomplish my task?
- Am I able to try new things to get the job done?
- Am I being paid the attention I deserve?

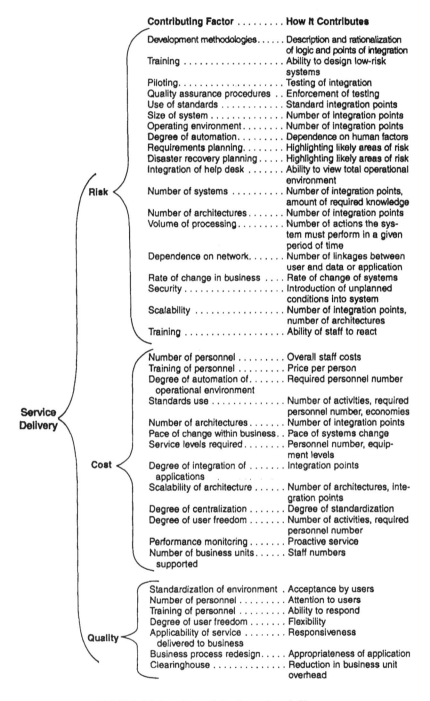

Contributing Factor	How It Contributes
Risk	
Development methodologies	Description and rationalization of logic and points of integration
Training	Ability to design low-risk systems
Piloting	Testing of integration
Quality assurance procedures	Enforcement of testing
Use of standards	Standard integration points
Size of system	Number of integration points
Operating environment	Number of integration points
Degree of automation	Dependence on human factors
Requirements planning	Highlighting likely areas of risk
Disaster recovery planning	Highlighting likely areas of risk
Integration of help desk	Ability to view total operational environment
Number of systems	Number of integration points, amount of required knowledge
Number of architectures	Number of integration points
Volume of processing	Number of actions the system must perform in a given period of time
Dependence on network	Number of linkages between user and data or application
Rate of change in business	Rate of change of systems
Security	Introduction of unplanned conditions into system
Scalability	Number of integration points, number of architectures
Training	Ability of staff to react
Cost	
Number of personnel	Overall staff costs
Training of personnel	Price per person
Degree of automation of operational environment	Required personnel number
Standards use	Number of activities, required personnel number, economies
Number of architectures	Number of integration points
Pace of change within business	Pace of systems change
Service levels required	Personnel number, equipment levels
Degree of integration of applications	Integration points
Scalability of architecture	Number of architectures, integration points
Degree of centralization	Degree of standardization
Degree of user freedom	Number of activities, required personnel number
Performance monitoring	Proactive service
Number of business units supported	Staff numbers
Quality	
Standardization of environment	Acceptance by users
Number of personnel	Attention to users
Training of personnel	Ability to respond
Degree of user freedom	Flexibility
Applicability of service delivered to business	Responsiveness
Business process redesign	Appropriateness of application
Clearinghouse	Reduction in business unit overhead

Exhibit 19.1. A model of service delivery

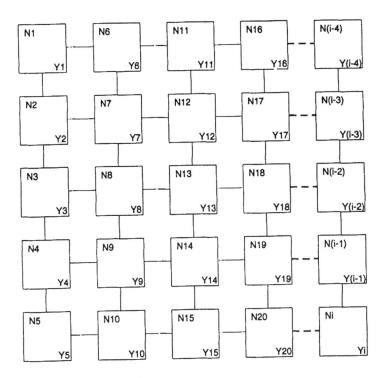

N   = Component number

Y   = Component risk

Given fully independent components, total network risk is equivalent to the sum of the individual component risks, 1 to i. Thus, the way to minimize risk is either to minimize i (i.e., to have a centralized computing environment) or to minimize Y for each component by standardizing on components with minimum risk profiles.

Exhibit 19.2   Optimization of risk in a network

One of the most important factors in the perceived quality of service delivery is the ability of the support technology to work unnoticed. Because of the similarities between this need and the way in which the U.S. telephone network operates (you pick up the phone and the service is invariably there), the term *dialtone* is used to describe such a background level of operation.

One problem with highly functional IS environments is that users must think about them to use them. This is not the case with the telephone system, which operates so dependably that we have integrated it into our routine working practices and use it without much conscious effort. The phone companies maintain this level of usefulness by clearly separating additional features from basic service and letting the customer add each new feature as the customer desires.

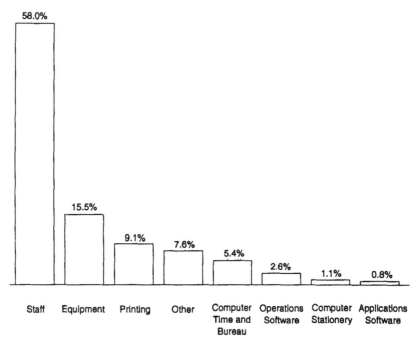

Note:
*Average of organizations studied; total IS costs
SOURCE: Decision Strategies Group, Greenwich CT

Exhibit 19.3.   Cost profile of the IS function

Contrast this with the typical business system that represents an attempt to deliver a package of functions on day one and to continually increase its delivered functionality. The impact on users is that they are forced to continually adapt to changes, are not allowed to merge the use of the system into the background, and must continually stop delivering on their jobs just to cope with the technology. This coping might be as simple as looking something up in a manual or changing a printer cartridge, or it may mean not working at all while the system is rebooted.

Does anyone ever call up AT&T and congratulate it for keeping the nation's phones working that day? Of course not. Yet IS organizations are continually disappointed when users do not seem to appreciate that they have delivered 99.99% availability and a 24-hour help desk.

Complexity: The Barrier to Service Delivery

In general, the basic driver to each of the three service factors is complexity. Complexity increases risk by increasing the number of interfaces

216

between system elements as well as the number of elements themselves. It increases cost by increasing the need for staff as the only way to deal with ill-defined environments. Finally, it affects quality by making it harder to provide those services upon which users base their perception of quality (i.e., dialtone and personal attention), in response to which even more staff are added.

This, then, is the paradoxical environment in which IS managers operate. To improve the quality of service, they find themselves increasing the risk and cost of the operation. Improved application delivery cycles result in more systems to manage. End-user development tools and business unit-led development increase the number of architectures and data formats. Increasing access to corporate data through networks increases the number of interfaces. Conversely, trying to improve the risk and cost aspects, typically through standardization of the environment, usually results in decreased levels of service delivered because of the constraints placed on user freedom. This paradox did not exist in the good old days of centralized computing, when the IS organization dictated the service level.

ADVICE FOR MANAGING DISTRIBUTED COMPUTING

The measure of success in a distributed computing environment is the ability to deliver service through optimizing for the factors of risk, cost, and quality while meeting the needs of both the business units and the corporation. It sounds like a tall order but it is not impossible. There are five key practices involved in corporate information processing:

- Manage tightly, but control loosely.
- Organize to provide on three levels.
- Choose one standard — even a single bad one is better than none or many good ones.
- Integrate data at the front end — don't homogenize on the back end.
- Minimize the use of predetermined architectures.

Manage Tightly, Control Loosely

The situation for the Allied paratroopers at the Bulge was grim. Vastly outnumbered, outgunned, and in a logistically poor location, they faced a greater likelihood of total annihilation than of any sort of victory. Yet they managed to hold out for days, waiting for reinforcements and beating an orderly retreat when they finally came.

In Korea, the First Marine Division at Chosin Reservoir and the Second Infantry Division at Kanu-ri faced the Chinese backlash from the UN decision to cross the 38th parallel. The marines retreated in good order, bringing their dead and wounded and all their equipment with them and disabling between a quarter and a third of all the Chinese troops along the way. The army in Korea, in contrast, suffered many casualties, lost most of its equipment, and escaped as a scattered bunch of desperate men.

What do these battle stories signify for the manager of a distributed computing environment? They highlight the need for flexible independence at the front lines, based on a solid foundation of rules and training and backed up with timely and appropriate levels of support. The army at the Battle of the Bulge reacted flexibly to the situation at hand; in addition, they were backed by rigorous training that reinforced standards of action as well as by a supply chain that made action possible. In contrast, the army in Korea suffered from a surfeit of central command, which clogged supply lines and rendered the front line troops incapable of independent action.

In the distributed computing environment, the users are in the thick of battle, reacting with the best of their abilities to events moment by moment. IS can support its troops in a way that allows them to react appropriately or can make them stop and call for a different type of service while the customers get more and more frustrated.

BPR and Metrics. Two tools that are key to enabling distributed management are business process redesign (BPR) and metrics. BPR gets the business system working first, highlights the critical areas requiring support, builds consensus between the users and the IS organization as to the required level of support, and reduces the sheer number of variables that must be managed at any one time. In essence, applying BPR first allows a company to step back and get used to the new environment.

Without a good set of metrics, there is no way to tell how effective IS management has been or where effort needs to be applied moment to moment. The metrics required to manage a distributed computing environment are different from those IS is used to. With central computing, IS basically accepted that it would be unable to determine the actual support delivered to any one business. Because centralized computing environments are so large and take so long to implement, their cost and performance are spread over many functions. For this reason, indirect measurements were adopted when speaking of central systems, measures such as availability and throughput.

But these indirect measurements do not tell the real story of how much benefit a business might derive from its investment in a system. With distributed computing, it is possible to allocate expenses and effort not only to a given business unit but to an individual business function as well. IS must take advantage of this capability by moving away from the old measurements of computing performance and refocusing on business metrics, such as return on investment.

Pricing should be used as a tool to encourage users to indulge in behavior that supports the strategic direction of the company. For example, an organization used to allow any word processing package that the users desired. It then reduced the number of packages it would support to two, but still allowed the use of any package. This resulted in an incurred cost to the IS organization due to help desk calls, training problems, and system hangs. The organization eventually settled on one package as a standard, gave it free to all users, and eliminated support for any other package. The acceptance of this standard package by users was high, reducing help calls and the need for human intervention. Moreover, the company was able to negotiate an 80% discount over the street price from the vendor, further reducing the cost.

In addition to achieving a significant cost savings, the company was able to drastically reduce the complexity of its office automation environment, thus allowing it to deliver better levels of service.

Organize to Provide Service on Three Levels

The historical IS shop exists as a single organization to provide service to all users. Very large or progressive companies have developed a two-dimensional delivery system: part of the organization delivers business-focused service (particularly applications development), and the rest acts as a generic utility. Distributed computing environments require a three-dimensional service delivery organization. In this emerging organization model, one dimension of service is for dialtone, overseeing the technology infrastructure. A second dimension is for business-focused or value-added service, ensuring that the available technology resources are delivered and used in a way that maximizes the benefit to the business unit. The third dimension involves overseeing synergy, which means ensuring that there is maximum leverage between each business unit and the corporation.

Dialtone IS services lend themselves to automation and outsourcing. They are complex, to a degree that cannot be well managed or maintained by human activity alone. They must be stable, as this is the need of users of these services. In addition, they are nonstrategic to the business and lend themselves to economies of scale, and hence, are susceptible to outsourcing (Exhibits 19.4 and 19.5).

Value-added services should occur at the operations as well as at the development level. For example, business unit managers are responsible for overseeing the development of applications and really understanding the business. This concept should be extended to operational areas, such as training, maintenance, and the help desk. When these resources are placed in the business unit, they will be better positioned to work with the users to support their business instead of making the users take time out to deal with the technology.

Common Operational Problem	Responsiveness to Automation
Equipment hangs	●
Network contention	◐
Software upgrades	●
Equipment upgrades	○
Disaster recovery	●
Backups	●
Quality assurance of new applications	●
Equipment faults (e.g., print cartridge replacement, disk crash)	○
Operator error (e.g., forgotten password, kick out plug)	○
Operator error (e.g., not understanding how to work application)	●

Responsiveness
High ●
Medium ◐
Low ○

SOURCE: Interviews and Decision Strategies Group analysis

Exhibit 19.4. Responsiveness of operations to automation

The third level of service — providing maximum leverage between the business unit and the corporation — is perhaps the most difficult to maintain and represents the greatest change in the way IS does business today. Currently, the staff members in charge of the activities that leverage across all business units are the most removed from those businesses. Functions such as strategic planning, test beds, low-level coding, and code library development tend to be staffed by technically excellent people with little or no business knowledge. IS managers must turn this situation around and recruit senior staff with knowledge of the business functions, business process redesign, and corporate training. These skills are needed to take the best of each business unit, combine it into a central core, and deliver it back to the business.

Dialtone Function	Applicability
Equipment maintenance	●
Trouble calls	●
Help desk	●
Installations	●
Moves and changes	●
Billing	◑
Accounting	◑
Service level contracting	○
Procurement	○
Management	○

Applicability
High ●
Medium ◑
Low ○

SOURCE: Interviews and Decision Strategies Group analysis

Exhibit 19.5. Applicability of outsourcing to dialtone

Choose One Standard

In the immortal words of the sneaker manufacturer, "Just do it." If the key to managing a distributed computing environment is to reduce complexity, then implementing a standard is the thing to do. Moreover, the benefits to be achieved from even a bad standard, if it helps to reduce complexity, will outweigh the risks incurred from possibly picking the wrong standard. The message is clear: there is more to be gained from taking inappropriate action now than from waiting to take perfect action later.

It should be clear that IT is moving more and more toward commodity status. The differences between one platform and another will disappear over time. Even if IS picks a truly bad standard, it will likely merge with the winner in the next few years, with little loss of investment. More important, the users are able to get on with their work. In addition, it is easier to move from one standard to the eventual winner than from many.

Even if you pick the winner, there is no guarantee that you will not suffer a discontinuity. IBM made its customers migrate from the 360 to 370 architecture. Microsoft moved from DOS to Windows to Windows NT. UNIX still is trying to decide which version it wants to be. The only thing certain about information technology is the pace of change, so there is little use in waiting for things to quiet down before making a move.

Integrate Data at the Front End

At the very core of a company's survival is the ability to access data as needed. Companies have been trying for decades to find some way to create a single data model that standardizes the way it stores data and thus allows for access by any system.

The truth of the matter is that for any sufficiently large company (i.e., one with more than one product in one market), data standardization is unrealistic. Different market centers track the same data in different ways. Different systems require different data formats. New technologies require data to be stated in new ways. To try to standardize the storage of data means ignoring these facts of life to an unreasonable extent.

The standardization approach also ignores the fact that businesses have 20 to 30 years' worth of data already. Are they to go back and recreate all this to satisfy future needs? Probably not. Such a project would immobilize the business and the creation of future systems for years to come.

Systems designed to integrate and reconcile data from multiple sources, presenting a single image to the front end, intrinsically support the client/server model of distributed computing and build flexibility into future applications. They allow data to be stored in many forms, each optimized for the application at hand. More important, they allow a company to access its data on an as-needed basis. These integration systems are an important component to successfully managing future growth.

Less Architecture Is More

To overdesign a systems architecture is to overly constrain the organization. Most architecture arises as a function of rightsizing of applications on the basis of where the data must be stored and used. Understanding this helps the IS manager size the network and associated support infrastructure.

The management of risk and impact also drives architecture by forcing redundancy of systems and, in some cases, mandating the placement of data repositories regardless of user preferences. Assessing project vs. operational risk helps to determine whether a system is built for central or distributed use.

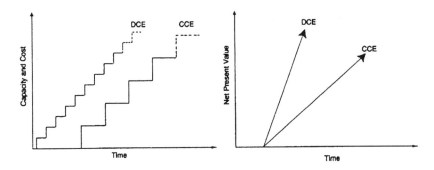

Distributed computing environment (DCE) has a higher net present value because its capacity can be used sooner relative to its marginal costs when compared with the centralized computing environment (CCE).

SOURCE: Decision Strategies Group, Greenwich CT

Exhibit 19.6. Net present value of distributed vs. centralized computing

---

This view is one in which the business needs drive the shape of the architecture. It results in a dynamic interconnection of systems that respond flexibly to business needs. Under a centralized computing environment, it was impractical to employ such an approach. It took so long and cost so much to implement a system that investment had to come before business need. This necessitated preplanning of an architecture as an investment guide.

The economics of distributed computing are different. Systems cost much less and can be quickly implemented. This means that their use can be responsive to business needs instead of anticipative. It also results in a greater net present value, for even though their operational costs might be higher, distributed computing environments are more immediately useful for a given level of investment (Exhibit 19.6).

CONCLUSION

For IS managers, there indeed exists a framework for managing the new computing environment, one that in fact more directly relates to the business than their old way of managing. If you are able to master it, you enhance your opportunities to become a member of the corporate business management team instead of simply a supplier of computing services.

Success in a distributed computing environment requires a serious culture shift for IS managers. They must loosen up their management styles, learning to decentralize daily control of operations. They must provide direction to staff members so that they can recognize synergies among business units. Some jobs that were viewed as low-level support activities (e.g., value-added services such as help desk and printer maintenance) must be recognized as key to user productivity and distributed. Others, viewed as senior technical positions (e.g., dialtone functions such as network management and installations), might be outsourced, freeing scarce IS resources.

Most important, IS managers must understand the shift in power away from themselves and toward users. The IS organization is no longer the main provider of services; it now must find a role for itself as a manager of synergy, becoming a facilitator to the business units as they learn to manage their own newly found capabilities.

Chapter 20
Improving Data Center Productivity and Effectiveness

John P. Murray

THE INTRODUCTION OF MORE easily understood technology gives managers with limited information technology experience more autonomy and confidence in managing that technology. That in turn has encouraged non-IT staffs, often urged on by vendors with an interest in installing their own brands of hardware and software, to assume increased responsibility for the management of their own processing environments. Given these circumstances, IS managers must show that the function is well managed and will continue that way, or they will become vulnerable to some form of reallocation of responsibilities.

Beyond the issue of relinquishing responsibilities is the issue of the general trend within organizations to reduce expenses whenever possible. Because the operation of the data center often represents a considerable line item in the IT budget, it can easily become a focal point for expense reduction. The well-prepared data center operations manager anticipates that possibility and begins to reduce expenses before being forced to do so.

Reducing expense through reductions in data center customer service, however, is not the answer. In fact, managers must reduce expenses while improving customer service levels. To meet this challenge, improvements in data center productivity and effectiveness must be made.

BEGINNING THE PROCESS

The issues of improved productivity, efficiency, and expense reduction almost always collide with cultural issues. First, IS staff members likely believe that current work is as productive as possible and if there was a need for improvements, they would already have made them. Second, the IS manager may believe there is a need for more money to make improvements, not less. Whatever the cultural issues, however, they must not

0-8493-9820-7/00/$0.00+$.50
© 2000 by CRC Press LLC

hinder taking action to move toward increased productivity and effectiveness.

To begin, managers must make the time and effort to ensure that staff members understand the benefits from a plan to make productivity, effectiveness, and expense management improvements. How the topic is handled depends on the manager's perception of the operation's status. For example, if the perception is that there are many opportunities to improve because of the poor quality of the current practices, an aggressive approach would be in order. The manager would clearly state the situation: changes must come about if the operation is to survive. Conversely, if the perception is that the department is well run, the approach would be to find opportunities to make improvements that enhance an already strong operation. In this example, the process is more a fine tuning than an overhaul.

The idea is to share with the staff the reasons for moving to improved productivity when possible and to work together to identify areas to reduce expenses. The goal is to gain staff support, which is critical in making the project as successful as possible. If everyone understands the purpose of the project and what its outcome means to each individual, there will be a much stronger likelihood of success. Sometimes, the message being sent is painful, but it is important to send the message. The reason for change should be obvious, no matter how difficult. To succeed, the IS manager needs the support of all the members of the IS staff. The benefit is that the success of the group ensures the success of the individuals.

MAPPING THE EXISTING PROCESS

The starting point for an improvement project must be to gain a clear understanding of current processes. Too often, there is a gap between the staff's perception and the reality of what the department is doing. The concern should be to determine accurately what is occurring, so any proposals produce the most benefit. Also, identifying current processes often reveals areas that are candidates for adjustment to bring about positive results quickly.

One effective method for gaining an understanding of what is occurring is to map the work flow within the data center. The procedure is to build a collection of process maps that track the flow of a particular piece of work from the time it enters the data center until it leaves. Each step in the flow is identified, recorded, and then connected to show how they relate to each other and to other processes. The result is a graphic representation of the entire work process as it moves through the center. One map should be completed for each set of processes.

Doing a thorough job creating and reviewing the maps provides the basis for changes that can both reduce processing time and effort and improve customer service. The value of the mapping process is to produce an objective analysis of the way work is being done.

Mapping need not be an onerous task, as there are microcomputer-based graphical application packages available that both create and modify process maps. These tools are inexpensive, flexible, and easy to use.

When the maps are completed, the staff meets to review them. All staff familiar with the work being reviewed (i.e., IS staff and data center customers) should attend, to contribute to the informed decisions on what is being done and what changes must be considered. Each map should be carefully reviewed within the context of the following questions:

- Is this function necessary? If not, can it be eliminated?
- Is it possible to combine several functions to reduce the work load?
- Are there more effective methods that produce the same, or better, benefits?

As a result of this review, there may be some discussion about the accuracy of the maps because of some staff assumptions about how the work is processed within the installation. Also, the amount of work that is either redundant or no longer necessary will quickly become apparent.

For example, in one data center, in reviewing the maps, the staff found that two production runs for two departments used files and programs that seemed to be identical. After further analysis, it turned out that two applications did almost the same processing for the different departments, the only difference being that the reports, though identical in content, were sorted and printed differently.

In this example, several minor adjustments were made to one of the applications, and the other was eliminated. Even though the initial processing increased the work load a bit, the net results are savings in processing time and increases in productivity and effectiveness.

As the review of the process maps moves forward, one goal should be to identify processes that do not add any value to serving customers. When these non-value-added processes are identified, they should be noted and marked for removal from the work flows. There may be an eagerness to remove the work immediately; however, it is important to make sure there are no links to other processes. Such links may not be obvious, so it will be important to understand what those links mean before any changes are made. This is an example of how it helps to involve people from the business areas of the organization who have an understanding of the applications.

Circumstances that would support not making the changes include having to alter a significant amount of code to effect the change. The effort and time involved might not justify the change. The idea is to get at as much of the unnecessary processes as possible and to understand that there is a cost to making the changes.

Once the links between processes are identified, however, one rule of thumb is that any processes that can be removed, should be. It may be that the removal of a particular process appears to produce a marginal effect on the efficiency of the operation, but it represents a significant cumulative benefit. As a rule, no matter how small the benefit, any candidate for removal should be deleted.

IT installations that have been in operation for some time — 10 or more years, for example — have applications that have outlived their usefulness. The development and review of the data center maps hold the promise in some installations for a considerable improvement in productivity and effectiveness. Taking the time for a careful analysis of those old applications is likely to produce several candidates for restructure or elimination.

IMPROVING ERROR RATIOS

The next area with potential for improvement in productivity, efficiency, and expense reduction is a review of operational errors. The purpose of such an investigation is not to place blame, although doing a good job here will probably highlight some areas or individuals that would benefit from improvement. Rather, the idea is to locate the causes of errors and to do whatever is necessary to stop those errors from occurring. An analysis of the cause of data center errors will show that there are only a few areas that create conditions for errors. These include

- Applications defects.
- Operations errors.
- Insufficient operator training and supervision.
- Vendor problems.
- Technical support errors or omissions.
- Inadequate, outdated, or incorrect operations documentation.

Again, depending on the particular operation, one or two categories of problems may be responsible for a large portion of the errors, or errors may be created in varying degrees by all of the conditions. Having identified the areas in which errors are occurring, the staff should assess the impact of those errors on performance.

The Impact of Data Center Errors

Several examples of various error conditions and their effect on data center performance illustrate the need to follow up on the errors and their causes. The most dramatic and usually the most expensive example of the negative effect of data center processing errors are those that could be termed *operating disruptions.* These are error conditions that slow, disrupt, or shut down the normal online data processing functions.

Any of the items in the preceding list fall into the category of operating disruptions because they can play a part, either by themselves or in combination with another condition, in disrupting normal processing operations. Sometimes the reasons for such circumstances are obvious and therefore easy to correct. An example is a production application that has insufficient editing capabilities. Because the edits are weak, inaccurate data enter the system and, later in the process, these data cause the application to fail. In other instances, the cause of difficulty may be much less obvious and, as a result, much harder to pinpoint and correct.

To obtain a strong return from addressing and correcting operating disruptions, the staff should identify as many of those instances of operating disruptions as possible. When the operating disruptions are identified, they should be categorized on the basis of their severity and the amount of time and effort required to make the needed corrections. One way to proceed is to develop a grid that includes a description of the error condition, the severity of that condition, and the estimated amount of time and effort required to bring about the desired corrections. In addition, there should be an estimate of the potential benefits to be obtained as the result of the correction. Those benefits should be considered in terms of both hard dollars and intangibles. It may be that improvements in customer satisfaction, as an example, carry as much value to the organization as dollar savings.

With the data produced in the grid, the error items can be ranked and schedules for the anticipated correction of the error conditions can be developed. By using the grid to both list the items and analyze the effort and timing of the corrections, the IS manager can move the process forward on several levels simultaneously.

DEFENDING THE NEED TO FINANCE CHANGES

When the IS manager begins to focus on correcting operations disruptions, it is not long before the topic of the expense associated with making the corrections arises. Making the corrections often depends on the concentration of resources, because applications development staff may have to correct errors in production applications and vendors must correct errors in purchased software packages.

Applications development managers might resist efforts to direct resources away from projects already in process. When challenged with flaws in its applications, vendors could be reluctant to make any changes, to avoid incurring expenses. This is more likely to be the case when the error condition appears to be isolated to one customer. When moving into these discussions, the manager should expect emotional battles for resources to arise.

An effective method to defuse the issue is to gather the facts beforehand to support the need for action. To do that, the manager should develop a process to assign costs to the organizations responsible for correcting the errors. Again, the use of the grid can be helpful in showing the costs, both tangible and intangible, of not making the corrections. Because many error conditions result in the loss of time, it helps, when practical, to relate the time lost to dollars lost.

Several examples of the effects of error conditions and their associated cost to the organization effectively build a case to gain the resources necessary to correct those conditions. For example, a batch processing system that had been working correctly is modified to add more processing capabilities. When the changed system moves to the production processing environment, the system aborts on occasion. When the problem is brought to the applications manager's attention, the manager installs a fix rather than repairing the problem, to enable the operators to restart the processing sequence when it fails.

The difficulty is that when the system fails, the restart process requires three hours of processing time to correct the error. The results are that data center production processing schedules are disrupted and online customer files are not available at the start of the work day. Placing the fix in the application does not solve the problem; it only provides a way to get around the problem, and the problem remains in the operations disruption category.

In addition, the organizationwide impact is that several departments must simply wait until files become available to start their work. This causes significant costs to the organization as lost productive work hours, lost revenue, and bad will among various stakeholders.

MAKING THE NECESSARY CORRECTIONS

Whereas the issue of lost productivity is an important item, it is hardly the only issue. The effect on department morale, coupled with the bad publicity for the IS department, are issues that must be considered. Beyond the internal harm suffered by the organization is the issue of the negative effect on the organization's customers. If these delays result in lower standards of customer service — and in today's world that is almost always the case — lost wages may represent only a very small sum.

If, however, it is not possible to obtain assistance from the applications department or the vendor, securing additional funding to address these items should be considered. Working with an outside firm to develop a plan to attack the items that create operational disruptions may provide the solution.

Another approach is to request adding programmer positions to the staff to work on the operational disruptions. Again, using the data from the mapping process and the estimates for the expense associated with uncorrected operational errors, the IS manager should not find it difficult to justify one or more programmers to address those problems. It should be made clear that these employees will correct the applications that are causing operations disruptions.

Documentation Difficulties

Errors in applications code are not, however, the only source of operations errors. Another source of errors may be found in the data center's operations documentation, which may be of poor quality or so meager as to be virtually nonexistent. In this case, the applications developers' reasons are usually that, because of impending implementation deadlines, there has not been time to complete the documentation. Under these circumstances, it is unlikely that adequate documentation will ever be provided.

Poor operations documentation can also be found within the data center because changes and updates to operations documents are not maintained or clearly written. Experienced operators may be able to work with poor documentation because they can process the systems from memory, but new operators must rely on faulty documentation, which causes operational errors. The worst-case scenario occurs when operations documentation has not been properly updated for some time and those operators who understand the processing environment leave the organization.

A third area of documentation difficulty is the delivery of poor quality documentation from outside vendors. To avoid this situation, all installations should include a standard to withhold approval of vendor payments until the documentation has been reviewed and approved by the operations personnel. That condition of purchase should be made clear to the vendor well in advance of any vendor marketing effort. The most effective way to carry out that review and approval is to process several runs of the applications and determine documentation quality.

The most easily resolved of these three documentation problems is faulty documentation from outside vendors. Avoiding difficulty in this area requires cooperation between the IS manager and those purchasing the software. As an example, the development manager purchasing application software should understand and agree that the purchase will not be completed without formal acceptance of the products, including their documentation, from the data center.

Regarding the other two documentation problems, the IS manager may have to consider several options. One effective approach to the problem of less-than-adequate data center documentation is to employ the services of a technical writer. This position can be full or part time, or the technical writer can be engaged on a contract basis. The technical writer's role should go beyond that of maintaining the documentation; the writer should also be willing to conduct periodic reviews to ensure that all data center documentation is maintained in accord with the established standards.

DEVELOPING THE IMPROVEMENT PLAN

The plan to address the topic of operational disruptions should include

- The identification of difficulties created by the current problems and the probable cause of those problems.
- An estimate of the cost, both in hard dollars and in reduction of customer service levels, associated with the occurrence of the operational disruptions.
- An approach to address the various problem areas and to develop a tentative schedule to remove the areas of difficulty.
- The estimates of the expense required to make the needed corrections.
- The anticipated benefits associated with the success of the plan. When doing this section of the plan, the IS manager must address benefits beyond those of hard dollars (e.g., improvements in customer satisfaction).

A part of the plan should deal with the topic of communicating the results of the improvement effort. The plan, once approved, should be published so anyone interested can find out what is going to be done. As results are achieved, they should be made known so that people throughout the organization can see that progress is being made.

CONCLUSION

Opportunities exist within many IS departments to bring about improvements in productivity, efficiency, and reduction of expense, without the requirement to move to radical changes. Taking the time to think through current practices, to identify areas for improvement, and to install those improvements on the basis of the adoption of an aggressive plan produces tangible results.

Moving to the most effective, efficient operation must become the goal of every IS manager. Finding the time to do this is something the IS manager must accomplish.

Chapter 21
U.S. Telecommunications Today*

Nicholas Economides

THIS CHAPTER EXAMINES the current conditions in the U.S. telecommunications sector (April 1999). It discusses the impact of technological and regulatory change on market structure and business strategy. The chapter touches on, among other issues, the impact on pricing of digitization and the emergence of Internet telephony. It also takes a brief look at the impact of the 1996 Telecommunications Act on market structure and strategy in conjunction with the history of regulation and antitrust intervention in the telecommunications sector. The author expresses concern about the derailment of the implementation of the 1996 Act by the aggressive legal tactics of the entrenched monopolists (the local exchange carriers), and he points to the danger that the intent of Congress in passing the 1996 Act to promote competition in telecommunications will not be realized. After discussing the impact of wireless technologies, the chapter comments on the wave of mergers in the industry and ventures into some short-term predictions.

INTRODUCTION

The U.S. Telecommunications sector is going through a revolutionary change. There are three reasons for this. The first reason is the rapid technological change in key inputs of telecommunications services and in complementary goods, which have reduced dramatically the costs of traditional services and have made many new services available at reasonable prices. Cost reductions have made feasible the World Wide Web (WWW) and the various multimedia applications that "live" on it.

The second reason for the revolutionary change has been the sweeping digitization of the telecommunications and the related sectors. The underlying telecommunications technology has become digital. Moreover, the consumer and business telecommunications interfaces have become more versatile and closer to multifunction computers than to traditional telephones. Digitization and integration of telecommunications services with computers create significant business opportunities and impose significant pressure on traditional pricing structures, especially in voice telephony.

The third reason for the current upheaval in the telecommunications sector is the passage of a major new law to govern telecommunications in the United States, the Telecommunications Act of 1996 (1996 Act). Telecommunications traditionally has been subject to a complicated federal and state regulatory structure. The 1996 Act attempted to adapt the regulatory structure to technological reality, but various legal challenges by the incumbents have so far delayed, if not nullified, its impact.

Before going into a detailed analysis, it is important to point out the major driving forces in U.S. telecommunications today.

- Dramatic reductions in the costs of transmission and switching.
- Digitization.
- Restructuring of the regulatory environment through the implementation of the 1996 Telecommunications Act coming 12 years after the breakup of AT&T.
- Move of value from underlying services (such as transmission and switching) to the interface and content.
- Move toward multifunction programmable devices with programmable interfaces, such as computers, and away from single-function, non-programmable consumer devices, such as traditional telephone appliances.
- Reallocation of electromagnetic spectrum, allowing for new types of wireless competition.
- Interconnection and interoperability of interconnected networks; standardization of communications protocols.
- Network externalities and critical mass.

These forces have a number of consequences:

- Increasing pressure for cost-based pricing of telecommunications services.
- Price arbitrage between services of the same time immediacy requirement.
- Increasing competition in long-distance services.
- The possibility of competition in local services.
- The emergence of Internet telephony as a major new telecommunications technology.

TECHNOLOGICAL CHANGE

The last two decades have witnessed (1) dramatic reductions in costs of transmission through the use of technology, (2) reductions in costs of switching and information processing because of big reductions of costs of integrated circuits and computers, and (3) significant improvements in software interfaces. Cost reductions and better interfaces have made feasible many data- and transmission-intensive services. These include many applications on the WWW, which were dreamed of many years ago but only now have become economically feasible.

The general trend in cost reductions has allowed for entry of more competitors in many components of the telecommunications network and an intensification of competition. Mandatory interconnection of public telecommunications networks and the use of common standards for interconnection and interoperability created a "network of networks" (i.e., a web of interconnected networks). The open architecture of the network of networks allowed for entry of new competitors in markets for particular components, as well as in markets for integrated end-to-end services. Competition intensified in many, but not all, markets.

Digital Convergence and "Bit Arbitrage"

Entry and competition were particularly helped by (1) the open architecture of the network and (2) its increasing digitization. Currently, all voice messages are digitized close to their origination and are carried in digital form over most of the network. Thus, the data and voice networks are one, with voice treated as data with specific time requirements. This has important implications on pricing and market structure.

Digital bits (zeros or ones) traveling on the information highway can be parts of voice, still pictures, video, or a database or other computer application, and they appear identical — "a bit is a bit is a bit." However, because some demands are for real-time services while others are not, the saying that "a bit is a bit is a bit" is only correct among services that have the same index of time *immediacy*. Digitization implies arbitrage on the price of bit transmission among services that have the same time immediacy requirements.

For example, voice telephony and video conferencing require real-time transmission and interaction. Digitization implies that the cost of transmission of voice is hundreds of times smaller than the cost of transmitting video of the same duration. This implies that if regulatorily imposed price discrimination is eliminated, arbitrage on the price of bits will occur, leading to extremely low prices for services, such as voice, that use relatively very few bits. Even if price discrimination remains imposed by regulation, arbitrage in the cost and pricing of bits will lead to pressures for a de facto elimination of discrimination. This creates significant profit opportunities for the firms that are able to identify the arbitrage opportunities and exploit them.

Internet Telephony

The elimination of price discrimination between voice and data services can lead to dramatic reductions in the price of voice calls, precipitating significant changes in market structure. These changes were first evident in the emergence of the Internet, a ubiquitous network of applications based on the TCP/IP. Started as a text-based network for scientific communication, the Internet grew dramatically in the late 1980s and 1990s, once not-text-only applications became available.[1] The Internet now reaches about half a billion computers, most of which are connected to it through the telephone network. Internet-based telecommunications are based on packet switching. There are two modes of operation: (1) a time-delay mode in which there is a guarantee that the system will do whatever it can to deliver all packets and (2) a real-time mode, in which packets can, in fact, be lost without possibility of recovery.

Most telecommunications services do not have a real-time requirement, so applications that "live" on the Internet can easily accommodate them. For example, a number of companies currently provide facsimile services of the Internet where all or part of the transport of the fax takes place over the Internet. Although the Internet was not intended to be used in real-time telecommunications, despite the loss of packets, telecommunications companies presently use the Internet to complete ordinary voice telephone calls. Voice telecommunications service started on the Internet as a computer-to-computer call. As long as Internet telephony was confined to calls from a PC to a PC, it failed to take advantage of the huge network externalities of the public switched telephone network (PSTN), and was just a hobby.

About four years ago, Internet telecommunications companies started offering termination of calls on the PSTN, thus taking advantage of the immense externalities of reaching anyone on the PSTN. In 1996, firms started offering Internet calling that originated and terminated on the PSTN (i.e., from and to the regular customers' phone appliances). The last two transitions became possible with the introduction of PSTN-Internet interfaces and switches by Lucent and others. In 1998, Qwest and others started using IP switching to carry telephone calls from and to the PSTN using their own network for long-distance transport as an Intranet.

Internet calls are packet based. Because they utilize the real-time mode of the Internet, there is no guarantee that all the packets of a voice transmission will arrive at the destination. Internet telephony providers use sophisticated voice-sampling methods to decompose and reconstitute voice so that packet losses do not make a significant audible difference. Because such methods are by their nature imperfect, the quality and fidelity of an Internet call crucially depend on the percentage of packets that are lost in transmission and transport. This, in turn, depends, among other factors on (1) the allocation of Internet bandwidth (pipeline) to the phone call and (2) the number of times the message is transmitted.[2] Because of these considerations, one expects that two types of Internet telephony will survive: (1) the low-end quality, carried over the Internet, with packets lost and low fidelity, and (2) a service of comparable quality with traditional long distance, carried on a company's intranet on the long-distance part.

Internet-based telecommunications services pose a serious threat to traditional national and international long-distance service providers. In the traditional US regulatory structure, a call originating from a computer to an Internet service provider (ISP) (or terminating from an ISP to a computer) is not charged an "access charges" by the local exchange carrier. This can lead to substantial savings.

The Federal Communications Commission (FCC), in its decision of February 25, 1999, muddies the waters by finding that "Internet traffic is intrinsically mixed and appears to be largely interstate in nature" on the one hand; while, on the other hand, it validates the reciprocal compensation of ISPs which were made under the assumption that customer calls to ISPs are treated as local calls. If Internet calls are classified as interstate (i.e., as long-distance data calls), the price that most consumers will have to pay to reach the Internet would become a significant per minute change and it is likely that the Internet will stop its fast growth. In fact, one of the key reasons for Europe's lag in Internet adoption is the fact that in most countries, unlike in the United States, consumers are charged per minute for local calls.

In response to the Internet telephony threat, in January 1998 AT&T announced that it would offer a new long-distance service carried over the Internet and AT&T's intranet. AT&T's service, offered at 7.5–9 cents per minute, will originate and terminate on the PSTN and therefore will appear to customers like a regular call; no computer will be required. Several months earlier, Deutsche Telecom (DT) introduced Internet long-distance service within Germany. To compensate for the lower quality of voice transmission, DT offered internet long-distance service at one-fifth of its regular long-distance rates. Internet telephony remains the most important challenge to the telecommunications sector.

THE TELECOMMUNICATIONS ACT OF 1996 AND ITS IMPACT

Goals of the Act

The Telecommunications Act of 1996 attempts a major restructuring of the U.S. telecommunications sector. The 1996 Act will be judged favorably to the extent that it allows and facilitates the acquisition by consumers of the benefits of technological advances. Such a function requires the promotion of competition in all markets. This does not mean immediate and complete deregulation. Consumers must be protected from monopolistic abuses in some markets as long as such abuses are feasible under the current market structure. Moreover, the regulatory framework must safeguard against firms exporting their monopoly power in other markets.

In passing the Telecommunications Act of 1996, Congress took radical steps to restructure U.S. telecommunications markets. These steps may result in significant benefits to consumers of telecommunications services, telecommunications carriers, and telecommunications equipment manufacturers. But the degree of success of the 1996 Act depends crucially on its implementation through decisions of the FCC and state public utility commissions and the outcome of the various court challenges that these decisions face.

The 1996 Act envisions a network of interconnected networks that are composed of complementary components and generally provide both competing and complementary services. The 1996 Act uses both *structural* and *behavioral* instruments to accomplish its goals. The 1996 Act attempts to reduce regulatory barriers to entry and competition. It outlaws artificial barriers to entry in local exchange markets in its attempt to accomplish the maximum possible competition. Moreover, it mandates interconnection of telecommunications networks, unbundling, nondiscrimination, and cost-based pricing of leased parts of the network, so that competitors can enter easily and compete component by component and service by service.

The 1996 Act imposes conditions to ensure that de facto monopoly power is not exported to vertically related markets. Thus, the 1996 Act *requires* that competition be established in local markets *before* the incumbent local exchange carriers are allowed in long distance.

The 1996 Act preserves subsidized local service to achieve "universal service" but imposes the requirement that subsidization is transparent and that subsidies are raised in a competitively neutral manner. Thus, the act leads the way to the elimination of subsidization of universal service through the traditional method of high access charges.

The 1996 Act crystallized changes that had become necessary because of technological progress. Rapid technological change has always been the original cause of regulatory change. The radical transformation of the regulatory environment and market conditions that is presently taking place as a result of the 1996 Act is no exception.

History

Telecommunications has traditionally been a regulated sector of the U.S. economy. Regulation was imposed in the early part of this century and remains until today in various parts of the sector.[3] The main idea behind regulation was that it was necessary because the market for telecommunications services was a natural monopoly, and therefore a second competitor would not survive.

As early as 1900, it was clear that all telecommunications markets were *not* natural monopolies, as evidenced by the existence of more than one competing firm in many regional markets, prior to the absorption of most of them in the Bell System. Over time, it became clear that some markets that may have been natural monopolies in the past are *not* natural monopolies any more, and that it is better to allow competition in those markets while keeping the rest regulated.

The market for telecommunication services and for telecommunications equipment went through various stages of competitiveness after the invention of the telephone by Alexander Graham Bell. After a period of expansion and consolidation, by the 1920s, AT&T had an overwhelming majority of telephony exchanges and submitted to state regulation. Federal regulation was instituted by the 1934 Telecommunication Act, which established the FCC.

Regulation of the U.S. telecommunications market was marked by two important antitrust lawsuits that the U.S. Department of Justice brought against AT&T. In the first one, *United States* v. *Western Electric*, filed in 1949, the U.S. Department of Justice (DOJ) claimed that the Bell Operating Companies practiced illegal exclusion by buying only from Western Electric, a part of the Bell System. The government sought a divestiture of Western Electric, but the case was settled in 1956 with AT&T agreeing not to enter the computer market but retaining ownership of Western Electric.

The second major antitrust suit, *United States* v. *AT&T,* was started in 1974. The government alleged that (1) AT&T's relationship with Western Electric was illegal, and (2) that AT&T monopolized the long-distance market. The DOJ sought divestiture of both manufacturing and long distance from local service. The case was settled by the modified final judgment (MFJ). This decree broke away from AT&T seven regional Bell operating companies (RBOCs). Each RBOC consisted of a collection of local telephone companies that were part of the original AT&T. RBOCs remained regulated monopolies, each with an exclusive franchise in its region.

Microwave transmission was a major breakthrough in long-distance transmission that created the possibility of competition in long distance. Microwave transmission was followed by technological breakthroughs in transmission through satellite and through fiberoptic wire.

The breakup of AT&T crystallized the recognition that competition was possible in long distance, while the local market remained a natural monopoly. The biggest benefits to consumers during the last 15 years have come from the long-distance market, which, during this period was transformed from a monopoly to an effectively competitive market. However, often consumers do not reap the full benefits of cost reductions and competition because of an antiquated regulatory framework that, ironically, was supposed to protect consumers from monopolistic abuses and instead protects the monopolistic market structure.

Competition in long distance has been a great success. The market share (in minutes of use) of AT&T fell from almost 100 percent to 53 percent at the end of 1996. Since the MFJ, the number of competitors in the long-distance market has increased dramatically. There are four large facilities-based competitors: AT&T, MCI-WorldCom, Sprint, and Frontier.[4] There are also a large number of "resellers" that buy wholesale service from the facilities-based long-distance carriers and sell to consumers. For example, currently, about 500 resellers compete in the California interexchange market, providing strong evidence for the ease of entry into this market. At least 20 new firms entered the California market in each year since 1984. At present, there are at least five "out of region" RBOCs providing service in California through affiliates. In California, the typical consumer can choose from at least 150 long-distance companies.

Prices of long-distance phone calls have decreased dramatically. The average revenue per minute of AT&T's switched services has been reduced by 62 percent between 1984 and 1996. AT&T was declared "nondominant" in the long-distance market by the FCC in 1995.[5] Most economists agree that presently the long-distance market is *effectively competitive.*

Local telephone companies that came out of the Bell system (RBOCs) actively petitioned the U.S. Congress to be allowed to enter the long-distance market, from which they were excluded by the MFJ. The MFJ prevented RBOCs from participation in long distance because of the anticompetitive consequences that this would have for competition in long distance. The anticompetitive effects would arise because of the control by RBOCs of essential "bottleneck" inputs for long-distance services, such as orginating access of phone calls to customers who live in the local companies' service areas to long-distance companies. Hence, RBOCs monopoly franchises.

A long-distance phone call is carried by the local telephone companies of the place it where originates and the place it terminates, and only in its long-distance part by a long-distance company. Thus, "originating access" and "terminating access" are provided by local exchange carriers to long-distance companies and are essential bottleneck inputs for long-distance service. Origination and termination of calls are extremely lucrative services.[6] Terminating access has an average cost (in most locations) of $0.002 per minute. Its regulated prices vary. A typical price is $0.032 per minute, charged by NY Telephone. Such pricing implies a profit rate of 1,500 percent.[7] Access charges reform is one of the key demands of the pro-competitive forces in the current deregulation process.

The great success of competition in long distance allowed the U.S. Congress to appear "balanced" in the 1996 Act by establishing competition in local telephony while allowing RBOCs into long distance after they meet certain conditions. However, the transition of local markets to effective competition will not be as easy or as quick as in the long-distance markets. This is because of the nature of the product and the associated economics.

Many telecommunications companies are presently trying to be in as many markets as possible so they can bundle the various products. Companies believe that consumers are willing to pay more for bundled services for which the consumer receives a single bill. Bundling also discourages consumers from migrating to competitors, which may not offer the complete collection of services, so consumer "churn" is expected to be reduced.

Entry in Local Services as Envisioned by the Act

At the time this chapter was written, the "last mile" of the telecommunications network that is closest to the consumer (the "local loop") still remains a bottleneck controlled by a local exchange carrier (LEC). The 1996 Act boldly attempts to introduce competition in this last bottleneck, and, before competition takes hold, the 1996 Act attempts to imitate competition in the local exchange.

To facilitate entry in the local exchange, the 1996 Act introduces two novel ways of entry other than through the installation of owned facilities. The first way allows entry in the retailing part of the telecommunications business by requiring incumbent local exchange carriers (ILECs) to sell to entrants at wholesale prices any retail service that they offer. Such entry is essentially limited to the retailing part of the market.

The second and most significant novel way of entry introduced by the 1996 Act is through leasing of unbundled network elements from incumbents. In particular, the 1996 Act requires that ILECs (1) unbundle their networks and (2) offer for lease to entrants network components (unbundled network elements, or UNEs) "at cost plus reasonable profit."[8] Thus, the 1996 Act envisions the telecommunications network as a decentralized network of interconnected networks.

Many firms, including the large interexchange carriers AT&T and MCI-WorldCom, attempted to enter the market through "arbitration" agreements with ILECs under the supervision of state regulatory commissions, according to the procedure outlined by the 1996 Act. The arbitration process proved to be extremely long and difficult, with continuous legal obstacles and appeals raised by the ILECs. By the time of this writing, just over three years after the signing of the 1996 Act by President Clinton, arbitrations have been concluded in only a few states, and entry in the local exchange has been minimal.

Entry of RBOCs in Long-Distance Service

RBOCs (Ameritech, Bell Atlantic, BellSouth, SBC, and US West) have 89 percent of telephone access lines nationwide. Most of the remainder belongs to GTE and independent franchise holders. Competitive access providers (who did not hold a franchise monopoly) have less than 1 percent of residential access lines nationwide. Besides providing access to long-distance companies, LECs also provide lucrative *custom local exchange services*, such as call waiting, conference calling, and automatic number identification. Basic local service provided by LECs is considered not to be particularly profitable.

The 1996 Act allows for entry of RBOCs in long distance once a list of requirements has been met and the petitioner has proved that its proposal is in the public interest. These requirements can be met only when the market for local telecommunications services becomes sufficiently competitive. If the local market is not competitive when an incumbent LEC monopolist enters into long distance, the LEC can leverage its monopoly power to disadvantage its long-distance rivals by increasing their costs in various ways and by discriminating against them in its pricing. If the local market is not competitive when an incumbent LEC monopolist enters into long distance, an ILEC would control the price of a required input (switched access) to long-distance service while it would also compete for customers in long distance. Under these circumstances, an ILEC can implement a *vertical price squeeze* on its long-distance competitors whereby the price to cost ratio of long-distance competitors is squeezed so that they are driven out of business.[9]

In allowing entry of local exchange carriers into the long-distance market, the 1996 Act tries not to endanger competition that has developed in long distance by premature entry of RBOCs in the long distance market. However, on this issue, the 1996 Act's provisions guarding *against premature entry* may be insufficient. Hence, to guard against anticompetitive consequences of premature entry of RBOCs in long distance there is a need of a deeper analysis of the consequences of such entry on competition and on consumers' and social welfare.

THE IMPACT OF WIRELESS (CELLULAR, SATELLITE AND PCS) AND OF CABLE TELEVISION

During the last 15 years there has been a tremendous (and generally unanticipated) expansion of the mobile phone market. This significant growth has been limited by relatively high prices resulting from (1) the prevention of entry of more than two competitors in each metropolitan area and (2) the standard billing arrangement that imposes a fee on the cellular customer for *receiving* (as well as initiating) calls.

However, during the last three years, the FCC has auctioned parts of the electromagnetic spectrum that will enable the transmission of personal communication services (PCS) signals.[10] The auctioned spectrum will be able to support up to five additional carriers in the major metropolitan markets.[11] Although the PCS spectrum band is different than the traditional cellular bands, PCS is predicted to be a low-cost, high-quality, mobile alternative to traditional phone service. Other wireless services may chip away at the ILECs markets, especially in high-capacity access services.[12] The increase in the number of competitors has already created significant decreases in prices of mobile phone services.

By its nature, PCS is positioned between fixed local service and traditional wireless (cellular) service. Presently there is a significant price difference between the two services. Priced between the two, PCS will first draw consumers from cellular in large cities and later on will be a serious threat to fixed local service. AT&T has recently announced that it will use some of the spectrum that it acquired in the PCS auctions to implement a fixed wireless service ("telepoint"), a close (and maybe superior) substitute to fixed wire service.[13]

Industry analysts have been predicting the impending entry of cable television in telephony for many years. Despite numerous trials, such entry in traditional telecommunications services has not materialized. There are a number of reasons for this. First, to provide telephone service, cable television providers needed to upgrade their networks from analog to digital. Second, they need to add switching. Third, most of the cable industry has taken a high debt load and is unable to make the required investments in the short run.

If and when it is able to provide switching, cable television will have a significant advantage over regular telephone lines. Cable TV lines that reach the home have a significantly higher bandwidth capacity than do regular twisted pair lines. This is not important for regular voice telephony, but it is crucially important for applications on the World Wide Web that require high bandwidth capacity. Companies such as @home and WebTV are utilizing this capacity to provide bundles of Internet and traditional TV services. Often these services do not allow for two-way communication but rather rely on a telephone line for transmissions from the home to the ISP which are expected to require only low bandwidth. The merged AT&T -TCI plans to provide telephony, broadband video, and Internet services over the cable line to the home.

THE CURRENT WAVE OF MERGERS

The various legal challenges have derailed the implementation process of the 1996 Act and have increased the uncertainty in the telecommunications sector. Because the arbitration process that started in April 1996 has resulted in final prices in only a handful of states, long-distance companies have been unable to enter the local exchange markets by leasing UNEs. As of this writing, no state has completed the implementation of the Telecommunications Act of 1996, and only 15 of the 50 states have adopted permanent prices for unbundled network elements.[14]

In the absence of final prices, given the uncertainty of the various legal proceedings, and without final resolution on the issues of nonrecurring costs and the electronic interface for switching local service customers across carriers, entry in the local exchange through leasing of UNEs has been minimal. Moreover, entry in the retailing part of the business through total service resale has also been minimal, because the wholesale discounts have been small.

In the absence of entry in the local exchange market as envisioned by the 1996 Act, the major long-distance companies are therefore buying companies that give them some access to the local market. For example, MCI has merged with WorldCom, which had just merged with Brooks Fiber and MFS, which in turn also own some infrastructure in local exchange markets. MCI-WorldCom is focusing on the Internet and the business long-distance market.[15]

AT&T has acquired TCG, which owns the local exchange infrastructure that reaches business customers. AT&T has also recently unveiled an ambitious strategy of reaching consumers' homes by using cable TV wires for the "last mile." With this purpose in mind, AT&T bought TCI with the intent of converting the TCI cable access to an interactive broadband, voice, and data telephone link to residences. AT&T has also entered in an agreement with Time Warner to use its cable connection in a way similar to TCI's, and in April, 1999, AT&T announced its bid for MediaOne, the cable spin-off of US West, which had earlier announced its merger with Comcast.

TCI cable presently reaches 35 percent of US households. Together with Time Warner and MediaOne, AT&T would be able to reach a bit more than 50 percent of U.S. households. Without access to UNEs, to reach all residential customers, AT&T would have to find another way to reach the remaining U.S. households. Further cable conversion is one strategy that can accomplish this. AT&T has also announced, but not yet implemented, a wireless telepoint technology, similar to cellular mobile technology, but only suitable to immobile or slow-moving receivers.

The provision of telephony, Internet access, broadband, data, and two-way video services exclusively over cable lines in the "last mile" requires significant technical advances, significant conversion of the present cable networks, and an investment of at least $5 billion (and some say $30 billion) just for the conversion of the cable network to two-way, switched services. Moreover, there is some inherent uncertainty in such a conversion, which has not been successful in the past. Thus, it is an expensive and uncertain proposition for AT&T, but, at the same time, it is one of the few remaining options of entry in the local exchange.

Early attempts of the RBOCs to maximize their foothold, looking forward to the time when they would be allowed to provide long-distance service, include SBC's acquisition of Pacific Bell and Bell Atlantic's merger with NYNEX , despite antitrust objections. SBC also bought Southern New England Telephone (SNET), one of the few companies that, as an independent (not part of AT&T at divestiture), was not bound by MFJ restrictions and had already entered into long distance.

Two additional significant mergers that were announced in 1998 are still being reviewed by antitrust and regulatory authorities at this time. Bell Atlantic announced its intention to merge with GTE, and SBC has announced its intention to buy Ameritech. At the present, the DOJ has conditionally approved the SBC-Ameritech merger, and the FCC has announced its own requirements to approve the merger. However, the GTE-Bell Atlantic merger may be much harder to approve as this merger may allow the combined entity to bypass existing rules. GTE is already providing long-distance service because it was not part of AT&T and is not bound by the MFJ restrictions. On the other hand, the Telecommunications Act of 1996, amending the MFJ, prohibits Bell Atlantic from offering long-distance service until a number of conditions are met and Bell Atlantic shows that its entry into long distance is in the public interest. One option is for GTE to spin off its long-distance voice and data assets. If the Bell Atlantic-GTE merger is approved without such a condition, the combined entity can engage in a vertical price squeeze, cross subsidization and raising rivals costs — all the reasons that led to the prohibitions of the MFJ and the 1996 Act.

If all the LEC mergers pass antitrust and regulatory scrutiny, the eight large local exchange carriers of 1984 (seven RBOCs and GTE) would be reduced to only four: Bell Atlantic, Bell South, SBC, and US West. The smaller ones, Bell South and US West, already feel the pressure, and have been widely reported to be in merger/acquisition talks with a number of parties. For example, BellSouth has announced a pact with Qwest to sell Qwest's long-distance service once BellSouth is allowed to sell long-distance service.

THE COMING WORLD

The intent of the 1996 Act was to promote competition and the public interest. It will be a significant failure of the U.S. political, legal, and regulatory systems if the interests of entrenched monopolists rather than the public interest as expressed by the U.S. Congress dictate the future of the U.S. telecommunications sector. The market structure in the telecommunications sector two years ahead will depend crucially on the resolution of the LECs' legal challenges to the 1996 Act and its final implementation.[16] Already, we have seen significant vertical integration into the cable industry, as AT&T found it extremely difficult to enter the local exchange market.

Whatever the outcomes of the legal battles, the existence of arbitrage and the intensification of competition necessitate cost-based pricing and will create tremendous pressure on traditional regulated prices that are not cost based. Prices that are not based on cost will prove unsustainable. This includes access changes that LECs charge to IXCs, which have to become cost based if the vision of a competitive network of interconnected networks is to be realized.

Computers are likely to play a bigger role as telephone appliances and in running intermediate size networks that will compete with LECs and intensify the arbitrage among IXCs. Computer-based telephone interfaces will become the norm. Firms that have significant market share in computer interfaces, such as Microsoft, may play a significant role in telephony.[17] Hardware manufacturers, especially firms such as Cisco, Intel, and 3Com, that make switches and local networks will play a much more central role in telephony. Internet telephony (voice, data, and broadband) is expected to grow fast.

Finally, I expect that, slowly but steadily, telecommunications will drift away from the technical standards of signaling system seven (SS7) established by AT&T before its breakup. As different methods of transmission and switching take a foothold, and as new interfaces become available, wars over technical standards are very likely.[18] Such wars will further transform telecommunications from the traditional quiet landscape of regulated utilities to the mad-dash world of software and computer manufacturing. This change will create significant business opportunities for entrants and impose significant challenges on traditional telecommunications carriers.

Notes

* For this chapter, "today" is April 1999. Portions of this article are based on "US Telecommunications Today," *Business Economics*, April 1998.

1. Critical points in this development were the emergence of GOPHER in the late 1980s and MOSAIC by 1990.
2. A large enough bandwidth increases the probability that fewer packets will be lost. And, if each packet is sent a number of times, it is much more likely that each packet will arrive at the destination at least once, and the quality of the phone call will not deteriorate. Thus, the provider can adjust the quality level of an Internet call by guaranteeing a lot of bandwidth for the transmission and by sending the packets more than once. This implies that the quality of an Internet call is *variable* and can be adjusted upward using the variables mentioned. Thus, high-quality voice telephony is immediately feasible in intranets because intranets can guarantee a sustained large-enough bandwidth. There is no impediment to the quality level of a phone call which is picked from the PSTN at the local switch, carried over long distance on leased lines, and redelivered to the PSTN at the destination local switch, using the recently introduced Lucent switches. For Internet calls that originate or terminate in computers, the method of resending packets can be used on the Internet to increase the quality of the phone call, as long as there is sufficient bandwidth between the computer and the local telephone company switch. The fidelity of calls can also be enhanced by manipulation of the sound frequencies. This can be done, for example, through the *elemedia* series of products by Lucent.
3. The telecommunications sector is regulated both by the federal government through the FCC and by all states, typically through a public utilities commission (PUC) or public service commission. Usually a PUC also regulates electricity companies.
4. Frontier is a new name for Rochester Telephone.
5. *See* Federal Communications Commission (1995).
6. These fees are the single largest cost item in the ledgers of AT&T.
7. Termination pricing varies. Pacific Bell, under pressure from the California Public Utilities Commission, recently had an access charge of $0.016 per minute, giving it a profit rate of 700 percent.
8. The FCC and state regulatory commissions have interpreted these words to mean total element long-run incremental cost (TELRIC) which is the forward-looking, long-run, (minimized) economic cost of an unbundled element and includes the competitive return on capital.
9. Avoiding a vertical price squeeze of long-distance competitors, such as MCI, was a key rationale for the 1981 breakup of AT&T in the long-distance division that kept the AT&T name and the seven RBOCs that remained local monopolists in local service. *See* Economides (1998, 1999).
10. Despite this and other auctions of spectrum, the FCC does not have a coherent policy of efficient allocation of electromagnetic spectrum. For example, recently, the FCC gave for free huge chunks of electromagnetic spectrum to existing TV stations so that they may provide high-definition television (HDTV). Some of the recipients have publicly stated that they intend to use the spectrum to broadcast regular TV channels and information services, rather than HDTV.
11. We do not expect to see five entrants in all markets because laxity in the financial requirements of bidders resulted in default of some of the high bidders in the PCS, prompting a significant dispute regarding their financial and other obligations.
12. The so-called wireless loop proposes to bypass the ILECs' cabling with much less outlay for equipment. Trials are under way to test certain portions of the radio spectrum that were originally set aside for other applications: MMDS for wireless cable and LMDS as cellular television.
13. The second impediment to wider use of mobile phones seems also likely to disappear. In January 1998, AT&T announced that it will offer mobile service with billing of incoming calls to the originator of the call.
14. These were Colorado, Delaware, Florida, Georgia, Kentucky, Louisiana, Missouri, Montana, New Jersey, New Hampshire, New York, Oregon, Pennsylvania, Texas, and Wisconsin. Of the states that have adopted permanent prices for UNEs, five are in the Bell Atlantic/ NYNEX territory (Delaware, New Hampshire, New Jersey, New York, Pennsylva-

nia). Also note that only four states have adopted permanent rates in arbitrations of entrants with GTE (Florida, Montana, Oregon, and Texas). For more details, see Hubbard and Lehr (1998).

15. The MCI-WorldCom merger was challenged by the European Union Competition Committee, the DOJ and GTE on the grounds that the merged company would have a large market share of the Internet backbone and could sequentially target, degrade interconnection, and kill its backbone rivals. Despite (1) a lack of an economically meaningful definition of the Internet backbone, the fact that (2) MCI was unlikely to have such an incentive because any degradation would also hurt its customers, and (3) it seemed unlikely that such degradation was feasible, the Competition Commission of the European Union ordered MCI to divest of *all* its Internet business, including its retail business, when it was never alleged that the merging companies had any monopoly power. MCI's Internet business was sold to Cable and Wireless, the MCI-WorldCom merger was finalized, and MCI-WorldCom is using its UUNET subsidiary to spearhead its way in the Internet.

16. In one of the major challenges, GTE and a number of RBOCs appealed (among others) the FCC (1996) rules on pricing guidelines to the Eighth Circuit. The plaintiffs won the appeal; the FCC appealed to the Supreme Court, which ruled on January 25, 1999. The plaintiffs claimed (among other things) that (1) the FCC's rules on the definition of UNEs were flawed, (2) the FCC default prices for leasing of UNEs were so low that they amounted to confiscation of ILEC property, and (3) that FCC's "pick and choose" rule allowing a carrier to demand access to any individual interconnection, service, or network element arrangement on the same terms and conditions the LEC has given anyone else in an approved local competition entry agreement without having to accept the agreement's other provisions would deter the "voluntarily negotiated agreements." The Supreme Court ruled for the FCC in all these points, thereby eliminating a major challenge to the implementation of the Act.

17. Microsoft owns a share of WebTV and has made an investment in Qwest.

18. A significant failure of the FCC has been its absence in defining technical standards and promoting compatibility. Even when the FCC had a unique opportunity to define such standards in PCS telephony (because it could define the terms while it auctioned Spectrum), it allowed a number of incompatible standards to coexist for PCS. This led directly to a weakening of competition and higher prices wireless PCS consumers have to buy a new appliance to migrate across providers.

Recommended Reading

Crandall, R. W. 1991. *After the breakup: U.S. telecommunications in a more competitive era.* Washington, DC: Brookings Institution.

Economides, N. 1996. The economics of networks. *International Journal of Industrial Organization* 14(2):675–699.

Economides, N. 1998. The incentive for non-price discrimination by an input monopolist. *International Journal of Industrial Organization* 16(March 1998):271–284.

Economides, N. 1999. The Telecommunications Act of 1996 and its impact. *Japan and the world economy* 11(September) forthcoming.

Economides, N., Lopomo, G., and Woroch, G. 1996. Regulatory Pricing policies to neutralize network dominance. *Industrial and Corporate Change* 5(4):1013–1028.

Federal Communications Commission. 1995. In the matter of motion of AT&T Corp. to be reclassified as a non-dominant carrier. CC Docket No. 95-427, order, adopted October 12, 1995.

Federal Communications Commission. 1996. First report and order. CC Docket No. 96-98, CC Docket No. 95-185, adopted August 8, 1996.

Hubbard, R. G., and Lehr, W. H. 1998. Improving local exchange competition: Regulatory crossroads, mimeo, February.

Mitchell, B., and Vogelsang, I. 1991. *Telecommunications pricing: Theory and practice.* Cambridge: Cambridge University Press.

Noll, R. G., and Owen, B. 1989. The anti-competitive uses of regulation: *United States v. AT&T.* In *The antitrust revolution*, edited by J. E. Kwoka and L. J. White. New York: Harper Collins, 290–337.

Chapter 22
Operating Standards for LANs

Leo Wrobel

THE FOLLOWING SCENARIO is common in many organizations: There are 200 local area networks (LANs) located across the country, in everything from small sales offices with a handful of people to regional distribution centers. The company does not know if these outlying locations handle mission-critical data. The company does not know with certainty who is running these LANs, because staffing ranges from office managers and clerical employees right up to seasoned IS professionals. A site that once had 10 salespeople now has nine salespeople and a LAN administrator. The company does not know how these sites are buying equipment, yet it is reasonably sure that they are paying too much, because they are not buying in bulk or enjoying any economies of scale in equipment purchases.

Locations are beginning to lean on IS for help-desk support because there is no way they can keep up with the rapid proliferation of hardware platforms, software, and special equipment being installed in the field. The telecommunications department is worried about connecting all of these locations together.

Although some attempts at standardization of these locations may be made, LAN managers in the field invariably consider standards to be an attempt by the IS department to regain control of the LAN administrators' environment. Because LAN managers seldom have had any input into what these standards would be, they were soundly rejected.

Today, there are literally thousands of companies fighting this same battle. This chapter offers some solutions to these problems. First, however, it is important to understand why standards are required and how IS can implement standards without stifling productivity or adversely affecting the organization.

WHY LANS REQUIRE STANDARDS

In an ideal environment, the LAN administrator can select exactly the type of equipment best tailored to do the job. LAN managers are historically close to the core business. For example, if the company is involved in trading stock, the LAN operations department can go out and buy equipment exactly tailored to trading stock. If the organization is engaged in engineering, the LAN administrator can buy equipment exactly tailored to engineering.

From the standpoint of operational characteristics, LANs are far more desirable than mainframes because they are closer to the business, they empower people, and they make people enormously productive by being close to the core business. This is not the whole story, however. It is equally as important to support LANs once they are in place. This is where the trade-offs come in.

Lessons from Mainframe Experience

Because mainframes have been around so long, there is a high degree of support available. When users in the mainframe environment call the help desk with a hardware or a software problem, the help desk knows what they are talking about. Help-desk staff are well trained in the hardware and the software packages and can quickly solve the users' problems.

As another example, in an IBM 3070 terminal environment, 100 terminals or more could be supported by a single technician. When those terminals became PCs, the ratio dropped perhaps to 50 PCs per technician. When those PCs became high-end work stations, the ratio dropped even further. The value of a mainframe level of technical support cannot be underestimated.

Mainframe professionals had 20 years to write effective operating and security standards. These standards cover a number of preventive safeguards that should be adopted in the operational environment to ensure smooth operation. These range from:

- How often to change passwords.
- How often to make backups.
- What equipment should be locked up.
- Who is responsible for change control.
- Defining the standards for interconnecting between environments.

In the mainframe world it was also easy to make very large bulk purchases. Because the mainframe has been around for so long, many advanced network management systems exist that provide a high degree of support and fault isolation.

Balancing Productivity and Support Requirements for LANs

Because LAN platforms are relatively new in comparison to mainframes, there has not been as much time to develop operating and security standards. This is especially irritating to auditors when mission-critical applications move from the traditional mainframe environment onto LANs and the protective safeguards around them do not follow. Something as simple as transporting a tape backup copy of a file between LAN departments can be extremely complicated without standards. What if everyone buys a different type of tape backup unit? Without standards on what type of equipment to use, bulk purchases of equipment become difficult or impossible.

Even though major improvements have been made in network management systems over the past five years, the management systems associated with LANs often lag behind those associated with mainframe computers. Again, this causes the company to pay penalties in the area of maintenance and ease of use.

One answer, of course, is to force users into rigid standards. Although this pays a handsome dividend in the area of support, it stifles the users' productivity. They need equipment well suited to their core business purpose.

An alternative is to let users install whatever they want. This may increase productivity greatly, though it is doubtful that a company could ever hire and support enough people to maintain this type of configuration. Worse, mission-critical applications could be damaged or lost altogether if users are not expected to take reasonable and prudent safeguards for their protection.

It is the responsibility of both users and technical staff to find the middle ground between the regimented mainframe environment and the seat-of-the-pants LAN environment. Through careful planning, it is possible to configure a set of standards that offers the advantage of greater productivity that is afforded by LANs, but also the advantages learned through 20 years of mainframe operations in the areas of support, bulk purchases, and network management.

The remainder of this chapter concentrates on exactly what constitutes reasonable operating and security procedures for both LANs and telecommunications.

STANDARDS COMMITTEES

One method for establishing LAN standards is through the formation of a communications and LAN operating and security standards committee. An ideal size for a standards committee would be 10 to 12 people, with representatives from sales, marketing, engineering, support, technical services

I. Objective: Defining Mission Critical

   1. For Non-Mission-Critical Support Systems
   2. For Mission-Critical Support Systems

II. Physical Security

   1. For Non-Mission-Critical
   2. For Mission-Critical

III. Operational Support Issues

   1. Standards for All LAN and Telecommunications Installations
   2. Documentation Standards for Software and Application
   3. Server and PBX Class-of-Service Indicator Backups

IV. Access Control

   1. Procedures for Passwords

V. Change Control Policy and Procedures

VI. Virus Protection Procedures

VII. Disaster Recovery Procedures

   1. For Non-Mission-Critical Equipment
   2. For Mission-Critical Equipment

Exhibit 22.1. Sample table of contents for operating and security standards document

---

(including LANs), IS and telecommunications, and other departments. It is important to broaden this committee to include not only technical staff, but also people engaged in the core business, since enhancement of productivity will be a key concern.

The actual standards document that this committee produces must deal with issues for both the operation and protection of a company's automated platforms. Exhibit 22.1 provides a working table of contents from which to begin to write a document. Subjects include

- Basic physical standards, including access to equipment rooms where PBX equipment is kept, what type of fire protection should be employed, standards for new construction, standards for housekeeping, and standards for electrical power.
- Software security, change control, which people are authorized to make changes, and how these changes are documented.

- The security of information, such as identifying who is allowed to dial into a system, determining how to dispose of confidential materials, determining which telephone conversations should be considered private, and the company's policy on telecommunications privacy.
- Weighing options with regard to technical support of equipment.
- Resolving issues regarding interconnection standards for the telecommunications network.
- Disaster backup and recovery for both LANs and telecommunications, including defining what users must do to ensure protection of mission-critical company applications.

Defining "Mission Critical"

Before all of this, however, the committee is expected to define and understand what a mission-critical application is. Standards are designed to cover both operational and security issues, so the business processes themselves must be defined to avoid imposing a heavy burden of security on users who are not engaged in mission-critical applications, or not imposing a high enough level of security on users who are.

Standards for equipment that is not mission critical are relatively easy. In practice, this means securing the area in which the equipment resides from unauthorized access by outside persons when there is danger of tampering or theft. It also includes avoiding needless exposures to factors that could damage the equipment, such as water and combustibles, and controlling food items around the equipment, such as soft drinks and coffee.

Because of the types of functions it supports mission-critical equipment, however, has a value to the company that far exceeds the value of the equipment itself. Determination of what constitutes a mission-critical system should be made at a senior management level.

LAN and telecommunications equipment that supports an in-bound call center for companies such as the Home Shopping Club would definitely be mission-critical equipment, because disruption of the equipment, for whatever cause, would cause a financial hit to the company that far exceeds the value of the equipment. Therefore, mission-critical equipment should be defined as equipment that, if lost, would result in significant loss to the organization, measured in terms of lost sales, lost market share, lost customer confidence, or lost employee productivity.

Monetary cost is not the only mission-critical measurement. If an organization supports a poison-control line, for example, and loss of equipment means a parent cannot get through when a child is in danger, it has other implications. Because financial cost is a meaningful criteria to probably 90% of the companies, it is the measurement used for purposes of this discussion.

There is not necessarily a correlation between physical size and mission criticality. It is easy to look at a LAN of 100 people and say that it is more mission critical than another LAN that has only 4 people. However, the LAN with 100 people on it may provide purely an administrative function. The LAN with four people on it may have an important financial function.

WRITING THE OPERATING AND SECURITY STANDARDS DOCUMENT

The following approach recommends that two distinct sets of standards be created for mission-critical vs. non-mission-critical equipment.

Network Software Security and Change Control Management

One issue that should be considered in this section is the group or people who are authorized to make major changes to LAN or telecommunications equipment.

There is a good reason to consider this question. If everyone is making major changes to a system, a company is inviting disaster, because there is little communication concerning who changed what and whether these changes are compatible with changes made by another person. Standards should therefore include a list of persons authorized to make major changes to a mission-critical technical system. It should also have procedures for changing passwords on a regular basis, for both the maintenance and operation functions of LANs and telecommunications. Procedures should be defined that mandate a back-up before major changes in order to have something to fall back on in case anything goes wrong.

Procedures should be established to include DISA (direct inward system access). Unauthorized use of DISA lines is a major cause of telecommunications fraud or theft of long-distance services. Automated attendants, for example, should also be secured and telephone credit cards properly managed. As a minimum, establish a procedure that cancels remote access and telephone credit to employees who leave the company.

Physical and Environmental Security

There should be a set of basic, physical standards for all installations, regardless of their mission-critical status. These might include use of a UPS (uninterruptible power supply) on any LAN server. A UPS not only guards against loss of productivity when the lights flicker, but also cleans up the power somewhat and protects the equipment itself.

There should be standards for physically protecting the equipment, because LAN equipment is frequently stolen and because there is a black market for PBX cards as well. There should be general housekeeping standards as far as prohibitions against eating and drinking in equipment areas and properly disposing of confidential materials through shredding or other means. No-smoking policies should be included. Standards for control of combustibles or flammables in the vicinity of equipment should also be written.

Physical standards for mission-critical applications are more intensive. These might include sign-in logs for visitors requiring access to equipment rooms. They may require additional physical protection, such as sprinkler systems or fire extinguishers. They may require general improvements to the building, such as building fire-resistant walls. They should also include protection against water from drains, building plumbing, sprinklers, roof leaks, or other sources, since this a frequent cause of disruption.

Technical Support

The standards committee ideally should provide a forum for users to display new technologies and subject them to a technical evaluation. For example, LAN managers or end users may find a new, innovative use of technology that promises to greatly enhance productivity in their department. They can present this new technology to the standards committee for both productivity and technical evaluations. The technologist on the committee can then advise users of the feasibility of this technology; whether it will create an undue maintenance burden, for example, or whether it is difficult to support.

If it is found that this equipment does indeed increase productivity and that it does not create an undue maintenance burden, it could be accepted by the committee and added to a list of supported services and vendors that is underwritten by the committee. Other issues include what level of support users are required to provide for themselves, what the support level of the help desk should be, and more global issues, such as interconnection standards for a corporate backbone network and policies on virus protection.

CONCLUSION

The LAN operating and securities standards document is designed to be an organization's system of government regarding the conduct and operation of technical platforms supporting the business. A properly written standards document includes input from departments throughout the organization, both to enhance productivity and to keep expenses for procurement, maintenance, and support under control. Standards also ensure that appropriate preventive safeguards are undertaken, especially for mission-critical equipment, to avoid undue loss of productivity, profitability, or equity to the company in the event something goes wrong. In other words, they are designed to prevent disruptions.

Use of a LAN operating and security standards committee is advised to ensure that critical issues are decided by a group of people with wide exposure within the company and to increase ownership of the final document throughout the organization. If properly defined, the standards document will accommodate the advantages of the mainframe environment and needs of LAN administrators by finding the middle ground between these operating environments. By writing and adopting effective standards, an organization can enjoy the productivity afforded by modern LAN environments while at the same time enjoying a high level of support afforded through more traditional environments.

Exhibit 22.1 listed examples of typical standards for LAN installations. It is recommended that readers use them as a baseline for developing their own standards documents.

Chapter 23
Virtual Networking Management and Planning

Trenton Waterhouse

FROM THE USER'S PERSPECTIVE, a virtual network is a data communications system that provides access control and network configuration changes using software control. It functions like a traditional network but is built using switches.

The switched virtual network offers all the performance of the bridge with the value of the router. The constraints of physical networking are removed by the logical intelligence that structures and enforces policies of operation to ensure stability and security. Regardless of access technology or geographic location, any-to-any communications is the goal.

The switch could be considered a third-generation internetworking device. First-generation devices, or bridges, offered a high degree of performance throughput but relatively little value, because the bridge's limited decision intelligence resulted in broadcast storms that produced network instability. Routers, the second generation of internetworking devices, increased network reliability and offered great value with firewalling capabilities, but the trade-off was in performance. When routers are used in combination with each other, bandwidth suffers, which is detrimental for delay-sensitive applications such as multimedia.

THE BUSINESS CASE FOR VIRTUAL NETWORKING

Both the business manager and the technical manager should find interest in this new virtual networking scheme. The business manager is usually interested in cost-of-ownership issues. Numerous studies from organizations such as the Gartner Group and Forrester Research have found that only 20% of networking costs are associated with capital equipment acquisition. The other 80% of annual budgets are dedicated to items such as wide area networking charges, personnel, training, maintenance and vendor support, as well as the traditional equipment moves, adds, and changes.

It is important for IS managers to remember that capital expenditure happens in year one, even though the equipment may be operating for another four years. Wide area network (WAN) charges can account for up to 40% of an organization's networking budget. For every dollar that the technical staff spends on new equipment, another four dollars is spent on the operation of that equipment. Therefore, focus should be on the cost-of-ownership issues, not necessarily the cost of the network devices.

Network Reliability

Business managers are also looking for increased reliability as the network plays a major role in the core operations of the organization. Networks have become a business tool to gain competitive advantage — they are mission critical and, much like a utility, must provide a highly reliable and available means of communications. Every office today includes an electrical outlet, a phone jack, and a network connection. Electrical and phone service are generally regarded as stable utilities that can be relied on daily. Networks, however, do not always provide comparable levels of service.

Network Accountability

Managers also can benefit from the increased accountability that virtual networks are able to offer. Organizational networking budgets can range from hundreds of thousands of dollars to hundreds of millions per year. Accounting for the use of the network that consumes those funds is a critical issue. There is no better example than WAN access charges. Remote site connectivity can consume a great deal of the budget, and the questions of who, what, when, and where with regard to network use are impossible to determine. Most users consider the network to be free, and the tools to manage and account for its use are increasingly a requirement, not an option.

THE TECHNOLOGY CASE FOR VIRTUAL NETWORKING

The IS manager's needs for higher capacity, greater performance, and increased efficiency can be met through the deployment of switched virtual networks. Each user is offered dedicated bandwidth to the desktop with uplinks of increasing bandwidth to servers or other enterprise networks. Rather than contending for bandwidth in shared access environments, all users are provided with their own private link. This degree of privacy allows for increased security because data are sent only to intended recipients, rather than seen by all.

The most attractive feature to the technical manager, however, may be the benefits gained through increased ease of operation and administration of virtual networks. A long-standing objective has been to deliver network services to users without continually having to reconfigure the devices that make up that network. Furthermore, many of the costs associated with moves, adds, and changes of users can be alleviated as the constraints of physical networking are removed. Regardless of user location, they can remain part of the same virtual network. Through the use of graphical tools, users are added and deleted from work groups. In the same manner, policies of operation and security filters can be applied. In a sense, the virtual network accomplishes the goal of managing the individual users and individual conversations, rather than the devices that make up the network.

VIRTUAL NETWORKING DEFINED

The ideal virtual network does not restrict access to a particular topology or protocol. A virtual network that can only support Ethernet users with Transmission Control Protocol/Internet Protocol (TCP/IP) applications is limited. The ultimate virtual network allows any-to-any connectivity between Ethernet, Token Ring, Fiber Distributed Data Interface (FDDI), Asynchronous Transfer Mode (ATM), Internet Protocol (IP), Internetwork Packet Exchange (IPX), AppleTalk, or Systems Network Architecture (SNA) networks. A single virtual network infrastructure under a single management architecture is the goal.

Network management software becomes a key enabling requirement for the construction of switched virtual networks. The greatest challenge network designers face is the separation of the physical network connectivity from the logical connection services it can provide. Many of the design issues associated with networks can be attributed to the physical parameters of protocols and the routers used as the interconnection device. A challenge for any manager is to remain compatible with existing layer 3 protocols and routers and still preserve the investment in existing local area network (LAN) equipment to the greatest extent possible.

Using Telephony as a Model

The principles of operation for switched virtual networks are concretely founded in the success of the global communications systems. Without doubt, the phone system is the world's largest and most reliable network. Built using advanced digital switches controlled by software, extensive accounting and management tools ensure the success of this highly effective means of communication. The connection-oriented switch is the key. End-to-end connections across multiple switches and various transmission types ranging from copper to fiber optics to microwave to satellites allow millions of calls per day to be successfully completed, regardless of the type of phone or from where the user is calling. The telephony model is used throughout this chapter to help illustrate the workings of a virtual network.

SWITCHING DEFINED

One of the more confusing terms in the networking industry today is the word *switch*. For the purpose of this chapter, switching can be broken down into three fundamental areas:

- Configuration switching.
- Packet switching.
- Cell switching.

The earliest form of switching enabled the network manager to assign an individual port or an entire group of ports to a particular backplane segment within an intelligent hub device. This port configuration switching allowed the logical grouping of users onto a particular segment without the need to physically travel to the wiring closet to move cables or connectors. In a sense, this offers an electronic patch panel function. Although the benefit is a reduction of moves, adds, and change costs, this advantage can only be realized within the confines of a single hub. The application of this type of switching is limited because it cannot extend beyond one intelligent concentrator. Although beneficial in the work group, the enterprise needs cannot be met.

Phone system operators in the 1940s manually patched user connections through to destinations and recorded call time and duration. Using configuration switching is similar to patching phone lines together. Just as the phone network grew at a pace that required the switching to be performed automatically without operator intervention, so too have data networks outgrown the limitations of configuration switching.

Packet switching isolates each port to deliver dedicated bandwidth to each user in the network. Fundamentally, a packet switch is any device that accepts an incoming packet on one port and then makes a decision whether to filter or forward the packet out another interface. There are two types of packet switch transports: connectionless and connection-oriented.

Connectionless Packet Switching

Connectionless devices are probably more familiar to IS professionals when described as bridges or routers. A bridge is a layer 2 (of the Open Systems Interconnection [OSI] reference model) switch that bases its decisions on the media access control (MAC) address of attached work stations. What many vendors describe as a switch is actually a wire-speed MAC layer bridge. Three methods of decision making in these types of devices are cut-through, modified cut-through, and store-and-forward.

The Cut-Through Switch. This switch reads a packet only until the destination address before it starts forwarding to the outbound interface. The benefit is an extremely low latency or delay in the forwarding of packets. The penalty is the propagation of errors, because the frame is being forwarded before it can be verified as valid, and the inability to support interfaces of different speeds that prevent high-bandwidth uplinks of FDDI or ATM on these type of devices.

The Modified Cut-Through Switch. This switch reads the first 64 bytes of a frame and then starts forwarding to the outbound interface, which greatly reduces the chances of propagating errored frames throughout the network. However, this method still requires all ports to be of the same type and speed.

Store-and-Forward Switch. The most flexible switch design uses a store-and-forward methodology that reads the entire frame before any filtering or forwarding decisions are made, thus ensuring that only packets that are error free are forwarded on the network. This method also allows packets to be buffered when transferring data between networks of different types, such as Ethernet to FDDI or ATM.

Bridges and Routers. A router is a layer 3 switch that bases its decisions on the network protocol address of attached work stations. Bridges and routers are considered connectionless because they forward and forget, requiring a decision to be made on every single inbound packet. The performance implications are that even though two communicating nodes on opposite sides of a bridge or router may be the only devices on their respective networks, the bridge or router must continuously make filter or forward decisions on every packet sent between the two nodes.

A connectionless transport is not capable of defining which path its payload will take, cannot guarantee delivery, and is generally slower than a connection-oriented system. When a node sends a packet through a bridged or routed network, it is analogous to dropping a letter into a mailbox. It is not apparent how the letter got to its destination. The arrival of a letter cannot be guaranteed (protocol prioritization techniques are comparable to sending a letter by express mail). If a letter is lost (or a packet dropped), determining where it was lost is often difficult. The only way the sender knows that the letter was received is if the recipient sends another letter back to the sender (i.e., frame acknowledgment).

In a sense, today's shared-access networks are like the party lines of the early telephone network. But just as the phone network evolved from party lines to dedicated lines as usage and deployment grew, so too must the data networks offer this same level of service guarantee and broad adoption.

Connection-Oriented Switches

The connection-oriented switch that the phone systems use offers immediate acknowledgment of communications when the person picks up at the other end. The exact path the call took as well as its time and duration can be logged. The destination needs to be dialed only once and information is exchanged until both parties hang up.

The idea of connection-oriented communications is not new. This type of switching provides a high degree of reliability and reduces operational costs. Multiple classes of service can be defined to support voice, video, and data transfer. Excellent bandwidth management through congestion control techniques is possible and security and access control are greatly improved. Connection-oriented switching, along with easy-to-implement policy-based management and accounting facilities, have enabled the phone system to become universally accessible.

Frame relay technology is centered around connection-oriented communications, as is the most promising future networking technology — ATM. ATM is the most desirable networking technology because it offers dedicated, scalable bandwidth solutions for voice, video, and data.

ATM Switching. ATM switching is connection-oriented. Communications in an ATM network can be broken down into three phases: call setup (analogous to dialing a phone), data transfer (talking on the phone), and call teardown (hanging up the phone). The use of fixed-length 53-byte cells for data transfer delivers fixed latency transfer times for constant bit rate applications such as voice and video. ATM addressing schemes are similar to a telephone number. In fact, the original designers of ATM technology had their roots in the telephony arena, so many analogies to the operation of the phone system can be made when referring to an ATM network.

Although the benefits of ATM networking are attractive, there are currently nearly 100 million networked personal computers that do not have ATM interfaces. Few organizations can afford to replace all of their existing desktop and server interfaces, not to mention network analyzers and troubleshooting equipment.

Through the preservation of existing interface technology, by merely changing the internetworking devices from being connectionless to connection oriented, many of the benefits of ATM may be realized without requiring the investment in all new ATM equipment. If LANs were designed to operate using the same principles as ATM, rather than making ATM compatible with LANs, users would benefit without significant capital investments in new equipment. By adding switching technology to the middle of the network, network administrators can be spared the trouble of upgrading numerous user devices, and users can be spared the inconvenience of rewiring and disruptions at their work site during an upgrade.

FEATURES OF SWITCHING SOFTWARE

The software that runs on switches is just as important as the switches themselves. A salesperson from Lucent Technologies, Fujitsu, or Northern Telecom does not focus the potential customer on the hardware aspects of the telephone switches. On the contrary, the salesperson conveys the benefits of the call management software, accounting, and automatic call distributor (ACD) functions. Switched virtual networks should also be evaluated for their ability to deliver value because of the software features.

The Virtual Network Server

Network management software has traditionally been thought of as software that passively reports the status and operation of devices in the network. In the switched virtual network, the network management software takes on a new role as an active participant in operations as well as configuration and reporting. A new middleware component known as the virtual network server (VNS) enforces the policies of operation defined by the network administrator through management software applications. The switches provide the data transport for the users of the network.

Directory Service. One of the software features in the VNS is the directory service. The directory service allows the identification of a device by logical name, MAC address, network protocol address, and ATM address, along with the switch and port that the user is connected to within the virtual network domain. The directory listing could be populated manually or dynamically as addresses are discovered. To fully realize the benefits of switched virtual networking, automatic configuration is absolutely essential. The directory service allows end nodes to be located and identified.

Security Service. The VNS security service will be used during call setup phases to determine whether users or groups of users were allowed to connect to each other. On a user-by-user and conversation-by-conversation basis, the network manager would have control. This communications policy management is analogous to call management on a telephone private branch exchange (PBX) where 900 numbers, long-distance, or international calls can be blocked. Users could be grouped together to form policy groups in which rules could be applied to individual users, groups, or even nested groups. Policies could be defined as open or secure, inclusive or exclusive.

A sample default policy can ensure that all communications are specifically defined to the VNS in order to be authorized. Policy groups can be manipulated either through drag-and-drop graphical user interfaces or programatically through simple network management protocol (SNMP) commands.

Finally, and most important, the directory service can work in conjunction with the security service to ensure that policies follow the users as they move throughout the network. This feature alone could save time spent maintaining a router access list, as occurs when a user changes location in the traditional network. However, it is important to realize that switched virtual networks ease administrative chores, they do not eliminate them.

Connection Management Service. The VNS connection management service is used to define the path communications would take through the switch fabric. A site may be linked by a relatively high-speed ATM link and a parallel but relatively low-speed Ethernet link. Network connections with a defined high quality of service (QOS) could traverse the ATM link and lower QOS connections could traverse the Ethernet. This connection management service allows for the transparent rerouting of calls in the event of a network fault. Connection management could also provide ongoing network monitoring in which individual user conversations could be tapped or traced for easy troubleshooting.

Bandwidth Service. The VNS bandwidth service is used during the call setup when a connection request is made. Video teleconferencing users may require a committed information rate (CIR) of 10 Mbps whereas the terminal emulation users may only require 1 Mbps. This is where ATM end stations and ATM switches negotiate the amount of bandwidth dedicated to a particular virtual circuit using user-to-network interface (UNI) signaling. Ethernet, Token Ring, and FDDI nodes do not recognize UNI signaling, but the switches they attach to could proxy the signal for the end station, thus allowing a single bandwidth manager for the entire network, not just the ATM portion.

Broadcast Service. The VNS broadcast service uses as its base the concept of the broadcast unknown server (BUS) that is part of the ATM Forum's LAN emulation draft standard. This is how broadcasts are flooded through the network to remain compatible with the operation of many of today's protocols and network operating systems. A degree of intelligence can be assigned to the VNS that would allow for broadcasts or multicasts based on protocol type or even policy group.

Virtual Routing Service. The VNS virtual routing service is one of the most critical components of a virtual network. Just as traditional networks required traditional routers for interconnection, virtual LANs will require virtual routers for internetworking between virtual LANs. In other words, routing is required, but routers may not be. Some protocols such as TCP/IP actually require a router for users on two different subnetworks to speak with each other. In addition, most networks today are logically divided based on network layer protocol addresses with routers acting as the building block between segments.

The difference in operation between a virtual router and a traditional router goes back to the connection-oriented vs. connectionless distinction. Routing allows for address resolution between the layer 3 protocol address and the layer 2 MAC address just as it happens through the address resolution protocol (ARP) process in TCP/IP networks. The VNS virtual routing service performs the address resolution function, but once the end station addresses are resolved, establishes a virtual connection between the two users. Two users separated by a traditional router would always have the router intervening on every single packet because the router would have resolved the protocol addresses to its own MAC address rather than the actual end station's MAC address. This VNS routing service allows the network to route once for connection setup and switch all successive packets.

Accounting Service. The VNS accounting service is beneficial because it allows the creation of the network bill. Similar to the way a telephone bill is broken down, the accounting service details connection duration with date and time stamp along with bandwidth consumption details. This is most directly applicable in the WAN. For many managers, WAN usage is never really accounted for on an individual user basis, yet it can consume up to 40% of the operations budget.

As usage-based WAN service options such as integrated services digital network (ISDN) gain popularity, accounting becomes that much more critical. Interexchange carriers (IXCs), competitive access providers, and the regional Bell operating companies (RBOCs) continue to deliver higher-bandwidth links with usage-based tariffs. In the future, they could install a 155 Mbps synchronous optical network (SONET) OC-3 link and only charge for the actual bandwidth used. Unless managers have tools to control access to and account for usage of WAN links, WAN costs will continue to rise. This service lets IS managers know who is using the WAN.

VIRTUAL NETWORKS VS. VIRTUAL LANS

Throughout this discussion, words have been carefully chosen to describe the operation of switched virtual networks. Many of the current vendor offerings on the market have as their goal the construction of a switched virtual LAN. These virtual LANs are interconnected using a traditional router device. However, the router has been viewed as the performance bottleneck. Routers should be deployed when segmentation or separation is the need; switches should be used to deliver more bandwidth. The virtual LAN (VLAN) concept is merely an interim step along the way to realizing the fully virtual network.

The ATM Forum's draft LAN emulation standard allows ATM devices to internetwork with traditional LAN networks such as Ethernet and Token Ring. However, it seems ironic that it essentially tries to make ATM networks operate like a traditional shared-access LAN segment. Although it is required for near-term deployment of ATM solutions into existing LAN architectures, its position as an end-all solution is questionable. A more logical approach uses ATM as the model that LANs must emulate.

CONCLUSION

Each vendor's approach to virtual networking features will vary slightly in implementation. Most vendors have agreed, however, that the router is moving to the periphery of the network and the core will be based on switching technologies with virtual network capabilities. The three critical success factors that a virtual network vendor must display to effectively deliver on all the promise of virtual networks are connectivity, internetworking, and network management.

Connectivity expertise through a demonstrated leadership in the intelligent hub industry ensures the user a broad product line with numerous options with regard to topology and media types. The product should fit the network, rather than the network design being dictated by the capability of the product. This indicates a vendor's willingness to embrace standards-based connectivity solutions as well as SNMP management and remote monitoring (RMON) analyzer capabilities.

Internetworking expertise ensures that the vendor is fully equipped to deal with layer 2 as well as layer 3 switching issues through an understanding of protocols and their operation. This is not something that can be learned overnight. The integration of these technologies is still unattainable.

Network management software is crucial — virtual networks do not exist or operate without it. The virtual network services provide all the value to the switch fabric. Users should look for a vendor that has delivered distributed management capabilities. Just as the telephone network relies on a distributed software intelligence for its operations, so too must the switched virtual network provide the same degree of redundancy and fault tolerance. Users also should consider whether the vendor embraces all of the popular network management platforms (e.g., SunNet Manager, HP OpenView, Cabletron SPECTRUM, and IBM NetView for AIX) or only one. Finally, users should make sure the vendor has experience managing multiple types of devices from vendors other than itself. It would be naive to think that all the components that make up a network are of one type from one vendor.

Chapter 24
Successful Network Implementations

Patrick McBrayer

TECHNOLOGY REFRESH is a very familiar term in today's organizations, especially when talking about network infrastructures. The lifecycle of today's average network infrastructure is only four to six years. The need for these network infrastructure changes is driven by application requirements. Switching from mainframe-based applications and terminal emulators to high-bandwidth client/server solutions and imaging technology significantly increases the demands put on the network infrastructure. Networks that are four years old or more and built using shared Ethernet, FDDI, or even switched 10/100 Mbps Ethernet technologies are not prepared to support these growing application demands. Therefore, corporations are looking for higher speed technologies that will scale to support their current and future application requirements.

The key to increasing the network lifecycle is conducting a comprehensive and successful network infrastructure selection and implementation. Experience will dictate the following four steps:

- Technology selection.
- Product selection.
- Contract negotiation.
- Testing and installation.

The technology selection must be focused on providing support for current and future application requirements. The product selection process involves selecting vendors to provide the products and services necessary to implement this technology. The contract negotiation process involves negotiating a contract that protects a company's time and resource investments, and testing and installation involve a thorough testing of a solution and well-designed installation plan that protects against user downtime and disruption. This chapter will provide some suggestions for completing these four phases of an implementation and includes some real-world examples to illustrate the processes.

0-8493-9820-7/00/$0.00+$.50
© 2000 by CRC Press LLC

TECHNOLOGY SELECTION

Selecting the appropriate technology for a network infrastructure requires analyzing the network requirements of current applications and future business plans. These requirements should be mapped to the bandwidth and functionality of available network infrastructure technologies. The trends toward client/server, thin client, imaging, and multimedia applications are considerably increasing the demand for bandwidth and functionality. These demands are driving implementations of leading edge network technologies such as Asynchronous Transfer Mode (ATM) and switched Gigabit Ethernet.

Choosing between ATM and Gigabit Ethernet is a common decision facing today's organization, with many convincing reasons for each technology. This chapter will not attempt to determine which technology is best for a particular organization; it will, however, identify some key decision-making criteria.

These decision criteria include scalability, maturity, complexity, functionality, and cost. Exhibit 24.1 provides a high level description of how each of these technologies supports these decision criteria.

Over the past several years, ATM appeared to be evolving as the dominant technology because of its scalability and functionality. However, many organizations have been turned off by the complexities of ATM, and have been turning to high-speed Ethernet as an alternative.

VENDOR SELECTION

The process for selecting a network electronics vendor should be similar to any vendor selection methodology. Typically, vendor selection is broken into two phases: narrowing to a short list of vendors and the final vendor selection.

Vendor Short List

The short list for network electronics vendors should be limited to those who actually have a working solution that supports the network requirements and selected technologies of the organization. In addition, these vendors should support the latest industry standards for the selected technology. With an ATM solution, the vendor should support LANE 2.0, UNI 4.0, and MPOA. With a switched Ethernet solution, the vendor should support Gigabit Ethernet, RSVP, 802.1 p/q, high-speed routing or cut-through switching. Proven support for these technologies and standards will limit the risks of selecting a vendor that cannot provide a successful solution.

As these technologies progress, new standards will be developed that will improve quality of service and efficiency of network infrastructures.

Decision Criteria	ATM Support	Gigabit Ethernet Support
Scalability	ATM is a scalable technology that currently supports 1.5, 45, 155, 622, 1200, and 2400 Mbps transmission speeds.	Ethernet technologies support 10, 100, and 1000 Mbps transmission speeds.
Maturity	ATM has been a growing technology for the past 10 years; standards have, however, been slow to mature and adoption of this technology has also been slow.	Ethernet technologies are very mature and have been widely adopted. Gigabit Ethernet has recently been standardized using similar technology.
Complexity	ATM is more complex than traditional Ethernet, Token Ring, and FDDI networks, and requires significant training to build an effective support organization.	Gigabit Ethernet is based on similar technologies as 10 and 100Mbps Ethernet. Many organizations are familiar with this technology and therefore, will require less training.
Functionality	ATM promises advanced functionality for quality of service for voice, data, and video transmissions. In addition, ATM is the primary Wide Area Network technology and end to end ATM should increase performance.	New standards are being developed to provide quality of service over Gigabit Ethernet including RSVP, 802.1 p/q and high-speed routing solutions. However, Ethernet's variable size packets and connectionless orientation may limit overall quality of service.
Cost	The cost of an ATM solution will vary based on the selected vendor. Vendors who are pushing ATM solutions have reduced their prices to compete with Gigabit Ethernet prices. Vendors who are pushing Gigabit Ethernet solutions have much higher ATM prices.	The cost for a Gigabit Ethernet solution is typically less than the equivalent ATM solution. Gigabit Ethernet is also newer technology and prices will continue to drop as implementation grows.

Exhibit 24.1. Decision Criteria

Therefore, it is important to limit this short list to vendors that have a long-term commitment to the selected technology. For example, there are several vendors that can provide ATM solutions, but whose primary research and development focus is on high-speed Ethernet solutions. If an organization is committed to ATM, it should ensure that vendors on its short list will continue to support leading edge ATM standards.

Final Vendor Selection

This involves selecting a vendor as a business partner to provide a solution that benefits both the company and the vendor. The selection criteria should be similar to any vendor selection and include previous investment, vendor relationships, cost, product availability, and product scalability. Most of these criteria are common practice and specific to an organization's environment. In addition to such standard evaluation criteria, special attention should be given to vendor product line, product availability, and installation and support services.

Selecting a vendor with a primary product line that fits your environment is a key success factor. Currently, vendors can be grouped into three categories:

- Vendors who support ATM as the primary backbone technology and high speed Ethernet as an edge technology.
- Vendors who support high speed Ethernet as the primary backbone technology and limit ATM to the Wide Area Network.
- Vendors who support both ATM and high speed Ethernet as a backbone technology and build solutions based on customer requirements.

It is critical to make sure the selected vendor will continue to support industry advances in the chosen technologies.

Product availability and product lifecycle are other very important decision criteria. A vendor usually cycles through a core product line every 3 to 5 years. An organization should not invest in a product at the end of this cycle because it may shortly become obsolete. However, an organization may not want to purchase product at the early stages of this cycle because it has not been installed and proven. Vendor selection should include careful analysis of the product lifecycle to identify the appropriate balance of risk from early product cycles and obsolescence of late product cycles. If an early product lifecycle is desired, it is important to be aware of the technology industry's history of announcing product availability well before the equipment is tested or released. Make sure the vendor has a solution that is actually in production, particularly if a product is in the Beta stage or is not yet shipping.

Installation and support services are very important when implementing new technologies like ATM or Gigabit Ethernet. Even if the installation is planned in-house (a decision that should be made with strong caution), extensive support services will likely be necessary to help troubleshoot any problems that occur. The arrangement for installation and support services can be negotiated in the contract; however, a vendor that has an internal support organization is better equipped than a vendor that relies on third-party vendors to provide their support for new product lines.

There is no "best" vendor; this depends on your environment. Using these selection criteria and mapping them to your organizational needs is the only way to determine the best vendor for your organization.

CONTRACT NEGOTIATIONS

There are several parts of a contract that must be negotiated. Most vendors have standard contracts, but those contracts are made to protect the vendor rather than the needs of the customer. Issues that should be ironed out in a contract are cost, installation and support services, installation timelines, and testing.

Cost must be negotiated based on the quantity of product purchased, the vendor, and the customer. These days, no one should pay list price for equipment; the percentage under list price generally varies between 15% and 50%. Some items can be sold at a higher discount rate for various reasons, such as an arrangement allowing the vendor to use your site as a reference or a marketing site. Additional discounts may also be available if you are implementing leading-edge technology and the vendor needs an early success story to increase its market share.

Installation and support services are always important when implementing new products. When requesting the vendor to install the equipment it is important to make sure they have adequate resources to support your project timeline. Even product manufacturers have a limited supply of ATM and Gigabit Ethernet resources, so the commitment for them needs to be made up front. When planning to do the implementation internally, support should be built into the contract with guaranteed response times. With new technologies, the vendor may be the only source for technical support, which heightens the need for advance arrangements.

Installation timelines go hand in hand with installation services. If the vendor is providing the product and installation services, the vendor can be held accountable for the project timeline. Extended project deadlines result in additional cost and resources to the customer; therefore, adding this to the contract transfers some responsibility and accountability to the vendor.

Testing is another component that should be included in the contract. Vendors usually do not like to include the actual test plan in the contract because that limits the flexibility of the test plan as the installation moves forward. This is acceptable, but at a minimum the test plan should be referenced and the areas of testing to be included in the plan should be defined, i.e., connectivity, interoperability, performance, management, failover, and application testing. A viable test plan should be developed and agreed to before the contract is signed. The contract should also specify that the test plan can only be changed if agreed to by all parties involved.

TESTING AND INSTALLATION

Until this point, most work has been vendor related, including the detailed network design based on how the product should work. This may or may not have included a site visit to see some of the equipment working in a production environment, but the customer probably has not seen the exact design being purchased working in a production environment. This is why the testing and implementation phase of the project is the most critical to the success of the roll-out. User disruption and downtime must be minimized for the project to be a success.

Testing

At this stage, experience in this area is critical; it is important to know where the potential for problems exists and what to look for in the testing phase to mitigate these potential problems. When Kaiser Permanente Health Plan of Georgia implemented its ATM network to support over 3000 users, a thorough test plan mitigated several problems with file server connectivity and application compatibility that saved days of downtime for the users. The test plan for an ATM implementation should be similar to any other technologies and include several phases. The phases should include pre-installation testing, post-installation testing, post cut-over testing, and operational testing.

Pre-installation testing tests the equipment as designed in a mock production environment. This should uncover any incompatibilities in the network electronics and network applications. Post-installation testing is done after the actual implementation of the equipment, but before cutting users onto the system. It should include performance and fail-over tests on the components that have been installed. Post cut-over testing can be done by the users or installation team and involves actual testing of applications on the end-user devices. Operational testing is done for a designated amount of time after cutting over users onto the new system to insure proper performance and availability.

When developing a detailed test plan that includes these phases for a high-speed network infrastructure installation, there are several areas of functionality that should be covered. Note that there is quite a bit of inconsistency across vendors and products within the following areas of ATM and Gigabit Ethernet functionality. These should be included in your test plan:

- *Application Testing* — Test all applications that use the network in any way. This includes applications loading from a network file server, using network resources, initiating a Telnet session, etc. In one ATM network implementation project, all applications worked except a LAB application that loaded a terminal emulation session from an ATM-attached Novell file server and initiated a Telnet session with a UNIX host. The ATM-attached file server loaded the session so quickly the application saw a delay in the response from the Unix server, which was across a T1 link. This Telnet application was not robust enough to handle that delay and would lock up the end-user device. Upgrading the Telnet application fixed the problem. In this example it is easy to see how even implementing a properly working solution can cause problems in a particular environment.

- *Connectivity Testing* — Test the connectivity of all network-attached devices. This is especially critical for ATM network implementations because it is a connection-oriented protocol. In order for two devices to communicate in an ATM network, a connection must be established through the LAN Emulation Server (LES). When that connection has no traffic for twenty minutes, it is taken down until another connection is established. Because ATM is connection oriented and takes these extra steps to provide connectivity, it is important to simulate a test environment that requires setting up and breaking down connections between all ATM equipment. In one project, the organization experienced incompatibility with the ATM switch LAN Emulation (LANE) code and the ATM card in the file server. The connections would establish without a problem, but after 20 minutes of inactivity, the connection would time-out in the file server ATM card but not in the ATM switch. This confused the ATM switch and the next time the file server wanted to communicate, it would not establish a connection. This type of problem can easily slip by in a lab environment if not specifically tested.

- *Virtual LAN and One-Armed Router Testing* — This test is appropriate for ATM and high speed Ethernet implementations. Test the capability to dynamically establish Virtual LANs and perform routing between virtual LANs through one connection to a router. Virtual LAN technology is a popular technology for ATM and Ethernet implementations. It allows users to be grouped into logical broadcast domains regardless of where they are geographically or physically located. This technology becomes very attractive when it is coupled with a connection in a router that can be assigned to multiple virtual LANs, allowing the router to have one high-speed connection to all virtual LANs. This technology has been an ATM standard for a couple of years but Ethernet support for this technology has recently been standardized. Because of this it deserves special attention during the testing process. A simple way to test a broadcast domain is to attach a sniffer to a virtual LAN port on the test network and broadcast traffic. One can see by the lights on most switches which ports are seeing that traffic. Then, by dynamically moving that port to separate virtual networks, one can test each network that has been established.

- *ATM and Gigabit File Servers* — If high-speed cards are being implemented in the file servers -whether it be Novell, NT, or some other operating system — it is critical to test extensively before implementation. This is the one area where many problems are not visible before a network is brought up in a production environment. In one case, problems in this area caused several hours of downtime before technicians could change the server back to 10Mbps Ethernet cards. In this case, the problem only occurred in the morning when more than 100 users came to work and turned on their work stations at nearly the same time. The high-speed card could not establish the connections quickly enough and could not handle the failed connections. This caused the server to stop communicating with the outside world and eventually lock up. The vendor was eventually able to get the original card to work by modifying the drivers but, during this time, technicians experimented with several high-speed cards and found problems with each one that was tried. It may be impossible to simulate 100 work stations in your environment; one option is to ask for references and do as much load testing as possible.
- *Redundancy Testing* — Testing the redundancy of the network design and individual components is very important for all network technologies. This should include simple things like testing redundant power supplies and controller modules, as well as testing complex things such as redundant switching fabrics and redundant network architectures. Testing redundancy is even more important when dealing with a new technology that is in high demand, because new technologies typically have more defective parts and it can be difficult to get replacements. The specific testing described above should be included whenever applicable, across every phase of the testing process. Depending on the specific network design, one will probably want to incorporate some other tests that would make sense for the particular environment. The importance of a thorough test plan to a successful implementation that minimizes user disruption and downtime cannot be stressed enough.

The Installation Plan

It is very important to carefully plan out the installation of a network infrastructure. Providing contingency plans throughout every phase of the installation is a must. However, even the most carefully thought-out test plan will not catch every problem experienced, and mitigating those problems as fast as possible is a must. In order to follow the phases of the test plan described above, several phases must be included in the installation plan as well. These phases include installation, cut-over, and system acceptance.

Installation. The installation phase is simply installing a portion of the network and connecting the components to the rest of the network. This provides a live burn-in and testing environment where the installation testing phase of the test plan can be performed. This is the last chance to troubleshoot problems without affecting the users.

Cut-Over. The cut-over phase is when the users migrate over to the new network. This would preferably be done after hours, providing an opportunity to perform cut-over testing before users are actually accessing the network. It is a good idea at this point to leave the existing network in place, if possible; in the case of a major problem with the network, one can always move users back. Providing this type of contingency plan saved one organization several hours of downtime when there were problems found with the ATM-attached servers.

System Acceptance. The final acceptance phase of the project should be a predetermined length of time after the system cut-over. Final acceptance involves monitoring the network for performance and availability. It is a good idea to associate some portion of the vendor payment to the completion of this final acceptance period in the event there are lingering problems after system installation and cut-over.

Every network environment is different and it may not make sense to implement every step described here. However, each implementation step should be carefully planned and have a clear contingency plan to minimize user disruptions.

CONCLUSION

New client/server and imaging applications are continually increasing demands on network infrastructures. Companies are looking for ways to implement scalable technologies that can maximize the network lifecycle. Furthermore, companies are demanding seamless integration of voice, data, and video on these networks to reduce costs and increase functionality. Implementation of these advanced technologies will increase risks of user disruption and network downtime. Following a comprehensive network implementation plan that includes a technology selection, vendor selection, contract negotiation, and testing and implementation will increase the chances of a successful network implementation that minimizes user disruptions.

Chapter 25
Integrating Electronic Messaging Systems and Infrastructures

Dale Cohen

IMPLEMENTING A MESSAGING SYSTEM infrastructure requires taking small steps while keeping the big picture in mind. The complexity of the endeavor is directly affected by the scope of the project.

If the goal is to implement an integrated system for a larger enterprise, multiple departments may need to communicate with their external customers and suppliers. The solution could implement a messaging backbone or central messaging switch. This approach allows the implementers to deploy common points to sort, disperse, and measure the flow of messages.

If an organization already has an infrastructure but needs to distribute it across multiple systems connected by common protocols, the goal may be to make the aggregate system more manageable and gain economies of scale. Implementations can vary widely, from getting something up and running to reducing the effort and expense of running the current system.

HOW TO ACCOMPLISH ROLLOUT AND MANAGE CONSTRAINTS

Messaging is a unique application because it crosses all the networks, hardware platforms, network operating systems, and application environments in the organization. Plenty of cooperation will be necessary to accomplish a successful rollout. The traditional constraints are time, functionality, and resources, though implementers must also manage user perceptions.

Resource Constraints: Expertise

It is easy to underestimate the expertise required to operate an efficient messaging infrastructure. Most IT departments are easily able to handle a single application in a single operating environment. Multiple applications in multiple operating environments are a different story.

Messaging systems must be able to deal with multiple network protocols, various operating systems, and different software applications — all from different vendors. Given these facts, it is difficult to understand why already overburdened LAN administrators would take on the significant systems integration responsibilities of a messaging system rollout.

Cross-Functional Integration Teams. The most efficient way to coordinate a rollout is through cross-functional teams. It is important to incorporate e-mail implementation and support into the goals of the individuals and the teams from which they come. Many organizations do this informally, but this method is not always effective. A written goal or service level agreement is extremely helpful when conflicting priorities arise and management support is needed.

When creating the core messaging integration team, it is very helpful to include individuals from WAN and LAN networking, systems, operations, and support desk staff, in addition to the individual application experts from each e-mail environment. Data base knowledge is very useful when dealing with directories and directory synchronization. A knowledge of tool development helps automate manual processes.

Functionality and Scope

At any point in the project, network administrators may find themselves trying to implement an enterprisewide solution, a new departmental system, a corporatewide directory service, or a solution for mobile e-mail users. When building a house, it is commonly understood that the plumbing and waste systems must be installed before hooking up the bath fixtures. This is not the case with messaging.

A messaging system rollout should start with a basic infrastructure "plumbed" for future expansion, and be followed directly with reliable user functionality. Results should be monitored and measured, and original infrastructure issues should be revisited as appropriate. Project success comes with regular reports on what has been delivered and discussions of incremental improvements in reliability and services.

Supporting Internal and External Customers

To satisfy user needs, the IT department should separate internal customers from external customers. Internal customers are those who help provide a service. They may be IT management, support personnel, or networking staff — they could be considered an internal supplier.

Because of the nature of most organizations, internal customers are both customer and supplier. They need to be provided with the means to supply a service. For example, IT management may need to create step-by-step procedures for the operations staff to carry them out. If the information technology group cannot satisfy the requirements of internal customers, it probably will not be able to satisfy the needs of external customers.

External customers are the end users. If they are in sales, for example, external customers may include the enterprise's customers from other companies. It is the job of the IT staff to provide external customers with messaging features, functionality, and reliability so they can do their job.

IMPLEMENTATION MODELS AND ARCHITECTURES

It is helpful for IS managers to know how other enterprises have implemented messaging systems. The next few sections describe the various components of the infrastructure, common deployment architectures, and how to plan future deployments.

Infrastructure vs. Interface

Often messaging systems are sold with the emphasis on what the end user sees. Experienced network managers know that this is only part of the real need. The behind-the-scenes components, which make the individual systems in an organization work as a near-seamless whole, include

- Network services.
- Message transfer services.
- Directory services.
- Management and administration services.

Network Services. The network services required for a messaging rollout involve connectivity between

- Desktop and server.
- Server to server.
- Server to gateway.
- Gateway to foreign environment.

It is not unusual to have one network protocol between a desktop device and its server and a second protocol within the backbone server/gateway/router environment. Servers may communicate via WAN protocols such as TCP/IP, OSI, DECnet, or SNA, and the desktops may communicate over a LAN protocol such as IPX or NetBIOS. WAN connections may occur over continuous connections or over asynchronous dialup methods.

The network administrator's greatest concern is loss of network connectivity. It is important to understand how it happens, why it happens, how it is discovered, and what needs to be done on an application level once connectivity is restored.

If the network goes down, e-mail will be faulted. Weekly incident reports should be issued that cite direct incidents (i.e., an e-mail component failure) and indirect incidents (i.e., a network failure) as well as remote site issues (i.e., a remote site lost power). Such information can help to clarify the real environment.

Message Transfer Services. The message transfer service (also termed the message transport system) is the most visible part of the messaging infrastructure. The message transfer service is responsible for moving a message from point A to point B. This service consists of one or more message transport agents and may be extended to include gateways and routers. The most popular services are X.400 and SMTP international standards, and IBM's SNA Distributed Services (SNADS) and Novell's Message Handling Service (MHS) proprietary industry standards.

X.400. More widely used in Europe than in North America, X.400 is popular because it:

- Provides universal connectivity.
- Has a standard way of mapping features.
- Is usually run over commercial WANs so it does not have the security problems associated with the Internet.

SMTP. Simple Mail Transfer Protocol's allure is its simplicity. Addressing is easier and access to the Internet is relatively simple compared with establishing an X.400 connection. Because it is simple, there is not much that can go wrong. However, when something does go wrong, it is usually monumental.

Directory Services. The directory service is critical to a company's e-mail systems, but it is also problematic. The problems are a result of the difficulty in keeping directories up to date, resolving redundant or obsolete auto-registered entries, and failures of directory synchronization.

The directory serves both users and applications. End users choose potential recipients from a directory. The directory should list enough information for a user to distinguish between the George Smith in accounting and the George Smith in engineering. Some companies include in their directory individuals who are customers and suppliers. The ability to distinguish between internal users and external users may be even more important in these cases.

Management and Administration Services. Management refers to scheduled maintenance and automated housekeeping procedures that involve system-related tasks such as reconfiguration and file maintenance. The constant I/O on messaging components leads to disk and sometimes memory fragmentation. Regular defragmentation procedures, including repro/reorg, tidy procedures, and checkstat and reclaim, are required. Whatever the environment, such procedures should be done more often than is recommended to prevent problems from occurring.

Alerts and Alarms. Alerts and alarms are extremely helpful because the system can tell the user if there is a potential problem. Alerts generally refer to warnings such as "too many messages in queue awaiting delivery." Alarms are a sign of a more serious problem, such as a disk full condition.

Mail Monitoring. Mail monitoring is typically an administrative function. One way of monitoring a system is to send a probe addressed to an invalid user on a target system. On many systems, the target system will reject the message with a "no such addressee" non-delivery message. When the initiating system receives this message, it indicates that mail flow is active.

Timing the round-trip provides a window to overall system performance. A message that does not return in a pre-established timeframe is considered overdue and is cause for further investigation.

Reporting. Reporting is used for capacity planning, measuring throughput and performance, chargeback, and statistical gathering. At initial implementation, network administrators will generally want to report breadth of coverage to demonstrate the reach of the infrastructure. Breadth can be measured by counting users and the number of messaging systems within each messaging environment.

Performance can be measured by reporting the volume — the average number of messages delivered per hour, or messages in each hour over a 24-hour period. This measure can be divided further by indicating the type of message (i.e., text only, single/double attachments, read receipts). This information gives network managers a measurable indication of the kind of features the user community requires.

For network planning purposes, it may be useful to measure volume or "system pressure," ignoring the number of messages sent and focusing on the number of total gigabytes sent per day.

IMPLEMENTATION SCENARIOS: A TIERED APPROACH

Manufacturing environments have long used a tiered approach to messaging for distributing the workload of factory floor applications. As environments become more complex, the tiered approach offers additional flexibility.

An entire enterprise can be considered a single department, indicating the need for a one-tier system where clients are tied into a single server or post office. Multiple departments in a single enterprise or a single department communicating with multiple enterprises require routers and gateways to communicate with the world outside. When multiple departments need to communicate with each other and with multiple enterprises, a messaging backbone or messaging switch is called for.

The following table summarizes the implementation scenarios discussed in this chapter:

	Enterprise	
	Single	Multiple
Single Department	One-Tier Single System	Two-Tier Similar Systems
Multiple Departments	Two-Tier Dissimilar Systems	Three-Tier Cross-Enterprise Systems

One-Tier Messaging Model

A single department in a single enterprise will most likely deploy a one-tier messaging model. This model consists of a single messaging server or post office that provides all services. It may be as large as an OfficeVision system on a mainframe or a Higgins PostOffice on a Compaq file server running NetWare. The department need only concern itself with following corporate guidelines for networking and any naming standards.

Caution should be observed when using corporate guidelines. It is often simple to apply mainframe conventions when standardizing PC LAN-based applications. Many large organizations tend to forget that the whole reason for deploying desktop computers is to move away from mainframe conventions (e.g., 8-character user IDs) that are nonintuitive for users. Exhibit 25.1 shows a typical one-tier model within a single department of an enterprise

Two-Tier Model: Multiple Servers

As the number of e-mail users grows, or multiple departments need to be connected, an organization will probably deploy multiple servers. This two-tier model can consist of integrating similar messaging systems from the same vendor or from different vendors. Exhibit 25.2 illustrates a con-

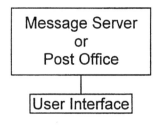

Exhibit 25.1.   One-tier model

284

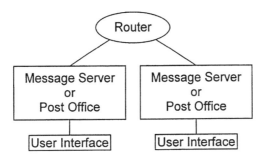

Exhibit 25.2.   Two-tier model

---

nection between two departments using the same vendor software connected via application routers.

In a typical PC LAN environment using a shared-file system such as cc:Mail or Microsoft Mail, the router acts the same way as the PC. The post office is completely passive. When users send messages, their workstations simply copy the message to the file server as an individual file or as an insertion into a file server data base. In either case the PC workstation actually does the work — the post office simply serves as a shared disk drive. The router is also an active component, but has no user moving messages. It periodically moves messages from one post office to another without user interaction.

Application Gateways for Integrating Dissimilar Systems

Many enterprises have different departments that have chosen their own e-mail systems without a common corporate standard. To integrate dissimilar systems, application gateways can bridge the technical incompatibilities between the various messaging servers (Exhibit 25.3).

A simple gateway can translate cc:Mail messages to GroupWise. A more complex gateway can bridge networks (e.g., Ethernet to Token Ring), network protocols (i.e., NetWare to TCP/IP), and the e-mail applications.

Converting one e-mail message to the format of another requires a lot of translation. Document formats (i.e., DCA RFT to ASCII), addressing formats (i.e., user@workgroup@domain to system::user), and message options (i.e., acknowledgments to read or deliver receipts) must all be translated.

Gateways can emulate routers native to each environment. They perform message translations internally. The alternative to this approach is to place the gateway between the routers as opposed to between the post offices — this is not an end-user design; it is merely a function of the vendor software (Exhibit 25.4).

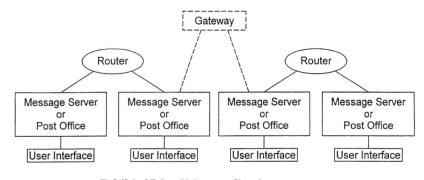

Exhibit 25.3. Using application gateways

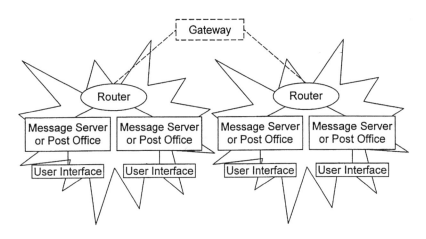

Exhibit 25.4. Placing a gateway between routers

If an enterprise is large, network administrators may want to make use of economies of scale to handle common administration, common gateways to X.400, and Internet networks. The network administration staff may simply need points in its network where it can measure progress. Gateways from each environment to every other environment can be provided, but this solution becomes costly and difficult to maintain. A better approach would be to use a central switching hub or a distributed backbone, as shown in Exhibit 25.5.

Distributed hubs. The central switch or hub allows for a single path for each messaging environment to communicate with all other messaging environments. The central hub, if it is relatively inexpensive, can be expanded into the distributed model. This is often done as the aggregate system grows and requires additional performance and capacity.

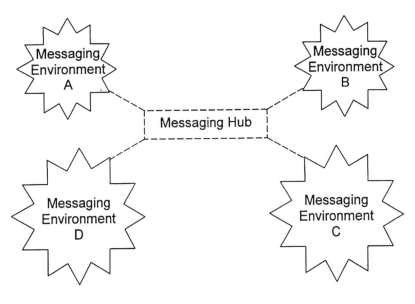

Exhibit 25.5.   A central switching hub

However, this implementation can be taken to an extreme, as seen by the number of companies that have grown PC LAN/shared file systems beyond their original design. It is inexpensive to grow these systems incrementally, but difficult to provide end-to-end reliability. Most organizations plug the technical gaps in these products with additional permanent and contract personnel to keep the multitude of routers and shared-file system post offices up and running.

Some organizations have taken this distributed hub approach to the point where they have multiple connections to the Internet and the X.400 world (Exhibit 25.6). Some organizations offer the single message switch for their global environment, and their messages are more well traveled than their administrators. A message sent from Brussels to Paris may stop in Los Angeles on the way because of the central switching mechanism. In addition to local switching, the distributed hub allows for redundancy.

THREE DEPLOYMENT ARCHITECTURES AND OPTIONS

Most companies deploy e-mail systems using variations of three architectures: a common platform, where all e-mail systems are identical; a multiple backbone where each e-mail environment has its own gateways; or a common backbone where all systems share common resources. The following sections describe these architectures along with the advantages and disadvantages of each.

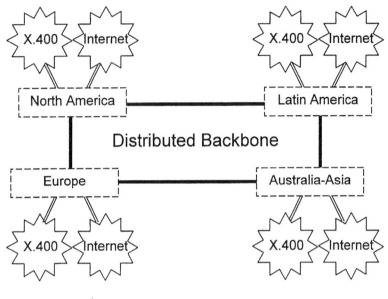

Exhibit 25.6. Worldwide distributed hubs

Common Platform Architecture

For years, a major automotive manufacturer delayed PC LAN e-mail deployment in deference to the purported needs of the traveling executive. Senior managers wanted to be able to walk up to any company computer terminal, work station, or personal computer anywhere in the world and know that they would be able to access their e-mail in the same manner. This implies a common look and feel to the application across platforms as well as common network access to the e-mail server. In this company's case, PROFS (OfficeVision/VM) was accessible through 3270 terminal emulators on various platforms. As long as SNA network access remained available, e-mail appeared the same worldwide. This IBM mainframe shop had few problems implementing this model.

The common platform model is not unique to IBM mainframe environments. Another manufacturer used the same technique with its DEC ALL-IN-1 environment distributed across multiple VAX hosts. As long as a DECnet network or dialup access was available, users could reach their home systems. The upside of this approach is that an individual's e-mail files are stored centrally, allowing for a single retrieval point. The downside was that the user had to be connected to process e-mail and was unable to work offline.

This strategy is not limited to mainframe and minicomputer models. A number of companies have standardized on Lotus Notes, Microsoft Mail,

288

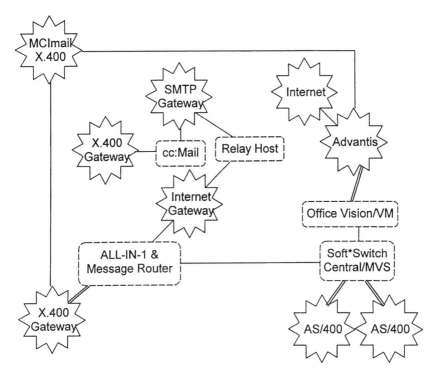

Exhibit 25.7. The multiple backbone model

or Novell's GroupWise. None of these products are truly ready for large-scale deployment without IT and network staffs having to plug the technical gaps.

Multiple Backbone Model

The multiple backbone model assumes that an organization integrates its e-mail systems as though it were multiple smaller companies. The OfficeVision/VM system may connect via Advantis to reach the Internet and X.400 world. The cc:Mail WAN may have an SMTP gateway for access to the Internet and an ISOCOR MTA for access to the Message Router/X.400 gateway. All the various e-mail environments may have a proprietary Soft*Switch gateway for access to the IBM/MVS host so that everyone who needs to can access their OfficeVision/400 systems (Exhibit 25.7).

On the surface, this hodgepodge of point-to-point connections may seem a bit unwieldy, but it does have advantages. Users of cc:Mail can address Internet e-mail users by filling out an SMTP template rather than waiting until the cc:Mail administrator adds recipients to the cc:Mail directory. OfficeVision/VM users can fill out a simple address block within the text of their message to reach an Internet user. AS/400 users can send mail

289

to an application that forwards the message on their behalf. The trouble occurs when the recipients of the AS/400 users try to reply — they end up replying to the application that forwarded the message rather than the original sender, or originator, of the message.

This architecture may still work. If each e-mail environment had its own gateway, network administration could offer multiple connections to the Internet.

Common Backbone

The common backbone takes two forms:

- A central e-mail hub or message switch on a single system that serves as the common denominator among all e-mail environments.
- A distributed model where all backbone components run a common software protocol.

The common hub involves a single switch that serves the users' applications, thus serving their needs indirectly. Each e-mail environment has an application gateway that converts its environmental format to that of the common hub. Other systems are attached to this hub in a similar manner. Messages destined for dissimilar environments all pass through this central point to be sorted and delivered to their final destinations.

The distributed backbone takes the central hub and replaces it with two or more systems sharing a common application protocol. This solution offers the ability to deploy two or more less expensive systems rather than a single, more expensive system. Any system connected to any point in the backbone can use any other service (e.g., gateway) connected to that same backbone.

IS managers may decide to purchase a single hub and gradually add systems to form a distributed backbone. Should you decide to use a common backbone protocol like X.400 or SMTP, there is an advantage. Because these protocols are available from a number of vendors, the cc:Mail/X.400 gateway could connect to an X.400 system running in an HP9000, DEC/Alpha, or Intel/Pentium system — all running the same protocols. It is possible to change distributed servers without having to change the gateways to these servers. Exhibit 25.8 illustrates three-tier flexibility.

A third approach is to use one central server or a distributed backbone of similar systems. In the central server/central hub approach, all e-mail environments use application gateways to connect to the central switch. There they are routed to their target environment.

Two-tier models may seem most convenient because they can use the offerings of a single vendor. One problem is that the system must use that

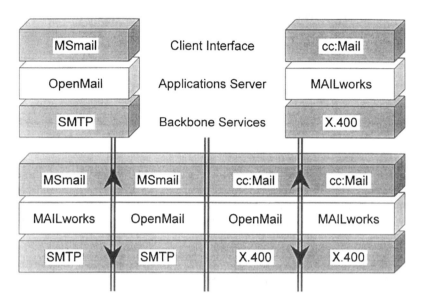

Exhibit 25.8.   Three-tier model.

vendor's protocols for a long time. Three tiers allow the layers in the model to be changed, which allows for ease of transition.

Under most application scenarios, changing one component of the messaging environment entails changing all the pieces and parts with which it is associated. It may be necessary to provide adequate support staff and end-user training or hire consultants to handle the need for temporary staff during the transition — a significant business disruption.

For example, in one environment, users have Microsoft Mail on their desktops and a traditional MSmail post office is used, as well as message transfer agents (MTAs), to route mail between post offices. The engineering department uses OpenMail. The IT group would like to begin consolidating systems. With minor changes to the desktop, IT can retain the Microsoft Mail user interface, remove the back-end infrastructure, and use the same OpenMail system as the OpenMail desktop users by consolidating the second tier and simplifying the support environment. The client changes somewhat because it is using a different directory server and message store, but it appears as a minor upgrade to the users — no significant training is necessary.

Likewise, IT can change the back end and still allow the OpenMail systems to communicate with the MAILworks and ALL-IN-1 systems without locking into a single vendor solution. This is a feasible option. Today, users can plug an MSmail client into a MAILworks or OpenMail server. Novell recently announced the ability to plug a cc:Mail or MSmail client into its GroupWise XTD server. A Microsoft Exchange client plugs into various servers, and Lotus's cc:Mail can plug into anything.

ESTABLISHING MESSAGING POLICIES AND PROCEDURES

An organization can prevent misunderstandings, conflicts, and even litigation if it publishes its policies and procedures for messaging applications at the outset. Most important are privacy and confidentiality.

Privacy

A privacy policy serves two purposes: to properly inform employees that their messages may not be private and to protect the organization from legal liability. Most organizations create a policy that cautions users as follows:

All electronic data is company property and may be viewed by designated personnel to diagnose problems, monitor performance, or for other purposes as the company deems necessary. While you normally type a password to access your e-mail and you may feel that your messages are private, this is not the case. The e-mail you create, read, or send is not your property nor is it protected from being seen by those other than you and your recipients.

Organizations can contact the Electronic Messaging Association (EMA) in Arlington, VA for a kit to aid in developing a privacy policy.

Proprietary and Confidential Information

E-mail appears to ease the process of intentional or inadvertent disclosure of company secrets. If this is a concern, an organization could try the following:

- Let users know that the IT department logs the messages that leave the company.
- Perform periodic audits.
- Apply rules or scripts that capture e-mail to or from fields, making it possible to search on competitor address strings.

Some systems insert a header on incoming e-mail that says: "WARNING: This message arrived from outside the company's e-mail system. Take care when replying so as not to divulge proprietary or confidential information."

A company may also specify that proprietary information should not be sent to Internet addresses if security measures on the Internet are inadequate for the company's needs. Users may be asked to confirm that only

X.400 addresses are used. It is helpful to incorporate any such e-mail ground rules — for example, that the transmission of proprietary information without a proper disclosure agreement is grounds for dismissal — as part of the new employee orientation process.

CONCLUSION

One of the most important elements of a successful messaging system rollout is a staff that is well versed in the workings of the network, operating system, backup procedures, and applications.

Network Connections

An implementation needs individuals who can set up network connections efficiently. A messaging system needs procedures in place to notify users when a network link is unavailable. If the network goes down, often one of the first applications blamed is e-mail. It is the job of the network staff to diagnose the problem quickly and have the right people remedying the problem.

Operating Systems

Many e-mail groups have their own systems and servers and operate them as their own. Consequently, many successful organizations pair systems programmers or senior software specialists with systems engineers who can provide installation services and upgrade support.

Backup

Most messaging support organizations are not set up to provide 24-hour support. It is important to borrow methodologies from the mainframe support environment and staff an operations center that can answer phone calls, fix problems, and backup and archive applications regularly.

Applications Support

This function demands staff members with:

- Excellent diagnostic skills.
- Excellent communication skills.
- Data base and business graphics experience.
- Cross-platform network experience.
- A basic understanding of the operating environment of each of the platforms.

E-mail integration by its nature involves cross-platform expertise. When staffing an implementation, the key is to match expertise across the various groups within the company. The team should be application-centric with contributors from across the enterprise. If an implementation is properly staffed, and the implementers keep in mind the big picture as well as the daily objectives, the messaging system rollout is far more likely to be a success.

Chapter 26
Data Warehousing Concepts and Strategies

Stefan M. Neikes
Sumit Sircar
Bijoy Bordoloi

MANY IT ORGANIZATIONS are increasingly adopting data warehousing as a way of improving their relationships with corporate users. Proponents of data warehousing technology claim the technology will contribute immensely to a company's strategic advantage. Predictions by consulting groups indicate continuing growth of the data warehousing market.

Companies contemplating the implementation of a data warehouse need to address many issues concerning strategies, the type of the data warehouse, front-end tools, and even the corporate culture. Other issues that also need to be examined include the responsibility over the maintenance of the data warehouse and the issues related to data warehouse access rights.

After defining the concept of data warehousing, this chapter provides an in-depth look at design and construction issues, types of data warehouses and their respective applications, data mining concepts, techniques, and tools, and managerial and organizational impacts of data warehousing.

HISTORY OF DATA WAREHOUSING

The concept of data warehousing is best presented as part of an evolution that began about 35 years ago. In the early 1960s, the arena of computing was limited by punch cards, files on magnetic tape, slow access times, and an immense amount of overhead. About the mid-1960s, the near explosive growth in the usage of magnetic tapes increased the amount of data redundancy. Suddenly, new problems, ranging from synchronizing data after

0-8493-9820-7/00/$0.00+$.50
© 2000 by CRC Press LLC

updating to handling the complexity of maintaining old programs and developing new ones, had to be resolved.

The 1970s saw the rise of direct access storage devices and concomitant technology of database management systems (DBMSs). DBMSs made it possible to reduce the redundancy of data by storing it in a single place for all processing. Only a few years later, databases were used in conjunction with online transaction processing (OLTP). This advancement enabled the implementation of such applications as automated teller machines and reservations systems used by travel and airline industries to store up-to-date information. By the early 1980s, the introduction of the PC and fourth-generation technology let end users innovatively and more effectively utilize data in the database to guide decision making.

All these advances, however, engendered additional problems, such as producing consistent reports for corporate data. It was difficult and time consuming to accomplish the step from pure data to information that gives meaning to the organization and a lack of integration across applications. Poor or non-existent historical data only added to the problems of transforming raw data into intelligent information.

This dilemma led to the realization that organizations need two fundamentally different sets of data. On the one hand, there is so-called primitive or raw data, which is detailed, can be updated, and is used to run the day-to-day operations of a business. On the other hand, there is summarized or derived data, which is less frequently updated and is needed by management to make higher-level decisions. The origins of the data warehouse as a subject-oriented collection of data that supports managerial decision making are therefore not surprising.

Many companies have finally realized that they cannot ignore the role of strategic information systems if they are to attain a strategic advantage in the marketplace. CEOs and CIOs throughout the U.S. and the world are steadily seeking new ways to increase the benefits that IT provides. Data is increasingly viewed as an asset with as much importance in many cases as financial assets. New methods and technologies are being developed to improve the use of corporate data and provide for faster analyses of business information.

Operational systems are not able to meet decision support needs for several reasons. First, most organizations lack online historical data. Second, the data required for analysis often resides on different platforms and operational systems, which complicates the issue further. Third, the query performance of many operational systems is extremely poor, which in turn affects their performance. Fourth, operational database designs are inappropriate for decision support.

For these reasons, the concept of data warehousing, which has been around for as long as databases have existed, has suddenly come to the forefront. A data warehouse eliminates the decision support shortfalls of operational systems in a single, consolidated system. Data is thus made readily accessible to the people who need it, especially organizational decision makers, without interrupting online operational workloads.

The key of a data warehouse is that it provides a single, more quickly accessible, and more accurately consolidated image of business reality. It lets organizational decision makers monitor and compare current and past operations, rationally forecast future operations, and devise new business processes. These benefits are driving the popularity of data warehousing and have led some advocates to call the data warehouse the center of IS architecture in the years ahead.

THE BASICS OF DATA WAREHOUSING TECHNOLOGY

According to Bill Inmon, a data warehouse has four distinguishing characteristics (Inmon, 1993):

1. Subject-orientation.
2. Integration.
3. Time-variance.
4. Nonvolatility.

As depicted in Exhibit 26.1, the subject-oriented database characteristic of the data warehouse organizes data according to subject, unlike the application-based database. The alignment around subject areas affects the design and implementation of the data found in the data warehouse. For this reason, the major subject areas influence the most important part of the key structure. Data warehouse data entries also differ from application-oriented data in the relationships. Although operational data has relationships among tables based on the business rules that are in effect, the data warehouse encompasses a spectrum of time.

A data warehouse is also integrated in that data is moved there from many different applications (see Exhibit 26.2). This integration is noticeable in several ways, such as the implementation of consistent naming conventions, consistent measurement of variables, consistent encoding structures, and consistent physical attributes of data. In comparison, operational data is often inconsistent across applications. The preprocessing of information aids in reducing access time at the point of inquiry.

Exhibit 26.3 shows the time-variant feature of the data warehouse. The data stored is about five to ten years old and used for making consistent comparisons, viewing trends, and providing a forecasting tool. Operational environment data reflects only accurate values as of the moment of access.

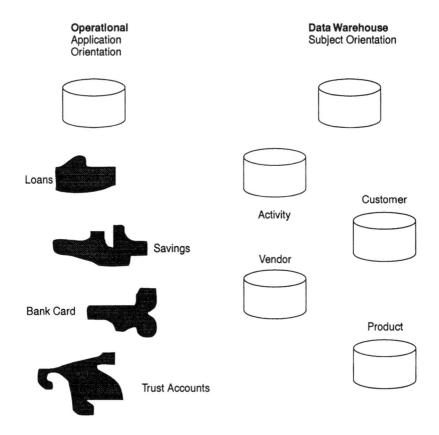

SOURCE: W.H. Inmon, *Building the Data Warehouse* (New York: John Wiley, 1993).

Exhibit 26.1. The data warehouse is subject-oriented

The data in such a system may change at a later point in time through up-dates or inserts. On the contrary, data in the data warehouse is accurate as of some moment in time and will produce the same results every time for the same query.

The time-variant feature of the data warehouse is observed in different ways. In addition to the lengthier time horizon as compared to the opera-tional environment, time-variance is also apparent in the key structure of a data warehouse. Every key structure contains, implicitly or explicitly, an el-ement of time, such as day, week, or month. Time-variance is also evi-denced by the fact that the data warehouse is never updated. Operational data is updated as the need arises.

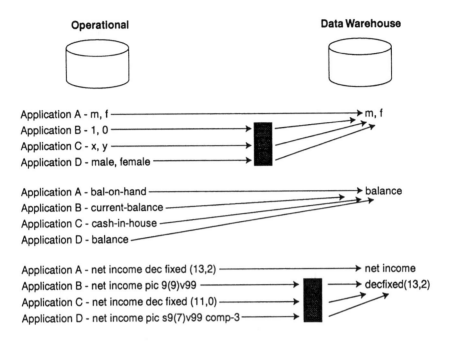

SOURCE: W.H. Inmon, *Building the Data Warehouse* (New York: John Wiley, 1993).

Exhibit 26.2. Integration of data in the data warehouse

Operational

Current value data:
- Time horizon—60 to 90 days
- Key may or may not have an element of time
- Data can be updated

Data Warehouse

Snapshot data:
- Time horizon—5 to 10 years
- Key contains an element of time
- Once snapshot is made, record cannot be updated

SOURCE: W.H. Inmon, *Building the Data Warehouse* (New York: John Wiley, 1993).

Exhibit 26.3. The data warehouse is time-variant

The nonvolatility of the warehouse means that there is no inserting, deleting, replacing, or changing of data on a record-by-record basis, as is the case in the operational environment (see Exhibit 26.4). This difference has tremendous consequences. At the design level, for example, there is no need to be cautious about update anomaly. It follows that normalization of the physical database design loses its importance, because the design focuses on optimized access of data. Other issues that simplify data warehouse design involve the nonpresence of transaction and data integrity as well as detection and remedy of deadlocks, which are found in every operational database environment.

Effective and efficient use of the data warehouse necessitates that the data warehouse run on a separate platform. If it does not, it will slow down the operations database and reduce response time by a large factor.

DESIGN AND CONSTRUCTION OF A DATA WAREHOUSE

Preliminary Considerations

Like any other undertaking, a data warehouse project should demonstrate success early and often to upper management. This ensures high visibility and justification of the immense resource commitment and costs associated with the project. Before undertaking the design of the data warehouse, however, it is wise to remember that a data warehouse project is not as easy as copying data from one database to another and handing

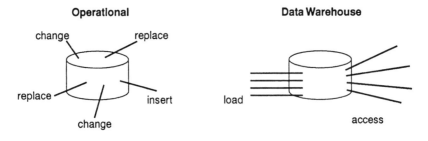

Operational

change   replace

replace   insert

change

Data is regularly updated on a record-by-record basis.

Data Warehouse

load

access

Data is loaded into the warehouse and is accessed there, but once the snapshot of data is made, the data in the warehouse does not change.

SOURCE: W.H. Inmon, *Building the Data Warehouse* (New York: John Wiley, 1993).

Exhibit 26.4. The data warehouse is nonvolatile

it over to users, who then simply extract the data with PC-based queries and reporting tools.

Developers should not underestimate the many complex issues involved in data warehousing. These include architectural considerations, security, data integrity, and network issues. According to one estimate, about 80% of the time that is spent constructing a data warehouse is devoted to extracting, cleaning, and loading data. In addition, problems that may have been undetected for years can surface during the design phase. The discovery of data that has never been captured as well as data that has been altered and stored are examples of these types of problems. A solid understanding of the business and all the processes that have to be modeled is also extremely important.

Another major consideration important to up-front planning is the difference between the data warehouse and most other client/server applications. First, there is the issue of batch orientation for much of the processing. The complexity of processes (which may be executed on multiple platforms), data volumes, and resulting data synchronization issues must be correctly analyzed and resolved.

Next, the data volume in a data warehouse, which can be in the terabyte range, has to be considered. New purchases of large amounts of disk storage space and magnetic tape for backup should be expected.

It is also vital to plan and provide for the transport of large amounts of data over the network. The ability of data warehousing to support a wide range of queries, from simple ones that return only limited amounts of information to complex ones that might access several million rows, can cause complications. It is also necessary to incorporate the availability of corporate metadata into this thought process. The designers of the data warehouse have to remember that metadata is likely to be replicated at multiple sites. This point to the need for synchronization across the different platforms to avoid inconsistencies.

Finally, security must be considered. In terms of location and security, data warehouse and non-data warehouse applications must appear seamless. Users should not need different IDs to sign on to the different systems, but the application should be smart enough to provide users the correct access with only one password.

Designing the Warehouse

After having addressed all the preliminary issues, the design task begins. There are two approaches to designing a data warehouse: the top-down approach and the bottom-up approach. In the top-down approach, all of an organization's business processes are analyzed to build an enterprisewide data warehouse in one step. This approach requires an immense commitment of planning, resources, and time and results in new information structure from which the entire organization benefits.

The bottom-up approach, on the other hand, breaks the task down and delivers only a small subset of the data warehouse. New pieces are then phased in until the entire organization is modeled. The bottom-up approach lets data warehouse technology be quickly delivered to a part of the organization. This approach is recommended because its time demands are not as rigorous. It also allows development team members to learn as they implement the system, identify bottlenecks and shortfalls, and find out how to avoid them as additional parts of the data warehouse are delivered.

Because a data warehouse is subject-oriented, the first design step involves choosing a business subject area to be modeled and eliciting information about the following:

- The business process that needs to be modeled.
- The fact that need to be extracted from the operational database.
- The level of detail required.
- Characteristics of the facts (e.g., dimension, attribute, and cardinality).

After each of these areas has been thoroughly investigated and more information about facts, dimension, attributes, and sparsity has been gathered, still another decision must be made. The question now becomes which schema to use for the design of the data warehouse database. There are two major options: the classic star schema and the snowflake schema.

The Star Schema. In the star design schema, a separate table is used for each dimension, and a single large table is used for the facts (see Exhibit 26.5). The fact table's indexed key comprises the keys of the different dimensions tables.

With this schema, the problem of sparsity, or the creation of empty rows, is avoided by not creating records where combinations are invalid. Users are able to follow paths for detailed drilldowns and summary rollups. Because the dimension tables are also relatively small, precalculated aggregation can be imbedded within the fact table, providing extremely fast response times. It is also possible to apply multiple hierarchies against the same fact table, which leads to the development of a flexible and useful set of data.

The Snowflake Schema. The snowflake schema depicted in Exhibit 26.6 is best used when there are large dimensions such as time. The dimension tables are split at the attribute level to provide a greater variety of combina-

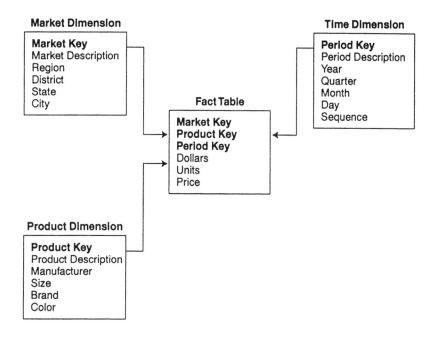

Source: N. Raden, "Modeling a Data Warehouse," *InformationWeek* (January 29, 1996), pp. 60-62.

Exhibit 26.5. The star design schema

---

tions. The breakup of the time dimension into a quarter entity and a month entity provides more detailed aggregation and also more exact information.

Decision Support Systems and Data Warehousing

Because many vendors offer decision support system (DSS) products and information on how to implement them abounds, insight into the different technologies available is helpful. Three concepts should be evaluated in terms of their usability for decision support and relationship to the so-called real data warehouse. They are virtual data warehouses, multidimensional online analytical processing (OLAP), and relational OLAP.

Virtual Data Warehouse. The virtual data warehouse promises to deliver the same benefits as a real data warehouse but without the associated amount of work and difficulty. The virtual data warehouse concept can be subdivided into the surround data warehouse and the OLAP/data mart warehouse. In a surround data warehouse, legacy systems are merely surrounded with methods to access data without a fundamental change of the operational data. The surround concept thus negates a key feature of the

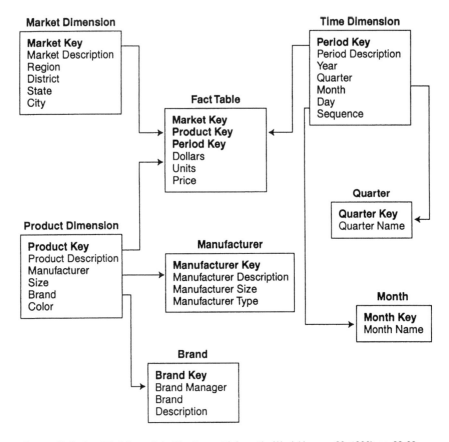

SOURCE: N. Raden, "Modeling a Data Warehouse," *InformationWeek* (January 29, 1996), pp. 60-62.

Exhibit 26.6. The snowflake design schema

real data warehouse, which integrates operational data in a way that allows users to make sense of it.

In addition, the data structure of a virtual data warehouse does not lend itself to DSS processing. Legacy operational systems were built to ease updating, writing, and deleting and not with simple data extraction in mind. Another deficiency with this technology is the minimal amount of historical data that is kept, usually only 60 to 90 days worth of information. A real data warehouse, on the other hand, with its two-to-five years worth of information, provides a far superior means of analyzing trends.

In the case of direct OLAP/data marts, legacy data is transferred directly to the OLAP/data mart environment. Although this approach recognizes the need to remove data from the operational environment, it too falls short of being a real data warehouse. If only a few, small applications were feeding a data mart, the approach would be acceptable. The reality is, however, that there are many applications and thus many OLAP/data mart environments, each requiring a customized interface, especially as the number of OLAP/data marts increases.

Because the different OLAP/data marts are not effectively integrated, different users arrive at different conclusions when analyzing the data. It is thus possible for the marketing department to report the business is doing fine and another department to report just the opposite. This drawback does not exist with the real data warehouse, where all data is integrated. Users who examine the data at a certain point in time would all make decisions based on the same data.

Multidimensional OLAP. Multidimensional database technology is a definite step up from the virtual data warehouse. It is designed for executives and analysts who want to look at data from different perspectives and have the ability to examine summarized and detailed data. When implemented together with a data warehouse, multidimensional database technology provides more efficient and faster access to corporate data. Proprietary multidimensional databases facilitate the organization of data hierarchically in multiple dimensions, allowing users to make advanced analyses of small portions of data from the data warehouse. The technology is understandably embraced by many in the industry because of its increased usability and superior analytical functionality.

As a stand-alone technology, multidimensional OLAP is inferior to a real data warehouse for a variety of reasons. The main drawback is that the technology is not able to handle more than 20 to 30 gigabytes of data, which is unacceptable for most of the larger corporations, whose need range in the 100 gigabyte to several terabyte range. Furthermore, multidimensional databases does not have the flexibility and measurability required of today's decision support systems because they do not support the necessary ad hoc creation of multidimensional views of products and customers. Multidimensional databases should be considered for use in smaller organizations or on a department level only.

Relational OLAP. Relational OLAP is also used with many decision support systems and provides sophisticated analytical capability in conjunction with a data warehouse. Unlike multidimensional database technology, relational OLAP lets end users define complex multidimensional views and analyze them. These advantages are only possible if certain functionalities are incorporated into relational OLAP.

Users must be removed from the process of generating their own structured query language (SQL). Multiple SQL statements should be generated by the system for every analysis request to the data warehouse; in this way, a set of business measurements (e.g., comparison and ranking measurements) is established, which is essential to the appropriate use of the technology.

The shortcoming of relational OLAP technology works well in conjunction with a data warehouse; by itself, the technology is somewhat limited.

Examination of the three preceding decision support technologies leads to the only correct deduction — that data warehouse is still the most suitable technology for larger firms. The benefit of having integrated, cleansed data from legacy systems together with historical information about the business makes a properly implemented data warehouse the primary choice for decision support.

Benefits of Warehousing for Data Mining

The technology of data mining is closely related to that of data warehousing. It involves the process of extracting large amounts of previously unknown data and then using the data to make important business decisions. The key phrase here is unknown information buried in the huge mounds of operational data that, if analyzed, provides relevant information to organizational decision makers.

Significant data is sometimes undetected because most data is captured and maintained by a particular department. What may seem irrelevant or uninteresting at the department level may yield insights and indicates patterns important at the organizational level. These patterns include market trends, such as customer buying patterns. They aid in such areas as determining the effectiveness of sales promotions, detecting fraud, evaluating risk and assessing quality, or analyzing insurance claims. The possibilities are limitless and yield a variety of benefits ultimately leading to improved customer service and business performance.

Data that is needed but often located on several different systems, in different formats and structures, and somewhat redundant provides no real value to business users. This is where the data warehouse comes into play as a better source of consolidated and cleansed data facilitating analysis than regular flat files or operational databases.

Three steps are thus needed to identify and use hidden information:

1. The captured data must be incorporated into view of the entire organization instead of only one department.
2. The data must be analyzed or mined for valuable information.
3. The information must be specially organized to simplify decision making.

DATA MINING TASKS

In data mining, data warehouses, query generators, and data interpretation systems are combined with discovery-driven systems to provide the ability to automatically reveal important yet hidden data. The following tasks need to be completed to make full use of data mining.

- Creating prediction and classification models.
- Analyzing links.
- Segmenting databases.
- Detecting deviations.

Creating Models

The first task makes use of the data warehouse's contents to automatically generate a model that predicts desired behavior. In comparison to traditional models that use statistical techniques and linear and logical regression, discovery-driven models generate accurate models that are also more comprehensible, because of their sets of if-then rules. The performance of a particular stock, for example, can be predicted to assess its suitability for an investment portfolio.

Analyzing Links

The goal of the link analysis is to establish relevant connections between database records. An example here is the analysis of items that are usually purchased together, like a washer and dryer. Such analysis can lead to a more effective pricing and selling strategy.

Segmenting Databases

When segmenting databases, collections of records with common characteristics or behaviors are identified. One example is the analysis of sales for a certain time period, such as President's Day or Thanksgiving weekend, to detect pattern in customer purchase behavior. For the reasons discussed earlier, this is an ideal task for data warehouse.

Detecting Deviations

The fourth and final task involves detection of deviations, which is the opposite of data segmentation. Here, the goal is to identify records that vary from the norm, or lie outside of any particular cluster with similar characteristics. This discovery from the cluster is then explained as normal or as a hint of a previously unknown behavior or attribute.

DATA MINING TECHNIQUES

At this point, it is important to present several techniques that aid mining efforts. These techniques include the creation of predictive models, and the performing of supervised induction, association, and sequence discovery.

Creating Predictive Models

The creation of a so-called predictive model is facilitated through numerous statistical techniques and various forms of visualization that ease the user's recognition of patterns.

Supervised Induction

With supervised induction, classification models are created from a set of records, which is referred to as the training set. This method makes it possible to infer from a set of descriptors of the training set to the general. In this way, a rule might be produced that states that a customer who is male, lives in a certain zip code area, earns $25,000 to $30,00, is between 40 and 45 years of age, and listens more to the radio than watches TV might be a possible buyer for a new camcorder. The advantage of this technique is that the patterns are based on local phenomena, whereas statistical measures check for conditions that are valid for an entire population.

Association Discovery

Association discovery allows for the prediction of the occurrence of some items in a set of records if other items are also present. For example, it is possible to identify the relationship among different medical procedures by analyzing claim forms submitted to an insurance company. With this information the prediction could be made, within a certain margin of error, that for treatment the same five medicine are usually required.

Sequence Discovery

Sequence discovery aids the data miner by providing information on a customer's behavior over time. If a certain person buys a VCR this week, he or she usually buys videotapes on the next purchasing occasion. The detection of such a pattern is especially important to catalog companies, because it helps them better target their potential customer base with specialized advertising catalogs.

Tools

The main tools used in data mining are neural networks, decision trees, rule induction, and data visualization.

Neural Networks. A neural network consists of three interconnected layers: an input and output layer with a hidden layer between (see Exhibit 26.7). The hidden processing layer is like the brain of the neural network

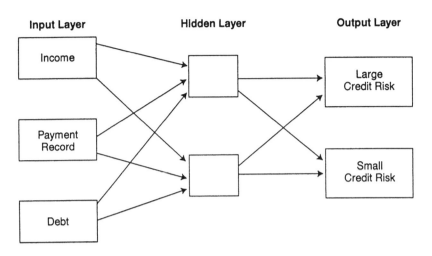

SOURCE: H. Edelstein, "Technology How To: Mining Data Warehouses," *InformationWeek* (January 8, 1996), pp. 48-51.

Exhibit 26.7. Neural network

---

because it stores or learns rules about input patterns and then producesa known set of outputs. Because the process of neural networks is not transparent, it leaves the user without a clear interpretation of the resulting model, which, nevertheless, is applied.

Decision Trees. Decision trees divide data into groups based on the values that the different variables take on (see Exhibit 26.8). The result is often a complex hierarchy of classifying data, which enables the user to deduct possible future behavior. For instance, it might be deducted that for a person who only uses a credit card occasionally, there is a 20% probability that an offer for another credit card would be accepted. Although decision trees are faster than neural networks in many cases, they have drawbacks. One of these is the handling of data ranges as in age groups, which can inadvertently hidepatterns.

Rule Induction. The method of rule induction is applied by creating nonhierarchical sets of possibly overlapping conditions. This is accomplished by first generating partial decision tress. Statistical techniques are then used to determine which decision trees to apply to the input data. This method is especially useful in cases where there are long and complex condition lists.

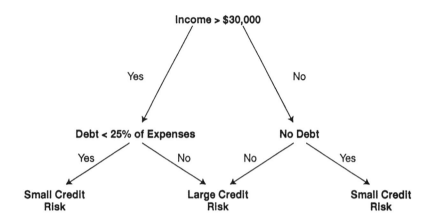

SOURCE: H. Edelstein, "Technology How To: Mining Data Warehouses," *InformationWeek* (January 8, 1996), pp. 48-51.

Exhibit 26.8. Decision tree

Data Visualization. Data visualization is not really a data mining tool; however, because it provides a picture for the user with a large number of graphically represented variables, it is a power tool for providing concise information. The graphics products available make the detection of patterns much easier than is the case when more numbers are analyzed.

Because of the pros and cons of the varied data mining tools, software vendors today incorporate all or some of them in their data mining packages. Each tool is essentially a matter of looking at data with different means and from different angles.

One of the potential problems in data mining is performance related. To speed up processing, it might be necessary to subset the data either by the number of rows accessed or by the number of variables that are examined. This can lead to slightly different conclusions about the data set; consequently, in most cases it is better to wait for the correct answer using a large sample.

MANAGERIAL AND ORGANIZATIONAL IMPACTS OF DATA WAREHOUSING

Although organizational managers eagerly await the completion of a data warehouse, many issues must be dealt with before the fruits of this new technology are harvested. This is especially true in today's fast changing enterprise with its quick reaction times.

The subject of economic benefit also deserves mentioning when dealing with data warehousing because some projects have already acquired the reputation of providing little or no payback on the huge investments involved. Data warehouses are sometimes accused of being pits into which data disappears never to be seen again.

Managers have to understand at the outset that the quality of the data is of extreme importance in a data warehousing project. The sometimes difficult challenge for management is to make data entering the data warehouse consistent. In some organizations, data is stored in flat, VSAM, IMS, IDMS, or SA files and a variety of relational databases. In addition, different systems that were designed for different functions contain the same terms but with different meanings.

If care is not taken to clean up this terminology during data warehouse construction, misleading management information results. The logical consequence of this requirement is that management has to agree on the data definition for elements in the warehouse. This is yet another challenging task. People who use the data in the short term and the long term must have input into the process and know what the data means.

The manager in charge of loading the data warehouse has four ways to handle erroneous data. If the data is inaccurate, it must be completely rejected and corrected in the source system. Data may also be accepted as is, if it is within a certain tolerance level and if it is marked as such.

A third option for handling erroneous data is the capture and correction of the data before it enters the warehouse. Capture and correction are handled programmatically in the process of transforming data from one system to the data warehouse. An example might be a field that was in lowercase and needs to be stored in uppercase. A final means of handling errors is to replace erroneous data with a default value. If, for example, the date February 29 of a non-leap year is defaulted to February 28, there is no loss in data integrity.

Another way that data warehousing affects management and organizations in general concerns today's business motto of working smarter, not harder. Today's data warehouse users can become more productive, because they will have the tools to analyze the huge amounts of data that they store instead of just collecting it.

Organizations are also affected by the invalid notion that implementing data warehousing technology simply consists of integrating all pertinent existing company data into one place. Managers need to be aware that data warehousing implies changes in the job duties of many people. For example, in an organization implementing a data warehouse, data analysis and modeling become much more prevalent than just requirements analysis. The database administrator position does not merely involve the critical aspects of efficiently storing data but takes on the central role in the development of the application. Furthermore, because it is a data model-oriented methodology, data warehouse design requires a development life cycle that does not fully follow the traditional development approaches: The development of a data warehouse virtually begins with a data model, from which the warehouse is built.

In summary, it must be noted that data warehouses are high-maintenance systems that require their own support staff. In this way, future changes are implemented in a timely manner by experienced personnel. It is also important to remember that a technically advanced and fast warehouse that adds little value will probably be abandoned by users from the start, reiterating the immense importance of clean data.

One of the most important issues that is often disregarded during the construction and implementation of a data warehouse is data quality. This is not surprising because in many companies the concern for data quality in regard to legacy and transaction systems is not a priority. Accordingly, when it comes to ensuring the quality of data being moved into the warehouse many companies continue with their old practices. This can turn out to be a costly mistake and has already lead to many failures of corporate warehousing projects. As more and more companies are making use of these strategic database systems, data quality must become the number one prerogative of all parties involved with the data warehousing effort.

Unreliable and inaccurate data in the data warehouse causes numerous problems. First and foremost, the confidence of the users in this technology is shattered and contributes to the already existing rift between business and IT. Furthermore, if the data is used for strategic decision making, unreliable data hurts not only the IT department but also the entire company. One example is banks that had erroneous risk exposure data on Texas-based businesses. When the oil market slumped in the early 80s, major losses were encountered by those banks that had many Texas accounts. In other cases, manufacturing firms scaled down their operations and took actions to rid themselves of excess inventory. Because of inaccurate data they had overestimated the inventory and sold off critical business equipment. Such examples demonstrate the need and the importance of data quality.

Poor quality of data appears to be the norm rather than the exception and points out that many technology managers have largely ignored the issue of quality. This is caused in part by the failure to recognize the need to manage data as a corporate asset. One cannot simply allow just anything to be moved into a data warehouse or it will become useless and might be likened to a "data garbage dump". In order to avoid data inaccuracies and their potential for harboring disasters, a general data quality awareness has to be made. There are critical success factors that each company needs to identify before moving forward with the issue of data quality.

First, senior management must make a commitment to the maintenance of the quality of corporate data. This can be achieved by instituting a data administration department that oversees the management of the corporate data resource. Furthermore, this department will establish data management standards, policies, procedures, and guidelines pertaining to data and data quality.

Second, data quality has to be defined. In order for data to be useful it has to be complete, timely, accurate, valid, and consistent. It does not simply consist of evaluation of its usefulness. The definition of data quality also includes the definition of the degree of quality that is required for each element being loaded into the data warehouse. If, for example, customer addresses are stored it might be acceptable that the four-digit extension to the zip code is missing. However, the street address, city, and state are of much higher importance. Again, this must be identified by each individual company and for each item that is used in the data warehouse.

A third factor that needs to be considered is the quality assurance of data. Since data is moved from transactional/legacy systems to the data warehouse, the accuracy of this data needs to be verified and corrected if necessary. This might be the largest task since it involves cleansing of existing data. Since no company is able to rectify all of its unclean data, procedures have to be put in place to ensure data quality at the source. Such a task can only be achieved by modifying business processes and designing data quality into the system. In identifying every data item and its usefulness to the ultimate users of this data, data quality requirements can be established. One might argue that this is too costly, but it has to kept in mind that increasing the quality of data as an after-the-fact task is five to ten times more expensive than capturing it correctly at the source.

If companies want to use data warehouse as a competitive advantage and reap its benefits, the issue of data quality has become one of the most important ones. Only when data quality is recognized as a corporate asset and treated as such by every member of the organization will the promised benefits of a data warehouse initiative be realized.

CONCLUSION

The value of warehousing to an organization is multidimensional. An enterprisewide data warehouse serves as a central repository for all data names used in an organization and therefore simplifies business relationships among departments by using one standard. Users of the data warehouse get consistent results when querying this database and understand the data in the same way without ambiguity. By its nature, the data warehouse also allows quicker access to summarized data about products, customers, and other business items of interest. In addition, the historical aspect of such a database (i.e., information kept for two to five years) allows users to detect and analyze patterns in the business items.

Organizations beginning to build a data warehouse should not undertake the task lightly. It does not simply involve moving data from the operational database to the data warehouse but rather cleaning the data to improve its future usefulness. It is also important to distinguish the different types of warehouse technologies (i.e., relational OLTP, multidimensional OTLP, and virtual data warehouse) and understand their fundamental differences.

Other issues that need to be addressed and resolved range from creating a team dedicated to the design, implementation, and maintenance of a data warehouse to the need for top-level support from the outset and management education on the concept and benefit of corporate sharing of data.

A further benefit of data warehousing results from the ability to mine the data using a variety of tools. Data mining aids corporate analysts in detecting customer behavior patterns, finding fraud within the organization, developing marketing strategies, and detecting inefficiencies in the internal business processes.

Because the subject of data warehousing is immensely complex, outside assistance is often beneficial. It provides organizational members with training in the technology and exposure, both theoretical and hands-on, that enables them to continue with later phases of the project.

The data warehouse is without doubt one of the most exciting technologies of our time. Organizations that make use of it increase their chances of improving customer service and developing more effective marketing strategies.

Suggested Reading

Inmon, W. *Building the Data Warehouse*. New York, NY: John Wiley. 1993.

Chapter 27
Data Marts: Plan Big, Build Small

John van den Hoven

DATA MARTS PROVIDE many decision support capabilities without incurring the cost and complexity associated with an enterprise data warehouse. With proper planning, they can be gradually consolidated to create a centralized warehouse that meets business needs and leverages improved technologies.

In today's global economy, enterprises are challenged to do more with less in order to compete successfully with a host of competitors: big and small, new and old, domestic and international. With less people resources and less financial resources with which to operate, enterprises need to better leverage their information resources to operate more efficiently and effectively. This requires improved access to timely, accurate, and consistent data that can be easily shared with other team members, decision-makers, and business partners.

It is currently acknowledged that data warehousing is the most effective way to provide this business decision support data. Under this concept, data is copied from operational systems and external information providers, then conditioned, integrated, and transformed into a read-only database that is optimized for direct access by the decision maker. The term data warehousing is particularly apt in that it describes data as being an enterprise asset that must be identified, cataloged, and stored using discipline, structure, and organization to ensure that the user will always be able to find the correct information when it is needed.

Data warehousing is a popular topic in information technology and business journals and at computer conferences. Like most new areas of information technology, data warehousing has attracted advocates who peddle it as a panacea for a wide range of problems. Data warehousing is just a natural evolution of decision support technology. Although the concept of data warehousing is not new, it is only recently that the techniques, methodologies, software tools, database management systems, disk storage,

0-8493-9820-7/00/$0.00+$.50
© 2000 by CRC Press LLC

and processor capacity have all advanced to the point where it has become possible to deliver an effective working product.

COMPARING DATA MARTS AND DATA WAREHOUSES

The term data warehousing can be applied to a broad range of approaches for providing improved access to business decision support data. These approaches can range from the simple to the more complex, with many variations in between. However, there are two major approaches that differ greatly in scale and complexity. They are the data mart and the data warehouse.

A data mart is a subject-oriented or department-oriented data warehouse. It is a scaled-down version of a data warehouse that focuses on the local needs of a specific department like finance or marketing. A data mart contains a subset of the data that would be in an enterprise's data warehouse since it is subject or department oriented. An enterprise may have many data marts, each focused on a subset of the enterprise.

A data warehouse is an orderly and accessible repository of known facts or things from many subject areas, used as a basis for decision-making. In contrast to the data mart approach, the data warehouse is generally enterprisewide in scope. Its goal is to provide a single, integrated view of the enterprise's data, spanning all the enterprise's activities. The data warehouse consolidates the various data marts and reconciles the various departmental perspectives into a single enterprise perspective.

There are advantages and disadvantages associated with both the data mart and data warehouse approaches. These two approaches differ in terms of the effort required to implement them, in their approaches to data supporting technology, and in the way the business and the users utilize these systems (see Exhibit 27.1 for more details).

The effort required to implement a data mart is considerably less than that required for a data warehouse. This is generally the case because the scope of a data mart is a subject area encompassing the applications in a business area versus the multiple subject areas of the data warehouse, which can cover all major applications in the enterprise.

As a result of its reduced scope, a data mart typically requires an order of magnitude (1/10) less effort than a data warehouse, and it can be built in months rather than years. As a result, a data mart generally costs considerably less than a data warehouse — tens or hundreds of thousands of dollars versus the millions of dollars necessary for a data warehouse. The effort is much less because a data mart generally covers fewer subject areas, has fewer users, and requires less data transformation, thus resulting in reduced complexity. In contrast, a data warehouse is cross-functional, covering multiple subject areas, having more users, and being a more com-

Effort	Data Mart	Data Warehouse
Scope	A subject area	Many subject areas
Time to Build	Months	Years
Cost to Build	$tens of thousands to $hundreds of thousands	$millions
Complexity to Build	Low to medium	High
Data		
Requirements for Sharing Sources	Shared (within business area)	Common (across enterprise)
	Few operational and external systems	Multiple operational and external systems
Size	Megabytes to low gigabytes	Gigabytes to terabytes
Time Horizon	Near-current and historical data	Historical data
Amount of Data Transformations	Low to medium	High
Frequency of Update	Daily, weekly	Weekly, monthly
Technology		
Hardware	Intel-based computers and minicomputers	Minicomputers and mainframe computers
Operating System	NT	UNIX, MVS
Database	Workgroup database servers	Large database servers
Usage		
Number of Concurrent Users	Tens	Hundreds
Type of Users	Business area analysts and managers	Enterprise analysts and senior executives
Business Focus	Optimizing activities within the business area	Cross-functional optimization and decision-making

Exhibit 27.1. Contrasts Between a Data Mart and a Data Warehouse

plex undertaking because it requires establishing a centralized structured view to all the data in the enterprise.

From a data perspective, a data mart has a reduced requirement for data sharing because of its limited scope compared to a data warehouse. It is simpler to provide shared data for a data mart because it is only necessary to establish shared data definitions for the business area or department. In contrast, a data warehouse requires common data, which necessitates establishing identical data definitions across the enterprise — a much more complex and difficult undertaking.

It is also often easier to provide timely data updates to a data mart than a data warehouse because it is smaller (megabyte to low gigabyte vs. gigabyte to terabyte for a data warehouse), requires less complex data transformations, and the enterprise does not have to synchronize data updates from multiple operational systems. Therefore, it is easier to maintain data consistency within the data mart but difficult to maintain data consistency across the various data marts within an enterprise.

The smaller size of the data mart enables more frequent updates (daily or weekly) than what is generally feasible for a data warehouse (weekly or monthly). This enables a data mart to contain near-current data in addition to the historical data that is normally contained in a data warehouse.

From a supporting technology perspective, a data mart can often use existing technology infrastructure or lower cost technology components, thus reducing the cost and complexity of the data warehousing solution. A data mart often resides on an Intel-based computer running Microsoft Corp.'s NT operating system. In contrast, a data warehouse often resides on a RISC-based (Reduced Instruction Set Computer) computer running the UNIX operating system or on a mainframe computer running the MVS operating system in order to support larger data volumes and larger numbers of business users. A data mart can also often be deployed using a lower cost workgroup relational database management system such as Oracle Corp.'s Workgroup Server or Microsoft Corp.'s SQL Server. In contrast, a data warehouse often requires a more expensive and more powerful database server such as one of the Universal Database Server products from Oracle Corp., Informix Software Inc., or International Business Machines Corp.

In addition to their different supporting technologies, the way in which business and users utilize these data warehousing solutions is also different. There are fewer concurrent users in a data mart than in a data warehouse. These users are often functional managers such as sales executives or financial executives who are focused on optimizing the activities within their department or business area. In contrast, the users of a data warehouse are often analysts or senior executives making decisions that are cross-functional and require input from multiple areas of the business.

Thus, the data mart is often used for more operational or tactical decision-making, while the data warehouse is used for strategic decision-making and some tactical decision-making. A data mart is, therefore, a more short-term, timely, data delivery mechanism, while a data warehouse is a longer term, reliable history or archive of enterprise data.

PLAN BIG, START SMALL

There is no one-size-fits-all strategy. An enterprise's data warehousing strategy can progress from a simple data mart to a complex data warehouse in response to user demands, the enterprise's business requirements, and the enterprise's maturity in managing its data resource. An enterprise can also derive a hybrid strategy that utilizes one or more of these base strategies to best fit its current applications, data, and technology architectures. The right approach is the data warehouse strategy that is appropriate to the business need and the perceived benefits.

For many enterprises, a data mart is often a practical first step to gain experience toward building and managing a data warehouse, while introducing business users to the benefits of improved access to their data, and generally demonstrating the business value of data warehousing. However, these data marts often grow rapidly to hundreds of users and hundreds of gigabytes of data derived from many different operational systems. Therefore, planning for its eventual growth should be an essential part of a data mart project.

A balance is required between starting small to get the data mart up and running quickly, and planning for the bigger data mart or data warehouse that will likely be required over time. Therefore, it is important to "Plan Big and Start Small." That is, to implement a data mart within the context of an overall architecture for the data, technology, and application that allows the data mart to support more data, more users, and more sophisticated and demanding uses over time. Otherwise, the enterprise will be implementing a series of independent and isolated data marts that recreate the jumble of systems and "functional silos" which data warehousing was trying to remedy in the first place.

CONCLUSION

The enterprise data warehouse is ideal because it would provide a consistent and comprehensive view of the enterprise, with business users employing common terminology and data throughout the enterprise. However, it remains an elusive goal for most enterprises because it is very difficult to achieve with today's technology and today's rapidly changing business environment.

A more cost-effective option for many enterprises is the data mart. It is a more manageable data warehousing project that can be focused on delivering value to a specific business area. Thus, it can provide many of the decision support capabilities without incurring the cost and complexity associated with a centralized enterprise data warehouse. With proper planning, these data marts can be gradually consolidated under a common management umbrella to create an enterprise data warehouse as it makes business sense, and as the technology evolves to better support this architecture.

Chapter 28
A Framework for Developing Enterprise Data Warehouses

Ali H. Murtaza

THE DECISION TO BUILD a data warehouse is not for the faint of heart — many critical issues must be understood early, or the project will fail. An enterprise data warehousing project is generally a huge, time-consuming investment. In many cases, the benefits are not immediately quantifiable and require a leap of faith to justify. While there are many reasons to build a data warehouse, the two most common reasons are to optimize control of current operations, or to gain significant competitive advantage. For instance, a complex, geographically distributed organization may decide that they need to identify their most profitable customer segments for target marketing programs. This is accomplished by extracting customer data from multiple production systems into a single, consolidated data warehouse. On the other hand, a niche company may architect a data mart as the first stage of a large data mining effort — revealing insightful purchasing patterns that could be leveraged for additional revenue. In both cases, the data warehouse defines itself as an integrated, non-volatile catalog of organizational data that is convertible into actionable information for strategic decision making.

There are numerous advantages of maintaining such a central perspective over the business that allows the end user to monitor both departmental and corporate performance, access all customer account information, increase managerial control, make proactive business decisions, and create sales opportunities. Although an IDC study reported an average data warehousing implementation cost of 3 million dollars (U.S.$), this expensive investment also produces a three-year average return-on-investment

0-8493-9820-7/00/$0.00+$.50
© 2000 by CRC Press LLC

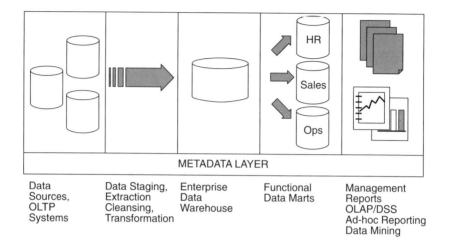

HR

Sales

Ops

METADATA LAYER

| Data Sources, OLTP Systems | Data Staging, Extraction Cleansing, Transformation | Enterprise Data Warehouse | Functional Data Marts | Management Reports OLAP/DSS Ad-hoc Reporting Data Mining |

Exhibit 28.1. Enterprise data warehouse model

(ROI) of 401%. Exhibit 28.1 shows a standard Enterprise Data Warehouse Architecture.

CONSIDERING THE CHALLENGES

An enterprise data warehousing initiative is one the most daunting projects an organization can tackle; a typical effort requires high levels of executive sponsorship, close cooperation between the business and IS communities, cross-functional expertise, and significant time and capital investments. In fact, the high risk of failure prompts experts to depict unsuccessful data warehousing projects as characteristic "rites of passage" for new project managers; experts state that approximately one out of every five DW projects actually runs to completion. This can easily make a project manager's decision to develop a data warehouse a risky move — often the key to success is the simple ability to neutralize the negative elements that could otherwise sabotage the project.

Before embarking on any data warehousing journey, a clearly defined enterprise strategy with specific goals and objectives must be presented to the project sponsors and stakeholders. Also, the project's objectives must align with those of the organization, or the project will fall short; the main driving force of any data warehousing effort is to assist decision making in achieving corporate objectives. Any project that focuses on achieving strategic objectives that differ significantly from the parent organization will be rejected by senior executives, leaving a painful lesson for the project manager.

A data warehousing venture differs from most technology projects by a high level of executive involvement. There should be no misconceptions about which group is driving a data warehouse project — the business users. Business users define the information requirements, validate the enterprise data model, and access the data for queries and reports. If the business user cannot easily navigate or understand the detailed, summarized, and historical data stored in the warehouse, the benefits are minimized. Frequent communication between the business and IS communities is mission-critical during all project phases to ensure that both groups are aligned and that the development plan meets the original business objectives.

Furthermore, the overall project structure and individual responsibilities must be clearly identified from the start, preventing any confusion among team members. If appropriate technical expertise is not available within the organization to staff the desired roles, the project manager should consider external consultants to fill in the skill gaps. Often, these consultants can provide valuable industry knowledge and vendor relationships important during the data modeling and tool selection stages. Regular meetings should be scheduled at all levels to keep everyone up to date and to uncover any potential roadblocks. A high level of sponsorship is mandatory, ensuring political support and reducing resistance from any of the business units. As the project progresses, the project manager must be aware of all organizational or resource issues, and raise them immediately to the project sponsor. Clear communication among the different project teams maintains high morale and strong levels of commitment to project objectives. As many data warehousing projects last over 18 months — albeit in manageable three to six month iterations — their benefits are realized even later, and maintaining the executive commitment and sponsorship becomes a serious challenge. The project manager must be aware of any cultural sensitivities to sharing data among the different functional units. Any political vendettas, power struggles or personal conflicts should be identified early and handled quickly before they become destructive. The key to success is constant involvement — business involvement in generating user requirements, creating the logical data models and choosing the end-user tools, and IS involvement for the hardware/software selection, data extraction, physical implementation and performance tuning.

A typical driving factor behind data warehousing projects is competition within the industry. As competitors take the lead in implementing their own corporate data warehouses and start to make sizable gains in market share and improvements in their bottom line, many companies naturally follow, expecting dramatic results in performance and significant gains in competitive advantage. Consequently, it becomes critical to understand the stability of the organization's industry — potential acquisitions or mergers could leave behind a lot of unfinished work, greater confusion surrounding corporate data, and wasted capital expenditures for both organizations. Today, many vendors are offering vertical solution sets for data-rich industries such as financial, telecommunication and health care services. These solutions are sought desperately by organizations for common business requirements and data models essential for effective analysis to be done. External consultants are also being leveraged for their vertical expertise and familiarity with vendor tools in addition to their project-related experience.

STAGE 1 — BUSINESS REQUIREMENTS

In the first stage of a data warehousing project, business requirements for enterprise information are gathered from the user community. This process generally consists of a series of interviews between the end users and the Information Technology teams in order to understand the informational needs and gaps in the organization. The consolidated results of these interviews drive the content of the data models and establish specific objectives for the new data architecture. The selection of business facts, dimensions, aggregations, level of granularity, historical depth, hierarchies, predefined queries, and standardized reports are all driven by the business users. Once the final version of the information requirements is approved by both the business and IS functions, functional data models are created with the granularity, historical detail, and summarization needed to allow end users access to the data while minimizing the performance effects of common table joins and complex queries. Specific vertical knowledge is most valuable here in customizing the data model to handle industry-specific analysis. Every piece of data in the target data model should have some business value attached to it, or it is useless to the business and should be dropped from the model. Lack of trust in the data raises a red flag, severely hindering the success of the project. However, the users must have realistic expectations of the kind of information that will be available to them with the data warehouse. Sample reports or vendor demonstrations can help in this stage to train inexperienced users to visualize the types of querying results and analytical capabilities of the data warehouse front-end tools.

The degree of summarization and size of the data being retained determines whether the data should be stored in a relational or multidimensional database. While the relational DBMS is well-established, commonly understood, and can support very large databases, the multidimensional DBMS is growing in popularity by offering quicker access to pre-aggregated data and multidimensional analysis capabilities. Multidimensional hypercubes are memory-intensive but reduce the number of physical joins for queries, and take advantage of hierarchical and historical information in the schema to "roll-up" through dimensions. Many organizations are discovering the need for a hybrid schema — both technologies are used by loading the data first into "near normal" relational models for longer term retention which are subsequently used to build specific views or dimensional models. All external feeds that are required for additional information must also be mapped into the enterprise model in this phase.

STAGE 2 — DATA SOURCING

Companies with data-intensive businesses typically have great difficulty in accessing their operational data. Somewhere in the depth of the multiple legacy systems lie valuable nuggets of business information that can never be capitalized, due to generally poor data quality and integrity. Consequently, this second stage involving extraction, cleansing and transformation of the data from the multiple sources to populate the target data warehouse is vital and often tends to be the most time-consuming part of the project. Further compounding this problem is the possible discovery that the technical resources supporting these legacy systems are no longer employed in the organization, leaving behind cryptic data definitions and programs to be deciphered for extraction when they are required. The task of cleaning up enterprisewide data from different functions and departments is often underestimated and can add significant delays to the project timelines. Increased complexity of the data makes the extraction process all the more difficult and laborious. Also, another issue to consider is the capacity of the transactional systems to scale to capture larger data volumes or external feeds that might be required in the target warehouse. Tool selection in this data staging layer must be well-researched to integrate well with the proprietary systems and the target warehouse.

STAGE 3 — TARGET ARCHITECTURE

The initial IS task to design a target architecture for the data warehouse can create religious, ideological wars among the architects; debates have raged over the tactical deployment of data marts and operational data stores as compared to the complete vision of an enterprise data warehouse. Some organizations will not take the risk of a failed project that could consume three years of their best resources. The scope of the business vision can also dictate the architecture approach: a short-term vision would require a lower budget, quick ROI implementation with small resource requirements offered by data marts, while more strategic objectives of long-term gain and full organizational control would necessitate the full-blown, enterprise data warehouse architecture. The most popular architecture choices outside the enterprise data warehouse model are the Operational Data Store, Virtual Data Warehouse, DSS Data Warehouse and the Data Mart.

An Operational Data Store is a rudimentary data store that provides a consolidated view of volatile transactional data from multiple operational systems. This architecture often provides real-time operational data that removes the redundancy and resource costs of creating a separate data warehouse. Analysis can be done with basic querying and reporting without impacting the performance of the production systems. This architecture also offers a shared view of the data, with regular updates from the operational systems. It contains current-valued data which is volatile yet very detailed. Unfortunately, operational data is not designed for decision support applications and complex queries may result in long response times and heavy impact on the transactional systems.

A Virtual Data Warehouse is quick to implement and usually less risky than a traditional data warehouse. It involves data access directly from operational data stores without creating a redundant database. This method gives the user "universal" access to data from any of the multiple sources; however, the extensive process of cleaning up the data to transform it into actionable information cannot be avoided. There are obvious time and cost savings by not consolidating the data or introducing infrastructure changes, but the tradeoff exists in the reduced usability of the data from the multiple systems. If there is a lot of data duplication in the various systems, this will easily confuse the end user and remove any confidence they have in the information. Also, if the data distribution across the legacy systems requires cross-functional information between non-SQL compliant data sources, the load, complexity and access time will be impacted on the OLTP systems and network, even if the query can be performed. This architecture also requires more intelligent analysis from the end user to understand the results of multiple queries instead of just one. Distributed query processing software must be in place to decide where and when the queries should be performed in the transactional systems. Once results are obtained, significant data validation may be required to make sense of the business information that was not cleansed or integrated. Also, the end user will not have access to historical "snapshots" which are one of the most valuable strategic decision-making tools offered by a data warehouse. Finally, the results will not be repeatable as the data is continuously changing.

The Decision Support Data Warehouse architecture simply consists of snapshots of corporate information consisting of low-level or highly summarized data. This method has the advantages of minimal infrastructure costs, access to non-volatile data, quick deployment time, and no repetitive data stores. However, the main flaw with this architecture is its inherent lack of flexibility to handle complex decision support analysis expected from a fully architected data warehouse; the data structures are not changed, merely stored periodically as "snaphots" for comparative analysis. This technique provides good historical information but fails to optimize access to the data. In fact, the snapshots of data are ideal for independent business intelligence and data mining approaches to unearthing customer patterns and trends.

Another potential architecture is the popular Data Mart or Functional Data Warehouse that captures a subset of the enterprise data for a specific function, business unit, or application. Data marts require less cost and effort to deploy, and provide access to functional or private information to specific organizational units. They are suited for businesses demanding a fast time to market, quick impact on the bottom line, and minimal infrastructure changes. Data marts are essentially mini-data warehouses without the huge cost, long time investment, high risk of failure, and high level of corporate approval; they are ideal for a rapid, iterative, prototype deployment. Data marts store non-volatile, time-variant, and summarized information used to serve the information needs of the business unit. However, data marts should not be used as a cheaper solution to a data warehouse; they should simply represent an initial step toward an enterprise data warehouse. If data marts are introduced first, they should be designed to integrate with a future enterprise data warehouse, or much rework will have to be done over the long term. As other business units notice the benefits, data marts must not be allowed to propagate freely throughout the organization, or the situation will spell disaster when attempting to integrate them into a single corporate warehouse. When data marts are introduced after the successful implementation of a data warehouse, they can be deployed quickly by replicating required subsets of the corporate database.

STAGE 4 — ACCESS TOOL SELECTION

The level of sophistication of the intended user should be a main driver in the reporting tool selection process. Exhibit 28.2 illustrates the many levels of query, reporting, and OLAP tools in the marketplace with functions ranging from basic management reporting to complex, drill-down, pass-through analytical processing. It is crucial that the user be comfortable in navigating through the newly consolidated data. Otherwise, this huge capital investment will result in the same scenario the organization started with, namely, lots of data with no perceived method to access it. Sample reports and demonstrations are good aids in assessing the results and the capabilities of the business intelligence tool.

In fact, careful training should be provided for the end users to ensure that they understand the various capabilities of the tools. Instead of producing monthly management reports, they should be encouraged to make ad-hoc queries and "slice and dice" through the multiple dimensions and navigate throughout the available information to isolate the specific set of information they require. Once the user taps into the metadata layer (see Exhibit 28.1) and understands the type of data and relationships that exist in the warehouse, he or she is are better equipped to perform meaningful analysis and extract valuable information about the business. Newly evolved data mining technologies promise to bring even greater benefits

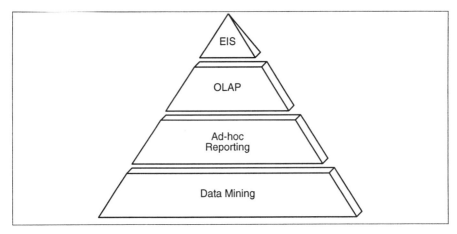

Exhibit 28.2. User access tools

by performing complex statistical analysis on historical records to uncover business patterns, customer trends, organizational inefficiencies and even potential fraud.

STAGE 5 — DATA WAREHOUSE ADMINISTRATION

One of the commonly neglected issues is the administration of the data warehouse after it is built. The appropriate technical resources must be assigned to monitor query load and performance, to handle dynamic changes to the data structures, and to ensure platform scalability with increased user demands. External data may be needed (e.g., stock feeds, Web downloads) and so the architecture must have an open interface to incorporate these new requirements. As users become more sophisticated in their use of the decision support tools, the frequency and complexity of the queries and reports will significantly impact the query performance. "Queries from hell" can destroy perceived levels of performance if they are not identified and managed carefully. Consequently, a dedicated administrator is needed to maintain constant supervision of the query performance and to prevent the data warehouse from grinding to a halt.

Generally, data warehousing projects use the prototype approach to development, and much of the initial success of the prototype will determine the overall success of the project. The data model should be designed against an extensive range of end-user queries and target reports showing enhanced analytical business information and should be designed to maintain buy-in from the executive sponsors during the pilot demonstration. Most importantly, the information must be accurate, or at least more accurate than the pre-data warehouse data to increase the user's confidence in the information. If the user has unwavering faith in the data, the project has a greater chance to succeed.

CONCLUSIONS

A common point of debate arises when measuring the overall investment impact of a particular project — the added value of "business information" is hard to translate into cost savings or generated revenue. The difficulty in quantifying these benefits is one of the most problematic issues facing the project manager in keeping corporate buy-in and team commitment. How can one measure business value? As shown in Exhibit 28.1, one answer lies in a well-developed metadata repository that allows the business user to easily understand and navigate through the large amounts of corporate-wide data contained in the new warehouse. Each piece of data selected for the new data model should be clearly defined in the metadata and perceived as adding business value. If the end user sees no value in it, he or she will not use it and it should be omitted from the new data model. The remarkable change in the business analyst's job is represented by the drastically reduced time needed to gather organizational data — much more time is dedicated to derive meaningful information that will drive the sustained growth and operational efficiency of the corporation.

The designed architecture of the metadata and data warehouse must be scalable enough to support future changes to information needs and analytical requirements (e.g., Web-based delivery). Ongoing management of the data warehouse with minimal adjustments to the data architecture and business users excited about their data are true indicators of project success. Business value is reflected by the enhanced corporate control, lowered costs, increased revenue, strong market share, and new opportunities that are all direct results of the information delivery architecture called the data warehouse.

References

Bachteal, Paul, "Data Warehouses: Professional management key to successful implementation", *Canadian Manager*, Vol. 22, No. 22, Summer 1997, pp. 20-21.

Barquin, Dr. Ramon C., *An Introduction to Data Warehousing*, Barquin and Associates, The Data Warehousing Institute, 1997.

Benson, Beth and Von Hollen, Cynthia, "Case Study III: Strategies For A Successful Data Warehouse," May 28, 1997.

Bischoff, Joyce and Alexander, Ted, *Data Warehouse Practical Advice from the Experts*, Prentice Hall, 1997.

Evans, Jim, "Need for analysis drives data warehouse appeal," *Health Management Technology*, Vol. 18, No. 11, Oct. 1997, pp. 28-31.

Foley, John, "Data Warehousing Pitfalls," *InformationWeek*, May 19, 1997.

Hackney, Doug, "Understanding and Implementing Successful Data Marts," May 28, 1997.

Stedman, Craig, "Turning to outside warehousing help," *ComputerWorld*.

Waltner, Charles, "Ready-made warehouses," *InformationWeek*, No. 655, Nov. 3, 1997, pp. 100-108.

Chapter 29

Data Mining: Exploring the Corporate Asset

Jason Weir

DATA MINING, as a methodology, is a set of techniques used to uncover previously obscure or unknown patterns and relationships in very large databases. The ultimate goal is to arrive at comprehensible, meaningful results from extensive analysis of information. For companies with very large and complex databases, discovery-based data mining approaches must be implemented in order to realize the complete value that data offers.

Companies today generate and collect vast amounts of data that they use in the ongoing process of doing business. Transaction data such as that produced by inventory, billing, shipping and receiving, and sales systems is stored in operational or departmental data stores. It is understood that data represents a significant competitive advantage, but realizing the full potential of it is not simple. Decision makers must be able to interpret trends, identify factors or utilize information based on clear, timely data in a meaningful format. For instance, a marketing director should be able to identify a group of customers, 18 to 24 years of age, that owns notebook computers who need, or are likely to purchase, an upcoming collaboration software product. After identifying them, the director sends them advance offers, information, or product order forms to increase product pre-sales.

Data mining, as a methodology, is a set of techniques used to uncover previously obscure or unknown patterns and relationships in very large databases. The ultimate goal is to arrive at comprehensible, meaningful results from extensive analysis of information.

HOW IS IT DIFFERENT FROM OTHER ANALYSIS METHODS?

Data mining differs from other methods in several ways. A significant distinction between data mining and other analytical tools is in the approaches they use in exploring the data. Many analytical tools available support a verification-based approach in which the user hypothesizes about specific data relationships and then uses the tools to verify or refute those presumptions. This verification-based process stems from the intuition of the user to pose the questions and refine the analysis based on the results of potentially complex queries against a database. The effectiveness of this analysis depends on several factors, the most important of which are the ability of the user to pose appropriate questions, the capability of tools to return results quickly, and the overall reliability and accuracy of the data being analyzed.

Other available analytical tools have been optimized to address some of these issues. Query and reporting tools, such as those used in data mart or warehouse applications, let users develop queries through point-and-click interfaces. Statistical analysis packages, like those used by many insurance or actuarial firms, provide the ability to explore relationships among a few variables and determine statistical significance against demographic sets. Multidimensional online analytical processing (OLAP) tools enable fast response to user inquiries through their ability to compute hierarchies of variables along "dimensions" such as size, color or location.

Data mining, in contrast to these analytical tools, uses what are called discovery-based approaches in which pattern matching and other algorithms are employed to determine the key relationships in the data. Data mining algorithms can look at numerous multidimensional data relationships concurrently, highlighting those that are dominant or exceptional. In other words, true data mining tools uncover trends, patterns and relationships automatically. As mentioned above, many other types of analytical methods rely on user intuition or the ability to pose the "right kind" of question. To sum things up, analytical tools — query tools, statistical tools, and OLAP — and the results they produce, are all user driven, while data mining is data-driven.

THE NEED FOR DATA MINING

As discussed, traditional methods involve the decision maker hypothesizing the existence of information of interest, converting that hypothesis to a query, posing that query to the analysis tool, and interpreting the returned results with respect to the decision being made. For instance, the marketing director must hypothesize that notebook-owning 18 to 24-year-old customers are likely to purchase the upcoming software release. After posing the query, it is up to the individual to interpret the returned results and determine if the list represents a good group of product prospects. The quality of the extracted information is based on the user's interpretation of the posed query's results.

The intricacies of data interrelationships as well as the sheer size and complexity of modern data stores necessitate more advanced analysis capabilities than those provided by verification-based data mining approaches.

The ability to automatically discover important information hidden in the data and then present it in the appropriate way is a critical complementary technology to verification-based approaches. Tools, techniques and systems that perform these automated analysis tasks are referred to as discovery based. Discovery-based systems applied to the marketing director's data store may identify many groups including, for example: 18 to 24-year-old male college students with laptops, 24 to 30-year-old female software engineers with both desktop and notebook systems, and 18 to 24-year-old customers planning to purchase portable computers within the next six months. By recognizing the marketing director's goal, the discovery-based system can identify the software engineers as the key target group by spending pattern or other variable.

In sum, verification-based approaches, although valuable for quick, high-level decision support, such as historical queries about product sales by fiscal quarter, are insufficient. For companies with very large and complex databases, discovery-based data mining approaches must be implemented to realize the complete value that data offers.

THE PROCESS OF MINING DATA

Selection and Extraction

Constructing an appropriate database to run queries against is a critical step in the data mining process. A marketing database may contain extensive tables of data from purchasing records and lifestyle data to more advanced demographic information such as census records. Not all of this data is required on a regular basis and should be filtered out of the query tables. Additionally, even after selecting the desired database tables, it is not always necessary to mine the contents of the entire table to identify useful information under certain conditions and for certain types of data mining techniques. For example, when creating a classification or prediction model, it may be adequate to first sample the table and then mine the sample. This is usually a faster, and less expensive operation.

Essentially, potential sources of data (e.g., census data, sales records, mailing lists, demographic databases) should be explored before meaningful analysis can take place. The selected data types may be organized along multiple tables. Developing a sound model involves combining parts of separate tables into a single database for mining purposes.

Data Cleansing and Transformation

Once the database tables have been selected and the data to be mined has been identified, it is usually necessary to perform certain transformations and cleansing routines on the data. Data cleansing or transformations are determined by the type of data being mined as well as the data mining technique being used. Transformations vary from conversions of one type of data to another, such as numeric data to character data, or currency conversions, to more advanced transformations such as the application of mathematical or logical functions on certain types of data. Cleansing, on the other hand, is used to ensure reliability and accuracy of results. Data can be verified, or cleansed, in order to remove duplicate entries, attach real values to numeric or alphanumeric codes, and omit incomplete records. "Dirty", or inaccurate data in the mining data store must be avoided if results are to be accurate and useful. Many data mining tools include a system log or other graphical interface tool to identify erroneous data in queries, but every effort should be made prior to this stage to ensure that it does not arrive at the mining database. If errors are not discovered, lower quality results and, due to this, lesser quality decisions will be the result.

Mining, Analysis and Interpretation

The clean and transformed data is subsequently mined using one or more techniques in order to extract the desired type of information. For example, to develop an accurate classification model that predicts whether or not a customer will upgrade to a new version of a software package, a decision maker must first use clustering to segment the customer database. Next, he or she will apply rules to automatically create a classification model for each desired cluster. While mining a particular data set, it may be necessary to access additional data from a data mart or warehouse, and perform additional transformations of the original data. The terms and methods mentioned above will be defined and discussed later in this chapter.

The last step in the data mining process is analyzing and interpreting results. The extracted and transformed data is analyzed with respect to the user's goal, and the best information is identified and presented to the decision maker through the decision support system. The purpose of result interpretation is to not only graphically represent the output of the data mining operation, but also to filter the information that will be presented through the decision support system. For example, if the goal is to develop a classification model, during the result interpretation step, the robustness of the extracted model is tested using one of the established methods. If the interpreted results are not satisfactory, it may be necessary to repeat the data mining step, or to repeat other steps. What this really speaks to is the quality of data. The information extracted through data mining must be ultimately comprehensible. For example, it may be necessary, after interpreting the results of a data mining operation, to go back and add data to the selection process or to perform a different calculation during the transformation step.

TECHNIQUES

Classification

Classification is perhaps the most often employed data mining technique. It involves a set of instances or predefined examples to develop a model that can classify the population of records at large.

The use of classification algorithms begins with a sample set of pre-classified example transactions. For a fraud detection application, this would include complete records of both fraudulent and valid transactions, determined on a record-by-record basis. The classifier-training algorithm uses these pre-classified examples to determine the set of parameters required for proper identification. The algorithm then encodes these parameters into a model called a classifier, or classification model. The approach affects the decision-making capability of the system. Once an effective classifier is developed, it is used in a predictive mode to classify new records automatically into these same predefined classes.

In the fraud detection case above, the classifier would be able to identify probable fraudulent activities. Another example would involve a financial application where a classifier capable of identifying risky loans could be used to aid in the decision of whether or not to grant a loan to an individual.

Association

Given a collection of items and a set of transactions, each of which contains some number of items from a given collection, an association is an operation against this set of records which returns affinities that exist among the collection of items. "Market basket" analysis is a common application that utilizes association techniques. Market basket analysis involves a retailer running an association function over the point of sales transaction log. The goal is to determine affinities among shoppers. For example, in an analysis of 100,000 transactions, association techniques could determine that "20% of the time, customers who buy a particular software application, also purchase the complementary add-on software pack."

In other words, associations are items that occur together in a given event or transaction. Association tools discover rules.

Another example of the use of association discovery could be illustrated in an application that analyzes the claim forms submitted by patients to a medical insurance company. The goal is to discover patterns among the claimants' treatment. Assume that every claim form contains a set of medical procedures that were performed to the given patient during one visit. By defining the set of items to be the collection of all medical procedures that can be performed on a patient and the records to correspond to each claim form, the application can find, using the association technique, relationships among medical procedures that are often performed together.

Sequence Based

Traditional "market basket" analysis deals with a collection of items as a part of a point-in-time transaction. A variant of this occurs when there is additional information to tie together a sequence of purchases. An account number, a credit card, or a frequent shopper number are all examples of ways to track multiple purchases in a time series.

Rules that capture these relationships can be used, for example, to identify a typical set of precursor purchases that might predict the subsequent purchase of a specific item. In our software case, sequence-based mining could determine the likelihood of a customer purchasing a particular software product to subsequently purchase complementary software, or hardware device such as a joystick or a video card.

Sequence-based mining can be used to detect the set of customers associated with frequent buying patterns. Use of sequence-based mining on the set of insurance claims discussed earlier can lead to the identification of frequently occurring medical procedures performed on patients. This can then be harnessed in a fraud detection application, also discussed earlier, to detect cases of medical insurance fraud.

Clustering

Clustering segments a database into different groups. The goal is to find groups that differ from one another as well as similarities among members. The clustering approach assigns records with a large number of attributes into a relatively small set of groups, or "segments". This assignment process is performed automatically by clustering algorithms that identify the distinguishing characteristics of the data set and then partition the space defined by the data set attributes along natural "boundaries". There is no need to identify the groupings desired or the attributes that should be used to segment the data set.

Clustering is often one of the first steps in data mining analysis. It identifies groups of related records that can be used as starting points for exploring further relationships. This technique supports the development of population segmentation models, such as demographic-based customer segments. Additional analyses using standard analytical and other data mining techniques can determine the characteristics of these segments with respect to some desired outcome. For example, the buying habits of multiple population segments might be compared to determine which segments to target for a new marketing campaign.

Estimation

Estimation is a variation on the classification technique. Essentially it involves the generation of scores along various dimensions in the data. Rather than employing a binary classifier to determine whether a loan applicant, for instance, is approved or classified as a risk, the estimation approach generates a credit-worthiness "score" based on a pre-scored sample set of transactions. That is, sample data (complete records of approved and risk applicants) are used as samples in determining the worthiness of all records in a data set.

APPLICATIONS OF DATA MINING

Data mining is now being applied in a variety of industries ranging from investment management and retail solutions to marketing, manufacturing and health care applications. It has been pointed out that many organizations, due to the strategic nature of their data mining operations, will not even discuss their projects with outsiders. This is understandable due to the importance and potential that successful solutions offer organizations. However, there are several well-known applications that are proven performers.

In customer profiling, characteristics of good customers are identified with the goals of predicting who will become one and helping marketing departments target new prospects. Data mining can find patterns in a customer database that can be applied to a prospect database so that customer acquisition can be appropriately targeted. For example, by identifying good candidates for mail offers or catalogs, direct-mail marketing managers can reduce expenses and increase their sales generation efforts. Targeting specific promotions to existing and potential customers offers similar benefits.

Market-basket analysis helps retailers understand which products are purchased together or by an individual over time. With data mining, retailers can determine which products to stock in which stores and how to place them within a store. Data mining can also help assess the effectiveness of promotions and coupons.

Last, fraud detection is of great benefit to credit card companies, insurance firms, stock exchanges, government agencies, and telecommunications firms. The aggregate total for fraud losses in today's world is enormous; but with data mining, these companies can identify potentially fraudulent transactions and contain damage. Financial companies use data mining to determine market and industry characteristics as well as predict individual company and stock performance. Another interesting niche application is in the medical field. Data mining can help predict the effectiveness of surgical procedures, diagnostic tests, medication, and other services.

SUMMARY

More and more companies are beginning to realize the potential for data mining within their organization. However, unlike the "plug-and-play", out-of-the-box business solutions that many have become accustomed to, data mining is not a simple application. It involves a good deal of forethought, planning, research, and testing to ensure a sound, reliable, and beneficial project. It is also important to remember that data mining is complementary to traditional query and analysis tools, data warehousing, and data mart applications. It does not replace these useful and often vital solutions.

Data mining enables organizations to take full advantage of the investment they have made and are currently making in building data stores. By identifying valid, previously unknown information from large databases, decision makers can tap into the unique opportunities that data mining offers.

Chapter 30
Data Conversion Fundamentals

Michael Zimmer

WHEN SYSTEMS DEVELOPERS build information systems, they usually do not start with a clean slate. Often, they are replacing an existing application. They must always determine if the existing information should be preserved. Usually the older information is transferred to the new system — a process known as data conversion.

Data conversion can involve moving data from flat file systems to relational database management systems (RDBMS). It could also involve changing from systems with loose constraints to new systems with tight constraints.

This chapter focuses on laying the groundwork for successfully executing a data conversion effort the first time around. It is assumed in this chapter that data modeling is being done and that relational data base technology is employed. At the logical level, the terms *entity set, entity,* and *attribute* are used in place of the terms *file, record,* and *field.* At the physical level, the terms *table, row,* and *column* are used instead of *file, record,* and *field.* The members of IS engaged in the data conversion effort are referred to as the data conversion team (DCT).

COMMON PROBLEMS WITH DATA

The difficulties of a data conversion effort are almost always underestimated. Usually the conversion costs many times more than originally anticipated. This is invariably the result of an inadequate understanding of the cost and effort required to correct errors in the data. Usually the quality of the existing data is much worse than the users and development team anticipate.

Problems with data can result from missing information and mismatches between the old model (often only implicit) and the new model (usually explicitly documented). Problems also result if the conversion effort is started too late in the project and is under-resourced. The most common sources of problems are data quality and incomplete data.

Costs and Benefits of Data Conversion

Before embarking on data conversion, the data conversion team should decide whether or not data really needs to be converted and if it is feasible to abandon the noncurrent data. Starting fresh is an option.

The customers may decide that the cost to preserve and correct old information exceeds the benefit expected. Often, they will want to preserve old information, but may not have the resources to correct historical errors. With a data warehouse project, it is a given that the data will be converted. Preservation of old information is critical.

The Cost of Not Converting. The DCT should first demonstrate the cost of permitting erroneous information into the new data base. It is a decision to be made by user management.

In the long run, permitting erroneous data into the new application will usually be costly. The data conversion team should explain what the risks are to justify the costs for robust programming and data error correction.

Costs of Converting. It is no easier to estimate the cost of a conversion effort than to estimate the cost of any other development effort. The special considerations are that there may be a great deal of manual intervention, and subsequently extra programming, to remedy data errors. A simple copy procedure usually does not serve the organization's needs. If the early exploration of data quality and robust design and programming for the conversion routines is skimped on, IS will generally pay for it.

STEPS IN THE DATA CONVERSION PROCESS

In even the simplest IT systems development projects, the efforts of many players must come together. At the managerial and employee levels, certain users should be involved, in addition to the applications development group, data administration, DBA, computer operations, and quality assurance. The responsibilities of the various groups must be clearly defined.

In the simplest terms, data conversion involves the following steps:

- Determining if conversion is required.
- Planning the conversion.
- Determining the conversion rules.
- Identifying problems.
- Writing up the requirements.
- Correcting the data.

- Programming the conversion.
- Running the conversion.
- Checking audit reports.
- Institutionalizing.

Determining if Conversion is Required

In some cases, data does not need to be converted. IS may find that there is no real need to retain old information. The data could be available elsewhere, such as on microfiche. Another possibility is that the current data is so erroneous, incomplete, or inadequate that there is no reason to keep it. The options must be presented to the clients so that they can determine the best course of action.

Planning the Conversion and Determining the Conversion Rules. Once the DCT and the client have accepted the need for a conversion, the work can be planned in detail. The planning activities for conversion are standard in most respects and are typical of development projects.

Beyond sound project management, it is helpful for the DCT to keep in mind that error correction activities may be particularly time consuming. Determination of the conversion rules consists of these steps, usually done in sequence:

- Analyzing the old physical data model.
- Conducting a preliminary investigation on data quality.
- Analyzing the old logical data model.
- Analyzing the new logical data model.
- Analyzing the new physical data model.
- Determining the data mapping.
- Determining how to treat missing information.

Analyzing the Old Physical Data Model. Some published development methods imply that development starts with a blank slate. As a result, analysis of the existing system is neglected.

The reverse engineering paradigm asserts that the DCT should start with the existing computer application to discern the business rules. Data conversion requires this approach for data analysis. The DCT can look at old documentation, data base definitions, file descriptions, and record layouts to understand the current physical data model.

Conducting a Preliminary Investigation of Data Quality. Without some understanding of data structures for the current application, it is not possible to look at the quality of the data. To examine the quality of the data, the DCT can run existing reports, do online queries, and if possible, quickly write some fourth-generation language programs to examine issues such as referential, primary key, and domain integrity violations that the users might never notice. When the investigation is done, the findings can be formally documented.

Analyzing the Old Logical Data Model. When the physical structure of the data is understood, it can be represented in its normalized logical structure. This step, although seemingly unnecessary, allows the DCT to specify the mapping in a much more reliable fashion. The results should be documented with the aid of an entity-relationship diagram accompanied by dictionary descriptions.

Analyzing the New Physical Data Model. The new logical model should be transformed into a physical representation. If a relational data base is being used, this may be a simple step. Once this model is done, the mapping can be specified.

Determining the Data Mapping. This step is often more difficult than it might seem initially. Usually, the exceptions are one old file-to-one new file, and one old field-to-one new field.

Often there are cases where the old domain must be transformed into a new one, an old field is split into two new ones, two old fields become one new one, or multiple records are looked at to derive a new one. There are many ways of reworking the data, and an unlimited number of special cases may exist. Not only are the possibilities for mapping numerous and complex, in some cases it is not possible at all to map to the new model because key information was not collected in the old system.

Determining How to Treat Missing Information. It is common when doing conversion to discover that some of the data to populate the new application is not available, and there is no provision for it in the old database. It may be available elsewhere as manual records, or it may never have been recorded at all.

Sometimes, this is only an inconvenience — dummy values can be put in certain fields to indicate that the value is not known. In the more serious case, the missing information would be required to create a primary key or a foreign key. This can occur when the new model is significantly different from the old. In this case, the dummy value strategy may be appropriate, but it must be fully explained to the client.

Identifying Problems

Data problems can only be detected after the old data structure is fully understood. Once it is determined what the new model will look like, a deeper analysis of the issue can be done.

A full analysis of the issue includes looking for erroneous information, missing information, redundancies, inconsistencies, missing keys, and any other problem that will make the conversion difficult or impossible without a lot of manual intervention. Any findings should be documented and brought to the attention of the client. Information must be documented in a fashion that makes sense to the client.

Once the problems have been identified, the DCT can help the client identify a corrective strategy. The client must understand why errors have been creeping into the systems. The cause is usually a mixture of problems with the old data structure, problems with the existing input system, and data entry problems that have been ongoing. It may be that the existing system does not properly reflect the business. The users may have been working around the system's deficiencies for years in ways that violated its integrity. In any case, the new system should be tighter than the old one at the programming and database level, should properly reflect the business, and the new procedures should not result in problems with usability or data quality.

Documenting the Requirements

After the initial study of the conversion is done, the findings should be documented. Some of this work will have been done as part of the regular system design. There must also be a design for the conversion programs, whether it is a one-time or an ongoing activity. First-time as well as ongoing load requirements must be examined.

Estimates should include the time necessary to extract, edit, correct, and upload data. Costs for disk storage and CPUs should also be projected. In addition, the sizing requirements should be estimated well in advance of hardware purchases.

Correcting the Data

The client may want to correct the data before the conversion effort begins, or may be willing to convert the data over time. It is best to make sure that the data that is converted is error free, at least with respect to the formal integrity constraints defined for the new model.

If erroneous information is permitted into the new system, it will probably be problematic later. The correction process may involve using the existing system to make changes. Often, the types of errors that are encountered may require some extra programming facilities. Not all systems provide all of the data modification capabilities that might be necessary. In any case, this step can sometimes take months of effort and requires a mechanism for evaluating the success of the correction effort.

Programming the Conversion

The conversion programs should be designed, constructed, and tested with the same discipline used for any other software development. Although the number of workable designs is unlimited, there are a few helpful rules of thumb:

- The conversion program should edit for all business rule violations and reject nonconforming information. The erroneous transactions should go to an error file, and a log of the problem should be written. The soundest course is to avoid putting incorrect data into the new system.
- The conversion programs must produce an audit trail of the transactions processes. This includes control totals, checksums, and date and time stamps. This provides a record of how the data was converted after the job is done.
- Tests should be as rigorous as possible. All design documents and code should be tested in a structured fashion. This is less costly than patching up problems caused by a data corruption in a million record file.
- Provisions should be made for restart in case of interruption in the run.
- It should be possible to roll back to some known point if there are errors.
- Special audit reports should be prepared to run against the old and new data to demonstrate that the procedures worked. This reporting can be done in addition to the standard control totals from the programs.

Running the Conversion

It may be desirable to run a test conversion to populate a test data base. Once the programs are ready and volume testing has been done, it is time for the first conversion, which may be only one of many.

If this is a data warehouse application, the conversion could be an ongoing effort. It is important to know how long the initial loads will take so that scheduling can be done appropriately. The conversion can then be scheduled for an opportune cutover time. The conversion will go smoothly if contingencies are built in and sound risk management procedures are followed. There may be a number of static tables, perhaps used for code lookup that can be converted without as much fanfare, but the main conversion will take time.

At the time planned for cutover, the old production system can be frozen from update or run in parallel. The production data base can then be initialized and test records removed (if any have been created). The conversion and any verification and validation routines can be run at this point.

Checking Audit Reports

Once the conversion is finished, special audit reports should be run to prove that it worked, to check control totals, and deal with any problems. It may be necessary to roll back to the old system if problems are excessive. The new application should not be used until it is verified that the conversion was correct, or a lot of work could be lost.

Institutionalizing

In many cases, as in data warehousing, conversion will be a continuous process and must be institutionalized. Procedural controls are necessary to make sure that the conversion runs on schedule, results are checked rigorously, rejected data is dealt with appropriately, and failed runs are handled correctly.

DATA QUALITY

A strategy to identify data problems early in the project should be in place, though details will change according to the project. A preliminary investigation can be done as soon as the old physical data model has been determined. It is important to document the quality of the current data, but this step may require programming resources. Customers at all levels should be notified if there are data quality issues to be resolved. Knowledge of the extent of data quality problems may influence the users' decision to convert or abandon the data.

Keeping the Data Clean

If the data is corrected on a one-time basis, it is important to ensure that more erroneous data is not being generated by some faulty process or programming. There may be a considerable time interval between data correction and conversion to the new system.

Types of Data Abnormalities

There may be integrity problems in the old system. For example, there may be no unique primary key for some of the old files, which almost guarantees redundancy in the data. This violation of entity integrity can be quite serious.

To ensure entity integrity in the new system, the DCT will have to choose which of the old records is to be accepted as the correct one to move into the new system. It is helpful for audit routines to report on this fact. In addition, in the new system it will be necessary to devise a primary key, which may not be available in the old data.

Uniqueness. In many cases, there are other fields that should also be unique and serve as an alternate primary key. In some cases, even if there is primary key integrity, there are redundancies in other alternative keys, which again creates a problem for integrity in the new system.

Referential Integrity. The DCT should determine whether the data correctly reflects referential integrity constraints. In a relational system, tables are joined together by primary key/foreign key links. The information to create this link may not be available in the old data. If records from different files are to be matched and joined, it should be determined whether or not the information exists to correctly do the join (i.e., a unique primary key and a foreign key). Again, this problem needs to be addressed prior to conversion.

Domain Integrity. The domain for a field imposes constraints on the values that should be found there. IS should determine if there are data domains that have been coded into character or numeric fields in an undisciplined and inconsistent fashion. It should further be determined whether or not there are numeric domains that have been coded into character fields, perhaps with some non-numeric values. There may be date fields that are just text strings, and the dates may be in any order. A common problem is that date or numeric fields stored as text may contain absurd values with the wrong data type entirely.

Another determination that should be made is whether the domain coding rules have changed over time and whether or not they have been re-coded. It is common for coded fields to contain codes that are no longer in use, and often codes that never were in use. Also, numeric fields may contain out-of-range values. Composite domains could cause problems when trying to separate them for storage in multiple fields. The boundaries for each sub-item may not be in fixed columns.

There may be domains that incorrectly model internal hierarchy. This is common in old-style systems and makes data modeling difficult. There could be attributes based on more than one domain. Not all domain problems will create conversion difficulties, but they may be problematic later if it cannot be proven that these were preexisting anomalies and not a result of the conversion efforts.

Wrong Cardinality. The old data could contain cardinality violations. For example, the structure may say that each employee has only one job record, but in fact some may have five or six. These sorts of problems make data base design difficult.

Wrong Optionality. Another common problem is the absence of a record when one should be there. It may be a rule that every employee has at least one record of appointment, but for some reason 1% of old records show no job for an employee. This inconsistency must be resolved by the client.

Orphaned Records. In many cases, a record is supposed to refer back to some other record by making reference to the key value for that other record. In many badly designed systems, there is no key to refer back to, at least not one that uniquely identifies the record. Technically, there is no primary key. In some cases, there is no field available to make this reference, which means that there is no foreign key. In other cases, the key structure is fine, but the actual record referred back to does not exist. This is a problem with referential integrity. This record without a parent is called an orphan.

Inconsistent Redundancy. If each data item is fully determined by its key, there will be no undesirable redundancy, and the new data base will be normalized. If attempts at normalization are made where there is redundant information, the DCT will be unable to make consistent automated choices about which of the redundant values to select for the conversion.

On badly designed systems, there will be a great deal of undesirable redundancy. For example, a given fact may be stored in multiple places. This type of redundancy wastes disk storage, but may in some cases permit faster queries.

The problem is that without concerted programming efforts, this redundant information is almost certainly going to become inconsistent. If the old data has confusing redundancies, it is important to determine whether they are due to historical changes in the business rules or historical changes in the values of fields and records.

The DCT should also determine whether the redundancies are found across files or within individual files across records. There may be no way to determine which data is current, and an arbitrary choice will have to be made. If the DCT chooses to keep all of the information to reflect the changes over time, it cannot be stored correctly because the date information will not be in the system. This is an extremely common problem.

Missing Information. When dealing with missing information, it is helpful to determine whether or not:

- The old data is complete.
- Mandatory fields are filled in.
- All necessary fields are available in the files.
- All records are present.

- Default or dummy values can be inserted where there is missing information.

Date Inconsistencies. When examining the conversion process, it is helpful to determine whether or not:

- The time dimension is correctly represented.
- The data spans a long enough time period.
- The data correctly reflects the state of the business for the time at which it was captured.
- All necessary date fields are available to model the time dimension properly.
- Dates are stored with century information.
- Date ranges are in the correct sequence within a given record.
- Dates are correct from record to record.

Miscellaneous Inconsistencies. In some fields, there will be values derived from other fields. A derived field might be computed from other fields in the same record or may be a function of multiple records. The derived fields may be stored in an entirely different file. In any case, the derived values may be incorrect for the existing data. Given this sort of inconsistency, it should be determined which is correct — the detail or the summary information.

Intelligent Keys. An intelligent key results from a fairly subtle data modeling problem. For example, there are two different independent items from the real world, such as Employee and Department, where the Employee is given a key that consists in part of the Department key. The implication is that if a Department is deleted, the employee record will be orphaned, and if an Employee changes Departments, the Employee key will have to change. When doing a conversion, it would be desirable to remove the intelligent key structure.

Other Problems. Often other problems with the old data cannot be easily classified. These problems involve errors in the data that cannot be detected except by going back to the source, or violations of various arcane constraints that have not been programmed as edit checks in the existing system. There may be special rules that tie field values to multiple records, multiple fields, or multiple files. Although they may not have a practical implication for the conversion effort, if these problems become obvious, they might be falsely attributed to the conversion routines.

THE ERROR CORRECTION PROCESS

The data correction effort should be run as part of a separate subproject. The DCT should determine whether or not the resources to correct the data can be made available. A wholesale commitment from the owners of the data will be required, and probably a commitment of programming resources as well. Error correction cannot be done within the context of rapid applications development (RAD).

Resources for the Correction Effort

Concerning resources for the correction effort, the best-case scenario would ensure that:

- Resources are obtained from the client if a major correction effort is required.
- Management pays adequate attention to the issue if a data quality problem is identified.
- The sources of the problem will be identified in a fair and nonjudgmental manner if a data quality problem is identified.

Choices for Correction

The effort required to write an edit program to look for errors is considerable, and chances are good that this will be part of the conversion code and not an independent set of audit programs. Some of the errors may be detected before conversion begins, but it is likely that many of the problems will be found during the conversion run.

Once data errors are discovered, data can be copied as is, corrected, or abandoned. The conversion programs should reject erroneous transactions and provide reports that explain why data was rejected. If the decision is made to correct the data, it will probably have to be reentered. Again, in some cases, additional programming can help remedy the problems.

Programming for Data Correction

Some simple automated routines can make the job of data correction much easier. If they require no manual intervention, it could be advantageous to simply put them into the main conversion program. However, the program may require that a user make the decision.

If the existing data entry programs are not adequate for large-scale data correction efforts, some additional programs might have to be written for error repair. For example, the existing system may not allow the display of records with a referential integrity problem, which are probably the very records that need correction. Custom programming will be required to make the change.

SPECIFYING THE MAPPING

Often, crucial information needed for the conversion will be missing. If the old system can accommodate the missing information, it may be a matter of keying it in from original paper records. However, the original information may not be available anymore, or it may never have been collected. In that case, it may be necessary to put in special markers to show that the information is not available.

Model Mismatches

It can be difficult to go from an non-normalized structure to a normalized structure because of the potential for problems in mapping from old to new. Many problems are the result of inconsistent and redundant data, a poor key structure, or missing information. If there is a normalized structure in the old system, there probably will not be as many difficulties. Other problems result from changed assumptions about the cardinality of relationships or actual changes in the business rules.

Discovered Requirements

The requirements of a system are almost never fully understood by the user or the developer prior to construction of the system. Some of the data requirements do not become clear until the test conversions are being run. At that point, it may be necessary to go back and revisit the whole development effort. Standard change and scope control techniques apply.

Existing Documentation

Data requirements are rarely right the first time because the initial documentation is seldom correct. There may be abandoned fields, mystery fields, obscure coding schemes, or undocumented relationships. If the documentation is thorough, many data conversion pitfalls can be avoided.

Possible Mapping Patterns

The mapping of old to new is usually very complex. There seems to be no useful canonical scheme for dealing with this set of problems. Each new conversion seems to consist of myriad special cases. In the general case, a given new field may depend on the values found in multiple fields contained in multiple records of a number of files. This works the other way as well — one field in an old record may be assigned to different fields or even to different tables, depending on the values encountered.

If the conversion also requires intelligent handling of updates and deletes to the old system, the problem is complicated even further. This is true when one source file is split into several destination files, and at the same time, one destination file receives data from several source files. Then, if just one record is deleted in a source file, some fields will have to be set to null in the destination file, but only those coming from the deleted source record. This method, however, may violate some of the integrity rules in the new data base.

It may be best to specify the mapping in simple tabular and textual fashion. Each new field will have the corresponding old fields listed, along with any special translation rules required. These rules could be documented as decision tables, decision trees, pseudo code, or action diagrams.

Relational Mathematics

In data base theory, it is possible to join together all fields in a data base in a systematic manner and create what is called the "universal relation." Although this technique has little merit as a scheme for designing or implementing a data base, it may be a useful device for thinking about the mapping of old to new. It should be possible to specify any complex mapping as a view based on the universal relation. The relational algebra or the relational calculus could be used as the specification medium for detailing the rules of the mapping in a declarative fashion.

DESIGNING THE CONVERSION

Before starting to design a computer program, reentering the data manually from source records should be considered as a possibility.

Special Requirements for Data Warehousing

Data warehousing assumes that the conversion issue arises on a routine, periodic basis. All of the problems that arise in a one-time conversion must be dealt with for an initial load, and then must be dealt with again for the periodic update.

In a data warehouse situation, there will most likely be changes to source records that must be reflected into the data warehouse files. As discussed previously, there may be some complex mapping from old to new, and updates and deletes will greatly increase the complexity. There will have to be a provision for add, change, and delete transactions. A change transaction can often be handled as a paired delete and add, in some cases simplifying the programming.

Extra Space Requirements

In a conversion, it will be necessary to have large temporary files available. These could double the amount of disk space required for the job. If it is not possible to provide this extra storage, it will be necessary to ensure that the conversion plan does not demand extra space.

Choice of Language

The criteria for programming languages are not going to be too different from those used in any other application area. The programming language should be chosen according to the skills of the IS team and what will run on the organization's hardware. The most appropriate language will allow error recovery, exception handling, control totals reporting, checkpoint and restart capabilities, full procedural capability, and adequate throughput.

Most third-generation languages are sufficient, if an interface to the source and target data bases or file systems is available. Various classes of programs could be used, with different languages for each. For example, the records may be extracted from the old data base with one proprietary product, verified and converted to the new layout with C, and input into the new data base with a proprietary loader.

SQL as a Design Medium. The SQL language should be powerful enough to handle any data conversion job. The problem with SQL is that it has no error-handling capabilities and cannot produce a satisfactory control totals report as part of the update without going back and re-querying the data base in various ways.

Despite the deficiencies of SQL as a robust data conversion language, it may be ideal for specifying the conversion rules. Each destination field could have a corresponding SQL fragment that gave the rules for the mapping in a declarative fashion. The use of SQL as a design medium should lead to a very tight specification. The added advantage is that it translates to a SQL program very readily.

Processing Time

IS must have a good estimate for the amount of elapsed time and CPU time required to do the conversion. If there are excessive volumes of data, special efforts will be required to ensure adequate throughput. These efforts could involve making parallel runs, converting overnight and over weekends, buying extra-fast hardware, or fine-tuning programs.

These issues are not unique to conversions, but they must not be neglected to avoid surprises on the day of cutover to the new system. These issues are especially significant when there are large volumes of historical data for an initial conversion, even if ongoing runs will be much smaller.

Interoperability

There is a strong possibility that the old system and the new system will be on different platforms. There should be a mechanism for transferring the data from one to the other. Tape, disk, or a network connection could be used. It is essential to provide some mechanism for interoperability. In addition, it is important to make sure that the media chosen can support the volumes of data and provide the necessary throughput.

Routine Error Handling

The conversion routine must support sufficient edit code to enforce all business rules. When erroneous data is encountered, there might be a policy of setting the field to a default value. At other times, the record may be rejected entirely.

In either case, a meaningful report of the error encountered and the resultant action should be generated. It will be best if the record in error is sent off to an error file. There may be some larger logical unit of work than the record. If so, that larger unit should be sent to the error file and that transaction rolled back.

Control Totals

Every run of the conversion programs should produce control totals. At a minimum, there should be counts for every input record, every rejected record, every accepted record, and every record inserted into each output file or table. Finer breakdowns are desirable for each of these types of inputs and outputs. Every conversion run should be date and time stamped with start and end times, and the control report should be filed after inspection.

RECOVERY FROM ERROR

Certain types of errors, such as a power failure, will interrupt the processing. If the system goes out in the middle of a 20-hour run, there will have to be some facility for restarting appropriately. Some sort of checkpoint and restart mechanism is desirable. The operating system may be able to provide these facilities. If not, there should be an explicit provision in the design and procedures for dealing with this possibility. In some cases, it may be necessary to ensure that files are backed up prior to conversion.

Audit Records

After the data has been converted, there must be an auditable record of the conversion. This is also true if the conversion is an ongoing effort. In general, the audit record depends on the conversion strategy. There may be counts, checksums (i.e., row and column), or even old vs. new comparisons done with an automated set of routines. These audit procedures are not the same as the test cases run to verify that the conversion programs worked. They are records produced when the conversions are run.

CONCLUSION

Almost all IS development work involves conversion of data from an old system to a new application. This is seldom a trivial exercise, and in many projects is the biggest single source of customer dissatisfaction. The conversion needs to be given serious attention, and the conversion process needs to be planned as carefully as any other part of the project. Old applications are fraught with problems, and errors in the data will be common. The more tightly programmed the new application, the more problematic the conversion.

It is increasingly common to make the conversion part of an ongoing process, especially when the operational data is in one system, and the management information in another. Any data changes are made on the operational system and then, at periodic intervals, copied to the other application. This is a key feature of the data warehouse approach. All of the same considerations apply.

In addition, it will be important to institutionalize the procedures for dealing with conversion. The conversion programs must be able to deal with changes to the operational system by reflecting them in the data warehouse. Special care will be required to design the programs accordingly.

Chapter 31
Quality Information Services

Joe R. Briones

THE IS MANAGER'S primary objective should always be to provide the customer with state-of-the-art information processing capabilities. To meet this objective successfully, managers must have a clear understanding of the customers' requirements. More often than not, IS managers make assumptions about customer requirements. Process improvements are generally based on what the data center management believes the customer needs or on historical customer requirements. Open communications with the customer, however, should be the foundation to ensuring overall customer satisfaction.

The IS manager's ability to monitor and gauge performance against customer expectations is a critical part of ensuring customer satisfaction. IS managers should establish what is generally referred to as service-level agreements. These agreements document the level of service that IS provides; they also identify the commitments that the customer makes to ensure that the information processing objectives are met. The fundamental concept of service-level commitments is that there is a two-way level of commitment. The customer as well as the information processing organization must put forth the effort to achieve their objectives. For the most part, however, it is the responsibility of the management team to drive the establishment and implementation of these service-level commitments.

IS management is responsible for ensuring that state-of-the-art processing techniques are used in the processing of the customer information. Such processes as report distribution, production turnover, and online viewing of reports are just a few of the processes that can be improved by incorporating the most advanced processing enhancements. This chapter discusses these processes and also the production software that is currently available on the market to achieve the processing improvements required to ensure that customer requirements are being met to the highest level of customer satisfaction.

0-8493-9820-7/00/$0.00+$.50
© 2000 by CRC Press LLC

DEFINING USER REQUIREMENTS

The IS manager can best determine user requirements by analyzing and understanding the user's obligation to the organization.

Because user requirements usually change suddenly and frequently, the IS manager must ensure some degree of flexibility in the production processing environment. Last-minute changes in the scheduling of computer resources and movement of development program modules from development libraries into production-controlled libraries are just a few of the changes that require quick and immediate support.

Tracking and evaluating job scheduling on a daily basis enable the data center to adjust to sudden changes. Another important factor to consider in supporting unplanned extended computer scheduling is the effect that it may have on hardware and software mainframe maintenance.

The IS manager must be aware of the customer's closing schedules (i.e., the obligations that the customers have to their suppliers, financial institutions, and government agencies). The customer depends on its computer processing support for the reports required to prepare the documents that are required for compliance with both private and government agencies.

Year-end processing creates an especially high degree of activity for the data center. Income statements and other federal and state documents are just a few of the documents that are produced during the year-end closing period. A clear understanding of the customer's year-end requirements helps ensure the successful and timely completion of the customer's processing requirements.

The success of IS is strongly dependent on how well the manager understands customer requirements; this should be the number-one priority.

ESTABLISHING STANDARDS AND MEASURING PERFORMANCE

IS managers must ensure that the information processing services provided by their organizations address and support user requirements. A service-level agreement between the user organization and the information processing organization establishes the standards by which the department's responsiveness and quality of work can be defined.

Development of a service-level agreement requires a statement of the user's workload requirements and a commitment to the standards of performance. The manager must keep in mind that service-level commitments are basically an understanding between the user and the information processing organization stating each party's responsibilities in the process of achieving the overall objective of quality performance.

It has been known that from service-level agreements the user and the information processing organization establish what is sometimes referred to as incentive performance objectives. Incentive performance objectives have direct costs associated with them. If the IS manager successfully meets the predefined incentive performance objectives, the manager is rewarded with some predefined monetary compensation. If, however, the IS department fails to meet the incentive objective successfully, it is subject to penalties that are paid to the customer organization.

CHANGES TO SERVICE-LEVEL AGREEMENTS

Although service-level agreements are generally negotiated annually during the customer contract negotiation period, changes to the service-level commitments must be incorporated as necessary. Some of the factors that drive a change in the service-level agreement cannot be postponed until the annual contract negotiation period. Any changes in a customer's workload or service requirements or changes in the data center's ability to provide the services and support required by the customer with the funding provided by the customer should be incorporated into a service agreement revision.

Circumstances that could initiate revisions to service-level agreements include

- Authorization for a new development project or the completion or cancellation of an existing project.
- Changes to authorized spending levels or revisions to capital or lease authorizations.
- Changes to computer hardware equipment configurations (including telecommunications lines and terminals) or operating system software.
- Changes to customer departments or department functions that result in the need for changes to the data center support and performance levels.

Changes should be incorporated into the service agreement as soon as reasonably possible following the mutual recognition and assessment of the impact of the change.

OPERATIONAL PERFORMANCE OBJECTIVES AND MEASUREMENTS

To ensure that the IS department is successfully meeting the information processing requirements of the customer, the IS department must establish operational performance objectives as well as a method or process by which these operational performance objectives can be measured and reported. Operational performance data is generally prepared and reported on a monthly basis and is used as a management tool to resolve current and prevent potential problems.

It is imperative that the IS manager define, document, monitor, and maintain standards and procedures to ensure that quality computer processing services are being provided to the user community. Some of the operational performance objectives that may be established may include the following (the specific percentages included are examples):

- *Online systems availability.* Maintaining database management availability at 98% or higher is imperative. In a typical data center environment, these systems include IMS, DB2, and CICS.
- *Mainframe systems availability.* This means ensuring that mainframe computer hardware and software are up and running 98% of the time or greater.
- *Time-shared option (TSO) availability.* This means ensuring that TSO response time is 90% less than two seconds.
- *Production abends.* This means ensuring control of production processing to see that production abends are less than 0.25% of the scheduled production workload.
- *Production reruns.* This means maintaining control of production reruns to ensure that production reruns are less than 0.35% of the scheduled production workload.
- *Report deliverability.* This means ensuring that batch report delivery is at 99% or higher. (The percentages for production abends and reruns should be confirmed, however, by checking the existing service level agreements.)

Depending on the computer processing installation and the specific requirements of the customer, additional performance objectives may be required.

OPERATIONAL IMPROVEMENTS

The IS manager must put forth an effort to improve the operational capabilities of the data center. Within the processing environment of a data center, several unique operational functions play key roles in producing customer deliverable products. This section presents the key functional processing elements within a data center. These functions are made up of both hardware and software components.

The operational elements focused on are

- Turnover of programs from development staging areas into production-controlled libraries.
- Report distribution.
- Incident reporting and problem resolution.
- Online viewing of production reports.

- Scheduling of production applications.
- Backup and recovery of production data.
- Contingency planning to ensure the recovery of customer critical applications.
- Retention of customer data.

Program Turnover from Development to Production

The IS manager must ensure that procedures are in place to secure the accuracy and quality of the programs being moved into production. Also associated with the turnover of programs is the turnover of the job control statements that drive the processing of the program application.

There are two important factors associated with the turnover of programs and job control statements. First, the validation of the application code and the integrity and accuracy of the job control statements. In addition, the IS manager must secure and restrict access to the libraries that store both the application programs and the job control statements. The objective of restricting access to the production libraries is to ensure the integrity of the application modules in production. Any modifications made to the program code must be made in the application development areas. Once the application module has been modified, movement of the module into the production library must be processed through the turnover process. This not only ensures the integrity of the module but also provides an audit trail of the changes made, why the change was required, and who made the change.

Report Distribution

The IS manager must assume full responsibility for providing customers with the output reports they require within the agreed-on delivery schedule. To ensure that this commitment is successfully completed, the IS manager must have a system that tracks the delivery time of the production reports. Although the delivery of nonproduction reports is important, managers must focus their attention on the delivery of production reports. This is because the service-level agreement commitments are directed at production reports and are not open-shop-level reports.

There are several software products on the market that provide managers with this tracking capability. Most of these products are online systems. Once installed in the production environment, they are easy to use and maintain. One such product, called Express Delivery, is marketed by Legent, Inc.

Incident Reporting and Problem Resolution

The IS manager must establish adequate procedures for reporting and analyzing both hardware and software production failures. The information that is captured at the time of the failure is critical to the timely recovery of the failed process. The accurate recording of facts and sequences of events contributes directly to the quality of the corrective action process.

The IS manager should do whatever is required to ensure that the failure will not reoccur. To make this happen, the technical staff must identify the root cause of the problem. This is often referred to as the RCA analysis process. To perform a successful RCA analysis, accurate information relative to the failed incident is required. The incident report information log should include such information as device address, failure time, vendor contact time, and any other pertinent information that would assist in identifying the cause of the failure. An RCA analysis should also be conducted if there is an application failure. As is the case of hardware failures, the information obtained at the time of the failure is also vital in identifying the root cause of the failure. The information required to support the resolution of application failures should include time of the failure, abend code, history of most recent program modifications, or job control modification.

The importance of incident reporting and application abend reports cannot be overemphasized. The time spent in preparing an incident report or an application abend failure report can prove instrumental in preventing the problem from reoccurring.

Problem Review Meetings

Regardless of the size of the computer installation, the quality and serviceability of the hardware and software depend on the level of support provided by the vendors and the data center's technical support organization. This is why the lines of communication between the data center operations organization and its support groups are critical. Problem review meetings provide an excellent means of informing the support organization of the problems and also provide the vendor or the technical support staff with a tool by which they can keep the data center's management informed on the corrective actions taken to resolve the problems at hand.

Online Viewing of Production Reports

Data center processes are subject to continual changes in processing technology. For this reason, the management team should ensure that the organization is keeping up with current technology. Improvements in the computing labs, such as the use of state-of-the-art hardware must always be pursued. This is especially true in the area of Direct Access Storage Device (DASD) and tape unit devices. Although in today's environment hardcopy printing is not as critical as it was in the late 1970s and 1980s, the need to produce high-quality, hard-copy output is still a customer requirement. Therefore, the data center should secure the latest technology in high-quality laser printing.

IS managers should acquire both hardware and software that will allow them, when possible, the capability of providing their customers with cost-effective production of computer-generated, paperless reports. Products being marketed today that provide for online viewing of production data include IBM Corp.'s Report Management Distribution System (RMDS) and Legent's Sysout Archival and Retrieval (SAR) system. Modern intranet implementations often include facilities for online delivery of reports.

Online viewing of production data eliminates or greatly reduces the costs associated with producing and handling hard-copy reports. Online viewing of production data also ensures that the customers have immediate access to their reports. In most cases, hard-copy reports arrive at the customer site an average of three hours after the data is produced. By eliminating unneeded paper, the organization saves filing space, computer processing time, and handling time. The faster a data center can process information, produce reports, and develop successful systems, the more competitive and prosperous the organization is.

Scheduling of Production Applications

As technological advances and operational improvements, and their impact on the data center, are identified and discussed, the scheduling of production jobs should be of major importance to the IS manager. Data centers today process an average 30,000 to 80,000 jobs per month. Of all of the jobs that the data center may process per month, only a small percentage is what could be classified as self-contained, jobs that create their own data files, use their own files, and neither pass nor receive data. The largest percentage of jobs processed by a data center today are what could be classified as successor- and predecessor-type jobs. In other words, the data files created by these jobs are passed on as input to other jobs. For this reason, the IS manager must provide a scheduling software package that automatically monitors the creation of input data files and submits the production jobs into the system when all required dependencies are met. In some cases, the job requirements may not be a data file, but rather a specific time of day. Due to the magnitude of the jobs being processed and their specific requirements, the manual scheduling of production jobs in today's data centers is highly discouraged.

There are several scheduling software packages available on the market today. IS managers should first identify their specific requirements and then purchase or lease a scheduling package that meets their requirements. Computer Associates and 4th Dimension are just two of the vendors that can provide this type of software.

Backup and Recovery of Production Data

The data center is responsible for ensuring the integrity of customer data. This level of accountability, however, also extends to protecting the data. To ensure that production data is secured, the IS manager must have documented backup and recovery procedures. The process for backing up data may vary from data center to data center, and the complexity of the recovery process depends on the amount of data being backed up. Regardless of the complexity level of backing up the data, managers must understand and take the appropriate measures to safeguard the data put in their trust.

Most data centers ensure the integrity of the data by performing what is generally referred to as stand-alone backup maintenance. Stand-alone backup maintenance means that the backup of all DASD volumes is performed when there is nothing else processing on the system. This type of backup ensures that the data being backed up is accurate to the point of the backup. There are ways to streamline the backup process, and improved processes should be discussed with the data center's storage management group or with the center's production control organization.

Off-Site Vaulting of Backup Data

As part of the production data backup process, the IS manager must ensure that the data center has the ability to store its critical production data in an off-site tape vault. The distance of the off-site tape vault facility is not of major importance. The key objective is to have the off-site facility away from the main processing lab and away from the production tape library. We should note that the primary emphasis of an off-site tape library is to support the recovery of the data center in the event of a major system outage. System restorations of this magnitude are generally supported by a disaster recovery hot-site data center. (The aspects of contingency planning and disaster recovery are discussed in more detail elsewhere in this book.) The primary emphasis of an off-site tape vaulting procedure, however, is to secure recovery of data in the event of a long-term system outage. Day-to-day recovery of data files should be provided by using the backup files that reside within the computing area's tape library. To help ensure this level of recovery, the current version of the production backups should be kept in the computing tape library for immediate access. The previous generation of the backup files should be stored at the off-site tape vault. The data center must work together with the storage management group and the customer to help determine and establish a suitable off-site vaulting tape rotation process.

The IS manager must also establish a process to audit the off-site tape vaulting process. This audit must focus on the support provided by the off-site tape storage vendor and the internal rotation process with the data center. The audit should be conducted at least on a quarterly basis.

Contingency Planning/Disaster Recovery

Assuming the role of data custodians for the data center customer incorporates the assurance that during periods of extended outages, customers are still provided with the capability of accessing their data, as well as the assurance that their critical applications will be processed as close to a normal schedule as possible.

To ensure that the customer is provided with this level of support, the IS manager must provide a contingency planning/disaster recovery plan. A workable disaster recovery plan must incorporate the following key components:

- *A disaster recovery manual must be established.* This manual must address the recovery process at the detailed level. This manual can be viewed as a how-to manual that not only identifies specific processes but the supporting parties, as well.
- *Critical applications must be identified by the customer.* The data center manager should never assume responsibility for identifying the critical applications. Defined as applications vital to the continued success of the customer's organization, these critical points are most of the time tied to financial or contractual requirements. The data center manager can assist the customer in identifying the critical applications, but the final selection should be in the hands of the customer.
- *The data center must select and subscribe to a disaster recovery hot site.* The hot site is used to process the critical applications identified by the customer. The hot site recovery center provides the following:
  — Network communications hardware and technical support.
  — Mainframe hardware as required to support the critical workload.
  — DASD and tape resources.
  — Printing capabilities.
- *The recovery plan must be tested at least annually.* Operational objectives should be established. The recovery test should support the accomplishment of the stated objectives.

Retention of Customer Data

Under normal processing standards, deletion of data files is generally controlled by system-controlled parameters. Simple data sets are generally marked for deletion by system-defined and -controlled expiration dates. Generation data groups (GDGs) are controlled by system-defined catalog indexes. Deleting of data files within GDG groups is managed by deleting the oldest data file in the index. The overall best approach in managing and controlling data files is to let the system manage the retention and deleting of files.

There are, however, times when operations personnel must override the system-defined controls. The IS manager must take every precaution possible to ensure that the customer data is protected. This is why manual overrides that delete a data file must be coordinated with the customer.

The simplest method of ensuring that the customer concurs with deleting of data files is requesting that the customer's representative sign the deletion request that is submitted to the operations organization. By no means should data files be deleted on a verbal request. All data file deletion requests must be in writing. It is suggested that the IS manager establish a data file deletion request form to incorporate and require data owner approval.

CONCLUSION

IS managers should carefully analyze the effectiveness of their organizations. All of the activities performed within the data center should have one primary key objective: to achieve total customer satisfaction at the lowest cost possible. The IS manager should establish and implement policies and procedures to ensure that customer objectives are being achieved. The customer and the IS manager must have a clear understanding of the commitments that each must make to achieve a successful long-term partnership. Once these commitments are established and understood, a service-level agreement should be developed to support the mutually agreed-on commitments and deliverables.

The IS manager should then implement a procedure by which operational performance metrics can be obtained and monitored. The primary objective of these is to confirm the data center's ability to meet customer requirements, but it also identifies shortfalls within the customer's commitments to the data center.

IS managers must realize that customer satisfaction can only be secured by providing the customer with state-of-the-art processing at a minimal cost. If the data center cannot achieve this, the customer will be forced to move its data center processing to a vendor that will meet its technological and cost targets.

Chapter 32
Information Systems Audits: What's in It for Executives?

Vasant Raval
Uma G. Gupta

COMPANIES IN WHICH EXECUTIVES and top managers view the IS audit as a critical success factor often achieve significant benefits that include decrease in cost, increase in profits, more robust and useful systems, enhanced company image, and ability to respond quickly to changing market needs and technology influences.

Both of the following are real and occurred in companies in which one of the authors worked as a consultant. In both situations, IS auditors played a critical role in not only preventing significant monetary loss for the company but also in enhancing the image of the company to its stakeholders:

- *Scenario 1.* One fine morning, auditors from Software Publishers Association (SPA) knocked on the doors of one of your business units. They wanted to verify that every copy of every software package that is in your business unit is properly licensed. The unit had 1,700 microcomputers on a local area network. Fortunately, information systems (IS) auditors had recently conducted an audit of software licenses in the business unit. This encouraged the IS auditors and business managers from the company to work closely with SPA auditors who reviewed the audit work and tested a sample of the microcomputers at the company's facility. The SPA auditors commended the business unit for its exemplary records and outstanding monitoring of software licenses. The investigation was completed in a few hours and the company was given a clean bill of software licensing audit.
- *Scenario 2.* Early in 1995, the Vice President of Information Systems of a Fortune 500 company visited with the Director of Audit Services and recommended that the company's efforts to be compliant with the

Year 2000 (Y2K) should be audited. The Vice President was sensitive to the fact that such audits, although expensive and time consuming, do not have any immediate or significant monetary returns. After considerable discussion, it was agreed that an initial exploratory audit of the current status of the Y2K problem should be conducted. The audit was to outline and discuss the implications of the Y2K problem on the company's profits and provide an initial estimate of the cost of conducting the audit. A few weeks later IS auditors presented a report to the Board of Directors which reviewed the findings and mandated IS managers and other managers throughout the company to invest resources where necessary to become Y2K compliant by December 1998.

Given the critical role that IS auditors play in the financial success and stability of a company, IS audits should not be only the preview of the information systems department. Instead, executives and other top managers should understand and support the roles and responsibilities of information system auditors and encourage their active participation at all levels of decision-making. A nurturing and supportive environment for IS auditors can result in significant benefits for the entire organization.

The purpose of this chapter is to present a broad overview of the IS audit function and its integral role in organizational decision making. The functions of the IS audit department are discussed and ways in which the IS audit can be used as a valuable executive decision-making tool are outlined. Recommendations for leveraging an IS audit report to increase organizational effectiveness are also outlined.

WHAT IS AN IS AUDIT?

Information systems audit refers to a set of technical, managerial, and organizational services provided by a group of auditing experts in the area of information systems and technologies. IS auditors provide a wide range of consulting services on problems, issues, opportunities, and challenges in information systems and technologies. The goal of an IS audit may often vary from project to project or even from system to system. However, in general, the purpose of an IS audit is to maximize the leverage on the investments in information systems and technologies and ensure that systems are strategically aligned with the mission and overall goals of the organization.

IS audits can be conducted in a number of areas such as utilization of existing systems, investments, emerging technologies, computer security, help desks, electronic commerce, outsourcing, reengineering, Y2K systems implementation, and Electronic Data Interchange (EDI). Other areas warranting an IS audit include database management, data warehousing, intranets, web page design and maintenance, business intelligence systems, retention of IS personnel, migration from legacy systems to client server environments, offshore software contracts, and developing strategic information systems plans. Given the dismal statistics on IS projects that are delivered within budget and on time, a number of companies are mandating audits of their information systems projects. Exhibit 32.1 identifies the different categories of IS audits.

TRADITIONAL APPROACH VS. VALUE-ADDED APPROACH

The traditional view of the IS audit function differs from the value-added view found in many progressive, forward-thinking organizations. In the traditional view, an IS audit is something that is 'done to' a department, unit, or project. On the other hand, in a value-added approach an audit is viewed as something that is 'done for' another department, unit, or project. This is not a simple play on words but is instead a philosophy that differentiates between environments that are controlling and nurturing; it exemplifies work places where people compete vs. cooperate. In the traditional approach, the audit is viewed as a product whereas in the value-added approach the audit is viewed as a service that enhances the overall quality and reliability of the end product or service that the company produces.

In the traditional environments, the auditor is viewed as an adversary, cop, and trouble maker. On the other hand, in a value-added environment the auditor is viewed as a consultant and a counselor. The IS auditor is viewed as one who applies his or her knowledge and expertise to leverage the maximum return on investments in information systems and technologies. The auditor is not someone who is out looking for errors but is instead

---

A. *Control Environments Audits:* Provide guidelines for enterprise-wide deployment of technology resources. Examples: business continuity (or disaster recovery) plans, PC Software Licensing, Internet access and control, LAN security and control.
B. *General Control Audits:* Review general and administrative controls for their adequacy and reliability. Examples of general controls: data center security, end-user systems access and privileges, role and functions of steering committees.
C. *Financial Audits*
    1. Review of automated controls designed as part of the systems. Examples: limit checks, compatibility checks, concurrency controls in databases.
    2. Provide assistance for financial audits. Examples: use of generalized audit software packages, and other computer-assisted audit tools to review transactions and their financial results.
D. *Special Projects:* Projects initiated to satisfy one-time needs. Examples: feasibility study of outsourcing of projects, processes, or systems, risk analysis for proposed offshore software development initiatives.
E. *Emerging Technologies:* Review and feasibility analysis of newer technologies for the business. Examples of technologies: electronic data interchange, Web technology, telecommuting, telephony, imaging, data warehousing, and data mining.

Exhibit 32.1. Categories of IS audits

an individual or a group of individuals who look for ways and means to improve the overall efficiency, effectiveness, and productivity of the company. Unlike the traditional approach where the auditor is viewed as someone who is on assignment, the value-based approach views the auditor as a long-term business partner. Refer to Exhibit 32.2 that summarizes the key differences between the traditional approach and the value-added approach.

ROLE OF THE IS AUDITOR

The role of an IS auditor is much more than simply auditing a project, unit, or department. An IS auditor plays a pervasive and critical role in leveraging resources to their maximum potential and also in minimizing the risks associated with certain decisions. An IS auditor, therefore, wears several hats to ensure that information systems and technologies are synergistically aligned with the overall goals and objectives of the organization. Some key roles that an IS auditor are outlined and discussed below:

Internal Consultants

Good IS auditors have a sound understanding of the business and hence can serve as outstanding consultants on a wide variety of projects. They can offer creative and innovative solutions to problems and identify opportunities where the company can leverage its information systems to achieve a competitive edge in the marketplace. In other works, IS audits can help organizations to ask critical and probing questions regarding IS investments.

Traditional Approach	Value-Added Approach
Something done to a unit, department, or project.	Something done for enhancing the quality, efficiency, and effectiveness of a unit, department, or project.
Audit is a product that is periodically delivered to specific units or departments.	Audit is an on-going service provided to improve the "quality of life" of the organization.
The auditor plays an adversarial role.	The auditor is a consultant whose goal is to leverage resource utilization.
The auditor is a "best cop."	The auditor is a house guest.
The primary objective of auditing is to find errors and loopholes.	The primary objective of auditing is to increase the efficiency, effectiveness, and productivity of the organization.
Auditing is an expense. Auditing is an investment.	The contribution of an auditor is temporary. An auditor is a life-long business partner.

Exhibit 32.2. Traditional approach vs. value-added approach to auditing

The consultant role includes a wide variety of issues including cost savings, productivity and risk minimization. IS audits can help firms realize cost savings and proactively manage risks that are frequently associated with information technologies. IS audits in many cases support the financial audit requirements in a firm. For example, one of the authors of this chapter audited the review of an offshore Y2K conversion project resulting in savings of $3.4 million to the company. The auditor interviewed over 35 technical and management staff from the business unit and from the offshore facility. Based on the recommendations of the IS auditor, the offshore software development process was reengineered. The reengineering resulted in a well-defined and structured set of functional requirements, rigorous software testing procedures, and enhanced cross-cultural communications. The implications of the IS audit were felt not only on the particular project but on all future offshore IS projects.

Change Agents

IS auditors should be viewed as powerful change agents within an organization. They have a sound knowledge of the business and this combined with an acute sense of financial, accounting, and legal ramifications of various organizational decisions make them uniquely qualified to push for change within an organization. For example, a company was having a difficult time implementing security measures in its information systems department. Repeated efforts to enlist the support of company employees failed miserably. Finally, the company sought the help of its IS audit team to enforce security measures. IS auditors acted as change agents and educated employees about the consequences of failing to meet established security measures. Within three months the company had one of the tightest security ships in its industry.

Experts

Many IS auditors specialize in certain areas of the business such as IS planning, Y2K, security, system integration, electronic commerce, and so on. These auditors not only have a good understanding of the technical issues but also business and legal issues that may influence key information systems and projects. Hence, while putting together a team for any IS project, it is worthwhile to consider including an IS auditor as a team member.

Advisors

One of the key roles of an IS auditor is to serve as an advisor to the business manager on IS issues that have an enterprisewide effect. The advisory role often spans both technical and managerial issues. Examples of situations where IS auditors could be used as advisors include software licensing management, establishing a standardization policy for hardware and software, evaluating key IS projects, ensuring the quality of outsourcing contracts, and so on. IS auditors not only monitor the progress of the project but also provide timely advice if the project is going haywire. It is worthwhile to always include a member from the IS audit team on IS ventures that have significant implications for the organization.

Advocates

IS auditors can serve as outstanding advocates to promote the information system needs and functions of business units to top management. As neutral parties who have a stake in the success of the company, their views are often likely to get the attention of top management. IS auditors cannot only serve as advocates of the technology and personnel needs of the business unit, but also emphasize the strategic role of information systems in the success of both the business unit and the organization at large. IS auditors also play a critical role in ensuring the well-being of the organization. For example, IS auditors have often played a leading role in convincing top management of the importance of investing in computer security, without which the organization may simply cease to be in business.

ROLE OF EXECUTIVES IN CAPITALIZING THE IS AUDIT FUNCTION

Successful and pragmatic companies view the IS audit function as an integral and vital element in corporate decisionmaking. Companies that view IS audit as an information systems function, or even worse, as merely an audit function will fail to derive the powerful benefits that an IS audit can provide. In this section we discuss how companies can use the IS audit to achieve significant benefits for the entire organization.

Be Proactive

IS audit should not be viewed as a static or passive function in an organization that is called to act on a need-only basis. Instead the IS audit function should be managed proactively and should be made an integral part of all decision making in the organization. The auditor is an internal consultant whose primary goal is to provide the information and tools necessary to make sound decisions. The auditor's role is not limited to one department or even to one project; instead, the goal of the auditor is to help each business unit make sound technology decisions so as to have a far-reaching and positive impact on the entire organization. However, this cannot be achieved unless companies are proactive in tapping into the skill set of its IS auditors.

Increase Visibility of the IS Audit

Executives who view the IS audit function as a necessary evil will be doing grave injustice to their organizations. Top management should take an active role in advocating the contribution of the IS audit team to the organization. Executives must play an active role in promoting the critical role and significant contributions of IS auditors. Publicizing projects and systems where an IS audit resulted in significant savings to the company or led to better systems is a good way to increase organizational understanding of IS audits. Many companies also mandate IS audits for all projects and systems that exceed a certain minimum dollar value, thus increasing the visibility and presence of IS auditors.

Enhance the IS Auditors Image

Encourage business units managers to view the IS audit not as a means to punish individuals or units, but as an opportunity to better utilize information systems and technologies to meet the overall goals of the organization. Include IS auditors in all key strategic committees and long-range planning efforts. Bring IS auditors early on in the development phase of a project so that project members view them as a team player rather than as a "cop."

Provide Resources

IS audit, like other audit functions, requires hardware, software, and training resources. Companies that recognize the critical role of IS auditors support their resource needs and encourage their active participation. They recognize that a good and robust audit system can pay for itself many times over in a short span of time. Given the rapid changes in technology, auditors not only need hardware and software resources to help them stay on the leading edge, but should also be given basic training in the use of such technologies.

Communicate, Communicate, Communicate

Effective communications between business units and IS auditors is vital for a healthy relationship between the two groups. Business unit managers should know the specific role and purpose of an IS audit. They should have a clear understanding of who will review the auditors' report and the actions that will be initiated based on that report. IS auditors, on the other hand, should be more open in their communications with business managers and communicate issues and concerns, both informally and formally. They should always be good team players and understand that their role is to help and support the organization achieve its full potential.

CONCLUSION

The IS audit is a critical function for any organization. What separates the successful organizations from the less successful ones is the ability to leverage the IS audit function as a vital element in organizational decision making. Companies in which executives and top managers view the IS audit as a critical success factor often achieve significant benefits that include decrease in cost, increase in profits, more robust and useful systems, enhanced company image, and the ability to respond quickly to changing market needs and technology influences.

Chapter 33

Key Factors to Strengthen the Disaster Contingency and Recovery Planning Process

Michael J. Cerullo
Virginia Cerullo

EARTHQUAKES, floods, bombings, and other natural and man-made disasters occur regularly throughout the U. S. and the rest of the world. These disasters inevitably shut down business operations. The longer a disaster shuts down a company's operations, the more likely it will never reopen for business. Thus, quickly recovering from a disaster is crucial to a company's survival as a going concern.

Studies have demonstrated time after time that a comprehensive disaster contingency and recovery plan must be prepared to survive a severe crisis. The plan provides guidelines that, if followed, enable a company to minimize damage and restore both its computer operations and regular business operations. A comprehensive disaster contingency and recovery planning process (DCRP) consists of emergency, backup, recovery, test, and maintenance plans. Key factors to include in each of these subplans are discussed. Also, six frequently overlooked factors to strengthen the overall DCRP process are examined, including continuity of general business operations, annual planning meeting, internal audit involvement, the human element, personnel awareness of their responsibilities in DCRP, and alternate telecommunications considerations.

The winter of 1996 brought 13 massive snowstorms across the upper Midwest and the resulting flooding in the spring of 1997 pushed 100,000 refugees from their homes. All the businesses in downtown Grand Forks, North Dakota, went underwater when the Red River overflowed its 60-yard channel and stretched 40 miles across. Total damages from this flood are estimated at $1 billion.[1] Although the Red River flood is not likely to recur for 500 years, it was only a few years before that another river, the Mississippi, was making headlines for record flooding in the Midwest. In the Great Flood of 1993, 150 primary and secondary levees failed in nine states, resulting in a total of $12 billion in damages. Many businesses in these nine states did not recover.

Great Western Bank with headquarters in Northridge, California, can testify to the variety of disasters a company may face. In 1992, Hurricane Andrew caused damages to their southern Florida branch operations. Later, the Big Bear and Landers earthquakes and the Laguna Niguel and Altadena wildfires struck in areas near company operations, and the major Northridge earthquake in 1994 had its epicenter only 1 mile from their primary service center for all operations. After the Northridge earthquake, 15 of 17 Great Western buildings were unusable. Fortunately, this company had a comprehensive disaster recovery plan that obtained on-site recovery and went live within 4 hours.[2]

Disaster contingency and recovery planning (DCRP) is a strategy for recovering from natural and man-made disasters that affect not only a company's computer processing capabilities but also its critical business operations. With support from top management, a DCRP should enable a company to respond to disasters without suffering irreparable damages.

Management and boards of directors have an additional incentive to establish a DCRP. If proper precautions for disasters are not taken, they may encounter a stockholder class-action suit alleging gross negligence in protecting corporate assets. Many organizations are required by federal legislation to develop and test disaster plans. However, the basic concepts of DCRP should be present in all companies, regardless of size or mode of processing — manual, computerized, or a combination of the two. Large entities should prepare a more formal and comprehensive plan, developing a separate plan in each of the five areas briefly reviewed below. In such companies, management should assign an internal task force to prepare the DCRP. In smaller companies, the DCRP process is likely to be less formal, less structured, and less comprehensive. In such companies, the owner/manager can prepare the plan, if qualified, or else hire a local consulting firm to assist in the plan's preparation.

COMPONENTS OF A DCRP

A comprehensive DCRP is presented as five component plans:[3]

- Emergency
- Backup
- Recovery
- Test
- Maintenance plan

These plans are listed as separate components but may actually overlap in certain areas. Considering the DCRP in five components will allow the division of responsibility and should emphasize the importance of each area in assuring an adequate overall DCRP.

Emergency Plan

The emergency plan provides guidelines to follow during and immediately after a disaster. Having a plan in place minimizes the necessity of making ad hoc decisions following a major disaster and provides confidence and assurance to employees facing a stressful situation caused by such an emergency. Some key factors included in an emergency plan are the following:

Prepare an organization chart, showing the chain of command involved in DCRP. Senior management should appoint a DCRP manager and a second-in-command to lead the DCRP. Senior management must be committed and involved in the contingency planning process. They must view contingency planning as part of the organization's culture. Senior management involvement ensures that qualified DCRP managers will be appointed and that they will have access to the resources needed to develop a successful DCRP.

Organizationally, the DCRP managers should report to the corporate audit committee. The DCRP managers should select key team members. These team members should represent each functional area and as many specific tasks as possible.

Conduct a risk analysis to rank relevant risks. The DCRP manager should conduct a risk analysis to identify and rank the significant relevant risks. The degree of technology within a company should be a major consideration in this risk assessment. If a company's critical operations are computerized, an analysis of whether or how long the organization could continue to operate without specific computer support should be considered. DCRP team members should collect information from the manager of each functional area. A comprehensive analysis may require inventories of both basic and specialized equipment. Special attention must be given to any items that are unique and would be difficult to replace. The output of the risk assessment should indicate which segments of the organization are more prone to particular disasters, what the costs are to protect them, and what the impact of such protection is on each segment. The DCRP manager should then rank each possible risk according to the need for recovery in the event of a particular disaster. The ranking should be based on the ability of the organization to achieve its mission. Mission-critical functions should be given the highest priority in terms of recovery.

Assign emergency responsibilities to specific personnel. The DCRP team must determine the specific measures necessary to ensure the safety of employees when disaster strikes. These measures include alarm systems, evacuation procedures, and fire suppression systems. A life-safety team should be organized to assure the safety of personnel. The team members should be given training in emergency first-aid. Specific team members should be given the responsibility to contact fire, police, and other agencies. Specific personnel should be selected to remain at company headquarters to lock doors, power-down computers, and perform other vital duties.

The DCRP team should prepare maps of primary and secondary evacuation routes and post these throughout the company. Finally, the emergency plan should include a method for communicating the "all-clear" signal that indicates when employees can return to headquarters or to the temporary business location.

Backup Plan

A backup plan ensures that key employees, vital records, and alternative backup facilities are available to continue business and data processing operations. Key factors of a backup plan include the following.

Store duplicates of vital information at appropriate off-site locations. The DCRP team must, with input from all functional areas, determine the definition of "vital" information. Vital information would normally include programs/software, data, and records that are critical to the company's mission. The primary procedure for backing up programs includes making working copies of all operating systems, utility programs, application programs, and related documentation. The working copies are then used for day-to-day operations, and the original programs are stored in a safe place. Choosing the location of the off-site storage facility can be critical, especially if the disaster incurred is a hurricane or earthquake.

Identify the personnel needed in the backup operations. The DCRP team must determine the full-time and part-time employees and temporary hirees who will be needed in the backup operations. Arrangements should be made to ensure that the temporary employees will be available when needed. Oftentimes, after a disaster strikes, key employees are injured or otherwise unable to temporarily perform their jobs. Therefore, key employees should be cross-trained to perform several duties.

Select the most appropriate type of backup system. Choose an alternate site for conducting regular business operations that is outside the area of anticipated destruction. Several options are available for resuming data processing operations. Manual backup systems may be feasible for small- and medium-sized companies that process low volumes of transactions. Decentralized firms with multiple compatible computer sites may choose to use an alternative company location as their backup site. A reciprocal arrangement can be made between two companies who contractually agree to provide backup for each other following a disaster. A third-party agreement to supply backup can be formed between the company and a data processing service bureau, university, or vendor's computer facility.

Other disaster recovery services for computer operations include cold sites, hot sites, cooperative hot sites, and flying hot sites. A cold site is an alternate data processing facility equipped with all the necessary resources, except for personnel, files, and computer equipment. Following a disaster, a prearranged plan is activated to move the company's personnel, vital files, and newly acquired or rented equipment to the cold site. A hot site is a fully staffed and equipped computer facility contracted to provide temporary and immediate off-site services to companies suffering disasters. Vital records are moved to this location and processed by the hot site's EDP staff and equipment. A cooperative hot site is similar to a hot site, except that the site is co-owned by two or more members who share operating expenses. A flying hot site is similar to a hot site, except that the site stores up-to-date copies of the company's vital records and software.

Recovery Plan

A recovery plan insures that a skilled recovery team is formed to reconstruct and restore full operational capabilities. The emergency plan provides the steps needed to protect employees and company resources during a disaster and to determine the personnel needed for the DCRP. The recovery plan emphasizes the steps necessary to ensure successful backup operations and to restore normal operations. Key factors to include in a recovery plan are the following.

Develop a strategy to monitor and assist operations at the backup site. An adequate backup plan will minimize the effort needed in this step. However, it is impossible to plan for every obstacle in maintaining critical operations in an emergency situation. For example, temporary personnel may have conflicting personalities that could lower morale or create a more stressful environment, resulting in critical mistakes. A member of the DCRP team should have the authority to make on-the-spot corrections/adjustments in the backup operations. Another major responsibility would be to ensure the security and control of these temporary operations.

Arrange for the recovery of lost or damaged resources. Arrange with vendors to have resources delivered to the alternate company site and the backup facility. This arrangement should be included in a comprehensive backup plan. However, unexpected resources may be needed and additional arrangements may be necessary.

After the emergency situation, an inventory of the resources destroyed or damaged due to the disaster should be taken. It is important to maintain a liaison with insurance companies to facilitate the assessment of damages and the speedy payment of compensation.

Establish a timetable for the recovery operations. An on-the-spot and frequently updated timetable for the recovery operations must be prepared and distributed to senior management. Future relations with customers and the general public may depend upon this timely notification.

Test Plan

The purpose of the test plan is to uncover and correct defects in the DCRP before a real disaster occurs. At random intervals a mock disaster, such as a fire, is simulated. The results are critiqued by test participants and management; gaps in the plan are identified and corrected.

Key factors included in a test plan include the following.

1. Choose a strategy to test the plan. Because comprehensive testing involves a substantial number of persons and necessarily interrupts normal business operations, companies may choose different levels of testing. These levels could be rotated and should result in comprehensive testing at regular intervals. The testing methods include the following:

   Think-through. This method is a paper testing or verbal undertaking of the contingency plan where participants are asked to state how the plan would guide their reactions.
   A walk-through. This method conducts partial tests. These tests may be announced or unannounced, or on-site or backup site tests.
   Demonstrations. A demonstration is an enactment of a disaster situation to insure that the contingency plan actually works. For example, an announcement is made that a disaster of a particular type (e.g., fire or hurricane) had developed and that all personnel are required to follow disaster procedures.

   Few organizations operationally test the complete disaster reaction cycle of activation, life-safety, damage assessment, mobilization, emergency operations using off-site files and backup resources and recovery planning. Only the data processing emergency operations area can be tested without involving a substantial number of persons during regular business hours.

2. Establish measurable objectives. Before testing begins, it is important to establish the objective(s) of the test. These objectives may be limited by the method of testing implemented. After objectives have been set, the DCRP team should predict the acceptable outcomes.

3. Document and critique the test results. After the testing, the results must be documented and compared to the predicted acceptable outcomes. The DCRP team and senior management should meet to discuss the results. Testing may reveal major weaknesses in the DCRP that can be corrected before a real disaster.

4. Conduct the simulations at random intervals. Business environments, including physical facilities and personnel, are constantly changing. The dynamic nature of the company requires that the DCRP be updated (discussed in the next section) and tested regularly. These tests should include announced and unannounced tests. The DCRP must be ready to handle any emergency situation.

Maintenance Plan

The final phase to DCRP is to prepare a maintenance plan, which devises guidelines insuring that the entire plan is kept up-to-date. Factors requiring revision of the DCRP include major changes in branch locations, key personnel, organization structure, vendor policies, hardware, and software. Any resulting updates to the DCRP should be reviewed by appropriate company officials before the DCRP is modified.

A maintenance plan should include the following key factors.

1. Prepare a set of guidelines with specific instructions on how to maintain the DCRP. Develop a flowchart or narrative description for maintaining the DCRP. This plan should include the information required from each of the functional areas to assess the need for revisions. Specific personnel should be assigned the responsibility for the maintenance of the DCRP.

2. Ensure that timely changes from the test simulations are incorporated into the DCRP. The ultimate objective of testing the DCRP is to identify weaknesses and to correct those weaknesses. The responsibility for incorporation of these corrections should be included under the maintenance plan.

3. Destroy earlier versions of the DCRP and replace these with the latest version of the DCRP; include at least one copy in an off-premise fireproof storage vault. Including this step in the plan emphasizes

the importance of replacing all the older versions of the DCRP. Companies may be tempted to only update the DCRP team's copies at regular intervals and update company-wide copies at less frequent intervals.

FACTORS FREQUENTLY
OVERLOOKED IN THE DCRP PROCESS

Companies often overlook a number of important factors when preparing a disaster contingency and recovery plan. Considering the important factors discussed below should result in a more effective DCRP.

1. Plan for the continuity of general business operations. A large percentage of disaster recovery plans still focus only on recovery of computer operations. A comprehensive DCRP must also consider the recovery of normal business operations. Many companies limit the backup plan to computer data processing operations. It is also important to select alternate sites for conducting regular business operating activities. In addition, a definite plan should be established to notify vendors and customers of the alternate business location and the length of time the company will be operating at this site. Arrangements should be made to have clean-up crews and repair services report to the damaged site as quickly as possible following the disaster.

2. Conduct an annual planning meeting with senior management. DCRP managers should meet with senior management to review the activities of the previous year and to discuss changes or improvements needed to update the DCRP.

3. Involve internal audit in all phases of the DCRP. The internal audit function should be involved in all phases of plan development. Internal audit should conduct an annual audit of the entire plan, periodically test it, and insure that the plan is updated as circumstances warrant. An internal auditor should visit the backup site to determine if the facility is properly maintained and check backups to determine if they are properly stored and controlled. In addition, internal audit should periodically evaluate insurance coverage on the company resources subject to significant risk from disasters.

4. Consider the human element. At times of disaster, the company should be prepared to provide assistance to employees and their families: for example, locating temporary apartments and providing transportation to work. A pay policy should be established before disaster strikes. For instance, all employees will be paid their regular salary as scheduled, regardless of whether or not they work for a designated number of days or weeks following the catastrophe. The human resources department should keep up-to-date information on all employees so they can be quickly reached during emer-

gencies. Guidelines that are in compliance with the American for Disabilities Act should be developed to evacuate disabled employees. Arrangements should be made to provide the recovery team members with food service and housing as close to the backup or operational sites as possible. Employees should be clearly notified when and where to return to work after operations have been restored.

5. Inform managers and employees of their responsibilities in the DCRP. Key employees should be given a complete copy of the current contingency planning documents and a summary of the DCRP should be distributed to all employees. Meetings should be conducted with employees to discuss the DCRP and to inform them of their responsibilities under the plan.

6. Consider alternate telecommunications backup. Keeping in contact at times of disaster is crucial to minimizing damage and saving lives. The disaster recovery manager cannot rely on any one source of communications. Several means of maintaining communications other than standard telephone service, such as cell phones, radio broadcasts, and two-way radios, should be investigated and incorporated into the DCRP.

SUMMARY

With proper planning, companies can be prepared for any disaster — floods, earthquakes, fires, or hurricanes. This chapter presents key factors that should be included in a Disaster Contingency and Recovery Plan (DCRP). Unfortunately, a large percentage of companies that prepare disaster contingency and recovery plans omit important considerations in the plan's preparation that are often discovered after a disaster strikes and the plan is activated. This chapter presents the DCRP as five component plans to highlight the importance of a comprehensive plan. First, the chapter briefly reviews key items to include in a successful DCRP. Second, it examines a number of factors frequently overlooked in the DCRP process. Inclusion of these key factors in the DCRP should result in a comprehensive plan that will work when disaster strikes, as it will sooner or later.

Notes

1. John McCormick, "Washed Away," *Newsweek* (May 5, 1997): 30.
2. Christy Chapman, "Before Disaster Strikes," *Internal Auditor* (December 1996): 22.
3. This section adapted from Joseph W. Wilkinson and Michael J. Cerullo, *Accounting Information Systems: Essential Concepts and Applications,* 3rd ed. (New York: John Wiley & Sons, Inc., 1997), chapter 9.

Chapter 34
Taking an Adaptive Approach to IS Security

Christopher Klaus

THIS CHAPTER PRESENTS a fresh perspective on how the IS security mechanism should be organized and accomplished. It discusses the unique characteristics of the Cyberspace computing environment and how those characteristics affect IS security problems. It describes three approaches to resolving those problems and analyzes the effectiveness of each.

THE CYBERSPACE ENVIRONMENT

In Cyberspace, one cannot see, touch or detect a problem. Most organizations find it difficult to allocate funds to address problems that their executives cannot directly experience. When an IS security problem occurs, all too often significant time elapses before the nature and extent of the damage is realized.

An information processing application or network looks the same (at least externally) from the time of an attacker's initial reconnaissance through penetration and subsequent attack on the application or network. If risks associated with the network are not adequately addressed, economic and operational harm may occur before the damage is discovered and remedied. The specific risk involved is defined by a combination of the threat to an information resource or the application that processes it, its vulnerability to compromise, the consequences of an assault, and the likelihood of such an attack.

Over the past few years a large number of commercial and government organizations have studied the challenges associated with reducing risk within such a complex environment. Both the U.S. Air Force and the U.K. Defense Research Agency (DRA) have pointed out that individuals responsible for defending information processing applications or networks are presented now with an operational risk environment in which the decision and response cycle has been reduced greatly. Within the physical domain, decision makers typically have minutes, hours, days, or even weeks to respond to potential or actual attacks by various types of intruders. This is not true in the world of Cyberspace.

The Four Categories of Human Threats

Four basic human threat categories exist in Cyberspace: internal and external, structured and unstructured.

Internal Threat: Unstructured. The unstructured internal threat is posed by the average information processing application user. Typically, this individual lacks awareness of existing technical computing vulnerabilities and is responsible for such things as device use errors and network crashes. These result from inadvertent misuse of computing resources and poor training. When these individuals exploit computing resources for illegal gain, they typically misuse authorized privileges or capitalize on obvious errors in file access controls.

Internal Threat: Structured. The structured internal threat is posed by an authorized user who possesses advanced knowledge of network vulnerabilities. This person uses this awareness to work around the security provisions in a simplistically configured network. An aggressive, proactive IS security mechanism must be deployed to counter the threat that this person's activities may pose.

External Threat: Unstructured. The unstructured external threat created by the average World Wide Web user is usually not malicious. Typically, this individual lacks the skills and motivation to cause serious damage to a network. However, this person's curiosity can lead to unintentional system crashes and the loss of data files.

External Threat: Structured. The structured external threat stems from someone with detailed knowledge of network vulnerabilities. This person has access to computer hacker tools that permit compromising most IS security programs, especially when the intruder does not perceive a risk of detection or apprehension.

The IS Security Issues of the Virtual Domain

Within the virtual domain, the entire sequence that may be associated with a network probe, intrusion, and compromise often can be measured in milliseconds. An attacker needs to locate only one exposed vulnerability. By contrast, the defenders of an application or network must address as many as 200 to 300 vulnerabilities. At the same time, these defenders must continue to support an array of revenue-generating or mission-enabling operations.

The virtual domain is not efficiently supported by conventional manual audits, random monitoring of information-processing application operations, and non-automated decision analysis and response. It requires sound insertion and placement of technical and procedural countermeasures as well as rapid, automated responses to unacceptable threatening and vulnerability conditions involving a wide array of attacks and misuse.

READY-AIM-FIRE: THE WRONG APPROACH

The primary challenges associated with bringing the network security domain under control result from its relatively new existence as a science and engineering discipline as well as the shortage of qualified professionals who understand how to operate and protect it. Some organizations have adequate and well-trained IS staffs. The norm, however, is a small, highly motivated, but outgunned team that focuses most of its energies on user account maintenance, daily emergencies, and general network design reviews. Few staff have time to study evolving threat, vulnerability, and safeguard (countermeasure) data, let alone develop policies and implementation plans. Even fewer have time to monitor network activity for signs of application or network intrusion or misuse.

This situation results in a ready-aim-fire response to IS security vulnerabilities, achieving little more than create a drain on the organization. This is the typical sequence of events:

1. IS executives fail to see the network in the context of the actual risk conditions to which it is exposed. These individuals understand the basic technology differences between such operating systems as Windows NT and Sun Solaris. They also understand how products such as Netscape, Internet Explorer, and Microsoft Word, Power-Point, and Excel enhance operations. However, these individuals typically have little knowledge about the vulnerabilities associated with the use of products and can allow threats to enter, steal, destroy, or modify the enterprise's most sensitive data.
2. IS safeguards are implemented in an ad hoc manner due to this incomplete understanding of the problem (Exhibit 34.1).There is no real traceability of security exposures to IS operational requirements, no study of their effects on either threats or vulnerabilities, and no analysis of the return on security investment. In other words:

    SECURITY = DIRECT TECHNICAL COUNTERMEASURES

    (The latter includes such things as firewalls, data encryption, and security patches.)
3. These organizations are left with a false sense of security (Exhibit 34.2). They believe that the risk has been addressed, when in fact many threats and vulnerabilities remain.

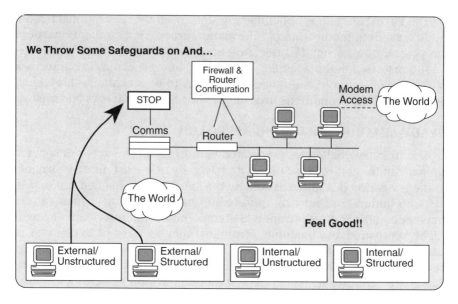

Exhibit 34.1. The ad-hoc approach to safeguard selection does not work

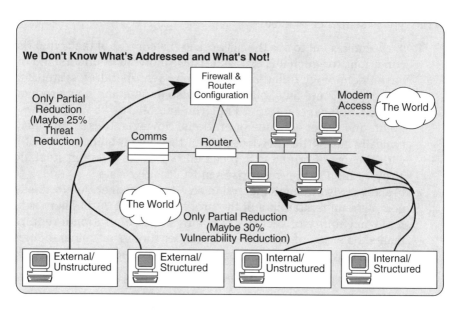

Exhibit 34.2. What the network really looks like

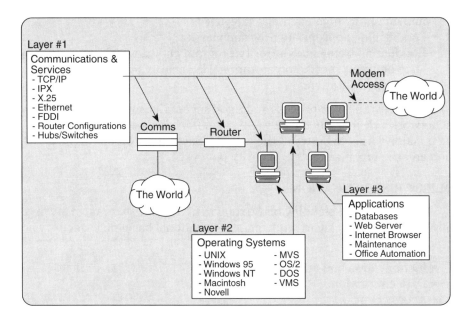

Exhibit 34.3. Vulnerabilities are located throughout the network architecture

4. As a result, risk conditions continue to degrade as users alter system and safeguard configurations and work around the safeguards.

LOOKING FOR MANAGEMENT COMMITMENT

The approach just described obviously is not the answer. As noted in Exhibit 34.3, network vulnerability conditions are complex and require more than token attention. Success within the virtual domain will depend on the acceptance and adoption of sound processes that support a sequential and adaptive IS security model. However, an attempt to obtain the commitment of the organization's senior executives to an investment in new IS security may be rejected. The key to obtaining support from senior executives is a clear presentation of how the organization will receive a return on its investment.

A GOOD START WITH WHAT IS UNDERSTOOD

The best place to start developing a new IS security solution is what is already understood and can be applied directly to the new problem domain. In this case, one starts with:

- Defining sound security processes.
- Creating meaningful and enforceable policies.

- Implementing organizational safeguards.
- Establishing appropriate program metrics.
- Conducting frequent IS security program audits, which evaluate variance between specific organizational IS security policies and their actual implementation.

Without established process and rigor, successful, meaningful reduction of network risk is highly unlikely. This situation also ensures that there will be a major variance between the actual IS security program implementation and the organization's IS security policy.

DIRECT RISK MITIGATION

Without an understanding of the total risk to their networks, many organizations move quickly to implement conventional baseline IS security solutions such as:

- Identification and authentication (I&A).
- Data encryption.
- Access control.

This approach is known as Direct Risk Mitigation. Organizations that implement this approach will experience some reduction in risks. However, these same organizations will tend to leave significant other risks unaddressed. The network security domain is too complex for such an ad hoc approach to be effective.

Incorporating risk analysis, policy development and traditional audits into the virtual domain will provide the initial structure required to address many of these issues. At a minimum, the IS security program must consist of well-trained personnel who:

- Adhere to sound, standardized processes.
- Implement valid procedural and technical solutions.
- Provide for audits intended to support potential attack or information application misuse analysis.

This approach is captured by the formula:

SECURITY = RISK ANALYSIS

+ POLICY

+ DIRECT TECHNICAL COUNTERMEASURES

+ AUDIT

If implemented properly, direct risk mitigation provides 40% to 60% of the overall IS security solution (Exhibit 34.4). This model begins, as should all security programs, with risk assessment. The results support comput-

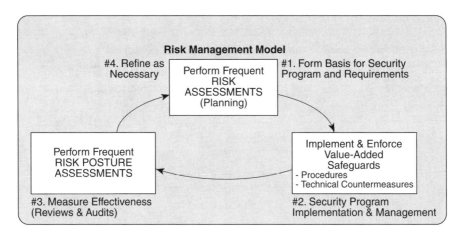

Exhibit 34.4. Implementation of a sound risk management process will ensure reduced risk

ing operations and essential enterprise planning efforts. Without proper risk analysis processes, the IS security policy and program lack focus and traceability (Exhibit 34.5).

Once a risk assessment has been conducted, the individuals responsible for implementation will acquire, configure, and operate the defined network solution. Until now, little has been done to ensure that clear technical IS security policies are provided to these personnel. The lack of guidance and rationale has resulted in the acquisition of non-value-added technical safeguards and the improper and insecure configuration of the associated applications once these mechanisms have arrived within the operational environment.

One other major problem typically occurs within the implementation phase. Over time, administrators and users alter system configurations. These alterations re-open many of the vulnerabilities associated with the network's communications services, operating systems, and applications. This degradation has driven the requirement represented within the final phase of the risk management cycle. Risk posture assessments (audits) are linked to the results of the risk assessment. Specifically, risk posture assessments determine the organizational IS security policy compliance levels, particularly as they define the variance from the policy. The results of such assessments highlight program weaknesses and support the continuous process of measuring compliance of the IS security policy against actual security practice. Organizations can then facilitate a continuous improvement process to reach their goals.

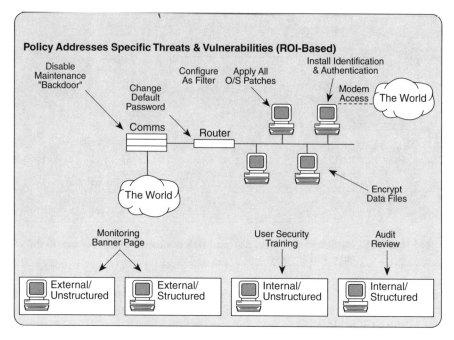

Exhibit 34.5. Ensuring a sound security policy

Risk Posture Assessment Results

The results of a risk posture assessment can be provided in a number of individual formats. Generally, assessment results may be provided to:

- Technicians and engineers in a format that supports corrective action.
- Security and network managers in a format that supports program analysis and improvement.
- Operations executives in a format that summarizes the overall effectiveness of the IS security program and its value to the organization.

This approach is sound, responsive, and simple to implement. But major problems still exist, and this approach addresses only 40% to 60% of the solution. Hackers do not care about this 40% to 60% — only about the remaining 40% to 60% that has been left exposed. Any success associated with this type of process depends on proper initial system and countermeasure implementation and a fairly static threat and vulnerability environment. This is not the case in most organizations. Normally, the IS security exposures not addressed by this approach include

- An active, highly knowledgeable, and evolving threat.
- A greatly reduced network security decision and response cycle.
- Network administrators and users who misconfigure or deliberately work around the IS security countermeasures.

- Low levels of user and administrator awareness of the organization's IS security policies and procedures — and the threats and vulnerabilities those policies are designed to detect and resolve.
- Highly dynamic vulnerability conditions.

The general classes of vulnerabilities involve:

- Design inadequacies in hardware and software.
- Implementation flaws, such as insecure file transfer mechanisms.
- Administration deficiencies.

Although direct risk mitigation is a good start to enhancing IS security, serious threats and vulnerability conditions can still leave the network highly susceptible to attack and misuse. The next level of response is described as adaptive information systems security.

ADAPTIVE IS SECURITY

The world of Cyberspace requires an adaptive, highly responsive process and product set to ensure ongoing, consistent risk reduction. This solution is the adaptive security model, which will be discussed further in this chapter. It is captured by the formula:

SECURITY = RISK ANALYSIS

+ POLICY

+ IMPLEMENTATION

+ THREAT AND VULNERABILITY MONITORING

+ THREAT AND VULNERABILITY RESPONSE

The adaptive security model consists of a proactive cyclic risk management approach that includes active network and systems monitoring, detection, and response. A network security management mechanism becomes a natural outgrowth of the network environment and provides overlapping, yet complementary, network management services. These performance and security management mechanisms are required to support an organization's overall operational requirements.

The network security management application supports the unique variables associated with the network security domain. Its architectural components address and support the following variables.

- *Attack Analysis and Response.* Attack analysis and response are the real-time monitoring of attack recognition signatures and other suspicious activities including viruses, probing activity, and unauthorized modification of system access control mechanisms. Real-time monitoring provides the ability to rapidly detect unauthorized hacker activity and respond with a variety of counterthreat techniques. The responses can range from simple IS security officer notification to dynamic reconfiguration of identified weaknesses or communications paths.

- *Misuse Analysis and Response.* Misuse analysis and response are the real-time monitoring of the internal misuse of network resources. Typically misuse is associated with activities that do not impact operational computing effectiveness, but are counter to documented policy regarding the acceptable use of organizational systems and resources. Automated response actions include the denial of access, sending warning messages to the offending individuals, and the dispatch of e-mail messages to appropriate managers.

- *Vulnerability Analysis and Response.* Vulnerability analysis and response consist of frequent, automated scanning of network components to identify unacceptable security-related vulnerability conditions. This unacceptability is determined by a failure to conform to the organization's IS security policy. The scanning includes automated detection of relevant design and administration vulnerabilities. Detection of the vulnerabilities leads to a number of user defined responses including automatic correction of the exposure, the dispatch of automated e-mail corrective actions, and the issuance of warning notices.

- *Configuration Analysis and Response.* Configuration analysis and response include frequent, automated scanning of performance-oriented configuration variables.

- *Risk Posture Analysis and Response.* Risk posture analysis and response include automated evaluation of threat activity and vulnerability conditions. This activity goes beyond basic, hard-coded detection and response capabilities. It requires and bases its response on the analysis of a number of variables such as asset value, threat profile, and vulnerability conditions. Analysis supports real-time technical modifications and countermeasures in response to dynamic risk conditions. These countermeasures may include the denial of access, placement of conventional decoy files, and mazing — setting up decoy files and directory structures to lock an intruder into a maze of worthless directories to track his activities and form a basis for possible prosecution.

- *Audit and Trends Analysis.* Audit and trends analysis include the automated evaluation of threat, vulnerability, response, and awareness trends. The output of such an examination includes historical trends data associated with the IS security program's four primary metrics: (1) risk, (2) risk posture, (3) response, and (4) awareness. This data supports program planning and resource allocation decisions.

- *Real-Time User Awareness Support.* Real-time user awareness support provides recurring IS security policy, risk, and configuration training.

This component ensures that users are aware of key organizational IS security policies, risk conditions, and violations of the policies.

- *Continuous Requirement Support.* The adaptive security model and its related technology components support organizational requirements to continuously ensure that countermeasures are installed and properly configured. Threats are monitored and responded to in a highly effective and timely manner, and vulnerability conditions are analyzed and corrected prior to exploitation. The model also supports the elimination of system misuse and increases general user and administrator IS security awareness.

With the inclusion of the model and its supporting technologies, the entire spectrum of network security is addressed and measured. Although reaching the 0% risk level is impossible in the real world of computing and telecommunication, incorporating adaptive IS security processes and mechanisms into the overall effort supports reaching and maintaining a 100% solution — that is, the best solution for any one specific organization. In addition to appropriately and consistently addressing these unique network security variables, these technology modules support the requirement for defining, collecting, analyzing, and improving the IS security program's operational metrics.

Section 3
Providing
Application Solutions

TWO DECADES AGO, the major responsibilities of the information systems function could be easily slotted into two buckets: computer operations and systems development. Just as operations responsibilities today have increased in complexity to include wide area and local networks, as well as enterprisewide distributed architectures, so too have the responsibilities for providing application solutions become more complex. The chapters selected for this section address these new application provisioning challenges as well as reaffirm the importance of established software engineering methods and techniques.

NEW TOOLS AND APPLICATIONS

We begin with four chapters that point to what's ahead for application developers as well as for application users. Chapter 35, "IT-Enhanced Productivity and Profitability," sheds light on why U.S. firms today are allocating up to 50 percent of their capital investments to information technology. Bottom-line payoffs are being realized from IT applications that involve integrated business process reengineering (BPR) and total quality management (TQM), global communications networks, the Internet and World Wide Web, integrated enterprisewide systems for mass customization and logistics, and data mining and warehousing. This short chapter ends with the warning that innovative IT people are needed to ensure that the IT productivity "paradox" of the past is finally laid to rest.

The use of intelligent agents for business applications is the focus of the next two chapters. Software agents, an extension of artificial intelligence, are autonomous software programs that work collaboratively and have some learning capabilities. Chapter 36, "The Use of Intelligent Agents for Decision-Making: An Analysis of the State of the Art," describes the conceptual attributes of intelligent agents, how they learn, and how they are being successfully used today for e-mail filtering and routing, data warehouse querying, Internet search engines, and other business applications. Several potential barriers to widespread diffusion are also discussed. Chapter 37, "Analyzing Agents for Electronic Commerce," focuses on the potential use of software agents for E-commerce applications. The author describes the concept of an object-oriented electronic commerce support system in which a collection of agents support business workers in coping with information overload, managing workloads, coordinating business processes, and providing negotiation support.

The intent of Chapter 38, "Java™: The Language and its Supporting Technologies," is to provide enough details about the Java programming language to enable the IS manager to evaluate its potential use in IS development projects. The chapter begins with a discussion of the concepts of architecture neutrality and object orientation. By the end of the primer, the reader should have a good grasp of why Java-related technologies are anticipated by many to become mainstream tools in the future.

SYSTEMS DEVELOPMENT APPROACHES

Four chapters that offer new perspectives on established systems development methods and techniques have been selected for this topic. The first one is concerned with paradigm shifts within software development environments. Chapter 39, "The Methodology Evolution: From None, to One-Size-Fits-All, to Eclectic," provides a historical overview of methodologies for systems development projects from an evolutionary perspective. Although methodologies in the past have sometimes been hailed by their proponents as "the holy grail," evidence from the field suggests that multiple methodologies are in fact typically customized for the problem situation at hand. The author advocates an eclectic, problem-centered view of methodology in contrast to a "one-size-fits-all" approach.

The remaining three chapters contain prescriptions for various methods and techniques. In Chapter 40, "Strategic Use of JAD," the use of joint application development techniques for enhancing employee participation and learning is related to the trend toward employee empowerment. The author argues that the facilitated group approach of JAD can be used to support the overall organization goals of group empowerment and organizational learning.

For an application to satisfy user needs, the human dimension of systems design must be attended to as well as the technical. Usability engineering, or user-centered design, is a framework of principles, methodologies, and techniques intended to help the analyst understand the user's perspective. Chapter 41, "User-Centered Design," describes in detail a user-centered requirements definition process and usability evaluation processes, as well as an assessment process to determine an IS staff's readiness to perform usability engineering.

The author of Chapter 42, "Database Development Methodology and Organization," takes a philosophical stance similar to that of the author of

Chapter 39. As a subset of a life-cycle methodology, a database development methodology is viewed as a flexible framework to be customized for a specific problem. The chapter describes some of the features, processes, deliverables, tools, roles, and pitfalls of a high-level methodology for database development.

PROJECT MANAGEMENT

Effective project management today not only involves meeting schedules and managing budgets but also a customer-oriented perspective. Chapter 43, "Project Success and Customer Needs," models systems project success as a function of the difference between the project outcome expected by the customer and the actual project outcome perceived by the customer. The authors present a framework for managing five typical performance gaps from a continuous improvement perspective.

The challenge of satisfying different constituencies is the focus of the next two chapters. In Chapter 44, "Win-Win Projects," Theory-W software project management principles are espoused as a way to manage project risks and user expectations. A case study is used to demonstrate how to (and how not to) use contracting and requirements definition processes that articulate win-win conditions for all stakeholders. In Chapter 45, "Managing the User/IS Relationship," proactive guidelines for making IS more "in tune" with its internal clients are provided from an IS consultant perspective.

Articulating the key implementation problems associated with reengineering projects in the 1990s is critical for understanding some of the pitfalls of enterprise resource planning (ERP) system implementations today. Chapter 46, "Reengineering Project Challenges," presents a categorization scheme for reengineering problems and an analysis of the five most severe problems discovered from a survey of companies in multiple industries. Four of the top five problems are categorized as change management issues. The authors conclude that business process reengineering projects require attention to organizational level factors that have not been associated with traditional systems projects of the past.

New skills for managing today's more complex systems projects are also called for by the author of Chapter 47, "Managing Development in the Era of Large Complex Systems." Based on a year-long field review of large, complex systems development efforts involving a Big 5 consulting organization, that were often tied to strategic client goals, the author identifies three factors associated with project success: business vision, system testing from a program management (vs. single project) perspective, and a phased rollout strategy. The author warns that eliminating system complexity does not appear to be a option; instead, IS managers need to devise strategies to manage project complexity and the inherent risks.

SOFTWARE QUALITY ASSURANCE

According to the authors of Chapter 48, "Meeting the Software Challenge," software development projects are still characterized by four problems: budget and schedule overruns, low quality, costly maintenance, and low reusability. A new type of systems development environment in which IT professionals continuously learn and adapt to new methods, techniques, and disciplines is proposed as the overall solution. The institutionalization of software development maturity models and standards is a key step toward this new learning organization paradigm.

A comprehensive introduction to software quality assurance in general is provided in Chapter 49, "Analyses of Software Quality and Auditing." The authors also present in detail the Software Engineering Institute's Capability Maturity Model (CMM) and the ISO 9000 set of quality assurance standards. Auditing practices for software quality assurance are also briefly described.

System testing is the last step in the software development process in which evidence is systematically collected about whether or not the right system has been developed and the system is working as intended; system testing is therefore a key software quality assurance task. Chapter 50, "Software Testing Basics and Guidelines," provides a comprehensive primer of software testing basics and debunks some testing myths. The author warns that testing requires substantial time, effort, and talent. As we approach January 1, 2000, the assessments of the IT profession's ability to do quality testing may become a matter of public record.

The implications of increased risks of financial loss or physical harm to users due to software defects is the focus of the final chapter in this section. Chapter 51, "Ethical Responsibility for Software Development," provides examples of lawsuits to increase the reader's awareness of the risks faced by companies in today's software industry. The implications are that not just organizations, but also individual software developers, need to be ethically responsible and demonstrate good-faith efforts to disclose known defects in software products. Again, as we approach the year 2000, the extent to which these ethical responsibilities have been embraced by IT professionals may become a matter of public debate.

Chapter 35

IT-Enhanced Productivity and Profitability

William R. King

MORE THAN FOUR YEARS AGO, I wrote that, "U.S. businesses have based their investments in IT more on faith than on demonstrated results," but that, "... IT investments may have finally begun to pay off."[1] Now, it is clear that the U.S. economy has been soaring and worker productivity has been increasing at a rapid rate, due in some large part to companies that are making effective and efficient use of information technology.

The old strategic management verities, which focused on paying high dividends to shareholders and planning long payback periods for large capital investments such as those in IT, have been thrown out the window in an era in which technology becomes obsolete very quickly. The nearly forgotten management philosophy of Andrew Carnegie, who relentlessly pursued cost reductions in steel production through new technology investments and his own 19th-century version of business process re-engineering, while paying few dividends to shareholders, has been re-adopted by many American businesses.

For instance, Owens Corning, in a flat market in which prices can't be raised, has thrown out its existing computer systems and is spending $175 million to link its 150 operating locations together in a effort at raising productivity and profits.

According to *Business Week*, "starting around 1995 ... companies began diverting bigger chunks of their capital budgets into computers, software and communications equipment."[2] Overall, American firms now allocate nearly 50% of capital investment to IT, with a rate of increase of IT investment that is nearly double that of other capital goods — a clear bet on IT's profitability- and productivity-enhancing potential.

0-8493-9820-7/00/$0.00+$.50
© 2000 by CRC Press LLC

DRIVERS OF THE PROFITABILITY AND PRODUCTIVITY REVOLUTION

While discussions of an "IT revolution" are trite, it is useful to assess the specific mechanisms that appear to be driving productivity and profitability increases. This is important because it is not just the omnipresent increases in computing speeds and capacities or decreases in computing costs, but new ways of using computers, that appear to be of paramount importance in these accomplishments.

Among the important drivers are the integrated philosophies of TQM and BPR, global communications networks, the Internet and the World Wide Web, intranets, enterprise systems, mass customization, integrated logistics, and data mining and warehousing.

The Integrated Business Process Re-engineering (BPR) — Total Quality Management (TQM) Philosophy

The pervasiveness of TQM and BPR appears to be a major driving force in productivity and profitability enhancement. Even though a significant proportion of specific TQM and BPR efforts are reported to be "failures," the mindset that the two philosophies jointly create — constantly improving the way in which things are done, applying IT to enhance productivity, empowering employees, redesigning entire business processes, measuring results, etc. — has led to revolutionary changes in business practices.

Most US companies are now emulating Carnegie, who would simply close down an underperforming steel mill department and restart it using new technology and methods rather than "making do" with mediocre performance. The net result of the integrated TQM-BPR philosophy has been a new attitude of "out with the old and the mediocre" and of continuous improvement through radical change — a new management philosophy that integrates the evolutionary notions of TQM and the revolutionary premises of BPR.

Global Communications Networks

Global networks, which were innovations a few years ago, are becoming commonplace. But, the important drivers of productivity and profitability are the uses to which they are put. For instance, many companies, such as Hughes Electronics, use these networks to allow engineers and designers to interact around the world. Hughes reports that this has reduced the time to develop and build a new satellite from 30 months to 18 months.

Texas Instruments uses its network to operate its chip factories around the world as a single integrated system, choosing which factories to assign which jobs on the basis of real-time data and according to its ever-changing desire to minimize cost, meet delivery schedules, produce various product mixes or any of a variety of other criteria. Its engineers can also use the network to remotely diagnose and solve production problems, thus reducing downtime and the need for time- and cost-consuming travel.

Overall, global networks have altered the focus of management attention from the "home office" to wherever skills and ideas are available. Centers of excellence and innovation now exist at various geographic locations because they can be recognized and utilized through the global networks.

The Internet and World Wide Web (WWW)

Although its widespread use is only a few years old, and despite the difficulties that many firms have experienced in figuring out ways to make a profit on the Internet, some companies are using the WWW to good effect in enhancing productivity.

Cisco Systems, for example, handles 70% of the support calls that it receives without human intervention. That use of the Web has saved about 1000 staff positions and is worth $125 million per year to Cisco.

Profitable businesses have also been created. For instance, Dell is selling computers at the rate of over a million dollars a day using the Web — an achievement that may lead to the creation of an entirely new business model for personal computer sales. Dell already possessed a cost advantage because of its direct sales model, and the Web sales channel can only reduce costs and increase sales.

Other companies have been successful in conducting business on the Web, although they may not yet be profitable. Amazon.com, the internet bookstore, has sold tens of millions worth of books electronically. Other booksellers have rushed to use the Web to augment their traditional approaches, fearing that the entire nature of book selling may be changing to this more highly productive channel that can offer discounts, ease of access, and availability to book buyers.

Firms in other industries are experimenting with Web-based models and entirely new businesses are being created at a rapid pace.[3]

Intranets

Just as the Internet has created new opportunities for firms, the in-house versions that are referred to as "intranets" have created the infrastructure that may make computer-supported cooperative work (CSCW) the normal way in which some businesses operate. The early intranet applications primarily served to disseminate information to employees concerning benefit plans, internal job opportunities and the like. They benefited everyone and enhanced productivity somewhat by allowing electronic selection of options. They may also have increased the morale and awareness of employees.

However, the critical use of intranets to support teams that are geographically dispersed, with some members working at home while others operate at various company locations and in different departments of the enterprise, all on different time schedules, has greatly enhanced the ability of some organizations to focus diverse talents and skills on solving a problem, performing a project, or developing a new product.

Enterprise Systems, Mass Customization and Integrated Logistics

The old days of producing a standard product, or many standard products, holding the finished goods in inventory and filling orders in a leisurely manner has given way to mass customization — producing products to achieve mass production economies, but meeting the precise needs and wants of the customer, including rapid delivery. Enterprise-wide systems have enabled various vertical functions to be integrated and coordinated.

Toyota can take an order for a car in Tokyo on Monday morning and deliver that specific model, color, and accessory package to a local customer before the week is out. This illustrates the increasing importance of time-based competition with customized products that is enabled by flexible manufacturing systems and integrated logistics to ensure that parts supplies and finished goods are available at the right place and right time. The same results can now be achieved on a global basis for high-value products by combining global networks to communicate orders with fast delivery by air.

Even companies that operate globally through the export of lower-value products can follow this strategy to some extent by achieving "pipeline visibility" — knowing exactly which products are at various stages of the delivery pipeline at any given time. While such firms may not literally produce to order, they may be able to promise delivery based on their knowledge of the goods that are already in transit around the world.

Data Mining and Warehousing

Warehousing and mining were traditional activities in the old economy. Now, they serve as metaphors for information-age activities.

Warehousing is a metaphor that can be applied to information in the context of data bases or "libraries" of information that record and relate the "bits" of business transactions at a level of detail that was previously unheard of. Data warehouses provide a uniformity of record keeping and relational data bases permit one set of records to readily be related to another set.

Mining is another metaphor for techniques that permit the analysis of large numbers of transactions so that critical management information which may previously have been "hidden" in a database can be unearthed.

For instance, data can be "cross tabulated" in terms of a large number of factors. How many blue Chevrolet Malibus have been ordered by customers in Pittsburgh with various combinations of options, for example? Or, which product categories, styles and sizes sell on hot days in Seattle vs. cold days in New York?

The two metaphors, jointly implemented through new software, can result in a rich treasure trove of management decision information. The combination permits decision makers to free themselves of the "chain of ignorance" that formerly permeated various decision areas — for example, the chain of production–inventory-distribution decisions.

Several decades ago, Jay Forrester at MIT used his "Industrial Dynamics" analyses to point out how business decisions at the factory level were often insulated from the realities of the marketplace by the layers of inventories at the in-process, finished goods, wholesale warehouse, and retailer levels, and the lack of certain and timely knowledge about the size and makeup of those stocks. This often resulted in marketplace changes being detected by the producer only after they had run their course and even after other, often offsetting, changes had occurred. The uncertainty and lack of timeliness of information that were created by the insulation of many levels of inventories sometimes resulted in the producer doing the "wrong thing at the right time" — e.g., increasing production and shipments when consumer demand was falling or adding production and shipments when demand was rising.

Now, with data at one level being related to that at another and with the capability for handling vast quantities of such data on a more-or-less real-time basis, such anomalies need not occur. With the availability of relational data bases (including newly introduced ones that can handle graphics), software to get data into warehouses, software to operate data warehouses and software for designing queries to probe data bases, managers have available a newfound wealth of relevant business information.

CONCLUSION

Taken together, applications of modern information technology — the management philosophy that has grown from TQM and BPR, global networks, the Internet, intranets, enterprise systems, mass customization and integrated logistics, and data warehousing and mining — have had significant impact on the profitability and productivity of businesses. Others might well produce a different, or longer, list to explain what has occurred, but whatever the list, it is important for IT people to recognize the cumulative impact that IS has had and is (finally) having and the growing critical importance of IT to every business that seriously wishes to compete in today's business environment.

PROVIDING APPLICATION SOLUTIONS

It is even more important that IT people serve as innovators in developing new business applications of new information technologies, since, without such applications, the "productivity paradox" that was referred to by IS-skeptics for so many years, will not finally be laid to rest.

Notes

1. King, W. R., "Forecasting Productivity," *Information Systems Management,* Winter, 1994, pp. 68-70.
2. *Business Week*, "How Long Can This Last?" May 19, 1997, pp. 29-34.
3. Clark, D., "Sampling of Start-Ups Shows How the Internet Inspires," *Wall Street Journal*, June 4, 1997, pp. B1 & B4.

Chapter 36

The Use of Intelligent Agents for Decision-Making: An Analysis of the State of the Art

Roberto Vinaja
Sumit Sircar

INTELLIGENT AGENT technology has evolved to become a promising technology used in aiding organizational decision making and information processing. Hence, a growing literature has appeared, although with limited focus on actual development for business applications. The goal of this chapter is to examine the state of the art and underline some business implications of the use of intelligent agent technology.

There is still much debate about the definition of an intelligent agent. Developers have not agreed on the necessary characteristics of an agent, its uses or its design. There is not even a common architecture to facilitate interaction of several agents across platforms. There is much confusion about the concept — each researcher has a changing definition of what the word means and how to go about implementing an agent. Each developer agrees as to the necessity of a consensus, yet no one can clearly define it in a way that achieves broad consensus. For this term to have any effectiveness, there must first be a universal definition that can be agreed upon and used consistently. One of the earliest and most accepted definitions is the one by Woolridge in the February 1996 issue of *The Knowledge Engineering Review*. An Intelligent Agent is "an autonomous, self-contained, reactive, pro-active computer system, typically with central locus of control, that is able to communicate with other agents via some Agent Communication Language."

0-8493-9820-7/00/$0.00+$.50
© 2000 by CRC Press LLC

BACKGROUND

In the last few years there has been a revolution in the tools for organizational decision making. The explosive growth of the Internet and the World Wide Web has encouraged the development and spread of technologies based on database models and artificial intelligence. The organizational information structure has been dramatically reshaped by these new technologies. The old picture of the organizational decision-making environment with tools such as relational databases, querying tools, e-mail, decision support systems and expert systems has to be reshaped to incorporate all the new technologies.

Several technologies must be incorporated into the framework of the organizational information system:

- The proliferation of GUI-based operating systems has changed the way humans interface with computers. Microsoft Windows has set the standard for user interfaces, and most decision support systems are GUI based.
- Data warehousing: Firms are strategically using their data to enable better decision making. Some data warehouses are so huge that it will be almost impossible for a user to obtain the relevant information without the aid of some "intelligent" technology.
- Groupware tools: Lotus Notes facilitates sharing data and implements work flow applications.
- The development and growth of the Internet and the World Wide Web.
- The rapid growth will expand the information available. In a short time, the amount of information available will be such that a single user will not able to make sense out of such an information overload.

As an example of intelligent agents' influence on a specific information systems category, David King and Daniel O'Leary of the University of Southern California, have proposed the following aspects in which the use of intelligent agents is reshaping the notion of executive information systems.

- Executive information systems now focus not only on internal data, but also on external data.
- The traditional focus has been on increasing communications capabilities, whereas the new paradigm is also bent on using technology to filter those communications so that only the important ones need to be addressed.
- Agents let executives browse resources, delegate searching and monitor several different settings, including data warehouses, business intelligence on the Internet, news findings, and internal qualitative database analyses.

- Traditional systems focused on getting information to the executive in a one-way communication process. Under current configurations, two-way communications and knowledge sharing are part of the use of information technology.

It is the heavy emphasis on external data that make EIS so amenable to the use of intelligent agents. However, these agents can be useful for information retrieval in organizations with very large internal databases.

ATTRIBUTES OF INTELLIGENT AGENTS

It is quite common in AI to characterize an agent using human attributes, such as knowledge, belief, intention and obligation. Some AI researchers have gone further, and considered emotional agents. Another way of giving agents human-like attributes is to represent them visually by using techniques such as a cartoon-like graphical icon or an animated face. Research into this matter has shown that, although agents are pieces of software code, people like to deal with them as if they were dealing with other people. Agents have some special properties, but miscommunication has distorted and exaggerated them, causing unrealistic expectations.

Intelligence

What exactly makes an agent "intelligent" is something that is hard to define. It has been the subject of many discussions in the field of artificial intelligence, and a clear answer has not yet been found.

Allen Newell defines intelligence as: "the degree to which a system approximates a knowledge-level system." By others, intelligence is defined as the ability to bring all the *knowledge* a *system* has at its disposal to bear in the solution of a problem (which is synonymous with goal achievement). A practical definition that has been used for artificial intelligence is "attempting to build artificial systems that will perform better on tasks that humans currently do better." Thus, at present, tasks like number addition are not artificial intelligence because computers easily do that task better than humans. However, voice recognition is artificial intelligence since it has proved very difficult to get computers to perform even the most basic tasks. Obviously, these definitions are not the only ones acceptable but they do capture the nature of Artificial Intelligence.

Recently, there has been an increased interest in an area of artificial intelligence that combines concepts from artificial intelligence, expert systems and object orientation. In many ways, agents are similar to objects but they go one step further. Like objects, agents are able to communicate via messages. They have data and methods that act on that data, but also have *beliefs, commitments and goals.*

Autonomy

Autonomy refers to the principle that agents can operate on their own without the need for human guidance. Self-regulated agents are goal-governed agents: when given a certain goal, they are able to achieve it by themselves.

Cooperation

To cooperate, agents need to possess a social ability, i.e., the ability to interact with other agents and possibly humans via some communication language. Agents may be *complex* or simple and either work alone or in harmony, creating a multi-agent environment. Each agent or group of agents has knowledge about itself and about other agents. The agent should have a "language" or some way to communicate with the human user, and other agents as well. The nature of agent-to-agent communication is certainly different from that of human-agent communication, and this difference calls for different approaches.

Openness

An open system is one that relates, interacts and communicates with other systems. Intelligent agents as a special class of open systems have properties of their own, but they share other properties in common with all open systems. These include the exchange of information with the environment and feedback. An agent should have the means to deal with its software environment and interact in the world (especially with other agents).

Bounded Rationality

Herbert Simon proposed the notion of Bounded Rationality to refer to the limitations in the individual's inherent capabilities of comprehending and comparing more than a few alternatives at a time. Humans are not optimal and only in some cases locally optimal. The *bounded rationality* concept can be also applied to describe the behavior of an agent that is nearly optimal with respect to its *goals* as its resources will allow. Because of limited resources, full rationality may not always be possible even when an agent has the general capability to act so. This is known as bounded rationality.

Purposiveness

The most distinctive character of the behavior of higher organisms is its goal-directness, its apparent purposiveness. Purposeful behavior is that which is directed toward the attainment of a goal, a final state. An agent is something that satisfies a goal or set of goals. That is, a degree of reasoning is applied to the data that is available to guide the gathering of extra information to achieve the goals that have been set.

Purposeful behavior pertains to systems which can decide how they are going to behave. Intentional attitudes, usually attributed to humans, are also a characteristic of agents.

Human Interaction and Anthropomorphism

An agent is a program which interacts with an end user and assists him or her. There are many viewpoints concerning the form of interaction between an agent and a human. There is still a controversy about whether or not agents should use facial expressions and other means of personification, i.e., anthropomorphism. There is a great debate over anthropomorphism in user interface design (utilizing a human-like character interface), and agents. Some designers think that providing an interface which gives the computer a more human appearance can ensure that a computer novice feels comfortable with the computer. On the other hand, some critics say that an anthropomorphic interface may be deceptive and misleading.

Adaptation

Adaptation is defined as the ability to react to environments in a way that is favorable, in some way, to the continued operation of the system. Autonomous agents are software components with some ability to understand their environment and react to it without detailed instructions. The agent must have some mechanism to perceive signals from its environment. The environment is constantly changing and modified by the user interaction. The agent should be able to adapt its behavior and continue toward the desired goal. Intelligent agents should be capable of constantly improving skills, adapting to changes in the world, and learning new information.

The agent should be able to adapt to unexpected situations in the environment and be able to recover and perform an "adequate" response. An example of this is Julia, a prototype conversational agent developed at MIT. The Julia agent has three alternative strategies to respond to an expression from the user:

- Try to understand the message and send a meaningful reply.
- Quote someone else on the same topic.
- If everything else fails, just start a different conversation topic.

Learning

Interface agents are software programs that assist a user to perform certain specific tasks. These agents can learn by interacting with the user or with other agents. The agent should be able to learn from its experience. This is related to heuristics and cybernetic behavior. Since people do not all do the same tasks, and even those who share the same task do it in different ways, an agent must be trained in the task and how to do it. Ideally, the structure of the agent should incorporate certain components of learning and memory.

According to Pattie Maes, a researcher at MIT, an agent has four learning sources: Imitation, Feedback, Examples, and Agent Interaction.

- *Observing and imitating the user.* The agent can learn by observing a repetitive behavior of the user over long periods of time. The agent monitors the user activity and detects any recurrent pattern and incorporates this action as a rule in the knowledge base.
- *Direct and indirect user feedback.* The user rates the agent's behavior or the agent's suggestion. The agent then modifies the weights assigned to different behaviors and corrects its performance in the next attempt. The web agent Firefly will choose certain web sites that may be of interest based on personal preferences. The agent asks the user to rate each one of the suggestions, and these ratings serve as an explicit feedback signal that modifies the internal weights of the agent.
- *Receiving explicit instructions from the user.* The user can train the agent by giving it hypothetical examples of events and situations and telling the agent what to do in those cases.
- *Advice from other agents.* According to Maes if an agent itself does not know what action is appropriate in a certain situation, it can present the situation to other agents and ask "what action they recommend for that situation". For example, if one person in the organization is an expert in the use of a particular piece of software, then other users can instruct their agents to accept advice about that software from the agent of that expert user.

BUSINESS APPLICATIONS OF INTELLIGENT AGENTS

Although agents seem to be a promising technology, they are still used within narrow domains. An agent can be targeted for a specific domain and at the same time have sophisticated capabilities. One example could be an agent for electronic commerce transactions.

Some of the latest applications of intelligent agents are e-mail filtering, calendar management, and news filtering. Researchers are developing prototypes for the following tasks:

- Collaborative meeting scheduling among multiple human attendees.
- Internet-based information retrieval.
- News filtering.

We will focus on how intelligent agents impact the other technologies, namely, how they are used in e-mail, GUI environments, data warehouse querying, and Internet navigation.

E-mail

Several applications have been developed for e-mail filtering and routing. An intelligent agent can help managers classify incoming mail based on the user's specifications. For example, we could specify that all incoming mail with the word "Confirmation" be stored in a folder with less priority. Also, the intelligent agent can learn that a user assigns a higher priority to mail personally addressed than mail received from a subscription list. After the user specifies a set of rules, the agent can use those rules to forward, send, or file the mail.

An artificially intelligent e-mail agent, for example, might know that all requests for information are handled by an assistant, and that a message containing the words "request information" is asking for a certain information envelope; as a result the agent will deduce that it should forward a copy of the message to the assistant.

An electronic mail agent developed by Pattie Maes (MIT) is an excellent example of a stationary, limited scope agent, operating only on the user's work station and only upon the incoming mail queue for that single user. This agent can continuously watch a person's actions and automate any regular patterns they detect. An e-mail agent could learn by observation that the user always forwards a copy of a message containing the words "request for information" to an assistant, and might then offer to do so automatically.

Data Warehousing

Data warehouses have made available increasing volumes of data (some data warehouses reach the terabyte size) that need to be handled in an intuitive and innovative way. While transaction-oriented data bases capture information about the daily operations of an organization, the data warehouse is a time-independent, relevant snapshot of the data.

Although several tools such as On-Line Analytical Processing (OLAP) help managers to analyze the information, there is so much data that the availability of such an amount of information actually reduces, instead of enhancing, their decision-making capabilities. Recently, agents have become a critical component of many OLAP and relational online analytic processing (ROLAP) products. Intelligent, autonomous software agents can be used to search for changes in the data and identify patterns, all of which can be brought to the attention of the executive. Users can perform ad hoc queries and generate multiple views of the data.

Monitoring

The routine of checking the same thing over and over again is tedious and time consuming. However, by employing agents to do this task, automated surveillance ensures that each potential situation is checked any time the data changes, freeing decision makers to analyze and act on the information.

This kind of an agent is essentially a small software program written to perform background tasks. They typically monitor networks or databases and other information sources and flag data they have been instructed to find.

News Filtering

One of the most useful applications of intelligent agents is helping the user to select articles from a constant stream of news. There are several applications that can generate an electronic newspaper customized to the user's own personal interests and preferences.

Push Technology and Agents

Push technology delivers information to the user without having him or her search for it. Push providers send information that is delivered and viewed by their customers. A related function for agents can be filtering information before it hits the desktop, so users receive only the data they need or get warnings of unusual data. Users may design their own agents and let them search the Web for specific information. The user can leave the agent working overnight and the next morning find the results. Another function can be to check a Web site for structure and layout. Every time that the site changes or is updated, the agent will "push" a notice to the user.

Searching

Search engines feature indexes that are automatically compiled by computer programs, such as robots and spiders, that go out over the Internet to discover and collect Internet resources. Well-known search engines include

- Lycos merges the results of its continuous WWW sampling into its catalog. The system uses a database with links in several protocols such as FTP, HTTP and Gopher. Its search mechanism ignores common stop words, and it searches the title, headings, links, keywords, and first 20 lines of Web pages. It also has the ability to search for sounds or images. The results are ranked according to its relevance score.
- WebCrawler allows document title and content searches of its database. It indexes the full text of the documents encountered and it operates with multiple retrieval agents in a server-breadth-first approach. To actually retrieve documents from the Web, the search engine invokes "agents." The response from the agent to the search engine is either an object containing the document content or a ratio-

nale of why the operation was not successful. Two methods are used to build the database for the WebCrawler search service: submission and a robot program. The robot runs on a regular basis, and visits sites in a random order. The database consists of both explored and unexplored Web pages. Results are returned in order of decreasing relevance in an unannotated, easy-to-browse list.

However, search engines are not an optimal way to find relevant information. The dramatic rate of web publishing is expanding the indexes and subject hierarchies at an exponential rate and the performance of these search engines is unpredictable from one day to the next. Some other problems derived from engines' uninformed, blind indexing are inefficiency and the waste of valuable Internet resources.

A potential solution for this problem is the use of intelligent search agents. Agents may interact with other agents when conducting a search. This will increase query performance and increase precision and recall. A user agent can perform a search in behalf of the user and operate continuously. This will save valuable time to the user and increase the efficient use of computer resources. An example of an search agent is the Internet Softbot, developed at the University of Washington under the direction of Oren Etzioni, one of the first agents showing adaptation to changes in the environment. Softbot is based on four main ideas:

1. *Goal oriented.* The user specifies what to find. The agent decides on how and when to find it.
2. *Charitable.* The Softbot tries to understand the request as a hint.
3. *Balanced.* The Softbot considers the tradeoff between searching on its own, or getting more specific information from the user.
4. *Integrated.* This program serves as a common interface to most Internet services.

Financial Applications

A financial analyst sitting at a terminal connected to the global information superhighway is faced with a staggering amount of information available to make a decision about investments and funding. The online information includes company information. Data is available for thousands of stocks. Added to this are online financial services and current data about companies' long-term projects. The financial analyst faces an important dilemma: how to find the information that is relevant to their problem and how to use that information to solve it. In the future, the information available through the network will be overwhelming, and the ability to appropriately access, scan, process, modify, and use the relevant data will be crucial.

A distributed agent framework called Retsina that has been used in financial portfolio management is described by Katia Sycara of Carnegie-Mellon University. The overall portfolio-management task has several component tasks: eliciting (or learning) user profile information, collecting information on the user's initial portfolio position, and suggesting and monitoring a reallocation to meet the user's current profile and investment goals. Each task is supported by an agent. The portfolio manager agent is an interface agent that interacts graphically and textually with the user to acquire information about the user's profile and goals. The fundamental analysis agent is a task assistant that acquires and interprets information about a stock's fundamental value. The technical analysis agent uses numerical techniques to try to predict the near future in the stock market. The breaking news agent tracks and filters news stories and decides if they are so important that the user needs to know about them immediately (for example, if a specific stock price might be immediately affected). The analyst tracking agent tries to gather intelligence about what human analysts are thinking about a company.

Users of a site that deals with stock market information, for example, spend a lot of time rechecking the site for new stock reports or market data. Users could be given agents that e-mail them when information relevant to their portfolio becomes available or changes.

Other Applications

The use of distributed agents in collaborative Internet-based information environment will assist information access and filtering, and can ease monitoring and incorporating retrieved information into decision-support tasks.

INTELLIGENT AGENTS AND THE INTERNET

As the World Wide Web grows in scale and complexity, it will be increasingly difficult for end users to track information relevant to their interests.

The number of Internet users is growing exponentially. In the early years most of its users were researchers; nowadays, most of the new users are computer novices. These new users are only partially familiar with the possibilities and techniques of the Internet. Another important trend is that more and more companies are offering services and information on the Internet, and not only companies but also the government is offering Internet services.

However, several factors have hindered the use of Internet for organizational decision making:

- The information in the Internet is located in many servers all over the world, and it is offered in different formats.

- The number of services and the amount of information are growing constantly
- The availability and reliability of the services offered are unstable.
- Since information is constantly updated and maintained, there is a source for errors.
- Information that is available today may not be available tomorrow.

These factors make it difficult for a single person to collect, filter, and integrate information for decision making. Furthermore, traditional information systems lack the ability to address this challenge.

In the past, information systems have delivered limited information about critical issues, such as competitors. However, the latest expansion of Internet and the WWW facilitates the ability to deliver business intelligence to the executive.

INTELLIGENT AGENTS AND INTRANETS

Intranets have recently become important mechanisms for intraorganizational communication. To facilitate capturing and sharing of important qualitative data, many organizations are implementing internal networks or intranets. Lotus Notes and other intranet software facilitates information sharing and group work. Intranets have become rich and diverse environments for a large number of different companies.

Beyond the convenient distribution of basic internal documents to employees, an intranet can improve communication and coordination among employees. Professional services and meetings can be scheduled through engagement management software and calendars on an intranet, thus providing input from all parties and communicating current status to the individuals involved.

Large amounts of a company's information are made available to executives of that organization. As a result, executives must be able to find relevant information on an intranet. It is in this area that intelligent support for information search comes to play an important role.

ISSUES SURROUNDING INTELLIGENT AGENTS

Several outstanding issues must be resolved before broad use of agent technologies can take off.

Marketing Issues

As with almost every new computer technology, the hype has begun. The people most cautious about overselling agent technology and its perceived ability to personify human behavior are the veterans of artificial intelligence work. The press has produced many articles about the intelligent agent concept and many companies are claiming that their product is an intelligent agent, when in fact it is not. Is this just a fashion? Is "intelligent agent" just a buzzword?

Many companies have started labeling their products as "intelligent agents" to increase sales. Everything that has the label "agent" sells. Like the words 'plus', 'super' and 'turbo', the term 'agent' sounds very enticing. The misuse of the term "intelligent agent" is diluting its meaning.

Because of the fact that in most cases current software agents have neither a very sophisticated nor a very complicated architecture, some wonder what qualifies them as "intelligent". In fact, some current commercially available agents barely justify the name.

Some other "agents" do not show any real intelligent behavior; typically, they just follow a set of rules specified by the user, a feature available in some software programs. This capability certainly does not justify the name "intelligent."

Implementation Issues

Unrealistic high expectations promoted by computer trade magazines and software marketing literature may affect the implementation of intranet/Internet systems and agent software. Before implementing a new Internet technology, managers and users should be aware that a new technology does not guarantee improved productivity just by itself. Implementing the most expensive or the more sophisticated intranet system may not necessarily provide benefits reflected in improved productivity; in fact, a less costly system may provide the same productivity level. There are instances where systems may be implemented as easily, without using sophisticated agents. It is really important to carefully plan agents' implementation to truly increase productivity and reduce the risk of implementation failure.

It has been proposed that internet delivery is a proven way to improve information deployment and knowledge sharing in organizations. However, more understanding is needed of the effects of information delivery in decision making and how information delivery is influenced by other variables. Many companies have implemented intranet sites with large economic investments expecting improved information deployment and ultimately better decision making. However, developers and implementers should take into account other issues in addition to the technical ones. It is important to train and educate employees and managers to take full advantage of agent technologies. Managers read articles that promise increases in revenue and productivity by implementing agent technology and they want to implement the same technologies in their companies. However, they may have no clear vision of how agents can enhance existing processes or improve information deployment.

There are many arguments supporting the claim that agent technology will lead to productivity improvements, but some of these arguments have not been tested in practice. Agents are not a panacea, and problems that have troubled software systems are also applicable to agents. If developers do not set appropriate standards and controls for agent development, a bad agent program may become an IS headache. Developers might potentially fill up a network with too many agents and crash an entire system.

Legal Issues

Both agency and commercial law fail to offer clear guidance on the role of intelligent agent technologies. Agent developers should be aware of the state of the law and agent technology.

Privacy

Some important issues confronting the use of intelligent agents are privacy and confidentiality. There is the possibility of a third party using some user's agent for their own personal profit. Donald Norman, of Nielsen Norman Group, has pointed out that we must address those issues now, not just in the technical sense, but in the local, national, and global legal systems.

Responsibility and Liability Issues

Should users be held responsible for the actions of their agents? It is important to protect private information about a user from being disclosed by an agent. Are there appropriate procedures to prevent potential privacy problems arising from multiple agent interaction? Another question to consider is whether a company is liable for damages caused by an employee's agent.

Ethical Issues

The extent to which intelligent agents will be used in the future is not really clear. However, what needs to be considered is whether or not their application in society conforms with the acceptable norms embodied in the morality of system design. While intelligent agents may benefit our quality of life, they also may have adverse effects. On the positive side, they may automate several functions, such as sorting e-mail, performing transactions in the Internet; on the negative side, intelligent agents have no conscience and may be programmed to cause damage to interests of human beings. A question of liability can be raised in this case. Christen Krogh, a researcher at SINTEF Telecom and Informatics goes beyond human beings and has considered the case when an agent violates the rights of another agent (or, more specifically, the rights of the owner of another agent). It is therefore imperative for designers to abide by the ethical norms of systems design to avoid detrimental side effects.

Miscellaneous Technical Issues

There are many other technical issues which will need to be resolved, such as the development of standards that facilitate the interaction of agents from different environments, the integration of legacy systems and agents, and security concerns regarding cash handling.

CONCLUSION

Leading-edge information systems managers and researchers should keep a close eye on agents. If agents fulfill their promise, within several years they could solve problems for both IS managers and the users they support according to Robert Scheier, a *Computerworld* columnist. Agents seem to be an excellent alternative for managing information. Corporate information technology managers and application developers are considering the potential business application of agent technologies.

Most agent programs today are site specific; companies are adding agents to their Web sites with knowledge and features specific to the business of that organization. At the most fundamental level, agents provide sites with value-added services that leverage the value of their existing content.

Some other companies that may benefit from agents are

- Information publishers such as news and online services, which can filter and deliver information that satisfies subscribers' personalized search profiles by the use of personalized agents.
- Companies implementing intranets which provide their employees with monitoring of industry news, product developments, sensitive data about competitors, e-mail, groupware software, and environmental scanning.
- Product vendors, who can provide customer support by informing customers about new products, updates, tips, and documentation depending on each customer's personalized profile.

Businesses could provide other agents that automate customer service and support, disseminate or gather information, and generally save the user from mundane and repetitive tasks. As the Web matures, these value-added services become critical in differentiating Web sites from their competition and maximizing the content on the site. The evolution of agents will undoubtedly impact future work practices. Current technology is already delivering benefits to users. By introducing more advanced functionality and additional autonomy to agents in an incremental way, organizations will benefit more from this technology.

Chapter 37
Analyzing Agents for Electronic Commerce

Shouhong Wang

ELECTRONIC COMMERCE involves more than online data processing and multimedia telecommunication. Software agents are playing a crucial role in supporting E-commerce. This chapter analyzes the roles agents play in supporting E-commerce. It examines eight types of objects that support activities leading to the effectiveness of E-commerce.

Electronic commerce (EC) is not to be perceived as just another example of the use of computers in business. Instead, the Cyberspacial dimension of EC gives it a distinctive character in contrast to other applications of information technology to business. Due to its infancy, few precise definitions of EC can be found in the literature. Broadly, electronic commerce is a contemporary methodology that addresses issues of improving the performance of business through the use of advanced information technology. More commonly, EC is associated with business processes via computer networks. However, the concept of EC is much broader than business on the Web in that the key to the online service is communicating, not commerce.

On the technology side, effective EC must be knowledge-based (not just communication-based and information-based) to cope with information overload and the complexity of business processes. As well, EC must be adaptive to meet the increasingly overwhelmed business needs and delivery quality self-service to the users. Software agent technology is the step toward the solution to the rapidly changing digital economy in the EC era.

A software agent is a software entity that functions continuously and autonomously in a particular environment, which often is inhabited by other agents and processes. Software agents carry out activities in a manner of human agents. Exhibit 37.1 illustrates an example of a group of software agents supporting a buyer in online purchasing. In this example, the purchasing rules agent gives advice about the internal rules and guidelines of the organization in purchasing. The merchandise search agent is actually an intelligent search engine that finds the merchandise that the buyer is

0-8493-9820-7/00/$0.00+$.50
© 2000 by CRC Press LLC

Exhibit 37.1. Software Agents that Assist a Buyer in Purchasing

looking for. The negotiation agent then represents the buyer to negotiate with the suppliers of the merchandise. The distributed inventory control agent helps the buyer to obtain inventory information to make a purchasing decision. Finally, upon the decision made by the buyer, the transaction is passed to the accounts payable agent for a payment arrangement. In this case, applications of software agents add much value to the entire business process.

The software agent is not a new concept, but it had not grown until the past decade when the Web created a perfect environment for EC, with its roots in problem solving and knowledge representation. Intelligent search engines and browsers, learning agents, and knowledge-sharing agents have begun to commercialize in the software market. However, specific business process workflow management agents and business intelligence agents most likely are built in-house. With the development and widespread availability of software agents, EC can accomplish much more than just multimedia telecommunication and online data processing. A collection of software agents engaged in EC is called Electronic Commerce Support Systems (ECSS).

To develop an ECSS, one must use a software tool(s). An agent-oriented approach[1] has been proposed for the set of activities necessary to create software agents. However, the agent-oriented approach has not demonstrated its ability for generating all kinds of agents. Currently the implementation of the agent-oriented approach still relies on traditional software development tools such as object-oriented languages. In fact, the agent-oriented approach can be thought of as a specialization of the object-oriented approach.[2] From this perspective, an agent is a set of objects that are integrated to achieve common goals by accomplishing tasks and coordinating activities. Hence, objects are the elementary units in the construction of ECSS. This chapter first discusses the role of ECSS in integrating business processes, and then proposes a generic object structure for ECSS based on a domain analysis. The domain analysis of ECSS identifies and formalizes fundamental objects involved in EC specification, especially intangible objects that are unique to ordinal types of information systems.

ELECTRONIC COMMERCE: INTEGRATED BUSINESS PROCESSES SUPPORTED BY SOFTWARE AGENTS

An ordinary business process can be viewed in three types of perspectives. Functional perspectives represent how the process elements are performed and how the product flows to these elements. Behavioral perspectives represent when process elements are performed, and informational perspectives represent what products (information) are produced or manipulated by a process. These essential perspectives in business processes are represented readily using the object-oriented methodology. That is, business processes can be modeled by using three fundamental types of object classes: physiomorphic, event, and document.

Physiomorphic objects are physically existing entities of person (e.g., customer), organization (e.g., department), or resource (e.g., machine). Generally, all entities targeted by traditional relational databases are called physiomorphic entities.

Event objects represent events of routine operations, such as order-processing or decision-making activities, such as credit approving. In the object-oriented paradigm of business process modeling, event objects explicitly describe the system timing dynamics.

Document objects are information entities that enter the system (e.g., order applications) or that are produced by the system (e.g., business reports). Web pages are typical document objects in the EC environment.

Without the support of ECSS, business processes are isolated at the individual organizational level even though they are supported by computers and telecommunication within individual organizations. Take the example in Exhibit 37.1 again. Without the help of a merchandise search agent, the buyer must search the Internet by him- or herself to find the suppliers. Although on the Internet there are many search engines, which might be viewed as extremely simple software agents, these search engines are inefficient because of their limited search capability and information overload on the Internet. The buyer would like to have an intelligent agent particularly related to his or her business and discover potential suppliers close to his or her needs. Also, without a negotiation agent, the buyer must negotiate with the person representing the supplier through telephone or e-mail. The buyer would like to give his or her current criteria to an intelligent agent and let the agent to negotiate with the suppliers. In fact, suppliers also can have their agents. The result of these software agents is the integration of business processes that cross the border between the organizations engaged in EC. This role of ECSS in integrating business processes for the networked organizations is illustrated in Exhibits 37.2 and 37.3. Exhibit 37.2 shows that, without an ECSS, the user in EC must deal with the local business process as well as the remote business process through the network by straining his or her own capacity. The ECSS can assist the user to cope with information overload on the Internet, make semi-unstructured decisions involved in the networked organizations, and maintain and improve the networked business process, as shown in Exhibit 37.3. In the next section, the authors analyze the existing conceptualizations and activity-specific instances of ECSS.

A DOMAIN ANALYSIS OF ELECTRONIC COMMERCE SUPPORT SYSTEMS

To determine the fundamental types of objects (or object classes) involved in ECSS, the domain analysis technique is used. Domain analysis has been defined as the process of identifying and organizing knowledge about some class of problems — the problem domain — to support the description and solution of those problems.[3] Domain analysis is applied primarily to analysis of software reuse.[4] For the author's purposes, analysis of the ECSS domain produces a generic object structure for the ECSS domain. Applying the domain analysis technique, a two-stage procedure should be conducted. First, a list of objects are extracted from the general literature of EC and software agents (see Recommended Reading for this).This is

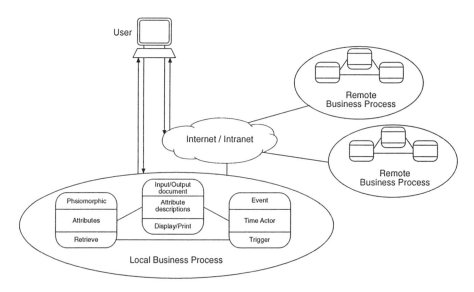

Exhibit 37.2. Electronic Commerce without the Support of Software Agents

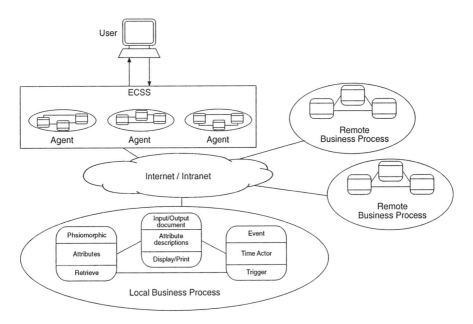

Exhibit 37.3. Software Agents to Support the User in Electronic Commerce

done through the identification of nouns in the descriptions of EC and software agent structures and uses, as well as operations. Next, a shorter list is abstracted by checking across the objects identified in the first stage. The purpose of this procedure is not to adhere to specific terminology or particular frameworks and architectures, but rather to explore the nature of objects in ECSS and to avoid ambiguity. The final set of elementary types of objects of ECSS derived is discussed next.

Goal

Software agents possess abilities such as autonomy, collaborative behavior, and inferential capability. A common characteristic of these abilities is that a software agent is goal-directed. Agents can initiate actions on their own without human intervention and explicit instruction. Hence, the central part of ECSS is the provision of goal descriptions for the software agents. If object-oriented specifications are applied, a goal or a subgoal is an object, and a goal structure is a type of assembly structure. Because a goal (or subgoal) is an object, it possesses its own attributes and operations. Attributes of a goal object include goal states, annotated histories, and strategies to achieve the goal. Technically, the strategies of a goal are general statements that can be used as a guideline for the design of the operations of the goal object. Operations of a goal object include knowledge apprehension related to the goal and evaluation of progress in the direction of the goal state. Knowledge apprehension retains the step-by-step behavior of the agent in reaching the goal. In Exhibit 37.1, suppose the negotiation agent has a goal of effective negotiation. The goal must have its measurements and evaluation methods specified by the object attributes and operations. This goal in turn has its subgoals, say, satisfying time constraints and high success rate. To support the agent in achieving these subgoals, the agent must be able to interact with other objects, as discussed next.

Operational Task

As a software program, an agent can be employed to perform a basic operational task(s). In Exhibit 37.1, the accounts payable agent can perform all the operations involved in the accounts payable task and then release the buyer from the paperwork. One of the most popular approaches to task descriptions is hierarchical task analysis.[5] It was intended to be a general approach to task descriptions and has been applied to a wide range of solutions. Using hierarchical task analysis, a task is described formally as a hierarchical structure, and a task can be represented by a tree of its subtasks. This philosophy is the basis of the traditional structured analysis. If object-oriented system specifications are applied, a task or a subtask is an object, and a task structure is an assembly structure. Generally, a task object can have more than one assembly structure to meet the requirements for the design of an agent.

Because a task (or subtask) is an object, it possesses its own operations, the set of computer procedures to accomplish the task. A task object can send messages to trigger other objects; it also can be triggered by other objects. Agents can be instructed to execute tasks at specific times or automatically wake up and react in response to system-generated events. That is, agents can make scheduled or event-driven actions. Consequently, in the object-oriented frame, the structure of a specific task is dynamic.

Cognizance

A software agent can demonstrate intelligent behavior if it possesses human knowledge or cognizance concepts. Cognizance concepts are powerful appliances to symbolize abstract knowledge in all organizations engaged in EC. A knowledge base is actually a set of cognizance objects representing production rules, semantic networks, cognitive maps, or other forms of knowledge. In Exhibit 37.1, the purchasing rule agent remembers all the rules and policies applied to the organization and provides a guideline of purchasing for the buyer and other agents. The negotiation agent might possess soft knowledge about personal characteristics of its negotiators, including emotion, belief, feeling, and culture. These descriptions of personal characteristics can be stored in a knowledge frame.

In a broad sense, cognizance concepts include problem solvers, which enable the agent to provide personalized assistance to the user. In this view, a traditional decision support system or expert system always can be viewed as a consulting agent.

Mnemonic Instrument

Currently, the Internet and intranets are growing at a rapid pace with the help of software agents. One of the missions of software agents in EC is to reduce information overload. ECSS needs several types of specific mnemonic functions, such as information filtering, knowledge acquisition, and case matching, which are independent of the knowledge objects. These mnemonic functions are the elementary instruments to support the agent in retrieving and retaining knowledge and are called mnemonic instruments. In Exhibit 37.1, a sophisticated Internet search engine might be a mnemonic instrument for the merchandise search agent to find a manageable list that provides most relevant suppliers for the buyer.

Decision Instrument

Software agent technologies have been introduced to decision support systems in the EC environment. In Exhibit 37.1, the distributed inventory control agent might use inventory control models to support the buyer in making a purchasing decision. A type of genuine elementary model that can be used for all kinds of decision support systems but not for a particular system is called a decision instrument. A decision instrument could be a statistical model, an operational research model (mathematical programming, networks, inventory model), a nondefinitional model (reasoning logic, simulation, production rule inference, cognitive maps, neural networks, suggestion model), an accounting/financial model (spreadsheet), or a visual model. In the object-oriented paradigm a decision instrument not only includes the algorithm defined by the model, but it also can contain various operations such as data conversion and output generation.

Work Flow Controller

Software agents work in a dynamic group form. Mobility is a characteristic of agents being able to migrate in a self-directed way from one host platform to another. In Exhibit 37.1, the distributed inventory control agent might travel to the individual remote server mainframe computers, located in corresponding warehouses, to check the inventory and bring inventory control information back to the buyer. The mobility approach of software agents is different from the current client/server computing approach. Using the mobility approach, the client computer sends agents to the server computer instead of making remote procedure calls. This not only reduces the communication workload required in the traditional client/server computing, but also makes it possible for the user to control the mission of the agent. In the EC environment, the journey of an agent might be complicated. One way that workgroup agents evolve to handle more complexity is to conduct travel based on explicitly represented workflows. Thus, a mobile software agent in EC must possess an object(s) of customized workflow controllers.

Learning Instrument

Just as people expect human assistants to learn as they work with them, people also will come to expect the software agents to learn from humans. To learn, the agent must possess a learning instrument(s). A simple learning instrument could be lines of computer programming, and the agent might learn by being given explicit instructions. However, more effective learning is accomplished by letting the agent observe and understand examples performed by the user. By building in learning instruments, an intelligent agent can adapt to different users as well as to multiple domains.

In Exhibit 37.1, the negotiation agent might learn negotiation skills from several buyers in dealing with various negotiators and under different circumstances. When the agent faces an unfamiliar situation, it would ask the buyer to give instructions and to learn from the case.

The increasingly competitive and information technology-enabled business world has decreased the time available for doing business. To survive in the EC environment, people increasingly are turning to advanced software agent techniques. In fact, artificial intelligence, with its roots in machine learning, now is experiencing a renaissance as new tools emerge to make EC more tractable.

User Interface

Interface descriptions specify the dialogue between the user and agents. There is much literature on the elemental description of interface design in the human computer interaction field. In a contemporary computer programming language, the programming environment often provides high-level interface implementation functions to allow easy development of a variety of interface formats for the user. In the object-oriented context, interface descriptions (windows or sound) are organized into a structure. There are two subclasses of a general interface object: one is requests for input, and the other is information presentation. Each subclass in turn has its subclasses of interface objects.

The human-like activities and characteristics of agents require special considerations in designing the interface between the user and agents. The interface should appropriately choose verbal message, graphics, and sound to ensure that the user feels in control of the agents and hides complexity while simultaneously revealing the underlying operations.

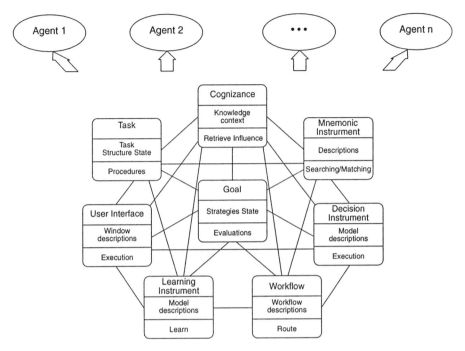

Exhibit 37.4. Electronic Commerce Support System: An Object-Oriented Perspective

Eight generic types of objects have been discussed in the ECSS context. An ECSS is composed of one or more software agents, and each software agent in turn is composed of one or more of these generic objects, as illustrated in Exhibit 37.4.

SUMMARY

In the author's view, one of the distinct characteristics of EC is the component ECSS that makes EC more than telecommunication and electronic data processing through the networks. Specifically, an ECSS is a set of software agents that supports the business in coping with information overload, managing workflows, coordinating business processes, and making decisions in negotiation and bargaining. To update these functions, ECSS must possess learning ability.

This chapter recognizes the needs of analysis for ECSS. Given the fact that the object-oriented approach is the base for ECSS construction, it is considered for modeling ECSS in this study. The proposed object-oriented ECSS structure has explored one theoretical approach to gaining a better understanding of ECSS. This structure integrates the eight aspects (goal, task, cognizance, mnemonic instrument, decision instrument, workflow controller, learning instrument, and user interface) of ECSS into a single object-oriented framework. This framework provides a base for the development of an ECSS in identifying and constructing elementary objects for software agents. Furthermore, the object-oriented framework can be specified in great detail, including descriptions of the dynamic supporting properties of ECSS by defining message connections between the objects. These detailed modeling diagrams can be used for various purposes including ECSS planning, analysis and implementation, as well as evaluation. Thus, this would make it possible to integrate ECSS modeling with computer-aided systems engineering.

Notes

1. Shoham, Y., An overview of agent-oriented programming, in *Software Agents*, Bradshaw, J.M., Ed., AAAI Press, Menlo Park, CA, 1997, 271.
2. Bradshaw, J.M., An introduction to software agents, in *Software Agents*, Bradshaw, J.M., Ed., AAAI Press, Menlo Park, CA, 1997, 3.
3. Arango, G. and Prieto-Diaz, R., Introduction and overview: Domain analysis concepts and research directions, in *Domain Analysis and Software Systems Modeling*, Prieto-Diaz, R. and Arango, G., Eds., IEEE Computer Society Press, Los Alamitos, CA, 1991, 9.
4. Stark, M., Impacts of object-oriented technologies: Seven years of software engineering. *Journal of Systems & Software*, 23, 163, 1993.
5. Annett, J. and Duncan, K.D., Task analysis and training design. *Occupational Psychology*, 41, 211, 1967.

Recommended Reading

Baecker, R.M. and Buxton, W.A.S., *Readings in Human-Computer Interaction: A Multidisciplinary Approach,* Morgan Kaufmann, San Mateo, CA, 1987, 427.

Bates, J., The role of emotion in believable agents. *Communications of the ACM,* 37, 122, 1994.

Bidgoli, H., *Decision Support Systems: Principles & Practice,* West, St. Paul, MN, 1989.

Bigus, J.P. and Bigus, J., *Constructing Intelligent Agents with Java,* John Wiley & Sons, NY, 1998.

Chen, H., Houston, A., Nunamaker, J., and Yen, J., Toward intelligent meeting agents. *IEEE Computer,* 29, 62, 1996, 62.

Date, C.J., *An Introduction to Database Systems,* Addison-Wesley, Reading, MA, 1986.

DeMarco, T., *Structured Systems Analysis and Design,* Yourdon, New York, 1978.

Elofson, G. and Konsynski, B., Delegation technologies: environmental scanning with intelligent agents. *Journal of Management Information Systems,* 8, 37, 1991.

Etzioni, O. and Weld, D.S., Intelligent agents on the Internet: Fact, fiction, and forecast. *IEEE Expert,* 10, 144, 1995.

Greif, I., Desktop agents in group-enabled products. *Communications of the ACM,* 37, 100, 1994.

Hinkkanen, A., Kalakota, R., Saengcharoenrat, P., Stallaert, J., and Whinston, A.B., Distributed decision support systems for real time supply chain management using agent technologies, 1996, *http://ecworld.utexas.edu/ejou/articles/art_1.html* [Accessed 1/30/98].

Huh, S.Y., Modelbase construction with object-oriented constructs. *Decision Sciences,* 24, 409, 1993.

Kalakota, R. and Whinston, A.B., *Frontiers of Electronic Commerce,* Addison-Wesley, Reading, MA, 1996.

Kolodner, J. and Mark, W., Case-based reasoning. *IEEE Expert,* 7, 5, 19926.

Lieberman, H. and Maulsby, D., Instructible agents: software that just keeps getting better, *IBM Systems Journal,* 35, 539, 1996.

Maes, P., Agents that reduce work and information overload. *Communications of the ACM,* 37, 31, 1994.

Norman, D.A., How might people interact with agents, *Communications of the ACM,* 37, 68, 1994.

O'Leary, D.E., The Internet, intranets, and the AI renaissance. *IEEE Computer,* 30, 71, 1997.

Riecken, D.M., An architecture of integrated agents. *Communications of the ACM,* 37, 107, 1994.

Selker, T., Coach: A teaching agent that learns, *Communications of the ACM,* 37, 92, 1994.

Shneiderman, B., *Designing the User Interface: Strategies for Effective Human-Computer Interaction,* Addison-Wesley, Reading, MA, 1987.

Sheth, B., and Maes, P., Evolving agents for personalized information filtering, in *Proceedings of the Ninth Conference on Artificial Intelligence for Applications.* IEEE Computer Society Press, 1993.

Wang, S., Object-oriented modeling of business processes. *Information Systems Management,* 11, 36, 1994.

Wang, S., Object-oriented task analysis, *Information & Management,* 29, 331, 1995.

White, J.E., Mobile agents, in *Software Agents,* Bradshaw, J.M., Ed., AAAI Press, Menlo Park, CA, 1997, 437.

Chapter 38
Java™:
The Language and
Its Supporting
Technologies

V. Ramesh

THE MID-1990s have seen the emergence of several computing technologies and paradigms that have transformed the way business is done. Examples include the Internet and World Wide Web, E-commerce, SAP, and Java.[1] The main focus of this chapter is the programming language Java, which has had an impact on the technologies mentioned above in addition to its own general impact on computing. This chapter introduces the reader to Java and the impact it has had on the development of systems and business applications software. The objective of the chapter is to provide the readers with sufficient details about the core aspects of Java for them to be able to evaluate its use in information systems development projects. The chapter will also discuss many of the supporting technologies that make Java a feasible alternative for developing large software systems.

JAVA

Java started out as part of a software development effort intended to create consumer electronics devices with software embedded in them (Gosling and McGilton, 1996). Numerous problems with writing embedded software using languages available at that time led the designers of the project to develop a new language. The result of this effort was the Java language, which had the following objectives: "a simple, object-oriented, network-savvy, interpreted, robust, secure, architecture neutral, portable, high-performance, multithreaded, dynamic language" (Gosling and McGilton, 1996).

The two best known features from this description are the architecture neutrality of Java and the object-oriented nature of the language. The first feature allows the same Java code to be run on different operating system platforms, such as Windows, Unix, or Macintosh. The object-oriented nature of the language leads to software systems that are easier to maintain and promotes code reuse. The majority of this section is devoted to a discussion of these two features.

Architecture Neutrality

The Java language is designed such that you can follow the Write Once, Run Anywhere™ model. This means that regardless of the operating system on which a software system was designed, developed, and tested, the system can be deployed on another platform without having to rewrite any pieces of the code. This is an immense benefit for corporations that support a diverse set of platforms. Traditionally, diversity in platforms has meant that software written for a specific platform (say, Windows) had to be ported to every other platform on which it needed to run. Porting required significant amount of code rewrites, which in turn required significant commitment of additional resources. Worse still, every time a new release of the software was developed, resources had to be allocated to incorporate the new changes into every platform supported by the software. Developing code in Java eliminates the need for porting code from one platform to another.

To understand how Java provides architecture neutrality it is important to take a deeper look at what happens when we develop systems using any other language. Let us assume that we are developing a new custom order-processing application program that is intended to run on the Windows platform. Let us further assume that we are going to write this program in C or C++. The system itself is probably going to consist of many program files. To create the graphical user interface, the code is likely to make several (probably thousands) calls to library functions specific to the Windows platform. For simplicity, we will assume that this is the only specific function the program uses. Running this program through a compiler will generate an executable file that is specific to the Windows platform. If we now decide to support the same application program on a Unix or Mac platform, at a minimum all the code that relates to calls made to the library functions will need to be modified to correspond to the libraries supported by Unix or Mac. Given the sheer number of such calls, this task will require a significant amount of development work. It will also require hiring people with a different skill set than the original developers. Exhibit 38.1 illustrates this scenario.

Let us now see what happens if we use Java to write this same program. The Java Abstract Windowing Toolkit (AWT) will be used to create the

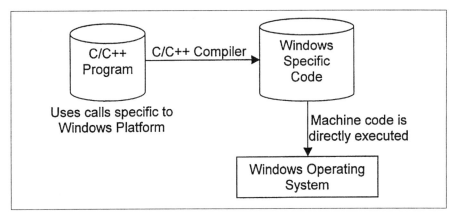

Exhibit 38.1. Typical Compilation and Execution of a Program

graphical user interface. The AWT is part of the Java language and is thus the same for whichever platform a program is going to eventually run on. Thus, the need to rewrite code for different platforms is eliminated, because compiling a set of Java files generates object code (called byte-codes) that is targeted to run on the Java Virtual Machine (JVM). The JVM is a piece of software that runs on top of the operating system (Windows, Unix, etc.). Thus, as long as the operating system supports the JVM, the code generated by compiling Java program(s) will be able to run on any platform without requiring any changes to the code. Exhibit 38.2 illustrates the process of how a Java program runs on a particular machine: the Write Once, Run Anywhere™ model.

To ensure the Write Once, Run Anywhere™ model it is important that programmers use 100% Pure Java™ in their programs.[2] This means that they should not use any extensions to Java that tie the code to a specific operating system platform. For example, Microsoft Visual J++ provides users with some classes that are specific to the Windows platform. Using these classes in an application would make these Java programs incapable of running on a Unix or Mac platform. This, of course, is one of the issues that is part of the *Sun v. Microsoft* lawsuit. Thus, if the ability to run on different platforms is important to a developer, it is critical to follow the guidelines for developing 100% Pure Java™ code specified by Sun (http://java.sun.com/100percent/).

Object Orientation

Object-oriented programming has for the past decade and a half been touted as the new paradigm for software development. Numerous papers and books have been written about the benefits of object-oriented systems development. Some example benefits include code reuse, robustness,

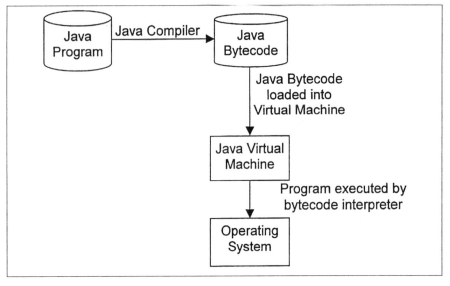

Exhibit 38.2. Compilation and Execution of a Java Program

adaptability to changing requirements, and easier maintenance of code. However, one of the key problems that plagued the object-oriented world in the past was that object-oriented languages were too difficult to use. I believe Java is an example of a simple yet powerful object-oriented language. The biggest advantage of Java is that features inherent in the language make it easy for programmers to create code that has object-oriented characteristics. For example, the simple act of defining variables as private in a class goes a long way toward enforcing encapsulation of objects. Using inheritance and polymorphism are also relatively easier in Java than in other languages. The end result is that programmers are less likely to violate object-oriented principles when writing their code.

Java is a language that allows novice programmers to write reasonably good code (somewhat unknowingly) and allows good programmers to write excellent code without wasting time on frustrating issues. For example, Java supports the notion of references (they are somewhat like pointers in other languages, without the associated headaches) and automatic garbage collection. These features relieve the programmer from hassles of memory management and pointer memory overruns, things that have plagued C/C++ programmers for years. Of course, the current generation of programmers who are using Java will not even get to experience the joys of tackling these problems.

Another example of how some of the built-in features of Java help novice programmers can be seen in its error/exception handling features. One of the most common mistakes made by novice programmers when writing programs that call system-level functions such as reading or writing to files, or network connections, is that they tend to not check to see if the calls actually succeeded. In Java, any pieces of code that perform functions that can lead to such errors are required to be put in a try/catch block. The catch part is mandatory and enables the programmer to deal with any errors that might occur when the program is run. By not allowing programmers to write code without dealing with the exceptions that may occur, Java forces programmers to write more robust code (mostly without much conscious effort from the programmer).

Java supports the basic tenets of object orientation including objects and classes, encapsulation, inheritance, and polymorphism. Java only supports "true" single inheritance; that is, it is possible to inherit properties *and* behavior only from a single superclass. However, it does allow developers to emulate multiple inheritance through the use of interface classes; that is, it is possible to inherit the behavior *alone* from multiple superclasses.

The Java development kit (JDK) comes bundled with a number of classes (grouped together into packages) that extend the power of the language. The current version of the JDK (1.2) has built-in support for creating graphical components (java.awt), using networking functions (java.net), accessing databases (java.sql), as well as common data structures such as hash tables, stacks, and a dynamic memory structure called vectors (java.util). In addition, it has built-in support for creating multithreaded applications through its thread mechanisms (java.lang.Thread) as well as distributed applications through remote method invocation (RMI). The following sections elaborate on the functions provided by some of these packages.

Remote Method Invocation

RMI provides the foundation for writing distributed computing applications using Java. RMI allows a Java object running on one machine to use the services provided by another object by calling the public methods in objects on remote machines. This communication is achieved through the use of an interface that hides the fact that the objects are actually located on a remote machine.

RMI-based applications (like other client/server applications) consist of a client object (running on a local JVM) and a server object (running on a remote JVM). Objects that want to provide services to other objects register themselves with an RMI registry. Clients that need to use them simply access the RMI registry and look for objects that provide the services they need. RMI also provides a mechanism for distributed garbage collection, that is, managing references to objects in the RMI server thus once again freeing up the programmer from memory management concerns.

JDBC

JDBC[3] is a set of classes that allows Java applications and applets to issue SQL (stuctured query language) requests to databases and process the results of queries. The JDBC application programming interface (API) provides support for establishing a connection, issuing a SQL statement, and processing the results. The JDBC API and SQL provide a standard database-independent mechanism for Java applications to communicate with a variety of databases.

To be able to connect to a database access to a JDBC driver is necessary. A JDBC driver provides the actual connection between your Java application (applet) and a database. Currently, the JDBC–ODBC bridge driver is used extensively because it allows developers to access any database that has ODBC drivers. However, pure Java drivers are also available for many of the popular databases.

Java Foundation Classes and Swing

Java 1.0 provided basic support for creating windowed applications through the AWT. However, the model for event handling was revised completely when Java 1.1 was released. This allowed programmers to create complex, graphical applications (and applets) using Java. However, these applications had their own unique look and feel. One could look or interact with a Java application and clearly identify it as being a Java program.

The new Swing classes are part of the Java Foundation classes that are bundled with the newest release of Java, JDK 1.2. The key characteristic of Swing classes is that they allow developers to control the look and feel of the application they are developing. Current users can choose between the Java look and feel, the Win32 look and feel, and the Motif look and feel. Developers can also design their own look and feel and then incorporate them in their applications. It should be noted that selecting a look and feel does not constrain the portability of the program. For example, when specifying the Win32 look and feel and trying to run a program on a Unix machine, the Swing mechanism will determine that the look and feel does not exist on that machine and will simply default to the cross-platform Java look and feel.

SUPPORTING TECHNOLOGIES

Java, the core language (as described earlier), has found its way into a number of application areas and has resulted in the development of a number of supporting technologies. These technologies have helped make Java a popular alternative to other development languages. This section takes a brief look at a number of these applications and technologies.

Java and the Web

Applets. A key reason for Java's rise in popularity has been the ability to embed small Java programs in Web pages. These programs, called applets, were initially used to "liven up" Web pages by adding graphical character-istics to an otherwise "drab" text-based Web page. Game and banner applets probably led this category of Java programs. Applets are special Java programs that have some restrictions on what they can and cannot do. In particular, they cannot (1) access files on the local machine, (2) spawn off any external programs, (3) communicate with any other host (Web server) other than the one they originated from, and (4) find out information about the machine they are running on. These restrictions were put into place to make it safe for users to download Java applets from Web servers on to their machines.

Although the majority of applets in use are currently still used to simply "beautify" Web pages, there is growing trend to use applets as the client tier in multitiered applications. By using applets and server-side Java tech-nology such as RMI or JDBC, one can create powerful multitiered applica-tions (including Web applications). Applets provide a simple alternative to complicated client-side software installation. To activate the client side of an application on machine, users simply have to download the Web page containing the applet. Thus, it is not surprising that this model is increas-ingly being preferred to the complicated software installations that are typ-ical of current client/server applications, especially E-commerce applications. Applets are also being used extensively as client front ends to legacy systems.

However, applets still have the drawback that they need to be download-ed across a network. Thus, the size of the applet (usually they are not very large) and the speed of the network are key factors in determining whether or not an applet-based solution is appropriate. This is perhaps why cli-ent/server applications using Java are more popular in high-speed corpo-rate intranets than across the (slower) Internet.

Servlets. Java has not only made an impact of the client-side of typical Web applications (through applets), but it has also made inroads into the server-side processing on the Web. To support server-side processing us-ing Java, Sun introduced the servlet API. Using the servlet API one can write Java programs that can process data from client applications that re-side on the Web browser. All input and output are achieved through HTTP style interaction between the browser and the programs. The servlet API provides an alternative to traditional CGI processing or other proprietary web applications development protocols. The benefit of using the servlet API over CGI is that you can advantage of the multithreaded nature of Java and create multiple threads to take care of multiple requests instead of creating a process for every request (as in CGI). Developers are also automatically able to take advantage of all the benefits of using Java such as its object-oriented features, advanced memory management, and exception handling capabilities, as well as to have access to all the Java packages and classes, including database connectivity through JDBC, discussed previously.

Given the lack of well-defined methodologies for developing Web applications and the subsequent nightmare of code maintenance that seems to be a staple of Web applications, using object-oriented design techniques on the server side certainly makes a lot of sense. As always, by using Java developers can ensure that their code remains portable across platforms as well as Web servers, as long as the Web server supports the servlet API. Currently, this list includes Sun's Java Web server, Apache Server, Web Logic Application Server, IBM Internet Connection Server, and Lotus Domino Go Webserver. Third-party add-ons are also available to enable servlet support on Web servers that only support the CGI protocol. Given the advantages of Java servlets, it is likely that they will play a key role in the development of E-commerce applications.

Java in Consumer and Embedded Devices

The discussion thus far has revolved around the use of Java on desktop or server machines that support various operating systems such as the Windows suite, Unix, or Mac. From the discussion in the previous section it can be seen that to run Java on one of these platforms, JVM combined with the core Java language and its supporting classes is necessary. These are commonly referred to as the Java application environment (AE) or the Java platform.

In keeping with the original intent of developing Java (i.e., to develop software that could be embedded in devices), specifications are available for developing and running Java programs on embedded and consumer devices. Examples of such devices include pagers, TVs, phones, personal digital assistants (PDA), routers, and so on. To serve the needs of these smaller devices, which typically have lower processor speeds and considerably less memory, three other Java application environments or platforms are available for use with different types of devices. They are the Personal Java, Embedded Java, and Java Card platforms. Each is tailored for a particular category of devices and applications. Essentially, each of these platforms uses a subset of the function of the Java API and has a corresponding virtual machine tailored specifically for it. It should be noted that this does not violate the Write Once, Run Anywhere™ model. Programs written for a device that supports one of the above platforms (e.g., a cell phone) is completely portable to other devices that support the same platform (e.g., a desktop phone), if it is so desired. Upgrades or changes in the hardware of these devices will not affect the software as long as the AE can be supported on the new hardware. Also, development of code for all the platforms described can be done using the JDK or other development environments (see the next section).

The Personal Java platform is intended for use by devices that are going to be used by business consumers. Such consumers will possibly need to run a variety of applications (a mini Web browser, e-mail, calendar software, etc.) on their devices. Examples of devices for which the Personal Java platform is intended include PDAs, Internet-enabled TVs, and advanced (multipurpose) mobile phones. The embedded Java platform is intended for use with such devices as cell phones, pagers, and printers and such networking devices as hubs, routers, and switches. These devices have specific applications needs and function. The Java smart card platform is intended for use in devices with severely limited memory and processor speeds. Examples include the Java Smart Card and Java ring. These devices are the electronic equivalent of the modern-day plastic cards.

Jini

The ability to embed Java into different types of devices (using the various Java platforms described previously) combined with the ubiquitous presence of networking technologies presents a great opportunity for creating a entirely new set of uses for these electronic devices. Sun's Jini technology represents the first step in facilitating the development of such new applications. Sun introduced the Jini connection technology in January 1999. The emergence of this technology is a measure of the strides that Java has made, both in its popularity as well as in its maturity.

Jini technology allows users to plug in different types of devices dynamically into a network. Devices that connect into a network publish the kinds of services they can provide to a lookup server. The process of looking up a server and registering services is done automatically. Jini defines the protocols that are used by the lookup server as well as the discovery and join protocols used by the individual devices. Jini technology is in turn based on Java and RMI (see the previous section). Thus, devices can be connected to the network with virtually no setup work. Devices can also join and leave the network at will without affecting the rest of the network. All that is needed is a connection to a network, a lookup server, and devices that implement Jini technology and are networkable.

Let us assume that you want to connect a laptop to a digital video camera and control the video camera from your laptop. We will assume that both devices are network compatible. Further, we will assume that a lookup server is in place on a network. Let us assume that the digital camera provides three types of services: move (up, down, left, right), take a snapshot, or take a series of pictures (at specified intervals). One way of setting up the two devices is to start by connecting the digital camera to the network. When the Jini-enabled video camera is connected to the network it would find the lookup server and then register its services (along with their interfaces) with the lookup server. Because each device can be treated as an object, the details of how a task is performed are known only to the individual device. Other devices (e.g., the laptop) need only be concerned with the services and interfaces provided by the device. If they want to use a particular service they would simply need to check with the lookup server on their network to see if any devices providing the services they need have registered with the server. Thus, in our example all a user would have to do is connect the laptop to the network. The laptop would find the lookup server and register itself with it. Because the laptop is a consumer of services (provided by other devices), the lookup server would provide a list of devices offering services (e.g., the digital video camera) to the laptop. The user of the laptop can then select the digital video camera from this list. This would cause the services and interfaces (Java objects) registered by the digital video camera to be downloaded from the lookup server, which then enables the laptop to communicate and use the camera through the network.

The key points in the previous example are (1) we did not have to set up the laptop with the drivers for the video camera. The laptop only needed to be concerned with the services provided (which it was able to download from the lookup server). The actual implementation of the service (the driver) is on the video camera. (2) The devices were able to "self-connect" themselves to the network, thus providing true plug-and-play technology; and (3) we did not have to concern ourselves with any network operating systems issues. As long as the devices (including the lookup server) were able to run Java and Jini we were able to hook them up to the network and use them.

Will Jini eliminate the need for complex operating systems? Will it eliminate the need to store separate device drivers for each device we want to use and free us from the need to update device drivers on a regular basis? Jini technology promises to do all of the above. However, it requires that vendors that produce different types of digital devices embrace the technology and make their devices Jini enabled.

JAVA DEVELOPMENT ENVIRONMENTS

What choices do I have if I want to develop Java applications? What does it take to run Java on a machine? What does it take to run Java on a browser? This section provides answers to these questions and more.

The easiest and cheapest way to develop Java applications is to download the JDK from Sun. The JDK is completely free and it comes with everything needed to create Java applications. The drawback is that the JDK is

entirely command line oriented. To date, there have been three major releases of the JDK: 1.0, 1.1, and 1.2. As mentioned previously, there was a
fundamental change in Java's event processing framework from 1.0 to 1.1.
JDK 1.2 had a lot of added function, such as the JFC and Swing classes.
However, unlike 1.0 vs. 1.1., there were no radical differences between 1.1
and 1.2.

Serious application development in Java will, however, require the use
of a graphical integrated development environment (IDE). Many vendors
such as IBM, Symantec, Borland, Sybase, and Microsoft provide IDEs that
provide a graphically oriented environment for developing, debugging and
testing Java applications. IBM's product is called Visual Age for Java, Symantec's Java toolkit is Visual CafÈ, Borland's produces Jbuilder, Sybase's
is called PowerJ, and Microsoft produces Visual J++. Each of these products has several editions (e.g., professional edition, database edition, and
standard edition) that are targeted toward various types of applications
developers. The version number of the product does not always reflect the
version of Java supported by the IDE. Thus, it is important to check whether the IDE supports 1.1 or 1.2 (or for whatever version of Java a developer
is trying to produce applications).

If one is not interested in developing Java applications but simply interested in running Java software on machines, all that is needed is the Java
runtime environment (JRE) for the platform. The JRE version numbers coincide with releases of Java. For example, JRE 1.2.1 supports Java 1.2.

To run Java-enabled Web pages in a browser, the browser software
needs to support the right version of the JVM. Because until recently the
timing of browser releases was usually not in sync with Java's releases, ensuring compatibility between the browser and applets has been a difficult
proposition. For example, Netscape version 4.0 only had support for Java
1.0 (Netscape 4.5 supports version 1.1). This means that applets developed
using JDK 1.1 could not be run on the browser. However, Sun has now released the Java plug-in that enables developers to run Java using the plug-
in and the corresponding JRE instead of a version of Java supported by the
browser. Using the plug-in will enable users to eliminate any compatibility
problems due to conflicts between the version of Java used to create applets and the one supported in the browser.

CONCLUSIONS

Java and its supporting technologies have had a significant impact on
computing in the 1990s. For the first time it is possible to develop applications for devices ranging from powerful work stations to digital cards, storage devices, high-end Web-enabled phones, and pagers using a common
language, Java. The use of this easy-to-learn object-oriented language results in code that is robust, portable, and easy to reuse and maintain. Writ-

ing code in Java enables developers to take advantage of the Write Once, Run Anywhere™ paradigm. For an IS project manager, the features mentioned previously mean that the overall cost of systems development, especially the cost of implementation, maintenance, and porting, will be lower. The portability of Java also means that IS organizations can develop software applications without making a long-term commitment to a particular Web server, database system, operating system, or hardware platform.

Early fears about Java that revolved mainly around the security and speed of Java applications have been put to rest. Applications written in Java are (for most practical purposes) as fast as applications written using popular languages such as Visual Basic, PowerBuilder, C/C++, and so on. Using Jini technology and current networking infrastructure, it has also become possible to plug in various kinds of devices as needed into a network and to facilitate cooperation among these devices.

Educational institutions and businesses are beginning to produce sufficient numbers of educated developers who can harness the power of the language. As long as Sun and its partners focus on the strengths of Java and continue to strive to bring Java into the mainstream of both systems and business software applications development, the future of Java and Java-enabled technologies looks very bright.

Notes

1. Java is a registered trademark of Sun Microsystems, Inc.
2. Write Once, Run Anywhere"! and 100% Pure Java are trademarks of Sun Microsystems, Inc.
3. It is interesting to note that JDBC is not an acronym for Java database connectivity, although that is essentially what it does.

Recommended Reading

A-Z Index of java.sun.com. http://java.sun.com/a-z/.
Java Platform Documentation. http://java.sun.com/docs/.
Gosling, J., and McGilton, H. The Java language environment: A white paper. http://java.sun.com/docs/white/langenv/.

Chapter 39

The Methodology Evolution: From None, to One-Size-Fits-All, to Eclectic

Robert L. Glass

Methodology — the body of methods used in a particular branch of activity
Method — a procedure or way of doing something
— definitions from the *Oxford American Dictionary*

TO USE A METHODOLOGY is to choose an orderly, systematic way of doing something. At least that is the message the dictionary brings us. But what does that really mean in the context of the systems and software field?

There has been a quiet evolution in that real meaning over the last few decades. In the beginning (the 1950s), there were few methods and no methodologies. Solution approaches tended to focus attention on the problem at hand. Because methodologies did not exist, systems developers chose from a limited collection of "best of breed" methods. Problem solution was difficult, but with nothing much to compare with, developers had the feeling they were making remarkable progress in solving application problems at all!

That "best of (primitive method) breed" approach persisted through a decade or two of the early history of the systems development field. And then, suddenly (in the 1970s), the first real methodology burst forth, and the systems development field would never be the same again. Not only was the first methodology an exciting, even revolutionary, addition to the field, but the assumption was made that this one methodology (structured

0-8493-9820-7/00/$0.00+$.50
© 2000 by CRC Press LLC

analysis and design, later to be called the "structured revolution") was suitable for any systems project the developer might encounter. We had passed from the era of no methodology to the era of best methodology. Some, looking back on this era, refer to it as the one-size-fits-all era.

But as time went by, what had begun as a field characterized by one single best methodology changed again. Competing methodologies began to appear on the scene. There was the information engineering approach. There was object orientation. There was event-driven systems development. What had been a matter of simple choice had evolved into something very complex. What was gong on here?

With this brief evolutionary view of the field, let us go back over some of the events just described to elaborate a bit more on what has been going on in the methodology movement and where we are headed today.

TOOLS AND METHODS CAME FIRST

In the early days, the most prominent systems development tools were the operating system and the compiler. The operating system, which came along in the mid-late 1950s, was a tool invented to allow programmers to ignore the bare-bones software interface of the computer and to talk to that interface through intermediary software.

Then came the high-order language (HOL), and with it the compiler to translate that HOL into so-called machine code. HOLs such as Fortran and COBOL became popular quickly; the majority of software developers had chosen to write in HOL by the end of the 1950s.

Shortly thereafter, in the early 1960s, a more generous supply of support tools to aid in software development became available. There were debuggers, to allow programmers to seek, find, and eliminate errors in their code. There were flow charters, to provide automated support for the drawing of design representations. There were structural analyzers, to examine code searching for anomalies that might be connected with errors or other problems. There were test drivers, harnesses for testing small units of software. There were error reporters, used for tracking the status of errors as they occurred in the software product. There were report generators, generalized tools for making report creation easy.

And with the advent of these tools came methods. It was not enough to make use of one or more tools; methods were invented to describe how to use them.

By the mid to late 1960s there was, in fact, a thriving collection of individual tools and methods useful to the software developer. Also evolving at a steady but slower rate was a body of literature describing better ways to use those tools and methods. The first academic computer science (CS) program was put in place at Purdue University in the early 1960s. Toward the end of that decade, CS programs were beginning to become commonplace. At about the same time, the first academic information systems programs began to appear. The literature, slow to evolve until the academic presence began, grew rapidly.

What was missing, at this point in time (the late 1960s), was something that tied together all those evolving tools and methods in some sort of organized fashion. The CS and IS textbooks provided some of that organization. But the need was beginning to arise for something more profound. The scene had been set for the appearance of the concept of "methodology."

THE METHODOLOGY

During the 1970s, methodologies exploded onto the software scene. From a variety of sources — project work done at IBM, analytical work done by several emerging methodology gurus, and with the active support and funding of the U.S. Department of Defense, the "structured methodologies" sprang forth. At the heart of the structured methodologies was an analysis and design approach — structured analysis and design (SA&D). There was much more to the structured methodologies than that — the Department of Defense funded IBM's development of a 15-volume set of documents describing the entire methodological package, for example — but to most software developers, SA&D *was* the structured methodology.

Textbooks describing the approach were written. Lectures and seminars and, eventually, academic classes in the techniques were conducted. In the space of only a few years during the 1970s, SA&D went from being a new and innovative idea to being the established best way to build software. By 1980 few software developers had not been trained/educated in these approaches.

What did SA&D consist of? For a while, as the popularity of the approach boomed, it seemed as if any idea ever proposed by any methodology guru was being slipped in under the umbrella of the structured methodologies, and the field covered by that umbrella became so broad as to be nearly meaningless. But at heart there were some specific things meant by SA&D:

- *Analysis*. Requirements elicitation, determination, analysis — obtaining and structuring the requirements of the problem to be solved.
  - The data flow diagram (DFD), for representing the processes (functions/tasks) of the problem, and the data flow among those processes;
  - process specifications, specifically defining the primitive (rudimentary or fundamental) processes of the DFD; entity/relationship (E/R) diagrams representing the data relationships.

- *Design.* Top-down design, analyzing the most important parts of the problem first;
  — transformation analysis to convert the DFDs into structure charts (representing process design) and thence to pseudocode (detail level process design).
- *Coding.* Constructing single entry/exit modules consisting only of the programming concepts sequence, selection, and iteration.

TOWARD THE HOLY GRAIL OF GENERALITY

An underlying theoretical development was also happening in parallel with the practical development of the concept: an evolution from the problem-specific approaches of the early days of computing toward more generalized approaches. The early approaches were thought of as "ad hoc," a term that in CS circles came to mean "chaotic and disorganized," perhaps the worst thing that could be said about a software development effort. Ad hoc, in effect, became a computing dirty word.

As tools and methods and, later, methodologies evolved, the field appeared to be approaching a Holy Grail of generality. There would be one set of tools, one set of methods, and one methodology for all software developers to use. From the early beginnings of Fortran and COBOL, which were problem-specific languages for the scientific/engineering and business/information systems fields, respectively, the field evolved toward more general programming languages, defined to be suitable for all application domains. First, PL/1 (sometimes called the "kitchen sink" language, because it explicitly combined the capabilities of Fortran and COBOL) and later Pascal and C/C++/Java were deliberately defined to allow the solution of *all* classes of problems.

But soon, as mentioned earlier, cracks appeared in this veneer of generality. First, there was information engineering, a data/information-oriented methodology. Information engineering not only took a different approach to looking at the problem to be solved, but in fact appeared to be applicable to a very different class of problem. Then there was object orientation (OO), which focused on a collection of data and the set of processes that could act on that data. And, most recently, there was the event-driven methodology, best personified by the many "visual" programming languages appearing on the scene. In the event-driven approach, a program is written as a collection of event servicers, not just as a collection of functions or objects or information stores. The so-called Visual languages (Visual Basic is the best example) allowed system developers to create graphical user interfaces (GUIs) that responded to user-created "events." Although many said that the event-driven approach was just another way of looking at problems from an OO point of view, the fact that Visual Basic is a language with almost no object capability soon made it clear that events and objects are rather different things.

If the software world only needed one Holy Grail approach to problem solution, why was this proliferation of competing methodologies occurring? The answer for the OO advocates was fairly straightforward — OO was simply a better approach than the now obsolete structured approaches. It was a natural form of problem solution, they said, and it led more straightforwardly to the formation of a culture of reuse, in which components from past software efforts could be used like Lego™ building blocks to build new software products.

But the rise of information engineering before the OO approaches, and event-driven after them, was perplexing. It was fairly clear to most who understood both the structured and information approaches, that they were appropriate for rather different kinds of problems. If a problem involved many processes, then the structured approaches seemed to work best. If there were lots of data manipulation, then the information approaches worked best. And the event approach was obviously characterized by problems where the need was to respond to events.

Thus it had begun to appear that the field was reverting to a more problem-focused approach. Because of that, a new interest arose in the definition of the term "ad hoc." The use of ad hoc to mean chaotic and disorganized, it was soon learned, was wrong. Ad hoc really means *focused on the problem at hand.*

TROUBLE ON THE GENERALITY RANCH

Meanwhile, there was additional trouble with the one-size-fits-all view. Researchers in another part of the academic forest began looking at systems development from a new point of view. Instead of defining a methodology and then advocating that it be used in practice — a prescriptive approach that had been used for most of the prior methodologies — they began studying instead what practitioners in the field actually did with methodologies. These "method engineering" researchers discovered that most practitioners were not using methodologies as the methodology gurus had expected them to. Instead of using these methodologies "out of the box," practitioners were bending and modifying them, picking and choosing portions of different methodologies to use on specific projects. According to the research findings, 88 percent of organizations using something as ubiquitous as the structured methodology were tailoring it to meet their specific project needs.

At first, the purists made such statements as "the practitioners are losing the rigorous and consistent capabilities that the methodologies were invented to provide." But then, another viewpoint began to emerge: researchers began to accept as fait accompli that methodologies would be modified and began working toward providing better advice for tailoring and customization and defining methodological approaches that lent themselves to tailoring and customizing. In fact, the most recent trend among method engineers is to describe the process of modifying methods and to invent the concept of "meta-modeling," an approach to providing modifiable methods.

This evolution in viewing methodologies is still under way. Strong factions continue to see the general approach as the correct approach. Many advocates of the OO methodology, for example, tend to be in this faction, and they see OO as the inevitable next Holy Grail. (Most data from practitioner surveys show that, in practice, the OO approaches have been very slow taking hold.) The structured methodology still seems to dominate in practice.

A PROBLEM-FOCUSED METHODOLOGICAL APPROACH

There is certainly a strong rationale for the problem-focused methodological approach. For one thing, the breadth of problems being tackled in the computing field is enormous and ever increasing. Do we really imagine that the same approach can be used for a hard real-time problem that must respond to events with nanosecond tolerances, and an IS problem that manipulates enormous quantities of data and produces a complex set of reports and screens? People who see those differences tend to divide the software field into a diverse set of classes of problems based on size, application domain, criticality, and innovativeness, as follows:

- *Size.* Some problems are enormously more complicated than others. It is well-known in the software field that for every tenfold increase in the complexity of a problem, there is a one hundredfold increase in the complexity of its solution.
- *Application domain.* There are very different kinds of problems to be solved:
  — Business systems, characterized by masses of data and complex reporting requirements.
  — Scientific/engineering systems, characterized by complex mathematical sophistication.
  — System programming, the development of the tools to be used by application programmers.
  — Hard real-time systems, those with terribly tight timing constraints.
  — Edutainment, characterized by the production of complex graphical images.
- *Criticality.* Some problem solutions involve risking lives and/or huge quantities of money.
- *Innovativeness.* Some problems simply do not lend themselves to traditional problem-solving techniques.

It is clear to those who have been following the field of software practice that it would be extremely difficult for any methodology to work for that enormously varied set of classes of problems. Some classes require formal management and communication approaches (e.g., large projects); others may not (e.g., small and/or innovative projects). Some require specialized quality techniques, such as performance engineering for hard real-time problems and rigorous error-removal approaches for critical problems. There are domain-specific skill needs, such as mathematics for the scientific/engineering domain and graphics for edutainment.

The fragmentation of the methodology field, however, has left us with a serious problem. There is not yet a mapping between the kinds of solution approaches (methodologies) and the kinds of problems. Worse yet, there is not even a generally accepted taxonomy of the kinds of problems that exist. The list of problem types described previously, although generally accepted at a superficial level, is by no means accepted as the definitive statement of what types of problems exist in the field. And until a generally agreed on taxonomy of problem types exists, it will be nearly impossible to produce that much needed mapping of methodologies to problems.

Even before such practical problems can be solved, an attitudinal problem also must be overcome. The hope for that Holy Grail universal solution tends to steer enormous amounts of energy and brilliance away from the search for better problem-focused methodologies. The computing field in general does not yet appear ready to move forward in any dramatic way toward more problem-specific solution approaches.

Some of the method engineering people are beginning to move the field forward in some positive, problem-focused ways. Others are holding out for another meta-methodology, with the apparent hope that there will be a giant umbrella over all of these specialized methodologies — a new kind of Holy Grail of generality.

THE BOTTOM LINE

My own storytelling suggests that the methodology movement has moved from none (an era when there were *no methodologies* at all and problem-solution approaches focused on the problem at hand) to *one-size-fits-all* (there was one single best methodology for everyone to use) to *prolific* (there were apparently competing choices of which "best" methodology to use) to *tailored* (methodology choices were back to focusing on the problem at hand).

Not everyone, however, sees the topic of methodology in this same way. There are those who still adhere to a one-size-fits-all-view. There are those who think that tailoring methodologies is wrong. There are those who point to a lack of a taxonomy of applications, or a taxonomy of methodologies, or an ability to map between these (missing) taxonomies, as evidence that the field is not yet ready for methodologies focused on the problem at hand. The methodology field, like the software engineering field of which it is a part, is still young and immature.

What does this mean for knowledgeable managers of software projects? First, they must stay on top of the methodology field, because its sands are shifting frequently. Second, for now, they must expect that no single methodology will solve the whole problem. They must be prepared for some technical, problem-focused tinkering with standard methodologies.

Further, many larger software projects today involve a three-tiered solution — a user interface (front end) tier, a database/Internet (back end) tier, and the application problem solution (middle) tier. Each of those tiers will tend to need a different methodological approach:

- The *front end* will probably be attacked with an event-driven GUI builder, probably using one of the Visual programming languages.
- The *back end* will likely be addressed using an information-based database system using SQL, or an object-oriented Internet system, perhaps using Java.
- The *middle tier* will be addressed by a problem-focused methodology, perhaps the structured approaches for process-oriented problems, information engineering for data-focused problems, or an object-oriented approach for problems that involve a mixture of data objects and their associated processes.

Event-driven plus information-based or object-oriented plus some combination of the above? Doesn't that mean that systems development is becoming enormously more complex?

The answer, of course, is yes. But there is another way of looking at this plethora of problem-solving approaches. The toolbox of a carpenter contains much more than one simple, universal tool. Shouldn't we expect that the toolbox of a systems developer be diverse as well?

Chapter 40
Strategic Use of JAD
Michael C. Kettelhut

INCREASING COMPETITION in the business environment has generated new management trends. One trend suggests that successful organizations are those that create environments that foster continuous learning, which in turn fosters continuous change.[1] Sharing knowledge empowers individuals to act.

There is a process that can help the IS department reap the benefits of this empowerment trend. Joint application development (JAD) is a facilitated process for effectively using groups of employees to generate information system requirements, which offers the promise of:

- Improving the quality of delivered information systems.
- Enhancing employee participation and learning.
- Yielding other advantages associated with employee empowerment programs.

Through a series of facilitated sessions, JAD provides an efficient process for collecting information and generating novel solutions to problems. The result is generally higher-quality applications and smoother project implementation.

This chapter briefly examines the JAD process and then suggests ways that JAD can be used to more tightly link the development of information systems to corporate strategy. It discusses the benefits of JAD for the IS department and the applicability of JAD techniques to broader organizational tasks.

THE PROCESS OF FACILITATION

Developed by Chuck Morris at IBM Canada, JAD methodology applies facilitation techniques to the development of system specifications. These techniques involve the use of formal procedures to prepare for and manage group sessions.

Although JAD is generally used by IS groups to generate detailed specifications, the methodology is useful as a general approach to managing group work across a broad range of organizational decision-making or systems development tasks. For example, team building is a facilitated process that uses a neutral facilitator or counselor to help organizational members define mutually supportive goals and processes. Facilitated sessions are useful when organizations begin to initiate the open dialogue necessary to form organizational strategies, create mission statements, or build common mental models of organizational processes and problems.[2]

The JAD process is straightforward. An executive sponsor approves a project and selects a neutral facilitator with the assistance of IS management. Other participants are selected for their functional business knowledge or their detailed task-specific knowledge.

All participants are interviewed and informed of the upcoming session. Information is collected to identify potential conflicts, requirements, operating assumptions, work flows, and system processes. Details of current reports, screen interfaces, menu structures, or other elements of the current system or work process are also documented. Identification of open issues (i.e., potential conflicts) is essential for later resolution during the sessions. The facilitator and scribe prepare an agenda, ground rules, lists of issues and assumptions, and lists of the basic requirements and functions of the proposed system.

Following the interviews, functional representatives participate in a group review of application requirements and design specifications. Participants are asked to adhere to specific ground rules during the sessions. For instance, attendance is mandatory — participants must attend a three-to-five-day group session.

Because consensus is a goal, decisions are based on a shared agreement. Consensus is defined as an agreement that all participants recognize as necessary and will support, even though some may not personally agree with what has been decided. Building consensus requires resolution of open issues. If an issue is not resolved, the facilitator assigns someone responsibility for its resolution.

The facilitator uses an agenda, charts, and visual aids to keep the process on track. If conflict occurs, the facilitator may invoke a ten-minute rule stipulating that disagreements not resolved in ten minutes are documented as open issues. The final documentation is similar to documentation developed in traditional systems analysis and design efforts.

Joint Requirements Planning

Facilitated sessions can be used to define strategic requirements, functional needs, user requirements, and implementation details. A project with distinct phases may involve a series of sessions with different participants in each phase. For example, the development process frequently begins with joint requirements planning (JRP). The facilitator interviews individual senior executives to identify their key requirements. Then a joint requirements review is held. The requirements review is a facilitated session, and the desired result is an approved set of clearly stated functional requirements. A signed document containing the requirements is forwarded to the executive sponsor for approval before initiation of the next phase.

Exhibit 40.1 depicts the potential series of requests and inputs used in successive sessions and the corresponding status reports provided to the executive sponsor. The executive sponsor and three groups are involved in the process: senior managers who define requirements, end users, and the development team. Numbers associated with information flows denote the possible sequence of events; each number represents one cycle, and appropriate subevents are denoted with letters. As indicated, decisions made by the executive sponsor trigger the process and are required for continuation from phase to phase.

To begin, the facilitator solicits input for definition of key requirements. If there is disagreement over the functional requirements, a JRP session may be held. Later in the development cycle, the user group may review screen designs and prototypes. At each iteration, participants determine acceptability of the current product and the facilitator reports their decision to the executive sponsor. The groups are empowered to make key decisions that they agree are essential. On the other hand, the sponsor retains veto power and can stop the development project.

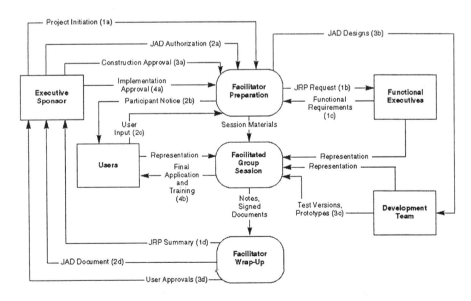

Exhibit 40.1. The facilitation cycle

This iterative group approach has three benefits:

1. The exchange of information and discussion of new points of view increases quality.
2. The sharing and documentation of knowledge increases organizational learning and reduces organizational dependence on individual employees.
3. The executive sponsor exercises control over the project as it progresses toward completion and has the opportunity at the conclusion of each phase to assess the group's work.

LINKING APPLICATIONS TO ORGANIZATIONAL STRATEGY

Use of an iterative group approach can increase the effectiveness of IS groups involved in implementing organizational strategies that depend on information technologies. An organization should begin by defining its strategic goals, competitive position, and critical success factors (CSFs). These lead to specific functional requirements that are detailed through decomposition. Decomposition provides task-level definition for organizational procedures. Implementation of business applications requires detailed, task-specific knowledge.

Suppose processing time in physical distribution is a CSF. Physical distribution functions may be decomposed into, for example, order processing, inventory, warehousing, packaging, and shipping. Organizations that focus on total quality may benefit from having the project manager, the facilitator, or the JAD team work directly with customers to determine which physical distribution tasks are most important to the customer.

As the project moves from requirements definition to detailed design, the knowledge required of participants shifts dramatically (see Exhibit 40.2). At project initiation, strategic perspectives address critical factors, the external environment, competitors, and strategic alternatives. These perspectives must be transformed into functional requirements and then into application modules, a process requiring knowledge of the functional processes under consideration and their relationship to other organizational processes. Staff with detailed knowledge of procedures is required at this stage to ensure accurate mapping of functional tasks to application modules. As processing steps for each module are defined, programming knowledge becomes more important.

Although Exhibit 40.2 depicts the level of expertise required through various phases, it does not clearly indicate the source of information used or the type of information required to implement new strategies based on changes in IT applications or architecture. Exhibit 40.3 presents a framework suggesting linkages between organizational hierarchy, key management responsibilities, and the functional requirements of organizational

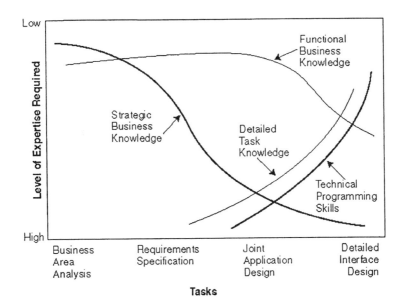

Exhibit 40.2. Knowledge/task changes in the development cycle

systems. Types of activities appropriate in facilitated sessions are also noted. As Exhibit 40.3 illustrates:

- Strategy is defined at the apex of the organization and implemented by executive management.
- For requirements definition, executive management translates responsibilities into performance standards.
- Requirements are translated into specific applications within functions and details of implementation are defined at the operational-task level of the organization.
- Task-specific user knowledge is required for specific application input, output, and processing requirements.

The participation of senior management ensures the transfer of strategic knowledge. This is particularly important when an organization's ability to compete depends on its ability to leverage information technology. The participation of middle management builds commitment and provides visible indication of support to end users. Finally, successful construction of an application requires end-user involvement to define system interfaces, tests of functionality, and prototyping of changes.

STRATEGIC BENEFITS

Studies report that use of JRP and JAD for system specifications reduces total project time by an average of 40%. Controlled experiments conducted

Organizational Level	Functional Responsibilities	Group Roles in the Development Process	Outcome	Development Phase(s)
CEO, Board of Directors, President	Strategic planning Product/market definition Profit planning	Workshops to define strategic use of technology Definition of critical business functions	Critical success factors Visible senior-management support	Project definition
Executive Management	Operational planning Organizational design Definition of functional responsibilities Product-line definition Capital management	Use senior staff to model the enterprise Joint requirements planning (JRP) workshop to define required functionality of a system	Standards for performance High-level requirements Visible management support	Feasibility study Requirements analysis
Staff/Middle Management	Budgeting Coordination Competitive analysis Market assessment Tactical planning Performance tracking	JAD sessions to accelerate design and define high-quality solutions End-user participation in validation and population of data models	Information requirements Standards for cycle times, data accuracy and currency Data definitions	Analysis Design Reviews and approvals
Production Organization	Production planning Scheduling Shipping Inventory management Credit evaluations Order processing Warehousing	End-user reviews of prototypes and specific implementation of interfaces JRP/JAD prototyping of maintenance changes Code reviews Structured walkthroughs	Screen definitions Interface design Menu structures Report designs	Detail Design Coding Prototype reviews Testing Reviews/approvals Implementation

Exhibit 40.3. Linking applications to organizational strategy

by CNA Insurance Co. found that JAD methods increased productivity in the analysis and design phases of a project by 50%. The real difference between JAD and traditional approaches may lie in the compression of the one-on-one interviewing process into a three-to-five-day meeting in which a group defines and approves the system specifications.[3]

Although saving time is important, JAD also provides a formal structure supporting group interaction in a participative environment. The group approach provides direct benefits:

- It reduces the probability of developing the wrong application.
- It reduces errors in specification that are one to two orders of magnitude more expensive to correct after implementation than during the analysis and design phase.
- It increases user acceptance and improves implementation.
- It broadens the base of participation and therefore furthers learning while reducing organizational dependencies on any single individual.

Learning is facilitated by a participatory, democratic environment, and workplace learning is maximized when people bring what they are learning into conscious awareness. Conscious awareness occurs during the questioning, reflection, and feedback that occur in the facilitated session. It permits deeper understanding to emerge from otherwise everyday activities.[4]

Good facilitators skillfully manage the interactive processes used in group sessions to help participants develop communication skills that focus on common meaning and encourage reflection about both the process and content of the discussion.[5]

Facilitated development should be viewed as a natural step in the evolution of applications development methodology. Just as quality circles have proven effective in improving the quality and efficiency of manufacturing processes, JAD contributes to the IS development process.

CSFS OF STRATEGIC IMPLEMENTATION

Some organizations adopt participative practices only superficially. These organizations may publicly state their philosophy, but closer examination suggests that groups are not really empowered and that participation actually means more meetings but not more autonomy for participants.

On the other hand, several organizations have built their reputation and success around participative management approaches and the use of teams. These organizations are frequently industry leaders.[6]

The strategies for moving to empowered organizations with self-managed teams are not complex. One common thread underlying the implementation of quality circles, JAD, empowerment programs, and other participative management initiatives is the creation of an appropriate communications environment.

Organizations that capitalize on their human resources follow specific communication practices. One of these is full disclosure of operating information, such as specifics on the organization's cost structure and earnings.

Many organizations create unique cultures or value systems that support participation and empowerment.[7] R.M. Schwarz suggests that organizations' value systems must ensure:

- The availability of valid information.
- Delegation of decision-making authority that lets employees make free and informed choices.
- A decision-making process that fosters internal commitment and choice.

The importance of these values to JAD is described in the following sections.

Valid Information

During JAD sessions, the facilitator reviews all the information collected from participants in the interviews that preceded the sessions. This public review lets participants challenge and validate the information. To maintain a focus on problem solving, the facilitator emphasizes the group's opportunity to start with a clean sheet of paper and discard the processes they have used in the past without respect to who designed them or how they were implemented.

Schwarz's values are reflected in these practices: information is shared with the help of the facilitator to ensure understanding. Furthermore, the independent presentation by the facilitator allows the group to validate information without regard to its source. Finally, the clean-sheet approach formally suggests the group's ability to change practices that result from previous decisions.

Free and Informed Choice

In well-orchestrated JAD projects, the support of senior management ensures that individuals who are selected as participants have relevant knowledge and interest. The participants are empowered to make decisions, and the facilitator helps prevent coercion or manipulation of any participant.

Internal Commitment to the Choice

Virtually all research examining commitment and participation suggests that involvement in the decision-making processes increases employee commitment. Furthermore, user participation in the development of information systems is one of three recurring themes in studies of successful development projects. The other two are clearly defined objectives and strong management support.

Organizations that adopt value systems such as those proposed by Schwarz empower their employees. One well-known organization that empowers its employees is Nordstroms, the Dallas-based high-service department store that outperforms most competitors. Nordstroms' value system is based on only one simple rule: "Use your good judgment in all situations. There will be no additional rules."[8]

The values prescribed by Schwarz suggest that organizations must avoid three dysfunctional behaviors:

- Misuse of participation. Such situations occur when participants recognize that there is a legitimate need to work as a team to solve a problem, but individuals are neither interested nor qualified.
- False participation. This behavior occurs when a leader invites a group to a meeting but proceeds to sell his or her own ideas or agenda without allowing real participation.
- Scapegoating. The organization finds fault with individuals or groups.

The first two behaviors lead subordinates to recognize the organization's initiatives as phony and to react negatively to them. The third contradicts the need for an organization using participative approaches, and specifically delegation, to be willing to allow individuals or groups to make an occasional mistake. When problems are identified, organizations must react proactively by focusing on finding solutions and learning how to prevent recurrence.

Proactive organizations that avoid these behaviors are better positioned to adapt facilitated approaches to systems development because participants recognize that they can make a difference during the process.

JAD AND CHANGE MANAGEMENT

Today's competitive business environment presents several challenges to IS departments. Foremost is the pressure to reduce costs: many corporations are still downsizing, rightsizing, or outsourcing. Many organizations that have outsourced the operations portion of their IS department must still complete the analysis and design tasks, if not the actual programming of new applications. This environment highlights the importance of

JRP and JAD for efficiently defining requirements and design specifications and producing what are often more effective, higher quality solutions.

Other business trends — service orientation, changing technology, TQM, teams, participatory management — are driving organizations to adopt a culture supportive of learning and change. These trends have also heightened interest in organizational reengineering.

Reengineering is a complex process. Reengineering projects that depend on leveraging information technology increase the pressure on the IS department. A great many reengineering projects have failed because of mismanagement of the change process. Participative approaches like JAD provide a formal framework for managing change by making affected groups part of the process and by building consensus.

The growing use of JAD reflects its potential in the area of change management. JAD sessions may make use of computer-aided software engineering (CASE) tools to capture information or group decision support systems to automate the brainstorming sessions. IS organizations that market facilitation services can extend the benefits of facilitation to other organizational tasks such as strategic planning, creating an organizational vision, or reengineering projects.

Organizations whose IS departments use and market JAD techniques can gain a competitive edge for the following reasons:

- They will develop systems faster, with fewer problems in specification, greater user acceptance, and smoother implementation.
- They will improve the quality of delivered applications and provide developmental opportunities for IS personnel.
- They will provide opportunities for IS developers to gain sorely needed business expertise.
- They will be better positioned to take advantage of new end-user technologies such as client/server computing, distributed data bases, and graphical user interfaces.[9]

These benefits accrue to the organization as a whole. In the IS department, the process leads to more stable application designs, less maintenance, and lower staff turnover. As turnover declines and maintenance requirements are reduced, organizations improve their capability to respond to environmental changes within their current resource constraints.

CONCLUSION

Two steps are required to realize JAD's potential. First, the organization must understand that implementation of JAD is a step toward employee team building and empowerment. The organization must be committed to changing its culture as needed to reflect values that support participation and empowerment.

The process of empowerment requires that management allow workers to take responsibility for their day-to-day tasks, including planning, scheduling, human resource decisions, quality control or quality assurance, and customer satisfaction. In essence, the process is one of building trust. The team at Corning asserts that there are eight key success factors for group empowerment:

- Start with a vision and clear goals.
- Ensure management commitment, visible support, and a willingness to take risks.
- Pay particular attention to middle managers and supervisors.
- Involve staff in all phases of the project.
- Communicate, communicate, and communicate some more.
- Keep your eye on the ball.
- Educate all those involved.
- Develop a reward system that promotes success.[10]

These factors also form the basis for the successful use of JAD techniques in the IS organization. However, JAD is usually viewed as a technique used by a development group for a specific project rather than as a process of group development/empowerment that can be institutionalized. Many organizations that use JAD establish new teams for each new project, and team membership usually changes. The creation of functional JAD teams responsible for the ongoing development, implementation, and maintenance of applications in a given organizational function is the first step toward the creation of empowered development groups.

Implementing JAD, a methodology with known benefits, supports the process of group empowerment and increases organizational learning. The structure used in JAD resembles the processes organizations have used for structured reviews of code.

IS managers will find useful information in several of the works discussed in this chapter, including information on where to receive training. Investing in formal training that prepares managers and analysts to act as facilitators in group sessions involves minimal risk and offers high returns that encompass more than the initial capital investment.

Notes

1. K. Watkins and V. Marsick, *Sculpting the Learning Organization: Lessons in the Art and Science of Systematic Change* (San Francisco: Jossey-Bass, 1993).
2. P. Senge, *The Fifth Discipline: The Art and Practice of the Learning Organization* (New York: Doubleday, 1990).
3. J. Wood and D. Silver, *Joint Application Design*, 2nd ed. (New York: John Wiley, 1995).
4. Watkins and Marsick, *Sculpting the Learning Organization*.

5. Senge, *The Fifth Discipline*.
6. J. Pfeffer, *Competitive Advantage Through People* (Boston: Harvard Business School Press, 1994).
7. R.M. Schwarz, *The Skilled Facilitator — Practical Wisdom for Developing Effective Groups* (San Francisco: Jossey-Bass, 1994.)
8. Pfeffer, *Competitive Advantage Through People*.
9. M. Kettlehut, "Group-Centered Systems Development: Improving the Development Process of High-Quality Systems," *Strategic Systems* 4 (June-August 1992), pp. 3-9.
10. H. Shrednick, R. Shutt, and M. Weiss, "Empowerment: Key to IS World-Class Quality" *MIS Quarterly* (December 1992), pp. 491-505.

Chapter 41
User-Centered Design

James J. Kubie
L. A. Melkus
R. C. Johnson, Jr.
G. A. Flanagan

USABILITY ENGINEERING, or user-centered design, is a framework of principles, methodologies, and techniques that maximize the likelihood that users will find an application solution useful and effective. Frequently, though, usability engineering is labeled as something that would be nice to do but is too expensive. Misleading impressions and the false sense of security created while pursuing other IT initiatives may also undermine efforts to implement highly usable systems. For example:

- *Reengineering.* Those believing that new streamlined processes somehow translate into usable, effective system solutions when computerized are frequently disappointed.
- *Object-oriented technology.* Techniques for object creation appear to provide adequate task and end-user focus by creating business objects that are linked to perform tasks. The risk is that usability engineering principles and adequate testing may not be undertaken to ensure that the user can easily and productively use these objects to accomplish key tasks.
- *Rapid application development (RAD).* The ease of producing alternative interfaces can blur project focus. A practical question is, when should developers stop prototyping? The answer is, when the requirements and performance criteria specified by the users have been met.
- *Graphical user interfaces (GUIs).* It is a myth that adhering to general GUI standards will produce an acceptable interface, much less the most productive solution.

Why is it important to create effective solutions? It is a simple matter of economics. A client might have incurred a $7 million increase in yearly operations costs just to match the service levels of an old command-line system. Why? Because task performance by average users on critical tasks was not established as a system objective. Instead, the company spent time and money working with exceptional end users during iterative prototyping. Although users had ample time to acclimate to the interface and build-up their performance times, the developers failed to focus adequately on specific, critical tasks. They overlooked the average user and did not recognize the importance of continual testing to confirm the achievement of performance objectives.

FITTING USABILITY TECHNIQUES INTO THE DEVELOPMENT CYCLE

Most design efforts focus primarily on technical, interface, and design validation issues. Effective end-user involvement is, however, one of the most critical factors in creating successful application solutions. The cognitive dimension of interface design deserves greater focus than the presentation, look, and feel of an application. In fact, it is estimated that 50% to 75% of the interface design effort should deal with the murky, difficult issues such as:

- Better task structuring to make the interface intuitive to most users.
- Improving data availability to minimize cognitive load.
- Enhancing screen topologies and screen flow to minimize errors.

This is also the time in the development cycle that the question of usability evaluation should be addressed. Determining what, how, and when evaluations should be conducted, as well as the number and type of subjects, can help maintain a user-centered focus.

Concentrating on the cognitive area of the design challenge produces solutions that are easier to learn and less error prone, which reduces user training and support costs. It also ensures that new processes are performed as designed and can potentially reduce project cost and cycle time.

A user-centered focus can be significantly enhanced by employing usability engineering techniques during all phases of the development cycle (see Exhibit 41.1). The next section discusses the requirements process and some useful techniques for identifying, validating, and ranking requirements quickly and cost-effectively. This work is critical to the definition of the user's conceptual model, which is needed to establish key tasks, quantitative objectives, and acceptance criteria.

THE USER-CENTERED REQUIREMENTS PROCESS

Understanding the users' perspective is integral to producing a system that users will accept. The user-centered requirements process provides a way to describe an application that is likely to be accepted and usable in tangible terms and that preserves the user's viewpoint during ongoing de-

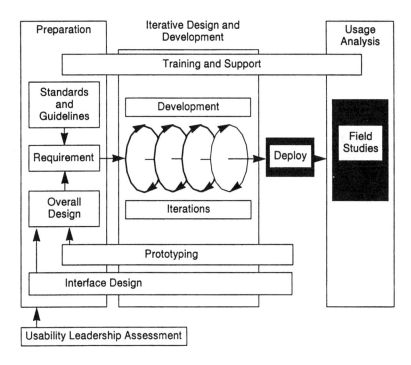

Exhibit 41.1. Incorporating usability engineering techniques during the requirements and design phases

sign and development. This tangible description allows the entire development team to share the user's model, which is a critical success factor.

Understanding How Users Work

The key to designing a successful user interface is understanding the user's conceptual model of the work domain being supported. The user's model has as much, if not more, to do with how users integrate work in practice than it does with the look and feel of a particular interface.

Project team members must share this model, so it must be expressed in some tangible form. By working with hundreds of end users on many projects, efficient methods for gathering and sharing end-user information with development teams have been refined over the past five years.

Model requirements come from multiple sources, primarily the business and technical points of view. IT is often faced with making tradeoffs among these requirements or filling in missing pieces in the translation between the intention and the end product.

The users' model is an additional framework used to evaluate the requirements. Given a team's commitment to maximize the application's success, the users' model provides a "lens" that focuses IT work on the key requirements for user acceptance and user performance. This lens acts as a guideline for making the tradeoffs in the design. As the design takes shape, the lens also provides a way to determine if an application's design has met the criteria that end users will use to judge the final product.

User-centered requirements keep the scope of the application in perspective. An IT team that is focused on developing one application can easily lose sight of the fact that users have many tools to perform work, and often the application is not the primary determinant of how easy a particular task is to perform. The amount of time required to perform a set of work tasks may be affected more by nonapplication factors (e.g., management policies or complexity of customer materials) than by an application's ease-of-use. User-centered requirements highlight the fact that any application is part of a larger whole from the users' perspective.

Describing the Work Task and Context

There are two primary types of information required to develop a user model. The first type is information about the work that users perform. The second type of information is the context in which users form opinions about an application. The context can be a set of expectations users have about a new application or a set of attributes users describe as being important. User-centered requirements are a combination of both types of information.

Task Information. Task information includes both procedural and evaluative components. Procedural information consists of descriptions of the process, the work objects, and the expected outcome of a task. It provides a basis for developing the set of objects with which users work. Evaluative information consists of judgments about the tasks, such as the importance, the difficulty, and the frequency of the task. It provides a way to rank the tasks according to their importance and to identify most probable paths and exception conditions.

Context. User-centered requirements address users' expectations. Users describe attributes of an application they would find satisfying. Through structured techniques, it is possible to refine this description to a set of measurement dimensions that are used to determine how well an application meets users' expectations. By using measurement dimensions, it is possible to measure existing applications and processes to determine a baseline on which the new application should improve.

Taken together, expectations, measurement dimensions, and baseline measures define measurable usability objectives for the new application.

Measurable objectives provide the IT team with a way to share the users' perspectives, make decisions about which requirements are likely to be perceived positively by the end users, and agree on when and how to address usability problems discovered later in the development cycle.

Identifying Representative End Users

The key difference between user-centered requirements and the more familiar business and technical requirements is that user-centered requirements come directly from representative end users who possess the same attributes as the general user population. They are not necessarily the most experienced in the population or the most technically capable.

Although the application must support very experienced and technical users, it is average users' skills that need to be apparent in the design. It must meet their needs and provide the support they require to perform work. It does not matter that an expert can perform a task 20% faster with a new application if the average user requires 10% more time to do it. To be valid, user-centered requirements must take into account the user population's demographics.

User-centered requirements are only as valid as the sample used to develop them. For example, job titles and years of experience often do not provide the required information to define a sample adequately. Geographic differences in experience with a new operating environment, in the types of customers the user supports, and in how the user is motivated to perform work can all affect the facets of the application the user attends to. It is important to create representative samples and to collect and treat the data appropriately to develop valid user-centered requirements.

Techniques for Developing User-Centered Requirements

Although most useful at the beginning of a project, taking the time to gather, validate, and rank user-centered requirements is beneficial for projects at any stage. Early in the development process, user-centered requirements provide a road map and decision-making framework on which to base the initial design. Even if a project is well into the design stage, applying user-centered requirements techniques to gather user feedback provides designers with a preview of how an application will be accepted. Having established the important tasks and expectations, users can evaluate prototype designs within a work context.

Several techniques can be used to develop user-centered requirements, including

- *Direct observation.* Direct observation is spending time with users who are performing the work tasks the application will affect.

- *Task-based requirements sessions.* These sessions can be conducted formally or informally and are similar to focus groups. Groups of users describe the work they do, assign priorities to their tasks, and develop the measurements that can be used to assess how well an application meets their expectations.
- *Gathering baseline measures of existing applications and processes.* Baseline measures are gathered by usability laboratory testing techniques.

Use of Electronic Meeting Rooms. Gathering user-centered requirements does not necessarily mean that a project will take more time. Tools such as Group Systems V allow significant reductions in the amount of time required to collect and analyze end-user feedback. Group Systems V is an electronic meeting room system that allows trained facilitators to gather user input in the users' own words and to structure meetings with greater consistency across sessions. With the electronic meeting room, users can provide ideas, organize them, and rank them in a single session.

The structure of a task-based requirements session depends on the project. Typically, cognitive psychologists play a role in developing a set of meeting agendas that let users express their needs in a way that is useful to the IT group. Cognitive psychologists are trained in methods of capturing users' perceptions, in creating an atmosphere that is conducive to honest user feedback, and in analyzing feedback in a way that preserves the users' point of view.

User-centered requirements must preserve the users' point of view, as opposed to framing users' ideas solely within the context of the IT group's view of the application. User-centered requirements provide a bridge between the end-user view of an application and the IT group. The bridge is in the form of the tasks, their priorities, and the measurable expectations users have of an application.

DESIGN AND DEVELOPMENT PROCESS

Another primary focus area of human factors professionals is testing or usability evaluation. These evaluations must be performed throughout the development cycle and not just before rollout, when the only remedies are adjustments to training and support or even delaying the rollout.

Usability Evaluation: Techniques for Software Developers

Software development organizations often display a somewhat ambivalent attitude toward usability: They acknowledge that usability is critical to the success of modern software applications, but they conduct few meaningful activities directed specifically at evaluating usability. Software developers may be unaware of usability evaluation techniques, or they may simply hold a mistaken belief that usability evaluation requires laboratory facilities or that usability cannot be measured.

In fact, usability evaluation is within the reach of most software development organizations. Techniques can vary, depending on organizational goals and resources, product capabilities, and the skills available. Applying these techniques can result in high-quality applications, which are more likely to generate client satisfaction.

Usability evaluation approaches fall into three major categories:

- *Heuristic reviews.* An application's usability can be analyzed by a usability or human factors expert.
- *Walkthroughs.* Potential users or project team members review all or part of an application and make judgments after seeing a demonstration of the system.
- *Laboratory tests.* An application is evaluated by potential users who make judgments based on hands-on experience with the application for a defined set of scenarios or functional area.

The choice of the most appropriate technique depends on such factors as:

- Project objectives.
- Desired level of precision.
- Development phase.
- Fidelity of application prototype to the end product.
- Time and schedule constraints.
- Cost.
- Available skills.
- Available facilities.

Heuristic Reviews

Heuristic reviews are the analysis of an application's usability. Heuristic reviews can be used at any stage of the development process — from initial design (when only paper descriptions of the application are available) to the prototype stage to the final product. They can range from informal to highly structured.

The informal review is judgment-based. An expert looks at an application and provides quick feedback about its overall usability. Factors such as consistency, navigation techniques, and screen design are considered. Execution of function focuses on the most common tasks.

At the other end of the spectrum, in a highly structured expert review, the reviewer bases the evaluation on a set of heuristics derived from user-interface design guidelines. These heuristics can be tailored to the particular requirements of an application. Sample heuristics include the following:

- Simple and natural dialogs.
- Use of user's language.
- Minimal memory load.
- Consistency.
- Feedback mechanisms.
- Clearly identified exit paths.
- Expert path.
- Effective error message.
- Prevention of catastrophic errors.
- Ability of the application to be specially tailored.

A highly structured and complete heuristic review presents an opportunity to analyze all functions, whereas walkthroughs or usability tests typically focus on major tasks or functions. The heuristic review may uncover problems spread out over the entire application instead of those focused on primary tasks, which might not be covered in usability laboratory testing. Heuristic reviews can also be an effective technique for comparing several similar applications.

Another important use of the heuristic review is identifying major usability problems before taking the application to users for their evaluation, thereby allowing them to focus on problems related to their expertise. For example, an expert review of an application might reveal a problem such as inconsistent exit techniques. Ideally, this problem would be corrected before involving users in extensive usability laboratory testing. Otherwise, users may become distracted by the difficulty of completing a function and might not provide feedback on how well the function corresponded to their business process.

Walkthroughs

Usability walkthroughs provide an opportunity for a set of participants to step through a series of screens for a task or a number of tasks. The set of participants can be one or more users of the application, programmers, or other members of the development team. The screens can be represented on paper, in a prototype application, or the application itself.

User Walkthroughs. In its simplest form, a user walkthrough occurs when a programmer sits down with a single user and step by step goes through a task or set of tasks. More often, the technique is used as an efficient means of gathering input from a group of users.

The evaluator is able to ask direct questions of users about what action they would take in response to the information on the screen, why they would take that action, and what they expect to happen onscreen next. The evaluator also asks if the users notice any problems, or if they have any questions about the information onscreen, being specific to gather comments from users about terminology, layout, navigation, and icons. Users should also be asked about the changes they would recommend.

The user walkthrough technique can yield qualitative data on the overall conceptual metaphor, screen layout, task flow, navigation issues, terminology, icons, and error-prone tasks. It does not provide precise quantitative data on task completion rates or error recovery rates. Because users are walked through a correct path, this technique does not let the evaluator see the kinds of errors that users might stumble into with a hands-on evaluation.

It is important that evaluators using the walkthrough methodology understand the rationale behind any user-suggested changes. Users are not designers, so initial analysis may reveal problems with the user-supplied solution. Further analysis of the underlying problem may supply a workable solution.

It is usually best to represent the system to walkthrough participants as faithfully as possible. It is best to use a prototype rather than paper renderings, or the product rather than the prototype. However, circumstances can dictate exceptions to this guideline. For example, in one study that involved both experienced and novice users of a complex product, novice users preferred using paper representations of screens during the initial walkthrough. When the walkthrough was done online, the experienced users requested many "side trips," which were confusing for novices. Using the paper screens allowed novices to focus on the functions under discussion. Another approach might have been to walk through the tasks online and have the facilitator defer any side-trip discussions until the end of the program.

Although assembling a group of users for a walkthrough offers the evaluation team a vast amount of data, much of that data is often lost because it is difficult to capture during an interactive session. The use of an electronic decision support center can assist the walkthrough session. Evaluators can capture verbatim comments from participants and structure activities for categorization and prioritization. The approach has been judged to be both efficient and cost-effective.

Walkthroughs by Project Team Members. The cognitive walkthrough and formal usability inspection are two specific implementations of the walkthrough methodology that assume participation by professionals including programmers and human factors specialists.

Based on a formal theory of exploratory learning, the cognitive walkthrough includes three components:

- *Problem solving.* Users select among alternatives according to the perceived similarity between their expectation of the consequences of an action and their current goal.
- *Learning.* After an action is executed, the user evaluates the system response and makes a decision about whether or not progress has been made. If so, the user stores the step in memory as a rule. If not, the user attempts to undo the action.
- *Execution.* If a rule is available for the given context, the user executes it; otherwise, the user engages in problem solving.

A sample worksheet to be completed by a participant in a cognitive walkthrough might include the following:

- Description of the user's task goals.
- Description of the series of actions a user might take, along with judgments about whether the actions are obviously available and appropriate.
- Description of how the user will learn what the action is. (For example, are all other available actions less appropriate? Why or why not?)
- Description of how the user will use the action and how the system will respond.
- Judgments about whether the user will understand the results of the action.

The formal usability inspection is a methodology to assist nonexperts in detecting usability problems. It assumes that there are four stages in the user's approach to a task and assigns analytic tasks to inspectors for each stage, as follows:

- *Perceiving.* Judgment about whether or not the user sees the need for information and can judge goal achievement.
- *Planning.* Description of previous knowledge on which the user would base actions.
- *Selecting.* Description of potential problems during selection process.
- *Acting.* Description of problems the user might incur while performing actions.

Both cognitive walkthroughs and formal usability inspections provide the kind of disciplined approach that can help a team assume the user's viewpoint for an objective evaluation of product usability. These techniques can be used alone or as a preamble to other usability activities in which the users themselves perform the evaluation. Like user walkthroughs, these techniques can be performed as standard group activities or conducted with the support of a trained facilitator and group decision-making software. In either case, success depends on the conscientious preparation of all participants.

Laboratory Usability Testing

Usability laboratory testing is an evaluation method that allows the test conductor or team to observe typical users performing defined scenarios in a simulated work environment. The test format allows for controlled scenarios, repetition of tasks across users/evaluators or applications, and precise measurement of factors such as time spent on the task, task completion rates, and error recovery times.

Usability laboratory testing is usually conducted in a two-room test suite. One of the rooms simulates the office or other work environment of the typical user; the other is a control and observation room for the test conductor or test team. The two rooms are divided by two-way glass, which appears as a mirror to the user/evaluator but allows the test team to look into the work room.

In the work room, one to three video cameras focus on the user/evaluator who is performing tasks that represent major activities for users of the system. In the observation room, a team member uses an electronic logging program that provides a time-stamped record of user/evaluator actions. The log, synchronized with the videotape, is an index to events on the tape and is an important tool in data analysis. If other observers participate in the control room, they may narrate the tape or control video mixing and switching equipment.

Laboratory usability can be a compelling educational tool for members of the development team because it allows unobtrusive observation of real users at work on typical tasks. By observing the users, programmers may modify their own expectations about what actions are simple or apparent to end users.

The laboratory testing method also achieves measurable usability objectives (e.g., an objective to be met might be that an employee can schedule a meeting using the electronic calendar in less than five minutes on the first attempt). If scenarios remain consistent, comparative measures can be made on successive releases of a product or across products when comparisons are necessary.

Strengths and Tradeoffs of the Techniques. Although usability laboratory testing is likely to uncover more usability problems and is better able to measure achievement of usability objectives, the other techniques offer different strengths — including the capability of a relatively quick evaluation or the ability to gather input from a group of users in a single session. The walkthrough/inspection methods may be superior for making numerous, low-level design tradeoffs.

Usability laboratory testing and expert review require the participation of trained human factors personnel. Walkthroughs can be pursued with limited or, in some cases, no human factors participation, although at least coaching-level participation from human factors personnel may be recommended.

The measurable results of usability laboratory tests and the videotapes of users at work are extremely useful tools for convincing software organizations that the usability problem data is valid. However, other methods can also be effective when the development team is appropriately involved.

Any of these methods will aid a project in producing a usable application. Exercising a combination of the methods at various times in the development cycle and choosing techniques, refinements, and tools that are best suited to the project and user organization, can greatly enhance the development organization's ability to implement a high-quality application for a satisfied user community.

ASSESSING DEVELOPER'S READINESS TO PERFORM USABILITY ENGINEERING

Whether a development organization is interested in causing a cultural shift in its focus on end users or simply wants to know how it compares to other organizations, an assessment may be helpful.

Early in the life cycle of any software development project, decisions are made about the methods, tools, and techniques to be employed. These decisions are crucial to the project and they are made with great care. For example, no organization would leave the choice of a development language to chance. At the very least, programmer skills and experience, along with an understanding of application, should influence this decision. Choosing an underlying technology, library system, change control system, tracking/reporting mechanism, life cycle methodology, or project standards and guidelines are all areas where explicit decisions based on knowledge of the organization's needs, skills, and capabilities have a profound effect on success.

To make equally informed decisions about the application of usability engineering methods — including the level of specific usability skills, the efficiency with which these skills are applied, and the effectiveness of usability-related development processes — the following Usability Leadership Assessment is recommended. This technique has been applied successfully at more than 50 organizations worldwide.

Usability Leadership Assessment Overview

The assessment (Exhibit 41.2) is conducted by a team of skilled assessors who have a thorough knowledge of both software development and

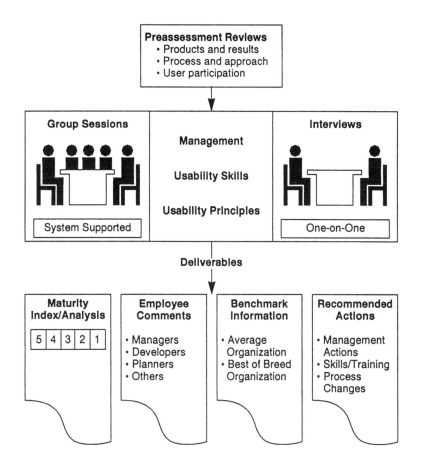

Exhibit 41.2. Usability leadership assessment

usability engineering. The assessment can be done for an entire organization, a cross-organization group, or a specific project group.

The assessors evaluate effectiveness in nine categories that are indicative of an organization's attention to usability issues. Three categories are collectively referred to as management issues:

- Usability awareness.
- Usability activities.
- Usability improvement actions.

Two categories collectively are referred to as usability skills:

- Character, vitality, and impact.
- Resource application.

Four categories are referred to as usability principles:

- Early and continual user focus.
- Integrated design.
- Early and continual user testing.
- Iterative design.

On the basis of their evaluation, the assessors develop an individual and an overall rating for each of the nine categories and a set of recommendations tailored to the assessed organization. The ratings are summarized on a grid (Exhibit 41.3) and the recommendations, which are linked to these ratings, are prepared to assist in action plan development. Typically, a follow-up assessment is scheduled for six to nine months to reassess usability attention and evaluate progress and the effectiveness of action plans, as well as provide additional recommendations.

		Usability Management Maturity					Action Plan Potential
		5	4	3	2	1	
Management Understanding and Awareness	Awareness						
	Activities						
	Improvement Actions						
Usability Skills and Resources	Character, Vitality, and Impact						
	Resources						
Usability Principles Applied in Development	Early and Continual User Focus						
	Integrated Design						
	Early and Continual User Tests						
	Iterative Design						

Overall Assessment						H - high M - moderate L - low
Participant Ratings						

Exhibit 41.3. Usability management maturity grid (UMMG)

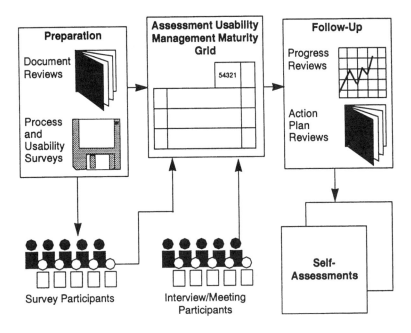

Exhibit 41.4. Assessment process in four phases

The Assessment Process

The assessment is conducted in four phases (Exhibit 41.4):

- *Preparation.* Before the actual assessment begins, a two-day visit by members of the assessment team occurs. During this visit, the team develops detailed plans and logistics and initiates a process analysis survey and a data-gathering survey when appropriate.
- *Assessment.* The assessment is typically conducted during an intense one-week period (Exhibit 41.5), culminating in a meeting with the sponsoring executive. During this week, the team completes all major assessment activities, summarizes the data, and prepares and presents a final report.
- *Follow-Up.* This activity is similar to the assessment week because similar techniques are used to gather, summarize, and report findings and recommendations. However, this phase focuses on action-plan effectiveness and potential and the progress made since the assessment.
- *Self-Assessments.* Some organizations choose to institute an ongoing, self-assessment program to ensure continued attention to usability and ongoing evolution of the action plans.

477

	Monday	Tuesday	Wednesday	Thursday	Friday
AM		Organization A and B • One-on-one interviews • Usability presentation • Survey kickoff meeting	Organizations A, B, and C • Survey results collected and summarized • DSC worksession Organization C • Management interviews • DSC worksession	Assessment Team • Data analysis and evaluation • Report preparation	• Executive Presentation
PM	Organization A • Survey kickoff with remote locations Organizations A, B, and C • Group interview with managers	Organizations A and B • One-on-one interviews • DSC worksession Organization C • One-on-one interviews • Survey results analysis	Organization A • Management interviews • Interview data analysis • Final survey collection and summarization	Assessment Team • Data analysis and evaluation • Report presentation	
EVE	Assessment Team • Review meeting • Identify focus team	Assessment Team • Review meeting	Assessment Team • Review meeting -Interview highlights -Survey summary -Initial findings	Assessment Team • Report preparation	

Contacts by Organization	Total
Design/Architecture	4
Development	25
Quality Assurance	7
End User Representatives	5
Delivery and Support	4
Total	45

Contacts by Type	Manager	Non-manager	Total
Interview	7	10	17
Survey	1	23	24
Other	3	1	4
Total	11	34	45

Exhibit 41.5. Intense One-Week Assessment Plan

The Assessment Activities

Depending on the organization being assessed, the process will include some or all of the following activities:

- *Documentation analysis.* This review of past or current project experiences and existing process documentation often occurs before the assessment week and is based on materials supplied by the organization being assessed.
- *One-on-one interviews.* Individuals meet with an assessor for about one hour to discuss experiences and perspectives on how usability engineering practices are applied. Participants represent all relevant disciplines and are a cross-organizational mix that includes both managers and non-managers.
- *Group interviews.* Small, functionally aligned teams meet with one or more assessors to discuss process and practice. During this interview, participants are free to discuss or debate the effectiveness of the existing approach.
- *Process-analysis surveys.* The process-analysis survey is used with organizations having a defined development process. It is completed by three to five team leaders who have considerable knowledge of the organization's development process and procedures.
- *Data-gathering surveys.* Size or geography may dictate the need for a survey where users participate in an introductory presentation (in person or over the telephone) and then complete a survey on existing process and practice.
- *System-facilitated group meetings.* Using laptop personal computers, a LAN, and decision support system software, groups of participants provide their comments and evaluations anonymously. During this session, the assessor chooses from several different tools to facilitate group interaction or brainstorming.

The Assessment Deliverables

The assessment's value is linked to the action taken by the sponsoring executive as a result of the assessment findings. Embodiment of the findings and recommendations are in the following deliverables:

- *Assessment team evaluation.* The assessment team's findings and conclusions form the assessment report and presentation. Included with the narrative is an assessment-team ranking displayed on grid (such as the matrix shown in Exhibit 41.3) that is used for benchmark comparisons.
- *Participant evaluations.* Quite often participant evaluations provide the most compelling incentive for management to accept the need for a usability improvement program. The insights gained through the

many interviews, direct quotations, and examples of specific activities are all included in the final report.

- *Benchmark data.* The summarized evaluations of all past assessments form a substantial comparison base for organizations to use as a benchmark. This information is included in the report presentation, and the assessed organization's ratings are compared to past assessments. Key characteristics of the top organizations are also presented at this time.
- *Recommendations.* Specific actions that the organization should take to improve its overall attention to usability engineering are presented.

CONCLUSION

There are proven, timely, and cost-effective principles, methodologies, and techniques in the field of usability engineering that can substantially assist development organizations in creating usable, productive systems that meet the needs of end users. Two areas that can produce significant benefits are the requirements process and usability evaluation.

Although the use of trained personnel is most beneficial, many inexpensive techniques can be learned and practiced by every development organization under the occasional guidance of a usability professional. A user-centered cultural change in a development organization can be accelerated by a usability leadership assessment. The primary result of this focus is the creation of application solutions that will truly assist a business in achieving its goals.

Chapter 42
Database Development Methodology and Organization

Sanjiv Purba

DATABASE DEVELOPMENT methodologies are a subset of full lifecycle methodologies that can be used to build databases from the requirements phase through to implementation. Database development methodologies that are iterative, with extensive user involvement, and that are packaged with reusable templates or deliverables offer a good opportunity for success. When selecting one for your organization, find one that is simple to learn, simple to use, and electronically deployed for quick access by project teams.

Database development is one of the fundamental objectives of the data management function, and certainly one of the end products of the process. In recent years, several trends have impacted the way that databases are built, and the role they play in the overall organization. Some of these trends include data warehousing, object-oriented technology, electronic commerce, and the emergence of very large databases (VLDBs). Other changes to the landscape include the popularity of complex data types (e.g., BLOBs, video), universal databases, and object databases. Despite this, the basis of many online transaction processing applications (OLTP) that run the business is still the relational database and the flat files. This fact is not going to change dramatically over the next few years. If anything, the relational database has proven its value as an enterprise enabler, and like the IBM mainframe is here to stay for the foreseeable future.

This chapter defines a database development methodology and approach that has proven successful on a variety of projects, as diverse as budgets from $100,000 to $15,000,000; architecture from mainframe to cli-

0-8493-9820-7/00/$0.00+$.50

ent/server to 3-tier with OO; and implementation mechanism from custom development to package implementation. This approach promotes viewing methodologies as flexible frameworks that are customized for every specific instance. This allows data-oriented teams to use their personal insight and experience alongside the best practices embedded in the methodology. This chapter also defines organizational roles for a data-oriented environment.

BENEFITS

The complexity that is inherent in constructing relational database solutions can be reduced by using proven database development methodologies on projects. Methodologies are an excellent combination of best practices and project lessons. Use of methodologies therefore reduces risk on development projects. Methodologies define activities and deliverables that are constructed in projects that were successful. Following these successful lessons can reduce project development time while increasing product quality. Furthermore, the use of methodologies simplifies the process of tracking project progress because there are clear benchmarks that can be reviewed by project managers. Methodologies that offer templates/deliverables also allow a quick start to the development process.

SELECTING A DATABASE DEVELOPMENT METHODOLOGY

Development methodologies with well-defined database development phases are commonly available in the marketplace. Some are freely available with modeling or project management tools, while others can be found on the World Wide Web. Many of the larger consulting firms have developed proprietary methodologies based on their corporate project experiences and proven best practices. These can be purchased separately, or they can be bundled with consulting/mentoring services retained from the firm. The following list identifies some of the features that should be included in any database development methodology that is being considered for deployment in an organization:

- *Linkage to a full lifecycle development methodology*: A full lifecycle methodology supports more than database development. The database development methodology you choose should either be a component of a larger full lifecycle methodology, or it should link seamlessly with one. Failure to do this could result in mismatched techniques or the development of deliverables that are not used.
- *Techniques*: Many popular development methodologies support a combination of techniques to streamline development of deliverables. The traditional "waterfall" approach involves producing deliverables in a sequential fashion. Deliverable B is not started until Deliverable A is completed and signed off. This approach, however, has historically

proven to be slow on many projects of all sizes. As a result of this experience, a Rapid Application Development (RAD) approach has gained popularity during the past ten years. RAD produces deliverables much faster than the older waterfall approach. Iteration and prototyping are cornerstones of most RAD approaches, as are teams that combine technical resources and users during the analysis and design phases of the project lifecycle. RAD has proven to be success on smaller projects, but has been problematic on the larger ones due to the complexity of the business requirements. A relatively new approach combines the best elements of both the waterfall and RAD approaches, and has proven valuable on larger development projects.

- *Support*: A development methodology (or a database development methodology) is a product, whether your organization has paid for it or not. As such, it is important for the methodology to be supported by the vendor into the future. An unsupported methodology becomes obsolete in short order. Some questions to ask the vendor include "How much research is being conducted to improve the methodology?","Is there a hotline for technical support?", and "When is the next version of the methodology being released?".
- *Price*: The price of the methodology should be considered in whole, in parts, and assessed against the value that is received. Consider the one-time cost, the training costs, upgrade costs, yearly license fees, costs per user, customization costs, hardware/software support costs, and costs for future releases.
- *Vendor*: Consider the stability and market share of the vendor providing the methodology. The vendor's references should also be checked to ascertain their support for clients. Vendors who are more stable and who have more market share are more likely to improve their methodology with new techniques in the future.
- *Proven Success*: One of the surest ways of selecting a suitable methodology is to check the references of organizations similar to yours that have used it successfully on development projects.
- *Electronic Availability*: The methodology should be available electronically through Lotus Notes, the internet, or CDROM. It should also be available on paper. This makes the methodology widely available to those using it across the organization.
- *Templates/Deliverables*: Reusable templates and deliverables are a good source of best practices that provide the means for quick starting development projects. Many methodologies are demonstrated with these, but the templates/deliverables are not provided to customers. In such cases, it is valuable to try to negotiate the inclusion of templates/deliverables as part of the transaction. If the templates/deliverables are still not offered by the vendor, but the rest of the methodology is acceptable, a pilot project should be used to create reusable templates and deliverables for future projects to use. While

this may slow the pilot project down in the short term, subsequent projects will run more efficiently. It is also desirable to select a methodology architecture that allows additional templates and deliverables to be added to the database on an ongoing basis.

- *Linkages to newer architectures*: The methodology should also support linkages with modules that support data warehousing, object technology, electronic commerce, and Web architectures. Flexibility in expanding the methodology directly or through deliverable linkages is desirable.
- *Ease of Learning and Use*: Methodologies that are easy to learn and use are more likely to be used on projects. Some methodologies are packaged with training courses from the vendor or other third parties.

It is not unusual to add to this list of features or to assign more weight to a handful of them because of their importance to a specific organization. Experience has shown that complicating the selection process does not necessarily improve the quality of the final selection. In fact, this can lead to wasted time and intense team debates or arguments that end in worthless stalemates. It is preferable to quickly build a short list of candidate methodologies by disqualifying candidates that are weak on one or two key features (e.g., not available electronically or purchase price is greater than $100,000). The short list can then be compared to maybe five or six of the features that are of key importance to the organization. It is also useful to conduct a limited number of pilot projects that test the value of a methodology before making a final selection. It is also not unusual to pilot two different methodologies in a Conference Room Pilot (CRP) before making a final determination. This process can take between 6 weeks and 6 months.

HIGH LEVEL DATABASE DEVELOPMENT METHODOLOGY

This section defines a high level methodology for database development. This methodology provides a good start for small to medium-size projects; however, a formal third-party methodology should be considered for projects that require more than six months of development effort. The activities discussed in this section are mapped to the standard project development framework which consists of the following main phases: Requirements, Architecture, Design, Development, Testing, Implementation, and Post-Implementation. These phases can be conducted in parallel or sequentially depending on the exact nature of the methodology, and are restricted to database specific activities.

The subprocesses that are described in this section fit into a larger full lifecycle methodology that would address such activities as corporate sponsorship for the project, project plan definition, organization building, team building, user interface development, application design, technology selection, acceptance testing, and deployment. It is assumed that these activities are completed outside the database development methodology phases.

- *Define Business Requirements*: Business requirements are captured for any system development effort. The requirements should also used to build the logical data model. They will feed such things as the number of entities, attribute names, and types of data stored in each attribute. These are often categorized by subject area.
- *Borrow or Create the Data Model*: With a solid understanding of the business requirements, it is a good idea to search the market for a data model that can be purchased from a third party. This can subsequently be customized for the organization.
- *Build the Logical Data Model*: The logical data model is built iteratively. The first view is usually done at a high level, beginning with a subject area or conceptual data model. Subsequent levels contain more detail. The process of normalization is also applied at this stage. There are many good books on normalization, so normal forms will not be covered here. Foreign key fields and potential indexes can also be considered here. It is not necessary to build the logical data model for performance at this time, and physical considerations are left until a later process.
- *Verify the Data Model*: The logical data model is iteratively validated with users, the fields of the user interface, and process models. It is not unusual to make changes to the data model during this verification process. New requirements may also be identified, which need to be fitted into the data model.
- *Build the Data Architecture*: The data architecture is defined in the context of the physical data environment. Issues such as the database server, distribution, components, and partitioning are considered in this step.
- *Build the Physical Data Model*: The logical data model is converted to a physical data model based on the specific database that is used. The physical data model will vary with the choice of database products and tools. The physical data model also contains such objects as indexes, foreign keys, triggers, views, and user-defined data types. The physical data model is optimized for performance and is usually denormalized for this reason. Denormalization can result in redundancy, but can improve system performance. Building the physical data model is not a one-step process. Do not expect to build a final version of the physical data model on the first attempt.
- *Refine the Data Model*: The physical data model is continuously refined as more information becomes available, and the results of stress testing and benchmarking become available to the database development team. The logical data model should also be maintained as the physical data model is refined.

- *Complete the Transaction Analysis*: Transaction analysis is used to review system transactions so that the physical data model can be refined for optimum system performance. Transaction analysis results are only meaningful after the business requirements and systems design are fairly solid. Transaction analysis produces statistics showing the access frequency for the tables in the database, time estimates, and data volumes.
- *Populate the Data*: After the database structure is established and the database is created, it is necessary to populate the database. This can be done through data scripts, applications, or data conversions. This can be an extensive set of activities that require substantial data mapping, testing, and parallel activities. It is expected that the details of this are include in the full lifecycle methodology.
- *Complete Testing*: Testing a database is usually done in the context of applications and is covered in the full lifecycle methodology. Some specific types of testing, such as stress testing, bench marking, and regression testing can be used to refine the performance of the physical data model. These require high volumes of data, testing tools, and distribution tools.

DELIVERABLES

Some of the important deliverables that are created from inception to the creation of a physical database are discussed in this section. It is useful to build a reference database that contains samples of each of these deliverables so that project teams know in advance what they are attempting to build.

- *Requirements Document*: This is the statement of the business requirements for the application being developed. This deliverable can contain narrative and any number of models or prototypes to capture and represent the business requirements.
- *Conceptual Model/Subject Areas*: This is a high level view of the business subject areas that are within the scope of the data model (e.g., Accounting, Administration, Billing, Engineering).
- *Logical Data Model*: Contains entities, attributes, and business rules within the subject areas. The model also shows relationships between the entities. Key fields and foreign keys can also be identified in this model.
- *Transaction Analysis*: A list of transactions supported by the system, the entities (and possibly the fields) that are accessed by the transactions, and the frequency with which they are accessed. A CRUD (Create, Read, Update, and Delete) matrix is a useful input for helping with this analysis.
- *Physical Data Model*: A denormalized version of the logical data model that is optimized for performance under a specific technical environ-

ment and refined through the transaction analysis results. The physical data model is usually refined throughout a development cycle and is not finished until implementation. The physical data model contains physical objects such as tables, fields, indexes, foreign keys, primary keys, views, user-defined data types, and rules.

- *Object Model*: An object model supports the logical data model. This often serves as an intermediate layer between an object-based user interface and a relational back-end database.
- *Validation Models*: This is a cross-reference of models, such as process models, to the logical data model to prove its validity. This often includes a mapping between the logical data model with a user interface and reports to identify gaps.
- *Conversion Strategy*: A statement of the strategy used to convert data into a new application. The level of detail can vary significantly. This could be anything from high level principles to detailed conversion scripts.

TOOLS

Modeling tools are critical for the database development process. There are a number of tools with various add-ons that can be used in this process. Modeling tools should offer support for both data models and process models. It is also becoming more useful for modeling tools to support object models, or link to other tools that do. Tools that support reverse-re-engineering from physical databases to generate logical data model or scripts are useful for organizations that require extensive changes to data structures (possibly following a corporate merger).

There are many other tools that are useful in the database development process. Some of these include CASE tools, conversion tools, testing tools, and database server tools.

ORGANIZATION

When staffing a project that involves a data initiative, it is necessary to fill specific roles. The roles defined in this section are generally specific to the data initiative. These roles are often complemented by other roles in full implementation projects. Projects that have high object-oriented content skew the organization toward object modeling skillsets.

- *Project Sponsor*: Projects should not be initiated or conducted without a senior project sponsor who is positioned to remove obstacles and ensure that the project team has the full support they require to be successful.
- *Project Manager*: The project manager is in charge of the entire project, including the data initiative.

- *Business User*: Provides the business rules for the application, which are used to derive the entities and attributes necessary to save the data.
- *Business Analyst*: Provides a critical link between the business user and the data architect by understanding the business requirements and translating them into technical words.
- *Data Architect*: Has the responsibility for defining the data architecture. This could be distributed, central, standalone, or integrated with a sophisticated overall architecture.
- *Data Analyst*: Works with the Business Analyst to build a consistent view of each element of the data. This person understands the linkage between the business and the individual items of data.
- *Data Modeler*: Works with the Data Architect to build a logical relational data model. May also get involved in transforming the logical data model into a physical data model.
- *Object Modeler*: Becomes involved in projects to build an object model, including messages and methods. This person may also be responsible for mapping the object model to the corporate data model.
- *Database Administrator*: Implements the physical database. Maintains and optimizes the physical environment. Restricts access to the database by controlling privilege levels for users. Offers advice to the development team for converting the logical data model to the physical data model. Holds the overall responsibility for running the database environment on a day-to-day basis.
- *Network Administrator*: Maintains the physical network. Has the responsibility for maintaining the integrity of the physical environment that supports the data environment. Operates at the operating system level and the hardware level. For example, this person would add more physical disks to support larger databases.
- *Developer*: Uses the database(s) for application development.

PITFALLS

Misuse or misinterpretation of how methodologies should be executed can result in significantly negative impacts to project timelines. It is not unusual for organizations to use methodologies as process charts or recipes without streamlining any of the activities. This can result in a considerable amount of wasted time as deliverables or activities are produced without an understanding of how they are leading toward a solution. Methodologies should be adjusted for specific projects. Activities or deliverables that are not necessary should be dropped from the project plan.

Methodologies that are too complicated or difficult to learn and use are frequently avoided by project teams. There are some methodologies that may contain information for thousands of project contingencies. However, they require thousands of megabytes of storage or dozens of manuals to store. During tight project timeframes, such methodologies are quickly sidelined.

It is important to update methodologies over time. New project experiences and best practices should be included in the methodology at specific intervals.

CONCLUSION

Database development methodologies are a subset of full lifecycle methodologies. Project teams can access a third-party database development methodology or follow the high level framework described in this chapter for database development. Database development methodologies should also support parallel development, iteration, high user involvement, and be accompanied by a database of reusable templates or sample deliverables.

Bibliography

Deloitte & Touche Consulting Group, *Framework for Computing Solutions*.
Maguire, Steve, *Writing Solid Code*. Redmond, WA: Microsoft Press, 1993.
Purba, Sanjiv, *Developing Client/Server Systems Using Sybase SQL Server System 11*. New York: John Wiley and Sons, Inc. 1995.
Smith, Patrick N. *Client/Server Computing*. 2nd Ed. Indianapolis: Sams Publishing, 1994.
Willian, Perry, *Effective Methods for Software Testing*. New York: John Wiley and Sons, 1995.

Chapter 43
Project Success and Customer Needs

Richard H. Deane
Thomas B. Clark
A.P. (Dennis) Young

IN MANY IS ORGANIZATIONS, the primary measure of project success lies in meeting some combination of project specifications, a project deadline, and a project budget. The tendency for the completion of one project to coincide with the start of another leaves little time for strategic and long-term measures of project success.

Because the ability of organizations to learn and improve faster than their competitors may be the only sustainable competitive advantage in the business world of the 21st century, successful learning organizations must do more than measure the end result of a project effort. In these organizations, project success involves a strategic question of whether or not project outcomes meet customer needs. The extent to which they do not is most often the result of one or more performance gaps in project planning and execution.

To ensure success, IS and project managers should link project planning to control actions that relate customer goals to end results. In other words, IS and project managers must envision and apply a model that translates customer requirements into a specific sequence of management actions. This translation and execution process should be measured, evaluated, and continuously improved so that ineffective practices are corrected or abandoned and effective practices are amplified.

This chapter presents a model that helps IS and project managers assess and ultimately narrow the gaps between customer needs and project outcomes. By identifying and reducing these intermediate project performance gaps, IS managers will systematically improve the project management process in a continuous learning cycle (see Exhibit 43.1).

Previous screen

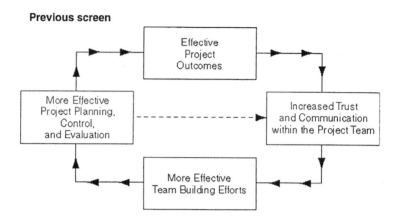

Exhibit 43.1. The learning cycle of effective IT project management

Responsibility for this improvement should not be delegated to a single individual but institutionalized throughout the organization.

THE PROJECT PERFORMANCE GAP

The project performance gap can be expressed as the difference between expected and actual project outcomes:

Project Performance Gap = Project Outcome Expected by Customer minus Actual Project Outcome.

IS and project managers who focus on strategic goals recognize that this equation must be modified to reflect the customer's perception of the delivered project outcome. Stated in terms of a performance gap, the new equation reads:

Project Performance Gap = Project Outcome Expected by Customer minus Actual Project Outcome *as Perceived by Customer.*

This second equation still does not ensure project success because it fails to take into account the true needs of the customer. A more representative equation of the project performance gap thus follows:

Project Performance Gap = *Actual* Project Outcome *Needed* by Customer minus Actual Project Outcome as Perceived by Customer.

A comprehensive model of project success driven by the third equation is presented in Exhibit 43.2.

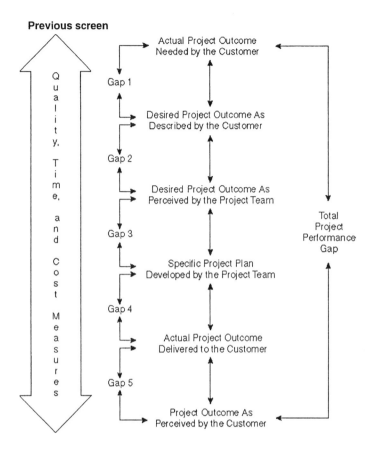

Previous screen

Q
u
a
l
i
t
y,

T
i
m
e,

a
n
d

C
o
s
t

M
e
a
s
u
r
e
s

Actual Project Outcome
Needed by the Customer

Gap 1

Desired Project Outcome As
Described by the Customer

Gap 2

Desired Project Outcome As
Perceived by the Project Team

Gap 3

Specific Project Plan
Developed by the Project Team

Gap 4

Actual Project Outcome
Delivered to the Customer

Gap 5

Project Outcome As
Perceived by the Customer

Total
Project
Performance
Gap

Exhibit 43.2. IT project performance gap model

PROJECT PERFORMANCE GAP MODEL

Exhibit 43.2 illustrates that an ineffective project result (i.e., total project performance gap) arises from five individual gaps in project performance. The following sections discuss these gaps and provide tips on how to manage them.

Gap 1: Ineffective Statement of Long-Term Customer Needs

The first performance gap occurs when the customer team is unsure, unclear, or unaware of the exact nature of the needed project outcome. Consider the example of a customer team that defines a project requirement for major revisions to a customer order-entry and tracking system. What the customer really needs, however, is a new automated order-entry system design and development effort (i.e., systems reengineering), not a revision to the existing system.

Managing Performance Gap 1. This gap involves a situation in which the project outcome fulfills stated or documented requirements but does not satisfy long-term customer needs nor provide the customer with a business advantage. In the example provided, a project that delivers a revised order-entry system, according to specifications, will not provide an effective solution to the customer's order management needs.

Gap 1 represents a frustrating problem for project teams that do not deal with the customer as a partner. A project team may suspect that the project requirements are improperly stated but be limited by organizational or contractual constraints on its information access or authority to seek clarification of the true project need. Such situations are more likely to arise in teams dealing with external customers (e.g., teams responding to an invitation to bid or a request for proposal), but they can and do arise with internal customers.

The keys to managing gap 1 are as follows:

- Ensuring that customers initiate interactions with the project team to describe how current business needs are being met (or not met). Likewise, the team should ask the customer to describe how the planned project outcome meets present or anticipated needs. The project team must therefore start the customer interaction process by discussing business needs, not specific project requirements. Customers should be asked to envision and specifically describe their operating environment in terms of what they are trying to accomplish and how they are evaluated.
- Asking key customers to describe the business needs of their own customers and how the project helps meet their needs.
- Using a project team charter to reduce any role ambiguity and conflicts among the project team, customers, and other project stakeholders. The team charter identifies team member roles and operating rules and clarifies how the team will function as it executes the project, particularly in interactions with customer and user groups. A team charter developed consensually and used consistently to guide team interactions actually serves to reduce all performance gaps.

Gap 2: Incorrect Perception of Customer Needs

Gap 2 occurs when the project team incorrectly perceives customer needs. In this instance, the customer correctly understands that a completely new design and implementation of an order management system is needed. However, the customer ineffectively describes the specific project scope, objectives, and constraints, or the project team is unable to understand these key project parameters as expressed by the customer. Often, the project team does understand the general project scope, objectives, and constraints but fails to understand which of these parameters are critical to the customer's interpretation of project quality. Gap 2 often occurs when the project team has a preconceived notion or preference for a given project definition that matches prior projects or its own capabilities.

For example, a project team meets with a customer to discuss a new automated order management system. The customer's primary need is a system that lets sales and marketing personnel verify the status of orders and provides local order-entry clerks real-time access to the order management data base. Furthermore, the project must be completed and the system fully operational by August 15, before the start of the Fall selling season.

The project team, however, interprets the customer's primary need as a system that generates daily reports with minimum computer processing time and provides the production division with two automated reports of new orders each day. The project team understands that remote access to the system and real-time access to the data base are desirable but incorrectly assumes that these are secondary objectives. Also, the team interprets the August 15 deadline as a target for system installation but fails to incorporate system testing and user training within the scope of the project that must be completed by that date.

Managing Performance Gap 2. Gap 2 problems typically involve an incomplete analysis or incomplete documentation of project requirements, resulting in an inaccurate or perhaps incomplete statement of project needs. IS managers can narrow this gap by:

- Making diligent use of the project charter. This three- to four-page document provides a word picture of the project scope, objectives, constraints, assumptions, concerns, risks, and users. Because it is written from a management not a technical perspective, the project chartering process should be used to lead the customer into commitment to the project definition. Diligent use of the charter is also a key tool in preventing scope creep once the project is under way. The project charter sections documenting project scope and objectives are especially important tools in managing gap 2.
- Using a classification of primary objectives vs. secondary objectives in the project charter. Primary objectives must be met in full for the project to be considered successful. Secondary objectives are desirable but are not direct determinants of project success.
- Ensuring that there is significant contact between the project team and the primary customers. Gap 2 problems are likely to arise when a project team is charged with implementing a project that has been negotiated and designed entirely by the customer and senior management.

- Ensuring that there is adequate communication between the project team and senior management. The project charter is an important step in this communication process.
- Periodically revisiting the project charter during project execution to ensure that the customer and project team do not lose sight of project objectives. A team may understand these objectives at project commencement but become distracted and lose sight of them over time.

Gap 3: Ineffective Translation of Customer Needs

Performance gap 3 results from ineffective translation of the customer's needs into the formal project plan. In other words, the project team understands the customer's needs and expectations but develops time, cost, and quality objectives and a project plan that do not fully reflect these needs.

Gap 3 is a common, and often wide, project performance gap simply because of the difficulty of developing a project plan that is directed toward multiple and sometimes competing objectives. The project team may also lack the skills or, equally important, the discipline to plan. Finally, gap 3 problems may arise because senior managers send signals that planning is unimportant; for example, they fail to proactively review project plans and recognize and reward project planning efforts.

The following examples illustrate this gap. The project team understands the importance of remote sales and marketing access to the data base as a desired feature in the order management system. It does not, however, establish specific software/hardware interface objectives and priorities that allow remote users reasonable access to the system during regular business hours. As a second example, project objectives for the new order management system might be clear but a functional rather than a cross-functional work breakdown structure is developed and a project network is not utilized. The resulting project plan omits important activities (i.e., documentation development and user training) or fails to recognize interdependencies among activities. The bottom line is an incomplete, unrealistic, and unworkable schedule. As a third example, the project plan may not include time for key activities necessary to ensure product quality, such as system testing, approvals, and rework as required.

Managing Performance Gap 3. The third performance gap arises when the project plan is inadequate to meet project objectives. Narrowing gap 3 starts with a careful comparison of the project plan with the project objectives for consistency. It is imperative that shortcomings in the plan be recognized before the plan is actually executed. The keys to managing gap 3 thus lie in:

- Using the work breakdown structure as a means of verifying the approach to meeting each customer need and objective. If each project objective in the charter cannot be associated with identifiable sections of the work breakdown structure, IS managers and project leaders must clarify how the objective is being met through the project. Conversely, they need to question the value added by each portion of the work breakdown structure that does not appear to be related to an identifiable project objective in the charter.

- Verifying consistency between the project charter, the work breakdown structure, the project network, the schedule, and the budget. Every project objective in the project charter should be related to identifiable activities in the project network. The project schedule and budget should be compatible with cost and duration constraints as stated in the charter.
- Verifying every task interaction among subprojects and submodules. Large, complex projects do not fail because there are too many details but rather because the project team and the customer fail to understand the interdependencies among activities and subprojects. The project network provides an excellent opportunity to foster discussions regarding the interaction of individual activities and subprojects.
- Using a team-based structured validation process for reviewing the baseline schedule and budget. The project team and customers should ask validation questions such as:
  — Is the critical path intuitive and logical in terms of its location, and is the project duration reasonable for this type of project? Are there surprise activities on the critical path? If so, why?
  — Has a resource plan been developed, and is it compatible with the schedule?
  — Is the budget reasonable based on projects of this type? Has a cash flow plan been developed and approved by management?
- Proactively discussing and evaluating decisions concerning time/cost tradeoffs. Even if the original baseline schedule is chosen, a discussion of time/cost tradeoffs raises vital issues, such as the financial and strategic value of reducing the project duration.

Gap 4: Ineffective Execution of the Project Plan

Gap 4 arises when the project work plan is adequate to achieve customer needs but the project team is unable to execute the plan. The numerous reasons why a project plan is not properly executed include:

- A flawed project control process.
- Inadequate technical expertise.
- Uncontrollable external interventions.
- Failure to prevent project scope creep.

In the case of the order management system, the project team is unable to execute what is an adequate plan because it lacks expertise in database design or the requisite hardware cannot be supplied in a timely manner by the customer or a vendor. Compounding slippage eventually causes project failure.

Managing Performance Gap 4. Implementation of an effective control process is, of course, essential to managing the problem of ineffective execution. Accurate measurement of progress is a necessary element of the control process for executing the project. The keys to narrowing gap 4 thus include:

- Ensuring that an agreed-upon set of metrics for measuring time, cost, and quality performance is consistently followed throughout the project.
- Regularly conducting project team meetings to evaluate progress, identify/diagnose problems, and develop corrective interventions.
- Remaining alert to environmental threats to the project effort and proactively responding to them. Because some external circumstances can make even the best planned projects go awry, a control system must be implemented that allows quick adjustment to the project effort after external threats to success are identified.
- Empowering project team members to report both good and bad results in control meetings. Because some managers seem to want to hear only good news in project meetings, poor intermediate performance results are swept under the rug or discussed offline.
- Developing a response to every deviation from the project plan, no matter how small.
- Updating the plan as required so that the team always has a current credible plan for the remainder of the project.
- Demonstrating commitment to the discipline of the project control process and ensuring commitment from upper management as well. Managers who routinely cancel project control meetings or ignore intermediate project status reports send the project team a signal that the control process is either unimportant or simply not worth the time and effort it requires.

Gap 5: Ineffective Communication of Results

Gap 5 represents the project team's failure to effectively communicate results to the customer. In other words, the team does a poor job of documenting or otherwise communicating that project outcomes do indeed meet customer needs. Gap 5 problems may arise from lack of communication or from miscommunication (e.g., overzealous promises). In most cases, the seeds of the gap 5 problem are planted during project planning or project execution, even though the gap is not recognized until project completion.

Continuing with the example provided, the project for the order-entry management system has successfully met the established and agreed-upon objectives and will serve the customer's real business need. However, the customer has received inadequate communication during project execution. Upper management in the customer's organization became actively involved with the project four times to resolve problems. The final project report is poorly written by the project manager based on the assumption that the new system is running and everyone seems satisfied. The result is a customer who does not understand what was actually accomplished.

Managing Performance Gap 5. IS and project managers should address the problem of ineffective communication throughout the project rather than at project end. The keys to narrowing performance gap 5 are

- Developing a specific customer communication plan. A regular channel of communication to the customer is coordinated with a plan to keep senior management informed. The communication plan identifies the format, timing, and distribution of project communications. Regular project status reports to customers must be concise and consistent.
- Establishing a horizontal communication plan among project team members. Simply stated, all project team members must be "playing from the same song book." IS and project managers can test the effectiveness of the communication plan by regularly surveying team members to determine if they feel informed regarding the project status.
- Ensuring that the final project report addresses each and every project objective as identified in the project charter, which should be used as a guide in writing the report.
- Celebrating project success.

The total IT performance gap thus implies a gap between the actual outcome needed by a customer and the customer's perception of the result. It can result from any one of the five single gaps or from a combination of them. Because the five gaps are always cumulative (i.e., they never offset each other), it is inadequate to measure only the total IT performance gap. Rather, the total gap must be analyzed and addressed through one or more of the other gaps.

Exhibit 43.3 provides a summary of how specific elements of the project management process should be used to prevent performance gaps.

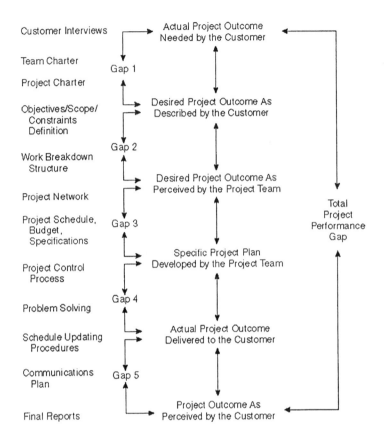

Exhibit 43.3. Project performance gap model

CONCLUSION

The framework provided in this chapter is designed to help IS managers create a learning project environment. By addressing intermediate gaps in the project planning and control process, IS managers will improve the entire project management process.

Although an overall gap in project performance is always the result of one or more of the five intermediate gaps, project team members are likely to disagree as to where gaps exist in a particular project. Addressing and resolving such a disagreement is the first step to improving the project management process, because it helps focus team thinking.

Chapter 44
Win-Win Projects
Stanley H. Stahl

IN THEIR PAPER "Theory-W Software Project Management: Principles and Examples," Barry Boehm and Rony Ross present a unifying theory of software project management in which a basic principle is to make everyone a winner. In the introduction of their paper, Boehm and Ross write:

> The software project manager's primary problem is that a software project needs to simultaneously satisfy a variety of constituencies: the users, the customers, the development team and management. Each of these constituencies has its own desires with respect to the software project. These desires create fundamental conflicts when placed together. These conflicts are at the root of most software project management difficulties — both at the strategic level (e.g., setting goals, establishing major milestones, and responsibilities) and at the tactical level (e.g., resolving day-to-day conflicts, prioritizing assignments, and adapting to changes).

Theory-W is a way to help project managers cope with the difficulty of simultaneously satisfying different constituencies. Theory-W has one simple but very far-reaching principle: Make everyone a winner by setting up win-win conditions for everyone.

THEORY W: BACKGROUND AND BASICS

How does Theory-W contrast with such earlier management theories as Theory X, Theory Y, and Theory Z? The Theory X approach to management originated in the work of Frederick Taylor at the beginning of the century. Taylor contended that the most efficient way to approach work was to organize jobs in a well-orchestrated sequence of efficient and predictable tasks. Management's responsibility was to keep the system running smoothing; this task was often accomplished by coercing and intimidating workers. For obvious reasons, Taylor's Theory X is inappropriate for managing software projects.

Theories Y and Z, dating from approximately 1960 and 1980, respectively, were intended as alternatives to Theory X. Theory Y's perspective is that management must stimulate creativity and initiative, which are important for a quality software project. The difficulty with Theory Y, however, is that it provides inadequate mechanisms for identifying and resolving con-flicts. Theory Z seeks to improve Theory Y by emphasizing the develop-ment of shared values and building consensus. The problem with Theory Z is that consensus may not always be possible or desirable; this can be the case with different constituencies that have their own unique set of individ-ual constraints and requirements.

If the Theory-X manager is an autocrat, the Theory-Y manager a coach, and the Theory-Z manager a facilitator, then the Theory-W manager is a ne-gotiator. The manager in the Theory-W model must proactively seek out win-lose and lose-lose conflicts and negotiate them into win-win situations.

Delivering software systems while making winners of all the stakehold-ers seems, at first glance, to be hopelessly naïve. Users want systems de-livered immediately; they also want them with all the bells and whistles imaginable. Management not only wants systems delivered on schedule and within budget, but also wants a short schedule and a low budget. De-velopers want technical challenges and opportunities for professional growth; they often do not want to document their work. Maintainers want well-documented systems with few bugs and the opportunity for a promo-tion out of maintenance. How can a project manager expect to successfully negotiate the conflicting needs of all constituents?

IMPORTANCE OF NEGOTIATING

Although it may seem like a naïve theory, there is an accumulation of ev-idence that Theory-W works. In fact, Theory-W can be seen as fundamental to project success. The objective in a win-win negotiation is for all parties to recognize each other's specific needs and to craft a resolution that al-lows all participants to share in getting their needs met.

In the absence of an explicit commitment to foster win-win relation-ships, software projects have the capability of becoming win-lose. For ex-ample, building a quick but bug-laden product may represent a low-cost win for an over-pressured development group, but it is a loss for the users and the organization as a whole. Alternatively, when management and us-ers force developers to add extra features without giving the development group the time and resources needed to develop the extra features, the re-sult may be a win for users and a loss for developers. Software mainte-nance personnel often lose as management, developers, and users fail to ensure that software is well-documented and easily maintainable.

At their worst, software projects can become lose-lose situations where no one wins. It is common for management to set unreasonable schedule expectations, and as a result, the development department tries to catch up by adding more and more people to the project. The result is, all too often, a poor product that comes in over cost and over schedule. In this case, everyone loses.

THE COST OF NOT NEGOTIATING: A LOSE-LOSE PROJECT

The following example illustrates how ignoring Theory-W affects a project. Although this example is fictional, it is based on actual experience.

A growing Retail Company had just hired a new chief information officer who was given the charter to modernize the company's antiquated information systems. The CIO was also told that budgets were extremely limited; the size of the IS staff would have to be decreased as new systems were implemented. The first task was to conduct a user-needs survey, which revealed that all but the company's payroll systems were viewed as inadequate. The inventory control system was barely usable, there was no integration across systems, and each system served, at best, only the limited needs of the department for which it had been designed. The survey also indicated that most users were unaware of the potential productivity gains from up-to-date information systems.

After the survey had been analyzed, the following four recommendations were made and enthusiastically approved:

- All existing systems should be replaced by client/server systems capable of supplying timely and accurate information to both operational personnel and senior management.
- The changeover should be implemented in stages. The first system should be a relatively simple, low-risk, standalone application.
- The system should be procured from an outside contractor, preferably a software house that had a package that could be used with minimal modifications.
- Training should be provided to middle managers to enable them to better guide the IS department in implementing the new systems.

Basic Planning Steps Were Ignored

A request for proposal (RFP) for a new inventory distribution management control system, which was everyone's favorite candidate to be implemented first, was requested. However, nothing was said about budgets, schedules, or personnel needs, and, in their enthusiasm, everyone seemed to forget about training.

Lack of User Input

The RFP was developed by the IS group with little input from distribution personnel, so it was rather open-ended and not very explicit. Eight responses ranging in price from $70,000 to $625,000 were received. After lengthy negotiations, a contract was awarded to a single company that would provide both hardware and software for the new inventory control system.

Unclear RFP

The contractor was a leader in inventory management systems, though its largest account was only half the size of the retailer. To land the account, the contractor promised to make any necessary modifications to the system free of charge. Based on the contractor's reading of the RFP, there was assumed to be little technical risk in the promise.

As it turned out, the contractor's interpretation of what was needed was deficient. The contract called for the system to be up and running in six months at a cost of $240,000, but a year later the contractor was still working on system changes to meet the client's needs. The users kept claiming that the system was not powerful enough to meet their needs, while the contractor argued that the system was in use by more than 200 satisfied companies. The IS department was continually at odds with both the users (distribution personnel) and the contractor over the capabilities of the new inventory system.

Costly Failure

At the end of the acrimonious year, the contractor and the retailer agreed to cancel the project. The contractor was paid more than $150,000. It estimated that its programming staff had spent more than 10-worker-months modifying the system. The retailer estimated that it had invested the time of one senior analyst as well as several hundreds of hours of distribution personnel.

HOW THEORY-W WOULD HAVE HELPED

Losers and the Consequences

The most apparent source of difficulty on the project was the explicit win-lose contract established between the retailer and the contractor. Establishing a contract in which the contractor had to cover any expenses incurred in modifying the system reduced the likelihood that the users would get the modifications they needed.

The IS department's relationship with senior management was also win-lose. Senior management wanted to decrease the size of the IS staff. The system had to be brought in on time and within budget, but the user community was ill-prepared to identify its system needs. The result was that neither the retailer nor the contractor had an adequate handle on the inventory system's requirements and consequently neither was able to adequately budget the project or schedule the implementation. Both the retailer's and the contractor's developers had invested time in a failed project.

The users lost the most. Not only did they not receive the system they needed and had been promised, but they wasted time and money and had diverted attention from their primary jobs to help develop an unimplemented system.

From a Process Perspective

The fault lies with both the contracting process and the requirements definition process. To improve these processes, Theory-W principles of software management can be used. The following three steps are adapted from "Theory-W Software Project Management":

1. Establish a set of win-win preconditions by:
   — Understanding what it is that people want to win.
   — Establishing an explicit set of win-win objectives based on reasonable expectations that match participants' objectives to their win conditions.
   — Providing an environment that supports win-win negotiations.
2. Structure a win-win development process by:
   — Establishing a realistic plan that highlights potential win-lose and lose-lose risk items.
   — Involving all affected parties.
   — Resolving win-lose situations.
3. Structure a win-win software product which includes
   — The users' and maintainers' win conditions.
   — Management's and supplier's financial and scheduling win conditions.

APPLYING THEORY-W TO THE RETAILER EXAMPLE

There are several actions the retailer's IS department could have taken to increase the project's probability of success. It could have trained user personnel in how to identify and articulate their needs, and then worked with these users to draft a more thorough RFP. After receiving RFP responses, the IS department could have involved senior management in identifying the limits on resources and schedules. It also could have foreseen the difficulties the contractor would have if significant program modifications were needed.

By identifying constituent win conditions, the IS department would then have been in a position to negotiate a fair contract that would have explicitly taken into account all the win conditions. Having done these critical up-front tasks, the IS department would then have been in a position to structure a win-win development process. Unfortunately, the IS department never set win-win preconditions.

In the absence of an explicit philosophy to make everyone a winner and an explicit process for accomplishing this, the IS department lacked the necessary support to identify the stakeholders' needs and negotiate a reasonable set of win-win objectives.

INTEGRATING THEORY-W INTO THE DEVELOPMENT LIFECYCLE

Theory-W can be easily integrated into the classical waterfall lifecycle. During requirements definition, for example, it can be used to ensure that management, users, and developers have their individual needs met in a way that supports the timely and cost-effective development of the system. During design phases, developers and maintenance personnel can work together to ensure that the system is able to be efficiently maintained. And throughout all phases, Theory-W is a natural mechanism for ensuring that all stakeholders are able to effectively articulate their individual win conditions.

Boehm and his colleague have also integrated Theory-W into Boehm's Spiral Model of system development. As originally conceived in the late 1980s, the Spiral Model is a four-step iterative model for system development that provides a better mirror of actual real-world development practices than the classical waterfall model, particularly in situations where it is difficult to pin down systems specifications in advance. The model shares similarities to other evolutionary models of system development.

In extending the Spiral Model to explicitly incorporate Theory-W, Boehm and his colleagues have produced the following iterative seven-step model (see Exhibit 44.1):

1. Identify next-level stakeholders.
2. Identify stakeholders' win conditions.
3. Reconcile stakeholders' win conditions. Establish next level objectives, constraints, and alternatives.
4. Evaluate product and process alternatives. Resolve risks.
5. Define next-level product and processes including systems-wide partitions.
6. Validate product and process definitions.
7. Review results. Establish commitments. Return to Step 1.

CONCLUSION

Theory-W has been shown to be successful in terms of both the paradigm it offers and its ability to help managers explicate and simultaneously manage the win conditions of all constituents and stakeholders. Theory-W

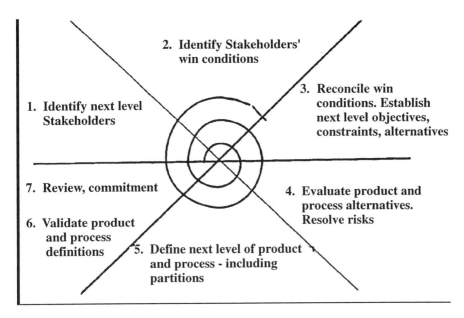

Exhibit 44.1. Theory-W extension to spiral model

has also proven itself to be of value for organizations embarking on a systematic program to improve performance whether it be more effective system deployment, improved productivity, better customer service, total quality management, or more effective processes. To be successful, performance improvement programs require the full and complete support of all stakeholders. Theory-W offers a robust theory, an effective process, and a practical model for getting and keeping this needed support.

Chapter 45
Managing the User/IS Relationship

Ann S. Angel

THE TECHNOLOGY GAP is closing between IS and its clients, but the communication gap is not. The IS professional who has spent a lifetime building programs on the mainframe with COBOL or FORTRAN is now confronted with clients talking in terms of macros built in Visual Basic and Object Linking and Embedding (OLE). In some cases, users are as sophisticated in their use of generic software as the IS professional is about languages and logic. In other cases, companies have moved systems analysts into the business unit to create a departmental technical staff person who is the interface between IS and the less-technical department management.

This chapter focuses on fine-tuning the relationship between IS and users. Thinking of users as customers or clients is at the heart of establishing a new relationship between IS and users. The techniques presented here can be successfully used by either in-house IS staff or contractors. We will use the generic term *IS consultant* to refer to both internal and external IS staff.

THE CLIENT-ORIENTED ORGANIZATION

There are options for making IS more in tune with its clients, more proactive in meeting their needs, and in the long run, better able to establish a win-win relationship. Many IS managers are under the impression that if there are no calls of complaint, there are no problems. This is not necessarily so. Some research shows that only 5% of people complain to management, 45% complain to the front-line person, and 50% never complain at all. These no-complaint people in an open marketplace simply take their business elsewhere. Clients may choose not to complain because they:

- Have the perception that it is not worth the time and trouble.
- Believe that no one really cares and that it will do no good.
- Have no formal channels for filing a complaint.

The number of complaints therefore has little bearing on whether or not clients are happy with services.

The chart in Exhibit 45.1 shows the changes in the focus, goals, and strategy when IS moves along the continuum from treating the end user as the consumer of products and services to the client.

FOCUS		Process	Satisfaction	Care
Consumer	**Focus**	Transactions	Customer	Relationship
⇓	**Goal**	Speed and Accuracy	Meet Expectations	Exceed Expectations
⇓	**Strategy**	Reduce Time	Convenience	Value
Client	**Viewpoint**	Consumer	Customer	Client

Exhibit 45.1. Moving from end user as consumer to end user as client

In a client-oriented organization, the IS consultant looks for opportunities to improve the working relationship between the service deliverer and the client. IS looks for chances to "identify and take away their pain", that is, to create new products and services that will make them more efficient, reduce costs, and increase profits. Clients want:

- Reliable products and services.
- Responsiveness to their individual needs.
- Assurances or guarantees that a solution will work.
- Empathy for their point of view.
- Tangible results.

IS consultants can benefit from frequently checking with their clients (the end users) to find out how expectations and requirements are being met. This is also an opportunity to ask about new projects or organizational changes that may be on the horizon. It is foremost a chance to strengthen the partnership between IS and the client. Many IS trainers solicit feedback from their students, or customers, in the form of course evaluations.

COMMUNICATION IS THE KEY

Establishing a line of communication and keeping it open, even in the face of possible conflict, is the critical key to a successful client relationship. Every business unit, including IS, has its own jargon. Some simple ground rules may be used to ensure clear communication.

Rules for Establishing a Common Vocabulary

The IS consultant should be an active listener whose goal is to achieve a common understanding with the speaker regarding the intentions, feelings, and beliefs the speaker is attempting to communicate. An active listener also gives frequent feedback and can help the speaker by:

- Stopping the conversation to ask for clarification of a term. Each person should understand the importance and impact of the terminology.
- Asking the client to develop a list of definitions common to that business unit that may have different meanings from the common usage of the words.
- Developing a dictionary to clarify computer terms that may be confusing to the client.
- Communicating the technology in terms that can be understood by non-technical people and giving them plenty of opportunities to ask for explanations.
- Setting up "dialog demos." Clients could arrange to have a tour of the systems department, including operations. IS could explain the systems development cycle and how IS professionals do their work. The client department could return the favor for the IS support team.

THE PHASES OF CONSULTING

When an IS consultant approaches a user group, department, or company for the first time to determine its requirements for new systems development, there must be a process to ensure success. Just as IS would not think of sitting down to write a program without some clear idea of what the end result needs to be, IS cannot define a client need without fully following the process.

When setting out to complete a project for a client, many IS consultants follow a process that includes contracting, diagnosing the problem, and providing feedback.

Contracting

Negotiating "Wants". The client may know what is needed to improve workflow and efficiency, but may not have a clear idea of the cost of programming or systems development. It is the job of the IS consultant to help clients determine what they can afford, what they can eliminate from their wish list and still meet the ultimate goals, and when they can use an alternative resource like a generic PC-based product. Exhibit 45.2 provides a diagram for navigating the initial client meeting.

Coping with Mixed Motivation. Office politics sometimes cloud people's perspective. The IS consultant should help the client see the big picture or the corporate perspective; this is a way for them to measure their individual needs against the whole. It is important to be diplomatic when informing a client that its needs are a lower priority than those of people in another department.

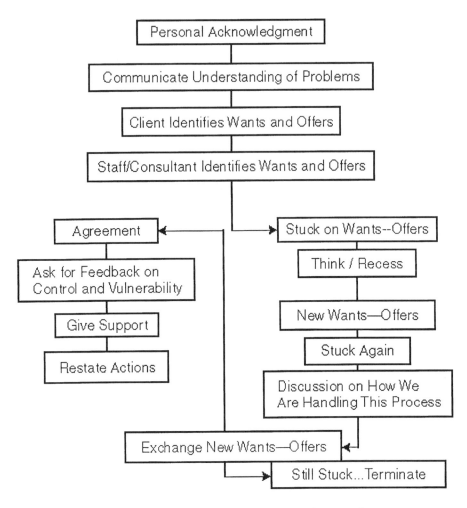

Exhibit 45.2. Navigating the initial contracting meeting

If a situation arises in which IS is used as pawn between disputing parties in departmental politics, the IS consultant should approach IS management and discuss possible solutions to the resolve the problem. It may also be necessary to involve the management of the client department.

Dealing with Concerns of Exposure and Loss of Control. When PCs and local networks first became practical tools of office automation, there was a great deal of concern about loss of data integrity and security. Time has proved that departmental processing is the most efficient, effective way to run the organization's business. PC software has broadened the scope of user productivity and lessened the demands on mainframes and development staff. The original concern resulted from a fear of loss of control and power, which is only natural. Many clients will express such fears when IS begins to change things.

Involving Users in Planning. Systems development should involve the primary users in the planning stage. All the users who are stakeholders should be involved in planning. This may include other departments that will rely heavily on the output of the current or planned system. It may be front-line users as well as management. All of the stakeholders should be in consensus before any decisions are finalized.

Diagnosing the Problem

Analysis. A thorough analysis of the workflow and processing requirements should be performed before any project is started. To do otherwise may result in a situation where IS recommends a solution, programs and implements the system, and finds that the staff is not using it because it did not do what they wanted it to do.

Resisting the Urge for Complete Data. Defining the scope of a project and staying inside the parameters are critical to project completion. However, it is helpful to consider opportunities for future developments while the system is being designed. This makes future additions and modifications easier.

Making the Diagnosis Process Client-Centered. The IS consultant should interview the clients in a department to find out why things are done the way they are, and then help the client see a different perspective and a better way of doing things, if necessary. Following are ways to make an interview client-centered:

- Concentrate on current workflow and task identification.
- Ask questions to clarify what is being done and in what sequence.
- Ask questions regarding duplication of work or record keeping.
- Without criticizing, determine if there are legitimate reasons for duplication of work; if not, try to get a buy-in for eliminating the duplicated task.
- Teach streamlining procedures and tasks before automating.
- Never assume that the client staff will eliminate a step in the task just because the computer system does not include it. The steps in a task should be fully explained to the clients.
- Do not make decisions about processing requirements without fully discussing the issues with management and staff, especially the primary users.

Providing Feedback

Funneling Data. After the analysis, IS should be able to give the client feedback about the systems they have requested, including costs and re-source availability. Often during the diagnosis, IS will uncover facts and fig-ures that might surprise the client. A feedback meeting, as early as possible in the life of the project, is the best time to bring all surprises to the table.

Identifying and Dealing with Resistance. IS may encounter resistance from some users to the change management is requesting. It is not impos-sible to change people's perceptions so that they accept the new ideas and systems, but management needs to be aware of the resistance so a strategy for dealing with it can be developed. IS may be unaware of certain reasons for resistance within a department; management may be able to shed light on user prejudices or preconceived ideas about the way things are done.

Decision Making. It is helpful for the IS consultant to learn the skills of getting people to reach a consensus in a group meeting. Once clients have heard IS feedback, everyone must reach a final decision about a project. All important parties should be in this meeting, otherwise the absent parties may try to unseat the decision later.

Focusing on Here-and-Now Choices. Clients should realize that they may need to choose the most critical pieces of the project for implementation in the beginning and wait on others until budget funds or resources are available. If they can see the plan for meeting critical needs now and even-tually getting most of the less important requirements addressed as well, they are more likely to accept the initial offerings.

Not Taking Things Personally. It is difficult for a presenter to remain com-pletely objective when pitching a plan for project completion. However, de-cisions are based on business, and the IS consultant cannot afford to take it as a personal affront if the client decides not to implement the recom-mendations. This is a critical time to keep a positive attitude for the sake of preserving any future relationship with the clients.

CONCLUSION

Following are tips for applying the principles discussed in this chapter to real-life situations:

- Teach the user how to streamline procedures by:
  — Analyzing current processes.
  — Being objective.
  — Eliminating any unnecessary steps and redundant record keeping.

- Get the client involved in the analysis and decision-making process by:
  — Defining the automation objectives.
  — Agreeing on what problems need to be solved.
  — Determining internal and external pressures.
  — Defining the tasks that need to be automated and setting priorities.
- Select appropriate off-the-shelf software by:
  — Setting standards for generic packages while remaining flexible.
  — Selecting packages that have a been on the market a long time and have an extensive user and support base.
  — Choosing packages written in languages that can be modified and supported locally, and where source code is available.
  — Choosing the product with the most training and support available.
- Define hardware platforms and requirements by:
  — Avoiding bias toward the mainframe. If the clients believe the IS consultant's knowledge is only on one platform, they may not trust suggestions.
- Ensure productivity gains by:
  — Making recommendations to the client that will ensure that his or her systems' investments are being used correctly and efficiently. He or she should also understand the requirements for training.
  — Arranging training for the client management team.
  — Encouraging users to learn more about their software and to use the upper-end functionality. Some outside costs can be eliminated simply by using equipment and software already in place.
  — Training and cross-training all users. A department should not be reliant on one person's expertise.

Chapter 46

Reengineering Project Challenges

Varun Grover

Seung Ryul Jeong

James T.C. Teng

BUSINESS REENGINEERING (BR) involves focusing on the business process as the prominent unit of analysis. The impetus for such programs has been reactive (financial crisis or competitive pressures) and proactive (improving corporate responsiveness). Common goals are improved customer service, reduced cost, compressed cycle time, increased productivity, and reduced defects. Although the concept of reengineering as "radical change" is already evolving to a more tempered and arguably more realistic stance, little data exist to evaluate implementation efforts of reengineering projects. This is of concern, especially given recent evidence that a large number of reengineering efforts result in failure.

Most of the "expertise" for BR has been developed through the experience of consultants, many of whom serve as external advisors to bring about fundamental change from within the organization.

In a similar vein, numerous trade articles prescribe approaches to reengineering based on proprietary expertise or anecdotal evidence. Systematic studies have been limited, even though many corporations have experienced both success and failure in reengineering projects and their collective wisdom can benefit future endeavors.

This chapter reports a study of a large group of companies that have undertaken reengineering efforts. Respondant rankings of more than 64 problems associated with reengineering projects reveal that change management challenges remain at the forefront of reengineering endeavors. Implications of the findings for implementation of future projects are discussed. The aim is to draw on these collective experiences to understand the implementation problems faced during reengineering.

0-8493-9820-7/00/$0.00+$.50
© 2000 by CRC Press LLC

PROBLEMS IN IMPLEMENTING BUSINESS REENGINEERING

BR is usually characterized by deliberate and fundamental change in a business process, conducted to achieve breakthrough improvements in performance. This change is typically (but not always) facilitated by information technology (IT). Most reengineering efforts described involve planned change, which requires an organization (generally in the form of a reengineering team) and an executive mandate to implement process change.

The cross-functional nature of most reengineering projects makes it challenging to integrate traditionally compartmentalized groups into integrated teams that focus on process outputs and customers rather than on parochial functional demands. Information technology, in its ever expanding role of assimilating and managing large amounts of data and enabling communication across time and space, can serve a powerful role in the integration required for reengineering. This can make reengineering analogous to a systems project in that its success requires careful management of people, technology, and the project. However, unlike systems projects, the change required is cross-functional or even organizational and, more important, it is usually radical, involving structural changes rather than automation of existing processes.

In this study, reengineering implementation involves all activities pertaining to planning, organizing, and conducting the reengineering project. This could involve developing a vision, analyzing the organization, identifying reengineering opportunities, evaluating information technology enablers, establishing commitment, allocating resources, managing the project, and evaluating results. Each aspect of implementation could have a potential set of problems.

A list of potential reengineering implementation problems was generated based on a review of literature on reengineering, information systems, change management, and project management. These problems were classified into six categories and verified through interviews with a number of practicing managers involved in reengineering. The categories are as follows:

- *Category 1 (Management Support Problems)*: Includes problems associated with top management's commitment and leadership for reengineering.
- *Category 2 (Technological Competence Problems)*: Includes problems related to the information technology expertise and infrastructure.
- *Category 3 (Process Delineation Problems)*: Includes problems in defining attributes and requirements of process reengineering.
- *Category 4 (Project Planning Problems)*: Includes problems in planning for reengineering.

- *Category 5 (Change Management Problems)*: Includes problems in getting people to respond positively to change.
- *Category 6 (Project Management Problems)*: Includes problems related to managing the reengineering team and project.

METHOD AND SAMPLE

This study mainly explored implementation problems of BR. The unit of analysis was chosen as a single reengineering project. Reengineering was described as a radical, deliberate (planned) change in a business process to achieve significant increase in performance. A separate sheet was included with descriptions of classic reengineering cases. Participants were asked to select a recently concluded reengineering project in which they had participated as a team member. They were asked to describe the project, the process being reengineered, and the performance criteria used.

The survey instrument listed the identified problems and the respondents were asked to rate the extent to which they have encountered each problem on a 5-point scale, where 1 = not a problem, 2 = a minor problem, 3 = a significant problem, 4 = a major problem, and 5 = an extreme problem.

For the present study, key informants were those who had actively participated in at least one reengineering project. Questionnaires were sent to members of the Planning Forum, which is the international business organization focusing on strategic management and planning. We requested that the recipients forward the questionnaire to a reengineering team member if they were not a team member. A total of 704 questionnaires was mailed. Each questionnaire was sent with a cover letter, a self-addressed stamped envelope, and a donation slip that offered a $2 donation to charitable organizations. A total of 239 usable responses were returned, resulting in a final response rate of 29.2%.

Of the 239 respondents, 105 (44%) had concluded at least one reengineering project and were able to respond to the entire instrument. Over half of the responding companies involved in reengineering were either in the manufacturing industry, the financial sector, or in the insurance industry. The remaining were involved in more than ten different industries. Therefore, in general, organizations in this survey represented a variety of industries. A size profile, as measured by the number of employees, revealed that more than two-thirds of the firms had over 1000 employees, with about a quarter having over 10,000. Another 28% had between 1000 and 5000 employees, and 16% had between 5000 and 10,000.

The most popular processes targeted for reengineering were the customer, product development, and order management processes (targeted by one-third of firms). Among these three processes, two (customer service and order management process) were customer-interfacing processes that extend into the customer organization. This result is not surprising because it has been widely recognized that processes at the customer interface are perhaps the most critical to an organization's success inasmuch as they are essential to a firm's cash flow and customer satisfaction. Further, among these three processes, customer service processes appear to be common across most industries.

Interestingly, but not unexpectedly, the major information technology enablers for the selected projects were database technology and telecommunication networks. Both these technologies serve to integrate and coordinate across functions, often critical to reengineering endeavors. Workflow software was also extensively used to manage process flow. Other technologies like imaging and expert systems also facilitate the compression of processes by offering repositories of information. Client/server architectures that enable information access and coordination were also used in numerous projects.

MOST SEVERE IMPLEMENTATION PROBLEMS

The items for the six categories of implementation problems are listed in Exhibit 46.1. For each problem item, we calculated a "severity score," which is the percentage of surveyed projects that experienced this as a major or extreme problem. The ranking of the problem's severity among the 64 items is indicated in the last column (identical rankings are assigned to items with the same severity scores). The five most severe problems are listed below:

1. Need for managing change is not recognized.
2. Top management's short-term view and quick-fix mentality.
3. Rigid hierarchical structures in the organization.
4. Line managers in the organization unreceptive to innovation.
5. Failure to anticipate and plan for the organizational resistance to change.

With the exception of the second problem, which belongs to the category of project planning, four of the top five problems are related to *change management*. These issues have been widely discussed both in the implementation literature and BR literature.

Upon implementation, programs like reengineering often encounter significant organizational resistance. People may fear that their expertise may no longer be valued, or that they will not be successful under the new regime. Subsequently, they may be afraid of losing their jobs. Often, reengineering implementation is considered a highly political process where stakeholders are more concerned about furthering their own self-interests than about contributing to their organization. This could be partly attributed to the rigid hierarchical structure (the third most severe problem)

	Severity Score (%)*	Severity Rank among 64 Problems
Category 1: Management Support Problems		
Manager's failure to support the new values and beliefs demanded by the redesigned process	21.7	16
Insufficient understanding about the goals of top management in relation to reengineering	18.2	24
Lack of senior management leadership for reengineering efforts	16.3	29
Top management's insufficient understanding about business reengineering	15.4	36
Lack of top management support in business reengineering efforts	13.5	41
Lack of BR project champion	8.7	56
Category 2: Technological Competence Problems		
Insufficient understanding about existing data, applications, and IT across the organization	25.3	6
Limited database infrastructure	22.2	11
Lack of expertise in IT in the organization	19.5	21
Limited IS application portfolio	18.6	22
Failure to aggressively use IT enablers	16.6	27
Failure to continually assess emerging IT capabilities	14.5	38
Lack of IS participation and assistance in the reengineering project	13.5	41
Limited telecommunication infrastructure	11.6	47
Category 3: Process Delineation Problems		
Difficulty in establishing performance improvement goals for the redesigned process	22.1	12
Failure to identify process owners who are responsible for the entire business process	16.3	29
Difficult to forecast human resources, financial, and other resource requirements	13.6	39
Focusing only on evaluation criteria that are easily measured and quantifiable	12.6	43
Failure to include process owners throughout the BR efforts	10.7	49
Scope of the reengineered process was defined inappropriately	10.6	50
Proposed changes to the process were too incremental, not radical enough	10.6	50
The approach to reengineering was too radical	2.9	64
Category 4: Project Planning Problems		
Top management's short-term view and quick-fix mentality	31.7	2
Lack of alignment between corporate planning and IT planning	23.3	7
Lack of strategic vision	22.1	12
Lack of experience in business reengineering	20.2	19
Failure to commit the required resources (financial, human resources, etc.) to BR efforts	17.6	25

Exhibit 46.1. Survey results

	Severity Score (%)*	Severity Rank among 64 Problems
Lack of authority given to reengineering team	16.3	29
Difficulty in financially justifying benefits of BR	13.6	39
Identification of candidate process for reengineering not based on strategic planning	12.6	44
Difficulty in finding business reengineering team members who have the required skills and knowledge	12.5	45
Lack of appropriate planning	10.6	50
Absence of appropriate training for BR team members	8.7	56
Failure to understand customers' viewpoints in the BR efforts	7.8	59
Lack of external consultant support for BR efforts	3.9	63

Category 5: Change Management Problems

Need for managing change is not recognized	31.8	1
Rigid hierarchical structures in the organization	30.1	3
Line managers in the organization unreceptive to innovation	28.8	4
Failure to anticipate and plan for the organizational resistance to change	27.7	5
Failure to consider politics of the business reengineering efforts	23.3	7
Failure to build support from line managers	23.0	10
Unreasonable expectations attributed to business reengineering as a solution to all organizational problems	22.1	12
Absence of management systems (e.g., incentive, training system) to cultivate required values	20.6	18
Difficulty in gaining cross-functional cooperation	20.1	20
Senior management's failure to commit to new values	18.5	23
Lack of appropriate employee compensation incentives in the new process	16.8	26
Failure to communicate reasons for change to members of the organization	16.3	29
Inadequate training for personnel affected by the redesigned process	16.0	33
Necessary changes in human resource policies for BR implementation were not made	15.9	34
Failure to consider existing organizational culture	15.4	36
Not enough time to develop new skills for the redesigned process	7.0	60

Category 6: Project Management Problems

The BR effort took too much time	23.1	9
Uncertainty about BR project time-frame	22.1	12
Difficulty in measuring reengineering project performance	21.1	17
Reengineering team members' conflict between team responsibilities and functional responsibilities	16.4	28

Exhibit 46.1. Survey results (continued)

	Severity Score (%)*	Severity Rank among 64 Problems
Poor communication between BR team members and other organizational members	15.6	35
Ambiguity in job expectations for team members	12.5	45
Failure to effectively monitor progress of project according to the schedule	11.6	47
Difficulty in gaining control of reengineering efforts	9.7	53
Difficulty in modeling and simulating the proposed changes to the business process	8.9	54
Failure to assess project performance in the early stage of BR efforts to provide feedback	8.9	54
Too much emphasis on analyzing the existing process	8.6	58
Lack of appropriate BR methodology	5.8	61
Poor communication among BR team members	4.8	62

*Percentage of projects that considered this a major or extreme problem.

Exhibit 46.1. Survey results

since organizations with this structure tend to be functional and hence parochial. As an assistant vice-president of reengineering at a major financial services company has indicated, line managers may support the idea of reengineering but insist that their area is one of few under control. Even with a high level of awareness of change issues, careful change management is needed to handle issues of turf and politics. In many cases, presenting employees with a prototype of how the reengineered organization will work and convening a sense of the project's urgency to employees may prove useful in overcoming resistance.

A severe problem (fourth) associated with change management concerns line managers. Line management provides resources to the change effort and bears major responsibility in implementing the changes. These line managers have a tendency to design systems for their domain of control. Thus, if they are unreceptive to new ideas and changes, the resulting innovation would be less than optimum. To avoid resistance by line managers who would have to make the changes work, their support is a critical ingredient for success.

The second most severe problem is top management's short-term view and quick-fix mentality. This issue has also been raised in previous studies concerning the implementation of IS planning. Because planning deals with the future, inadequate long-range perspective is said to lead to confusion in planning tasks and distrust of output. In the absence of a broad long-term vision, it is difficult to conceptualize a reengineering program aimed at radical improvements in productivity, service, and quality. The resulting reengineering efforts may become fragmented and stunted.

It is interesting, but not surprising, to note that rigid hierarchical structure was rated as one of the most severe (third) problems. Since the structural problem is more likely an overall context factor, it was not emphasized in the prior IS implementation research. However, in the reengineering literature, it has been widely recognized. Since reengineering is based on process orientation, redesigned processes often cut across existing organizational structures. Therefore, a strict hierarchical structure that supports management along individual functional hierarchies becomes a major obstacle for successful BR implementation.

One interesting finding is that among the top 20 most severe problems, only two problems are IT related. The finding suggests that, although IT plays a significant enabling role in projects, IT-related problems may not be critical to successful reengineering implementation. It reaffirms literature highlighting non-technical aspects of reengineering efforts. However, the results did indicate the importance of *understanding the existing IT infrastructure* (ranked sixth). For instance, a database shared by many different functions participating in the same business process facilitates a process-oriented approach. Thus, a *limited database infrastructure* can become a considerable obstacle (ranked eleventh).

CONCLUSION

James Hammer and Michael Champy view a business system as consisting of four major components: business processes, jobs and structures, management systems, and values and beliefs. They argue that it needs to be viewed as an integrated system where all four components must be changed together for successful reengineering. In a similar vein, a set of field case studies has demonstrated that, to achieve performance breakthrough, the redesign should fundamentally change a spectrum of related organizational elements: 1) roles and responsibilities, 2) measurements and incentives, 3) organizational structure, 4) information technology, 5) shared values, and 6) skills.

The top five problems resulting from our study are consistent with these previous research findings. For instance, existing values and beliefs may block innovative ideas (Problems 2 and 4) and heighten resistance (Problem 5). Rigid hierarchical structures (Problem 3) hinder cross-functional reengineering initiatives. New jobs and structures require a different management system to establish new measurement and incentive schemes. Careful design of a new management system reduces the chances of organizational resistance.

Although some commonly discussed inhibitors and facilitators were confirmed by this study, others were not. For example, a number of studies indicate unrealistic expectations as a critical inhibitor. The present study also rated this problem quite highly (twelfth). However, a number of authors have stressed the importance of appropriate project scope and this study found it to be one of the least important problems (tied at rank #50).

Our findings also reveal interesting differences between reengineering implementation and traditional IS implementation. A comparison of highly ranked problems in our results with findings from IS implementation studies shows that more than half of the problems we identified are *reengineering specific*. Although factors emphasized in IS implementation research include commitment to the project, the extent of project definition and planning, top management support, ease of use, attitudes and perceptions, situational and personal factors, and so on, this study highlights organizational structure, support from line managers, database infrastructure, experience in reengineering, cross-functional cooperation, appropriate management systems, etc. This shows that the reengineering efforts typically operate at a macro and organizational level, involving a multitude of structural, political, cultural, as well as technology factors. Further, these factors interact with each other in a complex manner, which is why researchers often label the change process as "sociotechnical" in nature. In comparison, traditional IS implementation endeavors generally cause less disturbance to the status quo and are relatively less complex.

The IS profession has, over the last 4 decades, witnessed and contributed to waves of tumultuous change in technologies and methodologies, such as the PC revolution, the rapidly evolving client/server platform, and the internet phenomenon. Many business reengineering projects are enabled by IT, and the participation of IS professionals in the project team should be critical to implementation success. Undoubtedly, the IS profession is now facing another great challenge that demands the continuing enrichment of IS professionals' knowledge and skill, particularly in the areas of process modeling, organizational analysis, and change management.

References

Bashien, B.J., Markus, M.L., and Riley, P.(1994). "Preconditions for BPR Success", *Information Systems Management*, 11, No. 2, pp. 7-13.

Caldwell, B. (June 20,1994). "Missteps, Miscues," *Information Week*, pp. 50-60.

Davidson, W H. (1993). "Beyond Engineering: The Three Phases of Business Transformation." *IBM Systems Journal*, 32, No. 1, pp. 65-79.

Hall, G., Rosenthal, J., and Wade, J. (1993). "How to Make Reengineering Really Work," *Harvard Business Review*, 71, No. 6, pp. 119-131.

Klein, M.M. *"The Most Fatal Reengineering Mistakes."* Information Strategy. The Executive's Journal, 10, No. 4, pp. 21-28.

Tyran, C.K. and George, J.E. (1993). "The Implementation of Expert Systems: A Survey of Successful Implementations." *Database*, 24, No. 1, pp. 5-15.

Chapter 47

Managing Development in the Era of Complex Systems

Hugh W. Ryan

As INFORMATION SYSTEMS do more and reach more users in more locations, complexity and size have become dominant factors in systems development. In this chapter, Hugh W. Ryan shares his experiences in developing large, complex systems and provides insight on how to manage their development.

To many, it appears that every move toward making technology simpler has been matched by a corresponding move toward increased complexity. This is a prime paradox of IT today: on the one hand, technology for the business user has become dramatically simpler as end users have been shielded from complexity; on the other hand, the actual development of systems architectures and business solutions has become far more complex.

Distributed computing environments and architectures that span the enterprise have meant that IT work is no longer a point solution for one department or division of a company. In most cases today, a systems development effort takes place with greater expectations that it will have a significant impact on the enterprise's book of business.

Where there is greater potential impact, there is also greater potential risk. Companies are making substantial investments in their technologies; they expect to see business value from that investment quicker, and they expect that the solution that is delivered will be robust enough to serve as a transition platform as technological change continues to compress years into months.

0-8493-9820-7/00/$0.00+$.50
© 2000 by CRC Press LLC

MORE PEOPLE, MORE YEARS

The new complexity of systems development can be seen in several ways. First, more people now are involved in development than was seen either in the mainframe development days or in the early years of client/server. Frequently, projects today may involve anywhere from 100 to 500 people, and this figure will continue to increase until thousand-person projects become common over the next several years.

Second, the number of years required to develop the more complex business solution also has increased. Enterprisewide solutions, delivered over several releases, may require three to five years or more to bring all aspects to fruition. This, in turn, adds additional complexities. For example, with longer development periods, the chances are good that management may go through at least one change during the course of the development project. If the project leader has not been careful to communicate and gain sponsorship at many different management levels, a change in management may put the investment at risk.

This new systems development environment is what the author's firm has come to call "large complex systems (LCS)." It is an environment where the solution

- Requires many years to develop
- Requires a hundred or more people to be involved
- Is expected to have a significant business benefit
- Has both a high potential value and a high potential risk

NEW MANAGEMENT NEEDS

The author recently has completed a year-long field review that looked in some detail at some of his firm's largest complex systems development efforts. Based on a set of going-in positions about the challenges of such efforts, extensive interviews were held with personnel at many different levels of the projects. From these interviews, definite repeated patterns about these projects began to emerge, and it became clear that it is possible to set forth a number of factors necessary for a successful implementation of a large complex systems effort. Although a full treatment of all these factors is outside the scope of a single chapter, this one focuses on several that have to do with new ways of leading and managing a large complex systems effort:

- Business vision
- Testing and program management
- Phased-release rollout plan

BUSINESS VISION

A vision of a new way of doing business that will result from the large complex systems (LCS) development is critical to the success of the LCS. Although intuition, as well as prevailing business management thinking, would indicate this is so, it was important to see the real benefit of business visions played out.

For example, one major project studied was one for a global stock exchange. There, the business vision was an integral part of the project — a crisp articulation of the eight essential capabilities that the final system was to provide. It was integrated into the project training and displayed in all essential documents of the project. Most important, all projects within the larger engagement had to be tied back to the vision and justified according to how they contributed to the realization of that vision.

Another development effort at a national financial institution also began with a business vision and a rollout plan that clearly delivered the long-term vision in a sequence of steps. The business vision and rollout plans have served as the basis of work since they were created. The vision deals with the concept of a "model bank" — a consistent set of processes and systems that permits customers around the country to get a standard high quality of service and also permits employees to move within the company without having to learn new processes. The vision is owned by the senior management of the bank and communicated to all employees in powerful yet simple ways.

Changes in management frequently can have a negative effect on the power of a business vision. For this reason, it is essential that the business vision be held by more than one individual. On a large complex system built in the United Kingdom, for example, there were several management personnel changes over the years required for the complete development. The key to success here was ensuring that, at any given time, there was a set of senior management personnel committed to the effort. As natural career progression took these people to other roles, there was always another core set coming in who continued to own the vision and push it forward.

TESTING AND PROGRAM MANAGEMENT

An LCS effort consists of a set of projects with many interdependencies. Many of these interdependencies may be rather subtle, but all of them must work. The traditional approach for determining whether or not things work is systems testing.

It is known that traditional testing works well for a single application. However, for an LCS with many projects and many interdependencies, the systems testing approach comes up against some real limitations. Experience in these efforts is showing that it is not reasonable to expect a single project leader to define, design, and execute all the tests that are needed to verify that the LCS works as a whole. It is not the responsibility of individual project leaders to test the LCS release as a whole. An architecture group typically does not have the application skills and user contacts to undertake the testing. In other words, the testing of a large complex system as a whole, using traditional approaches, is an undertaking that has no clear owner.

This creates a dilemma. Program management is not positioned to underwrite the quality of the timely delivery of an LCS effort. Individual project leaders cannot be expected to underwrite the quality of the LCS as a whole. At most, they can underwrite that their project works with its primary interfaces. An intense need today, therefore, is to develop the means to underwrite the quality and timeliness of an LCS release as a whole.

In practice, successful LCS efforts have found a way to resolve the dilemma. This approach, as it turns out, is actually a synthesis of program management and what is called the "V-model" testing strategy. This new synthesis in LCS engagements is called "engineering management."

Engineering management adds a testing responsibility to traditional program management. This testing role is charged with validating and verifying that the LCS effort works as a whole, as a system of systems, to meet user expectations of a release of an LCS. For example, it will test that when all the online applications are running as a whole, online response time, reliability, and availability meet service level agreements (SLAs). Individual project leaders can be expected to have confirmed that they meet their SLAs. The project leaders often, however, cannot confirm that they continue to meet SLAs when the entire LCS release runs. They do not have access to the rest of the LCS release. They may find it difficult or impossible to create a high transaction volume with multiple LCS applications running in a production-like environment. A more detailed discussion of engineering management will, perhaps, be the topic of a future chapter.

PHASED-RELEASE ROLLOUT PLAN

Finally, one of the critical success factors with LCS development involves a move away from a single release rollout strategy and toward a phased-release plan. Only one of the projects reviewed had attempted to use a big-bang strategy and, even in this case, it became apparent that the approach would prove problematic as the conversion approached. The effort encountered significant delays as it reworked the release plan and moved instead to the view that a phased release was most desirable.

The remaining projects followed a phased delivery. The phased-release approach serves a number of functions:

- *Reduced risk.* Using a number of releases with partial functionality can reduce the risk of implementation. At the global stock exchange, for example, initial discussions with the company's management were key in moving from the riskier single-release approach toward a phased rollout, even though the phased approach appeared to delay the benefits of the system. The balance was the reduced risk of achieving the benefits.
- *Early verification.* A phased approach permits early verification by the business user of essential components as they work with the system in their business. From the review work conducted, it appears that a first release tends to take from 18 to 24 months. Subsequent releases tend to occur in the range of six to 12 months after earlier phases. This is in contrast to a more typical three- to five-year development that a single-release approach may require. The result of the iterations is that the user has worked with the system and provided verification of the value of the system.
- *Ability to make midcourse corrections.* Inherent in the release approach is the ability to review the overall situation as the releases are rolled out, and thereby to make midcourse changes. As noted, an LCS effort can go on for many years, during which time a company and its business environment can go through a great deal of change. The release strategy can provide the means to deal with the changes in a controlled manner. It also can address issues in a long systems development where for periods of time the design must be frozen.
- *Closer user involvement.* Business impact can be seen faster when rollouts are provided to the user earlier through iterations. This allows the user to build up experience with and support for the system, rather than facing a sudden conversion at the end of a large development.

The downside of a phased rollout strategy is the significant increase in development cost. To the author's knowledge, there are no widely accepted estimates of the increase in cost caused by the phased-release approach. However, there have been some evaluations that showed more than a 50 percent increase in costs when a multiple release strategy was compared to a single release. This would seem to suggest not going with a multiple release strategy. The trade-off has a very high risk of failure in a single release combined with the benefits noted previously of a multiple release.

The points discussed are key to understanding the value of a release strategy. Phased releases allow a company to reduce risk, increase buy-in, and build a system that is closer to the company's business needs. The lower apparent costs may make a big-bang approach appear desirable, but the hidden costs and greater risks may prove unacceptable in the longer term. It is vital that management involved in this decision carefully weighs the costs and risks of either approach.

CONCLUSION

When the author began this review of large complex systems, his first thought was that the most important thing to do is simply to figure out how to eliminate the complexity. Based on the two years of review, he is convinced that eliminating the complexity is not possible. Complexity must be accepted as a part of the systems development world for the future. The size of projects that affect the enterprise as a whole tends to be large and will continue to increase. A project that affects the entire enterprise will increase complexity. Only when complexity is accepted can it be possible to come to grips with managing that complexity.

Finally, today's business environment — with its increasing focus on business partners, virtual enterprises, and the global span of business — makes complexity a reality that cannot be overcome. Delivering quality solutions in this environment must start with a recognition that complexity is inescapable. From that point, one initiates a set of strategies to manage the complexity and risk. There is no silver bullet in these strategies. The three points discussed in this chapter are examples of such strategies. Each of them is necessary, but none of them alone is sufficient to guarantee success. From a base of well-defined and -directed strategies, managing the ongoing complexity must become the focus on management in such large complex systems.

Chapter 48
Meeting the Software Challenge

Sami J. Albanna

Joe Osterhaus

As ECONOMIC AND TECHNOLOGICAL trends create spiraling demand for software resources, IS managers must increasingly weigh the risks of new technology against the costs of falling behind. In this environment, successful management of the IS organization depends less on the transfer of technological implements than on adopting the characteristics of a learning organization: a mature process, a culture supportive of continuous change, and effective management.

Beginning as a new discipline with no precedent in the scientific or industrial world, software has evolved in the last 50 years into one of the most strategic global industries, if not the most. By 1994, the value of the U.S. software market was estimated at $92.5 billion, only 10% of which was personal computer software.[1] The U.S. also provides most of the global software market.[2]

The revolution in business and government organizations brought about by information processing technology will last at least another 50 years, during which time, life as one knows it will be utterly transformed. New productive forces are emerging. Work relationships, the roles of information and knowledge, and the concept of the knowledge worker are the emerging elements that will be essential to the creation of economic success.

These changes have placed enormous burdens on — and created wide-ranging opportunities for — IS organizations. The success of government and private organizations is increasingly determined by the ability of an organization's information system to use new technologies to meet the needs of internal and external users.

This chapter describes the key factors IS managers must coordinate to enable their organizations' information systems to achieve critical goals. It identifies recent developments in organizational change and process engineering and presents a new paradigm that IS managers can use to address the critical issues in their organizations. In doing so, it frames central questions not usually addressed by IS management paradigms. The development and deployment of software in a business setting is extremely sensitive to process, culture, and organizational issues. This fact has enormous significance for IS managers who invest in and make decisions about software and related technologies.

The chapter assumes the following:

- The need to develop or enhance an organization's information systems is driven by the need of the business to improve services and deliver value to clients.
- IS management has the will and determination to make the necessary changes, deploy the relevant resources, and empower those who introduce and develop software products and related technologies.

The focus is on applications development and maintenance, with the assumption that the concepts discussed relate equally to other responsibilities of the IS organization, including information technology, data center management, network management, desktop management, and IT acquisitions and maintenance.

A STRATEGIC INDUSTRY MARKED BY RAPID CHANGE

Several large, interrelated global trends currently shape software technology and industry. One trend is the result of the large changes in nearly all disciplines and human endeavors that have resulted from computer-based information and control systems. These changes have matured to the point where the demand for more complex, integrated, robust, and resilient software-based systems is placing enormous demands on software development methods and technologies.

Adding to this trend are business and economic phenomena of the 1990s — including business reengineering, outsourcing, organization change, automated flexible production, and integrated communication services — which are also increasing demand on software development capacities. The impact of these phenomena on software technology and industry has been further heightened by the maturation of other delivery technologies, including multimedia, CD-ROM, publishing on demand, interactive television, and information highways such as the Internet and the World Wide Web.

The maturation, in the last decade, of several software development technologies is another global trend. The proliferation of these newer technologies has increased decision-makers' optimism about discovering effective solutions for the software dilemma. These technologies include object-oriented methods, and several others are also becoming more viable. We will explore these in the section on software technology.

The interrelationship of these trends increases their impact on the business environment exponentially, as shown in Exhibit 48.1. As software development creates new opportunities for business change by providing business solutions, the resulting transformations in the business environment place larger demands on software development capacities. Changes to the existing business that result from the introduction of new software eventually reach a level of major transformation. The transformed business also increases demand on software development capabilities because decision-makers expect software development to produce new applications that support the business in its transitional state. And, once the business successfully completes the transformation, it has new demands for software development. Software development technologies also add to this spiraling demand by adding new products and technologies that "raise the bar" on real and projected information systems performance.

To provide value to the overall enterprise, the IS organization must manage the acquisition, development, and deployment of these new technologies and software capabilities — and the changes they foster in the organization — in order to:

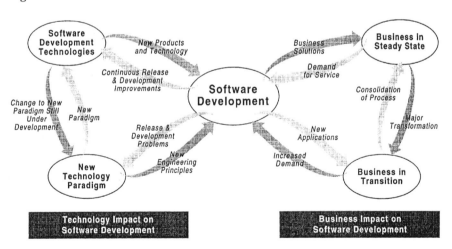

Exhibit 48.1. Forces Shaping the Software Development Environment

- Provide state-of-the-art systems that shorten time of business service and improve service quality, responsiveness to market, and service integration.
- Manage maintenance proactively by improving it and placing it under continuous development to enable system expansion.
- Reduce cost.
- Provide higher quality system solutions that offer better functionality and improved reliability.
- Make the information system expandable, resilient, and trustworthy for all users.
- Enable creation of new business opportunities.

Taken together, these economic and technological trends create demand for software resources that is orders of magnitude larger than what existed during the expansion of personal computing from 1976 to 1988. (Software resources comprise human resources, system engineering know-how, software development tools, maintenance processes, configuration management processes, and component repositories.) As a result, IS managers face increasingly difficult decisions about balancing new software development with the business needs of the organization and its customers. They must weigh the risks of new technology against the costs of falling behind.

The software dilemma was previously mentioned. While much progress has been made in bringing some engineering discipline to software development and production processes, the challenge remains daunting.

THE SOFTWARE DILEMMA

Software creation and production remain largely an art. Software developer training has yet to be codified and its certification is nonexistent. Moreover, software projects typically incur some of the worst cost and schedule overruns in the private or public sectors. For example, a milestone product like Windows 95 was released more than 18 months late and possibly more than 25% over budget. The development, publishing, and marketing budget for this product has been estimated at $1.25 billion.

Software development projects have four characteristic problems. These have existed for more than 30 years, yet still have no clear-cut solutions:

- *Budget and schedule overruns.* Software projects frequently exceed their schedules and budgets.

- *Low quality.* The quality of the software products when released is relatively low compared to other complex systems.
- *Costly maintenance.* Maintenance costs a disproportionate amount over the life span of the software. Typically, maintenance of major capital investments such as machinery and real estate is 10% of the original investment over a 10-year period. Software maintenance, on the other hand, doubles the original development costs within three years, making it unique among human artifacts.
- *Low reusability.* Typically, only a small percentage of released software products is reusable. Therefore, future developments are more likely to exceed their schedules and budgets.

History of Software Engineering

In the mid-1960s, maintenance of medium to large software systems generated approximately 75% of the total cost of the system. This phenomenon led to considerable industry research, which, in turn, led to Software Engineering. In simple terms, this discipline stated that software system products had to be planned, designed, constructed, and released according to engineering principles. Even then, controlling and managing schedules and costs of software projects were troublesome.

Ten years of extensive development of early structured techniques and construction tools, and several systems engineering developments, such as process and data modeling, improved the picture slightly. Some reports from the 1970s indicate that maintenance costs dropped to approximately 60% of the total life-span cost. But problems with cost and schedule control remained. The U.S. Department of Defense (DOD) reached the startling conclusion that the programming languages used to construct military software included more than several hundred dialects of more than 50 programming languages. This proliferation was the major contributor to the low reusability of systems, high maintenance costs, and low quality of system products. In the late 1970s, the DOD estimated that maintenance costs had again risen to approximately 75% of the system life-span cost. It also estimated that if that pace continued, the entire DOD budget would go to maintaining software by 2010.

There were multiple software breakthroughs in the 1980s — the glorious period of the growth of small and distributed systems. This decade also witnessed development of advanced structured methods and modeling and CASE tools, and widespread deployment and use of languages such as Ada and C. This work culminated in the object-oriented era of system engineering and construction tools at the end of the decade. The concepts of standards and process maturity also gained force during this period.

Real-World Effects of the Software Dilemma

The software dilemma results from the complex nature of software systems. "Software entities are more complex for their size than perhaps any other human construct, because no two parts are alike." Furthermore, the "complexity of software is an essential one, not an accidental one."[3] Changing requirements, rapidly evolving technologies, changing business environments, and the demands for more integration of processes and functions are also important contributing factors.

The software dilemma has caused significant business failures. The 1990s started with numerous development challenges. Measurements of numerous actual projects revealed that:

- Medium projects, classified as 1280 function points in size, have target completion spans of 18 months. These projects actually finish in 32 months and have a cancellation probability of 30%.[4]
- Large projects (10,240 function points) usually slip from 30 months scheduled time to 60 months. The cancellation probability of large projects is approximately 50% — with a total loss of project investments.[5]

The case-study literature of software failures is extensive; we cite one brief example here. On January 5, 1990, AT&T's massive long-distance network, the backbone of U.S. telecommunications, experienced a total shutdown that took more than 100 phone company personnel several hours to identify and fix. This calamity cost AT&T approximately $100 million. Estimates for what it cost the whole business community run as high as $10 billion. As the *Washington Post* reported, "The problem with AT&T's software turned out to be a mistake made in just one line of a 2 million-line program used to route calls ... The flawed line, or software 'bug,' in the AT&T program sent the call-processing mechanism to an incorrect place in the code, where the next instruction it encountered made no sense, thus disabling the equipment."

This is not an isolated instance, and it highlights the new issues facing IS managers. As software systems become more complex, they repeat the mistakes of the major systems that preceded them. Thus, AT&T's large system failure serves as a prototype for the present-day difficulties of IS organizations. As more organizations push to automate the production and delivery of their products and services, more IS organizations will find themselves within the realm of this type of large system failure.

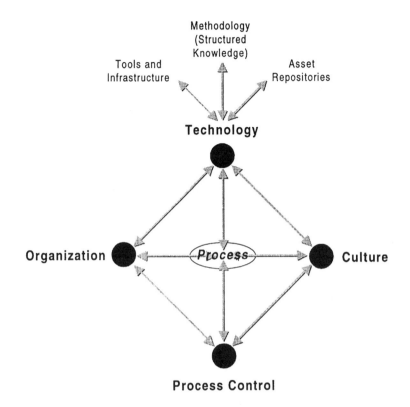

Exhibit 48.2. The Diamond of Change

To create value-added business change with software, addressing the dimension of software technology itself is important, but not sufficient. The evolution of stable, low-risk, and measurable development processes is as important as software technology itself to the production of high-quality software products and the overall success of the organization that uses such products. The next section reviews issues related to process and organization in the development of a software technology capacity.

PROCESS, ORGANIZATION, AND CULTURE

Exhibit 48.2, the diamond of change, is familiar to professionals who work on business reengineering. It represents the interrelated dimensions of change in an organization. Process is central to producing anything. It links organizational structure, technology, culture, and process control. As a result, a process change necessitates a change in the other dimensions, and change in the other dimensions necessitates process reengineering.

The diamond of change highlights new areas of concern for IS managers because current IS management paradigms do not address the dynamics revealed by the diamond. For example, current paradigms assume that managers have stable technology to develop applications. But, as described above, the rate of change in software development and related technologies means that IS managers face increasingly ambiguous technology choices. This, in turn, means that IS managers must make increasingly difficult decisions in the related dimensions of process, organization, and culture if they are to make their IS organizations responsive to the needs of the business.

IS managers must now focus on managing the other dimensions of the organization represented by the diamond: process control, organization, and culture.

- *Process control.* Change itself keeps changing. It is becoming increasingly complex, as is change management. Today, business processes change with almost every project.
- *Organization.* Organizational structure has also entered a state of constant change. In the previous business environment, rank, position, and role were linked. Bosses typically rose through the ranks and knew the content of the work they were managing. Today's project managers may not know the specifics of the work they manage and must draw on a different set of management skills.
- *Culture.* Traditional organizational theory assumes the organization has a definable culture. But because technology and related processes are in a constant state of flux, organizational culture is changing as well. The changes in technology mean that the ways people work together change continuously, often weekly.

Why should IS managers acknowledge and manage these issues? If they do not, their organizations will perish because they will not be able to respond to the needs of the business. Application development and maintenance must deliver the goods in months, not years; and some software must be replaced every 6 months.

And, even if the IS organization invests in technology or processes, the investments will not succeed unless the other dimensions are addressed as well. IS managers must manage all the dimensions of the diamond and create a dynamic balance between them. For example, investments in technology and process must be accompanied by management of the resulting changes in the culture.

IS organizations that are not managed this way will not survive. They will produce unstable systems that lack adequate functionality and that will not allow the business to stay competitive. To elaborate on the magnitude of these changes and to explore their impact on software technology, the meaning of the different dimensions of the diamond of change will be discussed.

The Learning Organization

Organization in the diamond of change refers to an organized structure of people and skills focused on achieving a mission or task. Organization may be defined as skilled people organized in a particular framework. Culture is the dimension that binds people together within the organization. It includes the habits, values, constraints, inhibitions, aspirations, dreams, and motivations that drive people to do what needs or must be done. What needs to be done is often different from what must be done. The tension that results from this difference is an important change engine in the organization.

An organization is most dynamic when:

- Members are innovative lateral thinkers. Edward de Bono's lateral thinking assumes that "thinking is a skill that can be improved by training, by practice, and through learning how to do better."[6]
- It has institutionalized knowledge acquisition and learning.
- Its structure and the culture support the difficult process of reflecting lessons learned into the organizational process, the habits of its members, and the thinking and expectation of its management.[6]

In short, a learning organization continues to learn, absorbs process improvement knowledge aggressively, and constantly seeks ways to perfect its techniques and products.

Process control represents management principles, guidelines, incentives, and behavior. Management refers both to organizational management and project management. Managers must be able to handle people, resources, and time. Effective management means delivering results on time, within budget, and at the highest possible level of quality. Effective managers have more than basic skills. They feature leadership, vision, a sense of mission, the ability to manage risk, and flexibility to respond to circumstances that change constantly.

Process refers to the processes required to perform work and deliver anticipated results. A mature process is an amalgamation of many levels of processes, all of which have to be "steady state." The way an organization achieves results and delivers value has to be documented, respected, and followed. This common process must be supported by a means of managing and incorporating change in the process itself. The guidelines for change must be derived from feedback of results, measurements of performance and delivery, and lessons learned. Achieving this state of continu-

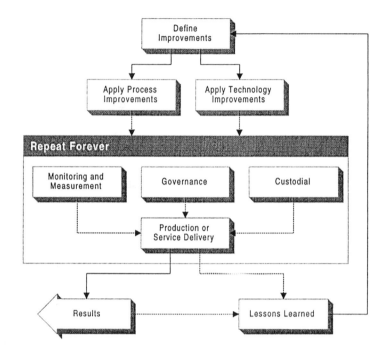

Exhibit 48.3. Production Process and Process Improvement

ous learning and process improvement is what is meant by balancing the dimensions of the diamond of change. Exhibit 48.3 is a schematic of mature business and improvement processes. When processes — shown as rectangles in Exhibit 48.3 — are stable, repeatable, and documented, a process is mature.

With regard to technology, one must assume that a learning organization, with a mature process and effective management, must possess proven technologies to deliver its results.

What do process, organization, and culture have to do with managing the IS organization? The short answer is: everything. This is the key to developing or acquiring software solutions that improve the organization's bottom line. In today's business environment, where the demands for software solutions are equaled only by the risks of undertaking such solutions, the management of process, organization, and culture in the IS organization is crucial to the overall success of the organization.

Industry Guidelines. Successfully managing the IS organization depends less on the transfer of technological implements than on the adoption of the characteristics of a learning organization; specifically, a mature process, a culture supportive of continuous change, and effective management. In other words, managing the IS organization involves more than buying packages, programming languages, or hardware. It involves implementing and following the concepts of the learning organization.

The U.S. Air Force, in collaboration with Carnegie-Mellon University of Pittsburgh, developed a model that can help organizations measure maturity in their software development processes, project management, and organization capability. The model, known as the Software Engineering Institute's Capability Maturity Model (SEI-CMM), was unveiled in 1991.

While the SEI-CMM does not explicitly promote the concepts of the learning organization, it overlaps considerably with these concepts. The model provides five maturity levels and several key practice areas within each maturity level. These practice areas can be assessed within an organization or a project. The underlying thesis of the model is that the higher the maturity level of the software process, the lower the risk of failure, which is defined as failure of the system product to meet costs, meet schedules, and produce high-quality system products. All organizations are assumed to be compliant with level 1. An organization is mature from the SEI perspective when it is able to document process knowledge and use that knowledge consistently, which is also a key characteristic of the learning organization.

A similar effort in the international and commercial arena was launched by the International Organization for Standardization when it extended the ISO 9000 standards to cover software production. Quality standards and process standards were proposed, again to help lower the risks of failure and improve product quality.

Today, in the U.S., there is a strong move to make software builders and contractors compliant with SEI-CMM and ISO 9000. The U.S. Air Force has mandated that all its software developers reach level 3 of the SEI-CMM by 1998. NASA is considering a similar policy. As of September 1994, 261 organizations had been assessed; 75% of these organizations were stuck in level 1, while 24% were at levels 2 or 3. Only two projects — not organizations — earned the highest rating of level 5.

In summary, compliance with the SEI model and ISO makes it much more likely that the organization is a learning organization and promotes higher levels of system engineering practice maturity.

EVOLUTION OF SYSTEMS ENGINEERING

Systems engineering comprises disciplined methods and techniques that pertain to the structure of system components, the functionality of each component, and the interaction between components. Systems engineering usually includes requirements engineering, also known as analysis; system architecture with layering and services; distribution schema; software design; work-flow design; and the logical design of data bases. Software engineering includes software metrics, modeling, methods, and techniques associated with the conception and detailing of the system before it is constructed. Prototyping, though it is dependent on tools, is included in the software engineering domain as well.

A methodology is a structured, integrated approach to the engineering of software and of the business. The methodology usually provides a coherent definition of components, activities, tasks, steps, work products, tips, techniques, and guidelines for achieving the development of software. The kernel of a methodology is a thought discipline referred to as systems engineering.

Classifications of systems engineering vary in the literature. A common approach is to use milestone technologies as the departure point for the evolution of the technology. A different classification scheme to present the evolution of systems technology is used here. This classification scheme focuses more on the set of ideas, practices, and techniques that prevailed in each school of thought. The classification is depicted in Exhibit 48.4 and described in the paragraphs that follow.

Artisan

The artisan approach prevailed in software development from the beginning of software engineering until the late 1960s. This school used limited modeling tools. Text was the only means of describing requirements or design aspects. Often, the process for software development processes was composed of a limited planning stage and then a long construction, or coding, stage. The construction stage incorporated the creation of the program codes as well as the creation of the architecture, design, and testing activities. Systems were created with limited or no documentation. Metrics to measure performance or create estimates were rarely used.

Early Structured

With the early structured school, software system practice took a giant step toward creating the foundations of an engineering discipline. Semantically richer models were introduced. This stage started in the middle 1960s and lasted until the end of the 1970s. In this stage, text remained the

EXHIBIT 48.4 Schema of the Evolution of Software Engineering Methods

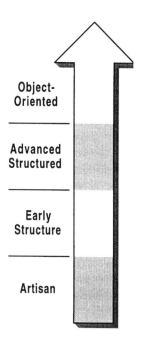

strongest descriptive tool. However, practitioners recognized that system documentation had to be created before the coding of the system. During this stage, analysis was also recognized as a phase within the development life cycle. Analysis techniques, however, were limited. This stage also distinguished between the design of the system and the design of the code. System architecture was not recognized as a concept, except toward the end of this stage when real-time system practice began to use the concept of system architecture, which was borrowed from hardware practices. Metrics were formal but limited. They were mostly a function of lines of code.

Advanced Structured

Numerous systems concepts were tested and developed from 1975 through the 1980s. The experience with early structured methods yielded a wealth of knowledge about systems engineering. The portfolio of system modeling techniques was greatly expanded. The set of modeling techniques now included event modeling, information modeling, data modeling, and process. Architecture was recognized as an important stage in the development of software systems. Analysis was enhanced with formal integrated essential models that provided views of the systems from several perspectives. Design was formally delineated from construction. The construction concept was expanded beyond coding to coding and assembly of components. Documentation became a design vehicle and documented the system. Metrics were formally recognized and some techniques were associated with metrics, such as the function point technique.

Object-Oriented

Object-oriented concepts existed in experimental programming languages since the early 1970s. These concepts matured into formal programming languages in the early 1980s. Some of the concepts were developed in engineering and special application systems. Interest grew by the mid-1980s with the expansion of graphical user interfaces and other developments in programming environments. By the late 1980s, a systems engineering approach to object orientation began to take shape.

Object-oriented methods involved the expansion of the modeling tool sets. Scenario building and verification promoted further development. Object-oriented concepts such as inheritance, assembly, and polymorphism encouraged the development of reusable component libraries. Object libraries, object containers of other objects, and object data bases now hold promise that an effective approach for reusable components might finally be at hand.

It is difficult to acquire systems engineering thinking and practice. They require continuous training and continuous learning from the lessons of both failed and successful projects. The essence of this process is a learning organization. Practitioners cannot acquire systems engineering practice by completing training and doing a few projects. There must be a systematic learning process that changes systems engineering thinking and improves the process.

CONCLUSION

This chapter uses the applications development environment within the IS organization to illustrate general changes currently facing IS managers. The main thesis is that these changes demand a radical shift in the IS organization's management paradigm. This shift entails moving from a paradigm focused on management of resources, skills, and technical implements in a hierarchical structure, to a paradigm that promotes a flat organization of knowledge workers who continuously learn and adapt new methods, technologies, and disciplines. This new paradigm not only fosters a state of perpetual learning in the organization, but also strong management ownership of and involvement in the operation and management processes. This paradigm shift must be accompanied by the use of process measures to enhance systems engineering practice and enable people to master increasingly complex systems and services.

IS managers should no longer consider technological solutions in isolation; the realities of the technology and the marketplace demand that such solutions be implemented as part of a larger process of rethinking and improving process, organization, and culture.

Notes

1. Gibbs, W. Wayt (1994). "Software's Chronic Crises." In *Scientific American*, September 1994, p. 90.
2. Brandt, Richard, Evan I. Schwartz, and Neil Gross (1991). "Can the United States Stay Ahead in Software?: America Still Dominates the Market, but Foreign Rivals Threaten." *Business Week*, 3202:98.
3. Brooks, Fredrick P. Jr. (1995). *The Mythical Man-Month: Essays on Software Engineering.* Reading, MA: Addison-Wesley. pp. 182.
4. Gibbs, W. Wayt (1994). "Software's Chronic Crises." *Scientific American*, September 1994, pp. 86–95.
5. Ibid.
6. de Bono, Edward (1970). *Lateral Thinking: Creativity Step-by-Step.* New York, NY: Harper and Row.
7. P. Drucker, (1993). *Post Capitalist Society*, 1st ed. New York: Harper Collins.

Chapter 49
Analyses of Software Quality and Auditing
David C. Chou
Amy Y. Chou

SOFTWARE QUALITY is a set of explicit and implicit requirements, standards, and characteristics that meets software users' needs and satisfaction. The utmost goal of producing quality software is to ensure that customers are satisfied with their deliverables. Customers' satisfaction will guarantee continued contracts to software shops. Software quality can be identified through software testing. Software testing is the process of ensuring that the software being tested actually meets its original specifications. The results of the tests provide a measure of the software product's quality. Therefore, software quality is defined as the "degree of compliance to specifications."

Software quality is one of the important ingredients of competitive advantages in the software industry. Software users ask for the commitment of software development companies to providing quality software. Because only zero-defect products can survive in today's competitive software market, software industries manage their software quality process to meet users' needs.

Delivering high-quality software is also paramount in internal software shops that design, generate, implement, and maintain their own software products. Here customer satisfaction relies on the following software attributes: quality (i.e., accommodating requirements specified by the customer), support (i.e., providing software services and assistance whenever needed), reliability (i.e., delivery of defect-free software), timeliness (i.e., delivery of software on schedule and on time), and cost (i.e., providing an affordable price to the customer).

The software quality assurance (SQA) process guides IS shops in delivering the high quality software customers demand. The SQA process is a technique of achieving software quality through the software engineering process. SQA activities include adopting analysis, design, coding, and testing methods and tools; applying formal technical reviews during each software engineering step; using a multitiered testing strategy; controlling software documentation and the changes made to it; implementing a procedure to ensure compliance with software development standards; and utilizing measurement and reporting mechanisms.

Two software process control methods are widely used in IS shops. They are total quality management (TQM) and the Capability Maturity Model (CMM). The International Standards Organization (ISO) has initiated another important SQA process for the European community — ISO 9000. The quality standards of ISO 9000 and its certification process ensure the quality conformance of an IS shop's product. An auditing process is needed for all three SQA methods to determine whether or not the elements in the quality system conform with stated quality objectives.

The ISO 9000 series is universally applicable to any total quality system, and the TQM or CMM program can be integrated into the ISO 9000 certification process. This chapter discusses how the software quality process, methodologies, and auditing process ensure software quality in the IS shop and reviews a framework and tool for implementing the ISO 9000 auditing process.

SQA PROCESSES AND METHODS

Software quality assurance (SQA) is based on three important premises:

- Software requirements are the foundation from which quality is measured.
- Specified standards define a set of development criteria that guide the manner in which software is engineered.
- There is a set of implicit requirements that often goes unmentioned.

The main goal of producing a quality product is to ensure that customers are satisfied with the product delivered. Although building a software product to meet customer requirements is not a difficult job, accommodating changes in the requirements and replying to problems in a timely manner are challenging tasks. Customers might want to add functionality or make other changes to reflect a changing business environment. These explicit and implicit requirements create uncertainty for the SQA process.

SQA Activities

SQA activities include the following seven tasks:

- Applications of technical methods.
- Conducting of formal technical reviews.
- Software testing.
- Enforcement of standards.

- Control of change.
- Measurement.
- Record keeping and recording.

SQA begins with a set of technical methods and tools that help the systems analyst and designer build high-quality software. The quality assessment process is implemented through a formal technical review procedure. The formal technical review is a meeting conducted by technical staff to uncover quality problems. Software testing includes a series of test case design methods that help ensure effective error detection. However, testing is not as effective as it should be for all classes of errors.

If formal standards do exist, an SQA activity must be conducted to ensure that they are being followed. Standards may be dictated by customers or mandated by regulation, although sometimes they are self-imposed by IS shops.

The change control process, a part of software configuration management, contributes directly to software quality by formalizing requests for change, evaluating the nature of change, and controlling the impact of change.

Measurement is an integral part of SQA. Various software metrics on technical and managerial measures must be collected for analytical purposes. Record keeping and reporting provide the vehicle for the collection and dissemination of software quality information.

Identifying Defects and Software Testing

Software testing is the process of ensuring that the software being tested actually meets its original specifications. The results of the tests provide a measure of the product's quality. Quality has been defined as the "degree of compliance to specifications." Software testing is also a process of identifying potential defects inherent in the software product.

The best way to identify software defects is through the use of walkthroughs, reviews and inspections. The most important quantifiable measure of goodness is the defect-discovery rate. Most SQA activities, including technical review, testing, standards enforcement, change control, measurement, and record keeping and reporting, are fulfilled through the three software testing methods of walkthroughs, reviews, and inspections.

Walkthroughs. Walkthroughs allow the developers, or authors, of a specific system to present their design in front of the design team and other reviewers. This process helps the other members of the team know more about the project. The reviewers' job is to spot problems or errors in the product under review.

Reviews. Two kinds of reviews are conducted: management reviews and technical reviews. Management reviews provide a means for managers to track the development progress, identify problems, recommend solutions, and ensure proper allocation of resources. These reviews establish a forum between the project team and management. Technical reviews are used to examine the project's development process and planning documentation. This includes the development plan, SQA plan, verification and test plans, and configuration management plans.

Inspections. Software inspection is a method of static testing to verify that software meets its requirements, including external product requirement and internal development requirements, and their standards. The benefits of software inspection include defect reduction, defect prevention, and cost improvement. In contrast to inspections, walkthroughs do not usually follow a process that is repeatable nor collects data, and hence the process cannot reasonably be studied and improved. The defect-detection efficiencies of walkthroughs are much lower than those of inspections.

The inspection process comprises the following six operation stages:

- *Planning.* The planning stage ensures that materials to be inspected meet inspection entry criteria and the availability of the right participants and suitable meeting places and times.
- *Overview.* Group training is conducted during this stage, and assignments are made to participants involved in the inspection process.
- *Preparation.* During the preparation stage, participants learn the material and prepare to fulfill their assigned roles.
- *Inspection.* The inspection stage comprises the defects-finding process.
- *Rework.* During the rework stage, the author reworks all defects.
- *Follow-up.* In this stage, the inspection moderator or the entire inspection team verifies all fixes made by the author. The ideal result is that no secondary defects are introduced.

The inspection process aims to identify defects in the software development process. Inspections are an element of a formal process where an intermediate product — such as a requirements document, design document, code element — is examined for defects by the producer's peers. The inspections should ensure conformance with applicable specifications and standards, identify logical defects, and identify problems with the internal and external interfaces.

TQM AND CMM

Two software process control methodologies are widely used in IS shops: total quality management and the Capability Maturity Model. The SEI's Software Maturity Framework (SMF) produced the Capability Maturity Model in 1991, which is used to guide the project management control and software quality control processes. Neither methodology provides specific implementation tools.

The functions, strengths, and weaknesses of TQM and CMM are discussed in the following sections.

THE TQM MODEL

TQM has three main components: quality planning, problem solving, and process management. The TQM process includes the following phases:

- *Quality planning.* During this phase, IS personnel incorporate the voice of the customer and the voice of the business in establishing IS quality objectives. These objectives drive an implementation plan for quality improvement activities.
- *Problem solving.* Based on the objectives, staff is trained in process management and the problem-solving process, initiating quality teams. If the process is measured and defined, a quality improvement team is initiated to improve the process. If the process is poorly defined or understood, process management is used to define and measure the process. Here benchmarking helps establish proven processes for software. As the team moves through the problem-solving process, the quality council reviews its progress and assists it in remaining on track.
- *Process Management.* Once the team has a proven solution to a quality problem, team members need to develop a process management system to standardize it. Then the quality council and IS management act to multiply the benefits by replicating the improved process throughout the IS shop. All three activities fit together in a system of continuous improvement.

SEI CAPABILITY MATURITY MODEL

The five levels in SEI's CMM for managing the software process are similar to the process maturity levels of SMF. The five levels are

- *Initial.* In the initial level, until the process is under statistical control, orderly progress in process improvement is not possible. Although there are many degrees of statistical control, the first step is to roughly predict schedules and costs.
- *Repeatable.* In the repeatable level, the organization has achieved a stable process with a repeatable level of statistical control by initiating rigorous project management commitments, costs, schedules, and changes.

- *Defined.* Here, the organization has defined the process as a basis for consistent implementation and better understanding. At this point, advanced technology can be introduced.
- *Managed.* Organizations at the managed level have initiated comprehensive process measurements and analysis. This is when the most significant quality improvements begin.
- *Optimizing.* At the optimizing level, the organization has a foundation for continuing improvement and process optimization.

The five levels were selected for the following reasons:

- They represent historical phases of evolutionary improvement.
- They provide achievable improvement steps in a reasonable sequence.
- They suggest interim improvement goals and progress measures.
- They provide immediate improvement priorities once an organization's status in this framework is known.

Key Process Areas of CMM Levels

Each CMM level except for the first includes key process areas (KPAs) on which organizations must concentrate in order to raise their software processes to that level. KPAs also serve as the threshold for achieving certain maturity levels.

The required KPAs for levels two through five are as follows:

- Level 2:
  — Software configuration management.
  — Software quality assurance.
  — Software subcontract management.
  — Software project tracking and oversight.
  — Software project planning.
  — Requirements management.
- Level 3:
  — Peer reviews.
  — Intergroup coordination.
  — Software project engineering.
  — Integrated-software management.
  — Training program.
  — Organization process definition.
  — Organization process focus.
- Level 4:
  — Software quality management.
  — Quantitative process management.

- Level 5:
—Process-change management.
—Technology-change management.
—Defect prevention.

Each KPA is subdivided into goals, commitment to perform, ability to perform, activities performed, measurement and analysis, and verification of implementation. Each area except goals is further defined by specific statements applicable to the area that are used to judge whether or not the specific software project meets the expressed criteria. For statements to be considered met, hard evidence demonstrating achievement of statement intent must be provided. An evaluation team requires hard evidence when judging the CMM level of a company.

The following sections discuss the two reviews conducted in the CMM process: the software process assessment and the software capability evaluation.

The Software Process Assessment

A software process assessment is launched by an IS shop to help improve its software development practices. This assessment is generally conducted by six to eight of the organization's senior software development professionals and by one or two coaches from the SEI or from an SEI-licensed assessment vendor. The assessment is conducted in six phases:

- *Selection phase.* During the selection phase, the organization is identified as an assessment candidate, and the qualified assessing organization conducts an executive-level briefing.
- *Commitment phase.* This phase encompasses the organizations' commitment to the full assessment process as evidenced by the signing of an assessment agreement by a senior executive.
- *Preparation phase.* In the preparation phase, the organization's assessment team receives training, and the on-site assessment process is fully planned. All assessment participants are identified and briefed, and the maturity questionnaire is completed.
- *Assessment phase.* The on-site assessment is conducted in about one week. Then the assessment team meets to formulate preliminary recommendations.
- *Report phase.* In the report phase, the entire assessment team helps prepare the final report and presents it to assessment participants and senior management. The report includes team findings and recommendations for actions.
- *Assessment follow-up phase.* During this phase, the assessed organization's team, with guidance from the assessment organization, formulates an action plan. After approximately 18 months, the organization

should conduct a reassessment to review progress and sustain the software process improvement cycle.

The Software Capability Evaluation

After the software process assessment, an organization establishes the CMM level it has reached. The organization then pursues a software capability evaluation (SCE), which is typically conducted by an outside organization such as the government or a software contractor.

Organizations that are candidates for an SCE first complete a maturity questionnaire. An evaluation team visits the organization and uses the maturity questionnaire to help select representative practices for a detailed examination.

This examination consists of interviewing the organization's personnel and reviewing the organization's software development-related documentation. It focuses on three important premises:

- The proposed processes will meet the acquisition needs.
- The organization will actually install the proposed processes.
- The organization will effectively implement the proposed processes.

The SCE is a judgmental process, and it is mandatory that all organizations for a single project be evaluated consistently. The SEI believes that the SCE method provides the necessary consistent criteria and method.

COMPARISON OF TQM AND CMM

TQM and CMM are the two important software quality methodologies used in IS shops both in the private and public sectors. However, CMM has been adopted by the U.S. government, especially in the Department of Defense (DOD), to evaluate contractors' capability maturity and as a qualification indicator for receiving and continuing DOD contracts.

Similarities

The process life cycles of TQM and CMM include all aspects of project planning, analysis, design, and development. For example, level 2 of CMM (i.e., repeatable) allows software projects to be repeatedly delivered on schedule with reasonable quality. At level 3 (i.e., defined), the software process is defined, trained, and followed by software engineers.

TQM's process management mechanism can be used at the repeatable level to define software processes. Once these processes are defined, IS shops can move to the next level (i.e., managed), where they begin to measure and analyze the process and its products. In addition, TQM's process management can help identify the measurements necessary to determine the stability and capability of the software process.

At the highest level, the optimizing level, all software engineers apply project management tools and principles of TQM to improve the software process. TQM's problem-solving mechanism can be used at all levels of CMM to identify and reduce the causes of customer dissatisfaction. Also, TQM's quality- planning mechanism links these project management tools and processes together to achieve breakthrough improvements in productivity and quality.

Dissimilarities

TQM's principles may affect all of an organization's projects, because TQM is a comprehensive mechanism for an organization's overall quality management. CMM, however, affects only software development projects. For that reason, CMM ignores the cultural dimension of organizational processes.

Weaknesses

Both the TQM and CMM approaches to software quality control are subject to failure from several inherent weaknesses:

- Lack of expertise in a particular application domain.
- Poorly implemented statistical process control.
- Confusion of a process's infrastructure and activity dimensions.
- Lack of recommended tools, methods, or software technologies.
- Lack of an automated implementation tool, particularly one supported by artificial intelligence (AI).

To remedy the flaws inherent in both methodologies and improve the effectiveness and efficiency of the quality control process, a competent, AI-enhanced CASE (computer-aided software engineering) auditing tool should be developed.

THE ISO 9000 SERIES AND ITS CERTIFICATION

The ISO 9000 series is a set of quality assurance standards. The first standard in the series, ISO 9000, is a guide to the other four standards. ISO 9001 is a standard for quality assurance in the design/development, production, installation and servicing areas. It applies to companies that design as well as manufacture products. The ISO 9002 standard applies to quality assurance in the prevention, detection, and correction of problems during production and installation. ISO 9003 is a standard for quality assurance in final inspection and testing. It applies mainly to manufactured products. ISO 9004 is technically not a standard because it contains guidelines on quality management and quality system elements.

ISO 9001, 9002, and 9003 must be certified through an external audit. ISO certification means only that a company has a system in place that enables it to meet the quality standards it established for itself. Because ISO 9000 does not specify quality criteria, each certified company sets its own quality standards. As long as companies conform to their own quality criteria, they retain ISO registration. ISO certification is not given to products or companies; it applies only to individual plant sites. It therefore does not guarantee that a company produces quality products. Rather, it certifies that a system of policies and procedures is in place to make the manufacture of quality products possible.

The ISO 9000 series is a uniform, consistent set of procedures, elements, and requirements for quality assurance that are universally applicable to any total quality system. A TQM or CMM program can be integrated into the ISO 9000 certification process; successful program can guarantee a successful ISO 9000 certification.

U.S. companies obtain ISO 9000 certification for four reasons:

- The European community legally requires suppliers of certain regulated products to have ISO 9000 certification. This requirement has a significant impact on American companies doing business overseas.
- ISO 9000 certification enables companies to compete for business from individual customers (both foreign and domestic) that contractually require their suppliers to be certified. The North Atlantic Treaty Organization and the U.S. Department of Defense also require suppliers to obtain ISO 9000 certification.
- Certification enables companies to differentiate themselves from noncertified competitors.
- Most importantly, many managers insist that the process of creating, documenting and establishing the controls for a quality system is a catalyst for improving quality.

THE AUDITING PROCESS

One way of assessing the quality control process is through auditing. Audits should be carried out to determine that the various elements within a quality system meet stated quality objectives.

A quality audit is defined by ISO as a "systematic and independent examination to determine whether quality activities and related results comply with planned arrangements and whether these arrangements are implemented effectively and are suitable to achieve objectives."

Audits are generally initiated for one or more of the following reasons:

- To initially evaluate a potential supplier.
- To verify that an organization's own quality system continues to meet specified requirements and is being implemented.

- To verify that the quality system of a supplier in a contractual relationship continues to meet specified requirements and is being implemented.
- To evaluate an organization's own quality system against a quality system standard.

An auditing process is thus initiated for internal or external purposes. It contrasts with other SQA methods, such as walkthroughs, reviews, and inspections, which are initiated purely for internal quality management purposes.

Auditors are responsible for many duties, including

- Complying with the applicable audit requirements.
- Communicating and clarifying audit requirements.
- Planning and carrying out assigned responsibilities effectively and efficiently.
- Documenting the observations.
- Reporting the audit results.
- Verifying the effectiveness of corrective actions taken as a result of the audit.
- Retaining and safeguarding documents pertaining to the audit: submitting such documents as required, ensuring documents remain confidential, and treating privileged information with discretion.
- Cooperating with and supporting the lead auditor.

The audit requirements and standards are set by internal and external sources. Most internal requirements and standards focus on maintaining product quality and meeting customer needs. The external sources of quality standards are usually identified by quality agencies, such as the International Standards Organization (ISO), American Society of Quality Control (ASQC), and Institute of Electric and Electronic Engineering (IEEE), and by such government agencies as the Food and Drug Administration (FDA), Federal Aviation Administration (FAA), Department of Energy (DOE), Department of Defense (DOD), and Environmental Protection Agency (EPA).

FRAMEWORK FOR SOFTWARE QUALITY AUDITING

Preparation

A software company begins its certification process by selecting the most appropriate ISO 9000 standard (i.e., ISO 9000, ISO 9001, ISO 9002, ISO 9003 and ISO 9004). After determining which ISO standard applies to its operations, the company seeks an ISO guidebook, such as the *ISO 9000 Handbook* or *ISO 9000: Preparing for Registration*, for preparing the process. These books provide guidance on documenting the work performed at every function affecting quality. They also identify the installing mechanisms to ensure that employees follow through on the documented procedures.

These books are available from the American National Standards Institute (ANSI).

A company seeking an ISO 9000 certification should form an internal team to identify its own software quality assurance criteria, standards, and procedures to implement its quality system, such as TQM or CMM. The entire company should follow the SQA methodology to analyze, design, and develop software. All software production should be based on the quality system and all related activities should be documented.

A qualified external audit registrar is invited to inspect the company's quality system (for information on registrars accredited in the U.S., contact the Registrar Accreditation Board, http://www.rabnet.com). This auditor conducts the auditing process and checks the actual practices and records to ensure that they are in compliance with the ISO quality system. If the results are appropriate, a compliance certificate is awarded. If any nonconformances are found during an audit, they must be corrected before certification can proceed. This certificate can be renewed every three to four years.

Stages of the Process

Auditing is divided into four stages: (1) preparation, (2) performance, (3) reporting, and (4) closure. The preparation stage starts from the decision to conduct an audit and includes the activities of team selection and on-site information gathering. The performance stage begins with the on-site opening meeting. It includes information gathering and information analysis through interviews and examination of items and records. The reporting stage encompasses translation of the audit team's conclusions into a tangible product. It includes the exit meeting with managers and publication of the formal audit report. The closure stage deals with the actions resulting from the report and the recording of the entire effort. For audits resulting in the confirmation of some weakness, the closure stage includes tracking and evaluating the follow-up actions taken to fix the problem and prevent its recurrence.

Corporate executives should review the effectiveness of the certification process. The results of certification guide them in setting up strategies for improving software quality and productivity.

A TOOL FOR THE AUDITING PROCESS

A CASE tool is a software package used to automate the system analysis and design process. An integrated-CASE (I-CASE) tool integrates all aspects of software development activity, including project management activities. It helps automate system analysis, design, and development. Its code generator generates usable programs for system implementation. Because the software quality assurance process requires computation of the metrics for software validation and verification, an AI-based CASE tool is well suited to making the software quality and auditing processes more efficient.

Organizations use the I-CASE tool for software development process. The software quality control can be an integral part of software development process by adding the software auditing capability into the I-CASE tool. This integrated CASE tool meets the following objectives:

- Monitoring SQA standards and procedures.
- Housing TQM or CMM operational standards in its repository for the auditing process.
- Generating assessment process harmony.
- Substituting paper documents with electronic data.
- Automating the generation of audit reports.
- Tracking weakness found during auditing.
- Automating the auditing process.

The main challenge to design such a tool is its knowledge base. This knowledge base stores various facts and rules for its information engineering processes, business goals, business strategies, operational models, programming structures and codes, design specifications and requirements for the systems, standards, criteria, procedures, and project management information for its basic process.

To include the capability of implementing the CMM methodology, the knowledge base of an AI-enhanced CASE tool must contain key process areas (KPAs) separated by maturity levels. If the company chooses the TQM method, the various elements for the Plan-Do-Check-Act (P-D-C-A) cycle must be included in the knowledge base.

The measurements and metrics collected from software process assessments and software capability evaluations are also stored in the knowledge base for future usage. Any weakness found during the auditing process is recorded for correction purposes.

CONCLUSION

Software quality assurance is a technique of achieving software quality through the software engineering process. The SQA process guides the IS shop in delivering the high-quality software demanded by customers. It is one of the important ingredients for gaining competitive advantage in the software industry. Total quality management and the capability maturity model are the two software process control methodologies used in the software industry. Neither provides specific implementation tools.

Software quality auditing is the process of determining whether or not the various elements within a quality system meet stated quality objectives. It is one way of assessing the quality control process in the IS shop. The ISO 9000 series is a uniform, consistent set of procedures, elements, and requirements for quality assurance that can be applied universally to any total quality system. Successful integration of the TQM or CMM methodology into the ISO 9000 process guarantees a successful ISO 9000 certification that enhances the competitive advantage of U.S. companies doing business in the international software market.

An AI-enhanced CASE tool automates software analysis, design, and coding and the performance of the SQA and auditing processes. It stores various data in its repository, such as business goals, business strategies, operational models, programming structures and codes, design specifications and requirement for the system, SQA criteria and methodologies (such as TQM and CMM), and auditing criteria and procedures for ISO 9000 certification. As a comprehensive software quality and auditing tool, it further enhances the competitive capability of the IS shop.

Chapter 50
Software Testing Basics and Guidelines

Christine B. Tayntor

ONE OF THE FIRST RULES of journalism is that a good chapter starts with the five w's – who, what, where, when, and why — adding "how" and "details" to complete it. Although software testing may seem worlds apart from chapter writing, the same careful planning and the same w's apply. This chapter defines the five w's of software testing and outlines an approach for successful testing.

WHY IS TESTING IMPORTANT

It is the bane of any application developer's existence, normally relegated to the end of the software development process, a task that is considered at best a necessary evil. But testing, which is sometimes referred to as quality assurance, is arguably the most important step in the software development process.

Despite careful requirements definitions and customer sign-offs, despite meticulous coding or the use of reliable code generators, it is possible that the system an IS organization develops is not the one its customers expected. Misunderstandings occur; mistakes happen. The discrepancies may be minute; they may be major. With testing, they can be resolved before a system is placed in production.

Testing proves that the system works as it was intended to; it demonstrates that the developers have understood and met customers' requirements; it shows that real people can use the product in the real world.

In an ideal project, half the development time is allocated to testing. In real projects, however, scope creep and other delays frequently jeopardize the overall delivery date. To meet the original schedule, testing is shortened. No doubt about it, this is a mistake. The test schedule should not be compressed. The reason is simple: a poorly or inadequately tested product is all too often a product that should not have been released.

Consider the paradox that savvy IS managers avoid the first release of commercial software, knowing that many version 1.0 products are little more than beta code, yet they deliver similarly immature code to their own customers. Unfortunately, in a corporate environment, customers rarely have the ability to refuse their IS department's 1.0 releases.

It is an axiom of software development that customers may forget late delivery of a system, but they will never forget poor quality. That's why testing is essential. Because it is the step that — if done properly – ensures excellence, testing should not be short-changed.

Almost all IS departments recognize the need for testing of newly developed systems and build testing time into the project schedule. Not all, however, have the same attitude toward system modifications. Small changes may be deemed too insignificant to require extensive testing. The second axiom of software management is that even the simplest change, the infamous one line modification that is so obvious that it does not need to be tested, may not work. Without testing, IS is subjecting its customers to potential malfunctions and itself to the reputation of delivering inferior quality products.

WHEN SHOULD TESTING BE PERFORMED?

When should testing be performed? The answer is two-fold: whenever a change — any change — is made to the software, and whenever the operating environment is altered. Although IS departments normally accept the need for testing when the application has been modified, they may not recognize the need for testing under the second circumstance. But today's software, particularly event-driven applications that run in a client/server environment, are affected by more than their own program code. Their operation can also be affected by changes in the desktop and network operating systems.

WHO SHOULD PERFORM THE TESTING?

One of the most critical aspects to effective testing is selecting the correct staff to perform it. Successful testing involves three groups: customers, developers, and professional testers.

Customers are a key part of testing, because they provide a real-world perspective. They are also the only group which can certify that the system will accomplish its goals. Customers are the people who verify that their needs have been understood and met, and their contribution to the testing process should not be underestimated. Similarly, system developers play a critical role in testing; however, the majority of the testing should be done by a quality assurance (QA) group. These are professional testers who have a singular mission: to assure software quality by testing. For maximum effectiveness, QA should be a distinct organization, separate from the software developers.

Many IS organizations have not established a separate group to perform testing, because they believe that testing is the responsibility of the developers. In part, they are correct. Developers should be responsible for initial testing of their software. They should deliver no code to QA until they are sure that it works perfectly. That's their job.

Why, then, is there a need for QA? The answer is simple. Developers cannot guarantee complete, impartial testing. Developers test to prove that their work is correct, while Quality Assurance tests to break the system. The difference is fundamental. Consider the example of a date field. A developer testing this field will typically enter valid dates, including checking that February has 29 days in a leap year. He or she may even enter 13 in the month field to demonstrate that invalid months are rejected. A QA tester will perform the same tests but will also enter blanks, alphabetic, and special characters in each field. QA will ensure that the system supports not just years later than 1999, but will also enter years less than 1000 to determine how an operator error would affect the system.

Because the nature of their work is different, the skills required for QA differ from those expected of system developers. Characteristics of effective QA staff are shown in Exhibit 50.1.

A good QA member is	Because
Detail-oriented	An effective test tests each and every field.
Logical	Testing requires thinking the way the developer did, then trying to find loopholes in that logic.
Able to recognize patterns	Testing involves finding problems, determining whether they are isolated or related to others, then checking all potentially related areas for other occurrences of the same problem.
Tenacious and not easily bored	Effective testing involves repeating the same cases multiple times until the problem is resolved.
An effective communicator	Problems must be described in sufficient detail that developers can understand what needs to be corrected.
Destructive	Testing involves trying to break software, and an effective tester will enjoy the process.

Exhibit 50.1. Characteristics of QA Staff Members

WHAT IS SOFTWARE TESTING?

Having discussed who should test, when, and why, it is important to answer the question, what exactly is software testing? All testing has the same objective – to ensure good quality. However, under the general term of software testing, there are several categories. In each of these, the scope of work being performed varies. Further variations exist, depending on whether this is a new or substantially modified system or it is a change to an existing program.

New Development

Although many IS departments consider testing to be the final step before implementing a new system, it should be a multi-staged process that starts early in the development cycle. There are actually seven categories of testing in the new development testing suite, each with a different purpose, and as shown in Exhibit 50.2, with different groups having responsibility for successful completion. These categories are discussed in the sections that follow.

Category	Primary Responsibility	When in Development Cycle
New Development		
Usability	Customers, people who will be regular users of the system	As early in the process as possible; typically uses prototype of software.
Unit	Developers	Once software has been compiled.
System	Developers	Once unit testing has been completed.
Functionality	Quality assurance staff	Once software has been compiled and beta tested.
Acceptance	Customers, including those who were involved in defining requirements	Following functionality testing and correction of bugs.
Volume	Quality assurance staff	Following acceptance testing.
Disaster Recovery	Quality assurance staff	After implementation.
System Modifications		
Regression	Quality assurance staff	Whenever a change is made to either the software or the operating environment.

Exhibit 50.2. Testing Categories

Usability. The first testing that should be performed is usability testing. Its goal is to prove that real people can use the system to do their jobs. Frequently working with a prototype version of the software, customers attempt to complete their daily tasks. This is the stage of testing where customers validate the overall system design and determine whether or not details like the order of fields on a screen are correct.

Although many development teams provide customers with mock ups of screen layouts during the requirements definition phase, usability testing provides the first opportunity for hands-on use of the system. Primary responsibility belongs to the customers, but members of the development staff as well as quality assurance staff may participate in the testing. At a minimum, QA personnel should serve as observers, recording the customers' comments and observing which portions of the software provoke frowns or grins.

Since it is not uncommon to discover at this stage that new fields and sometimes entire new functions must be added, project schedules should include sufficient time for both the usability test and resulting modifications to the software.

Unit. Unit testing is the first testing developers perform. As its name implies, it affects a single program or module, a unit of the whole system. Once the developers have completed their coding and have clean compiles, they test each program (or the group of programs in a system module) individually. Their objective is to demonstrate that the program or module functions as it was designed.

System. Once unit testing is complete, the developers conduct a system test, incorporating the new program or module into the entire system. This is sometimes referred to as integration testing. The goal of system or integration testing is to prove that the program functions correctly as part of a whole and that its addition has no negative effects on the overall system.

Functionality. Once the software developers have completed their initial testing of the system, it should be turned over to quality assurance for functionality testing. The goal of this testing is two-fold: to prove that the system does everything it was supposed to and to show that it is unbreakable. This is the most time-consuming testing phase, because it involves testing every logic branch.

Although developers may argue that they have already demonstrated system quality through their own testing, an independent group's assurance is critical. Methods of testing and some suggested test scenarios are detailed later in this chapter.

Acceptance. During acceptance testing, customers repeat the basic testing that they did during the usability phase. In addition, they simulate all cycles of work that the system will support, such as daily, weekly, and monthly. From a customer perspective, acceptance testing is the opportunity to approve the system or mandate changes before it is placed in production. Its objectives are to ensure that the system meets customers' requirements and expectations and to clarify any misconceptions about the software's capabilities. Since acceptance testing is usually preceded by training, it also allows the customers to verify that training materials and documentation are complete and correct.

Volume. Although customers may have completed their testing during the acceptance phase, the work of the quality assurance group continues. All previous test categories have involved a small number of persons entering limited quantities of data. In those phases, the focus was on the quality and variety of the test data. Volume testing, as its name implies, focuses on quantity. The goal of this type of testing is to prove that the system will not crash or suffer a brown-out under a heavy load.

Volume testing challenges the system's limits. If 50 concurrent users are considered the maximum, volume testing will begin with 51 users and continue to increase the number. If a thousand daily transactions have been defined as the maximum, a volume test might process 2,000 transactions. The objective is to determine the system's limits and to ensure that they exceed the customer's expectations.

Disaster Recovery. Testing does not end when the system is placed in production. A complete testing program includes a disaster recovery plan and a test to ensure that the plan works. The purpose of disaster recovery testing is to prove that, should a system (either hardware or software) fail, periodic backups are adequate to restore it. Typically disaster recovery testing involves simulating a system crash at key processing points, then applying the previously established plan to restore the system and validate its accuracy.

System Modifications

Although the testing for system modifications does not encompass as many categories as new development, it is no less crucial. In addition to unit and system testing, modifications should undergo functionality testing, whose goal is to prove that the change works as planned, and regression testing.

Regression. The objective of regression testing is to demonstrate that the most recent system modifications had no unexpected effects on the rest of the system. Like functionality testing in the development cycle, this is a time-consuming process, since it involves testing every branch of the software. Automated testing tools can shorten the time required for regression testing, since once a suite of test cases and expected results has been developed, the test tools can run them with little or no operator intervention.

WHERE SHOULD TESTING BE PERFORMED?

Most IS organizations have recognized the danger of testing using production machines and have established at least basic test environments that keep newly developed or newly changed software separate from production systems. This is an excellent first step; however, it is only the beginning. Just as there are categories of testing that should performed, there are different environments in which that testing should occur. The three primary test environments are lab, real world, and worst case.

The Lab Environment

A lab environment is one in which the system is isolated from as many outside influences as possible. In a typical lab, the software being tested runs alone. There are no other competing applications running on either the client or the server, assuming that this is client/server software. Note that in a mainframe environment cost considerations make it unlikely that the software could be isolated to that extent; however, separate regions can be established for testing.

The purpose of the lab environment is to ensure that any problems identified are caused by the system itself rather than by its interaction with other systems. Lab environments are typically used during the early stages of functionality testing. They are not appropriate for acceptance, volume, or disaster recovery tests, since each of those should simulate a real-world or worst-case environment.

The Real-World Environment

Real world, as its name implies, is a test environment that mirrors as much as possible the situation that will be encountered when the system is placed in production. If the system is client/server and will run on a server that also handles the company's E-mail system, a comparable system should be used for testing. If the client machines will have word processing and a spreadsheet program open at the same time as the new software, the test environment should be similarly configured. The purpose of real-world testing, which is typically used for the majority of functionality and all acceptance and disaster recovery testing, is to demonstrate that usual outside factors do not introduce any new problems.

The Worst-Case Environment

Worst-case environments, typically used in conjunction with volume testing, are designed to provide an additional stress test for the software. In them, if two other concurrent Windows-based applications are the norm, the QA group would load the client machine with four or five other applications. Similarly, the server would be loaded with more systems than normally expected. And if the system depends on network response time, bandwidth would be reduced and network usage increased to simulate a problem environment.

HOW TESTING IS ACCOMPLISHED: THE TESTING PLAN

The hallmark of successful testing is a plan. This should be a formal, written plan listing each case to be tested along with the expected results. Without such a document, there is no way to ensure that all possible combinations have been tested, and it is far more difficult to repeat the test. Although many organizations protest the time required to develop test cases and predicted results, this is an essential step. It also provides the framework for regression testing. A sample form for recording test cases is shown as Exhibit 50.3.

Case Number	Module	Function (Screen, Report)	Data to be Entered	Expected Results
30001	Accounts Payable	Vendor Data Entry	Vendor ID	Verify that the system will not allow you to enter a number but that it auto-assigns the next sequential ID when you cursor to the next field.
30002	Accounts Payable	Vendor Data Entry	Vendor Address (state)	Verify that the system provides a pick list of valid state and province codes. Verify that you can select a code from the list or can enter it without using the pick list. Verify that the system will not allow you to enter an invalid code.

Exhibit 50.3. Test Cases and Expected Results

The most difficult part of testing is constructing the test cases, but a few guidelines can simplify what is an undeniably time-consuming task.

Data Entry

1. Enter data for each field, trying to break the system by entering alphas or special characters in numeric fields.
2. If a field has a pick list of values, choose data from the pick list, enter a valid code without use of the pick list, and try to enter an invalid code.
3. When there is a range of data allowed, e.g., months, enter the lowest and highest value, then try to enter values below and above the range.
4. Create a record by filling in all fields.
5. Create a record by filling in only mandatory fields.
6. Try to skip mandatory fields.
7. Change each of the fields on each of the records created in steps 4 and 5.
8. Try to delete mandatory fields on a previously created record.
9. Delete each of the records.
10. Add another record. If record IDs are auto-numbered, determine whether or not an ID has been reused.
11. Test illogical combinations of fields, e.g., an employee's hire date is earlier than his birth date.
12. If the system is multi-user, have two people try to add the same record at the same time.
13. Have multiple people try to change the same record at the same time.

14. Have multiple people try to delete the same record at the same time.
15. If the system will be used outside the U.S., verify that the system allows European date formats (ddmmyyyy) and numbers (blanks or periods rather than commas to separate thousands).

Inquiry and Reporting

1. If there are online field prompts, verify that they are available and accurate.
2. If there is online help, verify that it is available, accurate and easily understood.
3. Ensure that all records can be retrieved for inquiry.
4. If there are varying security classes which allow selective inquiry, test each and verify that the correct fields or records are secured.
5. Try to break the security system.
6. If reporting allows ranges of records to be selected, enter illogical ranges, e.g., the starting date is greater than the ending date, or selecting all employees whose last name begins with K to D.
7. If date ranges are allowed, test both January and December.
8. Test ranges of dates that span the millennium.
9. If a range of values is expected, enter no range.
10. Verify that deleted records are not displayed on reports. (They may have been inactivated rather than physically deleted from the database.)

Once the test cases have been developed, the QA group is ready to begin testing. And, since it is inevitable that bugs will be found, it is important to have a formal mechanism for reporting those problems. Some organizations use a totally paper-based system for tracking defects. Others record the results in a spreadsheet or a simple database. Still others use the reporting mechanisms provided with testing tools. The method is less important than the data collected. Exhibit 50.4 shows a sample of fields to be recorded.

Note that the bug report references the test case number but also has its own bug number. In automated systems, the bug number may be auto-assigned. In the Exhibit 50.4 example, which is designed for manual tracking, the number is assigned manually and consists of the reporting person's initials followed by the next sequential number for that person's reports. This method provides a unique number for each bug but does not require coordination among individuals, since each tester has his own set of numbers.

It is also important to assign a priority to each bug, since testing will uncover problems that vary from system-halting to minor annoyances. Priorities are used to guide the developers, clearly indicating which changes must be made first. They are also useful in measuring system quality. Stating that 363 bugs were discovered is of little value, since a bug might be a

Bug Number	SMJ-1406
Date Reported	9/24/1998
Reported By	Susan Jones
Priority	2
Module	Accounts Payable
Test Case Number	30002
Bug Description	The Canadian province of Manitoba was not included on the pick list.
Attachments	None
Date Retested	9/30/1998
Retested By	Susan Jones
Retest Results	Province has been added.
Comments	
Date Closed	9/30/1998
Closed By	Susan Jones

Exhibit 50.4. Bug Report

spelling error in a help screen or a system crash. On the other hand, knowing that only six of those bugs were priority one demonstrates a measurable level of quality. (Whether six is good, bad, or average depends on the organization's standards as well as the size and complexity of the system.)

Since in most organizations more than one person will be testing, it is important to establish guidelines for assignment of priorities. Using a three-tiered priority scheme, for example, with one being the highest, an organization may decide that missing or erroneous help screens are priority three, while incorrect report headings are assigned priority two. Calculation errors would be a priority one. These guidelines should be documented in writing and given to all members of the QA and development staffs.

Note that it is helpful for QA staff and the developers to agree on both the priority classifications and the amount of time in which each class of bugs will be corrected. Typically, a priority one bug would be included in the next release of the software, whereas a priority two could be delayed until the release after that. A priority three item is often addressed only when the affected program is being modified for another reason.

CONCLUSION

Debunking the Myths

Like any component of system development, testing has its own set of myths. And, like all myths, they need to be exposed as such. The following sections cover the most important myths of software testing.

There Is No Need To Test Packaged Software

Adherence to this belief is sometimes called a career limiting event. Although an IS organization is justified in thinking that the software vendor has performed its own comprehensive set of testing, only a foolish organization would place a new version of software in production without doing its own testing. Depending on the vendor and the type of software, this testing may be minimal. Whereas a minor upgrade to a standard desktop application such as word processing would not require the same level of testing as a new release of a niche software product used for critical business functions, both should be tested.

Depending on the severity of the errors found and the organization's relationship with the vendor, it may be possible to have the bugs fixed immediately. If that is not feasible and the bugs are serious, IS should exercise its veto power and refuse to implement the new release.

Testing Need Only Be Done Once

Like not testing at all, this could be a career limiting event. Once a bug has been uncovered and the developers have corrected it, QA personnel must test again to prove that the fix was accurate and that it had no unplanned effect on any other portion of the software. Testing is repetitive. It must be performed each time a new piece of code is received until all bugs are corrected and the new program is placed in production.

Testing Tools Can Do Everything

Although some tool vendors might tout their products as the complete, single-source answer to an IS organization's testing problems, the fact is that tools cannot totally eliminate human effort. People are still needed to develop test cases and predicted results. Once that is done, the tools can be effective in automating subsequent tests and in verifying results against the predicted ones. As is true of most software products, testing tools are best used to eliminate repetitive tasks such as the actual entry of test cases. They should not, however, be relied on to perform the creative portion of testing; that is, determining what needs to be tested.

And the final, greatest myth: Testing doesn't take much time. It does. It requires substantial time, effort and talent. Testing is not easy, and it is not fast. What it is, is essential.

Chapter 51
Ethical Responsibility for Software Development

Janice C. Sipior
Burke T. Ward

RECENT EVENTS in the software industry signal a changing environment for development organizations in terms of ethical and legal responsibility should software malfunction and cause financial loss or physical harm to the user. Is it realistic for consumers to expect innovative software rich in both features and quality, and what are the implications for developers if users seek recourse for less than perfect products?

Computer-based systems have become ubiquitous in our daily lives. No longer limited to traditional data processing, software applications abound in the areas of air traffic and other transportation control, communication, entertainment, finance, industrial processes, medical technology, and nuclear power generation, among others. The resulting increase in demand for a diversity of applications has attracted development organizations to a lucrative commercial and retail market. Software may be mass-marketed, canned software sold at retail under a shrink-wrap, included as a part of turnkey systems, specially developed for systems designed to fulfill user's particular needs, or embedded as control devices.

Developing software for such varied uses outside the development organization increases the risk of financial loss or physical harm to users. If software does not function properly, do the users have any recourse? Are programmers, system analysts, IS managers, or organizations involved in development efforts ethically or legally responsible for poorly functioning software?

0-8493-9820-7/00/$0.00+$.50
© 2000 by CRC Press LLC

Media attention to reports of flawed software exemplify the mounting market expectations for software to function properly, underscoring the increasing potential for users to seek ethical responsibility through legal recourse. Are users justified in their expectations of properly functioning software? Can developers be held to a higher standard of software quality? This discussion focuses on software developed for sale as opposed to in-house development, because most actions would arise between a vendor and purchaser. Although the ethical and legal responsibility of software developers is currently unclear, the threat to seek recourse is nonetheless present and on the rise.

EXAMPLES OF MALFUNCTIONING SOFTWARE

Flaws, resulting in both trivial and severe consequences, have plagued software for decades. A classic example of a serious malfunction occurred in a U.S. nuclear missile warning system on October 5, 1960. Radar sensor input from Thule, Greenland, was erroneously interpreted as a massive attack by the then Soviet Union, with a certainty of 99.9%.[1] The actual cause of the warning system to issue the attack alert was identified, precluding nuclear warfare. The rising moon had caused echoes from the radar sensors, a factor overlooked during development.

Unfortunately, software defects are not always detected in advance. A series of tragic incidents occurred in a system developed by Atomic Energy of Canada Ltd. to control radiation doses delivered to cancer patients. Between 1985 to 1987, on-screen editing performed with the up-arrow key caused two modes of operation to be mixed, resulting in a radiation dose more than 100 times higher than the average. At least four patients believed to have received the erroneous radiation overdose died; others were seriously injured. Another malfunction in a medical application caused an overdose of Demerol to be delivered by a patient-controlled analgesic pump, designed to administer narcotic pain medication as needed. As a direct result, the post-elective surgery patient suffered respiratory depression, which caused a heart attack. After lapsing into a coma, the woman died a few days later. The cause was presumed to be an error in the software controlling the dosage by an infusion pump.

These life-critical cases have become classic examples in discussions of ethical standards in software development. The focus of concern, however, is no longer only on those applications wherein defects threaten life and safety. As the software industry matures, mounting market expectations are forcing greater ethical and legal responsibility in a diversity of application areas.

MARKET EXPECTATIONS

The software industry is now the third largest industry in the United States, generating revenues of $102.8 billion in 1996 according to a study conducted by Nathan Associates, an economic consulting firm in Arlington, VA. Since 1990, the industry has grown 12.5% annually, more than two and a half times faster than the economy as a whole. The total of direct employment, 619,400 individuals in the software industry, and indirect jobs, 1.44 million jobs in other industries, represents nearly 3% of U.S. workers. The leaders in the software industry, Microsoft Corp., Novell Inc., and IBM's Lotus Development Corp., are no longer the charming fledgling start-up companies they once were. The industry leader, Microsoft Corp., for example, has about $11.4 billion in sales and 22,000 employees worldwide, including a battalion of engineers, marketers, attorneys, and public relations personnel, to promote and deliver quality products to their customers, just like any other product manufacturer.

With such industry changes comes a difference in what the software market is willing to accept. One of the more well-known examples concerns Intuit's TurboTax, the company's leading tax assistance software. When problems in software use were revealed a few weeks before the 1995 individual tax filing deadline, Intuit initially argued that the defect would affect functioning adversely only in rare instances, involving particular financial considerations. However, market forces led Intuit to revise and replace TurboTax software free of charge. Further, Intuit promised to pay any Internal Revenue Service penalty, plus interest, resulting from errors attributable to TurboTax use. Intuit admitted that in any given year, about 1% of its users are affected by flaws.[2] The resulting cost to Intuit for the penalty guarantee is reported as less than $1,500 over three years.

In this case, Intuit simply had no time for extensive testing during systems development. The development schedule was dependent on Congress to finish annual tax code revisions and the release of final versions of federal and state tax forms by late December. User demand for tax preparation assistance has to be met by about the end of January to allow sufficient time for use before the personal tax filing deadline.

On Christmas day in 1994, mainstream America experienced just how far-reaching software problems can be, a problem characterized as "the first bug to affect popular culture."[3] The much anticipated CD-ROM version of the popular *The Lion King* was marketed for home use by Disney Interactive, the software unit of Walt Disney Co. With sales topping 200,000, Disney was deluged with communications from disappointed parents who unsuccessfully tried to install the children's multimedia entertainment package. Days and weeks went by before Disney responded to the calls, mail, E-mail, and bulletin board messages. The initial stance was to claim that problems were caused by novice users who did not know how to install the software properly because they did not read the message on the box and their equipment was obsolete. Within a month, Disney changed its tone and increased its product support staff from 8 to about 50, at an unanticipated expense. New versions of the CD-ROM were sent to customers who did not have the required sound card.

Disney later conceded that it released the CD-ROM even though it knew errors were present, believing only a small percentage of users would be affected. Outside developers, Media Station and Microsoft Corp., who produced portions of the code, informed Disney of the program's defects. Trying to capitalize on market demand, resulting from re-release of the movie on which the CD-ROM was based and the Christmas season, Disney decided to release it anyway.

More recently, a lawsuit, filed by Anthony Lefco against Microsoft, was poised to test the standard for acceptability of quality in software. After experiencing problems with the installation of Windows 95 in September 1995, Lefco filed a class action case against Microsoft, arguing the product did not deliver on the advertised claims of wide testing, high compatibility with existing hardware and other software applications, and easy installation. Attorneys for Microsoft related that Lefco ignored on-screen installation instructions and turned his computer on and off about 300 times, contributing to his problems. Further, after replacing his motherboard and monitor, he was successfully using the operating system. The class action status was denied on the basis that commonality or a pattern of problems was not experienced by a class of Windows 95 users.[4] Although the class certification was denied, this case demonstrates the heightened expectations for software capability and developer accountability within the marketplace.

A Shift from Caveat Emptor to Caveat Venditor

As software enters into more aspects of our lives, increases in the demand for a diversity of applications by both commercial and retail markets have changed the ethical and legal environment of development organizations. Many consumers are not sophisticated computer users. Programming is completely foreign to them and the idea that software could produce erroneous results is totally unexpected. Users, like any other consumers, are beginning to treat defects within the software industry as they do defects in other product purchases. If it does not work properly, take it back. If it causes financial loss or physical harm, seek monetary recovery through the legal system.

An ethical shift within the software market from the comfortable world of caveat emptor toward the high accountability of caveat venditor is occurring. The move along this continuum requires an associated increase in responsibility by software developers to users. Today, caveat emptor is no longer an acceptable stance for software developers. Although developers' motives still "often have more to do with marketing than with quality assurance," a shift toward the caveat venditor end of the continuum is evident.[5] Users now increasingly scrutinize software and have higher standards in evaluating the performance of purchased software. As market expectations force the software industry away from caveat emptor, developers correspondingly must continue to be more user oriented by initiating and continually enhancing business actions to improve user satisfaction through product quality.

CAN DEVELOPERS IMPROVE SOFTWARE QUALITY?

Software defects are more prevalent, not just because software itself is more prevalent. A widespread move away from highly standardized mini or mainframe systems to networks comprising various brands of hardware and software connected across long distances exists. Coupled with the complexity of such networks is more flexibility in user interaction, marked by the emergence of Microsoft's Windows. Various tasks can be performed with no predetermined sequence or combination of events, unlike old programs, which performed tasks through a structured series of command sequences. The new-style software requires exhaustive testing to assess every possible sequence, permutation, and combination of events, which is virtually impossible.

In response, the automated testing tool market experienced rapid growth, doubling sales in 1995 to $100 million. Automated testing tools capture the input of a human tester and generate test scripts to be run repeatedly. Errors are detected and testing resumes once the cause is determined and the fault repaired. However, each subsequent error is more difficult to detect and correct. What constitutes sufficient testing? When should the testing process end? Although automated testing tools are increasingly available, only about 75% of the code in the 60 leading products in the software industry has been tested.[6] In the overall development community, only about 35% of the code in a typical application is tested. The top four development organizations, however, are reported to be committed to quality development, detecting up to 95% of software defects before delivery to users. Should these developers be lauded or chastised for this error detection rate? Is this an acceptable rate of error detection or is software wherein 5% of its defects persist unacceptable?

Error detection focuses on correcting errors once they already exist within the software. A more comprehensive approach is to incorporate defect prevention throughout the development process. Hewlett-Packard Medical Group in Andover, MA, for example, utilizes special methods such as formal inspections, which require experts to analyze specifications and code according to strict rules and procedures. Another means is through causal analysis, wherein software errors are analyzed to identify their cause. Preventive measures, which extensively consider unusual events associated with the cause, are then incorporated into the development process. Error prevention and detection, however, can add time and expense to the development process. These methods certainly encourage a focus on quality software but may discourage developers from assuming the risk associated with research and development of new technologies, especially in safety-critical applications.

In the highly competitive software market, development organizations are driven to develop innovative software rich in both features and quality, within a tight schedule. Even developers with the strictest quality control may distribute software with some remaining defects. What defects remain may or may not be known by the developer before the software is released. Users have reported frustrating instances of hours wasted in attempting to get software to perform some simple task, only to have the development organization finally admit to a known problem.

Software developers themselves express greater optimism regarding their own abilities to avoid flaws in systems development. Yet, even software considered to be correctly programmed has had serious problems. NASA, for example, experienced several difficulties in life-critical applications, including a synchronization problem with the backup computer before the first Columbia launch, multiple computer outages on a subsequent Columbia mission, output misreading that caused liquid oxygen to be drained off just before a scheduled Columbia launch, Discovery's positioning problem in a laser-beam experiment, a reversal of shutdown procedures for two computers controlling Discovery, and difficulties in an Endeavor rendezvous with Intelsat due to not quite equal values being equated. Indeed, "there are no guaranteed assurances that a given system will behave properly all of the time, or even at some particularly critical time." Nonetheless, software developers must continue to strive to develop reliable software or be held ethically and legally responsible.[7]

IMPLICATIONS FOR RESPONSIBILITY

Responsibility, based either on voluntary initiatives or on legal requirements, promotes the quest for perfection in an imperfect world. However, we, as a society, seem willing to accept that software can never be perfect. The presence of flaws in commercial and retail software is simply the price we as users must pay for technological innovation. Those who suffer the consequences of software failure disagree. Are the financial loss and physical harm caused by software defects just random events for which no one is responsible?

Ethical Responsibility

The software industry has responded to the necessity to improve product quality and user satisfaction by continuously initiating business actions, which become norms and develop into industry practice. For example, technical support desks for users have become common in the software industry, although many organizations charge for this service. Such industry practices continue to develop and advance. Various entities, such as individual companies, industry groups, and professional organizations, formalize the industry practice for improving user satisfaction as ethical codes. The Association for Computing Machinery (ACM), for example, has adopted a Code of Ethics and Professional Conduct for its members. For software developers, this code advocates quality in both the process and the products. Ethical codes not only guide conduct within the industry but also demonstrate the presence of a mechanism for self-regulation.

A self-regulatory approach, however, may not always be viewed as sufficient, resulting in an extension of ethical codes into legal regulations. Further, these voluntary ethical codes may be used as a professional standard in a lawsuit. For example, in *Diversified Graphics, Ltd. v. Groves*, the court awarded $82,500 for computer malpractice. In its interpretation, the court recognized that the defendant, Ernst and Whinney, acting as IS consultants and not as CPAs, incorporated the AICPA's (American Institute of Certified Public Accountants) "Management Advisory Services Practice Standards" in its *Guidelines to Practice*. These standards are meant to provide guidance to accounting firms, not software development, and thus should not be used to establish a professional standard for IS services. Although this case is an aberration, it nonetheless presents a precedent.

Software developers who are not ethically responsible in business dealings with users may be held accountable through the legal system. To decide how much financial liability software developers should be exposed to, the legal system must address the ethical issues of distributive justice and consequence-based ethics. Distributive justice deals with risk sharing or allocation. As movement along the ethical continuum proceeds from caveat emptor toward caveat venditor, a distributive justice view increasingly places the risk for financial loss or harm caused by defective software on the developer. This increase in legal liability is actually a reflection of society's ethical beliefs, entirely consistent with the legal system's treatment of manufacturers of other products.

The twentieth century, especially the last half of the twentieth century, has seen a radical shift in risk allocation toward caveat venditor. Consequence-based ethics focuses on whether the consequences of such a liability shift are good or bad for society. Clearly, developers would develop and market software innovations more swiftly in a caveat emptor legal environment. Although this may be perceived as a societal good, an additional consequence may be a greater incidence of defective software, potentially causing financial loss or personal injury. The legal system eventually addresses the balance between the competing societal interests of innovation and safety.

Legal liability is a serious threat to software developers. The most threatening software bug, the millennium bug, is projected to lead to litigation costing $1 trillion in the United States alone, according to a mid-1990s' task force of Lloyd's of London. And it has been said that "more and more, Silicon Valley and business users are finding the newest high-tech growth industry to be — litigation."[8] Developers must thus be prepared for the heightened expectations of users, emphasizing the need for developers to understand the changing legal environment to which they are subject.

Legal Implications

A legal consequence of the argument that some level of software defects may be inevitable is the proposal for revisions to the Uniform Commercial Code (UCC). Under the current UCC Article 2, a software developer or vendor may be held liable for breach of an express or implied warranty (UCC article 2, §§ 313, 314, 315). If the proposed Article 2B of the UCC is enacted, disclosure of known defects could ultimately be required by law. Development organizations would usually not be held liable if they make a good-faith effort to appropriately disclose known defects.

This approach may be preferable to both developers and users. If known defects are disclosed appropriately, the developer's liability could be reduced because the user could read about and plan for any potential defects or incompatibilities in advance of software purchase or use. To disclose known defects may seem like a simple request, but what exactly is a defect, as opposed to a design decision, a feature, or a performance limitation? Because no standard exists in the software industry for certifying the quality of software, the determination remains a matter of personal opinion.

Regulations may also be directed toward specific types of software. For example, the Food and Drug Administration (FDA) has formulated a software policy proposal to regulate development procedures and reliability testing to minimize patient risk with health care applications. Current FDA regulation tightly oversees software-controlled medical devices, such as X-ray machines, exempting those that allow "competent human intervention" before patients are treated. Improved technology, such as software-controlled drug delivery to administer doses based on changes in a patient's condition, will render this exemption irrelevant.

CONCLUSION

The increasingly complex computing environment makes it more difficult to develop complex systems, correct in terms of the design specifications, with no defects. Even if it were possible, the development team would certainly be unable to foresee and accommodate all unanticipated circumstances that may arise during use. Many software errors have been attributed to human error rather than to the design. Must we accept an imperfect software world? Will users accept the inevitability of flawed software without seeking recourse, even in cases of devastating consequences?

Clearly, the ethical environment within which software operates has become more complex, and the potential for errors has increased. At the same time, pressure for software to function properly has been building within the computer software industry. A number of decades ago, the term "bug" was first applied to software defects. This cute little term subsequently became widely accepted, carrying with it both expectations for its occurrence and acceptability for its presence. However, the ethical sands have shifted under the industry's feet. Gone are the days when users were so delighted that the computer was able to do anything at all that they were willing to accept the inevitability of program bugs.

Notes

1. Belsie, L. "As Computers Proliferate, So Does Potential for Bugs," *The Christian Science Monitor* (February 16, 1994), p. 10.
2. Lewis, P.H. (March 24, 1995). "The Inevitable: Death, Taxes, Bugs," *The New York Times*, p. C1.
3. "Notorious Bugs," *Byte* (September 1995), pp. 125–128.
4. Lewis, P., "Judge Denies Class Status for Windows 95 Suit," *The Seattle Times* (March 3, 1997), p. WL (WestLaw) 3222483.
5. Vadlamudi, P., (Feb. 20, 1995). "Burgeoning Bugs," *InfoWorld*, 17 (8), pp. 1, 14.
6. Henderson, P. "Quality Crisis." *Datamation* (December 15, 1995), p. 84.
7. Neumann, P.G. (Feb. 1993). "Are Dependable Systems Feasible?," *Communications of the ACM*, 36 (2), p. 146.
8. Reid, W.S. (June 1996). "2001: A Legal Odyssey (The Millennium Bug)," *Computer Lawyer*, pp. 15–17.

Section 4
Exploiting Web Technologies

SINCE THEIR INCEPTION in the late 1980s, World Wide Web (WWW) technologies have had a dramatic impact on the development, maintenance, and utilization of information systems. Two relatively simple standards, Hypertext Transfer Protocol (http, a protocol for communication between web servers and clients) and Hypertext Markup Language (HTML, a page description language), together with a standardized data communications environment (networks utilizing the TCP/IP protocol), have created an unprecedented computing environment that supports document and data distribution between heterogeneous clients and servers.

From the simple beginning of the original text-based WWW implementation in 1989 we have quickly come to the current environment in which Web technologies increasingly form a part of the enterprise architecture, including enterprisewide systems and applications that link companies to customers and suppliers. Servers, browsers, languages, protocols, and telecommunications infrastructures have been developing at a rapid pace, and even though Web technologies are still in their infancy, they are being used today to build a variety of different systems: simple document distribution via the Internet as well as complex extranets for transaction processing and querying over a set of heterogeneous networking infrastructures. It is therefore vitally important for IS managers to understand the opportunities these Web technologies offer for the development and operation of information systems for both today and tomorrow.

At least one chapter in each of the prior sections has helped set the stage for this new application environment. The Internet is viewed as a dislocating technology (Chapter 4). Client/server architectures (Chapters 17 and 18) are enabling this global phenomenon to grow exponentially. Among the promising technologies for electronic commerce are intelligent agents (Chapters 36 and 37) and Java (Chapter 38).

The purpose of this section is increase the reader's understanding of some of the most important organizational uses of web technologies: external Web sites, intranets, extranets, and key issues associated with initial Web site development, Internet security, and acceptable usage policies.

E-COMMERCE OPPORTUNITIES AND CHALLENGES

The most visible and most widely discussed application of Web technologies is for electronic commerce with end-consumers via the Internet. Yet the applications with the largest potential for a bottom-line impact in the near future are those that enable business-to-business e-commerce. Chapter 52, "Creating Electronic Markets in Business-to-Business Commerce," describes and contrasts two forms of business-to-business e-commerce: interorganizational systems (which require buyer/seller agreements in advance) and electronic markets. This chapter provides short descriptions of five business benefits of electronic markets and the Internet features that they exploit. The author also presents lists of key questions that IT managers and business managers should jointly consider as they prepare to capitalize on today's electronic market opportunities.

For the average person on-the-street, however, the most visible application is the use of the Internet for electronic commerce between businesses and end-consumers. Chapter 53, "E-Commerce Issues for External Web Sites," discusses four categories of issues associated with conducting business with retail customers: technology infrastructure issues, online shopping concerns from the customer's perspective, product/service pricing issues, and as yet unresolved legal/regulatory issues.

INTRANET APPLICATIONS

Web-enabled changes *within* organizations have been as dramatic as the creation of new business opportunities on the Internet: Intranets, internal networks that utilize Web technologies for information distribution, interactive communication, and administrative applications have already had a strong impact on the ways organizations operate. Their standardized and easily understandable environment has made intranets affordable for even small and medium-size organizations, and their availability across platforms makes them very attractive for large corporations with heterogeneous environments,

The following two chapters focus on the same intranet issue from somewhat different perspectives. Chapter 54, "Developing Corporate Intranets," is a general overview to intranets that provides the reader with a good understanding of the issues that have to be taken into account when developing intranets for corporate usage, including security, development environments, scalability and reliability, and network infrastructure. Chapter 55, "Designing a Business-Justified Intranet Project," reminds us of the need to build a strong business case for any major IS project, including intranet implementation. It provides a broad-level methodology for justifying an intranet from the business perspective. Getting a successful start includes identifying a customer, articulating a goal for the intranet, planning and assigning resources, defining a measure for success, performing a cost/benefit analysis, and using a "proof of concept" approach to plan the implementation.

EXTRANET APPLICATIONS

Internal networks (intranets) that are expanded to include users from outside the organization are referred to as extranets. This definition includes an intranet that is opened to selected business partners and other external stakeholders, as well as an extranet for a group of corporations where all organizations participate as equal partners. Chapter 56, "Expanding the Reach of Electronic Commerce: The Internet EDI Alternative," describes the benefits for transaction processing applications that use electronic data interchange (EDI) standards. Chapter 57, "Implementing and Supporting Extranets," introduces the reader to the fundamental concepts and technologies underlying extranets and their implementation. The main focus is on the various implementation technologies: router-based filtering, application layer gateways, and virtual private networks.

POLICY AND DEVELOPMENT ISSUES

Security is an essential issue even within the organization. But when an organization's network is also linked to a public network (at this moment most often the Internet), security issues have a heightened level of importance. Chapter 58, "Internet Security and Firewall Policies," identifies the risks of being linked to the Internet, discusses the specific nature of potential attacks, and presents a set of defense mechanisms that organizations may choose to use to protect themselves. In addition. the chapter recommends several policies that help organizations maintain the security of their networks.

Another area of vulnerability is the management of external Web site projects. Because of the newness of the Internet as a commercial channel and the ease of use of Web authoring tools, companies may not initially impose a level of project management controls that are typical of traditional applications. This is one of the "lessons learned" from the comparison of two case studies presented in Chapter 59, "E-Commerce Initiatives: Case Studies of Implementation Management." The authors warn that internal pressures for creating a Web presence have in the past led to shortcuts that in the end prove expensive to unwary businesses, whether big or small.

A policy that defines the acceptable usage of the Internet by employees using company equipment and/or networks is the focus of Chapter 60, "Internet Acceptable Usage Policies." The author not only helps us understand the importance of well-defined, clearly communicated policies but also provides useful guidelines for drafting and implementing policies for acceptable usage. These policies have proven to be important safeguards against potential legal actions. In addition, they have the potential of improving productivity, as well as avoiding costly misunderstandings that can occur between employees and their managers in what is still an uncertain legal territory.

Chapter 52
Creating Electronic Markets in Business-to-Business Commerce

James A. Senn

CONDUCTING BUSINESS through electronic commerce, the handling of transactions over communications networks, continues to grow in a seemingly unabated fashion. The excitement surrounding the explosive growth of many Internet companies, coupled with a wide range of capabilities provided through the Worldwide Web are important drivers of this growth. So is a wide public awareness of consumer-oriented electronic commerce, including amazon.com the Internet bookseller and merchandiser, the Microsoft Expedia and Travelocity travel sites, and the online brokerage activities of E-Trade and Charles Schwab.

While the business-to-consumer side of electronic commerce (e-commerce) offers tremendous entrepreneurial opportunities, the impact of *business-to-business* commerce is even broader. For instance,

- Beginning late in 1996, the Boeing Airplane Company launched an e-commerce site on the Worldwide Web to assist its global airline customers in acquiring spare parts. They are able to check pricing and availability of parts, order parts, and track the status of their orders. Within a year of opening the site, 50 percent of Boeing customers were using the site for parts orders and service inquiries. Not only has usage of the site grown continually since then, but Boeing has also been able to grow the parts business with some 20 percent more shipments every month while maintaining staffing at 1996 levels.
- In late 1998, the city-nation of Singapore launched a plan to make it a global e-commerce hub. Adding to its long-established global leader-

ship in the use of electronic data interchange, the Singapore government envisions some $2.4 billion in products and services, and one-half of the nation's businesses trading via e-commerce in less than 4 years.

- Motorola, as well as Boeing and other companies have warned their suppliers that they must develop an ability to conduct business over the Web. The warning is explicit. Suppliers not changing to e-commerce over the Worldwide Web *within the next year* will probably be locked out as a supplier for the long term.

Business-to-business commerce is a fundamental shift in the manner by which firms are interacting with buyers and suppliers. It is much more than an Internet-based phenomenon. Rather, e-commerce is a restructuring of the very basis for conducting business. Unlike so many other business developments in the past, e-commerce is not an opportunity for only the large or multinational firms. Rather, the smallest entrepreneurial organizations can establish and build their businesses around e-commerce. As they do so, geographic distance disappears as a business barrier, for the global reach of underlying communications technologies becomes an easily accessible resource for all firms.

This chapter explores the two forms of business-to-business electronic commerce:

- *Interorganizational systems*, a long-established, but rapidly evolving part of business processes in so many firms.
- *Emerging electronic markets,* an extremely important vehicle for expanding the base of buyers and sellers.

For some firms, interorganizational systems are the basis for e-commerce activities as the underlying technologies are evolving to make these systems accessible to a greater number of firms—large and small—than ever before. Others will gravitate toward electronic markets, capitalizing on a new opportunity to create a product, deliver a service, or get in touch with potential customers. The public, global Internet, and its principle application, the Worldwide Web, provide a highly visible platform for electronic markets.

As this chapter illustrates, e-commerce merits careful consideration by executives and managers alike.

INTERORGANIZATIONAL SYSTEMS

Through interorganizational systems, buyers and sellers arrange for routine exchange of business transactions without the necessity of direct negotiation. Because information is exchanged over communications networks using prearranged formats (see Exhibit 52.1), there is no need for telephone calls, paper documents, or business correspondence to create and carry out transactions. Although interorganizational systems at one time involved proprietary communication links exclusively, throughout the last decade firms have opted to use public networks for these business-to-business systems.

Emergence of Interorganizational Systems

Interorganizational systems were driven by business needs and facilitated through information technology's continuing advances. The systems are a direct result of the growing desirability of interconnecting business partners to streamline business processes by:

- Reducing the costs of routine business transactions.
- Collapsing cycle time in the fulfillment of business transactions, regardless of geographic distance.
- Eliminating paper and the inefficiencies associated with paper processing.
- Creating application-to-application business processes between buyer and seller.

Networks that interconnect the diverse desktop and data systems facilitated pursuit of these objectives by business partners. Both proprietary network solutions and the services of value-added network carriers ensured that any firm wishing to link up could do so.

Types of Interorganizational Systems

The term *interorganizational system* describes a variety of business activities rather than a single entity. Following are five of the most prominent types of interorganizational systems:

- *Electronic data interchange (EDI)*. Computer-to-computer (or application-to-application) exchange of standard, formatted business documents transmitted over computer networks where translation systems overcome differences in information technology used by trading partners.
- *Electronic funds transfer (EFT)*. Automated exchange of money between parties in a commercial transaction or between banks representing businesses responsible for conducting the settlement portion of a business transaction.
- *Electronic Forms*. Online completion and transmission of business forms (e.g., claims forms and contracts, complete with electronic signature) that the recipient can route to the appropriate in-house destination for proper handling.
- *Integrated Messaging*. Delivery of electronic mail and facsimile documents through a single electronic transmission system; it may include

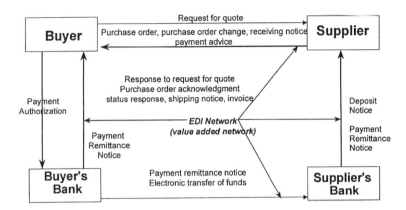

Exhibit 52.1.   Interorganizational system for electronic data interchange (EDI)

the combining of EDI, electronic mail, and electronic forms for transmission.

- *Shared databases.* Information stored in repositories shared between trading partners and accessible to both; such databases are often used to reduce elapsed time in communicating information between parties as well as to arrange cooperative activities.

Other types of interorganizational systems will undoubtedly evolve as businesses refine and capitalize on their IT capabilities.

Scope of Interorganizational Systems

All interorganizational systems share common characteristics (see left-hand column of Exhibit 52.2). The principal activities of the systems are business-to-business or business-to-government in nature. In many instances, intermediaries operate the networks that carry the information or provide transaction processing services or database access.

The communications infrastructure of an interorganizational system is predetermined. All parties know the links over which transactions will be transmitted and where and how they will be received, including the use of electronic mailboxes. Whether public or private networks are used varies from situation to situation.

Parties participating in electronic commerce interact on the basis of a relationship that is defined and preestablished. Terms and conditions of that relationship are often set forth either as contracts or in briefs that specify the expectations and responsibilities of each party.

Interorganizational systems are firmly established in business. The transfer of funds electronically is becoming the norm for such systems, both nationally and internationally. In the U.S. alone, approximately

Interorganizational Systems

Buyer Relationships

Buyer/supplier relationship is determined in advance with the anticipation it will be an ongoing relationship based on multiple transactions.

Electronic Markets

Buyer Relationships

Two types of relationships may exist:
- Buyer/seller linkage is established at time of transactions and may be for one transaction only (i.e., purchase transaction).
- Buyer/seller purchase agreement is established whereby the seller agrees to deliver services or products to buyer for a defined period of time (i.e., a subscription transaction).

Networks

Interorganizational systems may be built around private or publicly accessible networks.

When outside communications companies are involved, they are typically value-added carriers (VANs).

Networks

Electronic markets are typically built around publicly accessible networks.

When outside communications companies are involved, they are typically online service providers (which function as market makers).

Buyer/Seller Agreements

Advance arrangement results in agreement on the nature and format of business documents that will be exchanged.

Advance arrangement results in agreement on the nature and format of business documents that will be exchanged.

Joint guidelines and expectations of each party are formulated so each knows how the system is to be used and when transactions will be submitted and received by each business partner.

Buyer/Seller Agreements

Sellers determine, in conjunction with the market maker, which business transactions they will provide.

Buyers and sellers independently determine which communication networks they will use in participating in the electronic market. The network used may vary from transaction to transaction.

No joint guidelines are drawn in advance.

Exhibit 52.2. Distinguishing features of interorganizational systems and electronic markets

100,000 firms conduct business by way of electronic data interchange. Such well-known companies as Wal-Mart, The Home Depot, and Circuit City, known for dominating their business category, could not operate as they do without their EDI capability and interorganizational systems operating between them and their suppliers.

Although some businesses use the term *EDI* very broadly, electronic commerce encompasses capabilities much broader than EDI. All forms of interorganizational systems promise to continue growing at an accelerating rate.

Firms seeking to establish ongoing business relationships with buyers or sellers, where information will be exchanged regularly, should build interorganizational systems. If business-to-business activity, however important, is not recurring in a predictable manner, electronic markets may be a more appropriate tool.

THE BUSINESS CASE FOR ELECTRONIC MARKETS

Electronic markets are rapidly emerging alongside interorganizational systems as a vehicle for business-to-business e-commerce. A market is a network of interactions and relationships where information, products, services, and payments are exchanged. When the marketplace is electronic, the business center is not a physical building, but rather a network-based location where business interactions occur.

Exhibit 52.2 summarizes how electronic markets differ from interorganizational systems. In electronic markets, the principal participants—transaction handlers, buyers, and sellers—are not only at different locations, but they seldom even know one another. Nor are relationships between buyers and sellers likely to be predetermined by agreements. The means of interconnection varies between parties and may change from event to event, even between the same parties. The interactions themselves are managed by a broad array of IT applications (see Exhibit 52.3) .

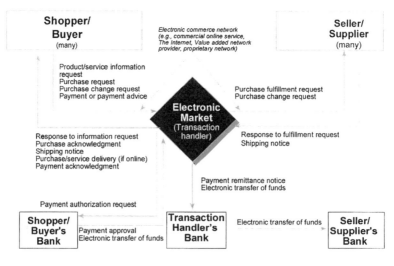

Exhibit 52.3. Electronic Markets

Executives and managers should evaluate the potential of electronic markets on the basis of five business benefits:

- Extending the firm's reach
- Bypassing traditional channels
- Augmenting traditional markets
- Boosting service
- Advertising

Each of these benefits is described below.

Extending the Firm's Reach

The ability of a firm to interact with customers or with business partners is defined by its reach. The ultimate objective is to be able to reach any potential buyers, regardless of location, without the need for prior arrangement. Even though they are valuable business tools, interorganizational systems cannot achieve this objective because they depend on predefined relationships and communications paths.

Firms are often limited in their ability to reach buyers by their sales and marketing processes. The size and location of their sales force, the breadth and depth of their distributor network, the extent of their dealer chain, the number of business locations, or the size and effectiveness of the mailing list all determine a firm's reach. These factors also determine the nature and extent of information exchange. On the other hand, the innovative use of communications networks for electronic markets can create the most dynamic form of reach: anyone, anytime, anywhere.

Bypassing Traditional Channels

Heightened competition and shareholder push for return on investments make it increasingly important for a firm to assess the value added, as well as the costs incurred, in working with its business partners. This is particularly true for distribution channels. If the services of a broker, representative, or distributor do not add value, firms will seek to bypass them to eliminate costs, delays, and other inefficiencies.

Largely for this reason, a growing number of firms are attempting to deal directly with manufacturers, passing along savings to buyers in the form of lower prices. Electronic markets facilitate bypass if they enable firms to deal directly with actual and potential buyers. Moreover, firms can enter the market even when they do not have, do not wish to create, or cannot establish access to traditional channels.

Augmenting Traditional Markets

Catalog companies have competed successfully against traditional retailers for many years by bypassing both traditional channels and markets where items are bought and sold (i.e., retail stores and other types of sales centers). Electronic markets are a natural evolution of catalog selling and direct dealing, except that both the catalog and order-entry process, and in some cases, actual fulfillment, are online. In fact, the best known catalog companies, including L.L. Bean, Lands End, and Spiegel, are expanding well beyond their traditional markets to compete in electronic markets.

Among the most effective electronic market alternatives are

- *Direct sales outlets*—Electronic storefronts where buyers deal directly with the supplier to create and carry out a sales transaction.
- *Online catalogs*—A special case of the sales outlet where companies can create databases that can be browsed by buyers and used by the firm to distribute information.
- *Direct service centers*—Electronic locations from which customer service, advertising, marketing, and technical support are provided.

Electronic shopping malls (cybermalls) have also been developed as some firms tried to emulate the traditional malls encompassing a variety of stores, services, and information guides. Business-to-business and business-to-consumer versions generally fail, an indication that traditional, non-electronic business forms, do not necessarily transfer to an e-commerce format.

Boosting Service

Service knows no boundary when markets are electronic. Time windows are eliminated because online services can be delivered 24 hours a day. Important buyer and supplier information is available around the clock. Yet inquirers need not wait for an assistant to provide the details. Careful and creative use of information technology also means that the information can consist of much more than narrative explanations, for drawings, photographs, animated descriptions, and full multimedia presentations are all within the scope of service support in the electronic market.

Other important service options include online sections that provide answers to the most frequently asked pre-and post-sale questions. Support can go well beyond troubleshooting concerns. Organizations have found that their descriptions of product updates or new service features can be much more detailed and offer better explanations when provided in this manner. Of course E-mail and fax-back responses are easily provided as well.

Even if a company chooses to never make a single sale by way of electronic commerce, it can still build its business. Boosting service by way of electronic markets has the potential to be much more than just another business tactic.

Advertising

Awareness, visibility, and opportunity—all-important benefits of advertising—take on special importance when markets are electronic. Firms are not constrained by the boundaries of a printed document or by the length of a time slot, both common constraints of advertising through conventional broadcast media.

Carefully chosen listings in online catalogs and databases enable a firm's buyers to learn about the company and its products even when they lack prior knowledge of their existence. Electronic links make it possible for shoppers to jump from the advertising spot to the firm's location in the market. There is a seemingly unlimited range of alternatives that can be used to inform, educate, and perhaps convince the customer of the company's capabilities. Product samples and colorful demonstrations, delivered electronically, are highly effective vehicles for gaining attention and garnering good will while building the business.

CREATING ELECTRONIC MARKETS USING THE INTERNET

There is little doubt that both the expanding reach of the Internet and the accelerating international interest in national information infrastructures will stimulate creation of electronic marketplaces. As more and more firms take steps to move the electronic marketplace from concept to reality, a broad array of innovations will emerge, making it possible for firms and individuals to capitalize on communications networks and overcome the traditional business barriers of time and distance.

Because the Internet has captured the attention of many IT users and observers, it is useful to examine the Internet's value in terms of electronic markets. The following sections explore the reasons why firms may want to include the Internet in their electronic market plans.

Internet Features

The characteristics of the Internet are widely documented, but a moving target (see Exhibit 52.4). Some have predicted that it will surpass the global telephone network by the year 2006. More than 80 percent of the CEOs in the world's largest companies expect e-commerce to significantly *reshape* the way the companies in their industry compete.

Eight key features are of greatest importance to businesses interested in participating in electronic markets.

Public Resource. The very public nature of the Internet is among its most important distinguishing features. Thus the vast majority of business practitioners are aware of the Internet and its widespread accessibility, even though many have not yet considered its business value. The sky-

Internet Growth and Usage

• Hosts on the Internet	44 million
• Estimated Internet users	150 million
• Worldwide percentage of Internet user population	United States/Canada 70% Europe 19% Asia 12%

• Rate of Internet growth	Number of pages doubling
	  annually since 1988
	Number of users estimated to
	  exceed 300 million (5% of global
	  population) by year 2000
	Expected to exceed size of global
	  telephone network by 2006

Business-to-Business Characteristics

E-commerce Sales Volume Forecast	1998/1999	2000
	($50 Billion)	($1.317 Trillion)
• Business-to-Consumer	30%	14%
• Business-to-Business	70%	86%

CEO Expectations

Price Waterhouse World Economic Forum; sample of 377 CEOs of world's largest 2,000 companies (1998)

• Global CEOs expecting e-commerce to significantly *reshape competition* in their industry80%	80% 28%
• European and Asian CEOs expecting e-commerce to *completely transform* their industries	16%
• North American CEOs expecting e-commerce to *completely transform* their industries	

Sources: CommerceNet Consortium/A.C. Nielsen; International Data Corp., The Internet Society; Vinton Cerf

Exhibit 52.4. Internet characteristics

---

rocketing attention to the Internet by the print and broadcast media is certain to fuel the growth in public awareness. Potential customers and business partners will expect firms to be accessible on the Internet.

Because virtually anyone can participate in the Internet as a business by making only a modest start-up investment, the number and diversity of firms participating will continue to increase rapidly. Moreover, the opportunities to announce new products and services and to reach potential customers or partners (television home shopping services pale by comparison) are abundant.

Global Reach. Approximately 30% of the worldwide Internet user population is estimated to originate from outside of the United States (see Exhibit 52.4). In addition, a substantial number of host sites reside in non-U.S.

cities, making it a truly international network. Both sectors are growing rapidly.

The broad international reach of the Internet means much more than business access to individuals and firms in developed countries, even though that alone is sufficient for many firms to integrate e-commerce over the Internet into their businesses. For the first time, individual shops in many underdeveloped countries can interact online as telephone links to the Internet make it possible to span vast geographic distances. No one knows how large this vastly undeveloped market will be.

Capability to Link. The Internet's capability to link firms has not been fully discovered. Many business users of the Internet still view it primarily as an electronic mail or publishing system—that is, a communications tool. Hence, only a fraction of companies connected to the Internet have sought to capitalize on its vast capabilities.

When viewed as a connection tool, rather than as a communications network, many other intriguing possibilities emerge. A variety of different business-to-business transactions can be passed through the network, and EDI documents are increasingly being transmitted through the Internet. Several traditional EDI vendors have developed capabilities to support Internet EDI.

Shared Ownership. No company, society, association, or individual owns the Internet. Rather, some thousands of independently owned and operated networks are interconnected to form the Internet. As a result, the Internet is distinguished by collaboration, not proprietary designs. The broad base of public participation means that new initiatives can be successful only if the majority of participants are interested in using them. Even more, it means that virtually every individual and firm, large or small, has the opportunity to participate.

Shared ownership does mean, however, that the Internet has some awkward features, especially in the areas of security and reliability.

Platform Flexibility/Diversity. There are few limits on the nature of the computing and communications that can be interconnected with the Internet. Companies are thus free to use the systems of their choosing (e.g., UNIX, NT, Windows, Linux, and Macintosh). Yet the choice of system platform places no restriction on others using the system or wishing to interconnect with them.

In many instances, the computing systems attached to the Internet are less sophisticated than those used in proprietary systems. Networking and applications software compensates for differences in systems capabilities even as they accommodate the diverse computing and communications platforms.

Cost Advantages. The cost of conducting business on the Internet is quite modest. The principal requirement is to create a business site, typically on the Worldwide Web (WWW) portion of the Internet. Getting on the WWW may cost as little as $100. Low-cost kits are readily available to construct the necessary features (such as home pages, online catalogs, and communication links). For a modest fee, the development of such features can be contracted.

Because of the many companies that have emerged to provide access to the Worldwide Web or other portions of the Internet, it is not necessary to even operate a computer network to be able to participate in business-to-business e-commerce (see Exhibit 52.5). These companies, which in effect function as "on ramps" to the network, will provide all services, at a cost that depends on the frequency of use for the service. Representative companies providing e-commerce service are listed in Exhibit 52.6. Some companies are investing heavily in their Internet resources, dedicating several staff members and a significant hardware and software investment into supporting their presence on the network. They are choosing to do so, because compared to other alternatives, including developing and maintaining a proprietary computer network or supporting a direct dial-up bulletin board, they view the Internet as a cost-effective resource.

CAPITALIZING ON THE INTERNET FOR ELECTRONIC MARKETS

Ongoing monitoring of firms using the Internet provides growing evidence that those who are capitalizing on the network's electronic market potential appear to follow several principles:

- The treat the Internet as a new medium.
- The use the Internet to leverage existing business and support capabilities.
- They formulate clear business objectives for Internet use.

The Internet as a New Medium

Many businesses tend to consider the Internet's features as supplementary to what they already do. Although this approach may offer attractive possibilities, greater opportunities may be found by taking a fresh approach to the Internet as a medium for reaching out, linking up, and delivering something entirely different. Hence, management should raise stimulating discussion by asking questions that will unleash creative possibilities, such as:

- What are the current limitations in linking up with business partners or supporting customers? What is the impact of those limitations?

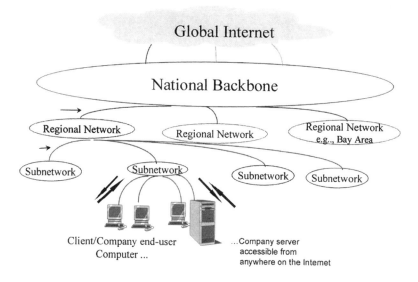

Exhibit 52.5. Architecture of the Global Internet

- What new products, services, or supports can be offered?
- What opportunities exist to aid the firm's customers in being more successful with their customers?
- How can the firm's current competitors turn the Internet into a competitive weapon that is detrimental to the firm?
- What new businesses can be developed as a means of offering Internet capabilities to others?

Leveraging Existing Business and Support Capabilities

Firms creating value through the Internet are doing so because they are able to leverage resources and expertise already present in the firm. Hence, it is vital that firms directly address these important questions:

- What is it that the firm does best—the products or services that it delivers—and how can they be leveraged into new business arenas or as new products and services to a different market?
- What important resources is the firm under-utilizing and how can they be put to new or extended use by making them available through electronic markets?
- How can the knowledge base of the firm be enhanced through access to new customers or business partners who are willing to share their insights and needs in an interactive environment?
- How can the knowledge base be leveraged into a product or service that will be accessible to virtually every individual firm through the power of electronic markets?

Firm	Worldwide Web Address
Best Internet Communications Mountain View, CA	http://www.best.com
CyberGate, Inc. Deerfield Beach, FL	http://www.gate.net
CTS Network Services San Diego, CA	http://www.cts.com
Icon CMP Corp. Weehawken, NJ	http://www.icon.com
The Internet Access Company, Inc Bedord, MA	http://www.tiac.net
iXL Enterprises Atlanta, GA	http://www.ixl.com
Macquarium, Inc. Atlanta, GA	http://www.macquarium.com
MCIWorldcom Jackson, MS	http://www.wcom.com
MindSpring Enterprises, Inc. Atlanta, GA	http://www.mindspring.com
Open Market, Inc. Cambridge, MA	http://www.openmarket.com
Teleport Internet Services Portland, OR	http://www.teleport.com
Web Communications Santa Cruz, CA	http://www.webcom.com
XMission Internet Access Salt Lake City, UT	http://www.xmission.com

Exhibit 52.6. Representative Commercial Electronic Market Providers on the Internet

Formulating a Business Case

Unless a company's journey onto the Internet is designed to be nothing more than an exploratory adventure or distraction, any rationale for moving onto the network should be formulated as a business case. This means establishing and then measuring against clear objectives, preferably with a timetable describing expected milestones. The business case should identify points of success, whether they be potential customer contacts, information inquiries, revenue generation, or profit margins. It should clearly answer two key questions:

- What will the company gain?
- How will success be measured?

It is all too easy to seek to justify new initiatives through such nebulous terms as visibility, public relations, advertising, and public awareness. Yet if these are important reasons for joining the network, as they often are, they should be cast in measurable business terms that will enable even the strongest (or weakest) supporter to gauge success.

CONCLUSION

Electronic markets and the Internet are in their infancy. Although it is not clear how either will evolve, both represent fundamental shifts in electronic commerce with significant implications for business in general. An ever-greater portion of business will be conducted online, with extensive reliance on communications networks.

Waiting to see how the promise and possibilities of electronic markets will evolve may appear the safest strategy in the short term, particularly for mangers averse to high risk. Yet, organizations must have ample time to gain insight into the potential of electronic markets and to create the necessary experience and knowledge to capitalize on the opportunities that may emerge. Organizations that begin learning early may gain long-term advantages that late-comers will never overcome.

Chapter 53
E-Commerce Issues for External Web Sites

Andrew Urbaczewski
Leonard M. Jessup

THE PROLIFERATION of the Internet and the World Wide Web (WWW) as a vehicle for and to end consumers has made electronic commerce a hot topic in the business world and in the popular press. It is now possible for individuals to purchase a variety of goods and services from firms that have established an Internet presence. According to Forrester Research, online sales to end consumers for 1999 are projected at over $18 billion, more than double 1998's $7.8 billion total. In 2003, sales could reach as high as $108 billion, approximately 6 percent of consumer retail spending. It is difficult to find a current newspaper or magazine without some mention of the Internet and electronic commerce. On the other hand, there were only about 87 million people in the United States and 154 million people worldwide connected to the Internet by February 1999 (http://www.nua.net/surveys), less than 4 percent of the world's population.

The objective of this chapter is to provide an overview of E-commerce issues of relevance for IT managers. For those just getting started with E-commerce initiatives, there is something to be gained especially from stepping back for a moment and evaluating some of the key issues posed by this new way of conducting business.

This chapter presents some of the critical issues in four major categories: technology infrastructure issues, concerns of potential customers, product/service pricing issues, and unresolved legal and regulatory issues. The discussion focuses on these issues from the perspective of E-commerce via external Web sites for conducting business with end consumers.

SOME TECHNOLOGY INFRASTRUCTURE ISSUES

As with any large-scale, networked information systems project, a well-planned, well-executed infrastructure is absolutely vital.

Bandwidth Issues

If a Web site is difficult to access and if content on the site is slow for visitors to download, it will frustrate users and may ultimately turn away customers. It is much easier to get "out of line" (i.e., remove yourself from a virtual queue) and change stores in cyberspace than it is in the physical world when one becomes frustrated with long waits. Internal testing should be required before implementing a site, using the system in the same way a consumer might, over a 28.8 Kbps modem. What loads quickly and looks flashy on a local hard drive may take so long over a modem that consumers will not bother with it and will instead try somewhere else.

Often sites can provide a graphical version and a text-only version of their sites to give users a choice based on the bandwidth available to them. Newer technologies that IT managers might like to use, such as streaming video, require large amounts of bandwidth that may not be readily available to their end consumers.

The amount of bandwidth available to a server is also crucial. When IT managers negotiate contracts with Internet service providers (ISPs) or WWW hosting services, T-1 (1.544 megabits per second) is probably the minimum bandwidth any server should have to conduct serious E-commerce. Many find that this slows down with even moderate usage, and they want to have several T-1 lines feeding the server, or perhaps even a T-3 (44.7 Mbps) connection. Response times from individual ISPs can vary even when supplying the same bandwidth "on paper," based on their proximity to Internet routers and their own bandwidth into the Internet backbone. Other bandwidth solutions could come from multithreaded application programming languages, such as Sun Microsystems' Java.

Platform Choices

Although the WWW is based on open technologies that suit E-commerce well, the technologies have inherent limitations. For example, HTML is good for displaying static text, pictures, and some animation, but the modifications necessary for complex database access and data retrieval tend to be slow. Because technology in this arena changes rapidly, as evidenced by the "Netscape-year" phenomenon, we can expect a replacement for HTML in delivering content to users, for example, Extensible Markup Language (XML).

For the first time in many years, there are vast choices in standard technology for use in electronic projects. From the most expensive Windows

NT™ implementation to free, open-source software such as Linux and Apache, managers can select a wide variety of platforms for their electronic storefronts. In evaluating open-source solutions such as Apache and Linux, one must consider whether or not they are willing to trade the advantage of consistently available support for a free product. The lack of accountability and support has been a barrier in the past to corporate acceptance of open-source products, but even this is changing now. Red Hat Software, a Linux vendor, is offering round-the-clock support packages for its Linux implementation, and corporations are now considering Linux for mission-critical applications.

Whatever platforms IT managers choose, they must consider the ability to scale their hardware and software for increasing capacity. If their Web site becomes more popular and applications are slowing down, they want to be able to simply increase hardware capacity without having to rewrite their applications, especially for a different platform. Scalability is a problem that has plagued Microsoft software at the enterprise level. In a speech at the November 1998 COMDEX, Oracle CEO Larry Ellison offered $1 million to anyone who could get a specific query to run on Microsoft's SQL Server database at 1/100 the speed that it runs on Oracle's enterprise database on the same hardware. Several months later, Microsoft technology caught up to this level (after Ellison had withdrawn the challenge), and its products may continue to become more scalable in the future.

Security Issues — Real and Perceived

A stumbling block to the acceptance of E-commerce by end consumers is the *perceived* lack of security with public networks. Encryption algorithms can be used to code and decode messages from sender to receiver. Yet well-publicized successes by graduate students in breaking supposedly unbreakable encryption schemes have caused consumers and information providers alike to reconsider the safety of data transmitted through public networks. It is not likely that E-commerce will ever be completely secure, much as there is no such thing as the "unsinkable ship" or "unrobbable bank," but there are much easier ways for a determined thief to steal credit card numbers than by deciphering coded Internet communications.

Firms should take advantage of the best products technology currently provides and still stay within budget. Secure HTTP (https) is one way of conducting secure business over the Internet. WWW browsers and servers establish a coded conversation that can only be understood by each other, completely transparent to the user. This is easily implemented today on server software that costs less than $1,000, a significant reduction from the $25,000 price tag of the first WWW Commerce server offered by Netscape Communications Corporation in 1994.

CONCERNS OF POTENTIAL CUSTOMERS

For the end consumer, communication, interaction, and relationships with the seller are all different in an electronic environment. This section describes some areas for concern from the customer perspective.

Privacy

People have always had a need to maintain some level of privacy or anonymity. With traditional commerce, this is possible through cash transactions at retail outlets, which generate little or no data linking a specific individual with those transactions. Most forms of E-commerce, on the other hand, generate data linking a specific individual with his or her transaction. Furthermore, consumers may have data gathered about them inconspicuously by organizations, through cookies or other means. This is often disturbing to users who wish their online pursuits to remain anonymous, as when a marketing representative of a firm is perusing another firm's WWW site for marketing intelligence or when a consumer is visiting electronic sites that he or she might rather not be associated with in public. As evidenced by the recent outcry over the digital IDs placed in Intel's Pentium III chips, many people are becoming fearful that "Big Brother" is constantly watching. Corporations should take responsibility for the information they gather about their potential customers, collecting only what is truly necessary and making sure that the users know these data are being collected about them. This will help companies be seen as responsible Internet marketers.

Social Benefits from Shopping

The direct-to-consumer model proposed by E-commerce is typically solitary. It is not likely that users will gather in front of the computer to shop online like they travel together to the shopping mall. Thus, direct-to-consumer E-commerce may not ultimately succeed with everyone, primarily because some consumers may shun its perceived convenience for the social benefits of shopping in person and interacting directly with sales personnel and other shoppers. Some E-commerce providers have offered social contact via online shopping by facilitating the creation of virtual communities. For example, at amazon.com, users with common interests in books can gather to exchange information, advice, and commentary.

Cost of Internet Access

At this moment, consumer access is rarely metered by the minute but, rather, is more commonly available for a flat monthly fee from an ISP. Some sites are still experimenting with charging the end user the equivalent of membership and/or subscription fees, but most sites are now paid for by the company completely as part of overhead, like the rent on the virtual storefront, and expenses are recouped through either purchases or advertising on the site.

The predominant consumer philosophy is that Internet access and information ought to be free. Having said that, however, there are instances in which consumers will pay for privileges. For example, several thousand users pay $13 monthly to James Cramer's TheStreet.com for timely information about stock market events. There are ways to make money on a Web site other than capturing eyeballs and then pushing in front of them ads that other firms pay you for the privilege of placing there. Sites such as TheStreet.com are discovering that people will pay for, visit, linger on, and revisit a "sticky" Web site that is fast and easy to use and has valuable, fresh content. We are by no means, however, close to perfecting the art of making money in this way on the WWW or determining reasonable, attractive prices for doing so.

Customer Service

Many of the advantages and efficiencies of electronic commerce, such as 24-hour-a-day availability and automation, also depersonalize the experience. This depersonalization or lack of customer service is a threat to the success of E-commerce. When one is shopping at the mall, it is easy to ask a salesperson questions about the product or to demonstrate it, or to try it out personally, as with a pair of jeans or a perfume. Questions about products such as warranty, form factor, and compatibility with other products, could be answered easily. Feedback from E-commerce sellers typically is not real time, requiring an E-mail message to be sent and replied, often taking several hours or days.

Companies utilizing E-commerce sites should make it a priority to maximize customer service. E-mails should be answered promptly. When sites generate enough traffic, it might be a good idea to assign a person or people as "sales representatives" who are able to answer questions in real time or as close to real time as possible. If relying on e-mail to field and answer questions, the organization should answer them promptly and accurately. Organizations with a separate 800-number customer support area may need to merge these operations with those for e-mail responses.

Customer Satisfaction

Testing an external Web site with focus groups before releasing it to the general public is a good way to get feedback before making a worldwide debut. Once implemented, metrics are needed to maximize system and site effectiveness. Companies with databases filled with electronic information about consumers and products are in a unique position to test and change their E-commerce approaches based on comparative analysis.

PRODUCT/SERVICE PRICING ISSUES

Electronic markets instantaneously connect buyers and sellers as well as enable buyers to compare prices for the same goods or services. Some of these markets are intentional, such as the NASDAQ stock market system. No physical market for NASDAQ exists; rather, it is an automated electronic system linking market makers with "bid" and "ask" prices on computers and enabling brokers to execute orders. Www.ebay.com is another good example of a collection of auctions assembled together in an intentional electronic market where anyone can offer, bid for, and/or trade anything they wish. On the other hand, some electronic markets are involuntary. For example, software programs called agents can be written to gather information from different vendors' WWW sites and then post current vendors' prices on a Web site where potential buyers can browse and choose a vendor. When the price an organization is offering for a given product can be captured accurately in real time, placed neatly in a rank-ordered list along with its competitor's products and prices, and displayed on demand for any consumer, the rules of the game are fundamentally changed. A quick visit to an online auction or to a site for comparison shopping is at once exciting and frightening in its implications for doing business in the future. Companies are also under pressure to have international pricing, whereas in the past pricing varied by regional area.

SOME UNRESOLVED LEGAL AND REGULATORY ISSUES

The introduction of a new technology usually raises legal questions that must be addressed by the courts. Computing and E-commerce have been advancing so fast that the laws cannot keep up with the technology. Some of these may be potential areas for concern that require organizational policies in advance of initiating a new E-commerce capability.

Responsibility for Information Accuracy

E-commerce enables and in some cases requires the business to store information about customers. This includes traditional information as required on invoices and billing statements, but also electronic information about the terminals used and digital signatures to authenticate a person's existence. *Who will be responsible when this information is incorrect?* For example, what if a CyberCash account has an incorrect balance? What if an online credit report has incorrect information? What if a digital signature is forged? It is not clear who will be responsible for accuracy in these contexts: the firm, the customer, the ISP, the software and hardware used to run the Web site, the outsourcing partner that helped to build the site, or somebody else?

Enforcing Local Standards

The openness of the Internet ignores both state and national boundaries. In cyberspace, it does not matter where a company is physically located; all that matters is its IP address. This openness facilitates international E-commerce. However, it also makes enforcing local standards and laws virtually impossible. Whose standards count is an important question for the courts and legal scholars.

The Communications Decency Act (CDA) was passed in 1996 as an attempt to shield the public from many "indecent" documents, pictures, and other material available on the Internet. The CDA was subsequently found to be unconstitutional as an unfair limit on free speech, but others in Congress are trying to pass versions of the bill that are less vague in definitions of "indecent." Is it legal for a WWW site to offer the services anywhere? Is it legal to use the services?

Inaccessible E-Commerce Sites

If a computer that hosts a company's external Web site goes down, it is equivalent to the front door being locked and business being closed. With E-commerce, it is not always clear why a computer is unreachable. Perhaps it is a problem with the computer, or it might be a problem with the network connecting the computer to other computers. If the external network is the problem, is the company's ISP or other service provider liable for lost profits and transactions? What recourse does the E-commerce-based shopkeeper have against this entity that has effectively locked the door to the commerce site? Or, is it the firm's responsibility to have backup connections ready in case the primary connection goes down, making its network fault-tolerant? Will the laws of telephone communications apply as they might to mail-order catalog companies, or will laws relating to more traditional forms of denial of entry apply?

CONCLUSION

E-commerce can mean boom or bust for a business. Some traditional catalog retailers, such as Dell Computer, now achieve about half their sales from the Internet. Chances are good that E-commerce will fundamentally transform a firm and an industry in one way or another. By ignoring the coming digital revolution, by not preparing oneself or one's firm for E-commerce, or by not properly managing and monitoring one's Web presence, IT managers put their companies at risk. It is time for IT managers to consider E-commerce as mainstream and to ensure that they and their firms thrive in a wired world.

Chapter 54
Developing Corporate Intranets
Diana Jovin

THE WEB is revolutionizing business practices. It provides a path to increased revenue and new customers while significantly lowering the cost of technology and the cost of doing business. Although much of the Internet hype has focused on what is visible — that is, what companies are doing on their external sites — the biggest impact is taking place behind the scenes, through intranets that are replacing paper and LAN applications as the vehicle for company and group communications.

Intranets play a key role in reducing costs and increasing effectiveness and efficiency of internal information management. Intranet applications serve as productivity, sales, service, and training tools that can be disseminated through the organization at much lower cost than traditional paper, client/server, or mainframe implementations. In addition, intranets enhance the capabilities of traditional applications by extending portions of the application to a wider audience within the organization.

THE INTRANET IMPACT — WHAT CAN AN INTRANET DO?

Applications made available on an intranet tend to fall into one of two categories — Web self-service and intranet reengineering. Web self-service applications make the process of information delivery more efficient by eliminating cost and redundancy from the information delivery cycle. Intranet reengineering applications, through the use of real-time information delivery, change existing business processes. These applications enable companies to offer new products and services and increase the effectiveness of the business decision-making cycle.

Web Self-Service

Web self-service applications allow users to access information more efficiently by eliminating an intermediary process or middleman whose sole function is facilitation of information access. These applications make information more readily available, accurate, and reliable. Examples include

0-8493-9820-7/00/$0.00+$.50
© 2000 by CRC Press LLC

- *Employee directories.* Directories provide basic personnel information, including phone numbers, extension, addresses, and job descriptions that allow employees to update information such as address changes themselves, without going through the process of filling out an information change request form.
- *Human resources benefits.* Human resources applications allow employees to review their status on vacation and medical benefits, look up current status of 401(k) contributions, and change allocation of contributions to 401(k) funds.
- *Technical support.* Technical support applications enable employees and business partners to look up answers to technical issues directly from a technical support database and extend service capabilities beyond working hours.

Intranet Reengineering

Intranet reengineering applications not only provide real-time information delivery, but they also impact existing business processes and how decision making feeds into them. The following sections describe sample applications.

Sales Force Automation. Web-based sales force systems provide the sales staff with immediate access to customer account status and activity. Whether in retail banking, brokerage, or other industries, viewing real-time status is a tool that the sales force can use to provide new products and better service. In some financial institutions, portfolio applications that make customer information immediately accessible to the sales force are replacing the practice of distributing customer account information in the form of monthly, paper-based reports.

Manufacturing and Inventory. Inventory systems that interface between manufacturer and distributors can significantly improve processes such as inventory location and price protection. An example application that manufacturers are providing to distributors is inventory tracking, which provides information on availability, price, and location. In industries with price volatility, Web applications allow manufacturers to respond more quickly to price protection issues by enabling distributors to enter sales and order information that is processed immediately rather than in batch mode.

Purchasing and Financial. Purchasing applications let employees submit purchasing requests directly from the Web. International companies can benefit from applications that provide the purchasing department with information on foreign exchange exposure and recommended cash position prior to purchase.

In these examples, real-time delivery of information can have a significant impact on a company's product and service offerings or its ability to respond more quickly to the customer. In some industries, the Web is redefining the competitive landscape. For example, banks, which have been losing share in back-office activities to software vendors such as Intuit, are using the Web to reclaim their market share with applications that allow customers to enter request-for-quote or payment initiation directly over the Web with an easy-to-use interface.

The Web as an Application Platform

The Web is compelling as an application platform because it provides both strategic and tactical benefits. Companies can harness the Web as a way to attract new customers and deliver new products and services. At the same time, companies can significantly reduce the costs of technology and doing business. These benefits combined make the Web an attractive platform over alternative implementations such as client/server or mainframe. Benefits include

- *Global availability.* Web applications can be made available on a global basis, providing companies with a mechanism to go after a new set of customers or to integrate remote offices or business partners without building expensive proprietary networks.
- *Instant application distribution.* Applications can be deployed instantaneously worldwide, eliminating the need for installation of client-side software or for printing, reproduction, and distribution of paper-based information.
- *Platform and version independence.* Applications are server based and can interact with any Web browser on any Internet-capable client. Applications are no longer tied to the client hardware platform and can easily be distributed across heterogeneous computing environments. Applications can be updated instantaneously, eliminating the hassle of version maintenance and support.
- *Reduced training costs.* Web applications have a common look and feel, which lowers training costs of applications traditionally presented in different types of GUI environments.
- *Increased data reliability.* Web applications can eliminate redundant data entry from paper forms. Reliability and availability of data is increased when the information holder can enter and update information directly.

With benefits that contribute to both increased revenue and decreased cost, the potential impact on a company's bottom line can be huge.

NEW MODEL FOR DISTRIBUTED COMPUTING

The Web's benefits derive from its architecture. A Web application is not merely a client/server application with a Web browser interface. "Web-native" applications take full advantage of this architecture. "Web-enabled" applications typically miss the full set of benefits because they are tied to an existing client/server-based architecture. Four key areas in which the Web architectural model differs significantly from that of client/server include: network infrastructure, client-side requirements, server-side requirements, and management of database login.

WAN versus LAN

Web applications are deployed over a wide area network (WAN), in contrast to client/server applications, which are deployed over proprietary local area networks (LANs). There are two immediate implications in this difference: reach and cost.

In the WAN environment, companies can communicate with anyone connected to the WAN, including customers and business partners worldwide. LANs typically have a smaller reach and are also often expensive to install and maintain. WAN applications provide a means for a company to communicate with business partners or employees worldwide without building a global private network as long as security considerations are sufficiently taken into account.

Application Publishing — Server versus Client

Web applications, in contrast to client/server applications, are primarily server-based, with a "thin client" front end. This thin client may do some business logic processing, such as data validation, but the bulk of the business logic is processed on the server side rather than on the client.

Client/server applications, in contrast, typically support "fat clients," in which the application is a sizeable executable running on the client. Although this model takes advantage of client CPU power for application processing, the client/server model does not provide the Web's primary benefit — instant application distribution. Web tools that provide client-side plug-ins typically call themselves "Web-enabled" as opposed to "Web-native" because they are not taking full advantage of the Web's architecture in instant distribution.

N-Tier versus 2- or 3-Tier

Web applications require a multi-tier, or n-tier, server architecture. Scalability takes a quantum leap on the Web, with a much larger application audience and greater uncertainty in the number of users who might choose to access the application at any given time.

Client/server applications hit the wall with a 2-tier architecture. To solve this problem, some client/server implementations have moved to a 3-tier architecture. Given the greater number of users who can access a Web application, even 3-tier models are not enough to sustain some of the heavy-duty applications being deployed today.

In addition, the Web provides the capability to move intranet applications, such as customer portfolio management, directly to the customer over the Internet. These applications can only migrate to the Internet environment if they have been designed to scale.

Shared Database Connection versus Individual Login

Web applications incur heavy CPU processing requirements as a result of the number of users accessing the application. As a result, well-designed systems provide users with persistent shared database connections. In this model, the user only ties up a database connection when he or she has pressed an action button, hyperlink, or image that requests data from the database. Once the data is returned, the database connection is free for another user, without requiring the database connection to be shut down and reopened for the new user.

In the client/server model, the user maintains an individual persistent database connection from the time he or she logs on to the time the application is exited. In this model, the database connection is inefficient because the user is logged onto the database regardless of whether a database action is taking place or whether the user is merely looking through the results that have been returned.

TECHNICAL CONSIDERATIONS

Although a Web architecture delivers significant benefits, it also introduces new technical challenges, particularly with respect to scalability, state and session, and security. When developing applications and selecting development tools, it is critical to understand these challenges and how they are being solved by different vendors in the industry today.

Scalability and Performance

Web-native applications (i.e., applications that are server-based rather than client-side browser plug-ins) that provide the highest degree of scalability are deployed through an n-tier application server. Application servers first appeared in the market in December 1995 and have rapidly gained acceptance as a model that overcomes the limitations of the common gateway interface (CGI) in execution of scalable applications.

In the early stages of Web development, applications were executed through CGI. In this model, the Web server receives a request for data, opens a CGI process, executes the application code, opens the database, receives the data, closes the database, then closes the CGI process, and returns the dynamic page. This sequence takes place for each user request and ties up CPU time in system housekeeping because of the starting and stopping of processes. System housekeeping involved in executing the application increases proportionally to the size of the application executable.

Application servers, in contrast, stay resident as an interface between the Web server and database server. In this model, the Web server passes the request to the application server through a very small CGI relay or the Web server APIs. The application server manages the application processing and maintains persistent connections to the database. Enterprise-level application servers multiplex users across persistent database connections, can be distributed across multiple CPUs, and provide automatic load balancing and monitoring.

State and Session Management

The Web is a stateless environment, meaning that information about the user and the user's actions are not automatically maintained as the user moves from page to page in the application. This presents obstacles to providing LAN-like interaction in the Web environment.

Some technology vendors have solved this problem by building session and state managers into the application server, which allows developers to build applications with persistent memory across pages. An early approach that also persists is to write "cookies" or files containing state information to the client browser. These files are read on each page access. This is a manual process that is less secure than server-based session and state memory.

Security

Security is a key to implementing business critical applications in the Web environment. The good news is that it is becoming easier to manage security on the Web.

In building a secure environment, it is important to understand first the intranet or intranet application's security requirements, and second the technology component of the intranet solution that is going to provide it. Exhibit 54.1 shows some of the components that might exist in an intranet environment and how they might contribute to different aspects of a secure solution.

Fine-grained security control appeared in the marketplace in mid-1996. Examples are control over navigation flow through the pages in the application and fine-grained user access control. For example, Acme Company may wish to grant Joe Smith access to a limited set of application pages

Technology Component	Contribution to Security
Web server	User authorization and data encryption
Application server	Page navigation flow control
Database server	Database login
Firewall	Internal network access control
DCE infrastructure	Centralized security login and rules

Exhibit 54.1. Some Components of an Intranet Environment and Their Contributions to Security

only between 9:00 a.m. and 5:00 p.m. It may wish to grant Joe CEO, however, full access 24 hours a day. Acme Company will require both users to enter the application at a specific page and step through in a predetermined sequence. Breaking the flow of the application exits the user from the application.

WHAT ABOUT JAVA?

Java is rapidly gaining momentum as the ideal programming language for the Internet, and one that can enhance client-side processing and GUI capabilities in a secure environment while maintaining Web advantages of platform independence and instant application publishing. Among its advantages are

- *Web-secure publishing.* Java is designed from the ground up to run in a restricted environment, such as a Web browser. Java provides developers with the ability to distribute client-side applets that contain programming logic while ensuring the security of the local PC's environment.
- *Platform independence.* The platform independence of Java code means that developers can easily move applications from platform to platform without recompiling code or mixing development and deployment platforms.
- *Simple, high-level, object-oriented language.* Java is a true object-oriented language with syntax that is very similar to C++. Java is, however, simpler than C++ and provides a higher level of functionality. For example, Java has no pointers to memory and provides automatic garbage collection. So all memory leaks and pointer manipulation problems that accompany C++ programs are eliminated with Java. Java also contains libraries providing built-in services such as thread support, string manipulation, I/O, networking, and graphical user in-

terface, allowing developers to focus on solving business problems rather than code manipulation.

- *Fast development cycle.* Java provides run-time linking. Thus, when a new class is written, only that class needs to be recompiled. This provides for a very fast compile link test development cycle, especially when compared with C or C++, where the entire project must be relinked before the program can be tested.
- *Application partitioning.* Java is the only language that can run on both a Web client and Web server. Thus, if both the client and server code are implemented using Java, the developer has the flexibility to push the application partitioning decision to run-time. Application logic can be run on either the client or server, depending on which location will optimize system performance.

Some concerns exist about the practicality of Java when there are so many developers versed in existing languages, such as C++. However, the growing number of Java developers and support being given to Java by all major players in the Internet space suggest that Java is on its way to becoming the standard language for the Internet and other networking environments. Evaluation of intranet tools and technologies should include consideration of how they leverage Java.

CONCLUSION

In addition to sound tools and technology, a successful intranet also requires a solid operational plan. These plans differ significantly from company to company, but issues that will need to be considered and addressed are

- Should the organization build in-house expertise or outsource Intranet development?
- Should purchases of tools and technology be centralized through one technology evaluation group, or dispersed throughout the company and individual business units?
- How should the company address training and education of the intranet?
- How can the company generate excitement and buy-in?

One common theme across companies, however, is to start with some simple but effective applications, such as employee directories. Successful operations plans use these applications to gain interest and excitement, and intranet champions within the organization take it from there.

Intranets can play a tremendous role in influencing or reflecting organizational culture, evident in the names being given to corporate intranets today. Examples of corporate intranets include

- AT&T — Unified Global Network.

- Booz Allen & Hamilton — Knowledge On Line (KOL).
- JCPenney — jWeb.
- Florida Power — Power Web.
- Silicon Graphics (SGI) — Silicon Junction.

The impact of intranets on corporate profits and productivity can be tremendous. The move to an intranet architecture requires rethinking some of the traditional assumptions of client/server architecture, but the benefits that can be reaped from the Web are enormous. Intranets are redefining the landscape of corporate America and can be a key to achieving or keeping competitive advantage.

Chapter 55
Designing a Business-Justified Intranet Project
Richard L. Ptak

THE UBIQUITY of both intranets and success stories about their rich returns on investment may provide solid foundation for their recommendation but does not lessen the need for a disciplined project and evaluation process. Using the methodology presented here for identifying and designing a business-justified intranet project helps minimize egregious errors and ensure the commitment, resources, and interest necessary for long-term success.

Today's enterprise intranets and accessible Web technologies provide business IT organizations a new technological hammer with which to address expensive communications, management, and application accessibility problems. New England radio waves and post midnight television deliver a barrage of advertisements promising a guide to fortune if not fame through intranet implementation.

Overview articles and anecdotal success stories have been verified by recent rigorous research describing rich returns on the investment for those who have already made the leap to intranet applications. Studies conducted and reported by sources ranging from research firms to industry magazines such as *PC Week* report over 90% satisfaction with project ROIs from leading edge implementers. Such referential evidence provides a solid foundation for recommendation but doesn't lessen the need for a disciplined process to make the business case before implementing a specific Intranet solution. The following methodology details a process for identifying and designing a business-justified Intranet project:

- Identifying the customer who has to be satisfied: For whom will the Intranet services be provided?
- Articulating the goal: What, specifically and incrementally, is to be achieved?

0-8493-9820-7/00/$0.00+$.50
© 2000 by CRC Press LLC

- Planning and assigning resources: Who should be responsible for what?
- Identifying and monitoring a specific performance metric: What is the measure of success?
- Performing a cost/benefit analysis: Does the benefit justify the investment?
- Planning for a phased implementation including a pilot.

Before these steps are discussed in detail, some additional success factors are reviewed.

GENERAL ISSUES FOR SUCCESS

Once established and available as tools, Web and the Intranet pages tend to release a storm of creativity and interest in customized presentation and use. Unmanaged, this risks the proliferation of an abundance of unrelated, haphazard and marginally useful sites, initiated with the best of intentions but quickly becoming irrelevant network clutter. New technologies and tools must support the needs of the business. Organizations which exist to deliver a service or product must do so in the most efficient and cost-effective manner. Few can indulge in technology for the sake of the technology. Every investment and effort must be associated with an improvement in competitive positioning or ability to compete. An intranet project is no exception.

Security and personnel relations both represent sensitive areas for an intranet project. Recent concerns expressed and discussed in the public sector regarding censorship, appropriate site access, quality of information, and so forth all hold true within the enterprise and must be addressed. Existing policy and monitoring procedures must be reviewed and revised to reflect the strengths, weaknesses, and capabilities of the intranet technology. The potential for misuse or abuse does not justify ignoring or avoiding the use of the technology but serves merely as a caution to think through the administrative and support infrastructure to manage an implementation process. Most enterprises will find a compromise between attempting to achieve complete central control and an anarchic, totally distributed, anything-goes administrative model.

It is important to plan for success and to determine early in the project process not only the start-up resources but also what is necessary for support and growth as the project succeeds. While most organizations make provision for unforeseen expenses and loads on networks, today's highly competitive operations running with thin margins make such resources typically available only for mission-critical situations. It is crucial to avoid having the project fail due to insufficient administrative resources or appear to fail because it cannot respond to the level of demand for implemented services.

Selecting the right individual to lead and manage the project is one of the most fundamental determinants of success. All too often, technical expertise overshadows more fundamental and valuable skills in project management, negotiation, people handling, and planning. A technically adept project manager, for instance, can allow technical elegance to outrank business justifications for decisions. Missing or inadequate management skills makes it much more difficult to gather together the range of support and cooperation needed for a successful project implementation. IS managers can avoid this risk by making the ability to manage complex relations, persuade, influence, and secure resources from skeptical, budget-strapped colleagues the foremost selection criteria for the project manager. Technology and technical experts must be part of the implementation and planning teams, but they should not be the lead managers.

To-Do List

Success at the outset depends on the following activities:

- Positioning the intranet and Web as a BUSINESS tool to solve a problem.
- Establishing a policy of self-policing and maintenance.
- Establishing a process to monitor use and plan for adequate resources.
- Selecting project leaders who are non-technical with project management and negotiation skills.

Pitfalls

The following pitfalls can hinder a project's success from the outset:

- Here's the hammer, what's the problem?
- Creation of pages for pages' sake without a business focus.
- Over-control inhibits use; under-control leads to chaos and clutter.

STEP 1: WHO IS THE CUSTOMER?

It is important first and foremost to determine the specific audience to be served. Potentially, the total enterprise represents a practical target. However, this will yield a far too large, varied, and unwieldy initial set of requirements to provide anything beyond a significant risk of failure. Although engineering may want and need a data- or document-sharing application, project management may be ripe for a project status and control display, and IT staff may want the ability to remotely monitor network status, the ready and automatic availability of Human Resource policies, benefits and choices to the entire employee population will conceivably provide a quicker and more measurable payback for an initial implementation. For this reason, it is wise to select a subsection with an identifiable and visible problem, one where the potential and actual benefits and savings promise to be readily monitored and documented.

Once the customers have been identified, involve them in the planning and requirements process. Experience and exposure to the Web and its capabilities have entered the popular culture to an amazing extent. Technical expertise complemented by the knowledge of the involved target population will result in a better project definition, while building a constituency of support for both the initiation and long-term success of the project.

To-Do List

- Select specific target customer with a specific problem.
- Involve the customer in planning and project definition.

Pitfalls

- Too broad a customer focus frustrates problem definition.
- Too narrow a customer focus yields a trivial problem.

STEP 2: WHAT IS THE GOAL?

A detailed and well-articulated statement of the goal and underlying problem to be solved represents a key success factor. More projects and technologies fail for lack of a specific and focused goal, growing expansively out of control and attacking a multitude of problems but resolving none. This is not to say that the purpose should be cast in unchangeable concrete. Flexibility and adaptability represent two of the greatest benefits associated with a Web-based solution. They also help to avoid a deliverable whose useful shelf-life will fall far short of the implementation cycle time.

Clearly established and specific objectives with fixed boundaries foster a crisp, relevant definition of content. Useful and relevant content depends upon both the design and application of suitable tracking mechanisms. These mechanisms must relate to and be supportive of appropriate measurements of success. Finally, these metrics must derived from and be linked to the identified business purpose.

Establishment of the business purpose and contribution of the intranet effort gives foundation to the project justification. If there is no linkage to an identifiable business problem that is a source of fiscal, administrative or management pain, then it is unlikely the commitment, resources and interest necessary for long-term success will be forthcoming. Serendipity happens, but success most often occurs as the result of significant effort and careful analysis.

Effort must be invested in determining a customer eager to participate, with a visible and painful problem, enduring a higher cost or quantifiable disadvantage that will be visibly affected by a successful project. These problems and customers are not all that obvious. This holds true especially because the point of most operational activity is the prompt delivery of a direct improvement to business competitiveness, not application of innovative IT solutions. Improvements are realized most often through faster, more efficient communication of information, reduction in the time required to close a sale, or faster delivery of the product to market.

It is also necessary at this point to consider the possible alternatives to intranet technology. Invariably, someone will ask about so-and-so technology already available in-house, which, with some minor effort can totally resolve the problem. Answering with 'the intranet is the greatest new thing, we need to use it' will not suffice.

Key here is the consideration of the strengths and weaknesses of the so-called competing technologies as well as how well the product strengths actually fit the goal and the problem. Especially in the area of distributed management tools, opportunities for a mismatch of tools and solutions abound. Much of the literature purporting to report the case of products which fail to deliver as advertised can be directly linked to a mismatch between the problem focus of the tool and the problem at hand. Choosing a solutions framework designed to support and implement distributed, dispersed management in an enterprise which wants a distributed capability but centralized management represents one frequent mismatch.

It is important to document the evaluation of other options and to include information to show why these alternatives were discarded. Excessive cost vs. benefit realized, conflicting problem focus, and mismatched architecture all represent solid reasons for cutting potential solutions.

To-Do List

- Clearly identify the goal of the project.
- Directly relate goal to resolution of a business problem.
- Identify strengths and weakness of possible technology alternatives.
- Understand the solution focus and the architecture of products and technologies considered.
- Document why alternative technologies do not give the best fit.

Pitfalls

- Avoid vague goal statements.
- Resist scope-creep.
- Resist protracted fights with internal technology advocates.

STEP 3: PLANNING AND ASSIGNING RESOURCES

Any project goes through phases where the specific focus changes. For an intranet these phases include

- Design.
- Implementation.
- Technology maintenance.
- Content maintenance.

Typically, during the initial phases of design and implementation, enthusiasm, interest, and visibility reach their highest level with individuals eager to contribute. Responsibility and authority during these phases are usually well established and clear. Unfortunately, after this first burst of activity, as the focus shifts to less visible and more mundane tasks of content and technology maintenance, the pool of once eager participants thins out. To minimize the decline in participation, managers must clearly identify and assign accountability, visibly linking individuals to the various responsibilities associated with each phase of design, implementation, technology maintenance, and content maintenance. The fall off in interest must be anticipated and individual responsibility for maintenance and monitoring of content and technology assigned. A system that automatically maintains high visibility and accountability for high quality performance of these responsibilities should also be implemented.

Above all, it is important to remember that too much success can bring its own problems. Both human and infrastructure resources may be swamped by access and content demands. Successful implementations of frequently accessed Web pages or applications can increase network bandwidth and management focus requirements at what threatens to be an exponential rate. An active Web page demands consistent, on-going content maintenance to ensure the currency, relevance, and accuracy of information appearing on it. For this reason, the project plan should provide for monitoring usage, changes in resource requirements should be projected, and appropriate adjustments budgeted.

To-Do List

- Associate and identify responsibility for maintaining content with the intranet page.
- Display and monitor dates of content change on each subject page (assuming time sensitive information).
- Identify page-masters responsible for maintaining link currency.
- Monitor resource consumption.
- Budget for adjustments to resources.

Pitfalls

- Monitoring tasks can become overwhelming.
- Avoid 'loading' the project with costs that should be shared (i.e., evolutionary network growth).

STEP 4: HOW WILL SUCCESS BE MEASURED?

Once the audience, goal, problem, and resources have been defined, it is important to establish the definition of success. A disciplined process should be applied when defining a metric. This includes documenting the current behavior in terms of the selected metric and forecasting improvement. Such a procedure will also provide additional opportunity to evaluate and validate the potential contribution to solving the problem. It is far too easy for technicians and project managers to get caught up in the excitement of their intentions, losing perspective on the significance of the more relevant importance that defines its contribution to resolving a business problem. Also to be considered is the risk of investing far too much resources and effort in attacking a problem which proves transient or merely exists as a symptom of a far more serious and fundamental inadequacy. Such a problem is probably more directly and efficiently attacked with a non-technical or alternative solution.

A generally accepted aphorism holds that one cannot manage what one cannot measure. The measurement of performance against a defined, document metric easily rests as one of the most talked about but truly neglected activities in modern management. All too frequently, a press of business argument provides sufficient excuse to avoid developing an accurate metric to judge success. Such a process will contribute to avoiding sites filled with pages of content-free HTML documents that create a big splash but quickly fade to irrelevancy.

A metric can be quantitative or qualitative, since some situations do not lend themselves to numeric evaluation. Be sure the measurement of the metric is unambiguous and well understood. Avoid soft metrics whose valuation can be manipulated or subject to misinterpretation. The best metrics will relate directly to an obvious business function. In this case, the number of hits or visits to a Web page doesn't translate to a business success, whereas a reduction in inquiries to a benefits administrator or in the number of support calls to the Help Desk would be a valid measure.

On the other hand, a metric should not be overcomplicated. Simplicity and appropriateness will finesse elegance and sophistication for payback and longevity. Just as diversity for the sake of diversity is a fool's end, sophistication for the sake of sophistication is wasteful, extravagant, and ultimately counterproductive.

To-Do List

- Select clear and explicit performance metrics.
- Establish a clear methodology for establishing the value (state) of the metric.
- Document the current value (state) of the performance metric.
- Set a metric target value (state) that indicates success.

Pitfalls

- Not all situations lend themselves to numeric performance evaluation.
- Avoid 'unintended consequences', i.e., assure the metric is valid (number of 'hits' on a page may reflect frustration in finding the correct path).
- Avoid 'soft' metrics with ambiguous interpretations.

STEP 5: COST-BENEFIT ANALYSIS

The potential and anticipated payback in terms of dollars saved, costs avoided or time gained needs to be identified. Today's business runs on financial terms so quantitative evaluations and comparisons of costs incurred, saved, and avoided provide fertile data. Care should be taken to ensure that costs incurred are properly allocated and that savings or cost avoidance can be documented.

For some projects, this entails documenting the payoff in terms of dollars saved in the collection or distribution of information. For example, a typical report costs from $15 to $35 per copy to deliver (counting request, routing, and distribution) per person. Given a reasonably sized enterprise, the savings with intranet distribution can be substantial. Web access and sharing of such dynamic reports as sales figures, production or inventory levels, the potential for savings as well as better informed employees should be obvious.

In addition to the information-sharing applications, leading edge firms experienced with using intranets suggest that automated software distribution, automation of high-cost data collection or sharing tasks, and applications for inventory tracking and ordering offer fertile ground for an intranet application. Supply and order fulfillment costs have been estimated to run between $25 to over $200 per order. Driving costs to the very low end of the estimate through intranet-based automation of the purchase process can yield significant savings and pave the way for eventual support of outside clients.

When determining the cost of implementing intranet solutions, the most frequently overlooked or underestimated costs tend to be

- Network capacity requirements

- Systems and network management
- Content maintenance

Not all network management, growth, and maintenance costs should be loaded on the intranet project. But in reality, the tendency has traditionally been to underestimate these costs. Also, there will be a tendency to blame new projects as being the prime cause of unexpected problems due to overloaded resources. Including an estimate of the growth in load accompanied by plans (and costs) of enhancing infrastructure and personnel resources will present a more accurate evaluation making it easier to get management approval in the future.

To-Do List

- Develop a cost model of project problem.
- Allocate current load as well as projected growth in resource and infrastructure.
- Include systems and network management costs.
- Include costs of monitoring, managing, and updating content.

Pitfalls

- Underestimating training/maintenance cost.
- Underestimating resource and upgrade requirements.

STEP 6: THE IMPLEMENTATION PLAN

The project implementation should be phased including a pilot as a 'proof of concept' test. In addition to such issues as responsibilities, equipment, and schedules, the plan should consider the following elements:

- *Underlying architecture.* This includes the Internet, the number of tiers (usually 3 or 4) as well as the enterprise.
- *Standards.* In this category, the relevant questions include which standards to embrace and at what level, who must decide what they are, and who must administer them?
- *Security.* Decisions need to be made regarding what information can be made available on the intranet as well as the need and the processes used to control access.
- *Maintenance.* Maintenance was discussed previously in terms of such areas as content and linking currency.
- *Management.* Management involves the initial server but increases as the intranet grows across the enterprise.

Each of these topics could be the subject of a standalone chapter. The following sections raise just some of the more pressing issues in each area.

Architecture

The Intranet has to meld into and support the existing corporate architectural plans for networks, access, administration, object (class libraries), and management. Nonexistent or incomplete architectural models need not delay the Intranet implementation except for obvious clashes such as network model; in most cases, however, reevaluation and possible modification to accommodate inconsistencies and conflicts at a later date can be provided.

Standards

Standards are an extensive area for decision and discussion. Standards for presentation of data, format of information, and technologies for presentation represent just some examples that have to be reviewed. The fundamental issue of how much control can realistically be applied must be settled. The decision will have to take into account the realities of corporate culture, customer sophistication and level of effort that can be justified. Typically, a realistic middle ground that allows significant discretion to web-masters is the default.

Security

The data that is made available as well as the personnel who will have access to it varies with project and application. Security management will quickly become an issue as more business transactions are conducted on intranets. When selecting the application package, care should be taken to avoid the very common mistakes made to save costs, mistakes which result in unexpected costs or failure to deliver expected, required functions.

Enterprise solutions require robust solutions with their associated price tag. There exist a limited number of vendors whose product technology, architecture, and implementation place them significantly ahead of the competition for policy-based, sophisticated security administration. Research invested in finding these vendors provides significant payback in terms of reduced problems and confident delivery of services. Any solution selected should automatically enforce adding as well as blocking access based on a user profile.

Maintenance

Staffing and implementing for post-installation maintenance represent a frequent source of problems. Addressing these in the plan won't entirely prevent their occurrence but will assure reasonable preparation has been made to deal with them.

Management

Automatic management of Web servers represents a unique problem and applications to address it exist from a variety of sources. These automatically perform operational tasks, administer firewall security, collect and report web performance, and monitor HTML links. Again, enterprise environments require robust solutions capable of scaling from local servers to workgroups to sites with thousands of servers.

CONCLUSION

Intranets, the Web, and browser technology have been around long enough so that they are no longer considered to be cutting-edge technology. Their omnipresence and resulting familiarity make them seem more commonplace and reliable than experience suggests. The trade press has many more stories of success than failure but sufficient cautionary tales exist to make prudent the application of a disciplined project and evaluation process. Thinking through this process also makes it much easier to justify the project since it would already be linked to an identifiable business need.

The benefits to be reaped from the reduced costs and increased efficiency in communicating information, automating transactions, and providing wide access to timely information promise to be sufficient justification for the plunge into the intranet technology. A step-wise, disciplined introduction will minimize egregious errors but unfortunately not eliminate them all. Common sense, a practical focus on business benefit, and a sense of humor should be considered mandatory accompaniments when commencing an intranet implementation. Finally, keep in mind, for any management justification the details of payback, longevity and fit will complement enthusiasm and technological interest in a cutting edge solution.

Chapter 56
Expanding the Reach of Electronic Commerce: The Internet EDI Alternative

James A. Senn

EXCHANGING BUSINESS TRANSACTIONS online through electronic document interchange is a well-understood practice. However, EDI's potential is limited by the inability of millions of companies to participate. That will change as the projected impact of Internet EDI means every company can become a trading partner.

The corporate mandate to "link up or lose out," increasingly common in business, has led many firms to develop interorganization systems whereby buyers and sellers share information electronically. These powerful systems are among the most important forces in business. Many have played a pivotal role in changing the business strategies and operational tactics employed in commerce and are causing the proportion of commerce conducted online by business to grow.

Electronic data interchange (EDI) has been the underlying technology of choice for implementing interorganization systems. Yet only a fraction of the firms who could benefit by online commerce are using EDI. Thus the full potential of interorganization systems and electronic commerce will be constrained until a substantially larger proportion of businesses is able to participate.

0-8493-9820-7/00/$0.00+$.50
© 2000 by CRC Press LLC

IMPACT OF EDI

Electronic data interchange is a computer-to-computer electronic communication method whereby trading partners (e.g., hub organizations and their spoke customers and suppliers) in two or more organizations exchange business transactions. The transactions consist of documents in structured formats that can be processed by the recipient's computer application software (Exhibit 56.1).

GROWTH OF EDI

The origin of EDI in the late 1970s opened the way for business to conduct a greater portion of the routine buyer-seller business activities online. Sensing the opportunity to reduce paperwork, automate key transaction-handling activities, reduce cycle time, and cut inter- and intra-industry coordination costs, the early adopters quickly gravitated toward EDI. Transaction formats were established within the U.S., followed rapidly by the emergence of international standards. Expectations were high that EDI would become the way of handling buyer/seller business transactions.

EDI has changed the landscape of business, even triggering the redefinition of entire industries. Well-known retailers, such as The Home Depot, Toys R Us, and Wal-Mart, would operate very differently today without EDI, for it is an integral and essential element of their business strategy. Thousands of global manufacturers, including Proctor and Gamble, Levi Strauss, Toyota, and Unilever have used EDI to redefine relationships with their customers through such practices as quick response retailing and just-in-time manufacturing. These highly visible, high-impact uses of EDI by large companies have been extremely successful.

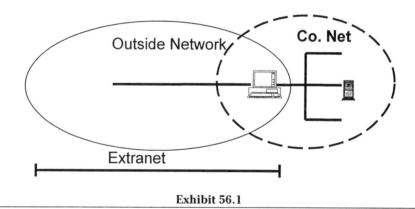

Exhibit 56.1

LIMITATIONS OF EDI

Despite the tremendous impact of EDI among industry-defining leaders, the current set of adopters represents only a small fraction of potential EDI users. In the U.S., where several million businesses participate in commerce every day, fewer than 100,000 companies have adopted EDI. In reality then, most businesses have not benefited from EDI or interorganization systems. Extensive interviews with company leaders revealed five principal reasons:

- *Significant Initial Resource Commitment* — Start-up costs associated with EDI implementation accrue from the need for software, network interconnections, new personnel, and typically contracting with an outside network service. Estimates for a hub company wishing to pursue EDI vigorously range from $100,000 to $250,000 just to get underway. The translation software needed to transform company data from internally used formats to the structure of standard industry transaction sets often requires an investment of $100,000. Hub companies are not the only ones accruing startup costs. Their trading partners also face expenses when they respond to EDI mandates, for they must purchase translators, augment communications links, and often add staff. It is repeatedly evident that hub and spoke companies both estimate technology costs better than startup staffing requirements. Frequently firms learn that true staffing requirements turn out to be more than double their original estimates.
- *Restructuring Business Processes* — In many firms, EDI touches every major business process — procurement, inventory management, manufacturing, order fulfillment, shipping, invoicing, payments, and accounting — and thus cuts across an entire company's practices. The business process changes needed to respond to a hub company's EDI requirements can thus disrupt well-ingrained practices. Since different hub firms often insist on unique procedures that fit their operations, a trading partner may ultimately have to support multiple versions of a specific process.
- *Start-up Challenges* — The challenge of implementing EDI requires months, not days, of startup efforts. Selecting and agreeing on the format of transaction sets, defining performance expectations, and negotiating legal matters not only taxes the best intentions of both parties, but can burn up hours of staff time.
- *Use of Private Networks* — Private value-added networks (VANs), constructed and operated by third parties, are used by most EDI trading partners as the principal means of exchanging transactions. VANs are useful to both hub and spoke companies because they provide the essential communication link. Yet neither company is required to invest in or maintain an EDI network. Each can use the VAN on a pay-as-you-go basis. However, if a dominant trading partner specifies use of a par-

ticular VAN, or when VANs will not agree to exchange transactions with one another, companies may have no choice but to work with multiple service providers. The result is extra expense, added process hassles, and sometimes multiple translation packages.

- *EDI Operating Cost* — Although EDI often reduces internal transaction costs, the process itself creates new expenses (beyond startup costs). If EDI volume is high, the ongoing transaction costs paid to a VAN accumulate to be a large expenditure, exceeding $100,000 annually for high volume users. Therefore, it is not surprising that heavy EDI traders are seeking ways to reduce these expenses for themselves, their current trading partners, and for potential new spoke companies.

EXPANDING EDI'S IMPACT

The preceding concerns suggest that traditional EDI, relying on formal transaction sets, translation software, and value-added networks, is not the enabling technology needed for the long-term solution. They are obstacles to expanding EDI's impact. For the proportion of commerce conducted electronically to grow more emphatically, four requirements must be met:

1. *Enable more firms to use EDI.* Across industries, the two largest trading partner segments not using EDI are (1) small business buyers and suppliers, and (2) important large and midsize companies who place few orders (regardless of their value) with a hub company. Firms in each group have shunned EDI, unable to justify the investment or convince themselves of the payoffs. Yet many managers in these firms acknowledge that lower costs would enhance EDI's appeal.

2. *Encourage full integration of EDI into trading partner business processes.* Paper and dual processing is still the norm for a substantial number of spoke company trading partners. Although they may *accept* EDI transactions, they do not *process* them, choosing instead to transfer the incoming transactions to paper and subsequently reentering the details into their own system. These firms have not developed the application-to-application interconnection that would enable them to share critical sales and inventory data electronically.

3. *Simplify EDI implementation.* The time it takes to bring new partners up to speed is considered excessive, further limiting EDI penetration. Hence, both hub and spoke companies seek more rapid, inexpensive implementation alternatives that will reduce the average implementation time from months to days.

4. *Expand online information exchange capabilities.* Because EDI has shown the benefits of electronic commerce to be substantial, it is not surprising that participating companies frequently seek to extend their capabilities to exchange more business information online. For example, hub and spoke companies frequently request

price lists, catalogs, and the capability to check supplier inventory levels available online. EDI's current structure of transaction sets and formatted standard business documents does not facilitate such a capability.

EDI OVER THE INTERNET

There is little question that the Internet, as one lane of an emerging global information highway, is a growing force influencing strategy for all forms of electronic commerce.[1] When considered as a channel for EDI, the Internet appears to be the most feasible alternative for putting online business-to-business trading within the reach of virtually any organization, large or small. There are five reasons for hub and spoke firms to create the ability to exchange transactions over the Internet:

- The Internet is a publicly accessible network with few geographical constraints. Its greatest attribute, large-scale connectivity (without the demand to have any special company networking architecture) is a seedbed for growth of a vast range of business applications. Only a few of the potentially attractive applications capitalizing on the Internet's capabilities and features for business-to-business exchanges have even been conceived to date.
- The Internet's global internetwork connections offers the potential to reach the widest possible number of trading partners of any viable alternative currently available.
- Powerful tools that make it feasible to interconnect traditional business applications to the Internet with a minimum of challenges are emerging rapidly. No end to this trend is in sight.
- Using the Internet to exchange EDI transactions is consistent with the growing interest of business in delivering an ever-increasing variety of products and services electronically (i.e., via electronic commerce), particularly through the World Wide Web.
- Internet EDI can complement or replace current EDI strategies.

The three principal channels for Internet EDI include the World Wide Web, FTP exchanges, and electronic mail (see Exhibit 56.2).

WWW EDI

The combination of World Wide Web (WWW or simply the "Web") and graphical browsers are the key reasons the Internet has become so easily accessible to the vast array of business and non-business users. This combination can do the same for EDI. Exchanging EDI transactions using the World Wide Web (i.e., Web EDI) capitalizes on its document format as the means for creating on-screen templates (see Exhibit 56.3) into which trading partners enter transaction details. Using this method, any standard

Channel	Description
WWW EDI	Using an ordinary browser, trading partner pulls down EDI transaction templates from a designated WWW server operated by:
	Value added network providers,
	Value added Internet service providers, or
	Hub companies.
FTP EDI	EDI transactions are accumulated as they are entered at the spoke company. Periodically the spoke company transmits the batch file to the hub company using the Internet's file transfer protocol.
E-Mail EDI	EDI transactions are inserted into an electronic mail message and transmitted over the Internet in the same way as all other e-mail.

Exhibit 56.2. The Three Principal Channels for Internet EDI

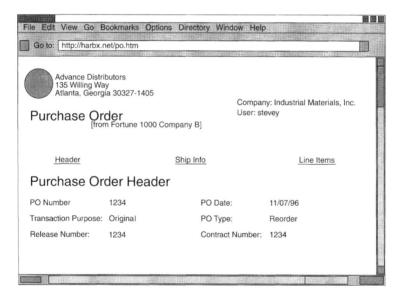

Exhibit 56.3 Purchase Order Template

business form (e.g., requests for quotation, purchase orders, or purchase order changes) can be displayed as a template.

HTML is the language of the WWW and therefore the means by which EDI templates are constructed, displayed, and processed. HTML allows designers to format each on-screen template in an easy-to-use layout and, if desired, even duplicate the design of paper forms. Color, image, and multimedia features may also be included to enhance appearance and usability.

Completed Web EDI forms are transmitted to the hub company over the Internet. Its route and any intermediate processing depend on which Web EDI alternative is used: by way of value-added networks, using Internet value-added service providers, or direct to hub company servers.

WEB EDI USING VALUE-ADDED NETWORKS

Sensing both opportunity and threat from the Internet and Web EDI, all value-added network providers (VANs) will roll out Web EDI services, with similar capabilities.[2] Although individual VANs will undoubtedly add special features, this method will function as follows: Users at spoke companies will access the designated VAN's Web site (by specifying the appropriate uniform resource locator (URL) — its Web address) where the hub company's transaction templates are maintained. The user's browser pulls down the template onto the desktop to enter transaction details.

A completed Web template is returned, via the Internet, to the VAN's Web server where the document's HTML code is translated into the EDI transaction format required by the hub company (see Exhibit 56.4). Then it is transmitted over the VAN to the hub company site where it is received and processed like any other EDI document.

Trading partners benefit by having a facility, at very low cost, for transmitting documents electronically without having to acquire or maintain special EDI software. Since most firms already have Internet access for other purposes, the intrusion into ordinary work processes is minimal (see Exhibit 56.5).

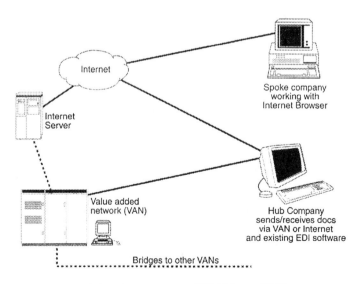

Exhibit 56.4. Internet EDI Using a VAN

Advantages	Disadvantages
• No special software is required if a trading partner is already using the Internet.	• Transmission delays over the Internet are not predictable.
• Converting new users to Internet EDI is relatively rapid when since the transaction is initiated using the familiar World Wide Web browser or e-mail formats.	• I VANs are not involved, transaction pickup and delivery actions are not logged nor are receipt notifications generated.
• Submission of EDI transactions is template-driven whereby trading partner staff members fill in on-screen templates using a World Wide Web browser.	• If VANs are involved, charges for their services are incurred.
• Hub companies can easily change business rules by adjusting EDI templates or altering translation and processing routines on their server.	• If a WWW front-end is not used with the FTP alternative, it is necessary to design and develop of a client/server front-end to create the transaction.
• If desired, the convenience and safeguards offered by value-added service providers can be incorporated into Internet EDI.	• Compared to other Internet EDI methods, the FTP alternative requires additional steps to accumulate and transmit batch files.
• VAN can build and maintain on-screen templates and server sites, freeing hub company staff.	
• Internet EDI can be integrated with traditional EDI as transactions are received from VAN.	

Exhibit 56.5. Advantages and Disadvantages of Internet EDI

The hub company benefits in three ways:

- It can use the simplicity of the WWW interface to induce more trading partners to initiate business transactions electronically.
- It can add new trading partners while sustaining current electronic relations with high volume trading partners already accustomed to EDI.
- It gains the capability to integrate standard transaction formats from both sets of companies into its electronic transaction processing stream.

WEB EDI USING INTERNET VALUE-ADDED SERVICE PROVIDERS

If the hub company chooses, Web EDI templates can be maintained by an Internet value-added service provider (VASP), e.g., America Online and Compuserve. With this alternative, the trading partner pulls down EDI forms from the VASP's server, enters transaction details, and returns them to the service provider who in turn transmits them to a VAN for translation and forwarding. The remainder of the process is the same as above.

WEB EDI USING HUB COMPANIES SERVERS

A hub company may also choose to bypass intermediaries entirely and maintain its own Web EDI server when following this method. A trading partner will point the browser at the hub's Internet URL to pull down the appropriate transaction template. When completed, the template is returned over the Internet to the hub's server where translation from HTML and processing occurs as described above.

The hub company must include in its Web server the capabilities to notify trading partners of the receipt and acceptance of transactions, a process that is normally an integral part of VAN services.

FTP-BASED EDI

A second Internet EDI option uses the file transfer protocol (FTP) capability. FTP EDI, which transfers entire files of transactions at one time, is useful when the sequence of collecting and sending batches of electronic transactions to hub companies is repeated frequently (see Exhibit 56.6). In the health care industry, for example, the claims submission process consists of health care providers (hospitals, physicians, and laboratories) who submit batches of claims forms periodically to insurers, and sometimes government agencies. With FTP EDI, providers can submit their claims, batched and in electronic form, over the Internet.

Using FTP EDI, a trading partner first prepares an individual EDI transaction set by filling in an electronic template on the computer screen. (In a client/server or LAN environment, multiple staff members are able to prepare transactions simultaneously.) As details are entered, they are formatted according to pre-determined EDI specifications. When the transaction is completed, it is added to the batch that is accumulated at the trading partner's site.

Periodically the batch is readied for transmission. The transaction sets are encrypted for privacy, if desired, prior to transmission. Digital signatures[3] may also be added, giving the recipient a means of authentication. Then the transaction file is transmitted over the Internet, using FTP, to the recipient's server.

The recipient EDI file first performs the authentication (if desired), normally on a server outside the recipient's fire wall. This protects the integrity of the hub site in the event the file has been altered or tampered with in any way prior to its arrival. Encrypted EDI files may be decrypted (i.e., returned to their original transaction set format for processing) on either side of the fire wall.

Once these steps are completed, processing of the EDI transaction can get underway.

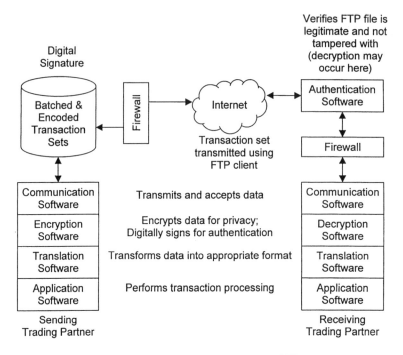

Exhibit 56.6. Internet EDI Using FTP

MIME AND E-MAIL EDI

The third Internet EDI alternative uses electronic mail. On the one hand, value-added network service providers have been augmenting their support of EDI using e-mail (via the X.435 mail standard[4]). At the same time, the Internet community is also aggressively developing another e-mail capability. Multipurpose Internet Mail Extensions (MIMEs) specify how EDI transactions can be sent as enveloped messages (Exhibit 56.7) using Internet Simple Mail Transport Protocol (SMTP), the principal method for sending and receiving e-mail over the Internet.[5] Trading partners can thus transmit messages containing EDI documents over the Internet to the mailboxes of hub companies. Transmission and arrival will occur in much the same way as any other e-mail message, with the EDI information embedded in the message.

The methods of identifying EDI transaction sets within a MIME e-mail message are under development by the EDI working group of the Internet Engineering Task Force (IETF-EDI). The work of the task force will be a principal factor in the emergence of E-mail EDI. Hence, it is highly plausible that other business applications will be expanded to accept or generate e-mail messages containing EDI transactions.

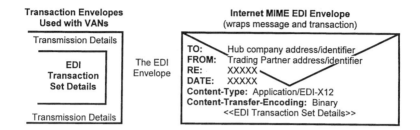

Exhibit 56.7. Internet EDI Using MIME E-Mail

INTERNET EDI AND ELECTRONIC COMMERCE STRATEGY

What does Internet EDI mean for business? It's increasingly evident that broadening the view of EDI is consistent with the creation of an electronic commerce strategy. Furthermore, incorporating the right set of objectives into that strategy can unlock a range of benefits even as it triggers new business opportunities.

BROADENING THE VIEW

Internet EDI's features should be treated as more than just a new generation of electronic data interchange. They can stimulate the creation of a broader array of services as well as trigger new business strategies even as they hold a key to increasing the number and characteristics of participating trading partners. Managers who view Internet EDI as no more than a technology foundation for online exchange of transactions will likely overlook important opportunities and face loss of business. Rather than a form of technology, Internet EDI is a new channel for conducting business. Therefore, it must be incorporated into an overall electronic commerce strategy.

COMPONENTS OF EDI STRATEGY

At a minimum, an EDI strategy should include five objectives. First, with cost and implementation barriers reduced, and multiple channels of interaction now available, companies should seek to use Internet EDI as a vehicle for bringing as many trading partners online as possible. The benefits — reduced cycle time, improved coordination mechanisms, elimination of paper documents, and more — will accrue to both hub and spoke companies.

Second, company objectives should include revenue generation, not just cost savings. Key features that make electronic commerce attractive to a hub company's upstream suppliers can also be beneficial to its downstream buyers and thus can lead to new revenue. These features can be an integral component in growth and market building strategies.

Since the exchange of documents electronically typically touches every major business process, implementation of Internet EDI should trigger renewed interest in cross-function redesign of business processes. Company intranets and extranets can readily be components of Internet EDI as well as embedded in internal processes. When online documents are evaluated with an eye toward simplifying business processes, the gains of deploying information technology in innovative ways are not only possible, but liberating. The result may transcend different business processes to the creation of new business models.

Fourth, companies should treat the Internet as a new front-end to their business. The same features that are attractive for enhancing EDI, including large-scale connectivity, wide geographic reach, a document paradigm facilitated by HTML, and the client/server structure mean the Internet can be integrated with current and planned mission-critical business applications and back-end support systems. The comfortable, multimedia interface of the WWW offers front-end opportunities that are at best challenging to create through traditional means.

Finally, companies should capitalize on the desirability of electronic payment and receipt. Streamlining invoicing and payment processing was responsible for triggering the business process reengineering revolution.[6] Companies quickly saw the benefits of not having to deal with traditional payment systems. It's time to realize that when business-to-business transactions can be created online they can also be settled online. Removing the two principal roadblocks — the mindset of trading partners and the commitment of financial institutions — will facilitate online settlement practices.

SUMMARY

There is little doubt that Internet EDI will become the method of choice for conducting business electronically, paving the way for the bulk of business-to-business EDI to be conducted over the Internet. Whether a company is large or small, the exchange of business information online will be an integral component of business strategy. Companies who fail to capitalize on Internet EDI are likely to miss opportunities even as they risk their current successes.

Notes

1. Senn, James A., "Capitalizing on Electronic Commerce," *Information Systems Management.* 13,3 (Summer 1996) pp. 15-24.
2. Prototypes of VAN EDI services suggest that companies seeking to use this form of Web EDI will pay a modest startup fee to the VAN and a monthly subscription fee entitling them to a specified number of transactions. Additional transactions will be billed on a per item basis. VANs will also charge hub companies to prepare and post each transaction template to the Web site.

3. A digital signature is an electronic code or message attached to a file or document for the intention of authenticating the record. It is attached, by software, in such a manner that if the contents of the message are altered in any way, intentional or accidental, the digital signature is invalidated. Laws governing the creation and use of digital signatures are emerging as business and government recognize they are essential to the growing reliance on electronic commerce.

4. In the 1980s, the X.400 standard was created to facilitate the exchange of e-mail messages between different systems. It has become the global e-mail standard. During the 1990s, a subset of the X.400 standard, designated X.435, was created as a standard for distinguishing EDI transaction sets within an ordinary e-mail message.

5. SMTP, which provides a common specification for the exchange of e-mail messages between systems and networks, is the method most users unknowingly rely on when transmitting mail over the Internet.

6. Hammer, Michael, "Reengineering Work: Don't Automate, Obliterate," *Harvard Business Review.* 68,4 (July-August 1990) pp. 104-112.

Chapter 57
Implementing and Supporting Extranets

Phillip Q. Maier

EXTRANETS have been around since the first rudimentary LAN-to-LAN networks which began connecting two different business entities together to form WANs. In its basic form an extranet is the interconnection of two previously separate LANs or WANs with origins from different business entities. This term emerged to differentiate from previous definitions of external "Internet" connection or just a company's internal "intranet". Exhibit 57.1 depicts an extranet with a Venn diagram, where the intersection of two (or more) nets formed the extranet. The network in this intersection was previously part of the "intranet" and has now been made accessible to external parties.

Under this design one of the simplest definitions comes from R. H. Baker, "An extranet is an intranet that is open to selective access by outside parties." The critical security concept of the extranet is the new network area that was previously excluded from external access now being made available to some external party or group. The criticality of the security issue evolves around the potential vulnerability of allowing more than the intended party, or allowing more access than was intended originally for the extranet. These critical areas will be addressed in this chapter from basic extranet set up to more complex methods and some of the ongoing support issues.

The rapid adoption of the extranet will change how a business looks at their security practices, as the old paradigm of a hard outer security shell for a business LAN environment has now been disassembled or breached with a hole to support the need for extranets. In many cases, the age-old firewall will remain in place, but it will have to be modified to allow this "hole" for the extranet to enable access to some degree for internal resources which have now been deemed part of the extranet.

Recognizing the growth of extranets as a common part of doing business today is important and therefore the business enterprise must be ready with architectures, policies, and approaches to handle the introduction of

0-8493-9820-7/00/$0.00+$.50
© 2000 by CRC Press LLC

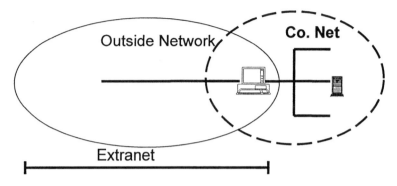

Exhibit 57.1. Venn Diagram of an Extranet

extranets into their environment. A few of the considerations are the business requirements vs. security balance, policy considerations, risk assessments, as well as implementation and maintenance costs.

As to the balance between requirements vs. security, the issue is the initial claim by business that extranets are an immediate need and absolutely must be established, "if we are to remain competitive." But from the perspective of security, such a drastic change to the environment, which may not have had any form of an extranet in place earlier, may well mean throwing their financial data assets out the door with the first implementation of an extranet. Therefore, security issues must be taken into account and put in balance with the claimed business need for an extranet implementation.

One of the first areas of review and possible update is the inner company's security policy. This policy most likely was not written with extranets in mind and thus may need modification if a common security philosophy is to be established regarding how a company can securely implement extranets. But the policy review doesn't stop with one company's review of their own policy, but must also be of the connecting company or companies on the outside. In the case of strategic business relationships that will be ongoing, it is important that both parties fully understand each others responsibilities for the extranet, what traffic they will and will not pass over the joined link, and what degree of access and by whom will occur over this link.

Part of any company's policy on extranets must include an initial requirement for a security risk assessment. The main question is what are the additional levels of risk or network vulnerability that will be introduced with the implementation of the proposed extranet? In addition to the vulnerability assessment, a performance assessment should be conducted to assist in the design of the extranet to assure that the proposed architecture not only addresses the security risk but also will meet performance expectations. Some of the questions to be asked in a combined security and performance assessment should be

- Data classification/value of data.
- Data location(s) in your network.
- Internal users' access requirements to extranet components (internal access design).
- Data accessibility by time of day (for estimating support costs).
- Protocol, access services used to enter extranet (network design implications).
- Degree of exposure by transmission mechanism (Internet, private net, wireless transmission).
- End-users' environment (dial-up, Internet).
- Number of users, total/expectation for concurrent users access (line sizing).
- Growth rate of user base (for estimating administrative costs).
- CONUS (Continental U.S.), international access (encryption implications).

The risk and performance assessment would, of course, be followed up with a risk mitigation plan, which comes in the form of selecting an acceptable extranet architecture and identifying the costs. The cost aspect of this plan is, of course, one of the critical drivers in the business decision to implement an extranet. Is the cost of implementing and maintaining the extranet (in a secure manner) less than the benefit gained by putting the extranet in place? This cost must include the associated costs with implementing it securely; otherwise, the full costs won't be realistically reflected.

Finally, the member company implementing the extranet must have a clear set of architectures that best mitigate the identified vulnerabilities at the least cost without introducing an unacceptable degree of risk into their computing environment. The following section reviews various extranet architectures, each with differing costs and degree of risk to the environment.

EXTRANET ARCHITECTURES

Router Based Extranet Architecture

The earliest extranet implementations were created with network routers which have the capability to be programmed with rudimentary "access control lists" or rules. These rules were implemented based solely on TCP/IP addresses. A rule could be written to allow external user A access to a given computer B, where B may have previously unreachable due to some form of private enterprise network firewall (and in the "early days"

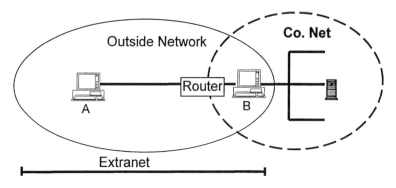

Exhibit 57.2. Basic Extranet with Router

this firewall may have been a router also). Exhibit 57.2 depicts this very basic extranet.

A more realistic rule may have been written where all computers in an "Outside Network" were allowed to access computer B in a company network, thus forming an extranet. This is depicted in Exhibit 57.3.

As network security architectures matured, routers as the sole network access control device were replaced by more specific security mechanisms. Routers were originally intended as "network devices" and not as security mechanisms and lost functionality as more and more security rules were placed in them. Additionally, the security rules that were put into them were based on TCP/IP addresses, which were found to be subject to spoofing/masquerading and thus deemed ineffective in positively identifying the real external device being granted access. Therefore, routers alone don't provide a wholly secure extranet implementation, but when used in conjunction with one of the following extranet architectures, can be a component to add some degree of security.

Application Gateway Firewalls

As network security architectures matured, the introduction of Application Layer Gateway firewalls, a software tool on a dedicated machine, usually dual homed (two network interfaces, one internal, one external) became the more accepted external protection tool. These software tools have the ability to not only perform router type functions with access control rules, but also provide user authentication services on a per user basis. This user authentication can take the form of an internal user authentication list, or an external authentication call to token-based authentication services, such as the ACE SecureID™ system. Exhibit 57.4 depicts this type of architecture set up to support an extranet using an

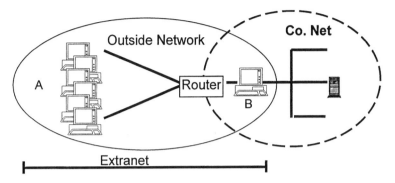

Exhibit 57.3. More Realistic Extranet

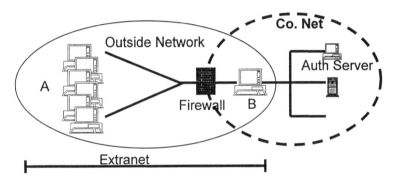

Exhibit 57.4. Extranet Using an Application Layer Gateway Firewall

application layer gateway firewall to enable authenticated users inward access to an enterprise in a controlled manner.

In addition to supporting access control by IP address and user, some gateways have the further capability to restrict access by specific TCP/IP service port, such as port 80 (HTTP), so the extranet users can only access the internal resource on the specific application port, and not expose the internal machine to any greater vulnerability than necessary.

Follow-on application layer gateway implementations have since emerged to provide varying additional degrees of extranet connectivity and security. One such method is the implementation of a "proxy" mechanism from an outside network to a portion of an internal company network. Normally a proxy performs control and address translation for access from an intranet to the external Internet. These types of "proxies" normally reside on the firewall, and all user access to the Internet is directed through the proxy. The proxy has the ability to exert access control over who in the intranet is allowed external access, as well as where they can go on the Internet. The proxy also provides address translation, such that the access packet going to the Internet, is stripped of the user's original internal address, and only the external gateway address of the enterprise is seen on the packet as it traverses the Internet. Exhibit 57.5 depicts these proxy functions.

The proxy provides both a security and network address function through the whole process which can be used in its reverse to provide an extranet architecture, because of its ability to provide access rules over who can use the proxy, and where these proxy users are allowed to go, or what resources they can access. Exhibit 57.6 depicts a "reverse" proxy extranet architecture.

Today, most proxies are set up for HTTP or HTTP–S access, though application layer gateway proxies exist for most popular Internet access services (telnet, FTP, SQL, etc.). One of the major issues with proxy servers, though, is the amount of cycle time or machine overhead it takes to manage many concurrent proxy sessions through a single gateway. With highly scaleable hardware and optimized proxy software, it can be carried to handle potentially high user demands but the system architecture must be specifically designed for high loads to be able to meet user response expectations, while still providing the security of an authenticated proxy architecture. On the "inward" proxy depicted in Exhibit 57.6, the proxy can be configured to only allow access to a single internal resource on a given TCP/IP port. Further protection can be added to this reverse proxy architecture by putting the target internal resource behind a router with specific access control rules, limiting the portion on the company intranet that inbound proxies can reach. This mechanism can assure limited access on the intranet should the internal machine ever be compromised, because

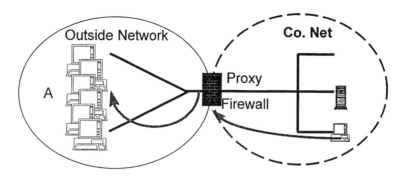

Exhibit 57.5 Outbound Proxy Architecture

now it cannot be used as a "jumping off point" into the rest of company intranet.

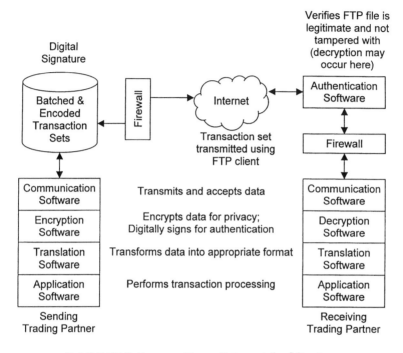

Digital
Signature

Verifies FTP file is
legitimate and not
tampered with
(decryption may
occur here)

	Transmits and accepts data	
Communication Software		Communication Software
Encryption Software	Encrypts data for privacy; Digitally signs for authentication	Decryption Software
Translation Software	Transforms data into appropriate format	Translation Software
Application Software	Performs transaction processing	Application Software
Sending Trading Partner		Receiving Trading Partner

Exhibit 57.6. Reverse Proxy Extranet Architecture

Under a somewhat "hybrid" architecture extranet, where some firewall controls are put in place but the external user is not granted direct inward access to an enterprise's internal domain has been evolving and put in place as a more popular extranet implementation. Under this architecture the external user is granted access to an external resource (something outside of the enterprise firewall), but still on the property of the enterprise. This external resource, in turn, is granted access to one or more internal resources through the enterprise firewall. This architecture is based on minimizing the full external access to the intranet, but still making intranet-based data available to external users. The most popular implementation is to place an authenticating WEB server outside the firewall, and program it to make the data queries to an internal resource on the enterprise intranet, over a specific port and via a specific firewall rule allowing only one external resource to have access to the one internal resource, thus reducing the external exposure of the intranet. Exhibit 57.7 depicts this type of extranet.

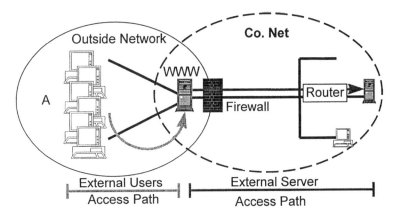

Exhibit 57.7. Extranet with Authenticating Web Server

Issues with this type of architecture include reliance on a single user interface that can be safely placed outside the enterprise firewall, which makes it vulnerable to attack. Additionally, the issue of whether or not tight enough access rules can be placed on the access method between the external user interface resource (the web server in this example) and the internal resources that it needs access to on the protected enterprise intranet. If these two issues can be safely addressed, then this form of extranet can be very useful for an enterprise extranet, with a high volume or varied user base, and a large intranet-based data repository.

The user front-end has been deployed as a web server, usually SSL enabled, to ensure data integrity and protection by encrypting the data as it passes over an external SSL link. Access to this external server is also associated with some form of user authentication, either a static ID or password over the SSL link, or more recently with client digital certificates, where each individual accessing the SSL-enabled site is issued their own unique digital certificate from an acknowledged certificate authority, validating their identity. Each client maintains their own digital certificate, with the Web server having some record of the public key portion of the client's digital certificate, either directly in the web server internally, or accessible from a standalone directory server (usually LDAP reachable).

Virtual Private Networks

The most recent entrant in the extranet architecture arena is the Virtual Private Network (VPN). This architecture is based on a software "tunnel" established between some external entity, either client or external network, and a gateway VPN server. Exhibit 57.8 depicts both types of VPN architectures. External network A has a VPN server at its border, which encrypts all traffic targeted for company network C (a gateway-to-gateway

VPN). Or, external client B may have client VPN software on his workstation which would enable him to establish a single VPN tunnel from his workstation over the external network to company C's VPN server.

Although both server-to-server VPN and client-to-server VPN architectures are offered in the industry today, this author's experience is the client-to-server VPN architecture is more popular, as it offers the most flexibility for the most diverse audience of external users. Though this flexibility does add to the complexity of the implementation, it can potentially involve a large number of external desktops, all with differing configurations. The benefit of VPNs, though, is the ability to safely traverse external public networks, with some assurance of data integrity and authentication as part of the VPN implementation. This architecture shows the most promise to meet the needs of extranets, and cost savings for a world hungry for connectivity over public/external networks, though it still has some growing pains to go through to reach full product maturity.

An emerging standard for VPNs is coming out of the ITEF's IPSec implementation, which draws a roadmap for the next generation TCP/IP security protocol. Under this protocol, standards are being drafted that will enable differing devices to securely communicate under a pre-agreed upon security protocol, including key exchange for encryption and standardized authentication. Today, there are IPSec-compliant products on the market, though the standard is still evolving, and tests are being conducted to evaluate differing vendors' compatibility with each other under the IPSec standards. One of the leading initiatives to evaluate this compliance is the Automotive Network Exchange (ANX) test which is intended to establish a large extranet environment between the core automotive manufacturers and their vendors.

In the meantime there is a wide variety of VPN product vendors on the market, some touting IPSec compliance and others with proprietary imple-

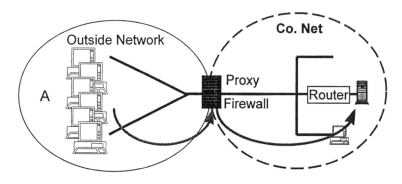

Exhibit 57.8. VPN Architectures

mentations, with IPSec in their future product roadmap, choosing to wait until the standard stabilizes. The recommendation is to either select a vendor offering IPSec if it has some degree of maturity within its own product line, or one that is planning on adopting the IPSec standard.

Regardless of whatever VPN solution is being considered for implementing secure extranets, a few technical considerations must be understood and planned for before selecting and implementing a VPN extranet architecture.

Scalability. Similar to proxy servers, VPN servers incur a fair amount of processing overhead, which consumes processing resources as high levels of concurrent VPN sessions pass through a single server. It is important to attempt to estimate your projected user base and current access to appropriately size your VPN server. Some servers are established on lower level processors for smaller environments, and should not be implemented where high concurrent access rates are expected. Although there is some benefit to physical load balancing (i.e., spreading the access among multiple servers), there is also a concern about implementing too many servers to easily manage. A balance has to be found between installing a single large server and creating a single point of failure vs. implementing many smaller servers and creating an administrative nightmare.

Multi-homed Intranets and Address Translation. In large intranet environments, many operate under a "split DNS" (Domain Name System) where intranet addresses are not "advertised" to the external networks, and external addresses are kept external, so as not to "flood" the internal network. Additionally, many larger intranet environments have multiple gateways to external networks. If one of the gateways is established with a VPN gateway and an external client makes a connection to the internal intranet, it is important that the tunnel comes in through the appropriate VPN gateway, but also that the return traffic goes "back out" through that same gateway so that it gets re-encrypted and properly returned to the external VPN client. Exhibit 57.9 depicts the correct traffic patterns for a multi-homed intranet with a single VPN gateway and an external VPN client.

VPN-Based Access Control. Many forms of gateway VPN servers offer the ability to restrict users access to a company intranet based on access groupings. This is especially important when intranets are being established for a diverse set of external users, and it is important to minimize their access to the intranet. This type of access control is, of course, critical in establishing secure extranets, which further highlights the importance of understanding VPN-access control capabilities.

User Authentication. Multiple options exist for user authentication, though the recommended option is to select a high level authentication

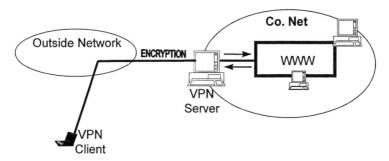

Exhibit 57.9. Traffic Patterns for Multi-Homed Intranet with a Single VPN Gateway and an External VPN Client

method, such as one-time passwords or time-synchronized password methods. Under the IPSec standard, client-side digital certificates are evolving as a standard, for high-level authentication. Unfortunately, initial implementations of client-side digital certificates for user authentication are wholly software based, eliminating the 2nd factor authentication, the "something the user physically has" in their possession. The return to true two-factor authentication under digital certificates will not really occur until physical "smart cards" become part of the authentication architecture. (Smart cards are credit card type tokens that have a physically embedded chip, which can be electronically read and written to, either with a portion of the client's digital certificate or the encryption algorithm used to "unlock" the digital certificate.)

IPSec Interoperability. Ultimately, when the IPSec standard stabilizes all vendors, following the established standard will allow different vendors VPN products to interoperate. Under this environment, a company may implement vendor A's VPN server, and their acknowledged clients can purchase and use an IPSec-compliant client to gain access to the company intranet once they are authorized.

SUMMARY

Secure extranets are becoming the external network of choice in today's business world. There are multiple implementation options as depicted in this document, each with varying degrees of risk and implementation complexity. Each implementation must be evaluated against a business case, using the recommended risk and performance analysis outline. The basic router-controlled extranets are only recommended for the least valuable data environments, while the more sophisticated VPN extranet architectures appear to be the future for extranets, especially when the IPSec standard matures and gains industry adoption.

Chapter 58
Internet Security and Firewall Policies

William Hugh Murray

ANY ATTEMPT to describe anything as dynamic, not to say unstable, as the Internet, is likely to make one look foolish. Describing the Internet can be likened to five blind men trying to describe an elephant. However, the elephant remains an elephant, it does not change during the examination and discussion. On the other hand, descriptions of the Internet that are only three years old are already out of date enough to be inaccurate if not dangerously misleading.

The Internet is already the most complex artifact in history. It may turn out to be important, or it may not. On the chance that it is or will be important, it makes sense to try to understand it, no matter how difficult and uncertain an explanation is likely to be.

THE CHARACTERISTICS OF THE INTERNET

The purpose of this section is to define and describe the Internet by its characteristics, which are all related. This section is a foundation on which subsequent sections on Internet security issues build.

Public and Open

Perhaps one of the most important characteristics of the Internet, at least from a security point of view, is that it is essentially public and open. It is public in the sense that, like the phone system, anyone can use it. One may have to go to a pay phone, a kiosk, or the public library, but anyone can use it. Libraries have been known to hand out user IDs with the same frequency as library cards. No requirements exist to be able to use the Internet, i.e., anyone can use it. In addition, as in broadcast TV, radio, or magazine advertising, most of the traffic is public. Its value increases with the number of people who see it. Although it has not always been so, most of the servers and services available on the Internet do not know or care who their users are. No user identification or authentication is required. The servers may count the accesses and they might like to know the demo-

0-8493-9820-7/00/$0.00+$.50

graphics of those who visit, but otherwise, the greater number of visits, the more successful the site is considered.

Similar to it being public, the Internet is open. Like the postal system and for the price of a postage stamp, anyone can send a message. For the price of an accommodation address, anyone can receive a message. Although there may be an agreement to pay, no other permission is required and, as a rule, payment in advance is not required. The Internet is also open in the sense that with a minimum of notice to or cooperation of others a connection can be made. A node at the edge of a network can be added easily and unilaterally, creating a new connection between networks. Therefore, it is difficult, nearly impossible, to know what the network looks like.

Although only a small percentage of the traffic on the Internet is sensitive to disclosure and most applications and services are free, almost all traffic is sensitive to contamination and most services are sensitive to interference. Moreover, although many who offer public information on the Internet want many people to see it, they want it to get through intact; they do not want it modified, they do not want it broken, and they do not want to be responsible for what they did not say. The public and open nature of the Internet makes this more difficult to achieve. It also makes it more difficult to achieve confidentiality and accountability for that traffic and those applications that require them.

Inclusive Network of Networks

By definition, an internetwork is a network that connects networks. Therefore, the Internet is a network of networks. It is one collection of all networks, and the economic advantage of a connection is so great as to be irresistible. Moreover, although isolated networks may exist in the short term, in the long term, the internetwork will be one. Isolated networks that persist will be so sparse, small, and temporary as not to be significant.

Mesh Topology

The Internet has a mesh topology, which means that, except at the edges, most nodes are connected to two or more other nodes. In addition, there are multiple paths between any two points on the network, because the topology maximizes the potential that a message will get through and maximizes the total message-carrying potential (i.e., bandwidth) of the network. On the other hand, at least by default, users do not know what path their traffic will follow or what nodes and links their messages will traverse.

Flat

Ideally, the Internet is flat, as opposed to hierarchical. Information flows directly from the origin to the destination rather than in, to a central switching point, and then back out to the destination. Therefore, the cost of sending a message between any two points on the network is the same as between any other two points. The time required for a message to move between any two points is roughly the same as for any other two points chosen at random. Finally, the bandwidth between any two points is roughly the same as for any other two points.

As expected, messages flow more quickly between nodes that are close together. However, it is possible for a part of a message to circle the globe, even when addressed to a nearby node. So, at least on average, across all randomly chosen pairs of nodes, the Internet is flat.

Broadcast

A node that desires to send a message to another node broadcasts that message to the remainder of the network. Depending on the routing algorithm used, the originating node may prefer nodes that it thinks are in the direction of the destination. However, it is possible for a message to traverse the globe even when addressed to a nearby node. Other nodes that receive the message look at the destination address in the message and forward it in the general direction of that destination. This is similar to a point-to-point network in which the path between two points is determined in advance and dedicated, at least for the instant, to carrying that message. Although every packet does not pass every node and it is possible for users to influence the path that their traffic follows, few users have the necessary special knowledge to take advantage of this capability. They do not know how to exercise the control or to distinguish one path from another. Such control, if used, would limit the paths and bandwidth available to the traffic and be achieved at the cost of a reduction in the chances that the traffic would get through quickly.

Different Types of Internet Connections

Three kinds of connections are available on the Internet.

Packet-Switched. Related to the idea of broadcast is that of packet-switched. A message is broken into packets, each packet is labeled as to its origin and destination and then is broadcast onto the network. Other nodes forward the packet in the general direction of the destination. It is possible that adjacent packets in a message will follow different paths to the destination. This is the opposite of circuit-switched networks, such as the voice network, in which a circuit or path is determined in advance and all parts of the message follow the same path. In a packet-switched network, an intervening node may see only a part of a message. On the other hand, it increases the number of nodes that may see a part of it.

Peer-Connected. Nodes on the Internet are "peer connected." No node dominates or controls another. Thus, by default, all nodes behave as if they trust all other nodes as themselves. The implication is that the level of trust is equal to that of the least trusted node.

Any-to-Any Connection. Like the postal system, and except as otherwise restricted, any device connected to the Internet can send a message to any other device. There is no requirement for an answer but, at a minimum, the destination device must recognize the message and make a decision about it.

Increasing Interoperability

If connectivity is the ability to send a message to any node, interoperability is the ability to get a meaningful answer back. Already, the Internet is better at answering questions than most individuals are at asking questions. The Internet can provide a report of freeway traffic in Los Angeles, hotel availability in London, or the schedule of every opera house in the world for the next two years. It can also locate all the bed and breakfast lodgings in most places in the world, and get an index to the treasures of the Vatican Library or of the British Museum. Individuals can locate and download graphics, moving images, and general and specialized software. A query on "Mona Lisa" returns references to both 1000 different prints of Da Vinci's La Gioconda and a sound clip of the Nat King Cole song. If the necessary software is unavailable to interoperate with another system at a particular layer, software can be downloaded at another.

As protocols and interfaces become more standard, they become more useful. As the use of a standard increases, so does the propensity to comply with it. The less standard an interface, the more it must include information about its intended or productive use.

No Central Authority

Although there are authorities such as the Internet Activities Board (IAB) and the Internet Engineering Task Force (IETF), which make architectural and design decisions for the Internet, no one is obliged to follow them. The individual networks are independently owned and operated. There is no central authority that is responsible for the operation of the entire network. Because the network is global, it is not even subject to the authority of any single nation-state.

INTERNET PROTOCOLS

The Internet can also be defined and described in terms of the communication protocols that it employs. One, somewhat pure, definition is that the Internet is a collection of interconnected networks that employ the Transmission Control Protocol and Internet Protocol (TCP/IP) and the TCP/IP suite of protocols. A more practical definition is that the Internet is the set defined above plus those networks connected to it by appropriate gateways. (For purposes of this definition, a gateway is a node that translates traffic from one protocol to another.)

The Internet Protocol

The fundamental protocol of the Internet is IP, the Internet protocol. IP is the network layer protocol for the TCP/IP Protocol Suite. It is fundamental in the sense that all other protocols are built on it. It is connectionless, best-effort, packet-switched, and unchecked. "Best effort" means that the network will do its best to deliver the packet, but there are no guarantees. "Unchecked" means that there is no redundancy in the protocol to enable either the sender or the receiver to know whether or not the packet was received correctly. There is no acknowledgement of the receipt of the message. The receiver cannot be sure that the message comes from where the origin address of the packet says that it comes from.

IP is to the Internet as the post card is to the postal system, limited in capacity, function, and intent. However, just as a message of any length can be sent by using multiple post cards, or by using one post card to acknowledge or to check on another, IP packets can be composed in such a way as to compensate for all of these limitations. These compositions make up the higher-level protocols.

The Transmission Control Protocol

The transmission control protocol (TCP) is the standard Internet protocol (IP) for the transfer layer. It defines how IP packets are sent back and forth between a sender and a receiver to provide many of the things that IP does not. However, even TCP does not provide security nor the reliability of origin and destination. Both the sender and the receiver know that they are talking to someone that is orderly and well behaved, but they do not know for sure that it is their intended party, and they do not know if any one is listening in.

The Oldest and Most Widely Used Application Protocols

The following are among the oldest and most widely used application protocols on the Internet:

- *Telnet.* This was originally intended for connecting host-dependent terminals to remote systems or applications. Today, it is used by terminal emulator programs on workstations.
- *File Transfer Protocol.* FTP is used to move files from one system to another.
- *Simple Mail Transfer Protocol.* SMTP is used for communication between e-mail servers.
- *Hypertext Transfer Protocol.* HTTP is used for communication between World Wide Web servers and browsers.

The applications of these protocols are discussed in subsequent sections.

Common Protocols on Lower Layers

In addition to those protocols previously discussed are the following, which operate on lower layers of the OSI model:

- *Serial Line Internet Protocol.* The serial line Internet protocol (SLIP) is used to exchange IP traffic with a device, usually a workstation, that is running the proper protocols but without a separate address. It is used to connect workstations to hosts or to Internet service providers through the dial-switched network. It is analogous to an extension cord or a remote.
- *Point-to-Point Protocol.* The point-to-point protocol (PPP) serves the same purpose as the Serial Line Internet Protocol, but it is newer and more versatile.
- *Network Time Protocol.* The network time protocol (NTP) is used to set and synchronize the system clocks of Internet nodes. It is able to synchronize all systems in a network to within milliseconds of each other, i.e., to within the accuracy and precision of the system clocks themselves.
- *Secure Protocols.* Recently, secure versions of these protocols have been specified, and reference implementations of these protocols are available for Unix systems.

INTERNET APPLICATIONS

Recall the analogy that describing the Internet can be likened to five blind men trying to describe an elephant. For most of the blind men, the Internet elephant looks like its applications. The Internet is open as to its applications. No real limit to the number of applications exists, and new ones are added every day. However, some applications are sufficiently significant that a description of those applications describes how the net looks to most users.

World Wide Web

The most widely used application on the Internet is World Wide Web, which within the last ten years has grown to become a versatile set of technologies that has dramatically changed the way people and organizations communicate with each other, retrieve information from public and private sources, follow news media, conduct business transactions, etc. Originally a simple set of protocols for linking documents together and retrieving them over the Internet, the WWW has become a complex set of intertwined, linked, and partially overlapping technologies that allow presentation and delivery of documents on the Internet and enable a variety of new interaction methods between individual users and organizations.

E-mail

Also a very widely used application on the Internet is e-mail. E-mail rivals television, copiers, and facsimile machines in its rate of growth. Moreover, as was the case with copiers and facsimiles, it is becoming difficult to remember how business was conducted before e-mail.

Internet e-mail uses the simple mail transfer protocol (SMTP) and the multipurpose Internet mail exchange (MIME) protocol for traffic between e-mail servers. MIME runs on top of SMTP to permit the exchange of files, programs, sounds, images, and moving images. E-mail is the most interconnected and interoperable application. Even those networks that have resisted connection to the Internet at other levels are connected at the e-mail layer.

E-mail is the most ubiquitous application in the Internet; it interoperates with many of the others. Several servers on the Internet that accept mail messages convert them into requests for other services, convert the answers to those mail messages, and send them back to the requestor. Thus, a user who has access to e-mail functionality, has access to most of the information on the network (i.e., Internet).

Logging on to a Remote System

One of the earliest and most obvious of Internet applications was to create a session between a terminal on one system and an application on a remote system. This kind of application used a client process on the origin system, the Telnet client. It is initiated by entering the command, Telnet, on the originating system. The parameters of the command specify the target system and any non-default characteristics of the connection request. The request is responded to by a Telnet server, a started process (a daemon in Unix parlance) on the target system. The protocol is also called Telnet. The user on the origin system sees a prompt from the answering server process, for example, the operating system or an application, on the target system. The user is usually expected to logon, that is, send a user identifier (i.e., user ID) and authenticating data (i.e., a password) to the target system. However, for the target system, the user identifier and password are optional.

File Transfer Protocol

The File Transfer Protocol (FTP) is used to exchange file system objects between systems. It is symmetric, and works in either direction. Either system may initiate a transfer in either direction. The FTP process (daemon in Unix parlance) must have access to the file system. That is, in systems with closed file systems, the process or the user on whose behalf it is operating must possess the necessary access rights (e.g., read, write, or create) to the file object or directory on which it wants to operate.

A convention called "anonymous FTP" permits the protocol to be used for public applications. The user can log on to the system with a user ID of anonymous, which requires no password. By convention, users are requested to put their origin system and user ID in the password field. However, the value in this field is not checked or validated in any way; a blank will work as well as the truth.

VULNERABILITIES ON THE INTERNET

The vulnerabilities on the Internet are closely related to its characteristics, its protocols, its uses, and its history. In addition, because the Internet is a broadcast network, messages are vulnerable to disclosure, replay, and interference.

The large number of components on the Internet makes it vulnerable to flaws in the implementation of those components. Because there may be many instances of a flaw, elimination of them is extremely difficult.

Many components in systems peer-connected to the Internet contain "escape" mechanisms. These are invoked by an otherwise unlikely character sequence to cause what follows this escape sequence to be handled, not by the component itself, but by the environment in which it runs, often with the privilege of the "escaped from" component. A famous escape mechanism, exploited by the infamous "All Souls" worm, was the debug feature of the sendmail mail handler. This option was invoked by an escape sequence in a message that caused what followed it to be passed through to Unix to be executed as a command. The worm used this feature, among others, to copy and execute itself.

Because nodes are peer connected and trust each other, compromise of one may result in compromise of many, perhaps all. In a peer-connected network, the level of trust in the network is equal to that of the least trusted node or link.

Many of the vulnerabilities described in the preceding paragraphs are features rather than flaws. In other words, they are desired and valued by some users and managers. Because of their value, their total elimination is unlikely.

Every node on the Internet has a system manager or privileged user. This user is not subject to any controls intended to ensure that users and their systems are orderly and well-behaved. In single-user systems, the only user is a peer of the privileged user in the multi-user system. That user is assumed to have the same motivation, training, and supervision as the manager of a multi-user system. The vast number of such users ensures that at least some of them will be disorderly and unreliable. Because they are all peers and because the systems are peer connected, it makes little difference which of them are trustworthy.

The Internet is so large and complex that no one, not the designers, not the implementers, not the operators, and not the users, fully apprehends it, much less comprehends it. Everyone is a blind man. Nonetheless, its immense scope and size make it unlikely that it will ever be perfect. Attackers look on it as a "target rich" environment. Although most nodes on the network are implemented, configured, and operated so as to resist attack, the great number of them ensures that there will always be some that are vulnerable to attack.

Finally, two of the vulnerabilities on the Internet, insecure links and insecure nodes, are fundamental. In other words, they are inherent to the Internet nature, use, intent, or at least its history. Contrary to popular belief, they are not the result of errors, flaws, or failures on the part of the designers, implementers, or operators of the network. Rather, these insecure links and nodes are the result of attempts to have the greatest chance of getting a message from point A to point B in the least amount of time. They are never going to go away; it is not simply a matter of time. Indeed, at least for the next five years, they are likely to get worse. That is, vulnerabilities will increase faster than the ability to fix them. Moreover, the number of insecure links and nodes in the network are growing at a much faster rate than the number of secure ones. This vulnerability is certain and extremely resistant to change.

ATTACKS ON THE INTERNET

The conditions for a successful attack include necessary access, special knowledge, work, and time. Because of its nature, all of these things are somewhat more available on the Internet than on other networks. Because the Internet is open, almost anyone can gain access. Most of the special knowledge in the world is recorded, encapsulated, and available on the Internet; naturally, permission is often required. Even much of the necessary work to launch a successful attack has been encapsulated in computer programs. Thus, they can also be perpetrated by those who lack skill and special knowledge and who are not prepared to do the work themselves.

Eavesdropping

As packets move through the net, they can be observed by privileged users of the nodes or by using special equipment to listen in on the links. These attacks are easily automated.

Packet and Password Grabbers

A packet grabber is an automated eavesdropping attack, a program that copies packets as they move through an intermediate node (i.e., a node between the origin and destination). A password grabber is a special case of a packet grabber that identifies and stores for later use user IDs and passwords as they pass through an intermediate node. Because, at least as a general rule, unprivileged processes cannot look at traffic in transit, password grabbers must be installed by privileged users. However, recent experience suggests that they are often placed in penetrated systems. Writing password grabbers requires special knowledge and work. However, at this moment so many copies of those programs exist that the attack can be used even by those without the knowledge and who are not prepared to do the work. The Internet has so may password grabbers that passwords in the clear are not sufficiently reliable for commercial or other sensitive applications, and the problem moves from the category of an attack to that of a pervasive problem.

Address Spoofing

The origin address on the IP packet is not reliable. The sending system can set this address to any value that it wishes. Nonetheless, by convention and for convenience, many systems rely on this address to determine where a packet came from and to decide how to treat it. Packets carrying the origin address of recognized systems may be treated as though they had originated on a trusted system. Again, with sufficient work and knowledge, it is possible to write a program to exploit this trust. Toolkits for building this kind of attack have been written and distributed within the hacker community.

Trojan Horses

A Trojan Horse attack is one in which a hostile entity, for example, armed warriors, is concealed inside a benign or trusted one, for example, a gift horse, to get it through a protective barrier or perimeter, in the original case, the walls of the city of Troy. In computer science, it usually refers to a malicious program included in another program or even in data. Although most systems are vulnerable to this kind of attack to some degree or another, and it has always been a concern, it was not a real problem until the proliferation of desktop computers and viruses.

As previously discussed, both node-to-node connectivity and trust and open file systems make the Internet particularly vulnerable. Trojan Horses can and do travel over any of the popular protocols and in any of the popular object types. For example, they can travel in files over FTP, as documents over MIME, or in arbitrary objects called by HTML scripts fetched from World Wide Web (WWW) servers by browsers. Although some browsers and interpreters (e.g., HotJava) are designed to resist such attacks, most are not. Even in situations in which the browser or interpreter is resistant, it is always possible to dupe some users in a large population.

Trojan Horses are easily executed because they have attractive names or descriptions or the names of frequently used programs. They may require a minimum of user cooperation. For example, the PRANK (virus) was implemented as a MS Word macro and could spread in any Word document. Simply asking Word to open an infected document would contaminate that copy of Word and any document that it subsequently opened. If an infected document were attached to an e-mail message, an act as simple as double clicking the icon for the document would be sufficient to execute the macro. Because such a macro can contain and call an arbitrary program, there is no limit to the sophistication of the program or the contamination it can cause.

Trojan Horse attacks are of special concern on the Internet because they compromise trust of end-point nodes, of the net, and of applications on the net.

Browsing

Browsing is going through the network to look at available, public, and accidentally and erroneously available data in search of something of value. Specifically, in an attack sense, this search method looks for special data that will reduce the cost of an attack against other nodes. For example, many systems implement or provide directory services. These directory services return the names of enrolled users, i.e., user identifiers. The information returned by these public services is used by the attacker to identify targets and thereby reduce the cost of attack. Attackers also use browsing to identify and download attack programs.

Exhaustion

When confronted with good security and when all other attacks fail, an attacker can always fall back on trying all possible combinations of data (e.g., user identifiers and passwords) until he or she finds one that gets through. Traditional systems resisted such attacks by disconnecting disorderly devices (i.e., devices that failed to successfully logon). Because the

Internet is a broadcast network, there is no connection to break. A system must look at every packet addressed to it and make a determination as to what to do with it. It is possible to spread the attack over time or across addresses so as to disguise the attack as errors or noise.

Denial of Service

Denial of service attacks are those that cause failures by overloading or consuming all available resources. On the Internet, this class of attack includes "spamming" or overloading a target with unwanted traffic. Although the target is not damaged in any permanent way, it may be unable to provide critical services to those intended to use it.

DEFENDING AGAINST ATTACKS ON THE INTERNET

A vast number of options exist that the implementers, operators, and users of the net can use to limit these vulnerabilities and the attacks against them. However, in considering them, keep in mind that these vulnerabilities are fundamental to the nature of the Internet. The only way to eliminate all of the risk is to either eliminate the Internet or alter it so fundamentally that it will lose its identity. Clearly, neither of these options are viable. Rather, the defenses should be balanced against the vulnerabilities so as to preserve essential trust. Discussions of some broad categories of defense mechanisms follow.

Isolation

Of course, the most obvious defense against network attacks is simply not to attach, to connect, or to participate in a network. Not only is this defense effective, it is also demonstrable to the satisfaction of third parties. However, the value of the security obtained rarely compensates for the lost value of connecting or participating in a network. Moreover, it has often been said that sensitive defense systems are safe because they are not connected to public networks.

Because the value of connecting to a network is high and because the cost of that connection is low, isolation is difficult to maintain. Even a very small system or a single desktop workstation can form a connection between networks.

Policies

In the presence of known connections, people can provide protection. They can recognize attacks and take timely and appropriate action. However, for this to be effective, it must be planned and pervasive. If management wishes to rely on individuals in advance, it must tell them what action to take. A policy is an expression of management's intention. It should contain a recapitulation of the user behavior that management relies on. It should also clearly delineate the responsibilities of employees and managers. Finally, it should specifically address the responsibility to report anomalies.

Bastions

Bastions are "projecting" fortifications. They are strong systems that can be seen from the outside (i.e., the public network), but which are designed to resist attack (e.g., by recognizing only a very limited repertoire of application-specific commands). Bastions normally hide the generality and flexibility of their operating systems from the network. A full-function gateway system that can be seen from the public network is called a bastion host. Such a gateway must be able to protect itself from its traffic. Finally, because most protective mechanisms can be bypassed or circumvented, all applications and services that can be seen from the network should be able to resist their traffic.

Filters

Filters are processes that pass some traffic while rejecting some other traffic. The intent is to pass safe traffic and to resist attack traffic. Filters may operate on headers or content. Many filters operate on the basis of the origin address in the header. They pass traffic that appears to have originated on recognized or trusted systems. They may also operate on a combination of origin, protocol, and destination. For example, they may pass mail traffic from unknown origins to the mail port on the post office machine and reject outside traffic addressed to the Telnet port on the same machine. Filters are important. For further information see the subsequent section.

Wrappers

Wrappers are proxy programs or processes. They can be viewed as traffic filtering programs. They are designed to protect the target from unintended traffic, known attacks, or to compensate for known weaknesses. They often assume the name of the process that they are intended to protect (i.e., common functions or known targets). For example, suppose that a privileged program is known to have a flaw or an escape mechanism that can be exploited by a packet or a message. A wrapper can be given the name of that program, placed ahead of it in the search order, and used to protect against messages of the dangerous form. After eliminating all messages of the dangerous form, the remainder are passed to the "wrapped" program as normal.

Using a wrapper is a preferable alternative and it presents a lower risk to cure a vulnerability than patching or replacing the vulnerable program. They have been employed to a great advantage in Unix systems in which it is often easier to use the wrapper than to find out whether the particular version of Unix or one of its subsystems that is being used has a particular problem. The most famous wrappers are a collection known as COPS. These are used to protect Unix systems from a set of known attacks and vulnerabilities.

FILTERS: THE MOST POPULAR DEFENSE

Filters are the most popular defense to ward off network attacks. The intent is to pass normal traffic while rejecting all attack traffic. Of course, the difficulty is in being able to recognize the difference between the two. Filters are normally based on the origin, the destination, and the kind of traffic. Traffic is permitted to flow from trusted or known sources to safe or intended destinations. Of course, most destinations will ignore traffic that is not addressed to them but will certainly listen to attack traffic that is addressed to them. Filtering on destination address can protect the system from seeing attack traffic at the expense of protecting it from all traffic.

Filters Implemented by Using Routers

In part, because networks are usually connected to each other through routers, routers are a favorite place to filter traffic. The same logic that is used by the router to decide where to send traffic can be used to reject traffic (i.e., to decide to send it to the "bit bucket"). For example, only those packets that appear to have originated on systems whose addresses are recognized (i.e., on a list of known systems) may be accepted.

Packets by Address: IP Address and Port

A filter must have criteria by which to decide which traffic to pass and which to reject. The criteria must appear in the packet. The most frequently used criteria are the IP origin and destination addresses. Typically, this is expressed as an address pair. In other words, traffic appearing to originate at A and addressed to B may pass this router. Although it could say all traffic originating at A may pass or all traffic intended for B may pass, this is significantly less rigorous or secure.

The origin and destination are usually expressed as IP addresses and may be further qualified by port. That is, traffic originating on the mail port of A may pass to the mail port on B, but to no other port.

Application Protocols

The application protocol is also visible in the packet and is useful for routing and security purposes. For example, the filter may pass traffic in the SMTP protocol to the mail server, while not allowing other IP traffic addressed to the same service to pass. Because the intent of the traffic is more obvious in the higher-level protocols, filtering by the application protocol can be very effective and useful.

Firewalls

It is beyond the scope of this chapter to provide instruction on how to build or even to operate a firewall. Within the allotted space, it is difficult to simply convey an understanding of their nature and use. A basic definition and discussion follows.

The *American Heritage Dictionary* defines a firewall as "a fireproof wall used as a barrier to prevent the spread of a fire." By analogy, a network firewall is a traffic-proof barrier used to prevent the spread of disorderly or malicious traffic. More specifically, a firewall is a special collection of hardware and software that connects two networks and that is used to protect each with regard to which side of the firewall a fire will start on.

Like most analogies, this one is instructive even at the extremes where it begins to break down. In the analogy, a firewall is assumed to resist fire equally in both directions. It is symmetric; it does not have to treat fire on one side of the wall differently from fire on the other. It must resist fire, but it must pass people. However, it is easy to distinguish people from fire, and all people and all fire, on either side of the wall, are treated the same. The task of the network firewall is to distinguish between threatening and non-threatening traffic and to do so differently depending on which side the traffic originates. In the presence of fire, a firewall need not pass people; resisting fire is more important than passing people. However, the network firewall will rarely be permitted to reject all traffic in the name of rejecting all attack traffic. It will usually be required to pass legitimate traffic, even in the presence of known attack traffic.

Moreover, a firewall is not is a box; it is not a product that can be purchased off the shelf. At time of this writing, more than 40 vendors offer products that are described, at least in part, as firewalls. Although similarities among them exist, there are also fundamental differences in their approaches. Even given a complete understanding of company requirements and security policy, gaining sufficient knowledge about tens of products to decide which one is most appropriate is a major challenge.

Firewall Policy Positions

Four fundamental policy positions are available to network operators. The firewall policy will be the result of these postures and of the applications on the network.

Paranoid. The first of these positions is called paranoid. It is motivated by extreme caution and probably fear, and characterized by the absence of a connection to the Internet.

675

Prudent. The second position is called prudent or restrictive. It also is motivated by caution, but also by a recognition of the value of connection to the Internet. It is characterized by the fact that everything which is not explicitly allowed is implicitly forbidden. For example, a private Internet user would have to be explicitly authorized to Telnet to a system on the public Internet.

Permissive. The permissive posture is the opposite of the restrictive policy. Under this policy, everything that is not explicitly forbidden is implicitly allowed. Obviously, it is the intent of this policy to forbid the necessary conditions for all known attacks. This policy is intended to provide a level of protection with a minimum of interference with applications. This is the policy most likely to be used when applying a firewall to an existing connection. It is particularly useful if little is known about the applications and if there is a strong desire not to interfere with or break those applications. It is the policy most likely to be recommended by Internet service providers who are motivated to maximize the value of the connection.

Promiscuous. The promiscuous policy is that anything goes. Under this policy, there are multiple connections and any legitimate packet can flow from any source to any destination.

Choosing a Firewall Policy

An interesting question is why would anyone want to be in postures one or four? Remarkably, position one is the default position for business. Most businesses have not yet connected to the Internet. Position four is the default policy for the Internet; all connections and traffic are tolerated in the name of maximizing the bandwidth and the potential for getting messages through.

If an Internet service provider is asked for guidance on a firewall policy, it will likely recommend that the position should be on the promiscuous side of permissive. The service provider will supply a list of restrictions to address all of the attacks that it knows about. However, this permits exposure to a large set of fundamental vulnerabilities. This is, in part, because the Internet service provider believes in the value of the net and does not wish to deny its clients any benefits without necessity.

In most cases reason dictates a position on the paranoid side of prudent or restrictive. In other words, permit only that traffic that is associated with a particular value for which the net is being used. The flow of all other traffic should be resisted.

A Conservative Firewall Policy

A conservative firewall policy is intended to position an institution or network on the paranoid side of restrictive. The intent is to protect not

676

only against known and expected attacks, but also against those that have not been invented yet. It is driven by fundamental vulnerabilities, rather than by known threats and attacks. It attempts to take only those risks that are necessary to accommodate the intended applications.

In addition, no information about the private network should be available on the public net. Private net addresses should never appear on the public net; they should be replaced or aliased to an address that the firewall owns. Addresses on packets and messages should be re-encoded at the firewall. Similarly, users' internal e-mail addresses should not appear on the public net. These private addresses should be replaced with the name of the site or enterprise at the firewall on the way out and replaced on the way in.

Application protocols should not traverse the firewall. Traffic should be decoded and re-encoded at the firewall. For example, a SMTP carrying a message should be decoded into a message and then re-encoded into another SMTP for transmission at the firewall.

Reusable passwords should not traverse the firewall in either direction. Incoming passwords may be replays and are not reliable evidence of the identity of the user. Outgoing passwords may be similar to those used by users on the inside, and their use across the firewall may compromise internal systems. A preference for Secure Telnet or FTP should be made. These protocols provide end-to-encryption for all traffic, including the password. Alternatively, one-time passwords (e.g., SecureID or s-key) could be used. Although these do not protect all traffic, they protect against replays.

Proxies should represent the public net to the private net. For example, when a user of the private net wishes to access a World Wide Web (WWW) server on the public net, he or she should be transparently routed through the WWW proxy on the firewall. This proxy should hide the user's address from the public net, and protects both nets and the user. The user cannot misrepresent his or her address to the public net, and a process on the public net can directly attack only the proxy, not the user.

Only a limited set of limited applications should be permitted. Under this policy, such a limited application as e-mail is permitted, and such a very general application as Telnet is discouraged. Telnet is very general, flexible, and its intent is not obvious. It is vulnerable as a target and useful for attack.

Those public applications that are intended for use on the public net should be placed there. The public should not be permitted to traverse a firewall simply for the purpose of gaining access to public applications.

677

Applications on the public net should be implemented on dedicated and isolated servers. The server should be dedicated to a single use; it should not rely on the operating system to protect the application. Public servers should not know about the private net. Any connection to the private net should be to an application and over a trusted path. Privileged access to such servers should require strong authentication.

The public should not be granted read and write access to the same resource. For example, if the public can read a web page, they should not be able to write to it. The ability to write to it would permit them to alter or contaminate the data in a manner that could prove embarrassing. If a directory is provided to which the public can send files, they should not be able to read from that directory. If they can both read and write to the directory, they may use it simply as storage in lieu of their own. They may also use it to store contraband data that they would not want on their own systems and which might also prove embarrassing.

ENCRYPTION

Encryption is the application and use of secret, as opposed to public, codes. It is a powerful defense that can deal with many of the problems related to vulnerable links and even some of those related to insecure nodes. It is inexpensive and effective. In addition, multiple implementations are available. However, it is limited in the open node problems that it can deal with and may require some management infrastructure. Exhibit 58.1 displays some of the encryption choices available for selected applications on the Internet.

Encryption is used for two fundamental purposes on the net. The first is to preserve necessary confidentiality on the net, which is the traditional use of cryptography. The second is to enable some confidence about with whom one is talking. In other words, if conversation is in a language that can only be spoken by one other, the correct parties are speaking to one another.

Application	Encryption
E-mail	PGP, SecureXchange, PEM, S-MIME
File	PGP, RSA Secure, Entrust
Application	DES, IDEA, stelnet, sftp
Client/Server	Secure Socket Layer (SSL)
Gateway-to-gateway	Digital, IBM, TIS
World Wide Web	s-http
Secure IP	S/WAN

Exhibit 58.1. Encryption on the Internet

Encryption can also be used to resist password grabbers and other eavesdropping attacks.

USING THE INTERNET IN A RELATIVELY SAFE ENVIRONMENT

The following are recommendations for using the Internet in a relatively safe way. Although few will follow all of these recommendations, there is risk involved in any deviation from the recommendations. Moreover, although complete adherence to these recommendations will not eliminate all vulnerabilities, it will address many of them. Finally, although complete adherence will not eliminate all risks, following these recommendations provides a reasonable balance between risk and other values.

- *Do not rely on the secrecy or authenticity of any information traversing the Internet in public codes.* Names and addresses, credit card numbers, passwords, and other data received from the public net may be replays rather than originals. Amounts and account numbers may have been tampered with.
- *Choose a single point of connection to the Internet.* Although the Internet is inherently mesh connected, and more than one connection may be necessary to avoid single points of failure, the more connections, the more points of attack and the more difficult it is to maintain consistent controls. The fewer the number or points of connection, the fewer the potential points of attack and the easier to maintain control.
- *Connect to the Internet only with equipment dedicated to that purpose.* When computers were expensive, it was economic to put as many applications as possible on the costly hardware. Communication software was added to connect existing multi-use, multi-user systems to the net. Attacks exploited this gratuitous generality. Because of less expensive hardware, hardware connected to the net should be dedicated to that use. All other applications should be run on other systems.
- *Choose application-only connections.* Many of the compromises of the Internet have resulted from the fact that the components were connected at the system layer and that attacks have succeeded in escaping the application to the more general and flexible system layer. If an attack encounters the e-mail service, it should see nothing else. If it escapes the e-mail application, it should see nothing. Under no circumstances should it see the prompt of an operating system that knows about any other system. In other words, the operating system should be hidden from the public net.
- *Limit the use of Telnet.* Telnet, particularly to the operating system, is a very general and flexible capability. It can be both used for attack and is vulnerable to attacks. Most of its functions and capabilities can be accomplished with safer alternatives.

- *Use end-to-end encryption for commercial applications on the net.* Although most of the applications and traffic on the public net are public, commercial and other private applications on the public net must be conducted in secret codes.
- *Require strong authentication.* Users of private applications on the public net or of the public net for commercial applications must use strong authentication. Two independent kinds of evidence should be employed to determine the identity of a user, and the authentication data must be protected from capture and replay.
- *Log, monitor, and meter events and traffic.* Given enough time, almost any attack can succeed. It is important to be able to recognize attack traffic and correct for it early. Attacks can usually be recognized by a change, often a sudden increase, from normal traffic patterns. It is useful to know what normal traffic looks like to be able to recognize variances on a timely basis, and to communicate the condition of those variances to managers who can take timely corrective action.

CONCLUSION

The Internet is as ubiquitous as the telephone and for similar reasons. It gives users such an economic advantage over nonusers that the nonusers are forced to become users. Pundits are fond of saying that no one is making money on the Internet. This position is fatuous and suggests that tens of thousands of enterprises are behaving irrationally. What is meant is that no one is conducting commerce on the Internet, at least not in the sense that they are selling, distributing, billing, and being paid over the Internet. Of course, many firms are doing one or more of these. Many others are making money, mostly by reducing costs. Many companies are using the Internet because it is the most efficient way to support customers.

The Internet holds out the promise to empower, enrich, and perhaps even ennoble. A minimum level of public trust and confidence must be maintained if that promise becomes a reality. That trust is both fragile and irreparable.

Because fundamental vulnerabilities on the network exist and because all possible attacks cannot be anticipated, a conservative policy and a responsive posture are required.

Chapter 59
Implementing the First Web Site

Lee A. Freeman
Leonard M. Jessup

DESPITE THE PROLIFERATION of electronic commerce, as evidenced by the recent surge in online spending, many companies are just in a beginning stage with their E-commerce initiatives and/or are still "feeling their way." Both technology and business managers need advice on how to be successful with the initial implementation of an E-commerce site. For the purposes of this short chapter, we are defining an E-commerce site as a Web site for access by business partners and/or potential customers.

By sharing the "lessons learned" from two early E-commerce projects, we will argue that the development and implementation of a Web site require just as much attention — if not more — than any other systems development and implementation project.

CASE 1: MID-CONSULTING

Mid-Consulting is currently among the 25 largest certified public accounting and consulting firms in the United States. Due to the nature of Mid-Consulting's business, there are many management levels throughout the organization. They range from junior consultant through analyst and up to senior partner. All these positions have at least some management responsibilities. As discussed, this hierarchy and complexity played an important role in the subsequent E-commerce initiative.

At the time this case began, many of the competitors within this industry already had external Web sites. These Web sites were receiving widespread attention in the media and within the consulting industry. Although Mid-Consulting had a systems and technology consulting group that consulted on Web-site development and other Internet-related projects, no effort had been made within Mid-Consulting to develop its own Web site.

Some key managers at Mid-Consulting wanted a "Web presence" quickly and decided to create a minimal site for the short term (i.e., just to focus on having an initial presence). In a rushed effort, two systems analysts got together and created Mid-Consulting's Web site. They did not take the time to formally gather business objectives or requirements. They also made an active decision to not benchmark their site against their competition. They launched a site that contained basic information about the services and products available to Mid-Consulting's clients, as well as a small amount of career opportunity and office location information.

Six months after Mid-Consulting's Web site went online, no updates had been made to the site, and few employees and even fewer clients were aware that the site even existed. An outside consultant was contracted to provide a feasibility study and a design proposal. An initial meeting was held with the project leader from Mid-Consulting to determine the scope and time line of the project.

After researching the company, the competition, and the industry, the outside consultant prepared to present a proposal to a team of several senior partners and analysts from the systems consulting and marketing departments. Due to scheduling conflicts (some of the team members worked out of offices in different states) and other priorities, this presentation did not take place until six weeks after the initial meeting. At this presentation, several of the team members introduced new goals and objectives for the Web site, and the whole team worked on amending and reprioritizing the original objectives. The decision to avoid benchmarking against the competition was also reaffirmed. The rationale was that Mid-Consulting needed to set themselves apart from the competition, especially the Big Five. The team also decided to deviate from some standard Web development guidelines, such as "short" pages that do not scroll extensively, in an attempt to differentiate themselves. As a result, a new proposal was needed and everyone agreed to meet again in another month.

New research was conducted and a new proposal was written. After two attempts at scheduling a meeting, it was decided that a meeting would not be possible. The proposal was sent to all the team members, and the project "ended" without a formal meeting. Eighteen months later an improved design had been implemented, but the site was still plagued with navigation problems (users were not sure where to go for information) and information overload on the main page. The sites of Mid-Consulting's major competitors were much cleaner in terms of style and much more active (and interactive) in terms of content and appearance.

CASE 2: CREATIVE COOP

The Creative Coop is a member-owned purchasing cooperative consisting of more than 300 small member organizations located throughout the United States and Canada. Creative Coop purchases mostly automotive parts, accessories, and electronics, which are then sold by the members to automotive dealers and individuals. There are approximately 25 managers, all working out of the headquarters, handling everything from information systems to marketing to product distribution.

To gain a competitive advantage over their competition, senior managers at Creative Coop felt that having a presence on the Web was vital. A corporate Web site could provide enhanced internal services for Coop members. Prior to this point, however, corporate management had not felt the need to have a corporate Web presence and several shop owners had created Web sites for their individual shops, mostly for advertising purposes. These Web sites varied greatly in content and complexity, and there was no integration across them. A corporate Web site would create a common E-commerce initiative for the organization.

Creative Coop decided to begin its E-commerce initiative with a full analysis of the options and possibilities for a Web site. They contracted a consultant to conduct a feasibility study and provide a proposal for the development of a corporate Web site. An initial meeting was held to determine the scope of the project and to gather information regarding the company, its products, its needs, and its vision for its Web site. An additional meeting was held several weeks later with representatives from different management groups (marketing, co-op membership, and product development).

A proposal for a Web site that would meet the initial needs and objectives of Creative Coop and also included a suggested plan for the physical design was presented to management at a final meeting approximately six weeks after the initial meeting that began the project. Creative Coop's Web site provided location information for all the member shops and detailed information on the major (most popular) products and services, as well as employment and membership opportunities. All the team members were in agreement with regard to the objectives of the project and of the Web site.

Creative Coop chose to use an outside consultant for the development of its Web site because there was no one internally with much Web expertise. There were no problems scheduling meetings, and the president went so far as to rearrange his own schedule to find a convenient time for the rest of the group. The Web site was physically implemented by an Internet design company and went online three months after the beginning of the project.

LESSONS LEARNED

There are valuable lessons to be learned here with respect to (1) the role of environmental pressures in shaping E-commerce initiatives; (2) how different implementation approaches, especially with regard to planning and oversight, can lead to good and bad outcomes; and (3) how wrong our prior assumptions might be about the predicted success of an E-commerce initiative if these assumptions are based on size or industry. Below we describe these lessons.

Creative Coop is a fairly low-tech firm within a relatively low-tech industry. Several people within the firm had been experimenting with the Web and the senior managers recognized that they should pull these experimental efforts together under one common E-commerce initiative. They made it a priority to agree rather readily on what to do and were able to implement a useful, working Web site in a very reasonable amount of time. Mid-Consulting, on the other hand, is a fairly high-tech firm in a relatively high-tech industry. It had all the right reasons, both internal and external, to justify and produce a useful Web site fairly quickly. The senior managers had trouble, however, making a Web site initiative a priority and reaching a consensus on the direction their E-commerce initiative should take.

Why didn't the E-commerce implementations of these two firms match more closely with what we would expect given their internal competencies and the contexts within which they each operated? Specifically, what worked for Creative Coop that wasn't working for Mid-Consulting? From our vantage point it appears that the informal culture at Creative Coop served it well for implementing this new kind of technology. There seemed to be an air of playful experimentation and a feeling that the company could beat its rivals to the Web given the fairly low competitive pressure. The implementation process was informal, the team worked well together, and there was free and easy communication among those people involved in the process. Despite its need to signal to the marketplace that it was competent in E-commerce-based technologies in particular and despite the pressures to match the already existing Web sites of its competitors, Mid-Consulting did not capitalize on its internal technological competencies to produce a Web site quickly and effectively. Team members did not object to the decision not to benchmark competitors' Web sites either because (1) they were aware of their competitors' Web sites but felt they had nothing to gain from analyzing their sites, or (2) they were simply unaware of their competitors' Web sites. It also appears that being large and complex got in the way of a smooth, successful implementation: There was a lack of a clear, agreed upon goal. The usage of an external consultant may also have been a poor choice, given the company's established rules and procedures and its internal expertise in Internet applications.

This suggests the following lessons learned for initial E-commerce initiatives:

- A complete business analysis is needed upfront. Promote experimentation and creativity throughout the company — possibly through a workshop-like atmosphere. This will help employees think "outside of the box" and be open to new ideas and methods. E-commerce initiatives require a willingness to give up on preset notions of what is good and what will not work.

- Set a clear vision, goals, and objectives for the E-commerce initiative. This focus is necessary to ensure that the team is always working in the right direction and in the same direction.
- The decision to not do what a competitor has done should be an information-based decision. If other industry leaders have already established a Web site, IT managers should take the time to analyze or benchmark what these competitors have done. The analysis should include both the content as well as the "look-and-feel" of these Web sites.
- A formal project team needs to be created, with appropriate business managers represented — including those who can speak for top management.

We believe that these short case studies are helpful in pointing out what seems to work well and what appears not to work well in implementing new E-commerce initiatives within firms. Web technologies are still a moving target, and the ease of use of today's Web tools means lots of potential expertise inside and outside the organization. However, good planning, development, and implementation approaches are still needed, even if the technologies are easy to use.

Conventional wisdom would *not* have accurately predicted the outcomes of these two cases: a company that we would expect to have an effective early Web presence did not. On the other hand, the conventional wisdom of sensing one's environment, conducting effective strategic planning, fostering creativity and innovation in the use of new technology, and keeping business management active in the project certainly prevailed in these two instances.

Chapter 60

Internet Acceptable Usage Policies

James E. Gaskin

THE JOB OF AN ACCEPTABLE use policy is to explain what the organization considers acceptable Internet and computer use and to protect both employees and the organization from the ramifications of illegal actions. This chapter describes how such policies are written, what they should cover, and how they are most effectively activated.

Now that an Internet connection is a requirement, IS executives are responsible for more work than ever before. One vital area on the to-do list is to write, update, or implement the company's Acceptable Usage Policy for Internet use. The company may refer to this as an Internet Use Policy, the networking portion of the Computer Use Policy, or the Internet addition to your Personnel Manual. No matter the name, the role of such a policy is the same: it lists the rules and standards the company believes are important for employees using computers, networks, and particularly the Internet. Although the Acceptable Use Policy can be incorporated into other existing documents, it is generally taken more seriously and provides more company protection if it is a separate document.

Why is the Acceptable Use Policy so important today? Legal liability for Internet actions can quickly shift from the employee to the employer. After all, if the Internet is filled with obscenity and other illegal temptations, the company should provide protections for the employees. If management knowingly allows access to inappropriate Internet sites without either warning the users or blocking that access, management climbs on the liability hook with the actual employee performing illegal actions.

WRITING AN ACCEPTABLE USE POLICY

You, or someone in your department, must write the Acceptable Use Policy. It is better to have the fewest number of people possible involved in writing the Acceptable Use Policy. The very best number of authors is one.

0-8493-9820-7/00/$0.00+$.50
© 2000 by CRC Press LLC

This may grate against corporate culture, where technical documents often see more hands than a public washroom sink. While there are few excuses for the amount of tampering and changing that goes on with technical documents, the Acceptable Use Policy goes beyond a product manual or marketing white paper. You and your management must consider the Acceptable Use Policy a legal document which binds the behavior of employees within certain boundaries explained within the document.

Limiting the number of authors limits the number of viewpoints within the Acceptable Use Policy. Your employees must have no doubt why they have been given the Acceptable Use Policy, what their responsibilities are in regard to Internet and computer use, and what the penalties are for misuse of company resources, including time. More authors, or up-the-line editorial changes, will muddy the Acceptable Use Policy. Internal contradictions within the Acceptable Use Policy will leave loopholes for employee lawyers to exploit.

After the Acceptable Use Policy is written, the committee to oversee employee compliance with the terms of the agreement should be created. The committee should meet and approve the Acceptable Use Policy before distributing the document. This is the time for any comments, suggestions, additions, or deletions to the Acceptable Use Policy. While all on the committee are welcome to offer changes to the document, only the author should implement those changes. Again, the consistency of viewpoint is important.

Legal review comes after the committee has approved the Acceptable Use Policy contents and related documents. This brings us to a philosophical decision: lawyers want long, complicated documents that spell out every possible infraction and associated punishment, while business managers want short documents that can be interpreted in the company's favor. Your decision on the Acceptable Use Policy length and completeness will reflect your corporate culture and the wishes of upper management.

Your Acceptable Use Policy will be considered part of the Employee Handbook. Some states regard these handbooks as a legal contract, and other do not. Your corporate counsel will be able to answer that question for the states where your company has operations.

If it matters, be aware that the number of employees who read your Acceptable Use Policy approaches zero as the document lengthens. Simply put, the longer the document, the fewer readers. In most states, employees are bound by the conditions of the Acceptable Use Policy regardless of whether or not they have read and signed the document. However, holding employees liable for a document they have not read will be seen as a cold, heartless corporate maneuver. Employees who feel betrayed contact lawyers far more often than those who feel they were treated fairly. Although it is legal in some states for companies to ignore the promises they make in Employee Handbooks, the antagonism generated within the employee ranks by that mode of operation guarantees more lawsuits than following your own written guidelines.

SCOPE AND OVERVIEW OF THE POLICY

Does your company already have policies concerning computer use? How about company telephone, fax, and U.S. mail use? Is there a security policy in place?

Some companies, remiss in providing policies in the past, try to cram everything into the Acceptable Use Policy. This is legal, but confusing to the employees. Your Acceptable Use Policy will be more valuable if targeted strictly to Internet and other computer-networking concerns.

E-MAIL

Since e-mail is the most popular Internet application, e-mail control is important. The good part of e-mail is that there is a strong analogy to something all users are familiar with, namely, physical mail.

One company includes the following excellent statement:

> Remember that e-mail sent from the company travels on the company's electronic stationary. Your e-mail appears to the recipient as if it were sent on company letterhead.

Your security policy, if separate, should cover information about e-mail accounts, such as forging identities (not good). If it does not, or you wish to put all e-mail information in your Acceptable Use Policy, feel free. You can easily make the argument that e-mail information belongs in your Internet usage document.

Here are a few more things different schools and companies warn clients about e-mail use:

- Sending harassing, obscene, and/or other threatening e-mail is illegal.
- Sending junk mail, for-profit messages, or chain letters is prohibited.
- Take all precautions against importation of computer viruses.
- Do not send or receive sexually oriented messages or images.
- Do not transmit confidential company information.
- Employee medical, personal, or financial information must never be divulged.
- Personal messages are prohibited (or limited, or freely allowed, depending on your policy).

The other important point users should be told is that you will, definitely, read e-mail messages at times. Whether or not an employee must be told

689

when the company monitors communications is advisable according to some lawyers, but not others. Either way, if every employee signs the Acceptable Use Policy saying they will be monitored on a random basis, there will be little wiggle room if they complain later. They will also pay more attention to following the rules when they know someone will be monitoring their messages.

Let me add one more bullet for the list two paragraphs earlier:

- Your e-mail messages will be kept and periodically reviewed before being deleted.

This should leave no doubt that messages from your users will be reviewed. Your user should have no expectation that their e-mail messages are private and protected by any type of privacy law. Make sure each user understands that some messages will be read, even if messages are only spot-checked. Employees must understand that every message they send or receive may be read by management.

Do not keep e-mail messages for longer than 90 days, if that long. Why? Lawyers are now routinely demanding e-mail archives during lawsuit discovery. If your company is sued for any reason, the opposing lawyers will try to read all internal and external e-mail messages for the time period in question. No e-mail archives means no embarrassing quotes and off-the-cuff remarks that will cost you in court. Some large companies refuse to back up e-mail files for this reason.

WORLD WIDE WEB RESOURCES AND NEWSGROUPS

The Web takes the brunt of criticism when the Internet is blasted as a giant productivity sink hole. Corporate mangers rank employee time wasted as their number two concern about Internet access, right behind security. Your management will also start wondering how many employees are frittering away hours at a time perusing the Web on company time using company equipment.

Newsgroups have somewhat the same reputation, since there are over 20,000 newsgroups, only a few of which pertain to your business. While newsgroups full of equivalent professionals in other companies provide great benefit to your company employees, the non-technical press focuses on the "alt.sex.*" hierarchy of newsgroups. Someone in your management will be determined to limit access to all newsgroups, just to keep the alt.sex.* groups out of the company.

Do not lie to management or employees in your Acceptable Use Policy. Yes, there are inappropriate Web servers and newsgroups. Yes, some Web servers and newsgroups are valuable. Yes, you can monitor and track each user of any network resource by name, date, time online, and amount of material downloaded from any inappropriate network source.

In other words, you can log the actions of each and every corporate user during each and every network communication. If you do not have the proper firewall or proxy server in place yet to monitor your users, get one. You can, however, get one after the Internet connection is available. Better late than never. After all, your employees will be told what the company considers inappropriate in the Acceptable Use Policy.

Realize that some time will be wasted on the Web, just as time is wasted reading through trade magazines looking for articles that apply to your company. Every profession has trade magazines that offer articles and information in exchange for presenting advertising to the reader. The Web, to some people, is becoming nothing more than a huge trade magazine, offering helpful information interspersed with advertising. In a sense, the Web is not new, it is just advertising delivered by computer rather than by magazine. Treat it similarly.

As some employees research information more than others, they will use their Web client more than others. Information-dependent employees will surf quite a bit; clerks and production employees should not.

You may mention your guidelines for the Web in your Acceptable Use Policy, or you may prefer to ignore the Web. Some sample restrictions may include

- Viewing, downloading, displaying, and/or distributing obscene images is illegal.
- While the Web encourages wandering, remember your focus during work hours remains business.

The first bullet point is not optional — remind your employees regularly that obscenity in the workplace will not be allowed. The second bullet point is optional, and should be modified to match your comfort level regarding employee use of the Web.

Let's see some of the restrictions other Acceptable Use Policies have listed for newsgroup activity, plus a few I have added:

- Downloading or uploading non-business images or files is prohibited, and possibly illegal.
- Sending harassing, obscene and/or other threatening posts is illegal.
- Sending junk posts or "for-profit" messages is prohibited.
- Post articles only to groups supporting that subject matter.
- Do not post company advertisements of any kind in any newsgroup.
- Posting messages without your real name attached is prohibited.
- Copying newsgroup information to any other forum is illegal (copyright infringement).

Newsgroups are where the majority of defamation happens; flame wars encourage angry responses rather than clear thinking. Often, other readers of the newsgroup will send copies of messages to the postmasters of the flame war participants. Whether the messages indicate a flame war that is getting out of hand or just unprofessional statements, it is best to visit your involved employee and counsel restraint. If kind words do not settle your employee, unplug them from the newsgroup access list. No sense risking a lawsuit when you know there is a good chance of things being said that have no positive value to your company.

Several Acceptable Use Policies address defamation somewhat oblique-ly. Here are some examples of the language included in those policies:

- ...including comments based on race, national origin, sex, sexual ori-entation, age, disability, religion, or political beliefs.
- ...inappropriate uses ... to send/receive messages that are racist, in-flammatory, sexist, or contain obscenities.

Whether these are politically correct or good business sense depends on the individual company. However, reading, "you can't understand, be-cause you're a [blank]" in a global forum such as an Internet newsgroup won't endear anyone to the employee making that statement. Your compa-ny will suffer loss of customer good will at the least, and may be sued for defamation. These same courtesy restrictions apply to e-mail, but e-mail lacks that extra edge brought when thousands of readers see your compa-ny name attached to the ranting of one overwrought employee.

IRC (Internet Relay Chat) and MUDs (Multi-User Domain) have not been mentioned because they have no redeeming professional use. No employ-ee use of such activity should be tolerated.

In case employees are confused about whether or not the company's rights to monitor employee activity extend to the computers, include a line such as this:

- All computer communications are logged and randomly reviewed to verify appropriate use.

Notice the words are appropriate use. If your Acceptable Use Policy says the words dirty pictures or indecent, your employees (and their lawyers) will argue about that wording. Dirty is in the eye of the beholder, as is inde-cent. Obscene, however, is a legal term that applies just as well to comput-ers as to magazines, books, and videos. Better to stick with inappropriate if possible, because that covers more activities than any other term.

Penalty for misuse should range up to and include termination. If an em-ployee must be terminated, do so for work-related causes, rather than mention the word Internet. Free speech advocates get involved when an employee is fired for inappropriate use of the Internet, but not when an employee is terminated for wasting too much time on the job and disobeying orders.

NETIQUETTE ADDENDUM

Some companies spell out appropriate e-mail, newsgroup, and Web communication guidelines within their Acceptable Use Policy. This is a noble endeavor, but slightly misguided. Your company guidelines toward Internet communications are likely to change more often than your restrictions on inappropriate Internet use and discipline for infractions.

Since the Acceptable Use Policy should be signed by each employee if possible, any changes to netiquette embedded in the Acceptable Use Policy will require a new signature. The logistics of this process quickly become overwhelming.

Put the rules of Internet behavior in a separate Netiquette Addendum, attached to the Acceptable Use Policy. In this way, changes to e-mail rules, for instance, will not negate the Acceptable Use Policy in any way, nor will anyone believe a new signature is necessary.

ACTIVATING THE POLICY WITH OR WITHOUT SIGNATURES

As briefly mentioned in the preceding section, getting signatures on the Acceptable Use Policy can be tricky. Small- to medium-sized companies can handle the logistics of gathering signed copies of the Acceptable Use Policy, although there will still be considerable amount of time expended on that effort. Large companies may find it impossible to ship paper policies all over the world for signatures and get them back signed, no matter how much time and effort they devote.

The best case is to get a signed Acceptable Use Policy from each employee before that person is connected to the Internet. Training classes offer an excellent chance to gather signatures. If software must be installed on client computers, the Acceptable Use Policy should be presented, explained, and signed during software loading.

Reality intrudes, however, and ruins our best case. Many companies already have granted Internet access before developing their Acceptable Use Policy. This is not the wisest course, but it is common. Other companies do not offer training or cannot physically gather signed copies.

It is important to send copies of the Acceptable Use Policy to each employee with Internet access. Copies should also be posted in public places, such as break rooms and department bulletin boards. Add the policy to the existing Personnel Manual or Employee Handbook. Send an e-mail to users every quarter reminding them of the Acceptable Use Policy and where they can read a copy if they have misplaced theirs. Public attempts will blunt any disgruntled employee contentions they did not know about Internet restrictions.

THE ACCEPTABLE USE POLICY COMMITTEE

The Acceptable Use Policy Committee should be carefully formed. Department managers should participate in the selection process for employees in their group, so as not to ruffle feathers or step into the middle of some other disagreement. Give each member plenty of warning before the first meeting and provide background information quickly.

Who should be included? The following list contains the requisite positions and their expected contribution:

- *Computer systems manager* — Technical details of Internet access and monitoring.
- *Company lawyer or Human Resources official* — Legal aspects of workplace rules.
- *Executive management representative* — Guarantees your committee will not be ignored.
- *Union representative* — Laws for union workers vary from those covering other employees.
- *The "One Who Knows All," or a general power user* — Provides employee concerns and input.

What is the committee responsible for, and to whom? Everything concerning the Internet, and everyone.

How often should the committee meet? At the beginning, every two weeks. Once the Internet connection is old news, once a month may be enough. The interval is dictated by the number of security incidents and employee discipline actions to be resolved.

In extreme cases, such as an employee action that could result in company liability or criminal prosecution for someone, the committee must meet immediately. The grievance policy in cases of Internet abuse should be clear and well known to all employees who care to ask.

It is important that all employees know who sits on the Acceptable Use Policy committee. Secret committees are repressive, but open committees can encourage good will within the company. Strongly consider setting up an internal e-mail address for your committee, and use it for questions and as an electronic suggestion box.

The most effective deterrent to misdeed is not the severity of discipline but the inevitability of discovery. Remember, your goal is to make the Internet serve the company, not to find excuses to discipline or fire employees.

After the first committee meeting, the following questions should be answered:

- Will employees be fired for Internet misuse?
- What is the penalty for the first offense? The third? The fifth?
- Will the police be called for stolen software or obviously obscene images?
- Where must your other employee policies be modified to support your Internet connection?
- Are any insurance policies in place to protect against hackers or employee misdeed? Should some be added?
- How often will employees be reminded of company Internet guidelines? How will this be done?

Discipline is particularly tough when discussing the Internet. After all, if an employee is wasting hours per day on the Internet, the department manager should be disciplined for improper management. Waste of time on the Internet is not a technology issue, but a management issue.

Even though the department manager should be disciplined, that same manager should be the one to discipline the employee. Outsiders with an executive mandate to punish miscreants are never popular and often are sabotaged by the very employees they should oversee. Keep the department managers in the loop as long as possible.

Exceptions to this approach include security violations and illegal acts. In those cases, the department manager must be informed, but company security or the local police will handle the situation. These cases are never pleasant, but do not be naíve. If you believe none of your employees could act illegally, you must be new to management.

CONCLUSION

The job of the Acceptable Use Policy is to explain what the company considers acceptable Internet and/or computer use and behavior. The committee dedicated to enforcing the provisions of the policy must publicize the Acceptable Use Policy and monitor employee compliance. Infractions must be handled quickly, or the employees will assume nothing in the Acceptable Use Policy is really important, and compliance levels will shrink. Proactive Internet management will drastically lower the chances of Internet-related lawsuits, arguments, and misunderstandings.

Section 5
Facilitating Knowledge Work

COMPUTER TOOLS for end-user computing have now been available for more than two decades. The diffusion of desktop productivity tools has continued to accelerate over the 1990s, aided by the maturation of many supporting technologies: local area networks, portable devices, Internet access options, and personal productivity suites. As we enter the new millennium, the typical knowledge worker is a savvy computer user who demands both efficient and effective support services for multimedia applications, both in the workplace and anytime/anywhere.

Yet, as personal technology columnists for business periodicals regularly remind us, today's PC tools continue to be complex and are being used not only for data management but also for document management. End-user technologies, as well as the skill sets that workers need to be productive, continue to be moving targets. This only heightens the need for IS managers to continue to pay attention to this critical IS management area. The key IS management issues, however, still belong to two major categories: support and control.

SUPPORT FOR END USERS

Providing reliable and effective user support has become a strategic IT capability. For many knowledge workers, the help desk and other technical support staff are their primary point of contact with the IS organization. Chapter 61, "Helping Users Help Themselves," describes three levels of user help and training, using both technology and people.

Supporting telecommuters and geographically dispersed team members is the focus of Chapter 62, "Supporting Telework." A comprehensive list of obstacles to virtual work arrangements is provided, followed by a discussion of technology resources and technical support that can be used to enable telework. However, the author cautions that technology-based solutions are necessary but insufficient. Successful telework support also involves careful attention to task design, reward mechanisms, and other adjustments to traditional work arrangements in order to address the needs of both employees and organizations.

A similar theme can be found in Chapter 63, "Information Sharing Within Organizations." Whereas the typical IS professional thinks first of groupware and Web technologies as solutions to information sharing needs across organizational employees, the author warns us that technological solutions are not enough: Behavioral norms and incentive systems can be major obstacles to information sharing.

CONTROLS FOR USER-DEVELOPED APPLICATIONS

The benefits of users developing their own applications are well documented and include direct user control as well as both faster and cheaper applications. Nevertheless, user-developed applications also pose significant risks to an organization, including weak data integrity and security controls, redundant systems, and inefficient use of organizational resources. Managing user-developed applications therefore requires a strong IS/user partnership.

Chapter 64, "End-User Computing Control Guidelines," presents an architectural approach to the control of end-user computing environments. The first component of this control strategy is a distributed management structure in which security management and internal auditing responsibilities are shared by IS and user groups. The author provides examples of enterprisewide policies and procedures, physical and system controls, network and communication controls, application and process controls, and continuity controls — all of which should be a part of an organization's information protection strategy.

The primary objective of Chapter 65, "Control Issues in End-User Computing and Applications," is to increase awareness of the risks associated with end-user development. The author describes in detail 12 specific risks and outlines the key elements of a control strategy. Chapter 66, "Reviewing End-User Applications," provides a comprehensive primer for establishing a review process for user-developed applications. The chapter includes detailed checklists of questions that can be easily adapted for organization-specific audits.

Chapter 61
Helping Users Help Themselves

James A. Larson
Carol L. Larson

PCS ARE AN INDISPENSABLE TOOL for most office workers and an integral part of business activities. In most organizations today, PC applications are used not only for word processing, but also for financial analysis, database management, e-mail, and Web browsing. Annually, business enterprises spend thousands of dollars in support for each PC used by employees.

Unfortunately, PCs are also more complex than they were just a few years ago because:

- *Software developers are creating more complex applications.* To remain competitive, software vendors are adding more functions to their applications. For example, basic word processors include spell checkers, grammar checkers, layout and formatting capabilities, and illustration and graphics capabilities. New versions of existing software appear almost annually.
- *Software developers are creating new applications.* New general-purpose applications are appearing, including desktop conferencing, document management, and simulation. New vertical applications are also appearing, providing new features and functions useful for specialized businesses.
- *Operating systems are more complex.* More functions common to multiple applications are finding their way into the PC operating system.

Because of the rapid evolution of PC environments and the lack of cooperation among software vendors, PCs frequently fail from software inefficiency, incompatibility, and instability. Most enterprises have help desk operations in which technical support agents answer users' questions and help with difficult tasks.

HELP DESKS AND TECHNICAL SUPPORT AGENTS

A typical help desk operation consists of one or more technical support agents who respond to telephone calls from PC users requesting help. For each request, a technical support agent creates a "trouble ticket," which is an entry in a "trouble log" that describes who requested help, the nature of the problem, and the location and configuration of the user's PC. After helping the user, the technical support agent records the diagnosis and the action taken to repair the problem and "closes" the trouble ticket. Help desk agents may examine the trouble ticket log to analyze the types of help being requested by users and to generate suggestions and responses to frequently asked questions, which are then made available to users.

Exhibit 61.1 illustrates three levels of help that can be made available to users. If users frequently experience delays when telephoning for help and are often placed on hold while the technical support agents help other users, the help desk function can be improved by providing:

Local PC help. This reduces help calls by using the PC to detect and resolve its own problems locally, often before the user is even aware of them.

Automated help. This reduces help calls by using intranet Web servers to provide help information directly to the user.

Personal help from technical support agents. This type of help should be the user's last resort. Personal help is still an integral part of the help desk function, however, and should still be performed regardless of other methods of help available.

Using PC Software to Reduce Help Desk Calls

The ideal place to tackle PC problems is at their source, before the problems result in technical support calls. With the appropriate amount of information and intelligence, the PC can detect and resolve many problems itself before the user is aware of them.

The following three types of technology supply a PC with intelligence:

- *Wizards.* These software devices help novice users by applying intelligence in the form of carefully crafted sequences of steps to perform difficult operations.
- *Expert systems.* These systems apply rules discovered by the technical support staff from the trouble log. The rules detect and resolve frequent PC problems. Call centers can build expert systems using case-based-reasoning inference engines.
- *Software agents.* These agents monitor the PC to detect and automatically resolve PC problems. Included in this category are applications that scan memory and detect viruses, examine memory utilization and make the appropriate adjustments, test the hardware, and recon-

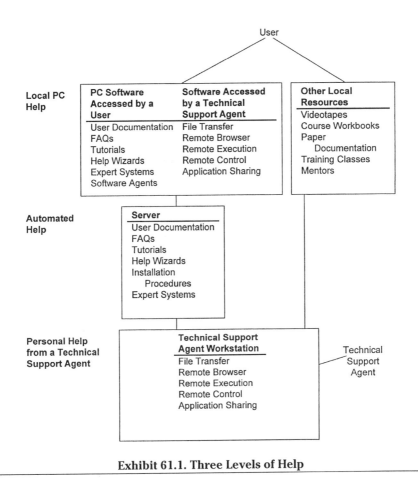

Exhibit 61.1. Three Levels of Help

figure the system automatically. Software applications that "tune-up" a PC are beginning to appear on the market. Tune-up applications examine and optimize environmental parameters so the PC works faster. An example of this is the adjustment of memory allocation.

Reducing Help Desk Calls with an Intranet Web Server

Another way to reduce help calls is to make help information easily accessible to users. Many call centers use intranet Web servers to store helpful information that users can access directly. Following are examples of automated help:

- Online user documentation, installation instructions, frequently asked questions (FAQs), and other advice that helps users solve their own problems.
- Installation files and software upgrades that users can download and install automatically onto their PCs.

- Expert systems that contain rules that may be more up to date than the rules in the expert system on the user's PC. When a local expert system cannot solve a particular problem, it is passed to the expert system on the Web server for resolution.

New Tools for Diagnosing and Resolving PC Problems

Certain tools enable technical support agents to remotely diagnose and repair software without having to travel to the user's site and work directly on the user's PC. These tools include file transfer, remote browsers, remote execution, remote control, and application sharing.

File Transfer. Technical support agents can use any of several file transfer applications, such as AUTOEXEC.BAT, SYS.INI, and CONFIG.SYS files, to upload and review users' files. The support agent edits the uploaded files and then downloads the updated files and device drivers back onto the user's PC. The technical support agent can also download new applications and updates to existing applications and install them remotely.

Remote Browsers. Remote browsers allow technical support agents to scan configuration and registry files in a PC directly from the help desk. The agents examine critical parameter values to diagnose problems on the user's PC. Most remote browsers also let technical support agents update parameter values on the user's PC.

Remote Execution. Technical support agents write scripts for downloading to the user's PC with the file transfer capability. Once the scripts are downloaded, the technical support agent can execute the script remotely to change the parameters and configurations on the user's PC. The remote execution capability is especially useful after downloading new software and the associated installation procedure. The technical support agent remotely initiates the installation procedure and verifies that it has been completed successfully.

Remote Control and Application Sharing. Remote control applications allow a technical support agent to remotely initiate and control the user's PC. The support agent sees the user's entire display and uses the mouse and keyboard on his own PC to drive the application executing on the user's PC. Application sharing allows a technical support agent to share the windows of an application executing on the user's PC — a user can thus demonstrate a problem to the agent, who in turn can demonstrate how to resolve the problem.

TOOLS FOR AUTOMATING PC SUPPORT

A typical application life cycle consists of software installation, user training, troubleshooting and maintenance, and replacement. Help desk operations attempt to minimize support costs by applying tools that automate many of these tasks.

Installing Software

Installing a new software package on hundreds of PCs can be a time-consuming process, especially if a technician must personally locate and install the software on every PC in the enterprise. By leveraging the connectivity provided by local area networks (LANs), this task can be minimized.

Initially, a new application is installed on a server. From their individual PCs, users can remotely invoke the application on the server and download the results back to their PCs for review. When users begin to execute the application more frequently, they may download the application directly to their PCs and use automated installation procedures to install the application.

User Training

After the new application is made available, users will most likely be anxious to learn when and how to use it. Most enterprises use at least two traditional techniques for user training — classes and mentoring.

Training Classes. Users attend scheduled sessions where an instructor explains when and how to use the application. However, it may be difficult to schedule training sessions convenient for all users. Instructors may also vary in their teaching effectiveness.

Mentoring. A knowledgeable user mentors a novice user in the operation of the application. However, this close working arrangement with the user may distract the mentor from other tasks, so novice users may have limited access to the mentor.

Some enterprises find it cost-effective to place more of the responsibility for training onto the user by enabling the user to self-train, if and when the user finds training necessary. Several self-training techniques, such as videotapes and course workbooks, online tutorials, online wizards, online help, user documentation, and FAQs, are useful.

Videotapes and Course Workbooks. A professional instructor prepares a videotape for novice users to watch at their convenience. The workbook focuses the user on critical concepts and actions. However, novice users may find sections of the videotape boring or out of date.

Online Tutorials. The novice user watches an online tutorial demonstrating when and how to use the application. Some online tutorials have interactive tasks for the novice to perform that reinforce critical concepts and actions. Users experienced with similar applications can bypass the online tutorial and focus on a"what's new and different" section instead.

Online Wizards. Novice users can invoke an online wizard that leads them through a series of steps and assists them in making choices and decisions to accomplish a high-level task. At the same time, the users learn how to perform the high-level task.

Online Help. The user requests assistance from a help system to perform a specific task. However, the user may be unable to locate the answer to his specific question if the help system designer failed to anticipate the user's particular question.

User Documentation. The user examines the help manual for instructions about the use of the application. However, paper documentation may be bulky, can be misplaced, can intimidate the user, and may be incomplete or out of date. Paper documentation can be avoided by distributing the documentation to the user via e-mail. More organizations are starting to place documentation on an HTML server so users can access it from any computer with an HTML browser. A single, centralized source of documentation has the advantage of providing one location where it can be updated.

Frequently Asked Questions (FAQs). Documenting and publishing frequently asked questions and their answers allows users to learn new techniques and solutions to common problems. FAQs should be incorporated into the online documentation as quickly as possible.

PROCTORING NEW OR DIFFICULT OPERATIONS

Even with the use of online tutorials, wizards, documentation, and FAQs, it is sometimes necessary for a user to seek help from a technical support agent. Through a sequence of verbal questions and answers, the agent solicits a description of the problem, diagnoses the problem, and leads the user through the steps to fix a problem. However, these telephone dialogs may be time-consuming, especially with novice users who may not be able to articulate precisely what the problem is or perform the necessary steps to correct the problem.

Application sharing and remote control enable both the user and the technical support agent to view the execution of a single application executing on the user's machine. The user demonstrates the problem to the technical support agent, who performs the appropriate operations to correct the problem. Alternatively, the agent demonstrates the appropriate steps to the user to correct the problem so the user learns how to correct the problem should it recur. Application sharing and remote control are powerful tools, especially when a technical support agent is also available to answer questions over the phone.

MONITORING USER ACTIVITY

Technical support agents may use LAN management software to remotely monitor possible trouble spots and resolve them before users notice the problems. LAN management suites such as Intel's LANDesk (see http://www.intel.com/com-net/sns/showcase/index.htm) include tools to monitor and resolve problems in the following components of an enterprise LAN:

- Network communication loads.
- Print queues.
- Printer availability.
- Server access.
- User computer software and hardware errors.

Monitors detect bottlenecks and broken components. Rule-based expert systems attempt to resolve problems by adjusting environmental parameters, such as queue lengths and active processes.

SUPPORT FOR TELECOMMUTERS

Many employees perform work-related activities on their home or portable PCs while on the road for their job. If the PC is able to connect to the enterprise's LAN via a modem, technical support agents may use file transfer, remote execution, browsing, remote control, and application sharing tools to diagnose and repair the PCs. If the user has access to a second telephone line, then the technical support agent and user may discuss the problem verbally while the support agent uses remote browsers, remote execution, remote control, and application sharing tools to resolve the user's problem. If the user's modem supports both data and voice transfer using protocols such as digital simultaneous voice and data (DSVD), then the user and the agent can talk through the problem while the technical support agent diagnoses and repairs it.

CONCLUSION

An enterprise should institute three levels of user help and assistance — local PC help, automated help from a server, and personal help from technical support agents. This gives users several lines of defense to turn to before their problem results in a trouble ticket.

Providing users with more sources of support allows the end-user computing staff to be more productive. The support staff can focus more energy on rolling out new software, troubleshooting, and training; the user can spend more time working because of reduced trouble-related downtime; and the entire enterprise can save money.

Chapter 62
Supporting Telework
Heikki Topi

SINCE THE INDUSTRIAL REVOLUTION, most organizations have been built around the model of bringing employees to centralized locations to perform work with a group of peers under the immediate supervision and control of management. For almost three centuries the general assumption among both managers and their employees has been that the employer assigns a place where the employee performs his or her work.

Today, advances in telecommunications technology and transportation have freed many workers from the traditional model of fixed place of work. Telework has become a widely implemented practice for two reasons. First, increasingly, many Americans have become *telecommuters* — spending at least a part of their regular business hours in home offices, satellite offices, or neighborhood work centers close to their homes. Current estimates of the percentage of Americans telecommuting either full- or part-time vary between 10 percent and 20 percent. Second, it has become increasingly common for work to be performed by *virtual teams* — where the membership of the team is not limited by the physical location of an employee's primary workplace or a team member's functional unit within the organization. Both of these kinds of telework require *virtual work arrangements*.

Research and practical experiences from a large number of organizations have shown that various types of virtual work arrangements are advantageous for both organizations and their employees (e.g., Davenport and Pearlson, 1998). When applied correctly, they provide the flexibility that allows companies to put together the best possible teams for various projects. They enable their employees to enjoy freedom from the restrictions set by a strictly defined place and time of work. Also, virtual work arrangements can provide significant cost reductions to both the employer and the employees.

The purpose of this chapter is to identify the obstacles that organizations face in implementing virtual work arrangements and to offer some practical solutions to alleviate these problems. The intention is to present a balanced view that includes both technological and managerial solutions.

0-8493-9820-7/00/$0.00+$.50
© 2000 by CRC Press LLC

OBSTACLES OF VIRTUAL WORK ARRANGEMENTS

The discussion that follows covers several categories of reasons why traditional work arrangements still are dominant. Some of these reasons are still valid but can be alleviated by advances in technology and management techniques. Other reasons are simply no longer valid. The extent to which obstacles exist naturally depends partially on the industry and the way the organization operates.

Task- and Resource-Related Obstacles

On many occasions, work has to be performed at a specific location because the physical objects being processed are there. Most manufacturing and construction jobs fall into this category, and with them, in most cases, it is either practically impossible or economically unjustifiable to spread the work between a large number of sites. Thus, the location of work is determined by the need to bring a team of workers together to a place that is suitable for the manufacturing operation or happens to be the site under construction.

In many service jobs the work has to be performed where customers are if they value face-to-face contact. The traditional model for retail sales, banking, repair services, hotels, and restaurants is based on the idea of attracting a customer to a specific physical location, and in most cases it is essential that employees are available in these locations, too.[1] Not only customers but also suppliers, financial institutions, government agencies, and other stakeholders assume that most organizations have a stable physical location where at least some of the employees can be found (this can, naturally, be a location of a parent or custodian organization). This assumption will probably not be radically changed in the near future. Also, in many cases the physical presence of an organization is a status symbol, and both buildings and the number of employees working in them are still used as indicators of success. In other situations, however, a mobile sales force is assumed; sales personnel are expected to interface with their customers at their own place of business.

The location of work is also often constrained by the need for specialized equipment or other resources. This is obvious in manufacturing: Often the work is where the machinery is. Also, in many industries, research and development work requires specialized laboratory equipment. For office workers, the location of work is often determined by the location of the documents that employees manipulate in their job: Much of office work still involves processing data on paper forms. Many times work takes place where access to physical archives of either organization-specific data or general knowledge is possible.

Reasons related to the nature of tasks and the availability of resources still anchor employees strongly to a specific physical location, even if technology significantly reduces these dependencies. For example, information technology can connect customers to virtual retail outlets or product experts and can make formerly location-specific resources (such as information sources and paper forms) available through networks.

Management-Related Obstacles

Many organizations require their employees to perform their jobs in a specific location even if they are not manipulating tangible objects in their jobs and they need no tangible resources to get their jobs done. This section will explore the reasons underlying these requirements.

Perceived Performance Advantages. Often managers perceive that the aggregated performance of all the employees working together in a specific location is higher than the sum of individual performances would be if employees worked separately in different locations (i.e., that co-location per se will create clearly beneficial synergies). People are brought together to work in the same location because management assumes that the support that employees give to each other improves their joint performance. The assumption is that co-location enables unplanned informal meetings, quick answers to unanticipated questions, idea generation, and problem-solving sessions.

It is important, however, to note that with advantages come disadvantages. Disruptions and interruptions are all too typical in office environments and can result in a lack of concentration; these include background noise, events unrelated to work being performed, and unnecessary and unproductive planned and unplanned meetings. Whether or not continuous co-location of a team is truly beneficial depends on a large number of factors such as the nature of the project and tasks, the stage of the project, the number of people involved, the cohesiveness of the project team and its ability to work together in different environments, the nature of the facilities allocated to the team, and the alternative communication mechanisms that are available. No organization should assume automatically that one arrangement is always better than the other; flexibility and freedom to look for the best possible alternative for a particular project organization at a particular project stage is the key.

Organizations' Need to Manage. Many organizations and individual managers still feel that they need their employees in a location where "management by walking around" or "management by example" philosophies can be applied literally, and where work behavior can be directly observed. Many managers are still uncomfortable with the idea of being responsible for a team if they are not able to be in face-to-face contact with team members regularly. Unfortunately, the problem is often the lack of trust between team members: many managers still have an expectation that they should be able to control an employee's contributions toward the goals of the team and/or the organization by observing his or her behavior. This is true specifically in cases in which the evaluation of results is difficult or the risk of failure is high.

Workers' Need to Be Managed. On the other hand, employees often feel the need to be managed, either because they want to show with their behavior that they are loyal and useful contributors to the organization's goals (and thus, for example, worth a promotion or a place among those who keep their jobs if employees are laid off) or because they simply need somebody to organize their work for them to get it done. Some employees also feel safer if they have the option of moving the responsibility for the most demanding decisions to somebody else.

Therefore, the needs to manage and be managed are strong reasons underlying the tenacity of the traditional work arrangements. Naturally, an important question is the validity and relevance of these needs and our ability to overcome these concerns with technology. On one hand, at least in some cases, it is possible to use modern communication technologies to implement mechanisms that would effectively produce the same results as traditional management techniques that require physical vicinity. On the other hand, it is possible (and increasingly often essential) that employees can feel that their performance is not (only) evaluated based on their behavior but based on their contributions to the organization's goals (i.e., their results).

Social Contacts and Support. Organizations also bring their employees together into one or several locations because often this is what their employees want. The physical workplace is for many an important social environment; many simply do not want to work outside the workplace (e.g., at home). Fears of social isolation and life without the variety of human contacts offered by traditional work arrangements are true and serious factors affecting the models of work that organizations are able to use. Partially, this is linked to the need to be accepted as a valuable member of an organization by managers and coworkers, and partially it is linked to the how social relations at the workplace often become a natural social network in addition to the extended family and close friends. For many, it is essential to be able to leave the home regularly and enter a different social and physical sphere.

Many employees also feel that the support given by coworkers in the immediate physical proximity is valuable and helps them perform their tasks better. A question or other request for help is at least interpreted to be less intrusive and more effective if presented in person than if presented using a communication technology such as phone, videoconferencing, or e-mail. Also, in an environment in which employees work in close physical proximity it is easier to find support with complex or in other ways difficult decision making.

REMOVING OBSTACLES WITH TECHNOLOGY

This section discusses a variety of technological tools and arrangements that can be used to enable virtual work arrangements and improve their utilization in organizations. Both tools and support of their usage are included because it is not sufficient to make technological resources available to employees; effective work arrangements require high-quality technology *support*. Later in the chapter we continue our discussion by emphasizing the importance of a variety of managerial actions: Even well-supported technology is not enough if it is not applied effectively.

Technology Resources

Virtual work arrangements are made possible by communication and computing technology. A well-functioning, efficient telecommunications infrastructure for voice, video, and data is one of the first requirements for a technology environment to support telework, whether telecommuting or virtual teams. In *voice communication*, the key characteristic of a support system for virtual workers is flexibility: The phone system of an enterprise should be able to connect a phone call to an employee with one number independent of his or her location, whether it is within company facilities, in the home office, or on the road with a wireless phone. Increasingly, wireless technologies form a natural basis for voice communication because they enable independence from location.

In *data communication*, it is important that virtual workers have access to all the same services that are available to employees with a permanent office, although often not at the same speeds. Virtual private networking and other remote access technologies have made a versatile way to access corporate data resources possible. The importance of sufficient bandwidth cannot be overemphasized: For any connection that is made regularly from the same location (as, for example, in telecommuting) integrated service digital network (ISDN), 128 Kbps is the minimum speed, and broadband options (asymmetrical digital subscriber line [ADSL], cable modems, satellite-based systems) should be used whenever possible. The additional cost compared to analog modem connections is small compared to the advantages: It does not make sense to lower the productivity of a highly paid professional because of low bandwidth and an unreliable connection if a faster and more reliable option is available at a marginal monthly cost of only $50–$100.

The promise of *videoconferencing* has not yet been fulfilled by widely available technologies except in large organizations, mostly because of the lack of sufficient bandwidth. Useful videoconferencing requires a circuit-switched or dedicated connection; the 128 Kbps bandwidth provided by an ISDN connection is the absolute minimum but, in practice, only 384 Kbps or higher bandwidth offers a connection that is sufficient for high-quality videoconferencing.

Existing and future telecommunications technologies such as increasingly fast Internet connections using ADSL and cable modems, the promise of ATM-based broadband ISDN, and coming third-generation wireless devices all mean significantly higher access speeds than those currently available. An organization that wants to seriously use the opportunities offered by virtual work arrangements should build a state-of-the-art telecommunications infrastructure and make it available for the employees who are applying the new model of work.

Technology Support

Providing the best of technology to employees who are doing their work outside the traditional work environment will not be sufficient if they are not trained and/or able and willing to learn to use the technology. Virtual workers are often far away from the traditional organizational support system and therefore need to have stronger technical problem-solving skills than do peers who are closer to the reach of the organized support. This area was often ignored earlier when employees interested in virtual work arrangements often were technology experts themselves. In the current situation, the need for technological survival skills is high enough to warrant a special training course for employees who are starting to telecommute or become members of virtual teams. The content should not only include standard software but also issues related to the telecommunications solutions used: The more dependent a teleworker is on the resources available on the network, the more important it is that the training enables the employee to troubleshoot and independently solve at least the most typical simple network problems.

However good the training, the importance of an excellent support structure cannot be overemphasized: Both telecommuters and virtual team members have their own special computing and telecommunications needs, and sufficient support should be available to address the relevant issues. For members of virtual teams, the most essential issue is the creation and maintenance of a proper environment for sharing information, an environment that allows efficient and effective file sharing and electronic conferencing among team members, wherever they are located. For telecommuters, it is vitally important that support personnel are easily accessible by phone (and videoconferencing, if used by the organization), and that they are able to provide help both with traditional software problems and telecommunications issues specific to telecommuters. The support organization should have the necessary expertise to help telecommuters choose the best telecommunications solution suitable for each individual from the set of available solutions.

REMOVING OBSTACLES WITH MANAGERIAL ACTIONS

The technology-based solutions reviewed previously are not, however, all that is needed. Especially for managers and knowledge workers focusing on technology-related projects it is easy to understand the technical solutions and to attempt to apply them to all problems. Technical solutions alone will, however, fail to bring the results that can be achieved by choosing a balanced approach that integrates appropriate technologies with carefully selected managerial tools.

Task Support

One of the problems with telework is the real or perceived lack of support for a variety of work-related tasks. Many employees find it problematic if they are not able to turn to their immediate coworkers or supervisors to ask for help with difficult decisions or problems requiring specialized knowledge that only few in the organization have. It appears that the problem is gaining somebody's immediate attention: Any teleworker has a variety of telecommunications media (e.g., phone, videoconferencing, electronic conferencing, and e-mail) for contacting the same coworkers they would be approaching to ask for help in a face-to-face setting, but every one of these media is easier to ignore than a direct person-to-person contact attempt in an office setting.

To alleviate the concerns regarding the lack of task support in a virtual work environment, clear organizational task support mechanisms should be available. First, either messaging and groupware tools such as Lotus Notes or other intranet technologies should be used appropriately to maintain organizational memory in the form of questions and answers or problems and their solutions. Second, teams and departments where at least some of the employees are working virtually should explicitly acknowledge the task support needs of the employees outside the permanent location and give them a priority when appropriate; this requires conscious effort especially from those working on the company premises. Third, whenever possible, regular face-to-face meetings with virtual employees present should be a part of the organization of work for all project teams and work groups; among other benefits, these meetings offer excellent opportunities for mutual learning and support. Fourth, in many situations it is good if the entire group or department learns to use asynchronous media (such as e-mail or electronic conferencing) for questions and answers that do not require an immediate answer; an additional benefit is that these media provide also an opportunity to store the questions and answers as part of the organizational memory.

Whatever the technical implementation chosen, it is important that the task support needs of the employees working in the virtual environment are taken into account and acknowledged in a way that reduces at least the perceived lack of task support.

Modified Reward Mechanisms

Successful telework requires organizational reward mechanisms that are adapted to suit the new models. If work behavior cannot be directly observed, it should not be a basis for evaluation either. This is, however, a tradition that is difficult to change; especially when direct results of an employee's work do not warrant a positive evaluation, managers often tend to rely on their impressions based on observations of work behavior. If an employee has successfully created the impression of hard work and strong dedication, it is much easier for a manager to attribute the unsatisfactory results to external causes, which were not under control of the employee. It is still much easier to create these impressions when co-located with the manager who performs the evaluation. (This is not to say that employees do not try to create similar impressions of dedication and diligence in virtual environments, too, for example, by creating work-related e-mail or electronic conferencing postings in the middle of the night.)

To a certain extent, visibility in the communication channels of the virtual world is also used as a behavioral criterion, and, thus, individual actions intended to create a positive image might be effective in some cases. Organizations should, however, find ways to move toward an evaluation model that in a fair and equitable way values contributions toward the organization's goals, not the number of hours spent or other similar activity-based measures. In many organizations, this is a clear cultural change, which is never an easy process, and it requires conscious effort by the management. Extra effort is needed to make sure that promotion decisions are fair and perceived to be fair. Virtual workers can aid this process by making sure that the results of their work are not hidden and that their supervisors understand what they are achieving.

Moreover, the external signs of rewards should also be available and visible in the virtual world if there are corresponding signs in the real world: For example, "Employee of the month" type of recognitions should be visible not only on the wall in company headquarters but also on the corporate intranet. If privileges that are only useful at the company premises (e.g., special parking or access to special facilities) are used as reward mechanisms, some corresponding rewards should be developed for those operating in the virtual world.

If the top management of an organization wants to support and encourage virtual work models, managers should express and communicate this explicitly to all employees using channels that are available also to those who are not physically present at the company locations. The best support is support by example, which requires that the top management is also able and willing to use the communication channels typically used by virtual workers. Also, it is important that the top management expresses the commitment to create and maintain a reward system that is fair for *everybody* because virtual work arrangements may create concerns regarding fairness among both those who participate in them and those who do not; the success of these arrangements requires that these concerns are addressed.

Maintaining and Enhancing Organizational Identity

Employees want to identify with the organization for which they are working, and it is important that teleworkers have enough opportunities to strengthen their organizational identities. Partially, this requires that organizational networks, particularly intranets, include information and symbolism that aids all employees with identification (e.g., statements regarding corporate values, mission, basic objectives, history, and future, consistent use of corporate colors and logos, or examples of achievements by the company and its employees). On the other hand, it is important that all employees without a strong permanent home within the organization are regularly brought together to social meetings in which they can learn to know their coworkers better, in a relaxed face-to-face setting, and to identify better with the entire organization.

One of the best ways to create and maintain a strong identification with an organization is to create an atmosphere of trust in which every employee can feel that he or she is trusted to contribute fully to the organization's goals without continuous observation and control by management. These feelings can be nurtured by explicit statements and other visible signs of trust, but it is even more important that employees can feel that management appreciates and accepts their decisions regarding their own work.

Responding to Other Social Needs

Organizations willing to use virtual work arrangements successfully should find mechanisms to respond to employees' social needs. For many employees, work is a justification to leave home regularly and meet other adults. Virtual teams, work at customer sites, and satellite offices fulfill this need, but for many teleworkers who work at home the advantages of freedom and flexibility are significantly challenged by the long hours alone without the opportunity to stop by at a colleague's office or have a lunch break together. Also, lack of face-to-face social contacts supports the feeling of being out of the loop and out of the core circle of employees.

One solution to this problem that also makes sense for other reasons is to make sure that all employees, however virtual their existence normally is, regularly attend face-to-face meetings with both their supervisors and their coworkers. If possible and mutually agreeable, one option is to implement part-time telework arrangements so that even telecommuters spend one or two days a week at central or satellite office locations. Naturally, if this option is chosen, logistical arrangements are necessary to make sure that cost savings related to the reduction of office and parking space are not entirely lost.

The developments in telecommunications technologies — especially relatively inexpensive high bandwidth solutions such as ADSL and cable modems with a flat fee pricing structure — make it possible to use a rich variety of communication options (including videoconferencing over IP networks) for business-related purposes. It is probable that active utilization of modern telecommunications technologies alleviates at least to a certain extent, but not fully, the feelings of being alone and far away from the center of action.

CONCLUSION

Many organizations have identified good reasons to make telework possible for their employees; the benefits include increased flexibility and cost reductions for both individuals and organizations. Yet many organizations are struggling to make these arrangements successful and widely available.

The lessons learned from this chapter can be summarized with two key points. First, advances in technology have dramatically expanded the possibilities for telework, but virtual work arrangements do not fit with all industries and all employee groups. Managers have to carefully evaluate the feasibility of telework for a given organization and given type of work. Second, the success of virtual work arrangements cannot be guaranteed with technological solutions only. In most cases, strong and clear managerial interventions are necessary.

The technical opportunities for virtual work arrangements continue to evolve; advances in wireless communication technologies, for example, are expected to have a strong impact. Yet even with future technologies, the benefits of telework may be elusive if due attention is not given to the careful design of work arrangements that fulfill the fundamental needs of both organizations and their employees.

Notes

1. Naturally, we acknowledge that computing and telecommunications technologies are in many cases changing the traditional model. E-commerce is increasingly often separating the place where a consumer makes a purchase decision from the location of the product or service that is being purchased. At the same time, consumers increasingly often accept that a salesperson or product support specialist is not physically present at the time of purchase or is not available for contact at a specific location.

Recommended Reading

Anonymous. 1998. Transcend the top ten telecommuting traps. *Byte* (July).

Belanger, F., and Collins, R.W. 1998. Distributed work arrangements: A research framework. *Information Society*, 14(April–Jun): 2.

Bresnahan, J. 1998. Why telework?. *CIO* 11(January 15): 7.

Davenport, T.H., and Pearlson, K. 1998. Two cheers for the virtual office. *Sloan Management Review* 39(Summer):4.

Hill, E.J., Miller, B.C., Weiner, S.P., and Colihan, J. 1998. Influences of the virtual office on aspects of work and work/life balance. *Personnel Psychology* 51(Autumn):3.

Mahlon, A. 1998. The alternative workplace: Changing where and how people work. *Harvard Business Review* 76(May–June):3.

Chapter 63
Information Sharing Within Organizations
Randall H. Russell

NEW TECHNOLOGY is making ever-mounting volumes of information more readily available, through more types of media and more recipients than ever before. However, the broadening array of communication channels that has eased information has coincidentally reduced the certainty that the message the sender tries to transmit will be received by the intended party.

These changes have complicated the jobs of those who manage their companies' information behavior, that is, the way their companies' personnel acquire and use information. This chapter explores the factors that affect information behavior and contribute to information sharing.

A DEFINITION OF INFORMATION SHARING

Information behavior is the way people act regarding the information they need to manage. This includes creating, retrieving, or modifying information, storing information, and providing access to information.

Information sharing is the voluntary act of making information available to others. It is not the routine reporting of information (e.g., the submission of a time and expense form at the end of a pay period), nor is it the routine exchange of information between intelligent devices.

Exhibit 63.1 highlights some of the differences between information sharing and reporting. Information sharing represents one end of a continuum of *information access*. It describes voluntary information access that takes place on an ad hoc basis. Together, information sharing and information reporting represent the two ends of the information access continuum.

The information access continuum is dynamic because information behavior changes over time. Consequently, when organizations have positive experiences with information sharing, they try to systematize this sharing into a more formal process (i.e., information reporting).

0-8493-9820-7/00/$0.00+$.50
© 2000 by CRC Press LLC

Information Sharing	↔	Information Reporting
Informal		Formal
Ad hoc		Periodic
Unstructured		Structured
Voluntary		Mandatory
Nonsystematic		Systematic
Implicit exchange		Explicit exchange
Value		Value

Exhibit 63.1. Forms of Information Access

For example, a large domestic oil company recently developed an operational model for the production of gas in one of its major fields. This new model, which was created only after its reservoir and facility engineers repeatedly shared information, was more accurate than the organization's past model. It also demonstrated to the oil company's business partner, the pipeline company, that it could ship more gas for the organization without reducing the volume of gas it had shipped for its other partners. Now that the new model has been accepted, the oil company has institutionalized information sharing: It has been acknowledged as a beneficial practice and is encouraged elsewhere in the organization.

THE IMPORTANCE OF INFORMATION SHARING

Information sharing has been seen to increase employees' commitment, improve decision making, quicken an organization's response to potential shortages or delays in production, and predict shifts in organizational structure. A study of collective bargaining processes found that in Japan, information sharing led to shorter and easier negotiation processes accompanied by the acceptance of lower wage increases by unions. In contrast, a similar study in the United States concluded that information sharing increased labor's bargaining power. Thus, sharing can result in undesirable consequences, depending on which side of the relationship the observer sits.

Experience shows that the information sharing within organizations does not occur easily. Because individuals try to maximize their individual gain, they may restrict their information sharing when they believe that their unique value to the firm is reflected in the information they control and selectively share. In the worst case, some employees share information only to advance their personal goals; they leak sensitive information to outsiders and withhold critical information from their managers.

THE IMPORTANCE OF CONTEXT

The context and content of information determine a lot about how and when it will be shared. Organizations must try to ensure that truly useful information is made available to those who will use it to serve the interests of the firm. Organizations can achieve this availability by using appropriate incentives for encouraging the sharing of this information. However, incentives, in and of themselves, are not enough. Other contextual matters play a role — namely, the explicit and implicit organizational rules and norms that help determine information behavior. These three factors — rules, norms, and incentives — are discussed in the following sections.

However, the following discussion also demonstrates that it is impossible to treat any of these factors in isolation. Two of the factors, behavioral norms and incentives, are always in evidence, regardless of whether formal or written rules are in place. Oddly, managers often focus on only the written rules of an organization when they attempt to change information behavior.

EXPLICIT RULES

All large and complex organizations use explicit rules to define their intended information flows. For information reporting, they use standard formats that specify information types and the frequency of the reporting required to systematically support decisions, trigger events, and in other ways drive organizational outcomes. For example, personnel in most large organizations must report time and expenses, evaluate themselves and others, monitor a project's status or sales activity, prepare and monitor budgets, develop strategic and tactical plans, and report on projects and initiatives. Organizational reports on quality achievements and measurements are increasingly being called for. Most of this reporting is in response to explicit rules that identify the information required to run the business.

Personnel, however, tend to only selectively adhere to such explicit reporting requirements. People comply more often when adherence is linked to incentives. Directly linking payment to the timely submission of time and expense reports, for example, is tremendously successful in increasing the percentage of reports delivered on time. (An inverse relationship exists between the number of reporting rules and the level of compliance.) People thus conform to rules selectively; those linked to outcomes of interest to the employee are best observed.

Explicit rules need not always be written. Official policy manuals often lag behind operational reality. Someone with senior-level authority can quickly change the rules that govern information access in a company simply by leading through example. For example, a senior manager of a corporate IT group wanted to impose a new software product as a communication vehicle. To enforce this rule, he refused to communicate through any other mechanism. He tied following the communications rule to the incentive of communicating directly with him. Further, as the manager introduced his official communication mechanism, he also encouraged staff members to use the formal rumor mill database for posting rumors or responding to posted rumors. Rumors include facts, beliefs, or mere suspicions. Intended to promote an environment of trust and openness, this mechanism provided a new formal opportunity for information sharing.

Following this experimental phase with the new software product, the bank merged with a financial institution that did not encourage as much communication among its personnel. The formal rumor mill conflicted with the underlying norms of the new organization. The executives of the newly created financial institution were concerned about how the automation of informal information flows would affect the regulation of the organization. In short order, this database was discontinued. Informal systems of information access (i.e., rumor mills) must support an organization's formal goal or chaos will ensue.

Information sharing can encourage organizational changes that may have little to do with an organization's formal structure. Because information sharing tends to flatten hierarchies and leads to further democratization, it may be strenuously resisted by those who expect to lose through such organizational changes. In turn, organizations considering the promotion of information sharing must decide whether or not organizational flattening, improved morale, and democratization are desirable potential consequences.

BEHAVIORAL NORMS — THE UNWRITTEN RULE OF THE GAME

Although the terms "organizational culture" and "behavioral norms" are often used interchangeably, they do not mean the same thing. "Culture" refers to the decision styles and customary forms of interaction that characterize an organization's work environment and significantly determine behavioral norms. Culture is ever present and can encourage or discourage desired changes in information behaviors.

Many people describe culture as "the way things work around here." This can include behaviors such as being polite to one's boss, not revealing personal information to staff members one does not know well, or leading a discussion only if one has the highest status in the room.

As Exhibit 63.1 suggests, explicit rules of access are typically associated with information reporting, but the explicit norms of organizations relate more closely to information sharing. Reporting, which is more formal and systematic, is defined by rules. Information sharing, which is more informal and ad hoc, occurs through the tacit agreement of people acting according to behavioral norms.

One commonly observed behavioral norm is that people prefer to share information associated with *positive outcomes*. In a recently reengineered R&D function within a major chemical company, for example, cross-functional teams were observed to be much more comfortable sharing information about the progress they were making, compared to any negative results teams or team members observed.

Another behavioral norm is the preference for contributing to an *ongoing exchange*. Seeding, a mechanism for encouraging the use of shared discussion databases, works because people like to share. When an organization seeds a database, it makes the data freely available in the expectation that users will, in turn, contribute to the database. The more useful, interesting, or rewarding the information in a seeded database is, the more people want to contribute information to it, to reseed it. Without such reseeding, a database declines in value, and sharing diminishes in a downward spiral of use and usefulness. Therefore, systems in which users receive information but do not contribute to it tend to be unstable and in decline.

The more useful, interesting, or intrinsically rewarding information is, the more valuable it is to share. The easier it is to share, the more an organization can rely on behavioral norms to ensure its communication. However, when information supports formally structured processes or when it can have a negative impact (e.g., the reporting of negative project results), organizations must systematize its communication by establishing formal reporting relationships and mechanisms. Information reporting is thus associated with increased formalization of the information access process.

INCENTIVES

When information sharing is not seen as risky and people depend on each other to accomplish work, the intrinsic value of information is often a sufficiently strong incentive to support an adequate level of information sharing. However, when traditionally conservative information behavior is entrenched, or when the information required is negative or mandated, organizations that want to encourage information sharing need to examine the value of the incentives they offer for it.

The evolution of customer support at Lotus Development Corp. provides a useful example of the important role that incentives can play in transforming an organizational culture and enforcing formal rules of behavior. Early customer service at Lotus was a cumbersome process in which a support representative would take a call, document the caller's problem, attempt to reproduce it, and develop a solution. The solution would then be documented and catalogued so that the next support representative who faced that problem would not have to recreate the solution.

One challenge in managing this support function was cataloguing the solutions in such a way that representatives could retrieve them; another challenge was changing the way representatives shared their knowledge. At the time, Lotus was actually unintentionally discouraging representatives from sharing information. This is because support representatives could get promoted by carving out a problem area and becoming such an expert in it that other representatives with questions about it would come to them for help. Representatives had learned that by hoarding information, by making other representatives come to them, they could appear more valuable to the company. Doing so, however, did not help the department achieve the goal of providing answers to customer problems as quickly as possible. To best support the customer, the department had to document all known solutions and rapidly make this material available.

Lotus now takes a two-pronged approach to customer service. Representatives are now supported by a combined groupware and database system that provides full text search and retrieval. This system helps them to determine rapidly whether or not a solution has already been developed for any specific problem. However, Lotus recognizes that a technical solution by itself cannot ensure optimal customer support. Therefore, it has instituted a formal performance evaluation standard whereby 10 percent of each support representative's annual appraisal involves a peer evaluation of how well he or she shares information. This is an example of how incentives can be used to modify sharing behavior.

WHEN DOES INFORMATION SHARING PAY OFF?

Information sharing is most appropriate when information behavior is not highly formalized or when individuals need to adjust their behavior to coordinate their activities to work with others. Information sharing is most useful to people who are reciprocally interdependent (i.e., who work together) performing nonroutine tasks. They need to communicate frequently in order to make mutual adjustments to complete their interdependent tasks effectively.

This type of environment exists during organizational transformations or when the external environment is changing rapidly. For example, if business process reengineering is disrupting formal information flows, information sharing can improve cohesion within and across processes.

The importance of informal information access can also depend on the type of work being done. For example, product development is one of the most promising places to implement work-group computing to support cooperative work. Here, data sharing and parallel development processes promise dramatic reductions in the development cycle. Other activities that can be improved through information sharing include the following:

- Conceptual design.
- Technology demonstration.
- Feasibility demonstration.
- Process capability demonstration.
- Design view.
- Production readiness.

The less structured activities for all these work tasks usually provide the best opportunities for information sharing. Information reporting is likely to be more useful within routine components of the process. The challenge, of course, is to properly align the organization's culture, rules, norms, and incentives to achieve the desired level of information sharing.

Chapter 64
End-User Computing Control Guidelines

Ron Hale

THIS CHAPTER EXAMINES end-user computing control within the context of an architecture based on quality. As end-user computing systems have advanced, many of the security and management issues have been addressed. A central administration capability and an effective level of access authorization and authentication generally exist for current systems that are connected to networks. In prior architectures, the network was only a transport mechanism. In many of the systems that are being designed and implemented today, however, the network is the system and provides many of the controls that had been available on the mainframe. For example, many workstations now provide power-on passwords; storage capacity has expanded sufficiently so that workers are not required to maintain diskette files; and control over access to system functions and to data is protected not only through physical means but also through logical security, encryption, and other techniques.

ARCHITECTURAL APPROACHES TO INFORMATION PROTECTION

Although tools are becoming available (e.g., from hardware providers, security product developers, and network vendors) that can be used to solve many of the confidentiality and integrity problems common in end-user computing, the approach to implementing control is often not as straightforward as is common in centralized processing environments. The goals of worker empowerment, increased functionality and utility, and the ability of end users to control their environment must be guarded. In many organizations, end users have the political strength and independence to resist efforts that are seen as restrictive or costly. In addition, networks, remote access, distributed data servers, Internet tools, and the other components that have become part of the end-user environment have made control a difficult task.

0-8493-9820-7/00/$0.00+$.50
© 2000 by CRC Press LLC

To address the complexity of end-user computing, an architectural approach is required. It helps to ensure that an organization's control strategy and technical strategy are mutually supportive. The components of an information protection architecture include management, confidentiality and integrity controls, and continuity controls.

MANAGEMENT STRUCTURE

Perhaps the best and most expedient means of bringing stability to the end-user platform is to develop an effective management structure.

Distributed Management

Because end-user computing is highly distributed, and because local personnel and managers are responsible for controlling the business environment where end-user solutions are implemented, it is appropriate that control responsibilities are also distributed. Centralized administration and management of security in a highly decentralized environment cannot work without a great deal of effort and a large staff. When authority for managing control is distributed within the organization, management can expect a higher degree of voluntary compliance; in particular, where adherence to policies and procedures is included in personnel evaluation criteria. If distributed responsibility is properly implemented, ensuring that the goals of the program are consistent with the requirements and goals of the business unit is more likely to be successful.

Distributing security responsibilities may mean that traditional information protection roles need to be redefined. In many centralized organizations, security specialists are responsible for implementing and managing access control. In a distributed end-user environment, this is not practical. There are too many systems and users for the security organization to manage access control. Even with the availability of network and other tools, it may not be appropriate for security personnel to be responsible for access administration. In many distributed environments where advanced networks have been implemented, access controls may best be managed by network administrators. In a similar manner, server, UNIX, and any other system security may best be managed by personnel responsible for that environment.

With many technologies that are used in distributed and end-user computing environments, no special classes of administration are defined for security. Administrators have access to root or operate at the operating system level with all rights and privileges. In such cases, it is not appropriate for security personnel to take an active role in managing access security. Their role should be more consultative in nature. They could also be involved with monitoring and risk management planning, which are potentially more beneficial to the organization and more in line with management responsibilities.

Security Management Committee

Because security in end-user computing environments is distributive, greater acceptance of policies and procedures can be expected if the organization as a whole is involved with defining the environment. To achieve this, a security management committee can be created that represents some of the largest or most influential information technology users and technology groups. This committee should be responsible for recommending the security policy and for developing the procedures and standards that will be in force throughout the enterprise.

Representation on the committee by the internal audit department is often beneficial, and their support and insight can be important in developing an effective security management structure. However, consideration must be given to the control responsibilities of audit and the need to separate their responsibility for monitoring compliance with controls and for developing controls as part of the security committee. In some enterprises, this is not a major issue because internal audit takes a more consultative position. If maintaining the independence of audit is important, then audit can participate as an observer.

Senior Executive Support

The internal audit department traditionally had an advantage over the security organization because of its reporting relationship. Internal auditors in most organizations report to senior executives, which enables them to discuss significant control concerns and to get management acceptance of actions that need to be taken to resolve issues. Security has traditionally reported to IS management and has not had the executive exposure unless there has been a security compromise or other incident. In a distributed environment, it may be beneficial to have the security department and the security management committee report to a senior executive who will be a champion and who has sufficient authority within the enterprise to promote information protection as an important and necessary part of managing the business. Such a reporting relationship will also remove security from the purely technical environment of information systems and place it in a more business-focused environment.

POLICY AND STRATEGY

The ability to communicate strategy and requirements is essential in an end-user computing environment. This communication generally takes the form of enterprisewide policy statements and is supported by procedures, standards, and guidelines that can be targeted to specific business functions, technology platforms, or information sources.

The Information Protection Policy Statement

An information protection policy statement should define management expectations for information protection, the responsibilities of individuals and groups for protecting information, and the organizational structure that will assist management in implementing protection approaches that are consistent with the business strategy. Because the statement will be widely distributed and is meant to clearly communicate management's and users' responsibilities, it should not take the form of a legal document. The effectiveness of the information protection policy depends in large part on its effective communication.

Classification of Information

To protect information, users and managers need to have a consistent definition of what information is important and what protective measures are appropriate. In any organization, local management will be inclined to feel that their information is more sensitive and critical than other information within the organization. From an organizational standpoint, this may not be the case. To ensure that the organization protects only to the appropriate level the information that has the highest value or is the most sensitive, a classification method must be in place.

In the mainframe environment, all information was protected essentially to the same level by default. In a distributed and end-user computing environment, such levels of protection are not practical and represent a significant cost in terms of organizational efficiency. The information protection policy should clearly identify the criteria that should be used in classification, the labels that are to be used to communicate classification decisions, and the nature of controls that are appropriate for each class of information.

Classifying information is a difficult task. There is a tendency to view variations in the nature of information or in its use as separate information classes. However, the fewer the classes of information that an enterprise defines, the easier it is to classify the information and to understand what needs to be done to protect it. In many organizations, information is classified only according to its sensitivity and criticality. Classes of sensitivity can be highly sensitive, sensitive, proprietary, and public. Classes of criticality can be defined in terms of the period within which information needs to be made available following a business disruption.

Monitoring and Control

A method of monitoring the control system and correcting disruptive variances must be established. Such monitoring can include traditional audit and system reports, but because the system is distributed and addresses all information, total reliance on traditional approaches may not be effective.

In an end-user computing environment, relying on business management to call security personnel when they need help is unrealistic. Security needs to be proactive. By periodically meeting with business managers or their representatives and discussing their security issues and concerns, security personnel can determine the difficulties that are being experienced and can detect changes in risk due to new technology, the application of technology, or business processes. By increasing dialogue and promoting the awareness that security wants to improve performance, not to block progress, these meetings can help ensure that business management will seek security assistance when a problem arises.

Standards, Procedures, and Guidelines

The other elements of effective management — standards, procedures, and guidelines — define in terms of technology and business processes precisely how controls are to be implemented. Standards could be developed for documenting end-user applications and spreadsheets, access controls and access paths, system implementation and design specifications, and other elements that need to be consistent across an enterprise. Procedures define how something is done, such as testing applications, managing change in end-user environments, and gaining approval for access to information and systems. Guidelines provide a suggested approach to security when differences in organizations make consistency difficult or when local processes need to be defined. Policies, procedures, standards, and guidelines are each a significant component in the information protection architecture.

CONFIDENTIALITY AND INTEGRITY CONTROLS

Confidentiality and integrity controls are intended to operate on physical, logical, and procedural levels. Because end-user computing is primarily business and user focused, security solutions need to be tightly integrated into the way the business is managed and how work is done.

Physical Controls

In early end-user computing solutions, physical security was the only available control to ensure the protection of the hardware, software, and information. This control helped to ensure the availability of the system as well as to prevent unauthorized access to information and functions.

With the spread of distributed computing and local networks, physical controls still maintain a certain significance. Devices such as data, application, and security servers need to be protected from unauthorized access; and continuity of service needs to be ensured. For example, the integrity of the system must be protected in cases where local users have been given access to servers and have installed programs or made modifications that resulted in service interruptions. Contract maintenance personnel should be prevented from running diagnostics or performing other procedures unless they are escorted and supervised. System code should be protected from unauthorized modifications. Vendor personnel should be monitored to ensure that any modifications or diagnostic routines will not compromise system integrity or provide unknown or unauthorized access paths.

The network represents a critical element of end-user computing solutions. Network devices, including the transmission path, need to be protected from unauthorized access. Protection of the path is important to ensure the continuity of network traffic and to prevent unauthorized monitoring of the traffic.

Last, media used with end-user systems need to be protected. As with mainframe systems, files on user workstations and servers need to be backed up regularly. Backup copies need to be taken off site to ensure that they will be available in the event of a disaster. During transit and in storage, media need to be protected from unauthorized access or modification. Media that are used with the local workstation may also need to be protected. Users may produce magnetic output to store intermediate work products, to provide local backup of strategic files, or to take home to work with. These media, and all media associated with end-user systems, need to be protected to the highest level of classification of the information contained therein.

System Controls

System security in end-user computing solutions is as significant as mainframe security is in centralized architectures. The difference lies in the tools and techniques that are available in the distributed world, which are often not as all-encompassing or as effective as are mainframe tools, and in the types of vulnerabilities.

Tools. In the mainframe world, one tool can be used to identify and to protect all data as well as system resources. For each device in the distributed environment, there may be an associated internal security capability and tool. Tools are often not consistent across platforms and are not complementary. They do not allow for a single point of administration and provide little efficiency from an enterprise standpoint. To gain this efficiency, additional security products need to be installed.

Even when a multiplicity of security tools is used, a decision needs to be made about where to place the locus of control. In some central management solutions, the mainframe becomes the center of access control and authentication. Distributed security management solutions may be practical for some of the many systems used in an environment, but may not address security in all environments.

Vulnerabilities. In some systems used to support end-user computing, problems in the design of the operating system or with the tools and functions that are bundled with the system have resulted in security vulnerabilities. For example, UNIX administrators have reported compromises of system integrity due to bugs in system software such as editors and main programs. These compromises have been well publicized and exploited by system crackers.

The lack of experience in effective system management has introduced other vulnerabilities. Distributed, open systems may be easier to break because they are open. Although UNIX is frequently pointed to as a security problem, similar vulnerabilities can be found in many systems typically used in the end-user or distributed system environment.

The task of security then is to identify areas of risk or technical compromise and to find ways to mitigate the risk or to detect attempts to compromise the integrity of the system. The risk of outsiders penetrating system security should not be management's only concern. Insiders represent a substantial risk, because they not only have all of the knowledge that is available to the cracker community but also understand the security environment, have increased availability to systems, and have potentially more time to attempt to break the system. Thus, an internal compromise may be more significant than an attack from outside of the organization.

Database controls. Access to the database represents another area of risk in a distributed environment. In mainframe systems, access paths to data are limited, and the security system can be used to control both the data and the paths. In distributed and end-user systems, data can be distributed across an enterprise. In many instances, the path to the data is expected to be controlled through the application. However, users frequently are given other software tools that can provide access through an alternate, unprotected path. For example, user access to data may be defined within client software provided on their systems. Controls may be menu driven or table driven. At the same time, users may be provided with interactive SQL products that can be used to define SELECTS and other database operations. If the database is implemented on top of the system level, and if access is provided through a listener port that will acquiesce to any request, users may have the ability to access, modify, and write anything to the database.

Network and Communications Controls

Access path controls also need to be implemented at the network level. In many environments, various access paths are used, each with different security characteristics and levels of control. One path may be intended for after-hours employee access. Another may be developed to provide system manager access for trouble shooting and testing. Vendors and support personnel may have an entirely different path. In addition, individual users may implement their own access path through internal modems using remote communication software such as PC Anywhere.

Multiple and inconsistent paths can create an opportunity for system compromise. Some paths might not be effectively monitored, so if a compromise were to occur, security and system management might not be aware of the condition.

Access path controls. To help ensure the integrity of the network, it is best to provide only limited access points. This helps both in detecting unauthorized access attempts and in correcting problems. Different levels of access may require different levels of security. Because system support personnel will be operating at the system level, they may require the use of one-time passwords. Individual users may be given multiple-use passwords if their access is not considered to be a significant security risk and if monitoring and detection controls are effective.

Access path schematic. If multiple access paths are provided, the cost of security may not be consistent with the risks or the risks may not be effectively controlled to support business protection requirements. To identify where control reliance is placed and the consistency of controls across an environment, an access path schematic should be used. This schematic depicts users; the path that they take to system resources, including data; control points; and the extent of reliance on controls. Often, it shows control points where major reliance is placed or where the control is inappropriate and the level of reliance is inconsistent with the general security architecture.

Some users (e.g., network support) may employ several diverse access paths, including dial-in access, Internet access, or private network access, depending on the type of maintenance or diagnostic activities that are required. For system and application access, reliance is placed at the control level on the use of shared identifiers and passwords. Routers that are accessed by network support may have two levels of access provided, one that permits modification of router tables and another that permits only read access to this information. This could represent a significant security vulnerability, particularly when certain routers are used as firewalls between the Internet and the internal network.

External users are provided with dial-back access to the network. At each level of access through the application, they are required to enter individual user identifiers and passwords, user authentication is performed, and an access decision is made. This may be a burden for the users and could provide ineffective security, particularly when password format and change interval requirements are not consistent. An excessive number of passwords, frequent changes, and a perception on the part of users that security is too restrictive may lead to writing passwords down, selecting trivial passwords, or using other measures that weaken the level of security.

Application and Process Controls

The last component of confidentiality and integrity controls is involved with applications and processes. Because end-user computing is generally highly integrated into the management of a business function, security solutions need to address not only the technology but also the process. Application development controls need to be consistent with the type and extent of development activity within the end-user area. At a minimum, spreadsheets and other business tools should be documented and the master preserved in a secure location. It may be appropriate to take master copies off site to ensure their integrity and recovery.

Workflow management software can be used to protect the integrity of processes. This software is generally a middleware system that allows management to develop rules that define what is expected or the limits imposed on a process as well as to create graphical images that define the process flow. For example, workflow rules can be developed that establish the organization's purchase authorization limits. If a purchase order exceeds the defined limit, the process flow will control what happens to the transaction and will automatically route it to the user with the appropriate signature authority. Through workflow management software, processes can be controlled, end-user solutions can be tightly integrated into business functions, and effective integrity controls can be ensured throughout the process.

CONTINUITY CONTROLS

Because much of the data and processing capability is distributed in end-user computing environments, continuity controls need to be distributed across an organization if systems are to be adequately protected. Centralized solutions for continuity may not be acceptable. Servers may be backed up by a centralized administration group, but this may not adequately protect work in progress or work that is completed on the user's work station.

In some instances, network backup strategies have been developed to periodically back up the user's work station. This can be a costly undertaking given the number of work stations and the size of local disk drives. However, with the availability of higher bandwidth networks, compression algorithms, and a strategy of periodically backing up only modified files, a centrally controlled process may be effective in such cases.

In many organizations, the risk of business disruption is not in the mainframe environment but in the systems that have been distributed across an enterprise. End-user computing systems need to be considered when the recovery and continuity strategy for an enterprise, and in particular the business function, is developed. Plans need to be developed to address the criticality of end-user systems to each business function and to determine the best approach to recovering these systems as defined by their importance to the overall enterprise.

CONCLUSION

End-user computing represents a significant departure from traditional data processing. It also represents a unique opportunity to integrate confidentiality, integrity, and continuity with business processes and with the use of information within business units. The following are the confidentiality, integrity, and continuity efforts that should be considered in the context of end-user computing.

- *Establish an enterprisewide information protection policy.* Because information and technology are distributed, responsibility for protecting information also needs to be distributed. A policy should define individual and organizational responsibility for protecting information, the classes of information that need to be protected, and the nature of the protection controls that are required. In addition, the policy should express management's concern for information protection and should provide the basic structure for achieving its goals.
- *Develop a management structure for information protection.* The role of traditional security organizations needs to change to support end-user computing environments. Security needs to be less involved with directly administering access control and more involved with designing controls. Protection management may need to be supported by an enterprisewide committee to represent technical groups as well as users' organizations. The security committee should be chaired by the security manager and should be responsible for managing changes to the protection policy and its implementation throughout the enterprise.
- *Develop appropriate technical components.* An appropriate technical architecture needs to be developed to support the distinct protection requirements of end-user computing. The use of new technologies,

increased dependence on networks, easy access to data, and the challenge of protecting end-user-developed applications must be addressed. From a network standpoint, external access points need to be consolidated for better manageability and increased control. Authentication and monitoring controls need to be implemented at the boundary point between the external and internal networks. Access paths to data need to be identified, and all access paths should be secured to the same level. Application development and change control processes need to be adjusted to reduce integrity and continuity risks. Within the end-user environment, controls must be implemented to ensure that access is authorized, that users can be authenticated, and that responsibility for individual actions can be assigned. Auditability controls, to help ensure that unauthorized actions can be detected, also need to be in place. New software solutions, including workforce management middleware solutions, may be used to help ensure that sensitive business processes are effectively controlled.

- *Provide an execution and feedback mechanism.* The end-user computing environment is characterized by rapid and frequent change. The systems that users have available, the software that can be used, and the utilities that can be purchased change daily. To manage change and to provide consistency and control, a means needs to be developed to detect changes either in business processes or requirements or in the technology or its use within an enterprise. To be effective, confidentiality, integrity, and continuity need to be considered in advance of change and throughout the life cycle.

Chapter 65

Control Issues in End-User Computing and Applications

Sandra D. Allen-Senft
Frederick Gallegos

END-USER COMPUTING AND APPLICATION development has taken on greater importance in organizations because of the perception that users can develop applications faster and cheaper than the Information Systems (IS) group. Many of these applications have become critical to sales, operations, and decision-making. However, there are many risks associated with end-user computing that need to be managed to protect resources and ensure information integrity. What's needed is a commitment to manage end-user computing to take advantage of speed and flexibility while controlling risks.

SPECIFIC RISKS IN END-USER COMPUTING

Because PCs seem relatively simple and are perceived as personal productivity tools, their effect on an organization has largely been ignored. In many organizations, end-user computing has limited or no formal procedures. The control or review of reports produced by end-user computing is either limited or nonexistent. The associated risk is that management may be relying on end-user developed reports and information to the same degree as those developed under traditional centralized IS controls. Management should consider the levels of risk associated with end-user applications and establish appropriate controls. Risks associated with end-user computing include

- Weak security.
- Inefficient use of resources.
- Inadequate training.
- Inadequate support.
- Incompatible systems.
- Redundant systems.

0-8493-9820-7/00/$0.00+$.50
© 2000 by CRC Press LLC

- Ineffective implementations.
- Copyright violations.
- The destruction of information by computer viruses.
- Unauthorized access or changes to data and/or programs.
- Unauthorized remote access.
- Reliance on inaccurate information.

Each of these risks is discussed in the remainder of this chapter.

Weak Security

Information systems security should be a concern of IS, users, and management. However, security, for many companies, is not a top priority. In a 1997 survey conducted by *Infosecurity News*, respondents indicated that information security has improved over the past two years and current year, but cited significant obstacles to reducing security risks. The most significant obstacles cited include lack of funds, lack of employee training, lack of end-user awareness, technical complexity, unclear responsibilities, lack of senior-management awareness, lack of senior-management support, and lack of good security tools.

The primary concerns in security involve educating management and end users on the exposures to loss through the use of technology. End-users' main focus is getting the work done, and management's primary focus is on the bottom line. The auditor's responsibility is to inform management and end users on how security can enhance job performance and protect the bottom line.

Inefficient Use of Resources

End-user development may at first appear to be relatively inexpensive compared with traditional IS development. However, a number of hidden costs are associated with end-user computing that organizations should consider. In addition to operation costs, costs may increase due to a lack of training and technical support. Lack of end-user training and their inexperience may also result in the purchase of inappropriate hardware and the implementation of software solutions that are incompatible with the organization's systems architecture. End users may also increase organization costs by creating inefficient or redundant applications.

For example, we see redundant data, inconsistent data, conflicting naming conventions, and data timing issues in these type of applications. In one financial company, EUC development systems were causing a problem with the general ledger system due to the timing of the transfer of transactions. Data was transferred late causing end of the month reports to be inaccurately stated. Managers who met to review reports of the prior month's activity noticed a shortfall of $50,000 in some accounts.

In another situation, auditors reviewed revenue reports from a department and noted some inaccuracies and questioned managers about the discrepancies. Discrepancies were traced to an EUC-developed support system which had been integrated into the overall reporting process. The manager stated that information provided by the centralized support system did not meet their need and their new system "was more" accurate. When the auditors checked the EUC-developed system, they found some questionable manipulation of the information not in accordance with the Company's reporting policy.

Inadequate Training

Organizations may decide not to invest in training by looking at the up-front costs alone. According to one study by the Gartner Group and a recent study by the U.S. National Institute of Standards and Technology, the cost of not training will far exceed the investment organizations will make to train both end users and IS professionals in new technologies. One reason for this paradox is that end users who are forced to learn on their own take as much as six times longer to become productive with the software product. Self-training is also inefficient from the standpoint that end users tend to ask their colleagues for help, which results in the loss of more than one individual's time, and they may also be learning inappropriate or inefficient techniques. Both studies also showed that an effective training program reduces support costs by a factor of three to six, because end users make fewer mistakes and have fewer questions.

Inadequate Support

The increasing complexity of technical environments and more sophisticated PC tools has fueled the increased demand for end-user support. Because traditional IS departments do not have the staffing or the PC knowledge to help end-user departments, end users have turned to "underground support" (i.e., support by peers or department-purchased outsourcing) to fill the gap. The previously mentioned studies found that the need for support is inelastic, and the gap between needed support and formal support is filled by underground support. This underground support accounts for as much as 30% of end-user computing costs). End users need "focal points" as "local" as possible for assistance. A focal point is a functional support person. Many times, the functional support person is an accomplished end user. However, without a central support organization, there may be limited coordination between end-user departments to ensure that procedures are consistent and that applications are compatible.

Incompatible Systems

End-user designed applications that are developed in isolation may not be compatible with existing or future organizational information technology architectures. Traditional IS systems development verifies compatibility with existing hardware and related software applications. Hardware and software standards can help ensure the ability to share data with other applications in the organization.

As mentioned earlier, inconsistent data, conflicting naming conventions, and data timing problems are very common types of problems which occur in EUC-developed systems. Inconsistent data often appears in the conflict between an EUC-generated report and a Corporate Report. Data used to create reports may be from different sources than the Corporate Reports, thus these "unofficial" reports are used for decision making which may conflict with Corporate interpretation.

Redundant Systems

In addition to developing incompatible systems, end users may be developing redundant applications or databases because of the lack of communication between departments. Because of this lack of communication, end-user departments may create a new database or application that another department may have already created. A more efficient implementation process has end-user departments coordinating their systems application development projects with IS and meeting with other end-user departments to discuss their proposed projects.

Redundant data can cause increased storage costs and require more processing complexity in resolving the redundancies. For example, mapping software was used to analyze an EUC-developed system in two different departments. These systems were 90% redundant. Discussion with staff indicated that the second system evolved because they wanted some changes made to the structure of the report but the other department did not have the "resources" to customize it.

Ineffective Implementations

End users typically use fourth generation languages, such as database or Internet Web development tools, to develop applications. In these cases, the end user is usually self-taught. And, they lack formal training in structured applications development, do not realize the importance of documentation, and omit necessary control measures that are required for effective implementations. In addition, there is no segregation of duties, because one person acts as the end user, systems analyst, developer, and tester. With sufficient analysis, documentation, and testing, end-user developed systems will better meet management's expectations.

The Absence of Segregation of Duties. Traditional systems application development is separated by function, tested, and completed by trained experts in each area. In many end-user development projects, one individual is responsible for all phases, such as analyzing, designing, constructing, testing, and implementing, of the development life cycle. There are inherent risks in having the same person create and test a program, because they may overlook their own errors. It is more likely that an independent review will catch errors made by the end-user developer, and such a review helps to ensure the integrity of the newly designed system.

Incomplete System Analysis. Many of the steps established by central IS departments are eliminated by end-user departments. For example, the analysis phase of development may be incomplete, and all facets of a problem may not be appropriately identified. In addition, with incomplete specifications, the completed system may not solve the business problem. End users must define their objectives for a particular application before they decide to purchase existing software, to have IS develop the application, or to develop the application themselves.

Insufficient Documentation. End users typically focus on solving a business need and may not recognize the importance of documentation. Any program that is used by multiple users or has long-term benefits must be documented, particularly if the original developer is no longer available. Documentation also assists the developer in solving problems or making changes to the application in the future, in addition to facilitating testing and familiarizing new users to the system.

Inadequate Testing. Independent testing is important to identify design flaws that may have been overlooked by the developer of a system. Often, the individual who creates the design will be the only one testing the program so that he is only confirming that the system performs exactly as he designed it. The end user should develop acceptance criteria that can be used in testing the development effort. Acceptance criteria help to ensure that the end users' system requirements are validated during testing. For example, the National Institute of Standards and Technology has created a forum of developers and users to exchange testing and acceptance criteria on new IS security products.

Copyright Violations

Software programs can easily be copied or installed on multiple computers. Organizations are responsible for controlling the computing environment to prevent software piracy and copyright violations.

The Copyright Act of 1976 makes it illegal to copy computer programs except for backup or archival purposes. Any business or individual convicted of illegally copying software is liable for both compensatory and statutory damages of up to $100,000 for each illegal copy of software found on the premises. Software piracy is also a federal crime that carries penalties of up to five years in jail. The Software Publishers Association (SPA) was established in 1988 to promote, protect, and inform the software industry regarding copyright issues. The SPA represents 1200 members with 85% of the PC software market share. The SPA receives information from disgruntled employees and consultants about organizations that use illegal software.

An organization faces a number of additional risks when they tolerate software piracy. Copied software may be unreliable and carry viruses. Litigation involving copyright violations are highly publicized, and the organization is at risk of losing potential goodwill. Furthermore, tolerating software piracy encourages deterioration in business ethics that can seep into other areas of the organization.

The key to controlling the use of illegal software rests with the end user. Organizations should inform end users of the copyright laws and the potential damages that result from violations of those laws. When users are given access to a personal or desktop computer, they should sign an acknowledgment that lists the installed software, the individual's responsibilities, and any disciplinary action for violations. In addition, written procedures should detail responsibility for maintaining a software inventory, auditing compliance, and removing unlicensed software.

The Destruction of Information by Computer Viruses

Most end users are knowledgeable about virus attacks, but the effect of a virus remains only a threat until they actually experience a loss. A virus is the common term used to describe self-reproducing programs (SRP), worms, moles, holes, Trojan Horses, and time bombs. In today's environment, the threat is great because of the unlimited number of sources from which a virus can be introduced. For example, viruses can be copied from a diskette in a floppy drive or downloaded from a remote connection through a modem.

A virus is a piece of program code that contains self-reproducing logic, which piggybacks onto other programs and cannot survive by itself. A worm is an independent program code that replicates itself and eats away at data, uses up memory, and slows down processing. A mole enters a system through a software application and enables the user to break the normal processing and exit the program to the operating system without logging the user off, which gives the creator access to the entire system. A hole is a weakness built into a program or system that allows programmers to enter through a "back-door," bypassing any security controls. A Trojan Horse is a piece of code inside a program that causes damage by destroying data or obtaining information. A time bomb is code that is activated by a certain event, such as a date or command.

Viruses can also be spread over telephone lines or cables connecting computers in a network. For example, viruses can spread when infected files or programs are downloaded from a public computer bulletin board.

Viruses can cause a variety of problems:

- Destroy or alter data.
- Destroy hardware.
- Display unwanted messages.
- Cause keyboards to lock (i.e., become inactive).
- Slow down a network by performing many tasks that are really just a continuous loop with no end or resolution.

A virus can consume processing power and disk space by replicating itself multiple times. The risk to organizations is the time involved removing the virus, rebuilding the affected systems, and reconstructing the data. Organizations should also be concerned with sending virus-infected programs to other organizations. Viruses cause significant financial damage as well as staff time to clean up and recipients may file lawsuits against the instituting organization.

Unauthorized Access or Changes to Data or Programs

Access controls provide the first line of defense against unauthorized users who gain entrance to a system's programs and data. The use of access controls, such as user IDs and passwords, are typically weak in user-controlled systems. In some cases, user IDs and passwords may be shared or easily determined. This oversight can subject applications to accidental or deliberate changes or deletions that threaten the reliability of the information generated. Programs require additional protection to prevent unexpected changes. To prevent accidental changes, users should be limited to execute only.

Unauthorized Remote Access

More and more users are demanding remote access to LAN services. The easiest method to provide security is to eliminate modem access completely. With weak access controls, a modem allows virtually anyone access to an organization's resources. To protect against unauthorized access, remote dial-up access should have a callback feature that identifies the user with a specific location. A more sophisticated solution is to have key cards with encrypted IDs installed on the remote terminal and a front-end server on the host. At a minimum, user IDs and passwords should be encrypted when transmitted over public lines. In addition, confidential data that is transmitted over public lines should be encrypted. The security solution depends on the sensitivity of the data being transmitted.

Reliance on Inaccurate Information

Accurate information is an issue whether the end user is accessing a database on the mainframe or a departmental database on a PC. End users may be asked to generate a report without fully understanding the underlying information, or they may not be sufficiently trained in the reporting application to ask the appropriate questions. Additional complications occur when end users download information from the mainframe for analysis and reporting. Departmental databases may have redundant information with different timeframes. The result is wasted time in reconciling two databases to determine which data is accurate.

END-USER COMPUTING CONTROLS

Strategy

Written strategy helps guide end users in implementing technology solutions that satisfy corporate objectives. A strategy document should include the future direction of the organization, how technology will be used, how technology will be managed, and what role IS and end users will fill. A high-level strategy guides in the acquisition, allocation, and management of technology resources to fulfill the organization's objectives.

Standards

Standards guide end users in selecting hardware, software, and developing new applications. Hardware and software standards ensure compatibility between user groups and ease the burden of technology integration and technical support. Application development standards help ensure that user requirements are adequately defined, controls are built-in, testing is thorough, users are trained, systems are adequately documented, and changes are adequately controlled.

Policy and Procedures

A policy statement should communicate the organization's stand on such issues as systems architecture, testing and validation of requirements/systems, and documentation. The areas are critical to establishing an institutional process for managing EUC applications. These Policies and Procedures should be developed by IT management and EUC groups to provide direction and governance over this area.

Systems Architecture is the foundation of any information system. Systems proposed should be upward compatible with the evolving architecture and within the strategic vision of the organization. Testing and validation of requirements/systems provide a structured process for systematically testing and validating the EUC-developed system to assure it meets Corporate and end-user requirements. Finally, documentation provides the means to capture the requirements and eventually improve corporate systems to meet the end users' needs.

Other major areas are unlicensed software, information privacy and security, virus prevention, and backup/recovery. The policy statement on unlicensed software should include the removal of unlicensed software and disciplinary action. Information privacy and security should include data classification, encryption policy, and procedures for users and remote access. Virus prevention should include standard virus protection software, regular virus definition updates, checking downloaded files and shared floppy disks. Backup and recovery procedures should define responsibility for data on all platforms (e.g., LAN, desktop). Once policy and procedures are completed, they need to be communicated to all users and enforced through periodic audits.

A number of professional societies have issued general guidance and guidelines to help and assist managers in this area. Organizations such as the Association of Information Technology Professionals (AITP), Society for Information Management (SIM), International Federation of Accountants (IFAC) and the Information Systems Audit and Control Association (ISACA) in their recent Control Objectives for Business Information Technology (COBIT) are examples of professional societies who recognize the need for general guidance.

CONCLUSIONS

End-user computing faces many of the same risks as traditional information systems, but without the benefit of management resources and controls that were developed over a long period of time for systems designed for mainframe computers. Additional risks, which should provide added reasons for managing and controlling end-user computing, are inherent in using PCs and distributed computing. End-user computing should be incorporated into the overall information systems strategy of the organization and be recognized as a resource that must be properly managed.

From the IT management perspective, the manager should ensure:

- That there are policy and procedures, and standards for end-user-developed applications.
- That end-user-developed systems are consistent with Corporate IT Architecture, short term and long term.

- That risks from end-user-developed systems are minimized through planning, review and monitoring to reduce organization-wide impact from incompatible systems, redundant systems, and other vulnerable areas cited.
- That an IT end-user committee be established to assist and support management of user-developed applications within the organization to facilitate communication at all levels.

The IT manager cannot ignore the increased number of end users developing complex applications and the corresponding reliance by management to base decisions on the data produced by these applications. This makes careful evaluation of end-user computing groups a must for any manager. A failed application can do serious damage.

Chapter 66
Reviewing End-User Applications
Steven M. Williford

IN MOST ORGANIZATIONS, sophisticated end users are building their own applications. This trend began with computer-literate end users developing simple applications to increase their personal productivity. End-user applications development has since evolved to include complex applications developed by groups of users and shared across departmental boundaries throughout the organization. Data from these applications is used by decision makers at all levels of the company.

It is obvious to most end-user computing and IS managers that applications with such organizationwide implications deserve careful scrutiny. However, they are not always familiar with an effective mechanism for evaluating these applications. The method for reviewing end-user-developed applications discussed in this chapter can provide information not only for improving application quality but for determining the effectiveness of end-user computing (and end-user computing support) in general.

A review of user-developed applications can indicate the need for changes in the end-user computing support department and its services as well as in its system of controls. In addition, such a review can provide direction for strategic planning within the organization and is a valuable and helpful step in measuring the effectiveness of end-user computing support department policies and procedures. Auditors might also initiate an audit of end-user applications as part of a continuous improvement or total quality management program being undertaken in their organization.

End-user computing or IS managers should also consider performing a review of end-user applications as a proactive step toward being able to justify the existence of the end-user computing support department. For example, a review may reveal that some end-user applications contribute heavily to increased productivity in the workplace. In an era marked by budget cuts and downsizing, it is always wise to be able to point out such triumphs.

0-8493-9820-7/00/$0.00+$.50
© 2000 by CRC Press LLC

DEFINITIONS AND CHARACTERISTICS

Each organization may use a different set of definitions to describe various aspects of end-user computing support, and it is important to have a common understanding of the terms to be used. The following definitions are used in this chapter.

- *Application.* An application is a set of computer programs, data, and procedures that is used to resolve a business-specific problem. For example, the accounting department may develop and implement an application that generates profit-and-loss statements.
- *Product.* Products are the software used to develop or assist in the development of computer systems. Examples are spreadsheets, word processors, fourth-generation languages (4GLs), CASE tools, or graphics packages. Tools is another common term for product.
- *System.* A system is a combination of computer applications, processes, and deliverables. During a review of end-user applications, it is important to determine the fit of the application within the system. An example is a budget system in which individual managers collect data from individuals using a manual process (e.g., paper forms), transfer the data to spreadsheets, and then electronically transmit the information to the accounting department, which consolidates the information and uses a budget forecasting application to create reports for senior management.
- *Work group.* This is a group that performs a common business function, independent of organizational boundaries, and is tied together by a system or process. The managers who collect data for the budget system make up a work group; they may all report to different managers in different departments, and each person is probably in more than one work group. Other work groups include project development and training.
- *Work unit.* This term is used for such organizational units as departments, divisions, or sections (e.g., accounting, human resources, and engineering). An application typically resides in a work unit (i.e., is run by that unit) but affects other units throughout the organization.

It is also important to review the unique characteristics of the end-user computing environment as they relate to user-developed applications:

- *Point of control.* In an end-user computing environment, the person using the application has either developed the application or is typically closer to the developer organizationally.
- *The critical nature of applications.* End-user applications tend to be valued less and are often not developed under the strict guidelines of traditional IS applications. Because of this, the impact of the application being in error or not working at all is often not considered until it is too late.

- *Range of measuring criticality and value.* End-user applications may range from trivial to mission critical. Applications created by IS have a much narrower range but are concentrated toward the critical end of the scale.
- *Development.* In an end-user computing environment, the people who handle any one application may be scattered organizationally; the applications may also be scattered over time and across products. For example, an application may originally be developed on a word processing package. If the math requirements for the application become too complicated, the application would be transferred to a spreadsheet product. Finally, the application may be converted to a database product to handle complex reporting requirements.
- *Quantity of applications.* There are more applications developed by end users than by the IS department, but they are usually smaller in scope and more tuned to individual productivity.
- *Type of products.* End-user development products usually provide a group of standard functions (e.g., Lotus 1-2-3 provides built-in functions). Creating a complex application using these products may require a high degree of knowledge about the development product or may necessitate using several development products to create a single application.

OVERCOMING MISCONCEPTIONS

In some organizations senior IS management initiates a review on behalf of user managers who may be concerned that their applications are getting away from them. In these cases, the end-user computing support department managers may be asked to help sell the idea to corporate managers. In most organizations, gaining any management commitment to reviewing end-user applications requires overcoming several obstacles. The following sections discuss common management objections to reviewing end-user applications and ways to overcome this mind-set.

End-User Applications are Not Significant

This is a typical misconception on the part of either corporate managers or senior IS managers. End-user applications may be perceived as transient, disposable, and not production oriented — therefore not significant. Traditional applications that are run by the IS department and cannot be tampered with in any way by anyone other than a technical expert are viewed as much more substantial, stable, and worthwhile. Senior management may be unwilling to approve an investment in reviewing what they perceive to be insignificant applications. To change this viewpoint and bring them up to date, end-user computing managers should make the effort to point out particular end-user-developed applications that are currently providing critical data or contributing more concretely to improved productivity and increased bottom-line benefits.

Ease of Use Results in Effective Applications

This is another common misconception of senior management and IS management. They may believe that the ease of use of end-user applications development products would prevent users from creating anything but the most effective applications. Again, managers would be reluctant to spend resources on reviewing applications that they feel are typically well created. This misconception has been amplified by sales promotions that vigorously emphasize the ease of use of these products. IS managers should point out to senior managers that development products have limitations and that ease of use not only cannot guarantee that applications do what they were intended to do but can contribute to end users creating unnecessary applications and duplicating effort.

The End Users will Not Cooperate with the Review

This is a common objection of user management and their employees. IS managers should promote the concept of an informal reviewing method (e.g., an inventory or statistics review, both of which are discussed in a later section) that would be less of an imposition on end users and therefore less of a threat to those users who are very protective of their current work processes.

In some organizations, end users react to a review of their applications in much the same way they would react to an audit of their personal finances by the IRS — that is, they view it as a hassle and something they would like to avoid at all costs, regardless of whether or not they feel they have anything to hide (e.g., pirated software). If this is the case, the IS department might want to consider setting up self-audit guidelines with the cooperation of the users, or have them participate in the first central review. Review guidelines explain what the review team will be looking for. When end users know what to expect and have a chance to evaluate their own applications using the same criteria the reviewers will be using, they are typically far more willing to cooperate with the actual review. In addition, involving them in the review can alleviate an us vs. them attitude.

PREPARING FOR THE REVIEW

The reviewing process follows a life cycle similar to that of any other project. The steps discussed in this chapter cover preparation for a review; they provide the background necessary to begin a review. These steps are designed as a general guideline. Not all companies may need all the steps, and early reviews (undertaken when end-user development is still relatively new to the organization) will usually not follow all the steps. Preparing for a review requires:

- Defining the review objectives.
- Defining the review method.
- Defining the scope and content of the review.

Each of these is discussed in the following sections and summarized as follows:

Define the Review Objectives. The audit may be designed to:

- Determine, identify, or resolve end-user applications problems.
- Evaluate end-user computing support group services.
- Respond to financial issues.
- Collect specific information.
- Provide input to strategic or long-range planning.

Define the Review Method. Four of the most effective methods are

- Formal audit.
- Inventory.
- Statistical review.
- Best-guess review.

Define the Scope and Content of the Review. Determining the scope and content helps:

- Define what the end-user computing department will consider as end-user computing.
- Define which environments a particular review will evaluate.

Define the Review Objectives

Review objectives help determine the results and essentially guide the process by defining the intent of the review. IS and user managers should define and agree to the objectives before proceeding. In general, reviews are more successful if they focus on a particular objective. For example:

Once it has been established that a review of end-user applications would be helpful or even necessary in a particular organization, careful preparation for conducting the review should begin. Although some more informal reviews may not require all the steps discussed in this chapter, for the most part, each step is an important and necessary component of a successful review (i.e., one that provides useful and valuable information). The following is a checklist of these steps:

- *Determine, identify, or resolve end-user applications problems.* This common objective ensures that the review will provide answers to such questions as:

- — Is there a problem with end-user applications (e.g., are particular applications proving to be error-prone, duplicating effort, or providing inaccurate data)?
- — What is the exact problem with a particular application (e.g., why is the application providing inaccurate data)?
- — How can this problem be solved? For example, what can be done to make this application more effective, or should a better set of checks and balances be implemented to validate end-user applications? A better set of checks and balances might involve comparing the results of an end-user application that reports sales volume by region to the results of a traditional IS application that tracks the same information.
- — What are the consequences of ignoring the flaws in this application?
- — Who should fix this application?
- — Is it worth the cost to fix the application, or should use of the application be discontinued? For example, end users might create an application that automates the extraction and compilation of sales data from a larger system. The cost of maintaining or repairing such a system could be prohibitive if the data from the larger system could just as easily be compiled using a calculator.

- *Evaluate end-user computing support group services.* When there are complaints from the user areas (e.g., users may feel that they are not getting enough support to develop effective applications) or when the end-user computing department takes on new levels of support, it may consider a review of end-user applications to help them evaluate current services. For example, such a review can reveal a large number of error-prone or ineffective applications, which would indicate a need for more development support. The review might reveal that a number of users are duplicating applications development effort or are sharing inaccurate data from one application. Users may have developed applications that are inappropriate or inadequate for solving the problems they were designed to address. Any of these scenarios would indicate an increased need for support of end-user applications development. Typical questions to be answered with this objective are
  - — Can the services be improved?
  - — Should new services be added?
  - — Should services be moved to or from another group of end users?
  - — Are resources being allocated effectively (e.g., is the marketing department the only user group without any productivity-increasing applications)?

- *Respond to financial issues.* This objective can provide pertinent information if budget cuts or competition within IS for resources threatens the end-user computing support department. A review of user-developed applications may lend credence to the need for end-user computing support of the development and implementation of valuable computer applications by pointing out an application that may be saving a great deal of time and money in a particular user area. A review with this objective provides information similar to the answers provided when evaluating services in the objective; however, the information is then used to answer such questions as:

— Can the end-user computing support group be reduced or eliminated?
—Can the services to user-developers be reduced?
—Can some budgetary efficiencies be gained in supporting end-user applications development?

- *Collect specific information.* Corporate or IS management may request information about end-user applications, especially if they receive data from them on a regular basis or if (as in applications run in the payroll department) many people would be affected by an inaccurate application. It is also not unlikely that user management would request an investigation of end-user applications in their area. Both of these cases are more common in companies that are committed to a continuous improvement or total quality program.

- *Provide input to strategic or long-range planning.* A review with this objective would highlight much of the same information found in a review to evaluate services or respond to financial issues but would add a more strategic element to the process. For example, this objective would answer such questions as:
  — Do end-user applications contribute to accomplishing corporate goals?
  — Are there end-user applications that might create strategic opportunities if implemented on a broader scale?
  — Are resources adequate to initiate or foster development of end-user applications that might eventually contribute to achieving strategic goals?

Define the Review Method

The methods of collecting data should be determined by the political climate, the people who will act on the results of the audit, and the resources available to perform the work. The following sections discuss five of the most common and effective methods for reviewing end-user applications and examine the most appropriate instances for using each of them.

Formal Audit. This method for auditing end-user applications is usually selected if the audit is requested by corporate management. They may be

concerned about applications that are built to provide financial information or about the possibility of misconduct associated with user applications. Because most organizations are audited in a financial sense,
corporate and user management are familiar with the process and the
results of a less formal method. However, a formal audit is more expensive
and often more upsetting to the participants (i.e., the end users).

Inventory. Taking an inventory of end-user applications involves gathering information about the products and applications on each work station.
Although an inventory is a less formal variation of an audit and may be perceived by corporate and senior IS management as less significant than a
formal audit, it provides much of the same information as a formal audit.
An inventory can be useful when the information will be used for improving
the user environment, preparing for later, more formal audits, or providing
feedback to management. The end-user computing support department
may initiate this type of review for purely informational purposes to
increase support staff awareness of end-user applications development
(e.g., the objective may simply be to determine the number of end-user
applications or to evaluate their sophistication). Inventories can be done
in less time and are less expensive than formal audits. In addition, they can
easily be done by the IS department without the consultation of a professional auditor. An inventory is more low-key than a formal audit, and taking
an inventory of applications is far less threatening to end users.

Statistical Review. Statistical reviewing involves collecting raw data from
the help desk, support logs, computer transactions, or similar sources.
This method of auditing is useful only if the support department generates
a statistically significant amount of readily available data. This implies a
large number of applications, a large number of users, and centralized support or centrally controlled computing resources (e.g., mainframes and
local area networks). A statistical review is most appropriate when minor
tuning of end-user computing services is the objective. This is an extensive
process that provides enough information to confirm or deny perceptions
or indicate the need to change; it has a product focus which can tell how
many people are using Lotus 1-2-3 or how many are using WordPerfect.
These statistics often come from LANs as users go through the network to
access the product. This product focus does not provide much useful information for deciding how to change.

Best-Guess Review. This is the most informal type of review. When time is
a critical element, a best-guess review can be performed on the basis of the
existing knowledge of the end-user computing support staff. This can even
be classified as a review of the IS department's impression of end-user
applications. Corporate or senior IS management may request a report on
end-user applications within the organization. Such a review can be useful

if support people and users are centralized and the support people are familiar with the users and their applications. The IS staff can also use the results to make changes within their limits of authority. Although a best-guess review does not gather significant unbiased data, it can be surprisingly useful just to get end-user computing staff impressions down on paper.

Define the Scope and Content of the Review

The scope defines the extent of the review and should also state specific limits of the review — that is, what is and is not to be accomplished. In most organizations and with most types of review, it may be helpful to involve users from a broad range of areas to participate in defining the scope. Knowledge of the review and involvement in the definition of the review scope by the users can be valuable in promoting their buy-in to the results.

The review may be limited to particular products, environments, a type of user, a work unit, or a specific application or system. Determining the scope and content focuses on the appropriate applications. As part of defining the scope and content of the application it is necessary to determine the types of end-user environments to be audited. This definition of environment is used to:

- *Define what the IS department considers end-user computing*, that is, to determine whether or not a particular application will actually be considered a user-developed application. For example, in some organizations a programmer's use of an end-user product to create an application would be considered end-user computing and the application would be included in a review of end-user applications. In most companies, however, applications that should be included in a review of end-user applications come from the point-of-origin, shared work unit, and work group environments. Applications in a turnover environment can also be included because, although development may be done by another group, end users work with the application on a daily basis. Each of these environment classifications is discussed at the end of this section.
- *Define which environments a particular review will evaluate*. For example, the application developed by the programmer using an end-user development tool would fit in the distributed environment, which is also discussed at the end of this section. However, the review might be designed to investigate only applications developed in a point-of-origin environment.

In each organization, end-user computing may consist of several environments. Each environment is defined by products, support, and resources. Although there may be a few exceptions or hybrids, an end-user computing environment can usually fit into one of the general categories discussed in the following sections.

Point-of-Origin Environment. In this environment, all functions are performed by the person who needs the application. This is how end-user computing began and is often the image management still has of it. These applications are generally developed to improve personal productivity. They are typically considered to be disposable — that is, instead of performing any significant maintenance, the applications are simply redeveloped. Redevelopment makes sense because new techniques or products can often make the applications more useful.

Shared Environment. In a shared environment, original development of the application is performed by a person who needs the application. However, the application is then shared with other people within a work unit or work group. If any maintenance is done to the application, the new version is also distributed to the other users in the unit.

Work Unit Environment. In this environment, applications development and maintenance are performed by people within an organizational unit to meet a need of or increase the productivity of the work unit as a whole (unlike point-of-origin and shared applications, which are developed for the individual). The applications are usually more sophisticated and designed to be more easily maintained. They may also be developed by someone whose job responsibilities include applications development.

Work Group Environment. In a work group environment, applications development and maintenance are performed by people within a work group for use by others in the work group. The developer is someone who has the time and ability to create an application that fulfills an informally identified need of the work group. In most cases, the application solves problems of duration (e.g., expediting the process) not effort (i.e., productivity).

Turnover Environment. In this type of environment, applications are developed by one group and turned over to another group for maintenance and maybe to a third group for actual use. There are many combinations, but some common examples are:

- The application is developed by the end-user computing support group and turned over to a work unit for maintenance and use. This combination is popular during end-user computing start-up phases and during the implementation of a new product or technology.
- The application is developed and used by the end user but turned over to end-user computing support for maintenance.

Distributed Environment. In a distributed environment, applications are developed and maintained by a work unit for use by others. The developing work unit is responsible for development and maintenance only. They may report to a user group or indirectly to central IS. The development products may be traditional programming products or end-user computing products. Although this is not typically considered an end-user computing environment, in some organizations the work unit is the end-user computing support group.

Centralized Development and Support Environment. In this environment, a programming group under the direct control of central information systems develops and maintains applications for use by end users. Although centralized programming groups in some organizations may use end-user computing products for applications development, in general, applications developed in this environment are not reviewed with other end-user applications.

Reseeded Environment. A common hybrid of environments occurs when a point-of-origin application becomes shared. In these instances, the people receiving the application typically fine tune it for their particular jobs using their own product knowledge. This causes several versions of the original application to exist, tuned to each user's expertise and needs. Maintenance of the original application is driven by having the expertise and time available to make alterations rather than by the need for such alterations. This reseeded application grows into another application that should be grouped and reviewed with point-of-origin applications. However, these applications should be reviewed to ensure that they are not duplicating effort. Fifteen to twenty applications may grow out of a single application. In many cases, one application customized for each user would suffice.

Determining the Application Environment

During preparation for the review, the scope and content phase helps determine which end-user environments should be included. For example, the IS staff may decide that only point-of-origin applications will be included in a particular review. The first step in actually performing the review is to identify the environment to which particular applications belong. To do this, it is necessary to isolate who performed the functions associated with the life cycle of the individual application. These functions are

- *Needs identification.* Who decided something needed to be done, and what were the basic objectives of the application created to do that something?
- *Design.* Who designed the processes, procedures, and appearance of the application?

- *Creation.* Who created the technical parts of the application (e.g., spreadsheets, macros, programs, or data)?
- *Implementation.* Who decided when and how the implementations would proceed?
- *Use.* Who actually uses the application?
- *Training.* Who developed and implemented the training and education for the application? Typically, this is an informal and undocumented process — tutoring is the most common training method.
- *Maintenance.* Who maintains the application? Who handles problem resolution, tunes the application, makes improvements to the application, connects the application to other applications, rewrites the application using different products, or clones the application into new applications?
- *Ongoing decision making.* Who makes decisions about enhancements or replacements?

The matrix in Exhibit 66.1 provides answers to these questions for each of the different end-user application environments.

Evaluating Applications Development Controls

This step in performing the review provides information about the controls in effect concerning end-user applications. It should address the following questions:

- Who controls the development of the application?
- Are there controls in place to decide what types of applications users can develop?
- Are the controls enforced? Can they be enforced?

Determining Application Criticality

This checklist helps determine the critical level of specific applications:

- Does the application create reports for anyone at or above the vice-presidential level?
- Does the application handle money? Issue an invoice? Issue refunds? Collect or record payments? Transfer bank funds?
- Does the application make financial decisions about stock investments or the timing of deposits or withdrawals?
- Does the application participate in a production process; that is, does it:
  - Issue a policy, loan, or prescription?
  - Update inventory information?
  - Control distribution channels?
- What is the size of the application? The larger the application (or group of applications that form a system), the more difficult it is to manage.

FUNCTION / ENVIRONMENT	Needs Identification	Design	Creation	Implementation	Use	Training	Maintenance	Ongoing Decision Making
Point of Origin	User	User	User	User	User only	User	User	User
Shared	Original User	Original user	Original user	Original user	Original user and users with similar needs	Original user or subsequent users	Original user and subsequent users	Original user
Work Unit	Work unit expert or manager	Work unit analyst and product expert	Work unit expert	Work unit expert	Someone other than the developer	Initially by work unit expert—later by user	Work unit expert	Work unit management
Work Group	Work group	Analyst and product expert	Work group expert	Work group	Work group	Initially by work group expert—later by user	Work group expert	Work group users
Turnover	User or work unit	Developing group	Developing group	Developing group and user	User	Developer	Developing group	Work unit management
Distributed	Work unit	Developing group	Developing group	Developing group and work unit	Portion of the work unit	Developing group, work unit expert	Developing group	Work unit management
Centralized	Work unit	Developing group	Developing group	Developing group and work unit	Portion of the work unit	Developing group, work unit expert	Developing group	Work unit management

Exhibit 66.1. Environment–Function Matrix for End-User Applications

Determining the Level of Security

This set of questions can help determine not only the level of security that already exists concerning end-user applications but the level of security that is most appropriate to the particular applications being reviewed. The following questions pertain to physical security:

- Are devices, work areas, and data media locked?
- Is there public access to these areas during the day?
- Is the room locked at night?
- Is access to the area monitored?
- Is there a policy or some way to determine the level of security necessary?

The following questions relate to the security of data, programs, and input/output and to general security:

- How is data secured? By user? By work unit? By work area? By device?
- Is the data secured within the application?
- Who has access to the data?
- Is use of the programs controlled?
- Are data entry forms, reports, or graphs controlled, filed, or shredded?
- Is there some way to identify sensitive items?

Reviewing the Use and Availability of the Product

Creating complex applications using an end-user development product often requires more product knowledge than creating them using a comparable programming language. The end-user developer may go to great lengths to get around end-user product limitations when the application could probably be created more easily using traditional programming or a different tool. The questions in the following checklist help evaluate the appropriateness of the development products in use to create specific applications:

- Are products being used appropriately? To answer this question, it is necessary to match user application needs to the tool used to create the application. This can help indicate the inappropriate use of development products (e.g., use of a spreadsheet as a word processor or a word processor as a data base).
- Is the user applying the product functions appropriately for the applications being developed or used? For example, a row and column function would not be the most effective function for an application designed to generate 10 or 15 reports using the same data but different layouts.

As part of this step, the availability of end-user applications development products should be assessed. The following questions address this issue:

- Which products are available to this user?
- Which of the available products are employed by this user?
- Are these products targeted to this user?

Reviewing User Capabilities and Development Product Knowledge

This step in conducting a review of end-user applications focuses on the end user's ability to develop applications using a particular product and to select an appropriate development product for the application being created. The questions to answer are

- Is the user adequately trained in the use of the development product he or she is currently creating applications with? Is additional training necessary or available?
- Does the end user understand the development aspects of the product?
- Is the end user familiar with the process for developing applications? With development methodologies? With applications testing and maintenance guidelines?
- Has the end user determined and initiated or requested an appropriate level of support and backup for this application?
- Is the end user aware of the potential impact of failure of the application?
- Are the development products being used by this end user appropriate for the applications being developed?
- If the user is maintaining the application, does that user possess sufficient knowledge of the product to perform maintenance?

Reviewing User Management of Data

Because the data collected using end-user applications is increasingly used to make high-level decisions within the organization, careful scrutiny of end-user management of that data is essential. The following questions address this important issue:

- Is redundant data controlled?
- Is data sharing possible with this application?
- Who creates or alters the data from this application?
- Is data from traditional IS or mainframe systems — often called production data — updated by end-user applications or processes? If so, is the data controlled or verified?
- If data is transformed from product to product (e.g., from spreadsheet to data base), from type to type (e.g., HEX to ASCII), or from paper to electronic media, is it verified by a balancing procedure?

- Are data dictionaries, common field names, data lengths, field descriptions, and definitions used?
- Are numeric fields of different lengths passed from one application to another?

Reviewing the Applications

This is obviously an important step in a review of end-user applications. The following questions focus on an evaluation of the applications themselves and assess problem resolution, backup, documentation, links, and audit trails associated with these applications:

- Problem resolution:
  — Is there a mechanism in place to recognize whether or not an application has a problem?
  — Is there an established procedure for reporting application problems?
  —Is there a formal process in place to determine what that problem may be or to resolve or correct the problem?
  — Are these procedures being followed?
- Backup:
  — Is the application backed up?
  — Is the data backed up?
  — Are the reports backed up?
  — Is there a backup person capable of performing the activities on the application?
  — Are backup procedures in effect for support, development, and maintenance of the application?
- Documentation:
  —What documentation is required for the application? Is the application critical enough to require extensive documentation? Is the application somewhat critical and therefore deserving of at least some documentation? Is the application a personal productivity enhancer for a small task and therefore deserving of only informal or no documentation?
  — If documentation guidelines are in place, are they being followed?
  — How is the documentation maintained, stored and updated?
- Links:
  — How are the data, programs, processes, input, output, and people associated with this application connected?
  — What is received by the application?
  — Where does the application send data, information, knowledge, and decisions?
  — Are these links documented?

- Audit trail:
  - — Are the results of this application verified or cross-checked with other results?
  - — Who is notified if the results of the application cannot be verified by other results?

GUIDELINES FOR IMPROVING END-USER APPLICATIONS DEVELOPMENT

Reviewing end-user applications requires that some resources (i.e., time and money) be spent. In most companies, these resources are scarce; what resources are available are often sought after by more than one group. A review of end-user applications is often low on senior management's priority list. Reducing the time it takes to collect information can greatly improve the IS department's chances of gaining approval for the review. However, reducing the need to collect information can decrease the need to conduct a review at all. This can be done by setting up and enforcing adherence to end-user applications development guidelines. It is a cost-effective way to improve the end-user applications development environment and help conserve limited resources.

To begin, general guidelines should be created and distributed before a planned review is started. The effectiveness of the guidelines can then be evaluated. The following checklist outlines some areas in which guidelines established by the IS department can improve end-user applications development:

- *Use of end-user development products.* Users should be provided with a set of hypothetical examples of appropriate and inappropriate uses of development products (i.e., which products should be used to develop which types of applications).
- *Documentation.* A checklist or matrix of situations and the appropriate documentation for each should be developed. This could also include who will review an application and whether review of the application is required or optional.
- *Support for design and development.* A quick-reference card of functions or types of problems supported by various groups can be distributed to end-user developers.
- *Responsibility and authority.* A list of responsibilities should be distributed that clearly states who owns the application, who owns the data, and who owns problem resolution.
- *Corporate computing policy.* Corporate policies regarding illegal software, freeware or shareware, and security issues should be made available to end-user developers.

One tactic to improve the quality of end-user applications development while avoiding some of the costs in time and money of a full-fledged review is to set up work group auditors. These people may report to a corporate auditing group or to the IS department on a regular basis concerning end-user applications development. This is particularly effective with remote users.

CONCLUSION

The increase in the number of end users developing complex applications and the corresponding reliance of decision makers at all levels of the organization on the data produced by these applications make a careful evaluation of the applications a necessary endeavor. In the current end-user environment, a failed application can seriously damage the business of the organization. To ensure that a review meets the objectives set out for it, IS managers must carefully plan the details of each aspect of the review. This chapter outlines the steps that should be taken before and during an actual review of end-user applications.

Index

A

Acceptable usage policies, 587, 687–695
  Acceptable Use Policy Committee, 694
  distribution to employees, 693
  e-mail, 689–690
  Netiquette Addendum, 693
  penalties for misuse, 692
  WWW resources and newsgroups,
    690–693
Acceptance testing, 567
Access path schematic, 734–735
Activity-based costing analysis, 139–140
Adaptation, 409
Adapters, 84
Adaptive security approach, 189, 391–392
Address spoofing, 670
Adopters, 84
Advertising, 597
Agents, *See* Intelligent agents
Air Products and Chemicals, 36
Alerts and alarms, electronic messaging
    systems, 283
All Souls worm, 668
Amazon.com, 401
American Airlines, 66
American Hospital Supply, 66
Ameritech, 242, 245
Analysis phase, 545
Anthropomorphism, 409
Antitrust lawsuits, 239
AppleTalk, 259
Applets, 437
Application, defined, 750
Application gateways, 285–287, 652–656
Application protocol-based network filters,
    674–675
Application servers, 618
Applications development, *See* Software
    development; Systems and
    applications development
Artificial intelligence, 395, 407, *See also*
    Intelligent agents
Artisan approach, 544
ASAP, 66
Asset management, 154, 164
Association discovery, 308, 335

Association for Computing Machinery
    (ACM), 581
Asynchronous transfer mode (ATM), 187,
    259
  successful network implementation,
    269–277
  testing, 275, 276
AT&T, 237, 238–240, 242, 244, 246, 538
Attack analysis and response, 391
Audits, 189, 365–372
  auditor's role, 368–370
  executive's role, 370–371
  outsourcing relationship, 182–183
  risk management function, 369
  software quality, 558–561, *See* End-user
    developed applications,
    reviewing; Software quality
    assurance
  traditional vs. value-added approaches,
    367–368
  Y2K compliance, 366
Automotive Network Exchange (ANX), 44,
    657
Autonomy, 408

B

BAAN, 74
Backup, plans and procedures, 376–377,
    568, 732, 735–736, 747
  electronic messaging systems, 293
  hot sites and cold sites, 377
  offsite vaulting, 362–363
  production data, 362
Bandwidth, telework support
    considerations, 711
BASEline analysis, 77–78
Bastions, 673
Behavioral norms, and information sharing,
    722–723
Bell Atlantic, 242, 245–246
Bell South, 242, 246
Boehm, Barry, 501, 506
Boeing, 589
Bounded rationality, 407
Brainstorming, 78
Bridges, 260, 261

Browsing, 671
Budget, *See also* Costs
    activity-based costing analysis, 139–140
    budget by deliverables, 137–140
    comparison, internal vs. vendor
        proposal, 136–140
    information technology investment
        portfolio, 78
    networking, 257
    outsourcing, 177
    planning, 59
    reviewing user-developed applications,
        754–755
    subsidy activity, 138–139
Business process, 60
    definitions, 57
    integration, software agents and object-
        oriented models, 421–422
Business process reengineering (BPR), 64,
        397, *See also* Organizational
        redesign
    advanced technology management,
        83–93, *See* Technology
        management
    business and IT management joint
        efforts, 16–17
    business system components, 524
    distributed computing enablement,
        218–219
    EDI and, 637, 646
    expertise for, 517
    implementation problems, 517–525
    information resource acquisition
        process, 159–160
    IT performance process, 170–171
    line manager roles, 523
    pilots, 92–93
    process, organization, and culture
        ("diamond of change") model,
        539–543
    strategic IS decisions, 53
    technology deployment and
        management, 89–93
    TQM and integrated information
        systems planning, 2, 63–72, 400,
        See also Information systems
        planning
    traditional IS implementation vs., 525
Business system components, 524
Business systems planning (BSP), 58
Business-to-business electronic commerce,
        586, 589–603
    advertising, 597
    capitalizing on the Internet, 600–603

emerging markets, 590, 594–603
interorganizational systems, 590–594
leveraging business and support
    capabilities, 601–602
market creation via the Internet,
    597–600
traditional market augmentation, 596

C

Cable television, 243–244
Capability Maturity Model (CMM), 398, 543,
    550, 552–557
    CASE tool support, 561
    TQM and, 556–557
Carnegie, Andrew, 399
CASE tools, 560–561
Cashiering, 66
Catalog retailers, 597
Causal analysis, 580
Cellular technology, 243
Centers of competency, 116–119
Centralized/decentralized organizations,
    7–10, 112
Centralized control issues, 73–74
Change management
    BPR implementation problems, 517–525
    creating atmosphere of change, 97
    integrated systems planning, 67–70
    joint applications development and,
        459–460
    transition to client/server environment,
        95–107
Charles Schwab, 66
Christensen, Clayton, 41
Cisco Systems, 401
Citicorp, 5
Classification model for data mining, 335
Client digital certificates, 656, 659
Client/server systems, 185–186, 191–199,
        201–209, 269, *See also* Distributed
        computing
    associated problems, 195–198
    benefits, 193–195
    corporate vs. IS management vs. end-
        user agendas, 191–192
    costs, 191, 193
    cross-functional teams and, 203–204
    cultural change, 201–209
    definitions, 192
    development teams, 99
    implementation considerations,
        198–199
    Java applications, 435, 437

limitations vs. Web applications,
616–617
operating system platforms, 192, 193
ownership problems, 197–198
resource acquisition process and, 159
resource reallocation, 195
security and control issues, 196–197
server tasks, 192–193
staffing requirements, 196
standards, 196
strategic IS decisions, 53
support tools, 197
technical changes, 202
technical support, 195
training, 198, 202
underperforming systems, 73–74
virtual network server, 263–264
Client/server systems, staff transition to,
95–107
commitment to staff retraining, 95–96
creating atmosphere of change, 97
IS departmental organization chart,
97–99
mapping current staff to future
positions, 102
partnering decision, 96
plan testing and execution, 105–106
position descriptions, 99
skills analysis, 102–103
skills and performance needed, 101
training or job assignment plan, 103–104
Clustering technique for data mining, 336
Cognizance, 424
Collaborative teams, 203–204
Comcast, 244
Common backbone architecture, 287,
290–291
Common gateway interface (CGI), 617–618
Common platform architecture, 287,
288–289
Communication skills, 206, 510–511
Communications Decency Act (CDA), 611
Community-of-interest-networks (COINS),
44
Compilers, 44
Complex systems, *See* Large complex
systems
Computer viruses, 744–745, 747
Conference Room Pilot (CRP), 484
Conferencing, 37
Confidentiality, *See also* Security
e-mail policies, 292
encryption, 678
end-user computing controls, 731–735

intelligent agents and, 417
outsourcing contract issues, 179–180
Connectivity testing, 275
Consulting phases, 511–514
Contingency planning, 363, 373–381, *See*
Disaster contingency and
recovery planning
Contract issues, 178–181, 269, 273
IS consultant concerns, 511–513
"lose-lose" example and Theory W
application, 503–506
service-level agreements, 355
Cookies, 618
Copyright violations, 743–744, 747
Cost-benefit analysis, intranet development
project, 625–626
Costs
budget comparison, internal vs.
outsourcing vendor proposal,
136–140
client/server systems, 194
data center performance, 225–232
data conversion, 339, 340
data marts, 316
data warehouses, 316, 321
database development, 483
distributed computing service delivery,
213
electronic data interchange systems,
637, 638
end-user development. 740–741
Internet access, 608–609
network infrastructure components,
273
networking, 247
new technology, 83
outsourcing and, 134, 175–176
phased rollout strategy, 531
productivity improvement efforts,
229–230
telecommunication trends, 235
total cost of ownership, 151
verification, 179
WAN access, 258
Web sites, 600
Creative Coop, 682–684
Crisis management simulation, 66
Crisis planning, *See* Disaster contingency
and recovery planning
Critical success factors (CSFs), 58, 78
Cross-functional applications, 60
Cross-functional teams, 203–204, 280
Culture, *See* Organizational culture

Customer-centered orientation, 149,
 355–364, 397, 509–510, *See also*
 Customer requirements and
 expectations
Customer/IS relationship, 509–515
Customer profiling, 33
Customer requirements and expectations,
 355–364
 acceptance testing, 567
 changing service-level agreements, 357
 data center operational improvements
  and, 358–364
 data retention, 363–364
 defining, 356
 information systems planning
  components, 65–66
 operational performance objectives,
  357–358
 project performance gap model,
  492–500
 project success and, 397, 491–500
 standards and performance
  measurement, 356–357
 understanding and meeting, 189
 user-centered requirements process
  (user model), 464–468
Customer service, E-commerce concerns,
 609
Customized products, 402–403
Cut-through switch, 261
Cybermalls, 596

D

Data backup, *See* Backup, plans and
 procedures
Data center, 6–7
 operational improvement, 358–364
 performance improvement, 225–232
Data conversion, 188, 339–354
 common problems with data, 339–340
 costs, 339, 340
 data mapping, 342, 349–351
 data mining process, 333–334
 data quality and error management,
  340–343, 345–348
 data warehousing requirements, 351
 database development model, 487
 design issues, 351–353
 determination of conversion rules, 341
 error correction, 343, 348–349
 identifying problems, 342–343, 345
 missing information and, 342, 349

programming, 344
 programming language, 351–352
 recovery from interruption, 353
 relational mathematics, 351
 routine error handling, 353
 steps, 340–345
 testing and running, 344–345
Data integration, 222
Data marts, 188, 303–305, 315–319, 327
 costs, 316
 data warehouse comparison, 316–318
 "plan big, start small" approach,
  318–319
 supporting technology, 318
Data mining, 188, 306–310, 327, 331–338,
 402–403
 analyzing and interpreting results, 334
 applications, 337
 data cleansing and transformation,
  333–334
 data selection and extraction, 333
 distinctive characteristics, 331–332
 need for, 332–335
 techniques, 335–337
 tools, 308–310
Data quality
 cardinality problems, 346
 conversion issues, 340–343, 345–348,
  See also Data conversion
 data warehousing considerations, 311,
  312–313
 date inconsistencies, 348
 domain integrity, 346
 E-commerce issues, 610
 end-user applications development
  problems, 746
 end-user applications review process,
  763
 erroneous data management, 311
 identifying data problems, 342–343, 345
 intelligent keys, 348
 joint applications development and, 458
 missing information, 342, 347, 349
 optionality, 347
 orphaned records, 347
 redundancy, 346, 347
 referential integrity, 346, 347
 routine error handling, 353
 types of abnormalities, 345–346
 uniqueness, 346
Data retention/deletion, 363–364
Data visualization, 310

Data warehousing, 187–189, 295–314, 315,
    402–403, 406, *See also* Data marts;
    Data mining
  basic technology and characteristics,
    297–300
  costs, 316, 321
  data conversion requirements, 351
  data mart comparison, 316–318
  data volume, 301
  decision support systems, 303–306, 326
  design and construction, 300–306
    bottom-up vs. top-down
      approaches, 301–302
    star schema, 302
  development framework, 321–329
    access tool selection, 327–328
    administration, 328
    business requirements, 324–325
    data sourcing, 325
    expertise required, 323
    risks and challenges, 322–324
    target architecture, 325–327
  development life cycle, 312
  functional data warehouse, 327, *See*
      Data marts
  history, 295–297
  importance of data quality, 311, 312–313
  intelligent agent application, 411
  managerial and organizational impacts,
    310–313
  measuring business value, 329
  motivation for building, 321, 323
  nonvolatility, 300
  "plan big, start small" approach,
    318–319
  ROI, 321–322
  snowflake schema, 302–303
  subject orientation, 297
  time-variance, 297–298
  virtual data warehouse, 303–305, 326
Database development, 396–397, 481–489
  benefits, 482
  business requirements, 485
  costs, 483
  data models, 485, 486
  deliverables, 486–487
  high-level methodology, 484–486
  organization and skill sets, 487–488
  pitfalls, 488
  selection, 482–483
  testing, 486
  tools, 487
  transaction analysis, 486
  "waterfall" vs. RAD approach, 482–483

Database management systems, and history
    of data warehousing, 296
Databases
  development, *See* Database
    development
  ownership problems in client/server
    environment, 197
  security controls, 733
  Web vs. client/server applications, 617
Decentralized organizational structure, 7–10
Decision support systems
  agents, 405–418, *See* Intelligent agents
  data warehousing, 303–306, 326
Decision trees, 309
Dell, 401
Desktop support services, 151–155, *See also*
    Support services
Deutsche Telecom, 237
Development life cycle
  data warehouse, 312
  Theory-W integration, 506
  usability techniques and, 464
Dialtone IS services, 215, 219
Diamond of change model, 539–543
Digitization, 235
Direct Access Storage Device (DASD), 360
Direct Risk Mitigation, 388–391
Directories, 282, 614, 671
DISA, 254
Disaster contingency and recovery
    planning, 189, 363, 373–381, 732
  backup plan, 376–377, *See also* Backup,
    plans and procedures
  critical applications, 363
  emergency plan, 375–376
  frequently overlooked factors, 380–381
  hot site, 362, 363
  maintenance plan, 379–380
  manual, 363
  mission-critical functions, 376
  off-site storage, 376–377
  recovery plan, 363, 377–378, 563
  risk analysis, 375–376
  simulation, 66
  test plan, 378–379
Discovery-based technology, 307–308,
    331–333, *See also* Data mining
Dislocating technology, 41–47
Disney Interactive, 577–578
Distributed computing, 42–45, 185–186,
    211–224, *See also* Client/server
    systems; Extranets; Intranets
  IS departmental shortcomings, 212
  Java applications, 435

management guidelines, 217–223
    architecture design, 222–223
    BPR and metrics, 218–219
    front-end data integration, 222–223
    standards, 221–222
    three levels of service organization, 219–220
    "tight management, loose control," 217–218
risk, cost, and quality, 213–215
service delivery model, 211–217
transition to, 95–107, 211–224, *See also* Client/server systems, staff transition to
Distributed hubs, 286–287
Distributed management, end-user computing control, 728–729
Diversified Graphics, Ltd. v. Groves, 581
Document objects, 421
Documentation issues, 231–232, 704
Dow Corning, 5, 18
Downsizing, 90
Drucker, Peter, 41

E

Eavesdropping, 670
ECONOMOST, 66
EDI, *See* Electronic data interchange
Electronic commerce, 586, 589–603, *See also* Internet and associated technologies; Web sites
    advertising, 597
    business case for, 594–597
    business-to-business, 586, 589–603, *See* Business-to-business electronic commerce
    capitalizing on the Internet, 600–603
    EDI applications, 587, 645, *See also* Electronic data interchange; Extranets
    emerging markets, 590, 594–603
    extending reach, 594–595
    intelligent agent applications, 396
    Internet access cost, 608–609
    interorganizational systems, 590–594
    leveraging business and support capabilities, 601–602
    local standards, 611
    market creation via the Internet, 597–600
    privacy concerns, 608
    security issues, 608, *See also* Internet security
    service enhancement, 596
    software agent applications, 419–428, *See also* Electronic Commerce Support System
    traditional market augmentation, 596
    Web site issues, 586, 605–611, *See also* Web sites
    case studies, 681–685
Electronic Commerce Support System (ECSS), 419–428
    business process integration, 422–423
    domain analysis, 422–427
    object-oriented methodology, 422
Electronic conferences, 37
Electronic data interchange (EDI), 60, 587, 591–594, 636–646
    business process redesign, 646
    costs, 637, 638
    definition, 636
    expanding impact of, 638
    history and growth, 636
    Internet and, 639
        E-commerce strategy, 645–646
        FTP exchanges, 643
        MIME and e-mail, 644, 667
        value-added networks, 641–642
        World Wide Web and, 639–643
    limitations, 637–638
    private value-added networks, 637–638
    standards, 636
    strategy components, 645–646
Electronic forms, 591
Electronic funds transfer (EFT), 591
Electronic meeting rooms, 468
Electronic Messaging Association (EMA), 292
Electronic messaging systems, 279–294, *See also* E-mail
    applications support, 293
    backup, 293
    deployment architectures and options, 287
        common backbone, 287, 290–291
        common platform, 287, 288–289
        multiple backbone, 287, 289–290
    directory services, 282
    implementation models and architectures, 281–283
    integrated messaging, 591
    integrating dissimilar systems, 285–287
    internal and external customer support, 280–281
    mail monitoring, 283
    management and administration services, 282–283

message transfer services, 282
network connections, 293
network services, 281–282
operating systems, 293
performance measuring, 283
policies and procedures, 292–293
rollout and constraint management,
    279–281
tiered approach to implementation,
    283–287
Electronic shopping malls, 596
Ellison, Larry, 607
E-mail, 279–294, 667, *See also* Electronic
    messaging systems
acceptable usage policy, 689–690
filtering, intelligent agent application,
    410, 411
Internet electronic data interchange,
    644
messaging policies and procedures,
    292–293
system implementation, 279–294
Embedded software applications, 431,
    438–439
Emergency plan, 375–376, *See* Disaster
    contingency and recovery
    planning
Employee directories, 614
Employee turnover, 130–131
Employees, *See* Human resources;
    Information technology personnel
Empowered development groups, 451–461
Enabler partnership role, 23–24
Encryption, 607, 678, 745
Ends/means analysis, 58
End-user applications development, control
    issues, 739–746, *See also* End-user
    computing control; End-user
    developed applications,
    reviewing; Systems and
    applications development
computer viruses, 744–745
copyright violations, 743–744
definitions and characteristics, 750–751
evaluating, for review process, 760
guidelines for improving, 765–766
inaccurate information, 746
ineffective implementation, 742–743
review of developed applications,
    749–766, *See* End-user developed
    applications, reviewing
security, 740, 745
support, 741–742
systems compatibility, 741–742

systems redundancy, 742
training, 741
unauthorized access to data/programs,
    745
use of resources, 740–741
End-user computing control, 698, 727–737,
    See also Security
application and process controls, 735
applications development, 739–746, *See*
    End-user applications
    development, control issues
architectural approaches to information
    protection, 727–728, 746
confidentiality and integrity controls,
    731–735
continuity and recovery controls,
    735–736
distributed management structure,
    728–730
information protection policy, 736
monitoring, 731
network and communication controls,
    734–735
physical controls, 731–732
policy and strategy, 729–730, 746
standards, procedures, and guidelines,
    731
system controls, 732–733
End-user computing environment, 757–759
End-user developed applications, reviewing,
    749–766, *See also* Software quality
    assurance
application criticality, 760
application environment, 759–760
applications development controls, 760
best-guess review, 756–757
data characteristics, 763
end-user computing environment,
    750–751, 757–759
financial issues, 754–755
formal audit, 755–756
inventory, 756
misconceptions, 751–752
product use and availability, 762
review method, 755–757
review objectives, 753–755
reviewing the applications, 764
scope and content, 757–759
security status, 762
statistical review, 756
support services, 754
user skills and knowledge, 763
End-user support services, *See* Support
    services

Enterprise productivity/profitability
    improvement, 399–404, *See also*
    Performance improvement;
    Productivity
Enterprise resource planning (ERP), 74, 397
Estimation technique for data mining, 337
Ethernet, 259, 264, *See also* Gigabit Ethernet
Ethical responsibility, 398, 575–583
    caveat emptor vs. caveat venditor,
        578–579, 581
    error-detection and defect-prevention
        capabilities, 579–580
    intelligent agents and, 417
    legal regulations, 581, 582
    life-critical software failures, 576
    market expectations and software
        malfunctions, 577–578
Etzioni, Oren, 413
Event-driven methodology, 446
Event objects, 421
Exchanges, 44–45
Executive management leadership, *See*
    Leadership issues
Exhaustion, 671–672
Experiments, 40
Expert systems, 700
Extended staffing, 141–142
Extensible Markup Language (XML), 606
Extranets, 44, 587, 649–659
    definition, 649
    multi-homed intranets, 658
    risk and performance assessment,
        650–651
    router-based architecture, 651–653
    security issues, 649–651
        application gateway firewalls, 649,
            652–656
        user authentication, 652, 656,
            658–659
    virtual private networks, 656–659

F

Facilitated systems development process,
    451–461
Federal Communications Commission
    (FCC), 239
    Internet telecommunications service
        and, 237
Federal Express, 11–12
Federalist organizational structure, 9–10
Fiber distributed data interface (FDDI), 259
File transfer applications, technical support
    applications, 702

File transfer protocol (FTP), 643, 666, 668
    anonymous FTP, 668
Filters, 673, 674–678
Financial portfolio management, 414
Firefly, 410
Firewalls, 43, 587, 691, *See also* Security
    extranets and, 649, 652–656, *See also*
        Extranets
Food and Drug Administration (FDA), 582
Forrester, Jay, 403
Frame relay, 262
Fraud detection, 335, 337
FTP exchanges, 643
Functional data warehouse, 327, *See* Data
    marts
Functionality testing, 567

G

Gartner Group, 151
Generation data groups, 363
Gibson, C. R., 58
Gigabit Ethernet, 187
    successful network implementation,
        269–277
Global markets, 599
Global networks, 400–401
Global trends in software development,
    534–535
Goal-directed agents, 423
Gould, Stephen Jay, 41
Graphical user interface (GUI), 202, 406, 546
    Java and, 432–433
    usability considerations, 463
Group management, joint application
    development, 451–461
Group Systems V, 468
Groupware, 54, 406
GTE, 245, 248
GUI, *See* Graphical user interface

H

Hammet, John, 25
Health care industry applications, 28,
    337–338
Help desk, 154, 697, 700–702, *See also*
    Support services
Hierarchical task analysis, 424
Hiring techniques, 102, 121–132, *See also*
    Information technology personnel
Holes, 744
Hughes Electronics, 400

Human resources, *See also* Information
    technology personnel
    Acceptable Use Policy Committee, 694
    client/server environment and, 95–107,
        See also Client/server systems,
        staff transition to
    continuing training, 129
    disaster planning, 380–381
    effective knowledge management and,
        37
    extended staffing, 141–142
    hiring techniques, 102, 121–132, *See also*
        Information technology personnel
    Internet acceptable usage policies, 587,
        See also Acceptable usage
        policies
    intranet applications, 614
    large complex systems requirements,
        528
    nine month review, 123
    outsourcing issues, 177, 180
    perceptions of reorganization, 109–110
    salaries, 123–124
    skills analysis, 102–103
    strategic issues, 3–4
    technology deployment guidelines, 90
    training or job assignment plan, 103–104
Hypertext Markup Language (HTML), 585,
    606, 640
Hypertext Transfer Protocol (http), 585,
    654, 666
    Secure HTTP (https), 607, 654

I

IBM, 24
Incident reporting, 359–360
Industrial Dynamics analysis, 403
Information behavior, 719
Information market economy model of IT
    environment, 75–76
Information mission and vision, 55
Information overload, 31
Information protection policy, 730, *See*
    Security
Information requirements analysis, 56–57
Information resource (IR) acquisition
    model, 158–159
Information resource planning, 56–59
Information sharing, 698, 719–725, *See also*
    Knowledge management
    appropriate environments, 724–725
    context, 721
    cultural support, 34, 39, 722–723

    definition, 719
    explicit rules, 721–722
    importance of, 720
    incentives, 723–724
    rumor mill database, 722
Information systems
    alignment with enterprise goals and
        processes, 1–3, 65, 77, 85–86, *See*
        also Strategic planning
    audits, *See* Audits
    consulting phases, 511–514
    managing user relationships with,
        509–515
    outsourcing, *See* Outsourcing
    partnering relationships, 19–26
    performance, *See* Performance
        improvement
Information systems planning (ISP), 63–65
    integration of BPR and TQM, 2, 63–72,
        400
        integrated process change
            management, 67–70
        IS management role, 70–72
        ISP, BPR, and TQM commonalities,
            65–67
        process change management steps,
            69–70
        success stories, 68–69
    measurement criteria, 71–72
Information technology architecture, 12–13,
    55–56, *See also* Information
    technology infrastructure
    development
Information technology infrastructure
    development, 5–18, 269–277, *See*
    also Network infrastructure
    implementation
    assessing value of, 5
    centralized/decentralized
        organizational structures and,
        7–10
    communication and education, 15–16
    corporate strategy, 11–12, 17–18
    definition, 6–7
    design and operation, 185–189
    enterprise market-responsiveness and,
        5–6
    funding, 16
    implementing and sustaining, 13, 14–17
    IT architecture, 12–13
    management elements, 10–14
    organizational systems and processes,
        14

partnership processes in development, 15

process redesign, 16–17

strategic IS decisions, 54

technology management, 16

Information technology investment, *See* Investment

Information technology leadership roles, *See* Leadership issues

Information technology management, 83–93, *See* Technology management

Information technology misuse, *See* Acceptable usage policies; Ethical responsibility; Security

Information technology personnel, 2–3, *See also* Human resources

client/server environment and, 95–107, 196, 201–209, *See also* Client/server systems, staff transition to

competition for, 121–123, 126

hiring and retention techniques, 121

candidate expectations, 128–129

criteria, 125–127

employee turnover issues, 130–131

salaries, 123–124

selling the organization, 130

skills, 126–127

Internet acceptable usage policies, 587

Information technology procurement process, 157–171, 269, 270

deployment processes, 161–163

Framework, 161–164

future research, 171

information resource acquisition model, 158–159

internal and external relationships, 168

key management issues, 164–168

management processes, 163–164

measurement, 168

performance metrics and benchmark, 169–170

process analysis and design, 159–160

process management, 168

reengineering tool, 170–171

roles classification, 170

training and education, 171

Information technology strategic planning, *See* Strategic planning

Infrastructure, *See* Information technology infrastructure development; Network infrastructure implementation

Innovator partnership role, 24

Installation physical security, 254–255

Insurance industry, 35

Integrated-CASE tools, 560

Integrated development environment (IDE), 441

Integrated process change management, 67–70

Integrated services digital network (ISDN), 265

Integrated systems planning, 2, 63–72, *See* Information systems planning

Integrity controls, end-user computing, 731–735

Intelligent agents (agents, software agents), 46, 395, 405–418, 419–428, 700

attributes of, 407–410

business applications, 410

data warehousing, 411

e-commerce, 419–428, 620

e-mail filtering, 410, 411

monitoring, 411–412

news filtering, 412

push technology, 412

searching, 412–413

business process integration, 421–422

cognizance, 424

definition, 405

goal-directed, 423

implementation issues, 416

Internet and, 412–413, 414–415

intranets and, 415

learning, 409–410, 426

legal and ethical issues, 417

marketing issues, 415–416

mnemonic instrument, 425

operational tasks, 424

productivity and, 416–417

user interface, 426

work flow control, 425

Intelligent highway systems, 46

Intelligent keys, 348

Interface design, usability engineering, 463–480

Internal customers model, 148

Internal marketplace model, 116, 117–119, 120

Internet and associated technologies, 406, 585–588, 597–600, 661–668, *See also* Electronic commerce; E-mail; Extranets; Intranets; Web sites

acceptable usage policies, 587, 687–695

access cost, 608–609

access path controls, 734–735
behavior rules (netiquette), 693
cable and, 244
capitalizing on for electronic markets,
    600–603
characteristics, 661–668
connections, 663–664
dislocating aspects, 41–46
EDI and, 639–644, *See also* Electronic
    data interchange
enterprise productivity/profitability
    enhancement, 401
industry-specific exchanges, 45
intelligent agents and, 412–413, 414–415
interoperability, 664
Java applets and servlets, 437–438
market creation, 597–600
mesh topology, 662
protocols, 665–666
security, *See* Internet security
strategic IS decisions, 54
value-added service providers, 642
Internet Protocol (IP), 259, 665
    TCP/IP, 236, 259, 265, 665
Internet Relay Chat (IRC), 692
Internet security, 661–680, *See also*
    Intranets; Security
    attacks on the Internet, 669–672
        address spoofing, 670
        browsing, 671
        denial of service, 672
        eavesdropping, 670
        exhaustion, 671–672
        packet grabber, 670
        password grabber, 670
        Trojan Horse, 670–671
    bastions, 673
    dedicated and isolated servers, 678
    defense strategies, 672–674
    encryption, 678
    filters, 673–678
    firewalls, 675–678
    isolation, 672
    policies, 672
    safe use guidelines, 679–680
    user authentication, 652, 656, 658–659,
        680, 735
    vulnerabilities, 668–669
    wrappers, 673
Internet Softbot, 413
Internet telecommunications, 236–237
Internet telephony, 246, 247

Internetwork Packet Exchange (IPX), 259
Interorganization systems, 635, *See*
    Electronic commerce; Electronic
    data interchange; Extranets
Intranets, 42–43, 247, 401, 586, 613–621, *See
    also* Distributed computing;
    Electronic data interchange;
    Extranets
    alternative options, 627
    business-justified project development,
        623–633
        cost-benefit analysis, 630–631
        goals and objectives, 626–627
        identifying target users, 625–626
        implementation plan, 631–633
        performance metrics, 629–630
        planning and resource allocation,
            628
        project phases, 628
    corporate intranet examples, 620–621
    intelligent agents, 415
    intranet reengineering, 613, 614–615
    Java applications, 437, 619–620
    maintenance, 632
    management, 633
    multi-homed systems, 658
    operational plan, 620
    ROI, 623
    scalability and performance, 617–618
    security issues, 618–619, 632, *See also*
        Internet security
    standards, 632
    successful planning, development, and
        implementation, 624–625
    technical support applications, 701–702
    Web as application platform, 615
    Web self-service, 613–614
    Web vs. client/server applications, 617
Inventors, 84
Inventory management applications, 403,
    614
Investment, *See also* Budget; Costs
    justifying, 58–59
    portfolio management, 78
    strategic planning, information
        technology investment portfolio,
        78
IPSec interoperability, 659
IRC, 692
ISO 9000, 398, 543, 550, 557–560
Iterative prototyping, 205

J

Java, 46, 396, 431–442, 450
    applets and servlets (Web
        applications), 437–438
    architecture neutrality, 432–433
    development environments, 440–441
    embedded software applications, 431,
        438–439
    Foundation classes, 435
    Internet and, 619
    intranet development and, 619–620
    JDBC and database connection, 436
    Jini connection technology, 439–440
    object orientation, 433–435, 619
    remote method invocation, 435
    supporting technologies, 436
JC Penney, 12
JDBC, 436
Jini, 46, 439–440
Job assignment plan, 103–104
Job scheduling, 356
Johnson & Johnson, 5, 8–9, 17
Joint application development (JAD),
    451–461
    change management and, 459–460
    implementation success factors,
        457–459
    iterative group approach, 453–454
    joint requirements planning, 452–454
    organizational strategy implementation,
        454–455
    strategic benefits, 455–457, 461

K

Kinney, Jim, 35
Knowledge base, 424
Knowledge management, 1, 27–40
    barriers to effective deployment, 33–34
    best practices examples, 34–37
    business case for, 30–33
    definition, 28–29
    examples of enhanced organizational
        effectiveness, 27–28
    IT management perceptions, 33–34
    planned experimentation and piloting,
        39–40
    prerequisites for successful
        implementation, 38–39
    quality considerations, 38
    successful deployment and outcomes,
        36–38
Knowledge preservation, 28, 31, See Data
    warehousing; Knowledge
    management
Kodak, 74
Kraft Foods, 34–35

L

Laboratory test environment, 569
LANDesk, 705
Large complex systems, 397, 527–532
    business vision and, 529
    personnel requirements, 528
    phased-release rollout plan, 530–532
    testing and program management,
        529–530
    time requirements, 528
Lawsuits, 433, 576–577, 581
Leadership issues, 1–40
    CIO-CEO relationship, 52
    CIO role as obsolete, 41
    dislocating technology and, 41–47
    intranet and, 43
    IT infrastructure development, 5–18
    knowledge management, 1, 27–40
    partnering relationships, 1, 19–26
    role in integrating ISP, BPR, and TQM,
        70–72
    strategic planning, 49–61
    transactional/transformational roles
        model, 1, 20–21
Learning capability, of software agents,
    409–410, 426
Learning organization, 30, 66, 533, 491–500,
    541–543
Lefco, Anthony, 578
Legal issues, 398
    acceptable usage policies, 687, 688
    E-commerce, 610–611
    intelligent agents, 417
    liability, 575, 577–578, 581, 582, See also
        Ethical responsibility
Lincoln National Reassurance Company,
    35–36
Line managers
    BPR implementation problems, 523
    role in strategic IT planning, 73, 75,
        76–79, 80
Link analysis, 307
Linux, 607
Load testing, 276
Local area network (LAN), 192, 616, See also
    Client/server systems; Intranets

LAN Emulation Server, 275
operating standards, 186–187, 249–256
security, 253–255
technical support, 255
virtual LANs vs. virtual networks,
265–266
Lotus Development Corp., 33, 723–724
Lycos, 412

M

Machiavelli, Niccolo, 209
Maes, Pattie, 410, 411
Maintenance support, 153, 282–283,
379–380, 732
Market basket analysis, 335, 337
Market economy model of IT environment,
75–76
Mass customization, 402
MCI-WorldCom, 242, 244, 248
MediaOne, 244–245
Media protection, 732
Medical devices, 576, 582
Mentoring, 703
Message transfer service, 282, 291
Messaging systems, 187, 279–294, *See*
Electronic messaging systems; E-
mail
Methodology, systems and applications
development, 396, 443–450,
544–546
Microwave transmission, 240
Mid-Consulting, 681–682
MIME, 644, 667
Mission, 55
Mission-critical applications standards, 253
Misuse analysis and response, 392
Modified cut-through switch, 261
Moles, 744
Monitoring
adaptive security approach, 391
end-user computing control, 731
intelligent agent application, 411–412
technical support applications, 702
Web users, 691
Morris, Chuck, 451
Motorola, 590
Multidimensional DBMS, 324
Multidimensional hypercubes, 324
Multidimensional OLAP, 305, 332
Multiple backbone architecture, 287,
289–290

Multipurpose Internet mail extension
(MIME), 644, 667
Multi-User Domain (MUD), 692

N

Netiquette, 693
Network computing, 42–46, *See*
Client/server systems;
Distributed computing; Extranets;
Internet and associated
technologies; Intranets
controls, 734–735
costs, 257
filters and firewalls, 673–678, *See also*
Internet security
monitoring, adaptive security
approach, 391
need for centralized control, 74
requirements for messaging rollout,
281–282
software security, 254
support services, 154
virtual networks, *See* Virtual networking
Network infrastructure implementation,
269–277
contract negotiation, 269, 273
installation and support services, 272,
273
installation plan, 276–277
technology selection, 269, 270
testing and installation, 269, 274–276
vendor selection, 269, 270–272
Network management software, 263–264,
266
Network security, *See* Internet security;
Intranets; Security
Network time protocol (NTP), 666
Neural networks, 308–309
New technology, *See also* specific
applications, technologies
deployment, 88–93
dislocating technologies, 41–47
management of, 83–93, *See* Technology
management
strategic IS decisions, 54
Newell, Allen, 407
News filtering, intelligent agent application,
412
Newsgroups, 690, 692
Nolan, R. L., 58
Nominal group techniques, 78
NYNEX, 245

O

Object-oriented technology, 446, 546
  database development methodology, 487
  JAVA, 433–435, 619
  software agents, 420–421, *See also* Intelligent agents
  usability considerations, 463
Obscenity, 691
OLAP (online analytical processing) tools, 303–306, 327, 332, 411
Online transaction processing, 296, 481
Online tutorials, 703–704
Online user-support tools, 703–704, *See also* Support services
Open system, 408
Operating system, 293, 444
Operational Data Store, 325–326
Organizational change, *See* Business process reengineering; Change management
Organizational culture, 205
  client/server-associated changes, 201–209
  customer-centered orientation, 149
  horizontal structure and process cultures, 206–207
  information sharing and, 722–723
  intranet and, 43
  joint applications development and, 458
  organizational history and, 206
  process, organization, and culture model of applications development, 539–543
  strategies for change, 207–208
  systems development model, 205
  support for information sharing, 34, 39, 722–723
  teamwork in, 31
Organizational learning, *See* Learning organization
Organizational memory, 30–31, *See* Knowledge management
Organizational redesign, 109–120, *See also* Business process reengineering
  employee perception of business strategy, 109–110
  information systems for determining roles and responsibilities, 113
  macrodesign structures, 111–113
  microdesign structures, 113–114
  objectives of, 110–111
  proposed model, 116–120

staff transition to client/server environment, 95–107, *See also* Client/server systems, staff transition to
  traditional IT hierarchy and, 115
Organizational structure
  centralized/decentralized, 7–10, 112
  federalist, 9–10
  organization chart, 97–99
  redesign, *See* Organizational redesign
Outsourcing, 3, 133–142, 143, *See also* Information technology procurement process
  accounting and, 177
  audit alternatives, 183–183
  budget comparison, internal vs. vendor proposal, 136–140
  continuing review and control, 181
  contract issues, 178–181, 269, 273
  control of, 173–184
  costs, 134, 175–176
  customer service quality vs., 173
  documentation issues, 231
  extended staffing alternative, 141–142
  internal service performance improvement alternative, 135–136, 143–155
  internal staff management and, 133
  IT procurement process, 157–171, *See* Information technology procurement process
  looking at options, 150
  motivating factors, 134–135, 144, 175–177
  organization-specific characteristics, 174–175
  personnel standards and, 180
  protective measures, 181–182
  results, 143–145
  security and confidentiality issues, 179–180
  service recovery, 178
  services, 174
  staff management and training, 177
  strategic approach to cost control, 153–155
  strategic IS decisions, 53
  strategic planning issues, 181
  support services, 151–155, 272, 273
  transition management, 177
  vendor claims and reality, 134–135
  vendor pricing, 140–141
  vendor selection, 269, 270–272
Owens Corning, 399

P

Pacific Bell, 68, 245
Packet grabber, 670
Packet switching, 236, 260–261, 663–664
Participative approach, facilitated system
    specifications development,
    451–461, *See also* Joint
    application development
Partnering relationships, 1, 19–26
    conversion to client/server
        environment, 96
    forms of partnerships, 20, 22–25
    infrastructure development processes,
        15
Password grabber, 670
Passwords, 677
PC LAN e-mail system, *See* Electronic
    messaging systems
Pentium III chips, 608
PeopleSoft, 74
Performance improvement, 225–232,
    358–364
    alternative to outsourcing, 135–136,
        143–155
    customer and service orientation,
        145–150
    data backup and recovery, 362
    documentation difficulties, 231–232
    error ratios, 228–229
    financing, 229–230
    implementing changes, 230–232
    improvement plan development, 232
    incident reporting and problem
        resolution, 359–360
    indicators of need for improvement,
        144–145
    information base, 148
    IT-enhanced productivity and
        profitability, 399–404
    online viewing of production reports,
        360–361
    operational performance objectives,
        357–358
    organization-specific factors, 146–147
    plan design, 148–149
    problem review meetings, 360
    process mapping, 226–228
    production application scheduling, 361
    program turnover, development to
        production, 359
    rationale and benefits of, 145–146
    report distribution, 359
    setting up, 147–148

Personal communication services (PCS),
    243
Pervasive computing, 45
Peters, Tom, 134
Phased-release rollout plan, 530–532
Physiomorphic objects, 421
Pilot operations, 40, 92–93
Pipeline visibility, 402
Planning, *See* Information systems planning;
    Strategic planning
Planning support services, 153
Point-to-point protocol (PPP), 666
Portal services, 43, *See* Intranets
Portfolio management, 414
Predictive models, and data mining, 308
Pricing
    internal technology management, 219
    network infrastructure components,
        273
    outsourcing vendor tactics, 140–141
    telecommunications sector
        developments, 246
    telephone services, 241
Printing capacity, 360–361
Privacy, 292, 608, *See also* Confidentiality
Private value-added networks, 637–638
Problem review meetings, 360
Process control, "diamond of change"
    model of applications
    development, 539–543
Process cultures, 206–207
Process mapping, 226–228
Process redesign, *See* Business process
    reengineering
Procurement process management,
    157–171, *See* Information
    technology procurement process
Product, defined, 750
Production library access, 359
Productivity, *See also* Performance
    improvement
    improvement, 225–232, *See*
        Performance improvement
    intelligent agents and, 416–417
    IT investment and, 399–404
    joint applications development
        methods and, 457
    LAN operating standards, 251
Profitability improvement, IT investment
    and, 399–404
Programmable agents, *See* Intelligent agents
Programming languages, 444–445, *See also*
    Java
Project performance gap model, 492–500

Prototyping, 71, 544
Proxies, 653–654, 677, 691
Punctuated equilibrium, 41–42
Purchasing support, intranet applications,
    614
Purposiveness, 408
Push technology, intelligent agent
    application, 412

Q

Quality, *See also* Performance improvement;
    Total Quality Management
    data, *See* Data quality
    distributed computing service delivery,
      213
    information services, 355–364
    knowledge management issues, 38
    outsourcing and, 173
    Procurement Process Framework, 164
Quality assurance, 189, 558–561, *See*
    Software quality assurance

R

Rapid application development (RAD), 205,
    483
    usability considerations, 463
Ray Hoving and Associates, 33
RCA analysis, 360
Reach, 594–595, 599, 616
Real-world test environment, 569
Recovery planning and procedures, 150,
    189, 362–363, 377–378, *See*
    Disaster contingency and
    recovery planning
Recovery team, 377
Recruitment and hiring techniques, 121–132
Redundancy, 276, 346, 347, 742
Regional Bell operating companies
    (RBOCs), 239, 242, 245, 248
Regression testing, 568
Regulatory issues, 234, 611
    software quality, 581, 582
Reinsurance industry, 35
Relational database management system,
    324, 339
Relational databases, 403, 581, *See* Database
    development; Databases
Relational mathematics, 351
Relational online analytical processing
    (OLAP), 303, 305–306, 411
Remote browsers, technical support
    applications, 702

Reporting
    distribution and tracking, 359
    electronic messaging systems, 283
    incidents, 359–360
    online viewing of production data,
      360–361
Retsina, 414
Return on investment (ROI)
    client/server systems, 194
    data warehousing, 321–322
    intranets, 623
Reusable software, 537, 546, 483
Risk assessment, 388–391
    emergency plan, 375–376
    extranet, 650–651
    risk posture assessment, 389–391, 392
Risk management, 189, *See also* Disaster
    contingency and recovery
    planning; Security
    information systems audits and, 369
Rockart, John, 58
Ross, Rony, 501
Routers, 257, 260, 261
    extranet architectures, 651–653
    gateway emulation of, 285
    network filters, 674
    testing, 275
    virtual LAN, 266
Rowland, Larry, 35
Royal Dutch Shell, 30
Rule induction, 309
Rumor mill database, 722

S

SABRE, 66
Salaries, 123–124
Sales force automation, 614
SAP, 74
SBC, 242, 245–246
Scheduling, 361
Schneider Logistics, 15
Schneider National, 9
Search application, 412–413
Secure HTTP, 607
Secure protocols, 666
Security, 189, 383–393, *See also* Internet
    security
    adaptive approach, 189, 391–392
    application and process controls, 735
    architectural approaches to information
      protection, 727–728, 736–737
    audit and trends analysis, 392

classification of information, 730
client/server and, 196–197
confidentiality and integrity controls,
    731–735, 737
continuity and recovery controls,
    735–736
cyberspace environment, 383–384
database controls, 733
direct risk mitigation, 388–391
distributed responsibilities, 728
E-commerce issues, 607
electronic messaging policies and
    procedures, 292–293
end-user controls, 727–737, 740,
    745–748, *See also* End-user
    computing control
end-user developed applications review
    process, 762
executive support, 729
extranets
    firewalls, 649, 652–656
    risk and performance assessment,
        650–651
    vulnerabilities, 649
human threat categories, 384
information protection policy
    statement, 730
intelligent agents and, 417
Internet, 587, 607, 661–680, *See* Internet
    security
intranet development considerations,
    618–619, 632
LAN operations standards, 253–255
management commitment, 387
management committee, 729
management structure, 728–730, 736
monitoring and control, 731
network and communication controls,
    734–735
network software, 254
outsourcing contract issues, 179–180
personnel, 388
physical controls, 731–732
policy and strategy, 672, 729–730, 736
production library access, 359
real-time user awareness and support,
    392
risk posture assessment, 389–391, 392
smart cards, 659
system controls, 732–733
tools, 732–733
user authentication, 652, 656, 658–659,
    680, 735
virtual networks and, 258
viruses and, 744–745, 747

vulnerabilities, 391–392, 668–669, 733
    wrong approach, 385
Security server, 263–264
Seeding, 723
Senge, Peter, 30
Sequence-based data mining, 336
Serial line Internet protocol (SLIP), 666
Service-level agreements, 355, 357, *See also*
    Contract issues; Customer
    requirements and expectations
Servlets, 437–438
Shell, 66
Silo cultures, 206
Simon, Herbert, 408
Simple Mail Transfer Protocol (SMTP), 282,
    644, 666, 667
Singapore, 589–590
SITA, 44
Skills, 126
    analysis, 102–103
    centers of competency, 116
    service orientation, 149
Smart cards, 659
Smokestack IT organization, 115
SMTP, 282, 666, 667
Snowflake schema, 302–303
Society for Information Management (SIM),
    157, 160
Software agents, *See* Intelligent agents
Software-controlled medical devices, 576,
    582
Software development, 533–547, *See also*
    Systems and applications
    development
    artisan approach, 544
    capability evaluation, 556
    CASE tools, 560–562
    economic trends, 534
    ethical and legal issues, 398, 575–583,
        See Ethical responsibility
    ethical responsibility, 398
    global trends, 534–535
    history of software engineering, 537–538
    methodologies, 396, 443–450, 544–546
    process, organization, and culture
        ("diamond of change") model,
        539–543
    process assessment, 555–556
    quality assurance, 398, *See* Software
        quality assurance
    testing, *See* Software testing
    the software dilemma, 535–539
        characteristic problems, 535–536
        real-world effects, 538–539

Software industry employment, 577
Software installation automation, 703
Software licensing audit, 365
Software market, value of, 533
Software piracy, 743–744
Software process assessment, 555–556
Software process control, 549–562, *See*
    Software quality assurance
Software Publishers Association (SPA),
    743–744
Software quality assurance, 398, 549–562,
    See also Software testing
  auditing, 558–561
  Capability Maturity Model, 552–557
  CASE tools, 560–561
  end-user application development,
    739–746
  error-detection and defect-prevention
    capabilities, 579–580
  formal technical review, 551
  ISO 9000 series standard, 557–560 *See
    also* ISO 9000
  processes and methods, 550–552
  standards, 550, 551
  TQM, 552–553, 556–557
  user-developed applications, 749–766,
    See End-user developed
    applications, reviewing
Software quality auditing, 558–561
Software testing, 274–275, 398, 549, 551–552,
    563–575, *See also* Software quality
    assurance
  automated tools, 579
  defect prevention, 579–580
  end-user applications development
    problems, 746
  error-detection and defect-prevention
    capabilities, 579–580
  ethical considerations, 579–580
  inspections, 552
  lab, real world, and worst-case
    environments, 568–569
  myths, 572–573
  personnel, 564–565
  reviews, 552
  system modifications, 568
  testing plan, 569–572
  types, 566–568
  usability, 566
  walkthroughs, 551
Spiders, 412
Spiral Model, 506
Split DNS, 658
SQL, *See* Structured query language

SRI, 89
Standards
  client/server systems, 196
  CMM, 552–557, *See* Capability Maturity
    Model
  distributed computing management,
    221–222
  electronic data interchange, 636
  end-user computing control, 731
  ethical and legal issues, 581
  integrating ISP, BPR, and TQM, 71
  Internet and local standards
    enforcement, 611
  intranet development considerations,
    632
  ISO 9000, 398, 543, 550, 557–560
  IT architecture development and, 12–13
  IT infrastructure development issues,
    16
  mission-critical applications, 253
  operational performance objectives,
    357–358
  security, 254–255
  service-level agreement, 356–357
  software quality assurance, 550, 551
  telecommunications technology, 246,
    248
    LAN operations, 186–187, 249–256
Standards committees, 251–253
Star schema, 302
Statoil, 5
Store-and-forward switch, 261
Strategic business unit, 111–113
Strategic information technology alignment,
    1–3, 77, 85–86
Strategic IT infrastructure development,
    11–12, 17–18
Strategic option generator, 78
Strategic planning, 49–61, 73–81, *See also*
    Information systems planning
  aligning technology strategy with
    business needs, 85–86
  basic elements, 50–51
  continuous planning cycle, 81
  dialectical approach, 75–76
  employee perceptions of
    reorganization, 109–110
  guidelines, 61
  information architecture and, 55–56
  information megatrends and, 53
  information services delivery, 54
  information technology investment
    portfolio, 78
  IS executive role, 52–55

IT management challenge, 74–75
justifying IT investments, 58–59
line manager's role, 73, 75, 76–79, 80
methodologies, 57–58
need for centralized control of IT, 73–74
outsourcing agreement issues, 181
planning horizon, 80–81
procedural guideline, 79–81
process and deliverables, 80
products of, 55–59
project characteristics and, 59–60
resource allocation, 56–59
reviewing user-developed applications,
    755
tactical bridge, 79
technology planning specialists, 86–87
Strategic planning team, 80
Strategic technology positioning, 84–85
Strategist partnership role, 24–25
Strategy-set transformation, 58
Structured analysis and design, 443,
    445–446, 544–546
Structured query language (SQL), 193, 196,
    202, 450
    data conversion application, 352
    relational OLAP and, 305–306
Subject-oriented database, 297
Subsidies, 138–139, 238
Sun v. Microsoft, 433
Support partner services, 155
Support services, 697, 699–705
    application sharing and remote control,
        702, 704
    client/server systems and, 195, 197
    economies of scale, 152
    end-user computing control issues, 741
    help desks and technical support
        agents, 700–702
    help documentation, 704
    integration of, 152
    intranet applications, 614, 701–702
    LAN operating standards, 251, 255
    network infrastructure implementation,
        272, 273
    outsourcing, 151–155, 174
    PC software, 700–701
    reviewing user-developed applications,
        754
    strategic approach to cost control, 153
    telework, 697, 705, 707–717, *See also*
        Telework support
    tools for automating PC support,
        702–704
    types of services, 153–155

"underground support," 741
Surround data warehouse, 303
Swing, 436
Switching technologies, 257, 260–266
Systems, *See* Information systems
    defined, 750
    development life cycle, 159
    housekeeping, 618
    specifications, *See* Customer
        requirements and expectations;
        Joint application development;
        Standards; Systems and
        applications development
    testing, 398, 567, *See also* Software
        testing
Systems and applications development,
    396–397, 533–547, *See also*
        Information systems planning;
        Software development
    Capability Maturity Model (CMM), 398,
        543, 550
    culture shifts, 205
    customer needs/expectations, 396
    database development, 396–397,
        481–489, *See also* Database
        development
    empowered development groups,
        451–461, *See also* Joint
        application development
    end-user applications, control issues,
        739–748, *See* End-user
        applications development,
        control issues
    end-user applications, reviewing,
        749–766, *See* End-user developed
        applications, reviewing
    enterprise resource planning, 397
    facilitated development, 451–461
    guidelines for improving end-user
        applications development,
        765–766
    integrated development environment,
        441
    intranets, *See* Intranets
    Java and, *See* Java
    large complex systems, 397, 527–532
    life cycle, 159
    methodology development issues, 396,
        443–450, 544–546
        "general" vs. ad hoc problem-
            oriented approaches, 446–448
        problem-focused approach, 448–450
        structured approaches, 443,
            445–446, 554–556

three-tiered solution, 450
process, organization, and culture
("diamond of change") model,
539–543
quality issues, 398, *See* Software quality
assurance
reengineering issues, 397, *See also*
Business process reengineering
Spiral Model, 506
terminology, 750
usability engineering, 396, 463–480, *See*
User-centered design
Systems engineering, evolution of, 544–546,
See also Systems and applications
development
Systems Network Architecture (SNA), 259

T

Tactical planning, 79
Tax assistance software, 577
Taylor, Frederick, 501
TCI, 244–245
TCP/IP, 236, 259, 265, 665
Teamwork, organizational culture and, 31
Technical skill sets, 126
Technical support, *See* Support services
Technological dislocation, 42–46
Technologist partnership role, 22–23
Technology deployment, 88–93
Technology life cycle, 85
Technology management, 83–93
    aligning technology strategy with
        business needs, 85–86
    IT deployment, 88–93
    process redesign, 89–90, *See also*
        Business process reengineering
    scope of, 84
    strategic positioning, 84–85
    technology planning specialists, 86
    tracking trends, 84–85, 87
    triad management, 86
Telecommunications Act of 1996, 234,
    238–243
    incomplete implementation, 244
Telecommunications sector, 233–248
    cable television, 243
    future of, 246
    Internet technology, 236–237, 246, 247
    mergers, 244–245
    model for virtual network, 259–260
    regulatory environment, 234, 238–243
    technical standards, 246, 248
    technological changes, 233–237
    wireless technology, 243

Telecommuters, 705, 707–717, *See* Telework
    support
Telework support, 697, 705, 707–717
    managerial support, 713–716
    obstacles of virtual work arrangements,
        708–711
    organizational identity and, 715
    reward mechanisms, 715
    social needs and, 715–716
    technological support, 711–713
Telnet, 666, 679
Testing, 563–573, *See also* Software testing
    contract negotiation, 273
    data conversion procedure, 344
    database development methodology,
        486
    disaster contingency/recovery plan,
        363, 378–379, 568
    large complex systems, 529–530
    network infrastructure, 269, 274–277
    software, 274–275, 398, 549, 551–552,
        563–575, *See* Software testing
    usability evaluation, 473–474
Texas Instruments (TI), 16, 68–69, 400
Theory W, 397, 501–507
Theory X, 501
Theory Y, 501
Theory Z, 502
Time bombs, 744
Time Warner, 244–245
Token Ring, 259, 264
Total cost of ownership, 151
Total Quality Management (TQM), 64, 550,
        See also Joint application
        development
    BPR and integrated information
        systems planning, 2, 63–72, 400,
        See also Information systems
        planning
    Capability Maturity Model comparison,
        556–557
    CASE tool support, 561
    software process control, 552–553,
        556–557
Training, 703, 712, 741
    assignment plan, 103–104
    client/server technology, 198, 202
    employee candidate expectations, 129
    IT procurement process, 171
    outsourcing, 177
    transition to client/server environment,
        95–96
Transaction analysis, 486
Transmission control protocol (TCP), 665

Transmission Control Protocol/Internet
    Protocol (TCP/IP), 236, 259, 265,
    665
Travelers Property and Casualty, 13, 17
Trojan Horse, 670–671, 744
TurboTax, 577
Tutorials, 703–704

U

Ubiquitous computing, 45
Uniform resource locator (URL), 641
Unit testing, 567
United Services Automobile Association
    (USAA), 65
United States v. AT&T, 239
United States v. Western Electric, 239
Universal relation, 351
UNIX security vulnerabilities, 733
Unlicensed software, 743–744, 747
US West, 242, 244, 246
USAA, 24
Usability engineering, 396, 463–480, *See*
    User-centered design
Usability testing, 566
User authentication, 652, 656, 658–659, 680
User-centered design, 396, 463–480
    requirements process (user model),
        464–468
    usability evaluation, 464, 468–474
        heuristic reviews, 469–470
        laboratory testing, 473–474
        walk throughs, 470–472
    usability leadership assessment,
        474–480
    usability principles, 476
    usability skills, 474, 475
User-developed applications, control
    issues, 698, 739–748, *See* End-user
    applications development,
    control issues
User-developed applications, reviewing,
    749–766, *See* End-user developed
    applications, reviewing
User interface
    anthropomorphism in design, 409
    software agent applications, 426
    usability engineering, 463–480, *See*
        User-centered design
User/IS relationships, 509–515
User model, 464–468
User requirements, 355–364, *See* Customer
    requirements and expectations
User support, *See* Support services

V

Value-added networks, 637–638, 641–642
Value-added service providers, 642
Value chain analysis, 78, 87
Vendor relationship, *See* Outsourcing
Video conferencing, 236, 712
Virtual data warehouse, 303–305, 326
Virtual LANs, 265–266, 275
Virtual networking, 44, 187, 257–267,
        656–659, 711
    business case for, 257–258
    definition, 259–260
    network management software, 263–266
    security, 258
    switching technology, 257, 260–266
    technology case for, 258–259
    virtual LANs, 265–266
Virtual routing service, 264–265
Virtual work arrangements, 707–717
    managerial support, 713–716
    obstacles, 708–711
    technological support, 711–713
Viruses, 670–671, 744–745, 747
Vision statement, 97
Visual programming languages, 446, 450
Visualization, 310
V-model testing strategy, 530
Voice telephony technology, 235, 247
Volume testing, 567
Vulnerability analysis and response, 392

W

WalMart, 8, 65
Waterfall approach, 4822–483
Waterman, Robert, 134
WebCrawler, 412
Web-enabled tools, 616
Web-native tools, 616
Web sites, 586, 587, *See also* Extranets;
        Internet and associated
        technologies; Intranets; Web
        technologies
    cost, 600
    E-commerce issues, 605–611
        bandwidth, 606
        customer concerns, 608–609
        implementation, case studies,
            681–685
        inaccessible sites, 611
        legal and regulatory issues, 610–611
        platform choice, 606–607
        pricing, 610

security, 607
security issues, 607, 618–19, *See also* Internet security
Web technologies, 585–588, 667, *See also* Internet and associated technologies; Web sites
electronic data interchange and, 639–643, *See also* Electronic data interchange
intranet applications, *See* Intranets
Java applets and servlets, 437–438
Wide area network (WAN), 258, 616
Win-win negotiation, 501–507, *See also* Theory W
Wireless technology, 243
Wizards, 700, 704
Work flow analysis, 226, 513
Work flow management tools, 425–426, 735

Work group, defined, 750
Work unit, defined, 750
World Wide Web, 401, 406, 667, *See* Internet and associated technologies; Web sites
acceptable usage policies, 690–693
Worms, 668, 744
Worst-case test environment, 569
Write Once, Run Anywhere, 432, 433, 438

X

X.400, 282
Xerox, 25, 68

Y

Y2K compliance audit, 366